ELEMENTS OF APPLIED PSYCHOLOGY

ELEMENTS OF
APPLIED PSYCHOLOGY

Edited by

Peter Spurgeon
University of Birmingham, UK

Roy Davies
University of Aston, Birmingham, UK

and

Antony J. Chapman
University of Leeds, UK

harwood academic publishers
Switzerland • Australia • Belgium • France • Germany • Great Britain
India • Japan • Malaysia • Netherlands • Russia • Singapore • USA

Harwood Academic Publishers

Private Bag 8
Camberwell, Victoria 3124
Australia

3-14-9, Okubo
Shinjuku-ku, Tokyo 169
Japan

12 Cour Saint-Eloi
75012 Paris
France

Emmaplein 5
1075 A W Amsterdam
Netherlands

Christburgerstrasse 11
10405 Berlin
Germany

820 Town Center Drive
Langhorne, Pennsylvania 19047
United States of America

Post Office Box 90
Reading, Berkshire RG1 8JL
Great Britain

Library of Congress Cataloging-in-Publication Data

Elements of applied psychology/edited by Peter Spurgeon, Roy Davies and Antony J. Chapman.
　　　p.　　cm.
Includes bibliographical references and index.
ISBN 3-7186-5120-3 Hard cover. 3-7186-5419-9 Soft cover.
1. Psychology, Applied. I. Spurgeon, P. (Peter) II. Davies, R.
Roy), 1948–　. III. Chapman, Antony J.
BF636.E45　1994
158--dc20   93-19277
　　　　　　　　　　　　　　　　　　　　　　　　　　　　　　CIP

CONTENTS

FOREWORD

This book contains a representative cross-section of the field of applied psychology. Other titles and other topics could have been substituted and the total content could have been differently distributed but the field is covered. It is interesting to speculate as to whether or not the country and decade of origin of this book are revealed by the Table of Contents and the answer is probably affirmative in both cases. These things are done rather differently in different countries for historical, cultural and economic reasons, although the field of knowledge is international. The titles and the topics change in time as well as with geography but we are not in the fashion trade. James, Ebbinghaus, Binet and Myers from their perspective at the beginning of this century would recognise and sympathise with the problems and achievements recorded by these authors and, for that matter, so would philosophers, scientists, policy-makers, leaders and others from much earlier times. People, the whole topic of study, do not change radically in the characteristics that govern their behaviour. They do change and differ in how they justify what they do and why but that is a different level of exploration. Proper psychology, applied or otherwise, pursues the bases as well as the remedies.

On the other hand what we have here is hardly an established fundamental discipline. Applied psychology is what applied psychologists do in practice and this shifts continually. In the current world community technology is one strong influence, for example, and there are at present many applied psychologists engaged with the ramifications of information technology. As Chapter 1 makes clear, applied psychology is strongly influenced by factors such as involvement in wars, fluctuations in employment levels, general economic well-being and government policies on education. Not surprisingly what affects the people affects the applied psychologists' activities. Nevertheless, the competent practitioners doggedly pursue the development of concepts which are independent of the *Zeitgeist*.

For this and many other reasons, it is a difficult field. The more so because positive progress is easy to dismiss as no more than common sense. No doubt this is because, as individuals, we can recognise what is pointed out, at least about other people if not ourselves, although most of us would not be able to reach these conclusions unaided by the insights of the professional practitioners.

In common with the disciplines that aim to provide a public service, applied psychology is in the permanent dilemma of needing standardisation to protect the recipient, but equally needing flexibility to encourage evolution. Certification and licensing are positive in diminishing charlatanism but negative in supporting the barely competent and in encouraging bureaucracy and ossification. Freedom and diversity have their own dangers but are essential for the encouragement of intellectual entrepreneurism. The answer seems to be to have yet more divisions between kinds and levels of practitioner functioning in different roles. This is unfortunate in what ought to be a seamless subject. As the editors point out, divisions of kinds of psychology and kinds of theory are still proliferating. Pessimistically this will continue indefinitely. Optimistically the bases will emerge to provide a secure foundation for practice, for theory and for education and training in the discipline.

In the meantime the editors and authors have presented what we do and what we know so far. Hopefully readers of this book will be encouraged to grasp the example, expertise and enthusiasm demonstrated and some at least will go on to make their own contribution. As in all sciences we stand on the shoulders of our predecessors. This is not to suggest that applied psychology is merely a science. In common with designing engineering it is also an art. Solutions do not appear solely as the product of logical education, there are always many possible ways forward and the good applied psychologist is distinguished by sensitivity and creativity in selecting remedies which fit neatly into the situation. Read on to see what I mean.

W.T. Singleton
Emeritus Professor of Applied Psychology
Aston University, Birmingham, UK

CONTRIBUTORS

F. BARWELL
The University of Birmingham, The Health Services Management Centre, School of Public Policy, Park House, 40 Edgbaston Park Road, Birmingham B15 2RT, UK

F. BLACKLER
Lancaster University, The Management School, Department of Behaviour in Organisations, Lancaster LA1 4YX, UK

P. BROKS
Royal Hallamshire Hospital, Neuroservices Directorate L Floor, Glossop Road, Sheffield S10 2JF, UK

M. CARROLL
Roehampton Institute, Department of Psychology and Counselling, Digby Stuart College, Roehampton Lane, London SW15 5PH, UK

A.J. CHAPMAN
University of Leeds, Department of Psychology, Leeds LS2 9JT, UK

D.R. DAVIES
University of Aston, Division of Applied Psychology, The Triangle, Aston, Birmingham B4 7ET, UK

J. ELLIS
University of Wales, School of Psychology, PO Box 901, Cardiff CF1 3YG, UK

A. GALE
University of Southampton, Department of Psychology, Southampton, Hampshire, UK

A. HEDGE
Cornell University, Department of Environmental Studies, I.C.H.C.A., New York, USA

P. HERRIOT
Sunbridge Park Management Centre, Plaistow House, Bromley BR1 3TP, UK

C.M. HICKS
University of Birmingham, Department of Continuing Studies, Winterbourne, Edgbaston Park Road, Birmingham, UK

D. JONES
University of Wales, School of Psychology, PO Box 901, Cardiff CF1 3YG, UK

S.E.G. LEA
University of Exeter, Department of Psychology, Washington Singer
Laboratories, Exeter EX4 4QG, UK

M.S. LIVINGSTON
University of Leeds, Department of Psychology, Leeds LS2 9JT, UK

S.P. LLEWELYN
The University of Edinburgh, Department of Psychiatry, Kennedy Tower, Royal
Edinburgh Hospital, Morningside Park, Edinburgh EH10 5HF, UK

V. PARFFREY
University of Exeter, Department of Education, Exeter, UK

J. PATRICK
University of Wales, Department of Applied Psychology, PO Box 901, Cardiff
CF1 3YG, UK

E. PICKARD
Consultant to TDA Consulting Group Ltd, Roehampton Institute, Digby Stuart
College, Department of Psychology, Roehampton Lane, London SW15 5PH, UK

V. SHACKLETON
University of Aston, Organisational Studies and Applied Psychology Division,
Aston Management Centre, Aston Triangle, Birmingham B4 7ET, UK

N.P. SHEEHY
University College Dublin, Psychology Department, Dublin 4, Ireland

P.C. SPURGEON
The University of Birmingham, Health Services Management Centre, School of
Public Policy, Park House, 40 Edgbaston Park Road, Birmingham B15 2RT, UK

P. WEBLEY
University of Exeter, Department of Psychology, Washington Singer
Laboratories, Exeter EX4 4QG, UK

J. WEINMAN
Guy's Hospital Medical School, Unit of Psychology as Applied to Medicine,
London Bridge, London SE1 9RT, UK

1

APPLIED PSYCHOLOGY: INTRODUCTION AND BACKGROUND

D.R. DAVIES, P.C. SPURGEON AND A.J. CHAPMAN

INTRODUCTION

The distinction between basic or 'pure' psychology and applied psychology reflects the attempts of psychologists to advance their subject both as a science and as a means of promoting human welfare. Basic psychology is primarily a research activity, mainly carried out in academic institutions, which aims to accumulate reliable and meaningful behavioural data and to devise and test theoretical explanations of why people (and, where appropriate, animals) think and feel and act as they do. The results and conclusions derived from basic psychological research form the backbone of the curricula adopted by universities and colleges providing first degree courses in psychology. Applied psychology comprises several areas of professional practice, for example, clinical psychology, educational psychology and occupational/industrial psychology. It is also a research activity, although the orientation and concerns of research in applied psychology are likely to be rather different from those of research in basic psychology. As Gale indicates in Chapter 18, basic psychological research is often described as being 'theory driven', while applied psychological research is held to be 'problem' or 'need' driven (Middleton and Edwards, 1985). Within applied psychology a distinction has also been made between 'applied' and 'applicable' research (Belbin, 1979). The former is mainly oriented toward the accumulation of knowledge within a particular area of applied psychology; an example would be the investigation of the relative importance of the various factors affecting work satisfaction. The latter is expressly directed at the solution of a particular practical problem; for instance the development of procedures to evaluate patient care and management in a psychiatric hospital (Watts, 1984) or to reduce labour turnover among guards on underground trains (Belbin, 1979). An important development in applied psychology in recent years, especially in the United States, has been the growth of policy oriented research, which aims to produce a more effective collaboration between psychologists and other social scientists on the one hand, and elected and appointed public decision making bodies on the other (Fischoff, 1990; Gallagher, 1990). Psychologists can attempt to influence policy at a conceptual level, by turning research findings into policy issues, by suggesting ways of thinking about policy initiatives, and by creating a common language in which to discuss them. In addition to policy formulation, psychologists and social scientists can contribute to policy evaluation by devising methods to determine the effectiveness of policy initiatives which have already been implemented (see Rossi and Wright, 1984, for a review of evaluation research).

Academically, psychology became an independent discipline during the 1870s, although it was not until after the Second World War that it was able to survive and prosper as a profession outside the universities. The pioneers of psychology in Europe, especially Germany, and in North America viewed psychology as a branch of the natural sciences, concerned with the discovery of fundamental truths about experience and behaviour in human and non-human organisms. But although psychology's principal task is generally acknowledged to be the investigation of experience and behaviour, in practice only a relatively restricted range of experiential and behavioural phenomena has been extensively examined, and only rarely have findings in different areas of psychology been related to one another. As Beloff (1973) remarked, in the preface to a review of modern psychology, "... soon as one attempts to say what psychology is about, it becomes clear that one is dealing, not with a single unified science, but with a collection of more or less affiliated disciplines, each with its own peculiar concepts and laws, its own methods and techniques' (p. ix). Because of the range of organisms, settings and behaviours with which it is concerned, it is extremely improbable that psychology will ever become a conceptually unified discipline (Koch, 1981; Koch and Leary, 1985), and increasing specialisation is generally regarded as inevitable (Bevan, 1982), with psychologists being divided into two cultures, one primarily scientific in orientation, and the other humanistic (Kimble, 1984), a distinction made over 50 years ago (Bruner and Allport, 1940).

The emergence of scientific psychology

Until about the 1860s psychology was essentially an 'armchair' subject, based on philosophical argument, anecdote and 'common sense'. The emergence of modern scientific psychology, with its emphasis on experimentation and research methodology, owes much to the enormous growth of scientific activity, the institutionalisation of science and the professionalisation of the scientist during the nineteenth century, all of which are largely attributable to the rise of the modern university, beginning in Germany in the early 1800s (Hearnshaw, 1987). German universities founded in the early nineteenth century, such as the University of Berlin, were characterised by a strong commitment to academic freedom, and by the vigorous promotion of research and graduate study in a wide variety of fields. Several thousand Americans studied in Germany during the latter half of the nineteenth century, and the German university model exerted a considerable influence on the development of the numerous American colleges and universities founded during this period.

The key figure in the establishment of psychology as an independent experimental science was Wilhelm Wundt, trained in medicine, a researcher in physiology, and professor of philosophy at the University of Leipzig from 1875 until his retirement in 1917 at the age of 85. Wundt's achievement was not simply to effect a marriage betweeen physiology and philosophy, as others had done before him, but to make "the resulting offspring independent" (Leahey, 1987, p. 182). Wundt found academic advancement easier to come by in the relatively static area of philosophy, while the more dynamic and competitive field of physiology offered greater prestige. He resolved the dilemma this career choice posed by inventing a new role for himself, "that of scientific psychologist, derived at least in part from the higher-status field of physiology, but investigating the questions of philosophy" (Leahey, 1987, p. 183). Four years after arriving at Leipzig, Wundt established his Psychological Institute, which is generally acknowledged to be the first experimental psychology laboratory, although it was not officially recognised by the university until a few years later. Wundt's laboratory was responsible for training the first generation of psychologists, many of them American (Leahey, 1987).

Once psychology had emerged as a distinct discipline, the number of qualified psychologists increased at a much faster rate in the United States than in any other country. William James had established an informal psychology laboratory at Harvard in 1875, which was officially recognised and financially supported by Harvard from 1885 onwards, thus becoming the first American psychological laboratory (Watson, 1968). James, like Wundt, a medically trained professor of philosophy, lectured in psychology from 1887 and in 1890 published his celebrated textbook, the *Principles of Psychology*, which charted the course American psychology was initially to follow. James shared Wundt's belief that psychology should become a natural science, effectively a branch of biology. But whereas Wundt was indifferent, or even hostile, to the potential applications of psychology, James believed that as well as being scientific, psychology should also be practical and should make a difference to people's lives (Leahey, 1987). He was, however, an accurate forecaster of the conflicts that might arise between psychologists as scientists and psychologists as practitioners

Most of the early American psychologists had studied with Wundt at Leipzig, although when they returned to the United States they tended to retain Wundt's methods, but to reject his approach to psychology, sometimes described as 'holistic', a psychology which had no place for individual differences. The majority of American psychologists followed James in adopting first a functionalist approach to psychology, derived from Darwinism, which rejected Wundt's emphasis on mental content in favour of an emphasis on mental function, and later a behaviourist approach, which focussed on observable behaviour rather than on mental activities. They also began to extend psychology's influence in America's rapidly expanding universities, and to enhance its status among the older established sciences. Their efforts were, in general, extremely successful, and by 1917, when the United States entered the First World War, 35 departments of psychology had been created in American universities, a figure not reached in Britain until the 1960s. Shortly after psychology had achieved its academic independence, therefore, the United States had established for itself a dominant poSition in world psychology, both with respect to the production of psychology graduates and the output of research. It has maintained this position ever since.

THE DEVELOPMENT OF APPLIED PSYCHOLOGY

It is currently estimated that there are about 500000 qualified psychologists in the world, over half of whom are based in the United States (see Rosenweig, 1992). Of this total, estimates and surveys suggest that world-wide about 15% of all psychologists can be classed as academics, who are engaged in basic or applied research as a primary or secondary work activity, mainly in research institutes, colleges or universities. The remaining 85% can be classed as practitioners, who are employed in various sub-fields of applied psychology, principally school/educational psychology, occupational/industrial/organisational - and clinical/counselling psychology. About half of the world's total number of academic researchers in psychology, and about the same proportion of the total number of psychological practitioners, work in the United States. North America, and particularly the United States, has been especially receptive to potential applications of psychology, in schools, in hospitals and clinics, in correctional/penal institutions, in business and industry, and in the military. As an American clinical psychologist has observed, "Throughout our history, in the schools, in mental health settings, in the military, in the work place, American psychologists have pressed the applications of psychology as far as they will go" Peterson, 1991, p. 422). The historical account which follows thus places greater emphasis on the development of applied psychology in the United States, where applied psychology first began and where it has spread most widely, although significant advances in Britain and other industrialised countries are also outlined.

The period from the emergence of scientific psychology to the end of the First World War was characterised by a high degree of social change, not only in the United States (which was transformed from a largely rural nation to a predominantly urban one) but in other countries too, especially in Europe. Many American psychologists were influenced by the Progressive movement, a leading social and political reformist movement of the time, and set out to professionalise psychology and to make it socially useful, if not an instrument of social control. A major step in the professionalisation of American psychology was the founding of the American Psychological Association (APA) in 1892 by Granville Stanley Hall, the President of Clark University, who had gained the first American doctorate in psychology under William James fourteen years earlier, and had founded the American Journal of Psychology in 1887. He had also been the first American to study with Wundt. There were thirty-one founder members of the APA, drawn from all over North America (Hilgard, 1978) and virtually all of them had, like Hall, worked with Wundt at Leipzig. Despite a long history of conflict between research/academic and practitioner members, sometimes resulting in the formation of rival organisations, by 1990 the APA had grown to a total membership of 108000, drawn from over 100 different countries (Fowler, 1991). Not only was the APA the first national organisation of psychologists to be established, the British and German equivalents were not formed until 1901 and 1904 respectively, but it was also founded at much the same time as national organisations of older established disciplines, such as the American Historical Association, the American Mathematical Society and the American Physical Society.

School/Educational Psychology

Psychology was first applied to education, partly because of the widespread progressive belief that educational reform was crucial for social reform, partly because of the enactment and enforcement of compulsory education laws in the United States and other countries during the late nineteenth century, which resulted in a huge expansion of school populations, and perhaps also because many of the pioneers of applied psychology, such as Hall and Lightner Witmer, had themselves been schoolteachers. The application of psychology to education took two forms, first the development of 'mental tests', and second what became known as 'experimental pedagogy' (Hearnshaw, 1987).

Mental Tests
In Britain during the 1880s Francis Galton initiated the measurement of individual differences by devising psychological tests to measure various abilities and, though trained as a physician, effectively became psychology's first practitioner (Forrest, 1981). In America mental testing was subsequently developed by James McKeen Cattell, who was the first to use the term, and by his student Edward Thorndike, by Herman Ebbinghaus, William Stern and others in Germany, and by Alfred Binet and Theodore Simon in France. Cattell, another of the pioneers of applied psychology, was the first American to gain a doctorate from Wundt's laboratory, in 1886, and also studied with Galton. He became the first psychologist to be elected to the US Academy of Sciences in 1900, and in 1921 organised the Psychological Corporation in order to promote the application of psychology.

The pressures of compulsory attendance resulted in many children attending school who had little or no previous experience of schooling, and for whom age was a poor predictor of where they should be placed within the educational system. Thus a major impetus to the growth of mental testing was the need to develop a method of classifying children in terms of their educational requirements. At first simple laboratory apparatus was used for this purpose, but in 1904 the French Ministry of Public Instruction decided to appoint a committee to inquire into the education of mentally retarded children. One consequence of this decision was that Binet was asked to devise a standard 'intelligence' test which would identify such children at an early age, so that they could receive remedial education. Various revisions of Binet and Simon's original test were made, and refinements were added by Cyril Burt and by Stern, who suggested that test scores should be expressed in the form of an intelligence quotient or IQ, the ratio of the child's 'mental age' as derived from the test score, to his or her chronological age. The Binet-Simon test, introduced to the United States by Henry Goddard, director of the Vineland Training School in New Jersey, was modified for American use by Lewis Terman, working at Stanford University in California, and the Stanford-Binet test, first produced in 1916, is still in use, albeit in revised form. As well as being used to select children for remedial education, in some countries mental tests alSo began to be used to select children for different kinds of secondary education, because tests were thought to be fairer than existing methods. In Britain, for example, mental tests were first employed for this purpose in Bradford in 1919, and Godfrey Thomson, among others, helped to refine the use of psychological tests as educational selection procedures.

Clinical Child Psychology
Following the introduction of compulsory schooling large numbers of schoolchildren were also found to be in poor health, suffering from physical or mental defects, and often presenting a variety of behavioural problems (see Fagan, 1992). In 1896 Lightner Witmer established the first psychological clinic at the University of Pennsylvania, and began to provide diagnosis, and to a lesser extent treatment, for children experiencing problems in school, who were generally referred by teachers, parents, or community agencies (see McReynolds, 1987). Witmer, who had studied with both Wundt and

Cattell, coined the term 'clinical psychologist' as a job description, although the range of services provided by Witmer and his followers was far more restricted than that provided by contemporary clinical psychologists (see Chapter 6), being mostly confined to the administration of psychological tests. Witmer's 'psychological clinic' led to the establishment of child guidance clinics, the first of which was attached to a Chicago juvenile court in 1909.

Experimental Pedagogy and Educational Research

Witmer was primarily interested in the particular problems encountered by an individual atypical child, in contrast to Hall, the leading American proponent of experimental pedagogy, who focussed on the common problems facing school-children, school administrators, teachers and parents in general (Fagan, 1992). Hall became the leader of the 'child study movement' and promoted research into child development, and methods of teaching and learning, laying the foundations of modern research in educational psychology. He also coined the term 'adolescence'. He founded an educational psychology journal, the *Pedagogical Seminary* (later the *Journal of Genetic Psychology*), in 1891 and became the first chief editor of the *Journal of Applied Psychology*, established in 1916.

Educational psychology was also the first branch of applied psychology to develop in many European countries. In Germany Ernst Meumann was an early advocate of experimental pedagogy, and like Hall founded a journal of educational psychology. Burt was appointed as the first educational psychologist in Britain by the London County Council in 1913. He promoted the development of child guidance clinics and made a number of contributions to educational testing (see Hearnshaw, 1979). The local authority psychological service was initiated in 1923 and by the 1930s the child guidance movement was well established.

Contemporary School/Educational Psychology

Currently, school psychologists in the United States are professional practitioners, who provide psychological services to the populations of schools, while educational psychologists tend to be involved in the research activities that form the knowledge base underlying professional practice. School psychologists devote over 50% of their time to assessment, over 40% to intervention and consultation, and less than 10% to research (Brown and Minke, 1986). The two major concerns of school psychology in the United States have been school learning and mental health in the schools (Bardon, 1983). Alpert (1985) quoted estimates suggesting that of the 63.4 million Americans then aged 18 and under, seven million would have major learning problems requiring educational intervention, and just over three million would have mental health problems requiring professional help. Fewer than half of those with learning problems, and only about 10% of those with mental health problems would receive the help they needed.

In Britain, educational psychologists may be either practitioners, or researchers, or both. British educational psychologists spend most of their time on individual case work (Topping, 1982), gathering information about learning and behaviour problems (see Chapters 2 and 3) of children who have been referred to them by the schools or other agencies, suggesting possible courses of intervention and, where appropriate, recommending special educational help. Educational psychologists are also involved in in-service training, providing courses for teachers on a range of psychological issues relevant to schools, and in research, evaluation and policy development. On the research side, educational psychologists can help to identify those aspects of the school environment which contribute to the effectiveness of schools, and considerable effort has been devoted to the examination of individual differences in learning, the enhancement of teaching and instructional skills, the cognitive analysis of subject–matter learning, the development of appropriate testing and assessment instruments, and the organisation, structure and management of schools (see, e.g., Glaser and Takanishi, 1986).

Occupational/Industrial Psychology

By the early 1890s William James had decided to concentrate on philosophy and recruited Hugo Munsterberg, an experimental psychologist from the University of Freiburg, and a former student of Wundt's, to succeed him as director of the psychology laboratory at Harvard. Although in Germany Munsterberg had been an active experimental psychologist, in America his interests turned towards applied psychology. An enthusiastic populariser, he attempted to increase public under-standing of psychology by organising exhibits, demonstrations and lectures at various World Fairs and Exhibitions held in the late 1890s and early 1900s. Munsterberg also had extremely varied interests. He was one of the first psychologists to consider the relation between psychology and law (see Chapter 17) and his book *On the Witness Stand* was published in 1908. Books on school psychology (*Psychology and the Teacher*, 1909) and on clinical psychology (*Psychotherapy*, 1909) soon followed. In 1913 he published one of the first textbooks on industrial psychology (*Psychology and Industrial Efficiency*), which emphasised the importance of individual differences. He divided industrial psychology into three broad areas: first, personnel selection, selecting the right person for the job through the use of psychological tests and vocational guidance; second, what would now be termed human factors or ergonomics, that is, ensuring that the individual worker's task or job was appropriately designed, that he or she was properly trained, and that the working conditions, such as lighting, ambient temperature, noise levels and so on, were optimal; and third, selling the products of work, through advertising and consumer research.

Personnel Psychology

American industrialists and managers were initially more interested in the potential contribution of applied psychology to the third of these areas, the advertising and selling of the products of industry, than in either personnel selection or work design (Rose, 1975). One of the first psychologists to apply psychology to advertising was Walter Dill Scott, who obtained his doctorate under Wundt in 1900, and eventually became President of Northwestern University in Illinois, where he had been a student. Scott published *The Psychology of Advertising* in 1908 and also directed various research projects into salesmanship. But Scott was also a keen promoter of personnel selection, and while an academic at Northwestern before the First World War provided a consultancy service for industry. His book *Personnel Management*, published in the early 1920s, went into several editions, and was still in use in the 1950s. One of Scott's most important contributions to personnel psychology was as Director of the Committee on the Classification of Personnel in the US Army during World War I, for which he received the Distinguished Service Medal (von Mayrhauser, 1989).

Scott's principal concern was to obtain results which would be of practical use to the Army and his committee devised officer promotion rating scales, developed techniques of skill assessment (producing proficiency tests for over 80 military jobs), and set up personnel departments in all US Army divisions, classifying well over three million men in the process (Driskell and Olmstead, 1989; Leahey, 1987).

The work of Scott's committee was to some extent complemented by that of a committee headed by Robert Yerkes, who, as APA president at the time America entered the war, had persuaded the Army to use mental tests in the selection of military recruits. Yerkes served as Chairman of the Psychology Committee of the US National Research Council, which put forward a plan for the psychological examination of recruits, in order to eliminate the 'mentally unfit' (Yerkes, 1918). An experimental/comparative psychologist with wide research interests, he aimed to collect scientific data on mental ability, as well as to assist the military. Although the US Army was reluctant to implement Yerkes's plan, following a pilot study it was agreed that all recruits should be psychologically tested. But since recruits were being inducted at a rate of around 180000 per month individual testing was impractical, and at Scott's suggestion Yerkes commissioned various test specialists to devise group tests of intelligence, which could be administered to large numbers of recruits simultaneously. By 1919 around 1.75 million men had taken either the newly developed Army Alpha, a verbal test of general mental ability, or the non-verbal Army Beta test, which was given to recruits whose command of English was poor. Although Scott's work was undoubtedly of greater value to the military, Yerkes's highly publicised introduction of mass psychological testing to the US Army gave a considerable boost to the standing of applied psychology.

Yet the subsequent analysis of the test results obtained from US Army inductees provoked considerable controversy, since it was discovered that the average mental age of a very large sample (c. 100000) of white American recruits was just over 13 years, well below the designated average adult mental age of 16, set by Terman in his development of the Stanford Binet intelligence test. Indeed Goddard had coined the term 'moron' to describe anyone with a mental age of less than 13 years (Leahey, 1987). Thus almost half of white American draftees would fall into this category, if the analysis and classification were to be accepted as correct. The interpretation of the US Army test results was cogently criticised by the political commentator Walter Lippman, and defended by Terman, in a long-running debate in the *New Republic* (see Block and Dworkin, 1977). But Lippman's criticisms were largely ignored, and the demand for mental testing from business and industry continued to rise. More importantly, it was also found that the test scores of immigrants were related to the number of years that they had lived in the United States, with those with less than five years' residence being classified as 'essentially feeble minded' (Kamin, 1977). Since many of those with less than five years' residence came from specific areas of Europe, and since it was assumed that intelligence tests were measuring innate mental ability, it was concluded that certain groups of immigrants were inherently intellectually inferior to 'native born' white Americans. These conclusions were reflected in the Johnson-Lodge Immigration Act of 1924, which restricted immigration by imposing quotas on particular countries, principally in South Eastern Europe.

There are now literally hundreds of psychological tests, assessing aptitudes, intelligence, interests, personality, social attitudes and so on, which are used in educational testing, personnel selection, clinical diagnosis, and for research purposes (see, e.g., Murphy and Davidshofer, 1988). Testing is thus ubiquitous; as Leahey (1987) observed, in the United States even golf pros are required to complete an aptitude test. In response to criticisms that psychological testing is susceptible to abuse and can be unduly intrusive, national psychological associations, such as the APA, have established technical and professional standards to be followed in the construction, evaluation, interpretation and application of psychological tests, and have laid down guidelines to be adopted in testing situations. Nevertheless, the debate about the social value of standardised tests, particularly intelligence tests, which erupted in the early 1970s (see Leahey, 1987), has not entirely subsided.

Productivity

In the United States the main impetus for improving methods of industrial production came initially from engineers rather than psychologists. The principal aim of 'scientific management', advocated by Frederick Taylor and others during the early 1900s, was to increase productivity and efficiency through the development of time and motion study methods and the creation of appropriate payment and production control systems. Proponents of scientific management assumed that workers should be studied as isolated units, arguing that the main factors affecting efficiency were fatigue, sub-standard environmental conditions or ineffective ways of performing the job which could be corrected by time and motion study, combined with incentive payment schemes designed to increase motivation. In essence, the scientific management movement viewed workers as 'greedy robots' impelled solely by the prospect of material gain, neglecting other potential social and psychological influences upon work output. Such influences were later given appropriate emphasis by the Australian sociologist Elton Mayo and his associates in the 'human relations school', mainly on the basis of their somewhat controversial studies conducted at the Hawthorne Electrical Works in Chicago during the 1920s and 1930s (see Rose, 1975).

   Interest in the factors affecting industrial productivity was also apparent in Europe, notably Britain and Germany, before the First World War, although the war gave a considerable impetus to this kind of research. During the war and the immediate post-war period a group of British industrial researchers emerged, known as the 'human factor movement' (see Rose, 1975), whose chief advocate was the Cambridge psychologist Charles Myers, the first president of the British Psychological Society. The industrial research conducted by members of the human factor movement, which comprised physiologists and economists as well as psychologists, primarily concerned with the physical influences on productivity and work behaviour, beginning with the effects of fatigue and hours of work on the productivity of munitions workers during World War I. In order to meet the Army's incessant demands for munitions the working hours of munitions workers had been markedly increased, to between 70 and 90 hours per week, with the result that health problems, absenteeism and accident rates all began to rise, while the quality of output fell. In the Autumn of 1915, Lloyd George, then Minister of Munitions, set up a Health of Munitions Workers Committee to investigate and advise upon health and productivity problems. Research conducted by this committee demonstrated that reductions in the length of the working day led to fewer accidents, less absenteeism and faulty work, and to higher output. These findings led to a reconceptualisation of the nature of fatigue by Myers and his colleagues (see Rose, 1975).

   Munsterberg's conception of industrial psychology was imported to Britain, and elaborated and extended, by an Australian psychologist, Bernard Muscio, who lectured in experimental psychology at Cambridge from 1914 to 1916, and in 1917 published a book, *Lectures on Industrial Psychology*, derived from a series of lectures given at the University of Sydney. Muscio came back to Britain in 1919 to work with the Industrial Fatigue Research Board, the peacetime successor to the Health of Munitions Workers Committee, but shortly afterwards returned to Australia to become professor of philosophy at Sydney, where he remained until his death in 1926, at the age of 39. Myers, who had spent much of the war in France, in charge of the British Army's psychological services, acknowledged that Muscio's book introduced him to the possibilities of industrial psychology (see Hearnshaw, 1964), which became his main professional interest. The National Institute of Industrial Psychology (NIIP) was founded in 1921, under Myers's direction, and devoted much of its research effort to the development of tests in the areas of personnel selection and guidance. Although it was later to be overtaken by more successful commercial rivals (Tizard, 1976), the NIIP also provided a consultancy service for industrial companies, business organisations and government departments, implemented an educational programme, and from 1922 published a journal, now known as the *Journal of Occupational Psychology*. Other research on industrial psychology was carried out by the Industrial Fatigue Research Board (IFRB), which had close links with the NIIP. The IFRB continued and expanded its earlier investigations of the physical aspects of work, such as lighting, environmental temperature, monotony, fatigue, the determination of the optimal length of the work spell so as to ensure maximum output, as well as the optimal number of rest pauses and their distribution through the work period (see Rose, 1975).

Contemporary Occupational/Industrial Psychology
In his inaugural address to the Industrial Section of the British Psychological Society in 1919, six years after Munsterberg's textbook on industrial psychology had been published, Myers identified four main areas in which psychology could be applied to industry: 'fatigue, movement, vocational guidance and management' (see Myers, 1920). Although much of the terminology has changed considerably, these areas still account for a large proportion of the activities of contemporary occupational/ industrial psychologists. While research on fatigue continues (see Craig and Cooper, 1992) the area has been somewhat eclipsed by that of occupational stress (Keita and Jones, 1990), and there is growing interest in techniques of occupational stress management and mental health counselling in industry (Murphy, 1984; Swanson and Murphy, 1991). The study of movement, which formed the basis of time and motion study, has diminished in importance and has been absorbed into the domain of ergonomics or human factors, an area broadly concerned with the relationship between individuals and their working environments (Murrell, 1965) and covering a wide range of issues bearing upon human-machine interaction and job design (Megaw, 1991). Much human-machine interaction in the current working environment involves information technology systems (see Chapter 13). Applied cognitive psychology, which has close links with ergonomics (see Chapter 12), has become a growth area in recent years, stimulated by work on a number of problems of attention, memory, decision-making and stress conducted by Broadbent and others at the Applied Psychology Unit in Cambridge, and by work on skill and human performance carried out by Fitts, Posner, Anderson and others in the United States, and by Bartlett, Craik, Welford and others, also at Cambridge. Occupational psychologists remain heavily

involved in the administration, analysis and interpretation of tests and other procedures for the purposes of personnel selection and assessment and occupational guidance and counselling (see Chapters 8 and 9), and in the development of training programmes and instructional systems (see Chapter 10). Many areas of psychology impinge on management, but 'management psychology' is perhaps best encapsulated in the terms 'organisational psychology' or 'organisational behaviour', discussed in Chapter 11.

Military Psychology

Partly as a result of its contribution to the selection and classification of army recruits in World War I, for a brief period in the 1920s psychology enjoyed considerable public esteem in the United States, with numerous articles about its achievements and potential appearing in popular magazines (see Benjamin, 1986). The demand for psychological services became so great that qualified psychologists were unable to meet it, and in consequence people without psychological training also began to offer such services. This inevitably led to some disillusionment, doubts were expressed by psychologists and others about the value of applied psychology to society, and public enthusiasm proved to be short-lived. Psychology did not escape the high levels of unemployment resulting from the Depression of the 1930s and the American psychological establishment became polarised between the 'restrictivists', who favoured a reduction in the supply of psychologists, and the 'expansionists', who supported an increase in the number of opportunities for employment (see Finison, 1976). The APA eventually adopted an expansionist programme just before the outbreak of the Second World War, and established an emergency committee to plan psychology's role in the war effort. Thus even before the United States formally entered the conflict, after the Japanese attack on Pearl Harbor in December, 1941, American psychologists had begun to mobilise themselves for the task ahead, in part because they believed that the expertise they could now offer to a variety of military areas would not only help to win the war, but would also enhance the status of psychology and shape future developments in the discipline. Certainly the potential applications of psychology became even more widely recognised during World War II, and between 1943 and 1945, about 1000 psychologists in America (about a quarter of the total) were working on some aspect of military psychology (Driskell and Olmstead, 1989). Moreover, psychology was the only social science to be cited as a 'critical profession' by the US War Department (Leahey, 1987).

The US military began World War II using essentially the same selection and classification tests that had been employed in World War I, even though much progress had been made in developing personnel selection tests for industry during the 1920s and 1930s. Procedures for the selection of military personnel were soon improved and refined, however, and extended from the army to the US Navy and Air Force. Britain also began to use selection procedures for officer candidates, and War Office Selection Boards were established in 1942. A significantly higher proportion of candidates selected in this way successfully completed officer training courses (Vernon and Parry, 1949).

Technological advances during the 1920s and 1930s meant that many new and highly complex weapons systems had been developed which military personnel had to be trained to operate effectively. Problems of human performance in relation to the operation of complex weapons systems first became apparent during the Second World War and significant attempts were made to solve them through improvements in equipment design and in training procedures (see Watson, 1978). Many prominent American social psychologists also became involved in war-related research during the Second World War, conducting the first extensive studies of military leadership, and of soldiers' behaviour during combat (for example, the *American Soldier* studies, subsequently summarised in the four-volume *Studies in Social Psychology* in World War II; see eg, Stouffer *et al*, 1949a, 1949b). The *American Soldier* studies systematically investigated soldiers' attitudes to various aspects of military life, with the aim of improving the formulation of US Army policy. Studies of combat behaviour in World War II also showed that relatively small numbers of soldiers, typically about 15% of company strength, actually opened fire on the enemy, even though those who did not fire exposed themselves to as much danger as those who did. The percentage of soldiers who opened fire was unaffected by the type of military action or by its duration, and in repeated actions the same soldiers tended to open fire (see Watson, 1978). Social psychological studies were also undertaken of the effects of strategic bombing raids on German civilian morale, which indicated that morale was most adversely affected by irregular moderate bombing rather than by regular heavy bombing raids. Other social psychologists were engaged on studies of the German national character and the appeal of Nazism, and of the personality of Adolf Hitler (see Hoffman, 1992).

The attempts to enhance the status of psychology during World War II and, at the same time, to set the agenda for post-war developments in the discipline were undoubtedly successful, particularly in the United States. Military psychology has developed considerably since 1945 and "has become a fully institutionalized part of the military community" (Driskell and Olmstead, 1989, p. 43). It has also exerted an important influence upon the growth of human factors and systems psychology, instructional psychology and personnel psychology, whose applications extend far beyond the military sphere. Funding for university-based research in applied psychology is also provided from military sources. The Second World War also radically altered the nature of clinical psychology, which during the 1920s and 1930s, still largely consisted of test administration and interpretation, and whose practitioners were effectively second-class citizens within the APA, being restricted to associate rather than full membership, which remained the prerogative of academic psychologists.

Clinical Psychology

The scientific study of psychopathology began in 19th century France with the work of Charcot, Taine and Ribot, which was continued in the early years of this century by Dumas and Janet (see Hearnshaw, 1987). A major theoretical and therapeutic advance was provided by Freud's system of psychoanalysis, which was continually being revised and extended until Freud's death in 1939. Freud's system influenced the development of a number of different psychodynamic approaches to the diagnosis and treatment of mental disorders. But until the Second World War the diagnosis and treatment of the 'mentally ill' remained almost exclusively the province of medicine, particularly psychiatry. Though proponents of the 'medical model' of mental illness emphasised biological and physical influences as causative factors, and preferred to adopt physical methods of treatment, such as drug therapies or brain surgery, some psychiatrists were sympathetic to psychodynamic approaches. In both the United States and Britain during the 1920s and 1930s clinical psychologists worked primarily with children, in child guidance clinics, and were very rarely involved in the assessment of adults. Adult psychotherapy was not considered to be part of the clinical psychologist's repertoire.

American clinical psychology was decisively changed first by a 1944 alteration to the APA membership rules, inspired by Robert Yerkes, which gave clinical and other professional psychologists full membership status, and at least for a time smoothed over the divisions which had arisen between practitioners and academics during the 1930s. Second, the return of some 16 million service personnel, including perhaps 100000 'psychiatric casualties' of the war (Peterson, 1991), necessitated urgent action by the US government, as part of its effort to ease the transition from military to civilian life. The Veterans Administration was responsible for supplying the psychological services that ex-service personnel required, and since many veterans, traumatised by war, were in need of psychotherapy, clinical psychologists were deputed to provide it. As few clinical psychologists were trained in psychotherapy the US government began to support training programmes in clinical and counselling psychology. Since the financial incentives were large, the universities, together with the APA, soon began to agree on what the objectives of such programmes should be, and what their curricula should contain (Peterson, 1991). At a conference held in Boulder, Colorado, in 1949, the 'scientist–practitioner' model of education for professional practice in psychology was adopted, and this model, despite the criticisms which have been made of it, has remained dominant ever since (O'Sullivan and Quevillon, 1992). With a generally accepted training model for professional psychologists in place, a major barrier to the expansion of applied psychology in the human services field was removed.

Currently, clinical and counselling psychologists tend to be involved in assessment, therapy, research and teaching (see Chapters 4, 5 and 6), though as the profession has developed, there has been a gradual shift away from providing assessments based on psychological test profiles, for use in diagnosis, toward therapy, and more recently, prevention and primary care. Since the 1940s, when psychodynamically oriented systems predominated, the number of therapies has proliferated, and clinical and counselling psychologists have become much more eclectic in their deployment of different therapeutic approaches. Moreover, while clinical psychology's main priority is mental health, there has been increasing interest in the behavioural factors affecting physical health and illness, and in interventions that may help to prevent disease and to promote and maintain health (see Chapter 16). There is also a sizeable research literature concerned with the vast range of behavioural problems that can arise from brain injury, such as disorders of language production and comprehension, of object recognition, and of memory (see Chapter 7).

THE GROWTH OF PROFESSIONAL PSYCHOLOGY

The unprecedented period of economic growth and restructuring that followed the Second World War provided abundant employment opportunities in the service sector, particularly for professional, scientific and technical workers, as expenditure on research and development rose dramatically. The demand for higher education increased and the universities expanded rapidly, with the student population in both Britain and America virtually quadrupling between 1945 and 1970. Psychology benefited greatly from this expansion, especially in the United States, where the number of qualified psychologists increased by 435% (from 17000 to 91000) between 1960 and 1979, a growth rate over four times as great as that for professional and technical workers as a whole (Pion and Lipsey, 1984). Until the early 1970s the major emphasis of American doctoral training programmes was academic research, although since then the number of doctorates awarded in this subfield of psychology has been far outstripped by the number awarded in the health service provider subfields, that is clinical, counselling and school psychology (Howard *et al.*, 1986). The most important development in applied psychology since 1945 has been the growth of professional psychology: as Benjamin (1986) observed, with reference to the United States, the work carried out by psychologists during the Second World War "changed the face of psychology forever, essentially establishing psychology as a profession that could thrive outside the halls of academe" (p. 945).

According to Ardila (1982a), "Psychology is now a profession that can be found in the list of occupations of almost any country, with the possible exception of some of the newer African nations" (p. 324). The number of psychologists in a particular country is likely to be related to the available opportunities for education, training and employment (Connolly, 1986). These will depend, at least to some extent, on the level of national wealth, since in most countries the activities of the majority of psychologists are publicly funded, as well as on historical and cultural factors which determine the public image of psychology and the priorities accorded to psychological services. Not surprisingly, therefore, the ratio of qualified psychologists to population is higher in rich than in poor countries and the growth of professional psychology has been especially vigorous in those countries where psychology was already well established before the Second World War. The professionalisation of psychology has progressed furthest in North America, Western Europe, Australasia and Israel, where the ratio of professional psychologists to population is among the highest in the world (Ben-Ari and Amir, 1986). But the memberships of national psychological organisations have also grown rapidly in a number of developing countries, such as the Dominican Republic and the Philippines (Rosenzweig, 1984).

Psychology as a profession

Perhaps the most important characteristic of a profession is 'the availability of a useful, communicable technology based in a reasonably coherent intellectual discipline' (Peterson, 1976a p. 572). The knowledge base underpinning professional psychology is derived from basic and applied research, and professional psychology also involves the application of a wide variety of techniques and skills, ranging from those involved in the design of working environments to the provision of guidance, therapy and counselling. Well established professions have carved out for themselves particular areas of expertise, for which they alone are responsible. Medicine, for example, is primarily concerned with the diagnosis, treatment, and prevention of illness. The profession of psychology has been defined as "the profession dealing with the problems of human coping effectiveness" (Fox, Barclay and Rogers, 1982, p. 308) and as being principally "concerned with the assessment and improvement of the psychological functioning of human beings as individuals, in groups and in social organisations" (Peterson, 1976b, p. 793). But the contrast between the position of psychology in society and that of medicine has been likened to that between the underdeveloped Countries of the third world and the major industrial powers (Tizard, 1976), and even in rich countries such as the United States and Germany physicians heavily outnumber professional psychologists (see Chapter 18).

Although in the past 15 years or so public opinion seems to have become gradually more aware of what psychologists do, the public image of psychology as a profession is somewhat confused, and the public perception of the scope of psychological activities is relatively narrow. The general public is largely ignorant of the nature of psychology as taught in first degree courses (Rose and Radford, 1986) and even prospective psychology students are not much better informed (Smith and Casbolt, 1984). Moreover, most people's experience of the impact of professional psychology is confined to the mental health services (Wood, Jones and Benjamin, 1986) and this perspective is reinforced by films and television programmes (Fishman and Neigher, 1982). Thus despite attempts to 'give psychology away', as advocated by Miller (1969), a view which is not without its critics (Koch, 1980), "the public does not appear to have the understanding of psychologists' activities and their potential impact that most psychologists would desire" (Wood *et al.*, 1986, p. 952).

Since professional work has principally practical objectives, almost all professions are regulated by professional associations or societies which function as 'gatekeepers' to the profession, determining the qualifications for entry, accrediting training programmes and implementing standards of ethical conduct and professional practice. Furthermore, in many professions, the professional title is legally protected. As the number of professional psychologists has grown, some countries, prompted by their national psychological associations, have introduced either certification laws, which limit the use of the professional title 'psychologist' to those with approved qualifications, or licensing laws, which not only regulate the use of the title, but also define the range of activities constituting the practice of psychology. A few countries have introduced both types of legislation. Although certification and licensure are primarily intended to provide protection for consumers of psychological services against fraud and unethical practice, some reservations have been expressed about their implications for the development of psychology as a profession (see, e.g., Danish and Smyer, 1981). Although at present relatively few countries have certification laws, and even fewer have licensing laws (see Fischer and Wittchen, 1980; Mcpherson, 1986), the adoption of one or other or both types of legislation seems certain to become more widespread.

The Training and Employment of Professional Psychologists

Training: Psychology graduates wishing to become professional psychologists usually specialise in one of the major branches of professional psychology, such as clinical psychology, educational or school psychology, or occupational/industrial psychology, although the demand for places on postgraduate training courses generally exceeds the supply. In Britain, for example, fewer than a quarter of psychology graduates are able to obtain professional training in psychology, or to become professional psychologists without a formal training course (Mcpherson, 1986; Rose and Radford, 1986). The availability, quality and duration of such courses vary from country to country

(Fichter and Wittchen, 1980), some being solely practitioner programmes while others also involve training in research skills, and the qualifications awarded upon the satisfactory completion of training differ too. Internationally, the most frequent qualification held by psychologists is the master's degree or its equivalent (Rosenzweig, 1992), and master's level courses are likely to require a dissertation and to emphasise methodological and statistical skills. Progress towards developing international standards for training in professional psychology has been slow, partly because of the wide variation in cultural and sociopolitical backgrounds among professional psychologists operating in different regions of the world (Nixon, 1990).

The distribution of professional psychologists: Internationally, psychologists are more likely to be employed in the provision of health services, either in the public or the private sector, than in any other employment setting. In the great majority of cases, psychologists working as 'health services providers' will be qualified as clinical psychologists. Clinical psychology is thus the largest area of specialisation within professional psychology, although there are considerable variations across countries in the ratio of clinical psychologists to population (Fichter and Wittchen, 1980). In Western Europe, the highest ratios of clinical psychologists to population are to be found in the Netherlands and the Nordic countries, where clinical psychologists comprise between 60% and 70% of all professional psychologists. This percentage is probably somewhat greater in the United States. But in some countries, such as Israel, the numbers of clinical and educational psychologists are about the same, and in others, such as Luxembourg, most professional psychologists work in the education services. In Belgium too, which has about 5000 professional psychologists, school psychology is the oldest and most familiar form of professional psychology (Richelle, Janssen and Brédart, 1992). In most countries the number of occupational/industrial psychologists tends to be smaller than the number of clinical or educational psychologists, and they are likely to be employed in a wider variety of settings, ranging from private practice as industrial or management consultants to working as personnel or human factors specialists either for industrial or commercial organisations, or for government agencies. In Latin America, however, government agencies, industry and commerce between them employ about 40% of all psychologists, a greater percentage than is found in the health or education services (Ardila, 1982b).

The role of research
There are now twice as many psychologists world wide as there were a decade ago (Rosenzweig, 1992), yet as psychology continues to expand, the gap between academics and practitioners continues to widen. While professional psychology is booming, especially in the health service provider fields, academic research in psychology is in relative decline, and fears have been expressed that if present trends are maintained the research base on which professional psychology depends may be gradually eroded (see Rosenzweig, 1992). One reason for the relative decline of academic research is obvious, the contraction of research funding, which affects all disciplines, not merely psychology, although psychological research is unlikely to be prioritised with respect to the distribution of scarce resources. Because research scholarships are severely limited, fewer psychology graduates are able or willing to register for higher degrees, thereby acquiring further training in research skills. Another is the increasing teaching and administrative workload encountered by

academics in many countries, as governments seek to raise participation rates in higher education without providing appropriate levels of financial support. A third is a possible change in the population of psychology students, the source of tomorrow's academic researchers and professional psychologists. Psychology remains a popular subject at first degree level, but there are indications that its appeal as a scientific discipline is on the wane. On the basis of several studies of British psychology students, Radford (1992) suggested that the "modal psychology student is female, 18 plus, and hoping to do some kind of caring work with people, often specifically clinical psychology. She likes social, developmental and abnormal/clinical psychology, and dislikes statistics and theoretical issues... She does not think... that psychology is very relevant to herself, nor is she interested in it 'as a science'" (p. 274). If this analysis is correct, then it appears that academic research has few attractions for the majority of psychology undergraduates, at least in Britain. Radford also suggested that male students, particularly those who have studied psychology at 'A' level, are more likely to be interested in psychology as a science, and pointed out that in the United States over the period 1974–1984 the number of psychology graduates fell by 20%, almost all of the reduction being attributable to a decline in the number of male graduates.

For the time being, however, applied psychologists continue to make significant contributions to research, not only in the existing core areas of professional psychology but also by accumulating knowledge which may provide the basis of future areas of professional practice, such as economic psychology (see Chapter 14), environmental psychology (see Chapter 15) and psychology and law (see Chapter 17). Additionally, applied psychologists have begun to contribute to interdisciplinary research on important societal problems such as global environmental change (see Stern, 1992, for a comprehensive overview) and the prevention, etiology and treatment of acquired immune deficiency syndrome (AIDS; see Morin, 1988; Pelosi, 1988). Much applied psychological research is relevant to issues of public policy, such as environmental issues (Fischoff, 1990), health care issues (Kiesler and Morton, 1988) and issues relating to children and families (Gallagher, 1990). Policies adopted by public decision makers determine the allocation of societal resources, and the interests of many disparate groups have to be carefully balanced. In addition, policy decisions often have to be made over a relatively short time span. Any information which reduces the chances of the wrong decision being made, however marginally, is likely to be highly relevant to the policy making process, particularly if an estimate of its reliability can be given, if it can be provided quickly, and if it can be tailored to fit the particular issue under consideration.

Ruback and Innes (1988) examined the factors determining whether psychological research is relevant to policy decisions, and whether its findings are likely to be used by policy makers, focussing on the issue of prison crowding. They pointed out that this issue has been the subject of much psychological research, and a number of policy decisions have been taken, but research and policy making remain largely independent of one another. Ruback and Innes suggested that the relevance of psychological research can be conceptualised in terms of two dimensions, first the number of policy variables investigated and second the usefulness of the dependent measures from the practitioners' point of view. Policy variables can in principle be controlled by policy makers, though various constraints may operate in practice; in the context of prison crowding examples of policy variables would be prison cell size and the number of inmates per cell. Dependent measures are more likely to be useful if they can be applied directly to the policy maker's situation and if they are taken at the system rather than at the individual level; examples of 'useful' dependent measures would be morbidity and mortality rates. Relevant research thus investigates the effects of one or more policy variables upon high utility dependent measures.

A criticism of relevant research is that the pursuit of relevance may result in psychological investigations dissolving into political activism or social engineering (Walker, 1970). But, as Leahey (1987) observed, psychology has always "perched awkwardly astride the dividing line between science and morals – between what is . . . and what ought to be"(p. 478). Political activism and social engineering are two extreme forms of asserting a set of moral values. Moreover, as Ruback and Innes (1988) acknowledged, investigations of issues such as prison crowding cannot be regarded as 'value free', since the attitudes and values of individual researchers determine both the nature of the research carried out and the uses to which any results are put. They also suggested that some investigators may in fact be deterred from conducting relevant research because of potential conflicts between their attitudes and values and the implications of any data they might obtain (see also Scarr, 1988). As a British philosopher/psychologist observed nearly 50 years ago, psychologists, unlike other scientists, cannot maintain 'a state of complete political neutrality' (Mace, 1946). The investigation of how people behave in particular situations inevitably leads to questions about the effects of situational influences upon behaviour, and in many applied psychological investigations sociocultural and political influences are likely to be relevant.

Much of psychology's effort to promote human welfare is concentrated on producing change in the individual, rather than in social conditions, even though social conditions presumably exert at least some effect on individual behaviour. The notion of the 'individual' may also be more important in some cultures than in others (Bloom, 1982). Furthermore, the views of 'human nature' advanced by some schools of psychological thought seem to offer little prospect for changing it, except perhaps in superficial ways. For example, Schwartz (1986), in a discussion of the portrayals of human nature given by economics, evolutionary biology and behavioural psychology, concluded that all three disciplines ultimately equate human nature with the pursuit of self interest, while also implying that human nature is fixed and immutable. Schwartz argued that these views arise through mistakenly treating "the particular social conditions in which we live as representative of the universal human condition. As a result, they have mistaken local and historical truths about people for natural laws. As a further result they have helped contribute to the perpetuation of these conditions by appealing to their natural inevitability" (p. 312). Similarly, Prilleltensky (1989) suggested that through its emphasis on the individual, psychology may well be "hindering the betterment of social conditions by guarding the interests of the status quo" (p. 795). Some of these issues are further discussed in Chapter 18, which considers possible futures for applied psychology.

REFERENCES

J.L. Alpert (1985). Change within a profession: Change, future, prevention, and school psychology. *American Psychologist*, **40**, 1112–1121.

R. Ardila (1982a). International psychology. *American Psychologist*, **37**, 323–329.

R. Ardila (1982b). Psychology in Latin America today. *Annual Review of Psychology*, **33**, 103–122.

J.I. Bardon (1983). Psychology applied to education: A speciality in search of an identity. *American Psychologist*, **38**, 185–196.

A. Baum & S.E.A. Nesselhoff (1988). Psychological research and the prevention, etiology, and treatment of AIDS. *American Psychologist*, **43**, 900–906.

E. Belbin (1979). Applicable psychology and some natural problems: A synopsis of the 1978 Myers lecture. *Bulletin of the British Psychological Society*, **32**, 241–244.

R. Ben-Ari & Y. Amir (1986). Psychology in a developing country: The case of Israel. *Annual Review of Psychology*, **37**, 17–41.

L. Benjamin (1986). Why don't they understand me? A history of psychology's public image. *American Psychologist*, **41**, 941–946.

J. Beloff (1973). *Psychological Sciences: A review of modern psychology*. London: Crosby Lockwood Staples.

W. Bevan (1982). A sermon of sorts in three plus parts. *American Psychologist*, **37**, 1303–1322.

N. Block and G. Dworkin (Editors) (1977). *The IQ controversy*. London: Quartet Books.

L. Bloom (1982). Applying psychology in the third world. *Bulletin of the British Psychological Society*, **35**, 143–146.

D.T. Brown & K.M. Minke (1986). School psychology graduate training. *American Psychologist*, **41**, 1328–1338.

J.S. Bruner & G.W. Allport (1940). Fifty years of change in American psychology. *Psychological Bulletin*, **37**, 757–766.

K. Connolly (1986). Psychology and the third world: A commentary on Moghaddan and Taylor. *Bulletin of the British Psychological Society*, **39**, 8–11.

A. Craig & R.E. Cooper (1992). Symptoms of acute and chronic fatigue. In A.P. Smith & D.M. Jones (Editors), *Handbook of human performance, Volume 3, State and Trait*. London: Academic Press.

S.J. Danish & M.A. Smyer (1981). License to help. *American Psychologist*, **36**, 13–21.

J.E. Driskell & B. Olmsted (1989). Psychology and the military: Research applications and trends. *American Psychologist*, **44**, 43–54.

T.K. Fagan (1992). Compulsory schooling, child study, clinical psychology, and special education: Origins of school psychology. *American Psychologist*, **47**, 236–243.

M.M. Fichter & H.U. Wittchen (1980). Clinical psychology and psychotherapy: A survey of the present state of professionalization in 23 countries. *American Psychologist*, **35**, 16–25.

L.J. Finison (1976). Unemployment, politics, and the history of organized psychology. *American Psychologist*, **31**, 747–755.

B. Fischoff (1990). Psychology and public policy: Tool or toolmaker? *American Psychologist*, **45**, 647–653.

D.B. Fishman & W.D. Neigher (1982). American psychology in the eighties: Who will buy? *American Psychologist*, **37**, 533–546.

D.W. Forrest (1981). *Francis Galton: The Life and work of a Victorian genius*. London: Elek Books.

R.D. Fowler (1991). Report of the Chief Executive Officer: A year of achievement. *American Psychologist*, **46**, 667–672.

R.E. Fox, A.G. Barclay & D.A. Rogers (1982). The foundations of professional psychology. *American Psychologist*, **37**, 306–312.

J.J. Gallagher (1990). Emergence of policy studies and policy institutes. *American Psychologist*, **45**, 1316–1318.

R. Glaser & R. Takanishi (1986). Creating a knowledge base for education: Psychology's contributions and prospects. *American Psychologist*, **41**, 1025–1028.

L.S. Hearnshaw (1964). *A short history of British psychology, 1840–1940*. London: Methuen.

L.S. Hearnshaw (1979). *Cyril Burt, Psychologist*. London: Hodder and Stoughton.

L.S. Hearnshaw (1987). *The shaping of modern psychology: An historical introduction*. London: Routledge.

E.R. Hilgard (1978). *American psychology in historical perspective: Addresses of the Presidents of the American Psychological Association 1892–1977*. Washington, DC: American Psychological Association.

L.E. Hoffman (1992). American psychologists and wartime research on Germany, 1941–1945. *American Psychologist*, **47**, 264–273.

A. Howard, G.M. Pion, G.D. Gottfredson, P.E. Flattau, S. Oskamp, S. Plaffin, D.W. Bray & A.D. Burstein (1986). The changing face of American psychology: A report from the Committee on Employment and Human Resources. *American Psychologist*, **41**, 1211–1327.

W. James (1890). *Principles of psychology* (2 volumes). New York: Holt.

L. Kamin (1977). *The science and politics of IQ*. Harmondsworth: Penguin Books.

G.P. Keita and J.M. Jones (1990). Reducing adverse reaction to stress in the workplace: Psychology's expanding role. *American Psychologist*, **45**, 1137–1141.

C.A. Kiesler & T.L. Morton (1988). Psychology and public policy in the "Health care revolution". *American Psychologist*, **43**, 993–1003.

G. Kimble (1984). Psychology's two cultures. *American Psychologist*, **39**, 833–839.

S. Koch (1980). Psychology and its human clientele: Beneficiaries or victims? In R.A. Kasschau & F.S. Kessel (Editors), *Psychology and society: In search of symbiosis*. New York: Holt, Rinehart & Winston.

S. Koch (1981). The nature and limits of psychological knowledge. *American Psychologist*, **36**, 257–269.

S. Koch & D.E. Leary (Editors) (1985). *A century of psychology as science*. New York: McGraw Hill.

T.H. Leahey (1987). *A history of psychology: Main currents in psychological thought* (Second edition). Englewood Cliffs, N.J.: Prentice Hall.

C.A. Mace (1946). Democracy as a problem in social psychology. Reprinted in M. Mace (Editor), (1973), *C.A. Mace: Selected papers*. London: Methuen.

F. McPherson (1986). The professional psychologist in Europe. *American Psychologist*, **41**, 302–305.

P. McReynolds (1987). Lightner Witmer: Little-known founder of clinical psychology. *American Psychologist*, **42**, 849–858.

E.D. Megaw (1991). Ergonomics: Trends and influences. In C.L. Cooper & I.T. Robertson (Editors), *International Review of Industrial and Organizational Psychology 1991, Volume 6*. Chichester: Wiley.

D. Middleton & D. Edwards (1985). Pure and applied psychology: Re-examining the relationship. *Bulletin of the British Psychological Society*, **38**, 146–150.

G.A. Miller (1969). Psychology as a means of promoting human welfare. *American Psychologist*, **24**, 1063–1075.

S.F. Morin (1988). AIDS: The challenge to psychology. *American Psychologist*, **43**, 838–842.

H. Munsterberg (1908). *On the witness stand*. New York: Clark Boardman.

H. Munsterberg (1909). *Psychology and the teacher*. New York: Moffat Yard.

H. Munsterberg (1909). *Psychotherapy*. New York: Moffat Yard.

H. Munsterberg (1913). *Psychology and industrial efficiency*. New York: Houghton.

K.R. Murphy & C.O. Davidshofer (1988). *Psychological testing: Principles and applications*. Englewood Cliffs, N.J.: Prentice Hall.

L.R. Murphy (1984). Occupational stress management: A review and appraisal. *Journal of Occupational Psychology*, **57**, 1–15.

K.F.H. Murrell (1965). *Ergonomics*. London: Chapman and Hall.

B. Muscio (1917). *Lectures on industrial psychology*. New York: Dutton.

C.S. Myers (1920). Psychology and industry. *British Journal of Psychology*, **10**, 177–182.

M. Nixon (1990). Professional training in psychology: Quest for international standards. *American Psychologist*, **45**, 1257–1262.

J.J. O'Sullivan & R.P. Quevillon (1992). 40 years later: Is the Boulder model still alive? *American Psychologist*, **47**, 67–70.

D.R. Peterson (1976a). Is psychology a profession? *American Psychologist*, **31**, 572–581.

D.R. Peterson (1976b). Need for the doctor of psychology degree in professional psychology. *American Psychologist*, **31**, 792–798.

D.R. Peterson (1991). Connection and disconnection of research and practice in the education of professional psychologists. *American Psychologist*, **46**, 422–429.

G.M. Pion & M.W. Lipsey (1984). Psychology and society: The challenge of change. *American Psychologist*, **39**, 739–754.

I. Prilleltensky (1989). Psychology and the status quo. *American Psychologist*, **44**, 795–802.

J. Radford (1992). The undergraduate curriculum in psychology. *The Psychologist*, **5**, 273–276.

M. Richelle, P. Janssen and S. Bredart (1992). Psychology in Belgium. *Annual Review of Psychology*, **43**, 505–529.

D. Rose & J. Radford (1986). The unemployment of psychology graduates. *Bulletin of the British Psychological Society*, **39**, 451–456.

M. Rose (1975). *Industrial behaviour: Theoretical development since Taylor.* London: Allen Lane.

M. Rosenzweig (1984). US psychology and world psychology. *American Psychologist*, **39**, 877–884.

M.R. Rosenzweig (1992). Psychological science around the world. *American Psychologist*, **47**, 718–722.

P.H. Rossi & J.D. Wright (1984). Evaluation research: An assessment. *Annual Review of Sociology*, **10**, 333–352.

R.B. Ruback & C.A. Innes (1988). The relevance and irrelevance of psychological research: The example of prison crowding. *American Psychologist*, **43**, 683–693.

S. Scarr (1988). Race and gender as psychological variables: Social and ethical issues. *American Psychologist*, **43**, 56–59.

B. Schwartz (1986). *The battle for human nature: Science, morality and modern life.* New York: Norton.

W.D. Scott (1908). *The psychology of advertising.* Boston: Small, Maynard.

W.D. Scott & R.C. Clothier (1923). *Personnel management.* Chicago: Shaw.

P.K. Smith & D. Casbolt (1984). Sixth formers and psychology: Fifteen years on. *Bulletin of the British Psychological Society*, **37**, 334–337.

P.C. Stern (1992). Psychological dimensions of global environmental change. *Annual Review of Psychology*, **43**, 269–302.

S.A. Stouffer, A.A. Lumsdaine, M.H. Lumsdaine, R.M. Williams, M.B. Smith, I.L. Janis, S.A. Star and L.S. Cottrell (1949a). *The American soldier: Combat and its aftermath.* Princeton, N: Princeton University Press.

S.A. Stouffer, E.A. Suchman, L.C. DeVinney, S.A. Star & R.M. Williams (1949b). *The American soldier: Adjustment during army life.* Princeton, NJ: Princeton University Press.

N.G. Swanson & L.R. Murphy (1991). Mental health counselling in industry. In C.L. Cooper & I.T. Robertson (Editors). *International Review of Industrial and Organizational Psychology 1991, Volume 6.* Chichester: Wiley.

J. Tizard (1976). Psychology and social policy. *Bulletin of the British Psychological Society*, **38**, 9–13.

K. Topping (1991). Psychology at work in education. In S. Canter & D. Canter (Editors), *Psychology in practice: Perspectives on professional psychology.* Chichester: Wiley.

R.T. von Mayrhauser (1989). Making intelligence functional: Walter Dill Scott and applied psychological testing in World War I. *Journal of the History of the Behavioral Sciences*, **25**, 60–72.

P.E. Vernon & J.B. Parry (1949). *Personnel selection in the British Forces.* London: University of London Press.

E.L. Walker (1970). Relevant psychology is a snark. *American Psychologist*, **25**, 1081–1086.

P. Watson (1978). *War on the mind: The military uses and abuses of psychology*. Harmondsworth: Penguin Books.

R.I. Watson (1968). *The great psychologists: Aristotle to Freud* (2nd edition). Philadelphia: Lippincott.

F.N. Watts (1984). Applicable research in the NHS. *Bulletin of the British Psychological Society*, **37**, 41–42.

W. Wood, M. Jones & L.T. Benjamin (1986). Surveying psychology's public image. *American Psychologist*, **41**, 947–953.

R.M. Yerkes (1918). Psychology in relation to the war. *Psychological Review*, **25**, 85–115.

2

THE CHILD AS LEARNER

C.M. HICKS AND P.C. SPURGEON

Psychology has made a significant contribution to educational practice in a wide variety of areas, for example in providing a knowledge-base for the principles of learning and teaching, as well as for child development, group and individual differences and the basis of measurement and evaluation. Consequently, the topic of educational psychology is diverse and extensively researched, factors which make its condensation into two chapters a difficult objective to achieve. This chapter will focus on the child in the learning process, with a consideration of some of the psychological models of this process and of other salient influences on individual school performance, while the main emphasis of the next chapter will be the wider context of learning, in particular the teacher and the school.

Central to the whole of the educational process is the child and the fundamental purpose of a child's attendance at school is to learn. While few would disagree with this, there is considerable dissent as to what should be learned and how. While much of this debate rests on the prevailing educational and political philosophy of the time (see Cosin, Flude and Hales, 1989), there is an almost universal and perpetual concern with the efficacy of the education process in teaching a child whatever is deemed necessary. Consequently, a considerable amount of research has been devoted to identifying those factors which facilitate learning and those which impede it.

While the teacher and the wider social and educational context play a salient role in determining the effectiveness of the learning process, it is the child with all the attendant individual characteristics who inevitably is the key figure. However, the current perspective on the psychology of learning is shifting away from the Piagetian view of the child as a solitary scientist, formulating and testing hypotheses about the world, to a perspective embedded in a social-interactional context, with the child learning through a complex system of interrelationships with peers, teachers and family (see Light, Sheldon and Woodhead 1991 for a review).

This chapter will consider a number of these issues: cognitive development and the learning process as distinct entities, the former being concerned with the maturational changes in physical and neural structures on which the learning process depends to a large extent; basic cognitive abilities, and group and individual differences in these. In this way, the shift in emphasis from the traditional solitary view of the learner to the social–interactional perspective will be traced.

The Development of Children's Cognitive Abilities

Undoubtedly, much contemporary thinking in education has been fundamentally influenced by Piaget's theory of cognitive development. While his work has been criticised largely on methodological grounds, there is little doubt that his epistemological approach has had an enduring and widespread impact on educational practices. In essence, Piaget's theory suggests that humans progress through four clearly identifiable stages in cognitive development from birth to maturity, each one characterised by a set of qualitative behaviours which are the product of underlying cognitive structures. Relatively little emphasis is placed on the role of social and cultural factors in this process (Piaget, 1970).

Piaget's highly complex theory of cognitive development centres on the notion that an individual continually strives to understand the world through a process of constructing and reconstructing their experiences of it, and that successful adaptation to this world is dependent on achieving a satisfactory equilibrium between the person and their environment. Basically, Piaget suggests that the invariant sequence of stages of cognitive development, through which all individuals pass, corresponds to changes in intellectual structures. These structures are mental operations, called schemata, which can be applied to any idea or event. The schemata develop and change because of the interplay of two adaptive procedures – assimilation and accommodation.

Assimilation is construed as a process by which the individual makes sense of experiences by incorporating them into their existing cognitive structures, while accommodation is a process by which the cognitive structure is altered to fit new experiences. Through this interactive procedure, the development of understanding occurs.

The first stage in this sequence of development is called the *Sensori–motor stage* and occurs from birth to around the age of 2 years, during which time the child starts to interact with the environment through the sensory system and motor activity. As these skills become more co-ordinated, so the child starts to develop the concept of cause and effect. Around the middle of this period the notion of object permanence develops, with its implicit assumption that things continue to exist even when they cannot be seen. Towards the end of this phase, the child starts to operate symbolically not only in play, but in thought and language.

There is a considerable body of research which confirms much of Piaget's theory of the first stage of intellectual development, although some studies suggest that some of the skills are attained at an earlier age than Piaget claims. For example, Bower (1981) conducted a series of experiments to test the concept of object permanence in babies and found evidence that from around 5 months they seemed to have some concept of the continued existence of objects even when they couldn't be seen.

The second stage in Piaget's theory of cognitive development is called the *Pre-operational stage* and lasts from around 2 years to 7 years. It is characterised by a rapid development of symbolic skills, most notably language, which Piaget sees as a direct product of enhanced cognitive capacities. In this regard, he differs from other theorists who consider conversely that thought is a *product* of linguistic ability. Another salient feature of this period is *egocentrism* – the child's inability to understand that another perspective, be it perceptual cognitive or affective, other than their own, can exist. However, the means by which Piaget derived these conclusions were complex empirical ones involving the child in a series of unusual tasks. Other researchers (e.g. Mossler, Marvin and Greenberg, 1976) have used alternative experimental techniques, incorporating activities which are likely to be familiar to the child and have found, conversely, that 4 and 5 year old children are well able to decentre their thoughts to encompass alternative perspectives. Clearly, then, Piaget's conclusions on the issue of egocentricity may be a function more of the methodology he used rather than the underlying cognitive skills of his subjects.

During the Preoperational stage, Piaget suggested that a child is capable of classifying objects in one way only and is incapable of alternative classifications or multiple classifications. For example, if a child is presented with a tray of 20 wooden beads of which 18 are brown and 2 are white, and is asked whether there are more brown beads than white beads, the child will correctly attest to a greater number of brown beads. If they are then asked whether there are more brown or more wooden beads, the child is unable to answer correctly; it would seem that if the colour-based classification has been made on the beads, the child is unable to reclassify them in terms of other properties.

A further, extensively researched feature also characterises this stage of development – a failure of conservation. Conservation refers to the capacity to retain the fundamental properties of an event or item, even if that event is altered. For example, 10 marbles remain 10 marbles whether they are arranged in a 10 inch line or a 30 inch line. A child at this stage of development has not achieved this concept of conservation, believing that either the short line or the long line has more marbles, depending on whether they have focussed on the density of the marbles or length of line. Similarly, the child does not perceive that a volume of water remains constant when it is poured from a tall, thin jar into a short, fat jar.

However, there is some evidence that the phrasing of the relevant questions during Piaget's experimental procedures may have been instrumental in producing these responses. If the questions are reworded, even slightly, then children are likely to demonstrate significant comprehension of the concepts underlying conservation tasks (e.g. Donaldson, 1978). Once again, it would seem that Piaget may have underestimated children's cognitive capacities at this stage as an artefact of the experimental procedures employed.

From around the age of 7 years, the child moves into the third stage of cognitive development – the *Concrete Operational stage*, during which time many of the problems that characterised the previous stage are mastered. For example, conservation concepts are now understood, such that in the row of marbles, density and length of line can be simultaneously processed as features of the situation, to enable the child to recognise that the number of marbles remains constant however they are arranged. This decentring of perception is also manifest in the decline of egocentricity such that the child at this stage of development can recognise the possibility of alternative viewpoints and perspectives besides their own, and as a direct consequence of this, social behaviour rapidly develops. Symbolic thought, especially of a quantitative, numerical nature increases, enabling the child to perform exclusively mental operations with numbers without recourse to concrete, visual aids such as counters or beads. Similarly, objects can be multiply classified in terms of several properties, such that an item can, for instance, be red, spherical, wooden, and large.

While many of the observations pertaining to this stage of development have been broadly corroborated, it is worth noting that experience of a socio–cultural nature may have a bigger role to play in the acquisition of some of the cognitive skills. For example, Jahoda (1983) found that concrete operational children in Zimbabwe had a highly developed understanding of abstract economic principles far in advance of a comparable British sample, a finding which could only be attributed to experiential factors within their own cultural context.

The final stage of development, from around 12 years to adulthood, is called the *Formal Operational stage*. Its principal characteristics relate to the existence of logical, abstract thinking including analysis, synthesis and evaluation, which are divorced from concrete contexts. The individual has the capacity to formulate series of alternative hypotheses for any given event and to text these out systematically and empirically.

However, subsequent research has suggested that this level of development may not be universal, but instead may be task, topic and individual specific. In other words, not everybody reaches this level of thought, nor is it attained in every domain. Its achievement appears to be more dependent on environment and experience than had previously been acknowledged (e.g. Shayer and Wylam, 1978).

Generally, Piaget's work has made an elaborate contribution to the knowledge – base of cognitive development, although criticism has been levelled at him for his qualitative, small–group methodologies which are not directly replicable because of the highly individualised techniques that he employed. Furthermore, there is consistent evidence that he underestimated children's intellectual capacities thereby calling into question his definitions of the various stages (Smith and Cowie, 1988).

All this notwithstanding, the theory has had a significant impact on educational procedures, most notably in junior school maths teaching and secondary school science. Underpinning Piaget's theory is the assumption that a child's thought processes are qualitatively different to the adult's and must therefore be accommodated in an appropriate child–centred teaching approach which emphasises active involvement between the child and the learning environment. In this way, the teacher acts as a facilitator to the learning process by providing age and stage – appropriate experiences from which the child can abstract knowledge, concepts and principles, as opposed to being a simple provider of information (e.g. The Nuffield Science Project). Moreover, there is some evidence that specifically teaching Piagetian cognitive operations can significantly help children who are behind in general attainment (e.g. Pasnak *et al.* 1991), thus confirming the general educational advantage achieved by mastery over certain key mental operations identified by Piaget. The reader is referred to Demetriou *et al.* (1992) for a fuller review on current thinking about Piagetian theory.

Another seminal theory of cognitive development is Bruner's (e.g. Bruner *et al*, 1966) which although not entirely distinct from Piaget's, does place more emphasis on cognitive function rather than structure. He also focuses on the way in which humans interact with their social environment as a process of cognitive development, forming internal representations of the world which are influenced by language, culture and education. In this way, the theory is more distinctly social interactional than Piaget's.

The central tenets of Bruner's theory suggest that cognitive development is dependent upon discovery learning through the continuous interplay between the individuals and their social, cultural and educational environment. He suggests that an individual can 'know' something in three different ways – the enactive way (motor and activity experiences which have been represented internally), the iconic way (sensory experiences which have been represented internally), and the symbolic way (linguistic and symbolic experiences which have been represented internally). These three ways of knowing something emerge throughout childhood, in the phase sequence just outlined and the age of their emergence is determined partly by the child's experiences and opportunities, as well as by their stage of development. The young child operates primarily in the enactive mode, while the older child can operate iconically and later symbolically, as their cognitive capacities develop. Therefore, the transition through these stages reflects an increase in complexity of function. The adult is capable of operating in all modes and thus illustrates the concept of the phases as integrative rather than self-contained.

These three types of representation enable the individual to transform incoming information and thus to make sense of the present by recourse to memories of past experiences. In order to do this, it is essential for the individual to interpret and classify information in order to understand it in their own terms. Insofar as Piaget also conceptualised cognitive development as a qualitative stage process, these two theories accord. However, Bruner's focus is more clearly on the function rather than the structure of cognitive development, as well as on the assumption that the stages are closely integrated and continuous.

Bruner's research approach typically involved providing children and adults with concept-attainment tasks, and by analysing the ways in which they attempted to solve the problems he set, he was able to identify how individuals were able to adapt their existing understanding to accommodate new information. Basically, Bruner found two principal strategies, focusing and scanning, which are a function of the individual's preferences and the situation in which they are operating.

Bruner's theory emphasises the importance of language in cognitive development, as well as the influence of education, culture and individual experience, and to this extent departs from Piaget. Bruner's conceptualisation of cognitive development has facilitated the way in which children acquire abstract learning skills as well as providing a more systematic plan of learning to take account of the nature of the learner, the material to be learned and the process by which it is learned. Piaget and Bruner have been major contributors to our understanding of how cognitive abilities develop. They, with many others, have also gone some way to a more general description of the whole learning process.

The Learning Process

Learning is generally defined as a relatively stable change in behaviour which is the result of experience rather than maturational factors. In order to optimise learning it is essential to understand the learning process. Unfortunately, a great deal of the information available on this topic is either directly translated from simple cause-effect experimental psychology which has little application to the complexities of the real-life classroom and its occupants, or alternatively it is derived from implicit informal theories – unsystematic educational folk-lore handed down through generations of educationalists which does not stand up to scrutiny or proper empirical evaluation.

Learning theories are concerned with the mode of acquisition of information, knowledge and concepts, but despite this common interest, the assumptions about the way in which the process operates is dependent on the theoretical stance adopted. One of the earliest learning theorists was Ebbinghaus who in an attempt to make a systematic study of learning, concentrated on the storage and retrieval of nonsense syllables, typically using himself as the subject. This approach was clearly a limiting one, confined as it was to a laboratory study of gibberish. However, Ebbinghaus' contribution to the study of forgetting as a function of the passage of time has been valuable. Essentially, he demonstrated that once information has been learned, the rate of forgetting is initially high, but thereafter slows down. While this may be because the learned material is not being used or practised, it is more likely to be the result of interference from other learned material. For example, recall of information may be prevented by the intrusion of material learned before (proactive inhibition) or by material learned subsequently (retroactive inhibition). The implication of these findings for educational practice is that children are unlikely to retain information they have learned through a process of rote memorisation unless it is both used and integrated with other material they have already assimilated. As a result, a system of associating new information within a framework of existing knowledge is more likely to facilitate retention and understanding. Consequently, then, Ebbinghaus' work formed the basis for a number of subsequent studies (principally on memory and forgetting) and learning theories, which were then extrapolated into the classroom.

Central to the Ebbinghaus tradition was the assumption that learning processes were general and operated in a similar way irrespective of the nature of the material being learned. This tenet formed the basis of one of the most influential of learning theories –associative learning or stimulus–response (S–R) theory, (e.g. Skinner, 1974) whereby an organism learns either to associate two stimuli (as in classical conditioning) or alternatively to associate a given response with a consequence (as in operant conditioning). Operant conditioning is of particular relevance to educational psychology, embracing as it does, issues of behaviour, both social and cognitive, relevant to the teacher. So essential is S–R theory to any psychology course that it is assumed that the reader will have encountered the details elsewhere. Suffice it to say, that this theory, derived from laboratory studies of birds and animals, emphasised the rôle of association between bits of knowledge or behaviours. In this way, for instance, previously linked information, through repeated pairings, would eventually become associated such that when one bit of knowledge was presented it would automatically evoke any bits associated with it.

The learning of these associations is dependent upon a system of reward and punishment – if the learner is rewarded for a given behaviour then that behaviour is more likely to be produced in the future. This reward can take the form either of the delivery of something desirable (for example, teacher praise, or merit awards) contingent on the production of the behaviour (positive reinforcement) or the removal of something undesirable, such as cessation of nagging or shouting (negative reinforcement). If the reward is later removed, then the behaviour that previously elicited it gradually diminishes or *extinguishes*. If the learner on the other hand is punished for doing something, for instance, by withdrawing something pleasant or desirable, then that behaviour is less likely to occur.

S–R theory has generated an enormous corpus of research which has direct application to both learning and classroom behaviour, through techniques of *behaviour modification*. This term refers to the systematic application of learning principles in order to effect a specified change in learning or general classroom behaviour. One of the main contributors to this area has been Skinner who used techniques of reinforcement to control human behaviour. These techniques employ empirically derived rules of reward referred to as schedules of reinforcement which can be applied systematically in order to promote target behaviours. For example, the frequent use of contingent reinforcement in the early stages of learning provides the child with immediate feedback such that the subsequent response can be modified accordingly.

Besides reward and punishment, of particular relevance to the issue of classroom learning are a number of processes which will be considered separately. *Modelling behaviour*, for example, is a process whereby the child copies behaviour observed in someone else. Dependent upon what happens to the model, the child's own behaviour may be altered, such that if, for instance, the model is observed to be escaping punishment for normally penalised behaviour, the child is less likely to inhibit that particular behaviour subsequently.

Shaping is a technique of building up a desired behaviour through successive reinforcement of a sequence of component parts of that behaviour. In this way, children who typically rarely demonstrate a specific target behaviour (for example, writing a passage of work) may be encouraged to behave more acceptably by rewarding actions which go some way towards the behavioural goal, such as then writing a sentence/paragraph etc. In this way, the regular reinforcement will act as a motivator and can ultimately be made contingent upon behaviours which more closely approximate the desired outcome.

Token economies are commonly used strategies of shaping behaviour, such that the child is presented with a tangible reward like a star, token, money, etc. upon the production of a specified behaviour. In essence, it is a simple principle, but many token economies have been elaborated to incorporate contract learning schemes, secondary reinforcement schedules, etc.

Perhaps one of Skinner's most notable contributions to educational psychology was the development of the teaching machine, which employed many of the basic principles of operant conditioning. Early teaching machines presented information to the learner in a sequence of frames, each of which contained new information and questions about it. Upon production of the answer, the learner checks the correctness of their response and moves on to the next frame. In this way, the teaching machine involves the pupil in active participation in the learning process and at a rate which can be customised to meet the individual's needs. Moreover, it provides immediate feedback on the student's progress. Although these early teaching machines have been superceded by more sophisticated techniques of Computer Assisted Learning (CAL), the basic principles remain similar.

While this conceptualisation of the learning process in S-R terms has aided our understanding of simple learning tasks, such as rote memorisation or classroom control through behaviour modification schedules, it clearly cannot account for much of the more complex mental processing involved in many classroom activities. Consequently, learning theories had to evolve further in an attempt to take account of this. Thus, in the 1960's, theories which represented learning as a hierarchical branching tree (e.g. Bower *et al.*, 1969) or complex networks of information (e.g. Quillian, 1968) were constructed. These theories began to take account of *concept formation*, in which the learner actively tests out ideas, rules and principles in order to make sense of incoming information. Thus, while Skinner and his associates conceived of the learner as mechanistically responding to events, other researchers such as Bruner *et al.* (1966) hypothesised that the learner interpreted and transformed any incoming stimulus in the light of previous experience. (See earlier section on Bruner).

The S–R theory of Skinner and the concept attainment theory of Bruner can be reconciled to some extent by the work of Gagné (1974) whose model of the learning process draws on both. Gagné suggested that learning was an 8-stage hierarchical process involving events both internal and external to the learner and which incorporate many different types of learning:

motivation
apprehending or attending (the learner perceives the relevant information)
acquisition (the learner codes the information)
retention (the information is stored in memory)
recall (the information is retrieved from memory)
generalisation (the information is applied to novel situations)
performance (or practice of what has been learned)
feedback (the learner receives knowledge of their performance)

Gagné argues that success at any one of these levels is dependent upon the learner's ability to perform the tasks at the subordinate levels. If a child fails to learn it is assumed to be the result of breakdown at one of these stages. Through the careful provision of learning objectives, cues and questions, Gagné argues that it is possible to reduce failure, and hence to optimise learning.

Over the last decade or so, these theories have been modified into a conceptualisation of the mind as computer. Under the generic title of artificial intelligence, the general view is that the mind is compartmentalised into a number of parts, each of which is specialised in dealing with certain types of activity. Each compartment, or "file", has a store of information, skills, expectations etc. which is based on experience, and which can be cross-referenced to other files. Within this framework, learning consists of modifying a file, through alteration or addition, creating new files, and improving the access to information stored on file, so that the most effective method of dealing with a given situation can be effectively accessed. There is a great deal of evidence to support this conceptualisation of learning. Shuell (1990) in a review of the learning literature, concludes that the learner passes through a number of stages of learning, the first of which involves the acquisition of isolated facts that are interpreted in the light of the individual's experience and schemata and then added to the existing body of knowledge. Gradually, these bits of information are assembled into new schemata or "files", providing additional conceptualising power. On this basis, it is possible, at least in theory, to facilitate the transition between the learning phases through the use of strategies (e.g. Christensen and Cooper, 1992). In other words, we can learn how to learn.

From this brief overview, it can be seen that there has been a change in the way in which learning is viewed partly as a result of the work on artificial intelligence and computer simulation models of the mind. Claxton (1989) has identified six major changes to the way in which learning is now conceptualised:

(a) a shift from thinking about discrete bits of knowledge, to looking at how knowledge is integrated.

(b) because of the interconnections in our knowledge, concepts are perceived as ill-defined or "fuzzy" rather than clear-cut.

(c) there is more interest in the thinking and learning *process* and less concern with trying to divide up the mind into hypothetical structures such as short-term and long-term memory.

(d) previously held assumptions about the existence of general mental processes which can be adapted to suit particular learning situations have given way to the notion that there may be purpose-built processes for specific skills.

(e) the conceptualisation of learning as involving the addition of new knowledge to an existing store may be inappropriate. What appears to be more relevant is the construction of knowledge as the modification and restructuring of information in the light of experience, and the superceding of knowledge which has been found to be incorrect.

(f) new models of the learning process specify that learning can only take place through what is already known, using existing information to make sense of incoming information.

Despite the large corpus of research which has pointed the way to a new, revamped model of the learning process, there is considerable evidence that these ideas have not yet infiltrated the majority of classrooms and that a number of traditional and perhaps outmoded educational assumptions and practices continue to dominate our schools. Claxton (1989) has outlined a number of key beliefs which still guide classroom activities; for instance, he argues that the long-held assumptions that the learner is a passive assimilator of objective knowledge and that the teacher's rôle is to present this knowledge in a clear and appropriate way, are still widely adhered to. In addition, the learning process continues to be seen as a homogeneous activity, whose success is almost entirely dependent on the amount of ability and effort the learner brings to the situation. Furthermore, the sort of knowledge still most revered is abstract and intellectual, which even though it may have no practical relevance, is construed as being intrinsically useful. Such beliefs are frequently challenged by the growing number of unemployed school-leavers, who claim that their school experiences have left them unprepared for the real world of work.

Ability

Central to the traditional view of the learning process is the construct of mental ability or intelligence.

Early definitions of intelligence were based on the assumption that ability was a monolithic construct, a general capacity which could be adapted to deal with a variety of events. Spearman (1904) defined intelligence as "the eduction of correlates", while Heim (1970) suggested that intelligent activity consisted of "grasping the essentials in a given situation and responding appropriately to them". More recent definitions have reflected a shift away from a single over-arching ability to a componential approach, based on an analysis of assumed underlying component processes. Sternberg's (1982) work is an example of this trend, and defines intelligence on the basis of its hypothesised structure. He suggests four critical components to intellectual ability:

(a) ability to think or profit from experience
(b) ability to think or reason abstractly

(c) ability to adapt to the vagaries of a changing and uncertain world
(d) ability to motivate oneself to accomplish expenditiously, the tasks one needs to accomplish.

Despite the differences in these definitions, most of them accord with respect to a view of intelligence as being stable and fixed, predictive, measurable and valuable. Such ideas have guided a number of educational policies and practices, for instance, the notion that ability is largely innately determined and relatively stable means that it is assumed that comparatively little can be done to modify the intelligence of someone perceived as having little of this attribute. While there is of course, extensive remedial provision for children deemed to be of low ability, many would argue that these children are, in reality, educationally written-off. This view also ties in with the notion of intelligence as predictive, which suggests that knowing a child's ability level means that prognoses about future performance can be made. Clearly, then if this is a widely-held construction of intelligence, then little investment will be made in "low-ability" children, on the grounds that their potential is relatively immutable. Clearly, much of this I.Q. malleability argument centres around the nature–nurture controversy of human intellectual ability (e.g. Locurto, 1988). Most of the evidence submitted to this debate is derived from studies which look at the correlation in I.Q. between people of differing degrees of genetic similarity. Overall, it appears that the closer the genetic relationship of the individuals (i.e. identical twins) the more similar their measured I.Q.'s. For example, the correlation in I.Q. between identical twins is around 0.86, between siblings, 0.47 and between cousins, 0.15 (Bouchard and McGue, 1981). However, despite the major contribution of inherited factors to I.Q., environmental influences do determine intelligence to some degree, in that when identical twins or siblings are reared apart from each other, the correlation in intelligence drops to 0.72 and 0.24, respectively, (Souchard and McGue *ibid*). Furthermore, Howe's (1988) conclusions on the effect of intensive early education or "hot-house" children support this. It would seem, then, that genetics do not prescribe an absolute ability level, but rather a range of likely responses to environmental influences known as the *reaction range*. Where an individual's I.Q. falls within this range depends on the quality of the environmental experiences, such that deprived circumstances will produce an I.Q. towards the bottom of the individual's reaction range and enriched circumstances an I.Q. towards the top. Findings such as these gave rise to pre-school enrichment programmes for underprivileged children, the aim of which was to compensate in educational terms, for the deprivation of the home background (see section on socioeconomic status).

These studies implicitly accept that intelligence is measurable. If it can be quantified then we can make decisions about a child on the basis of such measures. Allied to this is the assumption that children who score highly on these rather arbitrarily compiled measures of intelligence are rated more highly than those who don't score as well. Heated debates have long raged over the value of the notion of intelligence as an identifiable, measurable and useful construct (e.g. Howe 1990, Nettlebeck 1990) but it is true to say that despite this, many educational psychologists spend a considerable amount of their professional lives administering tests of intelligence (e.g. Swann 1982). Despite considerable internal pressure for change from within the professional body of Educational Psychologists (e.g. Wolfendale *et al.* 1992), there is a great deal of evidence to suggest that teachers have an expectation that the psychologist's role will be individual assessment – and intervention – oriented, and that this expectation exerts considerable influence over the operation of the Educational Psychologist's job. Given this, it may be appropriate to present a brief overview of the psychometric assessment of intelligence.

Theoretical perspectives as to how intelligence is structured determine to a large extent how it is measured. The growth of intelligence-testing occurred at the turn of the century with Binet's (1909) assessment schedule. Critical to Binet's test was the notion of mental age (M.A.), based on the assumption that a "normal" child's chronological age (C.A.) and mental age would be similar, with slow learning children having a M.A. below their C.A. and high ability children having a M.A. in excess of their C.A. Binet's original work, which had an enormous impact on educational policy and procedure, underwent several revisions, the most notable of which was the Stanford–Binet test, whose popularity was in part due to the easily understood I.Q. score it provided.

The Stanford–Binet test was superceded by the Wechsler Scales (e.g. Wechsler Intelligence Scale for Children or WISC) which introduced the notion of the deviation I.Q. which allowed the comparison of an individual child's I.Q. score with the population age-related norm. More recently, The British Ability Scales (B.A.S.), introduced by Elliott, Murray and Pearson in 1977, whilst retaining a number of the concepts fundamental to the WISC, have incorporated a Rasch scaling technique which allows the comparison of any two children who have been tested on this scale *independent of which items were included in the tests* – a property which does not feature in earlier I.Q. tests.

The use of I.Q. tests is undoubtedly a contentious issue, theoretically and politically. Opponents condemn such tests on the basis of the unproven assumptions underlying their construction, their accuracy (there is, for instance, some evidence that the complexity of an indivdual's mental activities may be unrelated to their performance on a formal I.Q. test, e.g. Ceci (1990) as well as their inherent bias against minority ethnic groups and children from lower-socio–economic classes (Stone, 1992). Undoubtedly, cultural background exerts an enormous influence on an individual's test performance, but, to date, any attempts to devise a culture–fair I.Q. test have not been promising. Those in favour of I.Q. testing regard it as a fairer means of assessing a child's ability and potential than the notoriously unreliable evaluations made by teachers, often on the basis of irrelevant characteristics such as facial attractiveness, (e.g. Rich, 1975).

Whatever the merits of either argument, there is little doubt that formal I.Q. testing remains a standard tool in educational assessment, particularly with children deemed to be exceptional. This notwithstanding, there has been a noticeable shift of interest away from the assumed monolithic notion of intelligence and the use of traditional I.Q. tests, towards a greater focus on the learning process and assessments of learning effectiveness. This, together with the implications of various Education Acts, has meant reduced emphasis on a child's underlying capabilities and more on what they know and can do at specified ages. The theoretical (as opposed to political) perspective underpinning this move is the assumption that successful school performance may depend less on underlying ability and more on teaching children appropriate and task–specific learning *strategies* relevant to the situation they are in. This more social–cognitive view of learning assumes that an individual's "ability" refers to the number and appropriateness of the available learning strategies they have, and this availability, in turn, depends on a variety of individual differences that the learner brings to the learning situation and which determine the pupil's predisposition to respond in a given way.

However, one ability which seems to differentiate successful from unsuccessful learners is their capacity to acknowledge and describe their particular learning difficulties. Inherent within this is the vital rôle of language. From the informal linguistic systems used in a social setting such as the playground, successful students can derive more appropriate verbal strategies for expressing both what they know and what they don't know in an academic context.

Another strategy of particular relevance to a considerable part of school learning, especially where exams are concerned, is verbatim learning – the rote memorisation of information which is often not fully understood by the learner. Given the usefulness of this sort of "knowledge" for passing exams, it is self-evident that if learners can adopt a strategy for making sense out of apparently meaningless material then they stand a better chance of exam success than those students who fail to do this. Howe (1984) has identified a number of useful strategies including acronyms, mnemonics, imagery, files and access routes, all of which exemplify the idea that learning strategies can be learned, and as such, masquerade as "ability" in traditional terminology.

Methods of Assessing Learning

Despite the historical emphasis on learning concepts and academic knowledge, there has been, in recent years, a move towards skills training. Central to this is the use of modelling strategies (watching how someone else performed the task and then attempting to emulate it), the value of performance feedback, experimenting and practising strategies. Similarly, monitoring and reflecting on one's performance are also essential learning strategies, in that they provide a feedback mechanism for modifying performance. Allied to this, is the whole of the assessment process in education, which besides providing feedback to the teacher and the student, also assists in a range of selection procedures (for good or ill) and can provide a qualification of some sort, e.g. a Bachelor's Degree, Diploma, etc. The most typical, if contentious method of assessing the efficacy of learning is the formal examination, a routine part of the education system which has been hotly contested, and in consequence has been replaced at least in part by continuous assessment. This latter technique has the merit of grading a student not on a single performance as with an exam, but over a period of time when any weakness in the student's grasp of a subject area is manifest, thereby enabling the teacher to modify the nature and content of teaching appropriately. However, continuous assessment does suffer from the possibility of subjective bias on the part of the marker, lack of uniformity in marking standards as well as from inability to gauge how far a piece of work is the sole product of the pupil. There are, of course, numerous other advantages and disadvantages of each system, and the reader is referred to Munby (1989) for a review of assessment in school.

One of the problems inherent within any assessment process is the issue of whether marking should be norm-referenced or criterion-referenced. The former refers to a grading system where any student's performance is marked by comparison with other similar students. The standard I.Q. test is a typical norm-referenced evaluation which assesses how well a child does relative to others in the appropriate age group. A criterion-referenced test, on the other hand, stipulates a fixed standard of performance above which a pupil is deemed to have passed, and below which, failed. This standard operates irrespective of the comparative performance of anyone else (e.g. a driving test). Thus the first approach can be construed as a *relative* measure and the latter, an *absolute* measure. Both have their uses and disadvantages, but it is probably fair to say that norm-referencing has fallen into disrepute over the last few years, at least within the British education system since it is clear that this approach could conceivably allow an uninformed or unskilled pupil to pass an exam provided the rest of the age group were also below standard. However, criterion referencing is a complex process to adopt in school exams, although with this as an ultimate goal, educationalists have moved some way towards its achievement through syllabus differentiation, despite the fact that this in itself, is not without problems. (See Nuttall, 1989).

While examinations continue to be criticised, they still form a dominant part of our educational assessment. Nonetheless, more innovative techniques are slowly infiltrating, such as records of achievement (characterised by a broader experimental and skills basis for evaluation) self-appraisal, contract grading schemes (whereby the student and teacher negotiate a reasonable grade for any given assessments), and graded assessments in which a series of progressively more difficult criterion-referenced grades is arranged to form a sequence of development, through which the learner moves at his/her own rate. This approach is gaining in popularity and forms the basis for the national assessment programme (Task Group on Assessment and Testing 1988) with all the attendant objections. This programme is intended to provide comprehensive and detailed feedback to students and teachers about the level of learning, through the publication of class, school and LEA results, and in so doing, would enable the consumers of the system to make more informed choices about schools. Objections to the scheme abound, however, and largely focus on concerns about the use of test results for selection purposes, the potential damage done to those schools whose pupils are at a social, economic or linguistic disadvantage and the fact that, in order to maintain publicly acceptable standards, the curriculum would be determined by the assessment, rather than the reverse. What remains clear, however, is that the most appropriate techniques of assessment will continue for years to be the subject of emotive debate.

Reading Ability

Central to the whole process of teaching and learning is reading. This is an enormously complex skill, depending as it does on a range of both specific abilities to translate symbols into sounds and to extract meaning from the words, as well as more general capacities such as memory and motivation. By studying the differences between the beginning reader and the fluent reader, it is possible to identify some of the processing which is inherent to the task, and which may be used to facilitate the teaching of reading at a variety of levels.

The study of reading has generated a plethora of research, spanning more than a century. Over this period there has been a shift in emphasis in the theories related to reading, from partial models which focused on the component skills, to more global models, which consider the entire process of reading as a gestalt, embedded in the acquisition of language rather than distinct from it.

In essence, models of reading have concentrated on internal information processing which operates between the stimulus input (the written word) and the response output (silent or spoken reading). These models have in general, fallen into two broad categories – top-down and bottom up processing systems – which relate to the way in which the brain is thought to deal with incoming information. Top-down analyses are concept-driven, such that the reader starts with an hypothesis about what the meaning of the sentence is likely to be, and this is checked against the printed stimuli. Subsequent stages in the process involve further hypotheses at the phrase, word and letter level in order to predict the most likely occurrences at these levels within the overall context of the sentence:

Top-Down Processing Model

World and Language experience
prediction of linguistic units
word recognition
letter recognition

(Sheldon, 1985)

Support for these theories has been derived from gap-filling tasks, where readers are asked to fill in missing words in a text. The capacity to do this is based on a series of predictions they make about the meaning of the passage and which have been derived from a generalised knowledge about the world which provides the overall context. In addition, an understanding of semantics (which words will make sense in a given phrase) and syntax (how words and sentences are constructed) facilitate this process of prediction.

This top-down schema has generated a number of models of the reading process such as Goodman's (1972). He proposed that the starting points of the reading process are the reader's predictions about the meaning of the text, and these predictions are derived from the graphic, syntactic and semantic information contained in the passage. The reader then tests these hypotheses against the information available in the text, the success of which depends largely on the reader's ability to anticipate critical aspects of the text. Goodman's evidence for this theory derives from the errors or miscues an individual makes when reading aloud, such that fluent readers are more likely to use contextual cues when predicting and anticipating, than are beginning readers, although this aspect of the model has been contested by a number of studies. For example, Allington and Strange (1977) presented good and poor readers with sentences in which some letters had been altered, thereby rendering the passage nonsense. However, the changes that were made bore a similarity in shape to the correct letter e.g. "He leaned too fan over the edge of the wall". If readers were relying on contextual cues, then a meaningful word would be substituted for the one that made nonsense of the passage. If, on the other hand, greater reliance was placed on graphemic input, then the reader would read the word as presented. Allington and Strange found that good readers were more likely to read the wrong word, suggesting a high dependence at the letter level, while poor readers tended to substitute meaningful words for the incorrect one, indicating reliance on context. This evidence, which is in direct contradiction to the predictions of the top-down model, has been corroborated by other studies such as that of Nicholson (1991) who also found that context was of questionable value especially to good readers.

In contrast to the concept–driven perspective of the top-down theorists, bottom-up theories are data-driven, in that they assume the beginning points of the reading process are letters, followed by words and word meaning.

Bottom-up Processing Model

use of words in language and the world
word meaning
word recognition
letter recognition

(Sheldon, 1985)

Within this schema, the reader attends to each individual letter, translating this into its sound equivalent, and building this into words and then sentences. This process of individual letter and word recognition is known as lexical access. While this process appears laborious, there is some evidence that it is not as time-consuming as would seem, since the initial recognition of the letter and word and their translation into sounds would appear to take place automatically within milliseconds. For example, using tachistoscopic techniques, subjects have been presented with words subliminally such that they have no conscious awareness of having seen them, and yet they are able to recognise the stimulus word from a list at a later point. Further support for the bottom-up theory comes from the capacity to read an unknown word or a nonsense syllable, a skill which is dependent upon analytical skills at the letter rather than meaning level.

It would seem, then, that each of the foregoing models can explain different aspects of the reading process without being able to explain the whole operation. However, the two models can be integrated to some extent, to take account of the available evidence. Stanovich (1980) suggests an interactive model of reading which proposes that the reader simultaneously derives information from different levels in the reading process, without necessarily starting from the letter recognition stage (bottom-up) or from the meaning (top-down). In this way the information flow is bidirectional rather than unidirectional as suggested by the two component theories. Depending on the skill of the reader, some levels of processing assume more importance than others, in that context cues may be of greater value at certain levels of reading development. Moreover, readers are able to compensate for deficiencies at any level of processing by extracting more information from the skill stages at which they have developed competence. Stanovich interpreted Allington and Strange's findings (ibid) as support for this idea, in that poor readers have to use alternative sources of information, i.e. context, in order to compensate for their poor symbol-to-sound skill.

Other interactive theories exist e.g. Rumelhart and McClelland (1982) which emphasize the role of memory. Their theory suggests that there are three basic types of information involved in word recognition-features, parts of letters, letters and words, each of which is represented in an interconnected memory store. In this way, if the stimulus input is "t", not only will the "t" memory traces be activated, but also all those for words containing the letter t. This means of course, that there has to be some selection process, since while many words with the letter t will be activated, only one will ultimately be accessed as the correct response to the stimulus. This selection process is dependent upon a similar activation process for all the other letter components of the stimulus word until a correct match has occurred. This process is clearly a bottom up one with feature recognition taking place first followed by letter and word. However, the interactive model suggests that a similar top down activation process can also occur, based on semantics instead. This enables the reader to supply missing words based on the context and not on any visual features. Therefore, at word level, access can be via the feature/letter route (bottom up) as well as the meaning/context route (top-down), allowing activation of the relevant memory stores to spread through all levels.

Clearly, one of the problems that faces the teacher is the wide range of ability to undertake these processes within any given group of pupils. These differences may be a function of a number of factors, such as lexical access skills, comprehension and level of parental support. For example, individual differences in knowledge affect reading comprehension, in that the reader can only make sense of the text by relating the content to his or her own knowledge base (Perfetti, 1985). In general, the greater the knowledge, and its application to the passage being read, the greater the reader's comprehension of the content. In addition, poor readers generally have a lower memory capacity than fluent readers (e.g. Goldman *et al.* 1980). The implication of this is twofold; firstly, essential words in the passage can be more readily recalled by good readers in order to understand the central theme of the text, and secondly, at the level of lexical access, good readers activate more quickly those features, letters and words represented in long-term memory which are necessary for bottom-up word recognition. (Perfetti ibid). At a more general level, the degree of parental involvement for instance, influences reading attainment. A study by Leach and Siddall (1990) found that if parents are involved in active reading instruction with their children, progress is significantly faster than if they simply hear them read. Level and type of involvement, rather than involvement per se, may well be a critical factor therefore in reading progress.

Gender appears also to relate to reading attainment in that boys are more likely to have a reading age significantly below their chronological age, a fact which may be a product of differential teacher expectations (Fergusson, *et al.* 1991). Other factors, however, such as language ability, motivation, general ability and cognitive style (e.g. Riding and Mathias, 1991) are also important influences on the reading process, points which serve to confirm the overall complexity of the task itself and the associated influences on it.

Reading Methods

Inevitably, one potential contributor to reading attainment is the method by which reading skills are taught. The methods can be broken down into three main approaches – analytic or code-oriented (breaking language and words down into their component parts), holistic (dealing with them as a gestalt) or a combination of both. Within these methods are many approaches, based on a variety of theoretical perspectives.

Of the analytic methods, perhaps the best known is the *phonic approach*, which is based on teaching the sounds rather than the names of letters (e.g. "ah" rather than "ay" for the letter 'a'). Once these are learned, the sounds can be blended to make words. However, it is clear from even a cursory glimpse at a text that the English language is phonetically very irregular (e.g. though, tough, thought) and for the phonic approach to succeed as a single method complete sound-symbol correspondence is essential.

By contrast, the holistic *look–say* approach teaches words as wholes, such that the reader learns to recognise a word by its shape rather than component parts. Thus, the reader is presented with a word and a picture of the object depicted by the word. After repeated exposures, the child is able to identify the word without the picture by recognising its global shape. This technique while allowing recognition of phonetically irregular words provides the child with no word analysis skills, rendering him or her unable to decode a word not previously encountered.

Combining both approaches overcomes to some degree the problems of each. The Language Experience Technique begins with child and teacher discussing some event of interest to the child. The teacher then writes down what the child has said and the child reads it back. In this way, the meaning and syntax are individual and entirely relevant to the child's own experience. Through a sequence of stages the child learns the inter-relationships between sound and symbol, as well as reading, speech and writing.

It would be fair to say that many comparative studies of reading approaches have yielded contradictory evidence concerning their effectiveness, perhaps because of the methodological difficulty in making comparisons between techniques which are so heavily dependent on the individual differences brought to the classroom by the teacher and child as well as the dynamic interaction between them. However, a recent overview by Vellutino (1991) concerning the relative effectiveness of code-based as opposed to whole-language approaches, found that, on balance, the evidence favoured the code-based techniques. Similarly, systematic letter-sound instruction produces faster progress in spelling as well as reading (e.g. Ehri and Robbins, 1992).

INDIVIDUAL AND GROUP INFLUENCES ON SCHOOL PERFORMANCE

Many individual and group differences will have an impact on school performance, for example, intellectual ability, motivation, learning styles, personality, sex, socio-economic background and race. General issues concerning ability have already been discussed; this section of the chapter will deal with sex, socio-economic background and race.

Sex Differences

Accompanying the rise of the women's movement have been debates concerning the bias against girls within education. Discussions of any form of educational inequality, be it due to selection procedures (such as the 11 +) class, race or gender are all founded on issues of equal opportunities, outcomes and treatment for the groups concerned. However, since all these topics are emotive ones it is consequently essential that any evidence for sex-based inequality in attainment be presented, at the onset, before possible explanations are put forward.

The Department of Education and Science regularly compiles statistics on examination performance, and close scrutiny of these suggests that while girls and boys do not differ in overall academic achievement, there is evidence that girls tend to do better at 'O' level and in arts subjects, and boys at 'A' level and in science subjects and furthermore, that while both sexes are equally likely to go on to tertiary education, more boys go on to study at degree level (e.g. Statistical Bulletin 11/84, 1984). Moreover, Archer (1992) found that those disciplines in which boys performed better were construed as "difficult", while those in which girls were superior were considered "easy". These constructions were particularly significant among girls, with boys being more likely to label the masculine and feminine subjects as interesting vs boring, respectively. What is particularly concerning about these figures is that the areas of lower achievement for girls (i.e. maths, science and technology) are now becoming increasingly valued by society as a whole, and that current trends towards co-educational schools serve to exacerbate these differences largely through a complex system of attitudes and expectations (e.g. Deem, 1984). Undoubtedly, the widely-held notion that boys do better in maths and girls in verbal tasks is supported by surveys such as that carried out by the Assessment of Performance Unit (APU) (1982a and 1982b) and which confirmed the existence of these gender-based differences. Although influential, this report founded its conclusions on mean test scores for both sexes which although statistically significant were so minimally different as to be of little educational importance. For example, the mean reading score for the boys was recorded as 54.4, while for the girls it was 55.0. Clearly, when interpreting findings of this sort it is essential to know what tests were used, how they were scored, the basics of descriptive and inferential statistics, and in particular, the variability of the data. Given that media reporting typically doesn't concern itself with such details, the usual sex-linked assumptions about performance will be promulgated with the consequent hardening of expectations. A great deal of research has also been directed towards identifying more fundamental differences between the sexes in terms of their intellectual abilities typically based on patterns of I.Q. test scores. In a seminal review of 1400 studies of gender differences, Maccoby and Jacklin (1975) reported that in general, males were superior in mathematical and visual-spatial skills, while females were better verbally. While this review is flawed in many ways (for example, the authors failed to take account of the quality of the studies) such conclusions not only fuel prejudicial judgements about each sex but also lead to expectations of subject-related achievement, which can exert considerable influence over a pupil's school performance. Of crucial importance here, however, is the question of whether these differences reflect true inherent and biological gender capacities, whether they are socially conditioned, or whether they result from an interaction of the two.

As with any nature vs nurture argument, the main causal factors of genetics and environment are almost impossible to isolate for systematic study. Nonetheless, these debates do have a feature in common – if any given attribute can be clearly demonstrated to be the result of genetic influences *only*, then there is relatively little that can be done to modify this attribute. In other words, if any gender differences can be ascribed to inherent biological dispositions, then there is little point in working towards gender equality on those differences. Conversely, if a given characteristic can be shown to be influenced or determined by environmental factors then there is some point in attempting to provide equal opportunities, at the very least, for development of this attribute. Such arguments can have a considerable impact on policy decisions; for instance, the Newsom Report of 1963 recommended a curriculum for 13–16 year old girls which would train them to understand the rôles of wife and mother since "the incentive for girls to equip themselves for marriage and home-making is genetic".

The evidence regarding the genetic determination of gender characteristics is far from conclusive. For example, while many theorists agree that boys and girls differ with respect to brain structure, there is minimal accord as to what this structure is, and how it manifests any differences. Regardless of this lack of consensus, there is little doubt that simply being male or female determines a number of developmental, educational and social outcomes, irrespective of the mechanism by which this is effected.

In terms of the contribution of nurture to the gender–distinction debate, much attention has been directed at the social conditioning of sex-roles and sex-appropriate behaviours. While there are a number of theories about the origins of sex-role identification (see Hargreaves & Colley, 1986), of particular interest here is the contribution of the classroom interaction in confirming these rôles (see Deem 1989 for a review).

It is widely acknowledged that through a complex interactional process, teacher expectation can exert a considerable causal effect on pupil attainment. Where a large network of people hold broadly similar expectations about an individual, the self-fulfilling prophecy is even more likely to occur. Delamont (1980) suggests that teachers, as a group, are rather more conservative in their opinions of what constitutes sex-appropriate behaviour than are other professions, and furthermore, teachers are very vulnerable to media scrutiny and criticism. Taken together, Delamont suggests that adverse societal reaction to any obvious change in teacher opinion on sex-appropriate behaviour means that teachers will remain confirmed in die-hard views on gender issues. The outcome of this leads to a prediction that where traditional views on sex-related skills and behaviours are apparent, then these lead to a confirmation of boys and girls in their assumed educational roles, and indeed, one early study by Palardy (1969) supports this. He found that teachers who believed girls to be better at reading than boys had pupils in their class whose reading attainment corroborated this belief; where teachers held no such gender assumptions, no difference in reading ability between boys and girls was found. Similar findings have been reported by Fergusson *et al.* (1991).

However, it appears that teachers have a more clear-cut set of expectations about classroom *behaviour* than about academic performance, believing girls to be neater, quieter and more conforming while at the same time being more tolerant of aggression when displayed by boys. Furthermore, it seems that any child, male or female, who is perceived by the teacher to possess traditional male characteristics is also perceived to be more intelligent and logical. These findings are further compounded by social class differences in expectations of gender.

There is then, little doubt that the sex of the pupil alters the way in which a teacher behaves towards them. Classroom management is often based on sub-dividing pupils into groups of boys and girls, and this division is so commonly accepted that it becomes entrenched in the thinking of pupils and teachers alike (see, for example, Morgan and Dunn, 1990). For example, Spender (1982) in a review of the literature found that if boys are given less than 2/3 the total teacher attention, then both the teacher and the male and female pupils assume that girls are being given more than their rightful amount. This assumption is based not on a belief that boys *should* get more attention than girls, but rather within a background of normative behaviour which is biased in favour of boys that any deviations from the norm towards the female pupils leads to an overestimation in the attention girls are thought to receive.

The overall result of these assumptions is that boys will typically be afforded more teacher attention, (and particularly in subject areas such as maths and physics) and that these differences, with all their attendant inequalities, will be accepted as normal by boys and girls alike. However, it should be emphasised that the greater attention boys receive is due, in large part to the degree of disciplinary action a teacher has to take with them.

This would suggest that the classroom is a more hostile environment for boys than for girls and yet as was pointed out at the beginning of this section, boys still do better in the school system, at least at 'A' level and subsequent types of tertiary education. At first it seems difficult to resolve this anomaly. However, attribution theory goes some way towards an explanation. If the negative attention boys receive is directed at their behaviour, this has no implicit criticism of their *ability*. Girls, on the other hand, receive less overall criticism, but that which they do receive is more likely to focus of the quality of their work (Dweck *et al.*, 1978). Therefore, girls develop less positive concepts about their capabilites. Lack of ability is then perceived as a stable attributional cause of failure which will then encourage girls to expect further failure with all the perpetuating self-fulfilling prophecies that this entails.

Other features of classroom interaction which have a definite gender bias are sexual harassment (for instance, the use of insulting terminology to describe girls) and language use. This latter has been most commonly researched with respect to reading materials, where sexism in both the wording and the images used is often apparent. However, it would be fair to point out that this corpus of literature has focused on the content and *assumed* impact of the content on boy and girl pupils; relatively little in the way of systematic evidence exists for any actual effect on subsequent performance or behaviour. Language in classroom interaction has also been subject to gender bias, with boys taking a more dominant, traditionally masculine rôle and women a supportive, subservient one (Deem, 1989).

While legislation and political movement towards gender equality may go some way towards recognising the problem of sexism, the education system is unlikely to be modified to a degree where male and female pupils truly have similar opportunities or learning experiences. Simply providing equal opportunities to learn does not counteract the negative effect of existing attitudes and expectations at least in the short-term. The reader is referred to Tutchell (1990) for a fuller review of the area.

The Family and Their Socio–Economic Status

It is obvious that children learn an enormous amount outside the classroom and it is the family rather than the school that offers the first learning experiences a child receives. Much of this learning is unstructured and informal and includes the conditioning of a set of attitudes and values in the child that will have a bearing on his/her subsequent school experiences. Given that the home and the school are the two main contexts in which most children function, with each exerting some influence on the other, it is hardly surprising that increasingly attention has been focused on the family as a principal agent in the educational process.

However, it is important to note that the home/school picture is a highly complex one. Just as there is a great diversity of school experiences, so is there a range of home situations too, with differences in family structure, child-rearing practices, personalities, attitudes and emotional climate all having some impact on the child as learner. This section will deal briefly with some of the salient family issues that affect school performance.

Generally, there does seem to be an overall link between patterns of child-rearing and subsequent school achievement, with authoritarian styles of parenting being associated with impeded social and intellectual growth. Perhaps the control that authoritarian parents exert over their offspring inhibits the development of self-reliant, age-appropriate and independent behaviour which clearly is essential for academic growth.

Family size and ordinal position appear to have some impact, too. First-born children seem to have an intellectual and educational advantage over their later-born siblings, perhaps because of the greater parental attention (and hence intellectual resources) that first borns receive (Zajonc, 1976). From this it follows that children from large families will also be at a disadvantage in terms of available adult attention and thus their academic performance will typically be lower than that of children with fewer siblings (e.g. Davie *et al.* 1972). It should be stressed, however, that while these trends are consistent they only account for about 5–10% of all individual differences in terms of educational attainment.

A number of researchers and Government reports have highlighted the issue of socio-economic status (SES) of the home in relation to educational outcomes, suggesting that there is a relationship between low SES and poor school performance, for a variety of reasons (see Lareau, 1989). These studies have emphasised the self-evident injustice of a system that affords educational opportunities on the basis of wealth rather than merit. Allied to this, is the notion that certain social classes get a significantly worse deal out of the education system than do others. Defining what is meant by "social class" however, is not straightforward. Classifications based on money are an oversimplification which take little account of differences in skill or responsibility. Nonetheless, the position of families within the economic framework will exert some influence on the school careers of their children. What is of fundamental importance to those interested in balancing the inequalities in education is how these influences are transmitted.

One salient contributor to this topic has been Pierre Bordieu (e.g. Bordieu, 1983). He suggests that middle and upper class children benefit to a much greater extent from "cultural capital" than do working class children. Using a series of economic analogies, the central tenets of Bordieu's hypothesis rest on the idea that schools implicitly assume how much their pupils know, and the more assumptions that are made, the more the child has to meet these assumptions before even starting to learn. Consequently, children from homes which fulfil the school's assumptions are placed at an automatic advantage, while those from homes at odds with the school will suffer a deficit. Evidence from Plewis *et al.* (1990) confirms this position, with their finding that middle class children spend more time on educational activities at home, which has a significant effect on their school performance. Obviously, the implicit equation here that "wealthy home equals school success" is much too simple, but Bordieu's argument has merit in that highlights a cultural mismatch between some homes and schools, which in turn creates a disadvantage for these children, in terms of the mutual requirements, expectations and abilities of each (e.g. Bordieu, 1983). In this way, the home and to some extent the school, provide a child with "cultural capital" which in turn partly determines educational achievement. What, though, constitutes this cultural capital? There are, of course, a number of factors, of which some will be discussed here.

Material conditions undoubtedly play a part. The Plowden Report (1967), like other research before it, drew attention to the correlation between poor school performance and poverty. More specifically, The National Child Development Study (Davie *et al.*, 1972) found that absent or shared amenities in the home, and overcrowding, are related to a reading retardation of 9 and 3 months respectively. Furthermore, social class is a reliable predictor of reading attainment, with the difference between children from social classes 1 and 2 and those from social class 5 being 27 months at age 11. While it is easy to speculate on why inadequate amenities, poverty and overcrowding might affect education, it is far more difficult to *establish* a causal link empirically, particularly since such factors often go hand-in-hand with other social problems and also do not affect all children equally. The conclusion that poverty in the home leads to poor educational attainment is a damaging one because of the negative and fixed assumptions that may be adopted once a child's home circumstances are revealed. Dubberley (1988) for example, in a study of a mining community in Yorkshire found evidence of unacknowledged teacher bias against working class pupils. In this way, teacher expectations based on class can contribute to school success or failure. Similarly, a study by Tizard and Hughes (1984) demonstrated that even at nursery school working class children were placed at an educational disadvantage by teachers who lowered their expectations and standards for these pupils.

The methods in which children are socialised within the family also influence the ease with which they adapt to the educational process and consequently contribute to the cultural capital. For instance, numerous studies have highlighted the different ways in which the various social classes control the behaviour of their offspring, with the general, if simplified, conclusion that middle class parents emphasise self control and working class parents emphasise control located in status or age-determined authority figures (e.g. Newson and Newson, 1970). Similarly Kohn (1969) found that working-class parents focus on behavioural control of their children, while their middle-class counterparts wanted their offspring to think independently and solve problems. The almost inevitable outcome, if this is the case, is that middle class children will develop the ability to regulate their own behaviour, while working class children rely more heavily on extraneous control. The trend towards schools where the process of learning is heuristic and informal may be entirely inappropriate for the working class child who requires greater specificity of behaviour direction. That teachers typically prefer a child who can operate independently, without constant teacher control, is support for the cultural capital hypothesis of Bordieu.

Parental attitudes towards education also play a part in determining the degree of cultural capital a child has. Despite an almost universal acceptance of education in its broadest sense, as beneficial rather than detrimental, there is considerable disagreement between some parents and educators as to its purpose and processes. Obviously a child from a home background at odds with the school is more likely to reject the educational system and to enjoy less parental support of scholastic activities. Such conflicts in ideas have been reflected in research on discipline standards and various school activities. Indeed parental attitudes have been held to account for scholastic success to a greater degree than variations in the quality of the home circumstances and the standard of the school (Bynner, 1972). While there is no one-to-one correlation between social class and the nature of attitudes to education, there appears to be a tendency for more supportive attitudes to be associated with non-manual, professional and managerial groups. Whatever the relationship to social class, what does seem to be unequivocal is the association between high levels of achievement and positive attitudes to education.

One particularly critical way in which socioeconomic status can influence school attainment is through the medium of language. Blatchford *et al.* (1988) in a longitudinal study of inner-city infant schools described a fairly general picture of classroom life, with the role of language being fundamental to the majority of classroom processes with around 2/3 of the time being taken up in talking. Obviously, if children differ in their experience, use and understanding of language then this must inevitably affect their school experiences. A great deal of contentious discussion has taken place over the last three decades over the differential use of language by the working and middle classes with Bernstein (1962), for example, suggesting that the working classes are linguistically deprived. In particular, Bernstein (1971) suggested that there are two language codes – the restricted and the elaborated, with the restricted code being particularistic and context-dependent with implicit meaning and the elaborated code being universalistic, context-independent and with explicit meaning.

Although Bernstein originally claimed that the restricted code was the language of the working classes, while the elaborated code was associated with the middle classes, he subsequently modified this rather rigid view, and suggested instead, that the middle classes had access to *both* codes, while some sections of the working classes are likely to have access only to the restricted code. Bernstein went to some lengths to explain that the restricted code is in no way defective, but he did suggest that the elaborated code is necessary to meet the conceptual demands of school. Such a claim engendered a number of reactions, some of which encompassed the highly distasteful view that the working classes are fundamentally ineducable, or at least would only benefit from remedial or technical educations. Inevitably such polarised opinions ultimately led to a wholesale rejection of Bernstein's hypotheses by some educationalists. But this, of course, denies some of the more valuable elements in the theory, for although there is virtually no evidence to support the idea that language can be broken down into two *mutually exclusive* codes, the fact remains that language can be described in the way Bernstein suggests, although any single utterance may not necessarily be one or ther other. Furthermore, there is evidence for a relationship between language and educational failure of which McKenzie (1981) provides just one example. He demonstrated that conceptual and reasoning abilities are affected by socioeconomic background and their associated linguistic codes, although lower cognitive skills which require no mental manipulation, such as short term memory, remain unaffected by different language skills. More recent interpretations, however, have suggested that rather than being deprived, the working classes are linguistically inhibited in the school context and this inhibition may serve to impair their school attainment even if only by giving the impression of reluctance and resistance (Tizard *et al.* 1988). Tizard and her associates additionally found that the home is a richer source of language learning than the school, irrespective of social class differences which, in turn, calls into question the value of compensatory pre-school education to equalise the educational experiences of the lower socio-economic groups.

These foregoing factors, then, all constitute ways in which the home background can negatively affect the child's potential adaptation to school before he or she even gets there. It would seem that in some way, the home environment conspires to predispose a child to benefit from school learning experience, by providing a degree of cultural capital which may accord to a greater or lesser degree with the school and its philosophy.

Mindful of these social and educational inequalities, remedial procedures for the disadvantaged have been developed. These have been of three types: homebased programmes which focus on the educational environment of the home, early education (pre-school) programmes which attempt to provide valuable educational experiences before going to school in order to maximise the child's chances of success and school based programmes which try to compensate for any cumulative disadvantage by providing additional remedial and educational provision.

Home based programmes focus on emphasising educational activities in the home and parental involvement in the child's educational activities. In general, they have achieved a considerable degree of success, with the child's improvement being maintained for several years after the conclusion of the programme e.g. Hewison (1988). Presumably, changes incorporated into the home as a result of these interventions may continue, thereby sustaining the improvement.

Early educational or pre-school projects are based on the assumption that if a child can be given adequate pre-school experience than the disadvantages on entering school will be minimised. The child is given a few hours help daily over a period of months, in a school setting. But despite the upsurge in these programmes, e.g. Project Headstart there is little corroboration over the results, primarily because of the different methods and processes involved. Moreover, it appears that any progress made disappears once the programme is terminated. This has led to lack of confidence in the ability of these programmes to overcome the problems experienced by the dis-advantaged child.

Most of the school based programmes have a number of common aims – language enrichment, perceptual and social skills training, stimulation by a variety of activities and materials, the provision of stability and the development of a more positive self-image. However, the outcomes have been inconclusive, leading some researchers, such as Bastiani (1987) to suggest alternative approaches, which rather than adopting a compensation model, focus instead on the complementary rôles of teachers and parents. Instead of denigrating the home for what it fails to provide, each party develops the experiences of the other in a cooperative venture.

Despite the laudability of the aims of these approaches, they are often a focus of objection by professionals who claim that families often lack the pre-requisite skills and knowledge (e.g. Bailey et al., 1992). Nonetheless where parents have been trained in specific instructional skills, the results are dramatic (e.g. Leach and Siddall, 1990). It would seem, therefore, that perhaps the most fruitful approach to compensatory education is via the home background, with a re-education of parents into providing a learning environment in the home which would help the child to succeed in school in much the way that Bastiani recommends.

Race and Education

Concern has frequently been expressed about the performance of British Afro-Caribbean and British Asian pupils within the education system (e.g. Swann Report 1985). For example, a series of studies (reviewed by Tomlinson, 1983) has suggested that ethnic minorities perform worse than white children in English, maths and verbal reasoning, with the Afro-Caribbean group doing least well. Moreover, it has been found that "immigrant" children comprise a disproportionately high percentage of the pupils in ESN schools (e.g. Coard, 1971) and are more likely to be unemployed after leaving school. Explanations for these disturbing facts cover a range of areas, from the mismatch between the prevailing school and ethnic cultures, to low expectations and overt prejudice. Before these explanations are reviewed it is essential to consider the notion of "Black under-achievement". The term is typically used to mean a level of performance by Black children which is comparatively lower than their white counterparts. Implicit within this definition is the assumption that both Black and white pupils have the same potential for achievement within an identical education system.

However, the whole concept of underachievement is beset by methodological problems. For example, a variety of different measures have been used to assess performance, from national exams to individual teacher ratings, and these assessment procedures are not comparable. Closer inspection of the research suggests that the performance of Black pupils is not uniformly worse throughout their period at school and that both Afro-Caribbean and Asian pupils are increasingly more likely to stay on in full-time education (e.g. Griffin, 1986). Related to this point is the fact that much research has taken little account of sub-groups within these ethnic minorities. When these generic groups are broken down, there is consistent evidence to demonstrate that African Asians and Chinese pupils have a higher level of performance which is at least comparable to and often better than their white counterparts. (ILEA, 1987). Furthermore, many of the assessment strategies contain considerable cultural bias, having initially been developed for the white majority, and so have less relevance for Black pupils, and are typically administered by white teachers, educational psychologists or researchers, a factor well-known to disadvantage Black pupils (e.g. Hegarty and Lucas, 1979). Moreover, there is growing evidence that the educational performance of Black pupils improves as a function of the length of time they have spent in this country. In consequence, the studies emerging from the 1960's and 1970's no longer reflect the current picture but serve rather to consolidate low expectations of Black pupils' performance. In this way, the entire operational procedure involved in collecting data about underachievement conspires to disadvantage Black minorities.

However, even taking these factors into account, there emerges a consistent picture of educational underperformance by some ethnic sub-groups, e.g. Bangladeshi children. One of the primary explanations for this derives from the persistent and very severe racial harassment directed towards this sub-group which has had a damaging impact on the psychological and physical well-being of its members (Gordon, 1986). Without doubt, persecution of this sort has had an adverse effect on the educational attainment of Bangladeshi pupils. Prejudice may be multifactorially determined, but has at its root, a tendency for some individuals to think in stereotypes, the nature of which depends on the cultural perspective of the individuals concerned. Stereotypy assumes that characteristics ascribed to an entire group also apply to each individual member, thereby not only exaggerating the uniformity of any given group but also increasing its distinctiveness from any others. In this way, discrete groups emerge, a process facilitated by any clearly observable differences the group may have in common, such as skin colour or style of clothing. When members of a majority group have high levels of aggression, this aggression may be displaced, in the form of scapegoating and racist attacks on minority groups. While stereotyping and prejudice lie more in the domain of social psychology, their relevance to the educational performance of some ethnic minorities is obvious and must be addressed both at a policy and individual level.

Another powerful explanation for the lower performance of specific groups is socio–economic status (SES). The previous section documented how levels of housing, income and parental occupation influenced children's school achievement in a complex but significant way. Given that levels of poverty and unemployment are higher amongst Black communities (Taylor, 1987) it is hardly surprising that children from these communities do less well than their middle-class counterparts. When SES as a constant error is controlled for, a change in the picture emerges, such that the differential attainment between Black and white pupils drops significantly, and often shows a superior performance by Black pupils. For example, Roberts *et al.* (1983), in a comparison of Black and white children in six inner ring areas, found that Black pupils, especially girls, left school with more qualifications than white pupils. In essence, then, any apparent underachievement by ethnic minorities may be the direct result of their geographical location, in that *all* the children in those areas and at schools which serve them underperform by comparison with national averages.

The earlier point concerning the superior school achievement of girls, raises again the issue of gender as a factor in school performance. It is clearly essential not only to control for SES when making comparisons of school achievement amongst ethnic minorities, but also for gender (e.g. Tizard *et al.*, 1988). When sex is taken into account, it would appear that both Afro-Caribbean and Asian girls have a strong commitment to the process and outcome of education, possibly as a means of controlling their futures, and which leads to better school performance in many cases (e.g. Fuller, 1983).

The foregoing evidence indicates that it is clearly wholly inappropriate to assume that Black children uniformly perform worse than white children, since school performance is always multi-factorially determined and cannot be attributed to single causal explanations such as racial origin. However, if these findings are taken at face value, it is quite conceivable that myths about Black under-achievement with all the attendant expectations will perpetuate. And, indeed, there is some evidence to suggest that the attitudes and expectations of white teachers towards their Black pupils may be a contributory factor to Black pupils' performance. Numerous studies (e.g. Eggleston *et al.*, 1986) have found that many teachers hold firm stereotypes about their Black pupils assuming, for instance, that Afro-Caribbean children are either lazy or aggressive, and Asian pupils are passive, industrious and pushed by their over ambitious parents. Scant regard is paid by a majority of teachers to the processes which operate to produce particular behaviours in particular pupils. These attitudes are likely to give rise to a host of unacceptable teacher behaviours based on their expectations of pupil characteristics. For example, Green (1985) found that some teachers gave less class time and attention to Black pupils, while other research has demonstrated, disturbingly, that Black pupils were more likely to be penalised in a variety of ways through misclassification of their abilities and behaviour (e.g. Cooper *et al.*, 1991). As an illustration, CRE (1985) found that Afro-Caribbean pupils were four times more likely to be suspended from school than their white counterparts, even when the original behaviours were comparable. In this way, teachers have the power to exclude ethnic minorities from a variety of educational experiences and opportunities and thus maintain, at least in part, a self-fulfilling prophecy. While this is damaging and divisive in itself, what may be more worrying is the fact that the real reasons for apparent underachievement which have already been noted, may be ignored and a set of erroneous explanations subscribed to instead.

Perhaps the most problematic of these is the notion of biological determinism, which implies that racial groups have some genetic and hence immutable characteristics which distinguish them and which justify discriminatory treatment. The foundation for this perspective was laid in the nineteenth century, when pseudo–scientific theories suggested that the entire human race could be subdivided on the groups of hair and skin colour, facial features and bodily structures, as well as in terms of personality and intellectual capacities which were, in themselves, determinants of achievement. Moreover, there was a rank ordering of status, such that the white races were considered to be superior to any other. Despite a large corpus of biological evidence which contradicts the assumption that individuals belong to genotypically and phenotypically separate races, research still continues which attempts to identify inherent differences between races on a range of characteristics, from brain weight and intelligence, through maturational rate, personality, size of genitalia and law abidingness (Rushton, 1990). Insofar as this research is accepted, it provides apparent justification for assuming the unalterability of numerous human characteristics on genetic grounds and the consequent discriminatory behaviour towards certain groups. This point can best be clarified by an example.

Racist arguments concerning intellectual ability have focused on the question of whether Blacks are inherently less intelligent than whites, and indeed, the available evidence would suggest that on standard IQ tests, Black groups do, in fact, achieve lower scores than white groups. However, some theorists argue that the cause of this discrepancy is genetic, in that the groups differ in inherent ability (e.g. Jensen, 1980), while others argue that environmental determinants are responsible (Kamin, 1976). There is, predictably, a wealth of evidence on this controversy (see Mackintosh and Mascie-Taylor, 1985 for a review), but is worth pointing out that these results may well be an artefact of the IQ tests used, which are typically devised for and validated on, white populations, rendering them comparatively valueless for any ethnic minority, since they have not been standardised on those populations. Not only is this a violation of proper psychometric practice, but it also has major implications for social policies based on individual and group test performance. Furthermore, children whose first language is not English are immediately disadvantaged not only in assessments of this kind, but in a wider educational sense through a process of home-school alienation. In addition when Black children are raised by high SES white families they score significantly higher on IQ tests than Black children brought up in their natural, but low SES, families (Scarr and Weinberg, 1976).

It seems fair to conclude then, that any observable differences in measured IQ between ethnic groups may be attributed to the complex determination of ability through an interplay of cultural and environmental experiences. Until a sound methodological technique can be found for eliminating the effects of environment on cognitive capacities, no conclusions can be drawn about genetically determined differences in ability.

A further, (erroneous), explanation for Black underachievement in schools concerns the assumed pathology of Black family structures, in particular, the Afro-Caribbean family. Rushton (1990) claims a high level of marital instability among negroid races, suggesting that Afro-Caribbean families may be characterised by a high percentage of female–dominated broken homes, with consequent instability and criminality. However, the real facts are in contradiction to these claims, since the majority of Afro-Caribbean children are raised in 2-parent families. Moreover, there is no conclusive evidence that single-parent families, in themselves, harm the educational achievements of the children (e.g. Phoenix, 1988). What seems to be operating instead within the family organisation are poor employment conditions and inadequate child–care facilities both of which combine to produce a system of disadvantage for any individual, Black or white, who fails within this group. In essence, then, any family who is materially disadvantaged may not have the resources to effect change and improvement in their children's educational experiences, and it is this, rather than racial origin, which maintains the current inequalities.

The literature on race and education is extensive, but is is possible to draw a number of conclusions. Firstly, the whole concept of Black underachievement is inappropriate, suggesting as it does a failure to meet certain universally prescribed standards, irrespective of the needs and abilities brought by the pupils to the learning situation. It would be better instead to encompass a diverse range of achievements in various disciplines which are not considered to be inherently superior or inferior to each other. Secondly, the evidence that exists to support the concept of lower levels of attainment among ethnic minorities is methodologically flawed by their failure to control for a number of variables such as SES, gender and sub-cultural differences within the minority groups. And finally, equality of educational opportunity for Black pupils may be hindered by persistent racist stereotyping by teachers and other pupils which may lead to a narrowing of educational options and outcomes for these pupils. The Swann Report recommended that pilot projects should be set up to implement multicultural and antiracist policies in education and almost every LEA in the country responded to these recommendations. In this sense, substantial reforms were made possible. However, it is worth pointing out that the 1988 Education Reform Act may operate against these objectives (e.g. Troyna and Hatcher, 1991) emphasising as it does, firstly, a National Curriculum which limits the possibilities for teaching core subjects in a multicultural way, secondly, open enrolment in schools which could conceivably lead to segregation by default, and thirdly, a mainly Christian religious education programme. There are, of course, other wide-ranging implications of the Act, but until the issue of race and education becomes a primarily educational as opposed to political item with a top-down as opposed to bottom-up implementation of multicultural policy it is unlikely that major gains will be made with the celerity required.

Conclusion

The effectiveness of the education system on the child's attainment depends heavily on the individual differences pupils bring to the learning situation, such as intellectual ability, motivation, etc. This chapter has attempted to explore some of these factors ranging from fundamental models of cognitive development to specific skill acquisition such as reading. However, it is inappropriate to focus exclusively on the child without taking into account the external influences or context within which any given child operates. In this sense, ethnic origin, social class, family background and the political framework are all influential in determining the outcomes of the education process. Consequently the interplay of the individual with the environment is critical, and can be thought of as an ecosystem. By trying to identify the many influences on a child's general and educational development, it is possible to go some way towards understanding how some children become disadvantaged within the school system and the means by which compensation for this can best be made. Some of these aspects have been illustrated here and they will be explored further in the next chapter.

REFERENCES

Allington, R. & Strange, M. (1977). Effects of graphemic substitution in connected text upon reading behaviour. *Visible Language* II 285–297.

Archer, J. (1992). Gender stereotyping of school subjects. *The Psychologist* 5(2) 66–69.

Assessment of Performance Unit (1982a) *Mathematical Development: Primary Survey Report No 2* London, HMSO.

Assessment of Performance Unit (1982b). *Language Performance in Schools: Primary Survey Report No 2* London: HMSO.

Bailey, D.B., Buysse, V., Edmondson, R. and Smith, T.M. (1992). Creating family-centred services in early intervention: Perceptions of Professionals in four states. *Exceptional children* 58(4) 298–309.

Bastiani, J. (1987). From compensation ... to participation? A brief analysis of changing attitudes in the study and practice of home–school relations. In: J. Bastiani. (Ed) *Parents and Teachers* Windsor, NFER Nelson.

Bernstein, B. (1962). *Class, Codes and Control, Vol. 1* London: Routledge & Kegan Paul.

Bernstein, B. (1971). *Class, Codes and Control, Vol. 1* London: Routledge & Kegan Paul.

Binet, A. (1909). *Les Idées Modernes sur les Enfants.* Paris: Flammarion.

Blatchford, P., Burke, J., Farquhar, C., Plewis, I. and Tizard, B. (1988). A Systematic observation study of children's behaviour at infant school. In Woodhead, M. & McGrath, A. (Eds) *Family, School and Society: a Reader* Milton Keynes: Open University Press.

Bordieu, P. (1983). The Forms of Capital. In: Richardson, J.G. (ed.) (1986). *Handbook of Theory of Research for the Sociology of Education* New York: Greenwood Press.

Bouchard, T.J. Jr. & McGue, M. (1981). Familial studies of intelligence: a review. *Science* 212 1055–1059.

Bower, T.G.R. (1981). Cognitive development. In M. Roberts & J. Tamburrini (Eds) *Child Development 0–5* Edinburgh: Holmes McDougall.

Bower, G.H., Clark, M., Lesgold, A. & Winzenz, D. (1969). Hierarchical retrieval systems in the recall of categorised word lists. *Journal of Verbal Learning and Verbal Behaviour* 8 323–43.

Bruner, J.S., Olver, R.R. & Greenfield, P.M. (1966). *Studies in Cognitive Growth: a Collaboration at the Centre of Cognitive Studies* New York: Wiley.

Bynner, J.M. (1972). *Parents' attitudes to education* Office of Population Censuses and Surveys: Social Survey Division, London, HMSO.

Campaign for Racial Equality (CRE) (1985). *Birmingham Local Education Authority and Schools: referral and suspension of pupils* London: CRE.

Ceci, S.J. (1990). *On intelligence ... More or Less: a Bio-ecological theory of intellectual development* Englewood Cliffs, N.J., Prentice Hall.

Central Advisory Council for Education (England) (1963). *Half Our Future* London: HMSO (The Newsom Report).

Christensen, C.A. & Cooper, T.J. (1992). The role of cognitive strategies in the transition from counting to retrieval of basic addition facts. *British Educational Research Journal* 18(1) 37–44.

Claxton, G. (1989). *Classroom Learning* Milton Keynes: Open University Press.

Coard, B. (1971). *How the West Indian child is made educationally subnormal in the British school system* London: New Beacon Books.

Cooper, P., Upton, G. & Smith, C. (1991). Ethnic minority and gender distribution among staff and pupils in facilities for pupils with emotional and behavioural difficulties in England and Wales. *British Journal of Sociology of Education* 12(1) 77–94.

Cosin, B., Flude, M. & Hales, M. (1989). *School, Work and Equality* Milton Keynes: Open University Press.

Davie, R., Butler, N. & Goldstein, H. (1972). *From Birth to Seven* London: Longman.

Deem, R. (1984) (Ed). *Co-education Reconsidered* Milton Keynes: Open University Press.

Deem, R. (1989). *Gender and Education* Milton Keynes: Open University Press.

Delamont, S. (1980). *Sex Roles and the School* London: Methuen.

DES (1967). *Children and their Primary Schools* (The Plowden Report) London: HMSO.

DES (1985). *Education for All* (The Swann Report) London: HMSO.

Donaldson, M. (1978). *Children's Minds* London: Fontana.

Dubberley, W. (1988). Social class and the process of school – a case study of a comprehensive school in a mining community. In Green, A. & Ball, S. (Eds) *Progress and Inequality in Comprehensive Education* London: Routledge.

Dweck, C.S., Davidson, W., Nelson, W. & Enna, B. (1978). Sex differences in learned helplessness: II. The contingencies of evaluative feedback in the classroom: III. An experimental analysis *Developmental Psychology* 14 268-276.

Egglestone, J., Dunne, D., Anjali, M. & Wright, C. (1986). (Eds) *Education for some: the educational and vocational experiences of 15–18 year old members of minority ethnic groups.* Stoke-on-Trent, Trentham Books.

Ehri, L.C. & Robbins, C. (1992). Beginners need some decoding skill to read words by analogy. *Reading Research Quarterly* 27 13-26.

Elliott, C.D., Murray, D.J. & Pearson, L.S. (1977). *The British Ability Scales* Windsor, NFER Publishing Co Limited.

Fergusson, D.M., Lloyd, M. & Horwood, L.J. (1991). Teacher evaluations of the performance of boys and girls. *New Zealand Journal of Educational Studies* 26 (2) 155-163.

Fuller, M. (1983). Qualified criticism, critical qualifications. In Barton, L. & Walker, S. (Eds). *Race, Class and Education* Beckenham: Croom Helm.

Gagné, R.M. (1974). *Essentials of Learning for Instruction* Hinsdale, Illinois, Dryden Press.

Goldman, S.R., Hogaboam, T.W., Bell, L.C., Perfetti, C.A. (1980). Short-term retention of discourse during reading. *Journal of Educational Psychology* 68 680-688.

Goodman, K.S. (1972). Reading: A psycholinguistic guessing game. In: H. Singer & R.B. Ruddell (Eds) *Theoretical Models and Processes of Reading* Newark, D.E. International Reading Assn.

Gordon, P. (1986). *Racial Violence and Harassment* London: Runnymede Trust.

Green, P. (1985). Multi ethnic teaching and the pupil's self-concept. In D.E.S. *Education for All* London: HMSO.

Griffin, C. (1986). *Black and White Youth in a declining job market* Leicester, Centre for Mass Communication Res.

Hargreaves, D.J. & Colley, A. (1986). *The Psychology of Sex Roles* London: Harper and Row.

Hegarty, S. & Lucas, F. (1979). *Able to Learn: the pursuit of culture – fair assessment* Windsor: NFER.

Heim, A.W. (1970). *The Appraisal of Intelligence* Slough, NFER.

Hewison, J. (1988). The long-term effectiveness of parental involvement in reading: a follow-up to the Haringey reading project. *British Journal of Educational Psychology* 58 184-190.

Howe, M.J.A. (1984). *A Teacher's Guide to the Psychology of Learning* Oxford: Blackwell.

Howe, M.J.A. (1988). "Hot-house" Children. *The Psychologist* 1(9) 356-358.

Howe, M.J.A. (1990). Does Intelligence exist? *The Psychologist* 3(11) 490-493.

ILEA (1987). *Ethnic Background and Examination Results 1985 and 1986* London: ILEA.

Jahoda, G. (1983). European 'lag' in the development of an economic concept: a study in Zimbabwe. *British Journal of Developmental Psychology* 1 113-120.

Jensen, A.R. (1980). *Bias in Mental Testing* London: Methuen.

Kamin, L.J. (1976). Heredity, Intelligence, politics and psychology. In Block, N.J. & Dworkin, G. (Eds) *The IQ controversy* New York: Pantheon.

Kohn, M.L. (1969). *Class and Conformity* Homewood, IU., Dorsey.

Lareau, A. (1989). *Home Advantage* Lewes, The Falmer Press.

Leach, D.J. & Siddall, S.W. (1990). Parental involvement in the teaching of reading: a comparison of hearing reading, paired reading, pause, prompt and praise and direct instruction methods *British Journal of Educational Psychology* 60 349-355.

Light, P., Sheldon, S. & Woolhead, M. (Eds) (1991). *Learning to Think* London: Routledge.

Locurto, C. (1988). On the malleability of IQ *The Psychologist* 11 431-435.

Maccoby, E. & Jacklin, C. (1975). *The Psychology of Sex Differences* Stanford: Stanford University Press.

Mckenzie, A.J. (1981). Level I and Level II abilities in primary school children *British Journal of Educational Psychology* 51(3) 312-320.

Mackintosh, N. & Mascie-Taylor, C. (1985). The IQ question. In D.E.S. *Education for All* London: HMSO.

Morgan, V. & Dunn, S. (1990). Management Strategies and gender differences in nursery and infant classrooms. *Research in Education* 44 81-91.

Mossler, D.G., Marvin, R.S. & Greenberg, M.T. (1976). Conceptual perspective taking in 2- to 6-year old children. *Developmental Psychology* 13 314-319.

Munby, S. (1989). *Assessing and Recording Achievement* Oxford: Blackwell.

Nettlebeck, T. (1990). Intelligence does exist. *The Psychologist* 3(11) 494-497.

Newson, J. & Newson, E. (1970). *Four Years Old in an Urban Community* Harmondsworth: Penguin.

Nicholson, T. (1991). Do children read words better in contexts or lists? A classic study revisited. *Journal of Educational Psychology* 83(4) 444-450.

Nuttall, D. (1989). *The assessment of learning* Milton Keynes: Open University Press.

Palardy, J. (1969). What teachers believe – what children achieve *Elementary School Journal* 69 370-374.

Pasnak, R., Holt, R., Campbell, J.W. & McCutcheon, L. (1991). Cognitive achievement gains for kindergartners instructed in Piagetian operations *Journal of Educational Research* 85(1) 5-13.

Perfetti, C.A. (1985). *Reading Ability* N.Y. Oxford University Press.

Phoenix, A. (1988). The Afro-Caribbean Myth *New Society* March 4.

Piaget, J. (1970). Piaget's Theory. In P.H. Mussen (Ed) *Carmichael's Manual of Child Psychology* (Vol. 1., 3rd Edition) New York: Wiley.

Plewis, I., Mooney, A. & Creeser, R. (1990). Time on Educational Activities at home and educational progress in infant school. *British Journal of Educational Psychology* 60 330-337.

Quillian, M.R. (1968). Semantic Memory. In Minsky, M. (Ed) *Semantic Information Processing*. Cambridge, Mass., M.I.T. Press.

Rich, J. (1975). Effects of children's attractiveness on teachers' evaluation. *Journal of Educational Psychology* 67 599-609.

Riding, R. & Mathias, D. (1991). Cognitive styles and preferred learning mode, reading attainment and cognitive ability in 11-year old children. *Educational Psychology* 11 (3 and 4) 383-393.

Roberts, K., Duggan, J. & Noble, M. (1983). Young, black and out of work. In Troyna, B. & Smith, D. (Eds). *Racism, School and the Labour Market* Leicester: National Youth Bureau.

Rumelhart, D.E. & McClelland, J.L. (1982). An interactive activation model of context effects in letter perception. Part II: The contextual enhancement effect and some tests and extensions of the model. *Psychological Review* 89 60-94.

Rumelhart, D.E. & Norman, D.A. (1978). Accretion, Tuning and Restructuring three modes of Learning. In Cotton, J.W. & Klatzky, R.L. (Eds) *Semantic Factors in Cognition*. Hillsdale, N.J., Laurence Erlbaum.

Rushton, J.P. (1990). Race differences, r/K theory and a reply to Flynn. *The Psychologist* 5 195-198.

Scarr, S. & Weinberg, R.A. (1976). IQ test performance of black children adopted by white families *American Psychologist* **31** 726–739.

Shayer, M. & Wylam, H. (1978). The distribution of Piagetian stages of thinking in British middle and secondary school children. *British Journal of Educational Psychology* **46** 164–173.

Sheldon, S. (1985). *Learning to Read* Milton Keynes: Open University Press.

Skinner, B.F. (1974). *About Behaviourism* London: Jonathan Cape.

Smith, P.K. & Cowie, H. (1988). *Understanding Children's Development* Oxford: Blackwell.

Spearman, C.E. (1904). "General Intelligence" objectively determined and measured. *American Journal of Psychology* **15** 72–101.

Spender, D. (1982). *Invisible women: The Schooling scandal* London: Writers and Readers Cooperative.

Stanovich, K.E. (1980). Towards an interactive-compensatory model of individual differences in the development of reading fluency. *Reading Research Quarterly* **16** 32–71.

Sternberg, R.J. (1982). (Ed) *Handbook of Human Intelligence* Cambridge: Cambridge University Press.

Stone, B.J. (1992). Prediction of Achievement by Asian-American and White Children *Journal School Psychology* **30** 91–99.

Swann, W. (1982). *Psychology and Special Education* Milton Keynes: Open University Press.

Task Group on Assessment and Testing (1988). *National Curriculum: A Report* (TGAT) London: D.E.S./Welsh Office.

Taylor, D. (1987). Living with unemployment. In Walker, A. & Walker, C. (Eds) *The Growing Divide: a Social Audit 1979–1987* London: Child Poverty Action Group.

Tizard, B. & Hughes, M. (1984). *Young Children Learning* London: Fontana Paperbacks.

Tizard, B., Hughes, M., Carmichael, H. & Pinkerton, G. (1988). Language and Social Class: Is verbal deprivation a myth? In Woodhead, M. & McGrath, A. *Family, School and Society: A Reader.* Milton Keynes: Open University Press.

Tomlinson, S. (1983). *Ethnic Minorities in British Schools* London: Heinemann.

Troyna, B. & Hatcher, R. (1991). 'British Schools for British Citizens?' *Oxford Review of Education* **17**(3) 287–299.

Tutchell, E. (1990). (Ed). *Dons and Dungarees* Milton Keynes: Open University Press.

Vellutino, F.R. (1991). Introduction to three studies on reading acquisition: convergent findings on theoretical foundations of code-oriented versus whole-language approaches to reading instruction. *Journal of Educational Psychology* **83**(4) 437–443.

Wolfendale, S., Bryans, .T, Fox, M. Labram, A. & Sigston, A. (1992). *The Profession and Practice of Educational Psychology* London: Cassell Education Ltd.

Zajonc, R.B. (1976). Family configuration and intelligence. *Science* **192** 227–236.

3

THE TEACHER AND THE LEARNING ENVIRONMENT

C.M. HICKS, P.C. SPURGEON AND V. PARFFREY

The Social Context

The education system is increasingly and fundamentally influenced by political perspectives, to the extent that many major developments in educational provision and school curricula are determined more by central government than by sound research or local individual needs. The agents of the education system, including schools, teachers, children and parents, operate and exert reciprocal influence within a total social system, which is largely determined by the prevailing educational policy and ideology of the time. For example the introduction of a national curriculum and the publication of a League table of examination performance results will undoubtedly influence the activities and focus of teachers.

Whilst acknowledging this broader social setting, it is, nonetheless, true to say that psychology as a discipline has traditionally adhered to an approach which focused on the individual, seeking to determine the factors influencing learning outcomes and to provide methods of coping with problems of behavioural adjustment at the individual level. The role of the educational psychologist, too, has typically been defined by the demand to assess and to initiate individual remedial programmes. Whilst this role is now altering somewhat in the U.K., there is still considerable emphasis on the individual within the system (see Wolfendale et al., 1992). The changing role of the Educational Psychologist will be dealt with at the end of this chapter. However, this rather narrow individual perspective is broadening to encompass more aspects of the whole social environment. Classroom behaviour is now more widely acknowledged as being the product of the person–environment interaction, which while not a novel hypothesis in itself, has not yet been widely adopted in the field of educational psychology (Burden and Hornby, 1989). Increasingly, however, constructs from social psychology are being assimilated into education with a consequent revision of the perception of classroom processes from an individualistic to a systems perspective. Concepts such as role, interaction, and ethos are now making inroads into educationalists' thinking (see Rogers and Kutnick, 1990). This chapter reflects this wider emphasis by looking at the impact of social factors within the classroom and deals with the major sources of influence within the education system.

The very fact that a body of literature now exists about events within the classroom is evidence of a fundamental change in relationships between schools and society. The classroom was once rather like the inner sanctum where only teachers and pupils dared set foot. Many teachers had, as individuals, long advocated a more open relationship which has now largely been achieved by the critical questioning and increased accountability of the education system. As a result, many schools now welcome parents into the school as a positive and valuable addition to their own activities and a previously closed system, shrouded in professional mystique, is now open and understood by many more people. The demand for democratisation and participation has led to parents and society as a whole requiring a rationale beyond that of the formal, professional status of the teacher to explain the methods and achievements of the school system.

Just as the child was the focus of the previous chapter here, because of the changes outlined above, it is the teacher and the wider context in which he/she operates, which form the central part of this chapter.

Teachers and Teaching

The teacher plays a crucial role in the development and socialisation of the child into society. Lindgren (1980) says:

> "The kind of future we and our children will experience is influenced more by teachers than any other professional group."

Given the degree of influence a teacher has on a child, it is hardly surprising that a great deal of emphasis has been placed on identifying central teacher functions and on the consequent development of "good teaching".

In terms of teacher functions, Davies (1971) sees teachers as managers of resources for learning and has identified four broad functions of the teacher's rôle:

1. Planning – establishing learning objectives;
2. Organising – arranging and relating learning resources so as to realise the objectives in the most effective, efficient and economical way possible;
3. Leading – motivating, encouraging and inspiring his/her students so that they readily realise the objectives;
4. Controlling – determining whether his/her organising and leading functions are successful in realising the objectives.

Whilst in other professions, such as medicine and law, there exists a definable expertise which limits the area of role activity, this is not the case in teaching, since the necessity of focusing on the needs of children means responding to very diverse requirements which require a broad role structure. Goals such as motivating the individual, transmitting values and awakening a sense of criticism are non-specific and as a consequence the activities of the role are highly diverse. This means inevitably, that successful teaching must depend on a wide variety of factors, and because of its dynamic nature cannot conform easily to a prescribed notion of cause and effect. As a result, it is immensely difficult to pin down what constitutes good teaching, or the "good teacher". Nonetheless, the current culture of performance-related pay has given rise to several attempts to do just this. For example, the Dept. Education and Science in 1982 outlined a four-fold profile of the good teacher as one who engages in good classroom management, who sets appropriate aims and objectives for the capabilities of classroom members, who matches pupil abilities and needs with work given and expected, and who uses language appropriately as a technique of instruction and development. Broad (1987) developed some of these issues in a blue-print for a "good teacher", citing five essential attributes:

professional behaviour (e.g. being reliable and co-operative)

personal qualities (e.g. being able to control the class, able to make use of a range of teaching styles)

organisational attributes (e.g. able to engage in short and long-term planning, able to encourage pupils' listening skills)

perceptive qualities (e.g. able to perceive and respond to pupils' individual differences, able to determine external factors which are affecting the individual)

information-gathering skills and evaluative skills (e.g. being skilled at identifying reasons for failure, being aware of temporary and permanent factors which may be affecting pupils' learning and behaviour)

Teaching Styles

Inherent within the above analysis is the notion of teaching style. At an intuitive level it would seem reasonable to suppose that particular teaching styles are related to good learning outcomes. While the corpus of research on the topic has generally endorsed this notion, the picture is more complex, necessitating an unambiguous system by which teaching styles can be classified, a definition of outcome which takes account of all the attributes a child brings to the classroom, and some understanding of the dynamic interaction between the two. Clearly, a simple cause and effect model is inadequate.

The starting point, however, is a classification system of teaching style, the best known of which is along a traditional–progressive, formal–informal dimension (Woods, 1989). Without doubt, over the last decade or two, teaching styles have become more flexible, open and informal, although this movement away from formal educational procedures has been extensively blamed for producing a generation of children who seem to lack mastery of the basic 3R skills. This debate has intensified attempts to link teaching style with pupil attainment in order to systematise procedures. However teaching styles cannot be so easily classified into traditional vs progressive, since teachers slip in and out of styles according to the pupil, problem and subject. Despite this, some links have been found between teaching style and pupil progress. For example, the Oracle project involved an in-depth study of the practice of primary teachers and their pupils. It identified six main teaching styles based primarily on the teacher's organisational approach, of which three were associated with better pupil performance in maths, comprehension and reading (Galton and Simon, 1980, Galton, 1987). However, on further analysis, the authors concluded that underlying these three styles was a high level of teacher–child interaction based on ideas–exchange and open-ended questioning, and it was this that seemed to engender greater attainment. What appears to emerge from this research is the notion that those factors deemed to be critical to pupil progress may be common to a number of different teaching styles and that a child's success is multifactorially determined.

Other studies have concentrated on the teacher's *cognitive* style rather than teaching style, which in turn has led to several attempts to explore personality variables associated with teacher performance. For example, Saracho and Dayton (1980) examined cognitive style as a variable influencing pupil performance. Field independent teachers whose cognitive style was felt to imply a more questioning, individualistic approach were reported as producing greater achievement gains than field dependent (more conventional, conforming) teachers.

Teacher personality has formed the focus of other research in this area. For example, Cattell's 16 PF measure has figured prominently in those investigations concerned with teacher personality and teaching ability, with McCabe and Savage (1973) reporting positive correlations between teaching practice grades and factors A (outgoing) and F (enthusiastic). Studies using the 16 PF have been reviewed by Sharples and Woodman (1972) and they list the following factors as having been found to be associated with good teaching performance on more than one occasion.

TABLE 1
16 PF factors found to be related to teaching effectiveness

Factor G	(Expedient v *Conscientious*)
Factor M	(Practical v *Imaginative*)
Factor H	(Shy v *Venturesome*)
Factor O	(*Self-Assured* v Apprehensive)
Factor Q₃	(Undisciplined v *Controlled*)
Factor F	(Sober v *Happy-go-Lucky*)
Factor L	(*Trusting* v Suspicious)
Factor N	(*Forthright* v Shrewd)
Factor Q₄	(*Relaxed* v Tense)

*The italic pole of the dimension being positively associated with good teaching.

But in contrast, Coletta (1975) compared open with traditional teachers on two standard personality measures (Edwards Personal Preference Schedule and Thurstone Temperament Schedule) and was unable to report any significant differences between the two groups at all. A slightly different approach was taken by Myers, Kennedy and Cruikshank (1979) who attempted to relate personality characteristics to types of problem issues perceived by the teachers themselves. They produced a series of personality profiles which appeared intuitively to form sensible links with the nature of the problems specified. For example, anxious, sensitive teachers were concerned about classroom control. This may present a promising direction for future research replacing static personality measures with rather more dynamic, individual problem identification.

In an important longitudinal study, Cortis (1979) suggested that personality characteristics become less and less clearly linked with teaching competence as teachers proceed through the professional ladder, with other professional experience–oriented criteria becoming more important in predicting future promotions.

Assessing Teacher Performance

The somewhat confused situation relating to personality variables can partly be explained by the variety of samples used (student teachers, qualified teachers, junior and secondary school teachers) and also by the fact that sex differences have usually been ignored. Perhaps most important though is the wide variety of assessment criteria employed. Indeed the entire area of determining teacher effectiveness is bedeviled by uncertainty as to how to evaluate teaching performance. Just what constitutes success, effectiveness or competence in a teacher? Does it depend on whether pupils are happy or miserable, whether the teacher gets promotion or whether pupils pass examinations? Techniques currently in use may be categorised under the following headings.

1. *Expert judgement*

The approach involves using experienced experts knowledgeable about teaching to make judgements about teaching performance. It is probably the most easily available technique but as a global and impressionistic procedure it has serious problems of subjectivity, bias and inconsistency.

2. *Rating scales*

Once again a judgement is made by an outsider with teaching experience but on this occasion moderated by a structure of teaching dimensions located onto rating scales. The scales consist of a list of qualities or abilities felt to be desirable in a teacher and by focusing upon specific aspects of teaching it is intended to increase the objectivity of assessment. The problem of interpretation of the meaning of specific factors still exists and a general 'halo' effect (an indiscriminate over or under rating of qualities by being unduly influenced by one factor in particular) cannot be avoided. Nonetheless the scales have proved useful in producing more consistency across raters.

3. *Pupil changes*

This approach concentrates upon trying to measure changes in pupil scores on specific achievement tests. This is perhaps the most appealing criterion available since it is fair to impute that teaching is directed toward bringing about some change in the learner. Therefore, measurements of any change provides the most suitable index of effectiveness and at least within the British education system will play an increasing part in determining a school's financial position. The simplicity of pupil change is, however, illusory. Assessment of pupil change is hampered by a number of important methodological limitations:

(a) if teachers are to be evaluated by pupil achievement then for each class pupils must be equated for ability and level of attainment;

(b) different rates of maturation mean that advances may not be attributable to the teacher;

(c) preparatory groundwork by a previous teacher may be as important as any current teaching contribution;

(d) the learning possibilities represented by friends, parents and books cannot be isolated sufficiently to attribute improvement to the teacher;

(e) achievement testing in the short term is susceptible to the impact of concentrated 'cramming' and this sort of success may really be less important than longer term grasp of principles which is less easy to assess;

(f) finally, the emphasis, within pupil change, on intellectual growth leads to the neglect of equally important affective development.

4. *Pupil opinion*

The approach here is inferential, is attempting to judge the quality of a teacher by seeking the views of those being taught. It is often argued that no-one is in a better position to judge the effectiveness of a teacher's performance than his/her pupils. They are certainly with the teacher more than anyone else, but just what sort of criteria do pupils use to judge their teachers and are these relevant to teaching effectiveness? Pupils, especially younger children, tend to judge in terms of liking, with the emphasis on personal rather than pedagogical characteristics. Thus, although the information may well be useful in understanding the classroom process, it would seem that this particular criterion is very indirect. (See Stones (1979) and Selmes (1989) for a review of teacher evaluation).

Part of the conflict in the results deriving from studies of teacher evaluation stems from differences in methodological approach, with some researchers focussing on product criteria (outcomes such as pupil achievements) while others concentrate on process criteria (specific teaching behaviours seen as having some inherent value in themselves). The diversity of measures no doubt contributes significantly to the lack of clear, agreed measures of teaching effectiveness. However, it is more realistic to acknowledge that as there is a host of different teaching contexts no teacher can be equally effective in each one; as de Landsheere (1980) concludes, "there is no single and universal type of good teacher". There is a virtually unlimited number of good teacher styles and the range of effectiveness criteria employed reflect this individual and situational variety.

Increasingly research efforts are moving from such broad-based associations of this kind to specific studies relating pupil/teacher characteristics to more precise effects. One such area attracting a good deal of current attention is teacher stress.

In a report by Cox and Brockley (1984) teachers were found to experience more stress than non-teachers, the nett outcome of which was an adverse effect on teachers' performance. It is inevitable, of course, that if teaching quality is impaired then so will pupils' learning outcomes, and some account has been taken of this by the escalation in stress management programmes for teachers (e.g. Bamford *et al.*, 1990). While the cause of high stress levels has been variously attributed to several factors such as workload, poor resources and demographic characteristics (e.g. Borg and Riding, 1991) undoubtedly disruptive pupil behaviour plays a part. Management of pupils with behaviour problems is therefore a central concern for most classroom teachers.

Managing Problem Behaviour

It is difficult to pin down exactly what is construed as disturbed behaviour particularly as the problem may be transient, selectively manifested and variously interpreted. For instance, Fontana (1988) defines problem behaviour as any behaviour which is unacceptable to the teacher, and consequently demonstrates the importance of the teacher in the assessment process. However, over-reliance on an individual teacher's standards of what is acceptable may lead to definitions of problem behaviour which largely reflect the teacher's own value system rather than an expression of the needs of the child. Thus if problem behaviour 'lies in the eye of the beholder', many incipient or established problems may well go unaided.

Perhaps more helpful definitions are those which make use of some observable effects on the educational process as a result of the behaviour problem. Lindgren

(1980) for example, suggests that problem behaviour is "any kind of behaviour that creates difficulties (interferes with the effective functioning of the student or the classroom group) or reveals the presence of difficulties (indicates that the student or group is not functioning effectively". This definition omits to label a *child* as disturbed, but identifies the *behaviour* as deviant instead, and thus affords a more constructive, problem oriented approach.

Inevitably, the definition adopted will influence the prevalence estimates of behaviour problems. A survey by Rutter *et al.* (1975) of 10–11 year olds in Inner London obtained a prevalence rate of 25.4%, while Wilson and Evans (1980) found that 10% of all school children were classified as having problems. Generally, from these studies it would appear that disturbed behaviour is related to age, gender, social class and culture or subculture to which the child belongs.

Taking these results at a more practical level, out of a class of 25–30 pupils, there are likely to be 3 with severe problems and between 6 and 10 who show sufficient disturbance to warrant intervention. As Swift and Spivack (1978) noted, this may mean that teachers may have to interrupt classroom activities on average every two and a half minutes in order to attempt some corrective action. Given, too, that the school achievement of the child with behaviour problems deteriorates significantly as the child progresses through school, this underlines the seriousness of the issue as an educational problem, as well as being a potent source of teacher stress.

Such a situation inevitably means that teachers are intimately involved in the identification and management of disturbed behaviour. However, this rôle is not always an acceptable one, for a number of reasons. For example, many teachers deny responsibility for dealing with the problem, pointing instead to their primary duty of teaching; in addition, their training typically does not equip teachers to detect problem behaviours and this is compounded by an absence of an adequate set of criteria for defining what is meant by disturbed behaviour. The outcome, then, is often one whereby those children usually acknowledged by other professionals as being most troubled (i.e. the silent and withdrawn pupil) are the very ones overlooked by the teacher because they pose few management problems in class. The current position requires teachers to act as an agent for screening problem behaviours and yet conspires to ignore those pupils most in need of help. Clearly, the situation would benefit from clearer assessment schedules of disturbed behaviour. If this could be achieved then it would afford educators information on the incidence, severity, nature, origin and treatment of the problem.

There are in existence a variety of such measures which can be classified under three headings

(i)   teacher assessments
(ii)   peer group assessments
(iii) self-assessments

Teacher assessments tend to take the form of a rating scale providing descriptions of behaviours on which the teacher rates the applicability to the child, e.g. Rutter's (1967) Children's Behavior Questionnaire. However, little concordance has been found between scores on various scales, thereby pointing to important psychometric issues about their reliability and validity as well as the possibility that they may be based on ill-founded classifications of behavioural problems (e.g. McMichael, 1981). On the pro-side, however, they are easy to use, and if they serve the purpose of initiating a full referral process, can be said to be more valuable than the even more unsystematic and subjective alternatives. Peer–group assessments are typically based on a sociometric approach whereby each member of a class of children is asked to nominate a child or children in the class with whom they would most like to be friendly. Sociograms are then constructed to identify the social isolates. The underlying assumption is that maladjustment is characterised by poor personal relationships – an assumption which may well be invalid since many isolates are stable, independent people. Furthermore, sociometric techniques may reflect the deviant norms of the majority of the class and are inappropriate for very young children. The third approach – self-assessment indices, require children to assess themselves by providing a description of their own characteristics. One example of this is the Mooney Problem Check List which has 210 items referring to a number of areas – home and family, school, relationships – thereby broadening the concept of disturbance outside the school boundary and giving indications of some of the possible causes. Such scales, however, require a degree of perspicacity which many children do not have.

The origins of disturbed behaviour have been a focus of great interest to psychologists and educators alike. As with any area of psychology there are a number of conceptual frameworks which can be applied to the study of this particular human behaviour and Docking (1980) has rationalised these perspectives with reference to behaviour problems. Of the variety of theoretical stances he discusses, three will be discussed here.

One of the most important explanations of causality are the Learning/Social Learning Theories. Learning theories of human behaviour developed out the S–R tradition of Watson and Skinner, amongst others, who claimed that 'what you do is influenced by what follows what you do'. Basically, the behaviourist would interpret disturbed behaviour as a set of learned responses to the environment, which have been acquired through reinforcement. Thus, the child who disrupts the class and who is reinforced by attention, is more likely to disrupt the class in future if the teacher chastises him. On the assumption that the inappropriate behaviour has been learned, it follows that it can also be unlearned, if a new set of environmental contingencies are applied. From this assumption, principles and practices of behaviour modification have been developed which aim to control environmental variables and hence, behaviour. In this approach, underlying causes for behaviour are irrelevant, the primary focus of concern being the shaping of the child's behaviour towards a desired goal, using operant conditioning techniques. The three main ways of modifying behaviour using this approach include the principle of, Rules + ignore + praise which involve the teacher in explaining to the children what is expected of them, then ignoring all undesired behaviour unless it harms another child, and finally praising all appropriate behaviour. The second method is known as a token economy system which use gold stars, coloured discs, etc., which the child earns for acceptable behaviour and then exchanges for a tangible reward; while the third approach uses contract systems which involve the teacher, child and sometimes parents in an agreement about the consequences of certain behaviours, such that behaviours considered desirable by the teacher have a pre-agreed positive pay-off for the child if he performs them, with negative behaviours carrying pre-agreed punishments. Because the child has some control over what each behaviour is 'worth', he has considerable responsibility for his own actions. While many successes have been claimed for behaviour modification programmes they are very demanding of the management skills of the teacher (see Merrett, 1981).

An alternative view of the origin of behaviour disturbances derives from the cognitive development theories of Piaget and Bruner (see previous chapter) who outlined the way in which the developing child interprets the world, accommodating new knowledge and thus promoting increasingly complex patterns of meaning. In this way, the child's behaviour is directed by cognitive ideas. While the theory was not initially formulated to account for behaviour problems, Wall (1973) has developed a Piagetian–type model to account for troubled behaviour. On the assumption that the child is constantly reconstructing his/her ideas of the world from new incoming knowledge and thereby develops his/her interpretations of events, it follows that if the incoming knowledge of *social* events is unpredictable, the child's interpretations of group behaviour and interaction will become increasingly idiosyncratic. On this basis then, the child's scheme of the world is unlikely to match that of those around him/her, by dint of its very idiosyncrasy. The child may then behave erratically, perceive himself/herself differently or feel rejected, all of which can lead to problems. One ramification of this is that children whose behaviour is disturbed need *educational* as well as therapeutic intervention, with the emphasis being on relearning in an environment of specially constructed learning experiences. While this theoretical perspective appears to be at odds with the Social Learning theorists, an amalgam of behavioural and cognitive approaches has even been successfully adopted and reported by Kendall (1984), and Kendall and Braswell (1982).

A more socially–related perspective comes from the Status theorists, who suggest that disturbed behaviour may simply be the expression of the values of a subculture rather than arising from any emotional or personality problems. Thus the child from a background characterised by mores, attitudes and behaviours which are at odds with those manifested by the school, is likely to fail in terms of the criteria of success defined by the school and may therefore demonstrate his rejection of these criteria by disruptive behaviour (Docking, 1980). Furthermore, the consequent discipline practices employed at the school often alienate the sub-groups further, instead of acting as an aid to helping the child adapt to the norms of the school (Reynolds, 1976). Interventionist strategies based on this approach focus on modifying the perceived cause of the problem e.g. the family, the classroom, child, etc. which while appearing valid, have considerable organisational implications. Allied to the status approach is the concept of labelling, which suggests that a child does not become deviant because he has transgressed the social norms, but is, instead, labelled deviant first, whereupon he assumes the appropriate role expectations, and in effect, the process is similar to the self-fulfilling prophecies mentioned later in this chapter.

From each of these theoretical perspectives on the causes of problem behaviour are derived relevant therapeutic interventions and despite protagonists from each area, the evidence suggests that most therapeutic techniques are useful. It is interesting to note that in a comparison of a variety of intervention approaches with disturbed children (counselling, play therapy, behaviour modifications, group therapy, etc) Kolvin *et al.* (1981) found that all therapies produced significant improvements, with little difference between them in terms of efficacy. However, it is self-evident from the foregoing discussion that many of the therapeutic techniques for problem behaviours are beyond the teacher's rôle and skill base. Consequently, many schools employ specialist full-time counsellors to deal with presenting difficulties of this sort.

This counselling approach has been criticised at a general level as being exclusively focussed on the child's interpersonal problems, without regard for the culture and environment in which they exist, and also at a more specific educational level, as undermining the teacher's traditional disciplinary and pastoral role. Because of these criticisms, it is essential that if the disparate goals of the school and counsellor are to be harmonised, then the counselling must be fully integrated with the ethos and administration of the school. Furthermore, there is a danger that any problems which are the result of teaching or of organisational aspects of the school may simply be overlooked, largely because the child is helped to adapt to the problem in preference to resolving the problems themselves.

A more common approach which is more specifically within the teacher's domain is direct help for the educational problems of the child. Although these problems may be secondary effects, their reduction often succeeds in ameliorating the behaviour disturbance. Insofar as problem behaviour can stem from repeated experience of failure and a consequent lowering of self-esteem, it is clearly essential that teachers develop a learning environment which maximises the child's scholastic competence. Hence, educational programmes geared specifically to the child's interests and needs can do much to alleviate behaviour difficulties. Docking (1980) recommends a two-factor educational provision for children with problem behaviours, which involves as a first stage, increasing the child's involvement in school work, by tailoring the task to the child's needs. In this way, discipline imposed from involvement in the task itself and not from the teacher, may act as a control on behaviour. The recommended model is a teacher–pupil interaction, with the child perceiving himself to be a valid contributor and the teacher acting as an active participant in the learning activity, although such an approach may have the disadvantage of being threatening to teachers who favour positional, rather than rational, authority. The second stage in Docking's two-factor model involves the development of social reasoning in the child, through discussion of moral issues and dilemmas. Consequently, desirable behaviour is not enforced by an adult, but arrived at through peer discussion.

In any discussion on problem behaviour, it would be naive to omit the topic of punishment. However, the concept of punishment is undoubtedly an emotive one, arousing heated arguments on both sides of the spectrum. It is not the role of this chapter to detail the moral and philosophical grounds for either viewpoint, but instead to discuss some of the psychological factors involved.

Essentially, punishment can take two forms – either the application of an aversive stimulus upon the production of an undesired behaviour or the removal of privileges. Punishment, if used responsibly may have a simultaneous deterrent and educational function, showing the child the gravity of behaving in an inconsiderate way towards others. However, this is an ideal notion. More often, punishment is used inconsistently, erratically and for a number of reasons and hence becomes counter-productive. Moreover, children, respond differently to castigation, depending upon their punishment history and may develop strategies to avoid punishment. This is obviously detrimental to the long-term development of the child, since it destroys the trust and quality of the teacher/child relationship. The child may also come to view punishment as a means by which the strong control the weak (Fontana, 1988). Interestingly, too, pupils and teachers differ in terms of the types of punishments they view as effective (Harrop and Williams, 1992). This may mean that the methods teachers typically use to control children are not those the pupils necessarily perceive as a particular deterrent, which may account, to some extent, for incidents of problem behaviour in those classes where this mis-match occurs. In addition, it should be pointed out that punishment used in an inappropriate way, presents the child with a less than ideal model of behaviour and furthermore only tells the child what he should *not* do and not what he should. With reference to this latter point, punishment, if it is to be effective, should be used in conjunction with some more constructive guidelines as to a more acceptable course of behaviour. (See Docking, 1987 and Wheldall and Glynn, 1989 for more detailed accounts of this area).

THE SOCIAL PSYCHOLOGY OF THE CLASSROOM

The whole issue of deviant or disturbed behaviour highlights the importance of the child-context relationship, and consequently may be perceived as part of a wider socio-psychological or systems perspective. The systems approach to education was highlighted earlier, and emphasised the translation of the social-psychological view of the person/situation relationship into educational psychology. Wilson (1977) captures the essence of the argument by stating the two assumptions of the approach as firstly, a belief that human behaviour is significantly influenced by the context in which it occurs and secondly, that in order for the social scientist to understand behaviour he/she must be aware of the framework within which subjects interpret their thoughts, feelings and actions. More recently an ecosystemic approach to classroom activities has been formulated, based on the premise that the origins and goals of behaviour are basically interactional (Cooper and Upton, 1990; Tyler, 1992). Pupil behaviour, then, is the product of the inter-relation between individual motivations (derived from previous social experience) and environmental influences. Thus manifest classroom behaviour is a function of simple or complex social interactions and any educational intervention must take account of the contribution of all factors to the situation from individual to institutional level. In these terms, the ecosystemic approach embraces previously held assumptions that the nature and quality of teacher–pupil interactions are in part responsible for a range of educational outcomes. Such an hypothesis serves to highlight the contribution of social psychology to our understanding of classroom processes, and will be considered in the next section.

Teacher–Pupil Interactions

It is self-evident that the educational research has been directed at identifying the possible impact of a variety of interactive patterns upon pupil performance. Inherent within any social interaction is the teacher's expectations and attributions and their impact on pupil performance. Because of the importance of these issues a short diversion to discuss the nature of expectations and beliefs may be useful.

Attribution theory (Kelley 1967) represents perhaps the most significant theoretical development in social psychology of recent years. The extension to this work by Weiner, *et al.* (1971) provides a useful vehicle for discussing the role of expectation in the classroom.

Attribution theory has been described as a cognitively–oriented personality theory whose basic tenets state that people have beliefs, reasons and explanations for the success or failure of events. These causal attributions will largely govern an individual's reaction to this outcome and also influence future behaviour in a similar context. For example, a student who believes a poor examination performance is due to an unfair paper is attempting to externalise the reason for the poor performance. Alternatively, if lack of revision is seen as a prime cause, the individual would experience more personal guilt and would probably be more highly motivated in a future examination situation.

The theory also allows for some predictions to be made about motivational states and emotional reactions, since, for instance, if a particular individual were to utilise primarily internal and relatively stable causal attributes then the repercussions are likely to be long standing. For example, ability is a relatively fixed capacity and if it was to be used as a prime source of explanation of success or failure in the classroom then individuals would increasingly come to expect success or failure. The circular nature of this expectation cycle is clear, particularly as internal attributes lead to stronger affective reactions. For example, successes attributed to ability or effort produce more personal pride than those attributed to luck, or ease of the task.

These fairly general formulations of attribution theory acquire more impact when the link between attribution style and other important characteristics is made. For example, levels of self-esteem in pupils have been linked to causal attribution, affiliation needs and type of school (Foon, 1988). Similarly, educational implications begin to emerge when attributional style is related to achievement motivation (Craske, 1988). Where a child is unclear about the cause of their own success or failure, poor subsequent achievement is likely to be the outcome (Butler and Orion, 1990). Bearing this in mind, it becomes evident that the teacher must frequently clarify reasons for academic outcomes as a standard classroom interation. However, expectations which derive from school performance whether emanating from teacher or pupils, can influence academic development. Consequently, research has been concerned to document interaction patterns in terms of how expectations communicate themselves and with what sort of impact.

The seminal work of Rosenthal and Jacobson (1968) served to highlight the extent to which teacher expectation can influence pupil behaviour. They attempted to manipulate teachers' expectations about pupil performance to see if these expectations would be fulfilled. On the pretext of developing a new achievement test the researchers identified to teachers pupils who were late developers and who should show significant intellectual progress in the near future. In fact, the children had been randomly selected. Although the results of an end of year test were somewhat inconsistent it was shown that certain of the identified group had exhibited markedly improved performance. The self-fulfilling prophecy effect of teacher expectations was offered as an explanation.

Much research followed this widely publicised finding, especially after Claiborn's (1969) failure to replicate the previous results. Good reviews of the area may be found in Brophy and Good (1974), and Rogers, (1982). On the whole it would appear that induced expectations (deliberate attempts to manipulate perceptions) do not produce expectancy effects while naturalistic expectations (formed through normal interaction) can be influential. The former situation enables the teacher to assess the source and credibility of the information rather more directly and hence reject its possible influence.

It is noteworthy that the original study of Rosenthal and Jacobson did not incorporate any observation of the classroom although such a procedure may have provided information concerning how teacher expectations may have been communicated to pupils. The prime focus of consequent research activities quite reasonably turned to investigating how this process may be operating within the classroom. Clearly, labelling children as "bright", "below average", "disruptive" or whatever has the effect of altering pupil and teacher behaviour to produce a range of types and quality of classroom interactions. The most likely mechanism through which these expectations are transmitted is a system of complex verbal and non-verbal cues. Good (1980) provides some concrete examples of how teachers may transmit their expectations in the classroom situation. Most studies have initially asked teachers to rank their pupils into high and low performers and have then attempted to describe and differentiate teacher behaviour towards the two groups. Typical differentiating behaviours include making less eye contact with low performing groups, seating them separately, calling on them less frequently for questions, waiting a shorter time when a question is attempted, and spending less time with them providing feedback. These patterns of behaviour are not exhaustive and indeed not all teachers demonstate consistently segregated response patterns of this kind. However, if all the behaviours listed were present in a teacher, they would characterise an over-reaction to low performance potential. Moreover, this over-reaction might be likely to exaggerate the discrepancy between high and low performers and thereby act to reduce motivation and the opportunity for learning in the low group.

These results have been extensively corroborated. For example, Fry (1987) noted that teacher interactions with children perceived as having behaviour problems were notably negative, which in turn acted as a determinant of the pupil's subsequent actions. As she notes:

> "A teacher's impression is formed on the basis of the child's behaviour and then functions
> as an interpretive framework within which the subsequent behaviour of the child is
> constructed, and leads to teacher expectations, which, in turn, help determine the child's
> subsequent behaviour".

Babad, Bernieri and Rosenthal (1989) corroborated Fry's results, but added an important feature – namely, that while teachers tried to compensate low-expectancy pupils, a significant amount of negative non-verbal emotion leaked out when dealing with them. In other words, they appeared to have control over manifesting their negative affect towards certain students, thereby making it increasingly probable that the cycle of the self-fulfilling prophecy will be perpetuated. Obviously, if these findings apply to most classrooms, and there is no reason to suspect that they do not, then they are of considerable importance. Lack of success for an individual pupil may be as much affected by the perception of others within the environment as by his/her ability and the downward spiral, once started, is difficult to counter. The result is similar to the findings concerning the impact of streamed classes (Barker-Lunn, 1970) when she reports great difficulty in a child changing his/her school position once assigned to a particular stream. This corpus of research serves to highlight the potential importance of the social environment and the interactions within it as determinants of learning outcomes.

However, just as the teacher creates evaluations and expectations of the child, so the child reciprocates. Kutnick (1988) points out that the social milieu of the classroom and the pupil's perception of, and relationship with, the teacher constitute a major factor in academic success. Typically, students report preferences for warm, friendly and supportive teachers who are simultaneously controlling of classroom behaviour (e.g. Brophy and Good, 1986; Crocker and Brookner, 1986) and where such an atmosphere exists, students are more receptive to teacher feedback, (e.g. Anderson et al., 1988).

Teacher Feedback

The issue of teacher feedback has been a fecund area of research, particularly in the light of recent increasing interest in behavioural approaches to teaching (see Schweiso and Hastings, 1987 for a review). For example, while there is considerable evidence to support the view that the use of systematic praise and punishment in the classroom is effective in increasing desirable student behaviours (e.g. Wheldall et al., 1989 Houghton et al., 1990) more naturalistic studies of the use of praise as feedback present a more complex picture.

Despite the general assent to the value of praise in the classroom the evidence is that it is used relatively unsystematically. There seems to be a greater likelihood of approval following appropriate academic behaviour while disapproval follows inappropriate social behaviour. (Schweiso and Hastings, 1987). Additionally, older children seem consistently to receive less approving and disapproving responses from teachers, while boys receive more approval and overall attention than girls (Schweiso and Hastings, 1987) although the nature of this attention appears to be dependent to some degree on the gender of the teacher (Merrett and Wheldall, 1992). Furthermore, even if all teacher praise was effective as reinforcement, there does not seem to be enough of it to exert a significant effect upon pupil performance (Glynn, 1987). Moreover, it appears that when used it is often used inappropriately. For example, Nafpaktitis et al. (1985) found that almost a third of the approvals they recorded followed inappropriate behaviours. Weinstein (1976) reports that praise is often directed to the lowest achievers presumably in a well-meaning attempt to encourage. It may not be given on merit and if pupils come to recognise this the result is likely to be both embarrassing as well as negative in terms of motivation and future credibility.

In the light of this rather more complex perspective it is perhaps not surprising that the link between pupil performance and the amount of praise given by the teacher has consistently been found to be rather weak. Children in the early school years, especially those finding it difficult to make progress do seem to be adversely affected by receiving limited praise, but praise seems to have little causal role is improving the performance of the average child in the everyday classroom. Attribution theory (discussed earlier) provides a valuable interpretation of this data. Young children typically internalise evaluative statements and are therefore more liable to be influenced by praise statements. As the child gets older, exactly the same statements will be interpreted quite differently depending upon an individual's attributional stance (Weiner, 1979). This may in part account for the inconsistent findings. The picture, then, looks confused, and is compounded by the fact that teacher approval can be manifest either verbally or non-verbally. The majority of studies have concentrated on the effects of verbal praise, but clearly non-verbal skills can also communicate approval. Comparatively little work has been carried out to date on the use of non-verbal communication alone to modify behaviour (see Neill (1991) for a review). However, it would seem fair to conclude that teachers should use praise sparingly making sure it is specific and contingent upon appropriate behaviours thus maintaining credibility and impact (see Fontana, 1988).

Peer interations

The didactic view of teaching and learning has so dominated our thinking about classroom events that anything other than teacher–child interaction, such as peer interaction, has been regarded more as a nuisance and a distraction than a potential contributor to a child's development. Interaction between the child and the teacher and between child and child is fundamental. Just as adult groups form roles and develop expectations so too do learning groups develop their supportive, functional structures as each member learns about his/her position within the group.

A normative sub-system of rules comes to regulate and order the behaviour of any fairly permanent grouping. These norms create expectations of behaviour and identify sanctions and rewards for diverging from or adhering to these expectations respectively. In certain situations such norms can actively hinder learning if they become antagonistic to academic goals. Hargreaves (1967) found that while some informal student peer groups valued academic achievement and looked down upon 'mucking around in class', other informal student peer groups valued obstructing teachers so that less material was covered in class; moreover they denigrated those pupils who co-operated with teachers' efforts to instruct.

In terms of influencing learning outcomes it has been advocated that teachers should attempt to foster positive group norms and a goal orientation appropriate to the class and task. Johnson and Johnson (1975) suggest three types of goal structures which may be operative. The first is a co-operative interdependence when children work together to achieve a common group goal and early research in this area has its roots in Piagetian Theory. The second is competitive interdependence when one pupil obtaining a goal operates to the detriment of others. The third structure is individualistic where pupils work to accomplish goals quite unrelated to the goals of others. The co-operative classroom is likely to minimise the possibility of being a 'loser' and has consequently been found to have a positive impact upon self-esteem of some children (Covington and Beery, 1976) as well as improving social integration among special needs students (Topping, 1992). The effect upon academic performance is less clear cut but there is a considerable body of literature which emphasises the value of peer tutoring particularly in areas such as reading (e.g. Topping, 1988) and increasingly in other areas such as French (Dean, 1990). In complex situations like problem solving co-operation does seem to produce better performance than competition, although the results are compounded by factors such as pupil age and ability and class size (see Topping, 1992 for a review).

Apart from direct effects upon outcome there are many more indirect contributions to pupil achievement that are derived from the social nature of classrooms. Peer relationships are also crucial in the process of socialisation. The emotive input and desire to be accepted means that a whole host of areas (e.g. values, attitudes, social roles) are susceptible to peer influence. Apart from the immediate acceptance within the social group it is clear that effective adjustment at this stage can be important to later adult psychological health. The inability to develop and maintain interdependent, co-operative relationships is often cited as a primary manifestation of psychological ill-health. Social isolation may subsequently be associated with adult aggression, poor social skills and high levels of psychological pathology (see Johnson and Norem-Hebeisen, 1977). In this way, then, it is important to know how the nature of classroom group dynamics influences individual social–psychological outcomes.

For example, competitive and individualistic goal structures are likely to result in little social interaction, low levels of trust and increased fear of failure, while supportive friendship seems to be promoted more in the co-operative classroom. Schmuck (1966) has reported that pupils who feel themselves to be liked and popular with their peers are likely to be much more positive about school goals. Friendship patterns can be influential not only between pupils but also by influencing the way pupils are seen by teachers. In summarising this area it may be useful to quote Johnson *et al.* (1980) who compared the effects of co-operative, competitive and individualistic learning situations on achievement in over 100 studies. They reported that co-operative learning promotes higher achievement across all age levels and all subject areas, and consequently can be construed as beneficial at both the individual and group level.

CLASSROOM CLIMATE

The *general* classroom climate and milieu can exert a considerable impact on learning outcomes. In order to evaluate the link between classroom ethos and a number of pupil and learning variables, various assessment techniques have been used, of which perhaps the most valuable is Fraser's Individualised Classroom Environment Questionnaire (ICEQ) (Fraser, 1986, 1987). This technique has the facility to gather information from students and teachers about their views of both their actual and ideal classroom environments. The ICEQ taps perceptions in five areas: Personal (teacher–child interactions on personal welfare etc). Participation (active involvement rather than passive recipients), Independence (degree of control students have over their own learning experiences), Investigation (the degree of emphasis placed on enquiring, problem-solving etc), and Differentiation (degree of individualised education each pupil receives). On all five scales the pupils and teacher can report what actually takes place and what, ideally, they would like to take place. Using this assessment of the prevailing classroom climate, it is possible to look at links between particular organisational styles and learning outcomes, the climate preferred by individual pupils or classes, and the mismatch between what is preferred and what actually happens. In this way, the classroom system can be negotiated to optimum effect. However, at a more concrete level, the way in which a classroom is physically structured may also influence learning and pupil satisfaction. Tricket (1983), for instance, in a comparison of open vs traditional classrooms found that classroom disturbance and achievement anxiety were higher amongst children, and particularly boys, in open settings, to a degree that could impede learning. Academic performance seemed to be unaffected. The results, however, are somewhat equivocal, since there is evidence that positive attitudes and affect among pupils may be related to open classrooms (see MacAulay, 1990, for a review). In general, younger children seem to prefer traditional organisations.

From an ecological perspective, the seating arrangements in the classroom appear to be influential to on-task behaviours. The general conclusion from the available literature points towards the beneficial effect of rows as opposed to clusters of seating in promoting pupil attention and acceptable behaviours (MacAulay, *ibid*). However, because there are discrepancies within the findings, Wheldall and Olds (1987) recommended experimenting with classroom seating plans as a mechanism for optimising the learning environment.

Leading on from this is the way in which the classroom organisation is managed and maintained. Successful management of the class has been cited as one of the primary concerns among new teachers. However, for once, the research findings generally accord. It appears that the key factors are the clear setting of behavioural limits, with fair and consistent enforcement of these. As MacAulay (1990) points out

> "The significance of a classroom climate which emphasises structure, order, rule clarity and organisation cannot be underestimated in school systems which are increasingly burdened with students' inability to conform to socially acceptable norms of behaviour".

From the classroom-environment literature, it would seem reasonable to conclude that if a match can be achieved between pupil preferences and classroom organisation, then a variety of learning and socio-emotional outcomes will be optimised. Where student preferences are taken into account, greater attention, and on task behaviours, as well as increased motivation have been observed (see MacAulay, 1990).

THE SCHOOL ENVIRONMENT

Besides the host of internal and micro-level factors which influence teacher performance there are a number of wider school issues too.

The school, as an institution imposes constraints, largely through the prevailing ethos. This rather vague term has been pinned down by Dancy (1980) to mean the values, aims, attitudes and procedures inherent within the school. That there is a link between ethos and educational outcome is virtually unchallenged. For example, Wragg, (1980) in an evaluation of Rutter *et al.*'s (1979) seminal work on school ethos, argues that there is remarkable consistency in pupil outcome as a function of the school's organisation. Indeed it would appear that the overriding school ethos is more important in determining pupil attainment and satisfaction than any of the individual school factors. What Rutter and his associates found to be critically important were the school's values and norms, the degree to which these are held consistently throughout the school and the extent to which the pupils accept them. Within these factors, expectations, staff relations, pupil involvement and consistency of approach all play a part. Since these variables have been correlated with pupil outcomes, it becomes self-evident that to optimise learning and pupil satisfaction, the *whole school* must be modified to promote positive change (Stratford, 1990). Using the school as the focus of intervention, a number of researchers have highlighted tangible areas which, if altered, could promote more effective pupil outcomes. For example, Mortimore *et al.* (1988) emphasise the involvement of teachers in school policy and decision making, while Stratford (1990) recommends a more specific approach of encouraging staff to identify problems and negotiating ways of solving them. Where resulting interventions are then tackled in a collaborative effort, changes in attitudes, values and general climate are likely to occur on a school-wide basis.

Whatever the approach, there is little doubt that the over-arching school ethos is of major importance in the determination of a variety of school outcomes and in this respect confirms the salience of a systems-view of education and psychology.

Techniques of Classroom observation

Much of the material discussed in this chapter has been derived from studies of classroom dynamics, made possible by an increased access to the classroom environment. A more open attitude from those involved in the educational process has also promoted an interest in the methods of recording classroom behaviour (for a review, see Sweetman, 1988). A brief comment upon the approaches that have developed may illustrate the means by which much of the foregoing evidence was derived.

The dynamic and complex nature of classroom interaction inevitably means that attempts to capture the patterns of behaviour which occur often seem rather restrictive in terms of the varieties of behaviour that are manifested. A more holistic approach is represented by the phenomenological perspective; here the basic tenet is that reality is subjective and the investigator's only route to what the classroom situation is actually like is via the 'cognitive maps' of its participants. The 'cognitive maps' are the perceptual structure of classroom events developed by pupils and teachers. Methodologically the phenomenological approach proceeds from a very open-ended brief to identifying characteristic themes of classroom life from the way pupils describe and feel about their situation. In this sense the approach lacks precision and generalisablity. However, as Lancy (1978) comments it can lead to a more complete and deeper understanding of what is happening, which can be used by teachers to conduct immediate analyses of how their classroom routines appear to pupils.

As indicated before, considerable research effort has been devoted to providing a satisfactory description of the effective teacher and the teaching process. Rating scales of personal qualities have been the main method of data gathering. The reliability of such techniques has been a problem in many research areas since they allow a considerable degree of latitude of interpretation by the observer. Such assessment techniques are described as 'high inference' techniques since they allow the observer to infer from the behaviour observed to an observational category. The subjective licence implicit in the approach has produced very unreliable data. The problems presented led to a pressure to develop 'low inference' techniques of observation where the focus is upon specific, denotable, relatively objective behaviours such as teacher statements. Almost inevitably this produced recording techniques heavily oriented to recording the teacher's verbal behaviour.

Simon and Boyer (1970) detail 79 such interaction schedules of which the most widely used is probably Flanders' (1963). It is no coincidence that this proliferation of techniques has happened alongside the growth of micro-teaching, the basic principles of which involve a teacher in a short lesson which is recorded. With the aid of the interaction analysis instrument immediate feedback is given to the teacher, the lesson is repeated in the light of this feedback and in this way patterns of teaching can be modified and improved whether it be trainees or experienced teachers. Full reviews of modification of the instruments and a variety of applications can be obtained in the review by McKnight (1980).

The availability of such systems with their increased reliability has had a significant impact upon our knowledge of classroom events. Specific teaching behaviours can be identified and linked to outcomes more effectively. Many of the studies quoted earlier have used some form of modified observational system. Whilst considerable progress has been achieved in terms of increased specificity it has been at the cost of comprehensiveness. Critics have argued that the provision of observation instruments is alien to the fluidity of classroom events and Smith (1979) stresses the importance of non-verbal communication noting that the verbally oriented scales omit a crucial aspect of teaching, namely non-verbal exchange.

This chapter has attempted to illustrate how the educational process encompasses a range of interactive situations where both educational and psychological knowledge can make a contribution to understanding the effects of the interplay of these different variables. This mixing of the educational/psychological world is best brought together in the role of the educational psychologist. This is a professional role that straddles the concerns of both chapters by being involved in individual aspects of the child's development as well as assisting teachers in a wider context.

The Role of the Educational Psychologist

The origins of the practice of educational psychology are closely linked to the growth of measures of ability. The liaison in the early years with the medical profession gave rise to a medical model where the cause of the problem was assumed to lie with the child. The use of tests to assess the degree of problem reinforced the strongly individualistic approach. The emphasis up until the 1950s both in the UK and USA was upon assessment rather than participation in remedial activities. The educational psychologist was reviewed as the gatekeeper to support services, special schools, etc.

The way the behaviourist movement developed within psychology generally provided the first movement out of this situation. Although, in general, behaviourism had been seen as quite limited it did allow educational psychologists to see that they could do something about individual problems by devising remedial programmes or advisory activities rather than simply assessing the child's difficulties. The fundamental importance of this shift was that it started to involve those in everyday contact with the child. Thus the psychologist was no longer just a technician but a provider of support and advice in the context of school or home (McPherson and Sutton, 1981).

The watershed of change came in the UK in the 1980s (slightly earlier in USA) when legislation sought to integrate the child with learning difficulties into the normal school setting. The teacher and the school became the main focus of intervention rather than the child.

Assessment remained a core activity but now as part of a multi-agency team of allied professionals. Moreover there was much more emphasis upon devising support programmes for individual teachers and parents, and also helping schools to develop their strategies for supporting the child. The intellectual basis underlying these changes also had a pragmatic element in that the supply of educational psychologists had failed to keep pace with demand, creating long waiting lists. The new approach involving others offered some way of apparently coping with more children more quickly. However, implementation was not easy (Ainscow, 1991). Both teachers and educational psychologists took time to adjust both in terms of skills and attitudes.

In many cases this tension remains unresolved with neither party able to fully undertake the role as described above. In the UK, at least, the advent of the National Curriculum has suddenly reverted educational psychology to a specialist test role again and has created much dissatisfaction within the profession. The future is uncertain, Jones and Frederickson's (1990) book 'Re-focussing Educational Psychology' offers exciting prospects of integrating new thinking into educational practice. However, in reality the role has been narrowed such that some private agencies are increasingly offering a limited assessment service. A more holistic provision remains an ideal for some but within a context of diminishing resources.

The future is further muddled by the development of the generic psychologist. Most of Europe operates a common training provision of 6/7 years for clinical, educational and organisational psychologists with specialisation, if at all, at the very end of the process. Only in the UK and USA is teaching experience and a specific educational psychology postgraduate qualification required. This may become a major deterrent to prospective applicants especially if the job appears to be increasingly limited. The future of educational psychologists appears to be bound up with wider issues about the generic v specialist nature of sub-disciplines of psychology. The generic approach would seem to offer much and currently seems to be winning the debate.

Final comments

The chapter has attempted to place the educational process in a wider social perspective and in so doing highlights the error of proposing simple causal statements about the nature of educational outcomes. Many variables are operate at the same time on teaching and learning and it is extremely difficult to allocate priority of influence to any one factor.

The psychologist can play a role in teasing out the nature of these influences and how they may be positively incorporated into an understanding of the teaching process. Perhaps the most important elements of this contribution is to improve methods and techniques for understanding classroom behaviour such that practitioners (the teacher, educational psychologist) will be aided in their task and the contribution of good applied studies will be received positively.

REFERENCES

Ainscow, M. (1991). Effective schools for all. Paper given at the DECP annual course, Torquay.

Anderson, L.M., Stevens, D.D., Prawat, R.S. & Nickerson, J. (1988). Classroom task environments and students' task-related beliefs. *Elementary School Journal* 88, 281–295.

Babad, E., Bernieri, F. & Rosenthal, R. (1989). When information is more informative diagnosing teacher expectations from brief samples of behaviour. *British Journal of Educational Psychology* 59, (3) 281–295.

Bamford, J., Grange, J. & Jones, P. (1990). An experimental stress management course for teachers. *Educational Psychology in Practice*, 6 (2), 90–95.

Barker-Lunn, J.C. (1970). *Streaming in the Primary School*, Slough: NFER.

Borg, M.G. & Riding, R.J. (1991). Occupational stress and satisfaction in teaching. *British Educational Research Journal* 17 (3), 263–281.

Broadhead, P. (1987). A blueprint for the good teacher? The HMI/DES model of good primary practice. *British Journal of Educational Studies* 35 (1), 57–72.

Brophy, J. & Good, T. (1974). Teacher-Student relationships: causes and consequences. NY, Holt: Rivehart & Winston.

Burden, R. & Hornby, T.A. (1989). Assessing classroom ethos: Some recent promising developments for the systems–oriented educational psychologist. *Educational Psychology in Practice*, 5 (1), 17–22.

Butler, R., & Orion, R. (1990). When pupils do not understand the determinants of their success and failure in school: relations between internal, teacher and unknown perceptions of control and school achievement. *British Journal of Educational Psychology* 60 (1), 63–75.

Claiborn, W. (1969). Expectancy effects in the classroom: a failure to replicate. *Journal of Educational Psychology* 60, 377–383.

Coletta, A.J. (1975). Personality characteristics held by open and traditional teachers. *Journal of Educational Research* 68, 250–252.

Cooper, P. & Upton, G. (1990). An ecosystemic approach to emotional and behavioural difficulties in schools. *Educational Research* 10 (4), 301–321.

Cortis, G. (1979). Twelve years on – a longitudinal study of teacher behaviour continued. *Educational Review*, 31 (3), 205–215.

Covington, M.V. & Beery, R.G. (1976). *Self-worth and school learning.* N.Y. Holt.

Cox, T. & Brockley, T. (1984). The experience and effects of stress in teachers. *British Educational Research Journal* 10 (1), 83–87.

Craske, M-L (1988). Learned helplessness, self-worth, motivation and attribution retraining for primary school children. *British Journal of Educational Psychology* 58 (2), 152–164.

Crocker, R.K. & Brooker, G.M. (1986). Classroom control and student outcomes in grades 2 and 5. *American Educational Research Journal* 23, 1–11.

Dancy, J.C. (1980). The notion of the ethos of a school. In "The Rutter Research – Perspectives 1": University of Exeter.

Davies, I.K. (1971). *The Management of Learning,* London: McGraw Hill.

de Landsheere, G.C. (1980). Teacher selection. *Prospects.* 10 (3), 318–324.

Dean, C.M. (1990). Peer-tutoring in French: improving performance amongst low achievers. *Evaluation & Research in Education* 4 (1), 11–16.

Department of Education & Science (DES) (1982). *The New Teacher in School.* London: HMSO.

Docking, J.W. (1980). *Control and Disciplines in Schools: Perspectives & Approaches.* London: Harper & Row.

Docking, J.W. (1987). *Control and Discipline in Schools.* London: Harper & Row.

Flanders, N.A. (1963). Intent, action and feedback: a preparation for teaching. *Journal of Teacher Education,* 14 (3), 251–260.

Fontana, D. (1988). *Classroom Control: Understanding and Guiding Classroom Behaviour.* London: Routledge.

Foon, A. (1988). The relationship between school type and adolescent self-esteem, attribution styles and affiliation needs: implications for educational outcome. *British Journal of Educational Psychology* 58 (1), 44–54.

Fraser, B.J. (1986). *Classroom Environment.* London: Croom Helm.

Fraser, B.J. (1987). Use of classroom assessments in school psychology. *School Psychologist International,* 8 (4), 205–220.

Fry, P.S. (1987). Classroom environments and their effects on problem and non-problem children's classroom behaviours and motivations. In Hastings, N. & Schweiso, J. *New Directions in Educational Psychology.* Lewes: the Falmer Press.

Galton, M. (1987). An oracle chronicle: a decade of classroom research. In Delamont, S. (Ed) *The Primary School Teacher.* Lewes: The Falmer Press.

Galton, M. & Simon, B. (1980). *Progress and Performance in the Primary School.* London: Routledge & Kegan Paul.

Glynn, T. (1987). Contexts for Independent Learning. In Hastings, N. & Schweiso, J. *New Directions in Education Psychology 2: Behaviour & Motivation in the Classroom.* Lewes: The Falmer Press.

Good, T.L. (1980). Classroom expectations = teacher–pupil interactions. In J.H. McMillan (Ed) *The Social Psychology of School Learning.* London: Academic Press.

Hargreaves, D.H. (1967). Reactions to labelling. In M. Hammersley & P. Woods (Eds) *The*

Process of Schooling: a Sociological Reader. London & Henley: Routledge & Kegan Paul. Open University Press.

Harrop, A. & Williams, T. (1992). Rewards and punishments in the primary school: pupils' perceptions and teachers' usage. *Educational Psychology in Practice,* 7 (4), 211–215.

Houghton, S., Wheldall, K., Jukes, R. & Sharpe, A. (1990). The effects of limited private reprimands and increased private praise on classroom behaviours in four British Secondary School classes. *British Journal of Educational Psychology* 60, 255–265.

Johnson, D.W., Maruyama, C., Johnson, R., Nelson, D. & Skon, L. (1980). The effects of cooperative, competitive, and individualistic goal structures on achievement: A meta-analysis. Psychological Bulletin: University of Minnesota.

Johnson, D.W. & Johnson, R.T. (1975). Learning together and alone: cooperation, competition and individualisation. Englewood Cliffs: Prentice-Hall.

Johnson, D.W. & Norem-Hebeosen (1977). Attitudes towards interdependence among persons and psychological health. *Psychological Reports.* 40, 843–850.

Jones, N. & Frederickson, N. (1990). *Refocussing Education Psychology.* Lewes: The Falmer Press.

Kelley, H.H. (1967). *Attribution theory in social psychology. Nebraska Symposium on Motivation.* Lincoln: University of Nebraska Press.

Kendall, P.C. & Braswell, L. (1982). Cognitive–behavioural self-control therapy for children: a component analysis. *Journal of Consulting and Clinical Psychology* 50, 672–689.

Kendall, P.C. (1984). Cognitive–behavioural self-control therapy for children. *Journal of Child Psychology and Psychiatry* 25 (2), 173–179.

Kolvin, I., Garside, R., Nichol, A., McMillan, A., Wolstenholme, F & Leitch, I. (1981). *Help Starts Here: The Maladjusted Child in the Ordinary School.* London: Tavistock.

Kutnick, P.J. (1988). *Relationships in the Primary School Classroom.* London: Routledge & Kegan Paul.

Lancy, D.F. (1978). The classroom as a phenomenon. In D. Bar-Tal & L. Saxe (Eds). *Social Psychology of Education.* N.Y.: John Willen & Sons.

Lindgren, H.C. (1980). *Educational Psychology in the classroom.* N.Y.: Oxford University Press.

MacAulay (1990). Classroom environment: a literature review. *Educational Psychology* 10 (3), 239–253.

McCabe, J.J.C. & Savage, R.D. (1973). Personality and assessment in colleges of education. *Durham Research Review,* 7 (31), 800–806.

McKnight, P.C. (1980). Microteaching: development from 1968 to 1978. *British Journal of Teacher Education.* 6 (3), 214–227.

McMichael, P. (1981). Behavioural judgements: a comparison of two teacher rating scales. *Educational Studies* 7 (1), 61–72.

Merrett, F.E. (1981). Studies in behaviour modification in British educational settings. *Educational Psychology* 1 (1), 13–18.

Merrett, F. & Wheldall, K. (1992). Teachers' use of praise and reprimand to boys and girls. *Educational Review.* 44 (1), 73–79.

McPherson, I. & Sutton, A. (1981). (Eds). *Reconstructing Psychological Practice.* London: Croom Helm.

Mortimore, P., Sammons, P., Stoll, L., Lewis, D. & Ecob, R. (1988). *School Matters: the Junior Years.* Wells: Open Books.

Myers, B., Kennedy, J.J., & Cruickshank, D.R. (1979). Relationship of teacher personality variables to teacher perceived problems. *Journal of Teacher Education* 30 (6), 33–40.

Nafpaktitis, M., Mayer, G.R., & Butterworth, T. (1985). Natural rates of teacher approval and disapproval and their relation to student behaviour in intermediate school classrooms. *Journal of Educational Psychology* 77 (3), 362–7.

Neill, S. (1991). *Classroom Non-verbal Communication.* London: Routledge.

Reynolds, D. (1976). The delinquent school. In Hammersley, M. & Woods, P. (eds). *The Process of Schooling: a sociological reader.* London & Henley: Routledge & Kegan Paul/Open University Press.

Rogers, C. (1982). *A Social Psychology of Schooling.* London: Routledge & Kegan Paul.

Rogers, C. & Kutnick, P. (1990). *The Social Psychology of the Primary School.* London: Routledge.

Rosenthal, R. & Jacobson, L. (1968). Pygmalion in the Classroom. (N.Y.: Holt, Rinehart & Winston).

Rutter, M., Maughan, B., Mortimore, P. & Ouston, J. (1979). *Fifteen Thousand Hours.* London: Open Books.

Rutter, M. (1967). A children's behaviour questionnaire for completion by teachers: preliminary findings. *Journal of Child Psychology and Psychiatry* **8**, 1–11.

Rutter, M., Cox, A., Tupling, C., Berger, M. & Yule, W. (1975). Attainment and adjustment in two geographical areas. 1 – prevalence of psychiatric disorder. *British Journal of Psychiatry* **126**, 493–509.

Schmuck, R.A. (1966). Some aspects of classroom social climate. *Psychology in the Schools.* **3**, 59–65.

Schweiso, J. & Hastings, N. (1987). Teachers' Use of Approval in Hastings, N. & Schweiso, J. (1987). *New Directions in Educational Psychology 2: Behaviour and Motivation in the Classroom.* Lewes: The Falmer Press.

Selmes, C. (1989). *Evaluation of Teaching Assessment and Evaluation in Higher Education.* **14** (3), 167–178.

Sharples, D. & Woodman, P.F. (1972). Multiple and task–specific models in the assessment of teaching. *Durham Research Review.* **6** (28), 627–634.

Simon, A. & Boyer, E.G. (1970). *Mirrors for behaviour II: an anthology of observation instruments.* Philadelphia. Research for Better Schools Inc.

Smith, H.A. (1979). Non-verbal communication in teaching. *Review of Educational Research.* **49** (4), 631–672.

Stones, E. (1979). *Psychopedagogy.* London: Methuen.

Stratford, R. (1990). Creating a Positive School Ethos. *Educational Psychology in Practice.* **5** (4), 183–191.

Sweetman, J. (1988). Observational research: a study of discourse and power. *Research. Papers in Education* **3** (1), 42–63.

Swift, M.S. & Spivack, G. (1978). *Alternative Teaching Strategies: Helping Behaviourally Troubled Children Achieve.* Champaign, Illinois: Research Press Co.

Topping, K. (1988). *The Peer Tutoring Handbook.* London: Croom Helm.

Topping, K. (1992). Cooperative learning and peer tutoring: an overview. *The Psychologist.* **5**, 151–161.

Trickett, P.K. (1983). The interaction of cognitive styles and classroom environment in determining first-graders' behaviour. *Journal of Applied Developmental Psychology* **4**, 43–64.

Tyler, K. (1992). The development of the ecosystemic approach as a humanistic educational psychology. *Educational Psychology* **12** (1), 15–24.

Wall, W.D. (1973). The problem child in schools. *London Educational Review.* **2** (2), 3–21.

Weiner, B., Frieze, I., Kukla, A., Reed, L., Rest, S. & Rosenbaum, R.M. (1971). *Perceiving the causes of success and failure.* N.Y.: General Learning Press.

Weiner, B. (1979). *Theories of Motivation: From mechanism to cognition.* Chicago: Markham.

Weinstein, R. (1976). Reading group membership in first grade: teacher behaviours and pupil experience overtime. *Journal of Educational Psychology* **68**, 103–116.

Wheldall, K. & Olds, D. (1987). Of sex and seating: the effects of mixed and same-sex seating arrangements in junior classrooms. *New Zealand Journal of Educational Studies* **22**, 71–85.

Wheldall, K., Houghton, S., Merrett, F. & Baddeley, A. (1988). The behavioural approach to teaching secondary aged children (BATSAC) two behavioural evaluations of a training package for secondary school teachers in classroom behaviour management. *Educational*

Psychology **9** (3) 185–196.

Wheldall, K. & Glynn, T. (1989). *Effective Classroom Learning.* Oxford: Blackwell.

Wilson, S. (1977). The use of ethnographic technique in educational research. *Review of Educational Research* **47** (1), 245–265.

Wilson, M. & Evans, M. (1980). *Education of Disturbed Pupils.* London: Methuen Educational Limited.

Wolfendale, S., Bryans, T., Fox, M., Labram, A. & Sigston, A. (1992). *The Profession and Practice of Educational Psychology.* London: Cassell Education Ltd.

Woods, P. (1989). *Teaching.* Milton Keynes: Open University Press.

Wragg, E.C. (1980). Theory into Practice: the implications for Schools & LEAs. In: The Rutter Research: Perspectives 1. University of Exeter.

4

COUNSELLING PSYCHOLOGY

E. PICKARD AND M. CARROLL

INTRODUCTION

What is a counselling psychologist and how does one become one? What distinguishes counselling psychologists from related professionals and where and how do they work? These are some of the questions explored in this chapter. A central issue is the client–practitioner relationship which is explored, by means of a case study, in relation to different theoretical orientations to counselling and the skills and personality of the counselling psychologist. The chapter concludes by considering possible future developments within this very popular and rapidly expanding profession.

COUNSELLING PSYCHOLOGY AND THE COUNSELLING PSYCHOLOGIST

Counselling psychology is an applied area of psychology. It has "an emphasis on the systematic application of distinctly psychological understandings of the client and the counselling process to the practice of counselling". (The British Psychological Society, 1989). These statements emphasise the fact that the practice of counselling psychology is rooted in psychology itself and help us to distinguish it from forms of counselling which do not appear to be underpinned by any clear psychological principles or methods. Counselling psychologists work with a range of human needs and issues which occur within the course of the human life-span. They include family and marital matters, gender identity, bereavement, divorce and depression, phobias and sexual abuse, redundancy and retirement. Some counselling psychologists specialise in particular groups or issues such as youth or student counselling, gay counselling or occupational counselling. On the whole, the counselling psychologist works with the less disturbed client and in non-medical settings. The emphasis of their practice is on well-being and self-actualisation and less upon sickness and maladjustment (Nelson-Jones, 1982). They speak of clients rather than patients, avoiding a language of illness and treatment, working instead to establish and develop counselling relationships within which clients will feel safe and free to explore the issues they bring.

It was Carl Rogers who brought to psychology a philosophy of person and of human relationship that provided a new basis for therapeutic interaction. Critical of the instinctive, irrational concept of person held by psychoanalysts and also of the behaviourists' controlling philosophy, he argued for a wholistic approach to the person whom he viewed as essentially good. As a therapist, his concern was to provide a therapeutic relationship which would facilitate personal growth (Rogers, 1961). It is the psychological exploration and elaboration of the client–counsellor relationship which is claimed by some to be the hallmark of the counselling psychologist.

The skills of the counselling psychologist are centred on the development and maintenance of this client–counsellor relationship. Fundamental is the ability truly to listen to clients, to be able to empathise with their perspective, to hear their story. Just as important is the ability to stand back in order to evaluate, make judgements, interpret and observe outcomes. The counselling process requires well developed inter-personal skills through which the counselling psychologist can provide a safe therapeutic environment for the client, be aware of his or her own influence upon the counselling process and of the influence of the client upon the process and the counsellor. The counselling psychologist needs to know when to refer a client to another professional, when to terminate a counselling relationship, as well as being able to recognise the limits of his or her professional competence. Counselling psychologists have to learn to deal with stress and emotions. In some circumstances it may be appropriate to employ psychological tests for which training is necessary and there are important administrative tasks, in particular the writing of client reports. Good counselling practice is nourished by the counsellor's reflection upon practice and by the insights of counselling theory and research.

Counselling psychology is a rapidly growing profession. In Australia, where it is well established, the last four years have seen the membership of the Australian Board of Counselling Psychology increase significantly. In the United States the number of practising counselling psychologists more than doubled during the nineteen eighties and in Britain, the profession is developing quickly and confidently, with the British Psychological Society's Special Group in Counselling Psychology being one of the fastest growing sections of the organisation (Allen, 1990). However, establishing the numbers of counselling psychologists is a difficult task because they are closely related to other professional groups, such as psychotherapists and occupational psychologists and may well function under a working label other than counselling psychologist. There is also the issue of whom to include under the label of counselling psychologist. In Britain, for example, there are two major professional bodies engaged in counselling. The membership of the British Association for Counselling rose from 3,612 in 1988 to 7,028 in 1991. During the same period, membership of the British Psychological Society's Special Group in Counselling Psychology grew to well over one thousand. However, these different professional bodies have different membership criteria and beyond them are many smaller organisations with yet different criteria. There is no doubt about the rise of interest in counselling and counselling psychology but the figures currently available from professional bodies may lead us to underestimate it.

The surge of interest in counselling and the growing demand for counselling services from both public sector organisations and private companies are providing more employment opportunities for counsellors (Reddy, 1987). Some work with large companies, counselling staff and running development and training programmes for those at management level. Though counselling psychology is not, like clinical psychology, for example, built into the financial structure of the British Health Service, some hospitals have begun to employ counselling psychologists and a good number work in educational institutions either teaching and researching or counselling staff and students. Some work as one of a team in a general medical practice. At present, many counselling psychologists work privately, setting up their own practice (B.A.C., 1990). Kagan and Armsworth (1988) associate counselling psychology in the United States with similar practice settings. They also consider new practice settings which are likely to emerge in response to changing social conditions and expect settings for the elderly to be a growing need.

Organisations use counselling in very different ways (Lane, 1990). Some may view it as an intervention to deal with the pathology of the person. In situations of this kind the counselling psychologist is likely to deal with individuals who refer themselves or, in some cases, are encouraged by their management to see the counselling psychologist. Management might encourage the referral of staff perceived as problematic to the organisation, though the counselling service will remain confidential to the client. In a context of this kind the counsellor may be perceived as offering solutions to problems. In organisations espousing a different philosophy, the counsellor and the counselling processes may be viewed as an intrinsic part of the common life and development of the organisation. In such settings the counsellor is more likely to be involved in the dynamics of the organisation facilitating change and innovation or the management of particular difficulties, for example, redundancy. Whilst the counsellor may work with individuals as well as with the management process, this type of context will enable a more systemic approach, the client being understood within wider, working relationships. Between these two organisational approaches to counselling, the one adopting a welfare perspective with counselling perceived as distinct from the main purpose of the organisation, the other construing counselling as a creative intervention to facilitate both personal and organisational development, there is a range and mixture of organisational philosophies.

Historically, qualifications in counselling have often been gained in institutions outside the university sector. This separation of the so-called applied and academic aspects of psychology in both Britain and the United States (Whiteley, 1984) was due, in the main, to prevailing attitudes as to what constituted a science and is referred to in the literature as the 'scientist–practitioner' divide (Howard, 1986). When counselling did find its way into higher education it was most often through education and extra-mural departments. About eighty per cent of counselling programmes approved by the American Psychological Association are housed either partly or wholly in education colleges. Recently, however, counselling psychology has become more established in mainstream psychology programmes in higher education. In Britain, the British Psychological Society (1989) has addressed the question of training and accrediting counselling psychologists. Developments of this kind are further testimony to the rapidly growing interest in counselling psychology and to the improved dialogue between the scientist and the practitioner.

In the United States the scientist–practitioner model is the explicit paradigm for the education and training of counselling psychologists. The model emphasises the importance of a reflexive interaction between research and practice. In Britain, the programme proposed by the British Psychological Society (1989) reflects the same stance. The starting point for most counselling psychologists is a graduate qualification in psychology. For some students this initial programme in psychology may, for various reasons, be experienced as very academic or non-applied either because of the orientation of the particular course or because they themselves have yet to appreciate the application of psychology as a professional task. It is in postgraduate training that the significance of graduate education becomes more evident. Developmental psychology is a core component of graduate psychology programmes and an important preparation for intending practitioners of counselling psychology because it raises questions about the extent and significance of early influences upon the client, about processes and conditions influencing human development, the extent to which human development can be viewed as falling into stages and the implications of all this, if any, for the counselling process. In social psychology the study of interpersonal skills prepares the psychologist for the dynamics of the counselling process while courses dealing with historical and philosophical aspects of psychology provide an understanding of developing concepts of person as understood by various psychologists within changing historical contexts. Research methods is a core element of graduate psychological programmes and a sound preparation in both quantitative and qualitative methodologies is essential to post-graduate education in counselling psychology. A graduate programme will usually offer options in abnormal psychology, evaluation and assessment, personality and, more recently in some institutions, counselling psychology itself will form part of the curriculum. A post-graduate programme in counselling psychology will build upon this knowledge, extending the student's knowledge of counselling theories and of theories relevant to counselling.

Given the significance of the practitioner–client relationship in the counselling process it is not surprising that personal development and supervised client practice are central to post graduate training in counselling psychology. Programmes require trainees to be in personal counselling at some stage of their training. Developing awareness of self, increasing insights into one's own blocks and limitations, and an opportunity to work on personal issues are important elements in the training of counsellors. Personal counselling may facilitate some of these developments. It also provides the trainee with the experience of being a client. Supervision is the forum used to help trainees reflect upon their work with clients so they might learn to be more effective in their practice. Supervision of client work concerns itself with the applied therapeutic side or, as Lambert (1980) puts it, "that part of the overall training . . . that deals with modifying actual in-therapy behaviour". Its purpose is twofold: to ensure the welfare and safety of clients and to facilitate the progressive development of trainees. On completion of post-graduate training, which may be full or part-time, the counselling psychologist is ready to work as a professional. However, unlike other applied psychologists but like, for example, psychotherapists and counsellors, counselling psychologists will continue to seek some form of supervision for their client work. This is because of the significance of their role in the client–practitioner relationship and the need, therefore, for counselling psychologists to remain aware of their own ongoing personal changes and developments and their impact, if any, upon their clients.

Though counselling psychology is the youngest of the applied psychologies, its elements have existed for some time in other applications and many of its underpinning theories and principles have influenced other kinds of applied psychologists. Clinical psychologists, for example, might be distinguished from counselling psychologists on the basis of their behavioural tradition (Pilgrim, 1990), the influence of the medical model upon their practice and the non-requirement for personal counselling in their training. However, as the chapter dealing with clinical psychology in this text indicates, there is a growing interest amongst some clinical psychologists in the work of psychodynamic and humanistic practitioners. Further, though it is not a requirement of their training, some clinical psychologists are engaging in personal counselling or therapy in order to enhance the quality of their work with their patients.   These and other influences of counselling psychology can be found in occupational and educational contexts.

THE CLIENT AND THE COUNSELLING RELATIONSHIP

How does the would-be client find an appropriate counselling psychologist? How do clients find out about their specialisations, interests and expertise? For some clients the choice of counselling psychologist may be made by the referring agent, for example their doctor or friend. Others may approach organisations and centres known for their counselling practice. There is also available a series of registers in which the experience and expertise of counsellors are listed. The British Association for Counselling, for example, publishes a directory (1990) listing available counselling services and the British Psychological Society is in process of compiling a Directory to help intending clients in their search. Once a counsellor is located and an appointment agreed, there is usually an initial, assessment interview on the basis of which the counsellor and client will or will not agree to work together. The client may, for example, be uncomfortable with the therapeutic style of a particular practitioner and prefer to make another choice. Alternatively, the practitioner may prefer to refer the client to a colleague with a specialism that would be helpful to the client.

Once the client and the practitioner have agreed to work together, the ground rules of the counselling contract can be drawn up. Confidentiality is an issue around which clear agreements need to be made early in the counselling relationship. The client must be able to trust the confidentiality of the counselling relationship. However, both client and practitioner must be clear, at the outset, about circumstances under which confidentiality might have to be broached and about how this would be negotiated. Agreements about the termination of the counselling relationship are also made at this stage. Some counselling relationships are intended to be short-term and this will also be made clear at the outset. Others can be very long-term indeed. Related to the management of the counselling relationship are practical issues such as when and where to meet, arrangements for payments, and the cancellation of appointments. The cost of counselling varies from one organisation or individual to another. Some operate sliding scales on income related fees. Others may ask for a donation or have a clearly stated fee. Though these practical issues may appear to be small matters they can have a strong, controlling effect upon the counselling relationship and need clear, purposeful management.

Like psychologists in general, counselling psychologists hold different views on the nature of person, on human development and on factors affecting human change. Their different philosophies have implications for the kinds of therapeutic relationships they attempt to establish and facilitate. Some classify approaches to counselling into three main types: the psychodynamic, the humanistic, and the behavioural or cognitive–behavioural. However, since an increasing number of counsellors designate themselves as 'eclectic' and because there are a number of 'integrative' frameworks as well as the 'systemic' therapies, it may be somewhat simplistic to force new approaches to join old frameworks. In order to explore some of the implications of different theoretical approaches for the client–practitioner relationship, it might be useful to consider the following case of a fictitious client in a range of counselling contexts characterised by different philosophies and relationships.

The Case

M.R. is 34 years of age, single and lives alone in a small flat which she bought with the money she inherited on the death of her mother three years ago. She is a quiet, unobtrusive person, who dresses somewhat formally and in rather dull colours. She uses little make-up. She is an only child.

Her mother was caring but distant and more interested in her career than in her daughter. Her father was warm and close whilst she was a child and at early school but as soon as she showed signs of growing up and becoming sexual he withdrew from her, leaving her feeling rejected and hurt.

M.R. approaches her doctor and tells her about her depression, her anxiety, her lack of friends, and a general lack of purpose in her life. After a relationship which had lasted approximately one year, she parted from her boyfriend a week previously. The doctor suggests she talks with the counselling psychologist who is part of the G.P. practice and refers her with a brief note outlining the symptoms.

In her first session with the counsellor M.R. outlines the pattern of her life, and in particular her relationships with men. Typically, she finds she is attracted to a man and forms a close and warm relationship which promises well for the future. After about six months she finds herself becoming critical and demanding. Eventually the relationship breaks up. The break-up is usually initiated by the man and M.R. is left feeling hurt and abandoned. She wonders if she will ever be able to form an ongoing and lasting relationship with a man. She would like to marry and have a family.

If the counselling psychologist working with M.R. were psychodynamic in orientation then he would establish a 'transference' relationship with his client by revealing very little about himself, by remaining somewhat remote and by allowing M.R. to 'transfer' onto him feelings that rightly belong to her father. Positive transference usually occurs within the first few weeks of counselling. M.R. might find herself enjoying a session all to herself on whatever she wishes to talk about. She would also enjoy the undivided attention of the counselling psychologist who would offer her security through appointments at the same time and in the same place each week, and through his consistent way of working with her. Eventually M.R. might begin to feel like the little girl close to her father with the time and attention she wants from him. She might begin to think that she is as important to M.R. as he is to her. She may fantasise about how she would like to spend more time with him. The counselling psychologist would accept these feelings and try to help M.R. to see that they really relate to her earlier relationship with her father.

Negative transference might occur when M.R. has been working with her counselling psychologist for some time and is feeling positive about the relationship and the work achieved. The the discovery that her counselling psychologist is to take three weeks annual leave, might leave her feeling hurt and rejected even though she knows that he will return. She might begin to blame herself for his absence even though she knows that it is not caused by her. The counselling psychologist would help M.R. to explore these feelings and enable her to see how they relate to earlier experiences with her father.

The counselling psychologist will have feelings for and reactions to his client, M.R. In psychodynamic literature these are referred to as 'countertransference'. Defined at one stage as the unconscious reactions of the therapist to the transference of the client, the concept has been widened to include all feelings and reactions of the therapist towards the client. These feelings are used by the counselling psychologist to enable him to interpret M.R.'s behaviour. He may, for example, feel punitive towards her. He may be reacting against her demands for extra time and sessions and find himself experiencing some of the emotions experienced by her boyfriends. On the other hand, he might find himself becoming protective of her. The countertransference may be a fatherly reaction to the hurt little girl he sees in her. However, unlike M.R.'S boyfriends, he would not remove himself from the relationship. Instead, he would work with this experience, enabling M.R. to understand the patterns she establishes and the ways in which they relate to her experiences with men.

These instances of transference and countertransference are a source of information to the counselling psychologist. Through them, M.R. could be enabled to see that she is relating to men as if they were her father and not as individuals in their own right. By making these feelings conscious and by understanding them, therapist and client can work towards enabling M.R. to relate, not as a twelve year old girl, but as a mature woman. Jacobs (1988) illustrates the stages of setting up, maintaining, and terminating a therapeutic relationship of a psychodynamic kind.

If the counselling psychologist were to come from a behavioural or a cognitive–behavioural background then the relationship he would wish to establish with M.R. would be akin to a 'working relationship or alliance' in which they would negotiate how to work together and what roles would be used by each. The counsellor would encourage neither a personal nor a transference relationship but would focus on the work to be done, in this case helping M.R. build up the skills and abilities needed to initiate and maintain a relationship with a man. The counsellor might point out the 'irrational beliefs' underlying M.R.'s behaviour e.g. "I must have a man in my life" or "I must get married", or "I am to blame if relationships break up". He may explain what effective thinking is about, how we learn our behaviour from antecedents and consequences and how we can unlearn and relearn new behaviour through systematic programmes. He may then work with M.R. on a programme designed to help her learn how to relate and maintain a relationship with a man. This programme could include assertiveness skills training to enable M.R. to ask for what she wants without being overdemanding. She might be asked to keep a diary recording events which upset her. The counselling psychologist would explore with her the conditions that trigger particular reactions and behaviour patterns. The action programme may include rehearsing the first argument with her new boyfriend so that M.R. can be enabled to argue without destroying her relationship. M.R. may also be taught how to reward her constructive behaviour so that she could maintain and develop it. Thinking skills, for example recognising negative self-talk, challenging self-oppressive directives and changing misattributions, may be added to the programme. Nelson-Jones (1990) describes effective thinking skills and ways of developing them.

In the light of these learning experiences M.R. would establish personal goals. She may be taught relaxation and use visualisation as a way of rehearsing events that might come about. What becomes evident in this particular counselling context is the fact that M.R.'s problems are seen as behavioural ones, particularly as deficiency in skills and competences and the counselling psychologist's task is one of re-shaping behaviour and of teaching skills. Dryden and Spurling (1989) have written extensively on approaches of this kind.

The client, M.R., may work with a counselling psychologist from a humanistic background. Here the counsellor would relate to M.R. in a more 'realistic' way, that is not just a working relationship or a transference relationship, but one of genuineness and equality. He would share more about himself, try to enter her inner world, and offer unconditional positive regard (Rogers, 1961), that is, an unconditional acceptance of who she is just now. The counsellor would be genuine, sharing his thoughts and feelings in ways that might help her explore her own situation, and would connect the events of her life so that she could understand what is happening to her. This real relationship would have boundaries of time and place but would offer her the security to become her real self.

Humanistic approaches aim to enable the client to see that she has responsibility for herself and can change what she needs to change. The 'self-concept' is a key notion and would be explored with the client. In practical terms the person-centred counsellor would try to enter the world of M.R. and see life from her perspective. Being understood and being accepted for what she is could allow M.R. to explore her thoughts and feelings. The counselling psychologist would accept her tears and her sense of loss as she worked through the grief consequent upon the loss of her father when she was a teenager. He would not be alarmed by any anger or other strong emotions which she might express.

Because this counselling psychologist believes that M.R. has within herself the resources needed for personal change, his objective would be to create a warm and trusting relationship within which M.R.'s issues could be explored. He would listen carefully and encourage her to express her feelings, to articulate her fears and stay with her doubts. He would provide genuineness and congruence in the relationship. The sessions would end when M.R. was in touch with her feelings and her real self and able to express both in a constructive way. In summary, the humanistic counsellor would work with empathy (understanding and communicating understanding to the client), unconditional positive regard (accepting the client) and congruence (the counsellor being genuine and real with the client). Mearns and Thorne (1988) have an excellent exposition of the concepts and techniques of person-centred counselling and their application to work with clients.

This brief consideration of three approaches to the counselling relationship makes it clear that counselling psychology envelops a multitude of philosophies, values, and methods even though we talk about it as if it were a unified and single approach to helping people. Karasu (1986), who surveyed the therapist, found a:

> "proliferation of widely diverse theories, schools and clinical techniques. According to one recent count, which literally runs the gamut 'from A' (Active analytic therapy) 'to Z' (Zaraleya psychoenergetic technique), there are more than 250 varieties now competing on the psychotherapeutic scene". (p. 325)

Not only are there different approaches to the counselling relationship, there are also different ideas about the function and significance of the relationship itself in the counselling process. For some, the relationship between counsellor and client is, in itself, viewed as the counselling. In this therapeutic relationship the client grows not by instruction, information or insight into self but by the actual experience of being in relationship with the counsellor. Rogers (1961), the prime exponent of this approach to the therapeutic relationship, wrote of its purpose as follows:

> "No approach which relies upon knowledge, upon training, upon the acceptance of something that is taught, is of any use ... the most they can accomplish is some temporary change ... change appears to come through experience in a relationship ... if I can provide a certain type of relationship, the other person will discover within himself the capacity to use that relationship for growth, and change and personal development will occur" (pp. 32–33).

Not all counselling psychologists give the same degree of centrality to the therapeutic relationship itself. Some view the relationship as an essential ambiance but one within which learning can take place. Techniques may be introduced to help clients with their thinking skills (Nelson-Jones, 1990) or there may be visits to the past to come to terms with 'unfinished business' or, as in transactional analysis, there may be instruction to facilitate the client's understanding of the counselling process. Social influence theorists perceive the relationship as helpful to counselling but primarily as a vehicle for teaching and learning and it is the tasks of the counselling process, for example, expression of feeling or dealing with irrational beliefs, which are given priority. Further, in this theoretical framework, the relationship between counsellor and client is an unequal one. Dixon and Clairborn (1987) summarise the social influence approach to the therapeutic relationship:

> ... the counsellor first creates a relationship in which the client perceives the counsellor to be an influential source ... having established social power the relationship with the client, the counsellor influences the client, via a variety of interventions ... (p. 84)

In many of the cognitive–behavioural approaches to counselling priority is also given to the tasks and the therapeutic interventions rather than to the relationship in itself. Finally, some believe that there are circumstances where relationship might be perceived as a hindrance to effective counselling. Wessler and Ellis (1980), both rational–emotive practitioners, point out that:

> "... an intense therapist–client relationship can also be iatrogenic in several ways: (1) It can interfere with therapy if the therapist is fearful about confronting the client because it might 'harm the relationship'. (2) It may encourage the client to develop intense feelings about the therapist and focus on these rather than on uncovering and disputing irrational beliefs about the client's outside relationships and affairs. (3) It can provide so much reassurance and direct advice giving that the client becomes dependent on the therapist and thereby increases his/her disturbed needs for love and approval" (p. 184)

Because the understanding of relationship is central to the therapeutic task of the counselling psychologist, its exploration and interpretation is an ongoing task with new insights being merged with older ones to offer new conceptualisations. Clarkson (1990) proposes a set of relationships available to the counsellor which reflect both established and more recent insights.

The client–practitioner relationship is influenced by factors other than the philosophy of the counselling psychologist. This is one of the few areas of life where the personality of the helper may be used to facilitate change. Some researchers have looked at the qualities needed by the practitioner. Freud (1905) considered the personality of the therapist as primary in the therapeutic endeavour: "... diseases are not cured by the drug but by the physician, that is by the personality of the physician". Jung (1934) was of a similar mind: "the personality and attitude of the doctor are of supreme importance." Rogers (1951) talked about the "core conditions necessary for a therapeutic relationship" and saw three of these as directly related to the person of the therapist: genuineness/congruence, unconditional positive regard and empathy. McConnaughy (1987) surveyed the literature on this subject and concluded that:

"the person of the therapist is the primary determinant of the type and quality of the psychotherapy offered to a client" (p. 304).

It is imperative, if the personality of the counsellor plays such an important role in the outcome of the therapy, that the counsellor knows himself or herself well. Some researchers have examined the motivations involved in becoming a counsellor. Burton (1972) asked twelve therapists to write about how they lived and actualised themselves. He isolated a number of issues that led to their becoming psychotherapists one of which was having to be a caretaker in their family of origin. The findings of Corey and Corey (1989) support this claim:

"From childhood on I attended to the needs of my brothers and sisters. At age 8 I was made almost totally responsible for my newly-born brother. I not only took care of him but also attended to other members of an extended family" (p. 10).

What does research reveal about the effects of different counselling styles upon actual outcomes? And to what extent do factors such as the personality of the practitioner influence outcomes? Eysenck's (1952) highly critical review of the effectiveness of psychotherapy triggered an interest in studies of the effects or outcomes of therapy. In spite of the research generated by this review, the literature indicates that there are still few firm conclusions to guide the counsellor or intending counsellor on the relative efficacy of different therapeutic approaches. (Stiles, Shapiro and Elliot, 1986). Some studies of clients (McCohnaughy, 1987) suggest that it is the personality of the practitioner and not the theoretical orientation or technique which influences the client's choice and which plays a central role in the therapeutic alliance. Frank (1979) however, suggested that the largest proportion of variation in outcomes in therapy is explained by the personal qualities of the client. Clients with high motivation and high positive expectations of the therapeutic process are more likely to be associated with outcomes discerned to be successful. But this claim is also problematic because of the controversy that exists around the criteria by which therapeutic outcomes, including successful ones, are to be defined. (Kazdin, 1986). Why is it that research in counselling and related therapeutic processes is in this state of uncertainty and what steps might be taken to resolve some of the difficulties?

Counselling and other therapeutic processes are difficult to research because of the complexity of the processes involved and the problems of establishing appropriate methodological controls. Lane (1990), rightly emphasised the need to retain and develop the scientific base of counselling psychology in order to overcome some of the existing confusion and uncertainty but practitioners will argue that it is not always easy to establish these controls. The referral process, the entree to the counselling relationship, is determined largely by the preferences of the client or the referring agent, as is the process of matching client and therapist. So, from its inception the counselling process may escape some of the basic principles of psychological investigation. Once established, the counselling relationship is often concerned with complex, subjective, interpersonal issues which are extremely difficult to investigate (Reason and Rowan, 1987) and for which appropriate methodologies need to be generated (Barkham, 1990). Further, the outcomes of these processes are often open to interpretation (Kazdin, 1986). Greenberg (1986) makes the point that the therapeutic processes themselves are in need of more systematic investigation if we are to understand how the therapies produce change.

What are the ways forward for counselling research? Firstly, it is important to make the point that many of these methodological concerns are not peculiar to counselling (Howard, 1986). Developmental and clinical psychologists, for example, also struggle with issues of transition and change. Secondly, attention is being given to the development of methodologies appropriate to the questions and issues of counselling and related processes. Thirdly, practitioners and researchers who have too frequently worked in isolation, the one concerned with clinical treatment issues, the other with theoretical and methodological ones, are beginning to collaborate. This scientist-practitioner divide (Howard, 1989) has prevented an interaction between ideas, hypotheses and theories on the one hand and the actual, human situation, as worked and investigated by the practitioner, on the other. Counselling psychologists are well aware of these issues and the literature indicates the growing efforts to overcome them. (Reason and Rowan, 1987).

THE FUTURE OF COUNSELLING PSYCHOLOGY

Counselling psychology, the youngest of the applied psychologies, would appear to have a positive future. In the United States, it is already well established. Tyler (1972) highlighted the main changes that have taken place in counselling psychology in the United States since it emerged in 1951. She observed shifts in its central emphasis from personal counselling, organisational and behavioural counselling to work with groups. Shifts of emphases and developments of this kind are part of identity development. In Britain, counselling psychology has achieved professional identity, its training programmes are expanding and have become integrated into the university sector and there is a growing demand for counselling services. It is too early to anticipate the kinds of shifts that might take place in its central emphasis as the profession continues to develop its identity in Britain, but a number of issues merit consideration. As a newcomer, in name if not in its practices, to the line-up of applied psychologies, counselling psychology is still in process of establishing its relationships with close professional neighbours (Allen, 1990).

However, in the United States where for some time now Whiteley (1972) has been urging greater co-operation amongst closely related professionals, there are discussions about the possibility of merging specialities into an integrated human service delivery (Woolfe, 1990). This idea is beginning to emerge in discussions in Britain. Watts (1986), for example, rehearsed the possibility of 'core-professions'. Whiteley (1972) also considered the effects of innovations and social change upon the identity of counselling psychology, anticipating that counselling psychology will need to take greater account of environmental change and ageing populations. Counselling psychology in Britain can learn from the history and experience of the United States, but it will create its own future. In doing so it is likely to cause related professionals to re-evaluate their own professional identities and boundaries and lead the search for a new structure for the applied psychologies.

REFERENCES

Allen, J. (1990). *Counselling Psychologists and Counsellors: New Challenges and Opportunities.* British Journal of Guidance and Counselling. **18** (3), 321–325.

British Association for Counselling (1990). *Counselling Psychotherapy Resources Directory.*

British Association for Counselling (1990). *Careers in Counselling.*

British Psychological Society (1989). *Report of the Working Party on the Diploma in Counselling Psychology.* Leicester: B.P.S. Publication.

Burton, A. (Ed.) (1972). *Twelve Therapists: How they live and Actualise themselves.* London: Jossey-Bass.

Clarkson, P. (1990). A Multiplicity of Psychotherapeutic Relationships. *British Journal of Psychotherapy,* 7 (2), 148–163

Corey, M. & Corey, G. (1989). *Becoming a Helper.* Pacific Grove, Calif.: Brooks/Cole.

Dixon, D.N. & Clairborn, C.D. (1987). A Social Influence Approach to Counsellor Supervision. In J.E. Maddux, C.D. Stoltenberg, R. Rosenwein (Eds.) *Social Processes in Clinical and Counselling Psychology.* New York: Springer-Verlag.

Dryden, W. & Spurling, L. (1989). *On Becoming a Psychotherapist.* London: Tavistock/Routledge.

Eysenck, H.H. (1952). The Effects of Psychotherapy: An Evaluation. *Journal of Consulting Psychology.* **16**, 319–324.

Frank, J.D. (1979). The Present Status of Outcome Studies. *J. of Consulting and Clinical Psychology.* **47**, 310–316.

Freud, S. (1905). On Psychotherapy. In J. Strachey (Ed.) *The Complete Psychological Works of Sigmund Freud.* Standard Edition, Vol. 7. London: Hogarth Press.

Greenberg, L.S. (1986). Change Process Research. *J. of Consulting and Clinical Psychology.* **54** (1), 4–9.

Howard, S. (1986). The Scientist–Practitioner in Counselling Psychology: Towards a Deeper Integration of Theory, Research and Practice. *The Counselling Psychologist.* **14** (1), 61–105.

Jacobs, M. (1988). *Psychodynamic Counselling In Action.* London: Sage.

Jung, C. (1934). Civilisation in Transition: The State of Psychotherapy. *Collected Works,* 10, Princeton, N.Y.: Princeton University Press.

Kagan, M. & Armsworth, M.W. (1988). Professional Practice of Counselling Psychology in Various Settings. *The Counselling Psychologist.* **16** (3), 347–365.

Karasu, T.B. (1986). The Psychotherapies: Benefits and Limitations. *American Journal of Psychotherapy,* **40** (3), 324–343.

Kazdin, A.E. (1986). Comparative Outcome Studies of Psychotherapy: Methodological Issues and Strategies. *Journal of Consulting and Clinical Psychology.* **54** (1), 95–105.

Lane, D. (1990). Counselling Psychology in Organisations. *The Psychologist,* 3 (12), 540–544.

Lambert, M.J. (1980). Research and the Supervisory Process. In A.K. Hess (Ed.) *Psychotherapy Supervision: Theory, Research and Practice.* New York: Wiley.

McConnaughy, E.A. (1987). The Person of the Therapist in Psychotherapeutic Practice. *Psychotherapy,* 24 (3), 303–314.

Mearns, D. & Thorne, B. (1988). *Person–Centred Counselling in Action.* Sage: London.

Nelson-Jones, R. (1982). *The Theory and Practice of Counselling Psychology.* London: Holt, Rinehart and Winston.

Nelson-Jones, R. (1990). *Effective Thinking Skills.* London: Sage Publications.

Pilgrim, D. (1990). British Psychotherapy in Context. In Dryden, W. (Ed.) *Individual Therapy.* Open University Press: Milton Keynes.

Reason, P. & Rowan, J. (1987). *Human Inquiry: A Sourcebook of New Paradigm Research.* Wiley.

Reddy, M. (1987). *Counselling at Work.* Leicester: British Psychological Society.

Rogers, C. (1961). *On Becoming a Person: A Therapist's View of Psychotherapy.* London: Constable.

Rogers, C. (1951). *Client–Centred Therapy.* Boston: Houghton Mifflim.

Stiles, W.B., Shapiro, D.A., Elliot, R. (1986). Are All Psychotherapies Equivalent? *American Psychologist.* **41** (2), 165–180.

Tyler, L.E. (1972). Reflections on Counselling Psychology. *The Counselling Psychologist.* **3** (4), 6–11.

Watts, F. (1986). The Core Professions. An Unpublished paper given at the "Rugby Psychotherapy Conference."

Wessler, R.L. & Ellis, A. (1980). Supervision in Rational Emotive Therapy. In A.K. Hess (Ed.) *Psychotherapy Supervision: Theory, Research and Practice.* New York: Wiley.

Whiteley, J.M. (1972). Counselling Psychology in the year 2000 A.D. in *The Present and Future of Counselling Psychology.* J.M. Whiteley and B.R. Fietz (Eds).

Whiteley, J.M. (1984). A Historical Perspective on the Development of Counselling Psychology as a Profession. In S.D. Brown & R.W. Lent (Eds.) *Handbook of Counselling Psychology.* Wiley.

Woolfe, R. (1990). Counselling Psychology in Britain: An idea whose time has come. *The Psychologist.* **3** (12), 531–535.

5

THE NATURE OF ABNORMAL BEHAVIOUR

F. BARWELL

INTRODUCTION

In the course of their work, doctors, social workers, police, and probation officers often have to deal with individuals whose behaviour challenges the accepted social norm. They (or the distressed individual themselves) may decide that the scale or persistence of the aberrant behaviour is sufficiently "abnormal" to warrant the attention of clinical psychologists, psychiatrists or other "mental health" professionals. Unfortunately, even for these professionals, assessing the intensity or potential harmfulness of abnormal behaviour is not always an easy or reliable procedure. Nevertheless, these judgments must be made since they have considerable consequences for the subsequent medical or legal treatment which the individual may receive.

As Gale and Chapman (1984) have pointed out, it is recognised across all contexts of applied psychology that psychological knowledge and theories are not static and unfluctuating. There are many and varied conceptual frameworks and models of human behaviour and the ways in which these are conceived and scientifically evolve should influence the manner in which the practitioner deals with abnormal behaviour. Enhancing the quality of life of those with behavioural abnormalities is a mission which must be based on a sound understanding of the practical implications of an evolving theoretical base.

The purpose of this chapter is to briefly examine a number of current perspectives on abnormal behaviour. This necessitates that the wealth of potential material that could be included is approached in a very selective way. Within the confines of a single chapter it is simply not possible to do justice to all the pertinent approaches and consequently the chapter is a compromise between three conventional ways of partitioning the "abnormal" subject–matter. The traditional approach is to organise discussion around the psychiatric classification system, so that separate sections of text are devoted to each major disorder. Two excellent texts which adopt this approach are those by Davison and Neale (1982) and Miller and Cooper (1988).

Nonetheless there is real concern that the clinical classification systems are outmoded and have limited validity and this misgiving has provoked other authors to partition the abnormal subject–matter along different lines. The functional approach attempts to break away from the traditional clinical boundaries and uses instead various disturbances of psychological functioning (i.e. disorders of attention, memory, language etc.) as an organising framework. However, a great deal of abnormal source material is based upon clinical categories and this material does not fit comfortably into a functional framework. Consequently, even in functionally-based discussions clinical categories and classifications have a tendency to "re-surface" through the functional veneer. For example, one excellent review of the application of cognitive psychology to the investigation of emotional disorders (Williams *et al.*, 1988) still concentrated on discussing anxiety and depression since most studies in the area had used these clinical categories.

An alternative approach to either the "clinical categories" or "functional framework" perspectives is to focus upon the so-called "basic issues" which crop-up on a regular basis in studying abnormal psychology. These ongoing debates revolve around such issues as formulating the criteria for abnormality, evaluating the reliability and validity of classifications of abnormality, assessing the value of the concept of "mental illness", and understanding the role of social factors in the development and maintenance of psychological disorders.

The organisation of this chapter is a compromise between these three approaches. It is not assumed that any particular approach, perspective or school of psychology, psychiatry or psychotherapy is the single best way of viewing abnormal behaviour. In this way the contribution of various theories and approaches are freely drawn upon as required. Although the chapter adopts a structure which is loosely based upon traditional psychiatric categories, this is for convenience only and does not imply that the psychiatric perspective is necessarily seen as the best approach. For the sake of brevity, the chapter generally confines itself to adult psychopathology enabling abnormal behaviour in children, the mentally handicapped, and those with neurological disease to be omitted. Finally, some contemporary issues in abnormal psychology are introduced at various points.

THE CONCEPT OF ABNORMALITY

Many extreme behaviours are so appalling they seem impossible to comprehend. In recent years, cases such as the random massacre of fifteen people in Hungerford by gunman Michael Ryan, Dennis Nilsen's horrific murder and mutilation of fifteen young men and the dismemberment and cannibalism of seventeen victims by the American serial killer Jeffrey Dahmer appear to defy explanation. Psychopathology is concerned with abnormal behaviour but mapping the extent of its domain is particularly difficult because of the variability of human behaviour (both "normal" and "abnormal") and the numerous shortcomings in current theoretical perspectives. Consequently, human behaviour is often viewed as a spectrum – from "normality" at one end to extreme deviation at the other. The boundary between normal and abnormal behaviour is vague and ill-defined and to complicate matters further it may be that even extremely deviant or bizarre forms of behaviour have counterparts in so-called "normality" (an issue recently discussed by Herschel Prins; (1990).

Over the years various criteria for determining abnormality have been proposed and these typically fall into three "camps"; the statistical, the cultural, and those to do with personal distress. Behaviour may be deemed to be abnormal because it is infrequent, rarely observed or deviates from a statistically–defined norm. This normative approach assumes that psychological characteristics are known and can be reliably and validly measured. For instance, mental handicap is usually viewed from the statistical perspective with the lowest 2% (equivalent to an IQ below about 70–75) generally deemed to be mentally handicapped. Such statistical criteria are usually applied in a lop-sided fashion and instances of positive deviance are not included into the definition of abnormality. It is clear that the exceptionally intelligent (those with IQs above 130) are as statistically abnormal as the mentally handicapped but are generally not labelled or treated as deviants.

In contrast to statistical criteria, culturally-based criteria of abnormality may be adopted. Here behaviour is judged to be normal or abnormal based upon society's standards. Unfortunately, society's standards may not be stable; different cultures have different standards and even within the same culture, what is considered acceptable behaviour may change considerably over time. For example, until recently in Britain, homosexuality was generally condemned, prohibited by law and seen as a form of psychopathology. Since the Sexual Offences Act in 1967, male homosexuality is no longer considered a crime if both partners are over 21, consenting and the behaviour takes place in private. However, defining normality with respect to sexual preferences remains a contentious issue and many mental health professionals still consider that homosexuals experience a great deal of psychodynamic conflict which requires resolution if maturity is to be reached. Others consider that many homosexuals are not necessarily in psychological distress and should be considered as "normal" as the heterosexual population.

Personal distress is the third type of criteria which has been proposed as a means of distinguishing between normality and abnormality. Carr (1978) has suggested that psychological disorder is indicated when a person's life is disrupted to an extent that the sufferer finds it unacceptable. Not surprisingly, those people who present themselves for professional help are frequently suffering from severe personal distress. With disorders related to anxiety and depression the individual is generally acutely miserable and may be experiencing dramatic changes in bodily functions, cognitions and behaviour. In these cases it is relatively easy to recognise and diagnose those neurotic disorders which have adverse effects for either the individual or society. Unfortunately, the personal distress approach is less clear-cut when applied to many manic, psychopathic or paranoid personalities who can appear perfectly self-content or blame others for their difficulties. Clearly, none of the above approaches provides a watertight means of distinguishing normal from abnormal behaviour. Ideally, mental health professionals should consider the individual's behaviour from the statistical, the cultural and the personal–distress perspectives before contemplating assigning any label suggesting "abnormality".

Clearly, the unambiguous definition of "abnormality" is difficult although it is equally problematic to define "normality". Traditionally, "normality" has been tackled by examining an individual's degree of "adjustment" to their social and occupational environment. However, some psychologists think that use of "adjust-ment" criteria leads to a tendency to equate adjustment with conformity. Since many neurotics can suffer a great deal from constricted over-conforming the use of adjustment criteria may carry negative connotations. To complicate matters further cultural (and sub-cultural) norms may themselves be psychologically "unhealthy" and consequently represent an inappropriate metric for defining "normality".

An alternative, more positive approach to understanding "normality" is through the identification of positive traits associated with "mental health". Although, attempts to erect universal standards of mental health do not clearly differentiate between the normal and the abnormal, they are useful insofar as they highlight those traits which normal people tend to possess to a greater degree than abnormal people. For example, most psychologists would agree that the mentally healthy individual has a realistic perception of reality, is self-aware, can voluntarily control his or her behaviour, is socially effective, has adequate self-esteem, is able to form affectionate relationships and is actively productive. Different "schools" and different therapies emphasise the importance of different aspects of mental health and consequently focus on different therapeutic means to achieve their various treatment goals.

PERSPECTIVES ON DISORDERED BEHAVIOURS

In any discussion of disordered behaviour, terms such as mental illness, psychological disorders, maladaptive behaviour, personal distress and so on are often loosely used, sometimes in an almost interchangeable fashion. The number of roughly synonymous terms reflects the fact that the domain of abnormal behaviour is both extensive and complex enough to be viewed from a number of different perspectives. Potential psychological disorders can occur in a wide range of human systems and processes and the emotional, motivations, cognitive and behavioural systems are all susceptible to disturbance. In the numerous attempts to provide a framework for viewing the causes and cures of abnormal behaviour different psychological processes and systems tend to be emphasised by protagonists of various "schools" of thought. Sometimes their explanatory frameworks are referred to an "models" since they may aspire to the status of theoretical structures. Several of these approaches have been usefully introduced in other chapters and these will not be described again here. What is clear is that there is no single best model of abnormal behaviour, although each has enhanced facets of our understanding.

The role of such conceptual frameworks, models and theories is essential in shaping our perceptions of abnormal behaviour and it is important for the practitioner that the assumptions and the implications of different approaches are made explicit. Erecting frameworks, building models and constructing theories all involve searching for patterns and identifying generalisations so that explanations are enhanced and more accurate predictions can be made. The central activity of psychological science is understanding and predicting human behaviour and the scientist is concerned with understanding and representing "reality" so that explanations and predictions about behaviour can be made. As Rivett (1972) has pointed out model-building takes place in stages; initially by classifying both the causes which operate on the "reality" to-be-modelled and by classifying the states of the system. Subsequently these causes and states are linked to form hypotheses which can be tested and revised as necessary.

The various models of psychopathology differ not only with respect to the sorts of causes which are suggested to operate on the individual but also with respect to the identification and defintion of the various abnormal individual "states". For example, the medical model takes the view that abnormal behaviour is caused by disturbances in the nervous system (either genetic or biochemical) whereas the sociocultural model focuses on those familial, social or cultural factors which may be causally implicated. In reality, the identification of the causes of abnormal behaviour is problematic because it is difficult to disentangle whether any observed differences between "abnormals" and "normals" is a cause or a consequence of the abnormal state. With respect to the identification and definition of abnormal "states", many see the medical perspective as misleading because it implies not only that there is a clear-cut division between normal and abnormal behaviour but more specifically suggests that by examining symptoms a diagnosis can be made, the course of the disorder predicted and the appropriate treatment specified.

Over thirty years ago the American psychologist Meehl (1962) pointed out that minimally significant data supporting psychodynamic views of schizophrenia were generally accepted without serious question whereas much higher standards of evidence were demanded when genetic data were examined. Since then contemporary approaches to psychopathology have increasingly stressed the value of research using controlled experimentation and have criticised the psychodynamic procedure of observing and interpreting evidence based on single clinical cases. As a result, the status of approaches based on experimental psychology have become enhanced whilst much psychodynamic theorising has come increasingly into question. This is not surprising since many psychodynamic hypotheses have not (some would say can not) been put to controlled test.

Although many psychologists have been particularly critical of non-experimental approaches to psychopathology, both the behavioural and cognitive traditions tend to retain the conventional view that an individual with behavioural difficulties is "disturbed" and needs to be returned to a state of personal comfort through building conventional behaviour patterns. The behavioural approach emphasises the effects of early learning (rather than genetics or biochemistry) on adult behaviour. From this perspective, either failure to learn or learning of the wrong things may result in abnormal or maladaptive behaviour. For the behaviourist, most psychiatric disorders result from traumatic or inappropriate conditioning and the behaviourist assumes that anxiety reactions or phobic fears may be traced back to earlier learned association between the triggering event and negative emotional feelings. For example, a child punished for masturbation may become a sexually-anxious adult. The strict behaviourist assumes that abnormal behaviour can be effectively dealt with without considering any underlying psychological disturbance or conflict. By replacing maladaptive behaviour with "normal" responses the "illness" is considered cured.

In the subsequent chapter, you will see that much of the applied professional work of clinical psychologists involves the application of behavioural therapies. Although these have been successful across a wide range of clinical problems, the approach has often been criticised for embracing a simplistic and mechanistically crude model of abnormal behaviour. As a reaction to these criticisms, the cognitive approach is becoming increasingly popular. Essentially, the cognitive approach does not restrict itself to dealing only with observable behaviour and instead postulates "faulty" thinking patterns as an important determinant in abnormal behaviour. Whereas behavioural theories emphasise changes in motivation with accompanying changes in activity levels, cognitive theories stress changes in thinking as the primary cause of abnormal behaviour. It is suggested that many of those with emotional disorders are preoccupied with negative thoughts about bad experiences they have had although the relationships between cognition and the emotions are as yet far from being fully understood.

THE ROLE OF STRESS IN ABNORMAL BEHAVIOUR

Social aspects of abnormal behaviour have created a great deal of interest since the 1950s and many different social characteristics have been found to be important in the onset, prevalence and maintenance of various abnormalities. Although there have been numerous investigations of the part social factors play in abnormal behaviour, the major disorders of psychotic depression and schizophrenia have received the greatest research attention although little consensus has been reached about the implications of these studies for potential approaches to treatment.

Studies in depression have tended to focus upon onset and risk factors (e.g. gender, class, race, unemployment, and other stressors) whereas studies in schizophrenia have tended to focus upon social factors implicated in the course of the disorder (e.g. familial, social networks and other cultural factors). Recently, interest has focussed on examining the value of directly reducing the impact of social and other forms of stress in controlling both depression and schizophrenia.

Not all abnormal behaviour is activated by the direct or indirect effects of stress. Nevertheless, some people appear to be particularly vulnerable to stress-induced psychological disorder due to adverse social circumstances coupled with a lack of available coping mechanisms. Laing (1967) views disordered behaviour as a means by which some individuals come to terms with their role in society and Cochrane (1983) has pointed out that mental illness itself is a means of coping with stress when other coping strategies have failed. Indeed, Laing has argued that schizophrenia may be a mask behind which individuals conceal their emotional problems.

For all of us, the first line of defence against stress is our level of self-esteem. Whereas negative experiences can result in low self-esteem and may make people vulnerable to stress, positive experiences can enhance self-esteem and may act as antidotes to stress. These positive experiences may be linked to material resources such as wealth or possessions or may derive from stimulating and rewarding leisure activities. The feelings of value and personal worth engendered through intimate personal relationships or through the friendship and social support of others also strengthen favourable self-perceptions. Seeking these positive antidotes to the effects of stress are all socially acceptable ways of coping; other responses which are usually seen as deviant include drink and drug abuse, depression and suicide. As Kaplan (1972) has suggested, those who are unable to maintain their self-esteem in the face of threatening experiences are more likely to become anxious and depressed and indulge in deviant behaviour.

In addition to variations in the individual response to stress, some groups tend to have low levels of self-esteem and consequently are less able to handle stress than others. Women typically have lower levels of self-esteem than men and are about twice as likely as men to become depressed or even suicidal (Weissman and Klerman 1985). The increased risk of depression in women is probably due to a variety of factors including, greater exposure to stressful life events, restricted role opportunities, and possibly less opportunities to learn effective coping strategies.

Similarly, those with low social status such as the unemployed and minority ethnic groups may have particular difficulties in maintaining adequate levels of self-esteem and consequently may also be at risk. There has been a consistent finding that people in lower social classes are at greater risk to depression disorders, and stressful social factors associated with social status (e.g. poverty, poor housing, and poor working conditions) are usually seen as key causative factors. However, this social causation hypothesis has not been fully proved and a possible alternative view is that it is the individual's psychological impairment rather than social disadvantage which limits social achievement.

Race or ethnic origin is not in itself a major predictor of level of psychiatric symptoms in the United States (Steele, 1978; Ilfield, 1978) although two community studies of symptom rates in different ethnic groups in Britain (Cochrane and Stopes-Roe, 1979; 1980) have revealed some interesting differences between natives and immigrants.

Unemployment among men has been consistently found to be associated with increased risk of psychiatric disorder. In an extensive review, Warr (1984) concluded that unemployment was causally implicated in producing psychological disorder. As many as 20%–30% of men report an increase in abnormal psychological symptoms following job-loss (Warr and Jackson, 1985). For women, it appears that there is a more complex relationship between paid employment and psychological well-being. In a review of the evidence, Warr and Parry (1982) concluded that for single women there is a strong positive association between paid employment and psychological well-being but for married women no simple association holds between employment and mental health.

THE NATURE OF CLASSIFICATION

The fundamental activity of any science is classification since this means that complex systems can be made more manageable and more amenable to systematic inquiry. It has often been observed that Linnaeus's classification of plants provided the necessary antecedent knowledge vital to the subsequent development of evolutionary theory. Similarly, Mendeleef's classification of chemical elements greatly facilitated subsequent understanding of atomic theory. Classifying a subject matter in this way has two major outcomes; first it enables effective communication to take place about the entities which are classified and second, because entities with common characteristics are grouped together, it enables general theories and laws to be determined. The value of a good classificatory scheme is clear although a taxonomy based upon incorrect assumptions can severely hinder future developments. For example, Kendall (1983) has pointed out that for many years progress in understanding diseases was hindered by their ancient clasification as deficiences or excesses in the four Galenical "humours".

The foundations of modern psychiatric classification were laid by Kraeplin in 1896. Kraeplin believed that psychiatric disorders originated in hereditary, metabolic or endocrine disturbances and he assumed that there were a fixed number of "diseases" each of which was associated with a distinct cause and a distinct set of symptoms. Despite a great deal of criticism that this sort of "physicalist" medical approach is inappropriate for psychological disorders, even today most classification systems in common use are based upon medical psychiatric categories. Currently, the two best known classifications are the ninth revision of the International Classification of Diseases (ICD-9) and the American Psychiatric Associations third edition of its Diagnostic and Statistical Manual in 1980 (DSM–111). Both systems of classification are based upon the aetiology, symptomatology and prognosis of disorders although the DSM-111 uses a "multi-axial" approach and assesses the patient along five axes, rather than placing an individual in one diagnostic category. Both the ICD-9 and the DSM-111 aim to provide a standardised means by which effective communication can take place between professionals.

Miller and Morley (1986) have presented a useful outline of contemporary psychiatric classification and this is included below.

TABLE 5.1

	FUNCTIONAL		ORGANIC
Psychoses	Neuroses	Miscellaneous and personality disorders	
Schizophrenia	Phobias	Psychopathy	Senile dementia
Manic–depress. psychosis	Anxiety states	Addictions (drugs, alcohol, etc.	Arteriosclerotic dementia
Depression (psychotic)	Depression (neurotic)	Sexual deviations (e.g. paedophilia)	Toxic confusion states
	Obsessional disorders		Huntington's chorea
	Hysteria		Myoedema (hypothoiroidism etc.)

The outline shows that psychiatric conditions can be broadly divided into the functional and the organic. "Functional" means that there is no obvious organic damage and functional disorders include a wide range of conditions where the individual's problems are largely a result of coping and adapting to life's difficulties. If these problems persist then over time the person may become chronically neurotic. Traditionally schizophrenia and the affective psychoses have been considered to be due, at least in part, to a biochemical anomaly but are nevertheless included in the functional category of disorders. "Social" disorders such as psychopathy and delinquency are largely "functional" as are neurotic disorders although this does not excluded physiological factors playing a part. In contrast, organic conditions are those where there is clearly a direct association between psychological abnormality and an organic condition. These can include a great many causes including brain injuries, neurological disorders, toxic states and infections.

In later life organic psychiatric disorders are fairly prevalent and dementia represents one of the most specific abnormal processes in the elderly. Estimates of the prevalence of dementia range from 5% to 15% of the over 65s to between 20%–40% for those over 80 years old (Levy and Post, 1982). Dementia is a clinical syndrome which is characterised by a general impairment of memory, personality and skills without clouding of consciousness. Typically the condition is irreversible and progressive. Some investigators have argued for a more specific breakdown of dementia into numerous subtypes, although overcategorisation can itself lead to confusion. In general, there appears to be two major groups. One is cerebro-vascular or "multi-infarct" dementia and this is associated with raised blood pressure and characterised by "steplike" deterioration resulting from ischaemic lesions. The other is the most common form, known as senile dementia of the Alzheimer type (or SDAT for short) and this appears to be caused by cerebral atrophy as a result of degeneration of brain tissue. Unlike multi-infarct dementia, SDAT is characterised by a progressive deterioration in abstract thinking, visuo-spatial orientation and memory for recent events. Space precludes a detailed discussion here and the reader is referred to texts such as Hanley and Hodge (1984) and Woods and Britton (1985) for a general review of clinical psychology in relation to the elderly.

PROBLEMS IN CLASSIFYING ABNORMAL BEHAVIOUR

Classifying abnormal states is fraught with problems and there is a great deal of disagreement about making diagnoses. In one study, Schmidt and Fonds (1956) found that although psychiatrists were fairly reliable when using a broad threefold classification (i.e. organic, psychotic or characterological diagnoses), they were much less reliable when more specific diagnoses were required. Another difficulty with psychiatric diagnosis is that, unlike diagnosis of physical ailments, the diagnosis often provides little reliable indication of the course, duration or possible recurrence of the so-called "disease".

One of the biggest stumbling blocks in the classification of abnormal behaviour lies in the logic of an ideal classificatory system. The ideal system should be comprised of mutually exclusive and exhaustive subclasses, and each subclass should be defined by the necessary and sufficient conditions for membership. Unfortunately, for most abnormal states it is not possible to specify the necessary and sufficient conditions for membership of a diagnostic category. In practice, diagnostic decision-making is always complicated by determining not only whether any isolated symptoms are severe enough to link an individual to a diagnosis but also whether the combination of symptoms are characteristic of any diagnostic label.

Two other serious problems with current approaches to classification can be called the "diversity of classificatory principles issue" and the lack of "homogeneity within the classification categories" issue. Briefly, the diversity of classificatory principles issue arises from the fact that the categories used in psychiatric classification are not confined to clinical symptoms; in some cases aetiology and response to treatment are seen as more important than the presenting behaviour in determining a diagnosis. The lack of homogeneity within categories issue refers to the problem of defining which common features should be used to define membership of a classification category. For example, some have advocated the use of the separate category of "paranoid psychosis" rather than the more inclusive "schizophrenia" category since they consider that relatively high intelligence and late onset typical of paranoid psychosis warrants a distinct and separate diagnostic group. Others judge that those in the "paranoid psychosis" sub-group are sufficiently similar to others in the broader "schizophrenic" category not to require separate categorisation. Clearly, unstable classificatory principles and the confusion surrounding category membership seriously undermines the value of any classificatory scheme. The reader is referred to Mackay (1975) for a fuller description of these issues with respect to classifying abnormal behaviour.

THE LABELLING ISSUE

Although classification systems are intended to do more than simply label people, there is a long-standing concern about the damaging effects which diagnostic labels can have. The potential dangers of misusing classifications are serious since crude and insensitive "labelling" of individuals may undervalue important idiosyncrasies of human behaviour. In the latest version of DSM-111, common disorders as well as more unusual and severe forms of abnormal behaviour are included. This strategy has been criticised as over-inclusive since it increases the dangers of stigmatising those with relatively mild difficulties as "abnormal". Turner (1984) has pointed out the dangers in the misuse of classification and has summarised the following reasons for taking an anti-classification position; labels are unidimensional whereas people are multidimensional; labels stereotype people and minimise their individuality; labels have a tendency to be self-fulfilling; labels may lack adequate theoretical or empirical support and therefore give a false sense of understanding to both client and professional.

Although it is patently clear that no single classification category can adequately describe an individual, it is this very complexity of behavioural phenomena which necessitates systematic analysis and classification if our understanding of abnormal behaviour is to be furthered. More precise diagnosis must be based on reliable nomenclature and in turn improved diagnosis should lead to more effective therapeutic intervention.

THE NATURE OF NEUROTIC BEHAVIOUR

The World Health Organisation (1977) has defined neuroses in the following way;

> "mental disorders without any demonstrable organic basis in which the patient may have considerable insight and has unimpaired reality testing, in that he usually does not confuse his morbid subjective experiences and fantasies with external reality. Behaviour may be greatly affected although usually remaining within socially acceptable limits, but personality is not disorganised."

It is often claimed that all of us are neurotic to a greater or lesser extent. Through introspection most people are aware that they have neurotic patterns of thought and these have been usefully captured by Sims (1983) in the following way;

(i)   a lack of self-acceptance and low self-esteem in which the neurotic individual sees themselves as ineffectual, deficient, immature or even deformed.
(ii) a dichotomy between "myself as I know myself to be" and the fantasy self "myself as I wish I were".
(iii) a desperate attempt to hold the self together against perceived crushing forces.
(iv) a longing to belong coupled with a self-centred, self-consciousness which inhibits authentic relationships with others.
(v)   a lack of ability to give or receive sufficient affection despite aspirations otherwise.

Whereas the so-called normal person will occasionally feel these things, the neurotic person feels them to a greater degree or with a greater persistence. Whether an individual is diagnosed as having a neurotic illness or is considered to be an essentially normal person with a "touch" of neurosis is a matter of clinical judgment. Some common neurotic disturbances are described in the ensuing sections.

ANXIETY STATES

Although anxiety is a normal reaction to stress, it becomes pathological when it is not attributable to real threat or when it persists long after the removal of threat. Fear of the unknown or fear of separation appear to be the two major precursors for anxiety, and although anxiety states appear to be more common in females than males, they may occur in either sex at any age. The symptoms of anxiety may be psychological or physiological and these reactions may occur together or on their own. Psychological symptoms include feelings such as tension, worry, nervousness and uneasiness. Physiological correlates of the anxiety experience are associated with arousal of the sympathetic autonomic nervous system and may include choking sensations, increased blood pressure, palpitations, trembling, cold sweats, dry mouth, panting, stomach churning and so on.

Anxiety may occur in acute panic attacks or it may be chronic and persistent. A panic attack may last only a few seconds or may persist for over an hour. Typically, perceived threat precipitates an intense anxiety reaction in the individual. Often panic attacks are associated with over-breathing (hyperventilation) which has the effect of reducing the pressure of carbon dioxide in the blood which in turn leads to a range of secondary symptoms. These secondary symptoms include dizziness, faintness and pins and needles (paraesthesia) and often themselves further alarm the sufferer so that anxiety is raised and the momentum of the attack increased. Unlike the anxiety state of a panic attack, persistent anxiety is an ongoing anxiety trait and does not appear to be triggered by external circumstances. "Chronic worriers" do not appear to react to particular precipitants but rather display this symptom as a permanent feature of their personality. The causes of generalised anxiety may prove much more difficult to identify.

Anxiety often occurs with tension, agitation, frustration, and irritability and frequently plays a major role in other neurotic conditions such as phobic reactions, obsessive–compulsive behaviours and somatoform disorders (physical ailments for which there is no organic basis). Several types of neurotic conditions are discussed below although space precludes any discussion of the less common neuroses such as neurasthenia (chronic lack of energy), depersonalisation and derealisation (persistent sense of unreality of the outside world), and hypochondriasis (complaining about ailments without physical cause).

NEUROTIC DEPRESSION

The most common of all neurotic syndromes is neurotic depression although it has never been precisely defined. It's main features include a painful negative mood state although anxiety, restless agitation, sleeping or eating disturbances may be the main complaint which the patient presents to the mental health professional. Depression is a potential threat at every age and phase of development, and it is estimated that more than 12% of adults will become sufficiently depressed to require treatment.

Traditionally, practitioners have attempted to make a distinction between neurotic and psychotic depression; neurotic depression is often seen as reactive whereas psychotic depression is seen as endogenous. This separation of neurotic from psychotic depression based upon the presence or absence of external causes has been frequently questioned although the issue of whether depression should be regarded as a unitary disorder has not yet been resolved. Although neurotic depression commonly occurs following misfortunes, especially losses, it is often very difficult to separate acute reactions to stress and grief (i.e understandable states of unhappiness) from neurotic depression which, as a further complication, can itself share many symptoms of affective psychosis. Generally, neurotic depression is disproportionate to the distressing triggers and appears as a general manifestation of a neurotic condition that often merges in it's presentation with other neurotic features such as obsession, irritability, loss of self-esteem, hysteria or hypochondriacal ideas.

A diagnosis of neurotic depression is usually based on symptoms such as, unhappiness, lack of energy, difficulties in concentration, reluctance to face the future, sleep problems and pre-occupation with unpleasant thoughts. Although some depressives look slumped and gloomy, many do not appear to be depressed and can keep up a good front by taking an active role in conversations, telling jokes and smiling and laughing at appropriate times.

PHOBIC DISORDERS

A phobia is characterised by an irrational and abnormally intense fear of an object or a specific situation. Although many individuals experience apprehension or even panic when confronted with certain things (e.g. snakes, mice and spiders), the diagnosis of phobic states is usually confined to those who are experiencing significant personal distress or dysfunction on a day-to-day basis.

Anxiety, fear and avoidance are the central features of the phobic reactions. Clearly anxiety can be avoided by avoiding the feared object or situation in which this anxiety has become attached. The variety of objects and situations from which people may become phobic is very large. Agoraphobia (etymologically the "fear of the market place") is the occurrence of feelings of anxiety or threat on leaving a situation of familiarity and safety or on entering a public space. Agoraphobia accounts for more than 60% of all phobias and is the most important category of phobic disorder. Depression, depersonalisation, anxiety, panic attacks and loss of control are experienced by many agoraphobic individuals. These feelings may occur on public transport, or in shopping areas, open spaces, theatres or other crowded places.

Another important category of phobias are the social phobias. In these conditions, the individual suffers anxiety in those situations which involve social interaction. Eating in public places, speaking before groups, or even sharing lifts with strangers can be associated with excessive feelings of fear. Often being watched by an authority figure or walking into a crowded room is a particular source of discomfort or anxiety. Animal phobias are another phobic category, more common in children than adults, although fear of flying, heights, lifts, storms, winds and many other specific phobias have been identified. Since they can be more easily avoided, specific phobias are less common and less disruptive to the individual than the more prevalent diffuse phobias like agoraphobia and social phobias.

OBSESSIVE–COMPULSIVE DISORDERS

These conditions are those where the most prominent behaviour is characterised by involuntary and uncontrollable "obsessions" (i.e. recurrent and persistent thoughts or ideas) or "compulsions" (i.e. repetitive overt or covert behaviours performed in a stereotyped manner). The condition is characterised by strong feelings of subjective compulsion coupled with a desire to resist which itself results in intense or persistent distress. Traditionally, obsessive–compulsive disorders are seen as a unitary phenomenon although the clinical manifestations can be very diverse. Often compulsions involve hand washing, repetitive checking, counting of numbers, or repeating words or phrases in the head. Frequently obsessive thoughts are anti-social, aggressive or sexual; for example, a mother may fantasise about strangling her children, or a priest of exposing himself in church.

The apparent bizarreness of many obsessive–compulsive symptoms has encouraged some to believe that these symptoms may be a defence against psychotic breakdown although there is little clear evidence that obsessive–compulsives ultimately become schizophrenics (Rachman and Hodgson 1980). In fact, many of the symptoms of obsessive–compulsive disorders are also very prevalent in the non-clinical population and appear to serve the same purpose of protecting the person from overwhelming anxiety.

HYSTERIA

The term "hysteria" was coined by Hippocrates (460–377 BC) and was thought to be due to movements ("wandering") of the womb. Originally treatment attempted to encourage the womb to return to it's proper place in the female body. The obvious absurdity of the ancient explanation has not stopped the use of this label to the present day. Its resilience is probably due to the phenomena of hysteria being occasionally encountered in clinical practice although many practitioners have attacked the conceptual and explanatory status of hysteria (e.g. Szasz, 1961; Slater, 1976). Although, hysteria is one of the oldest it is also one of the most confused of the classificatory categories.

Broadly there appear to be two types of hysterical neurosis. The first type is commonly called "conversion hysteria", a term derived from classical Freudian theory and which refers to those conditions where individuals develop symptoms which cannot be linked to any underlying organic pathology. According to Freud, the anxiety elicited by unresolved sexual conflict at the Oedipal stage of development is repressed, carried into adult life and finally "converted" into physical symptoms. Although this psychoanalytic explanation of hysteria would find limited support from contemporary clinicians, many would agree that hysterical symptoms frequently benefit the individual in several ways. Developing hysterical symptoms not only delivers release from underlying psychological tension but also provides the patient with attention from others or escape from an unpleasant situation. The physical symptoms of conversion hysteria may be sensory (e.g. loss of sensitivity to pain, hysterical blindness or deafness), motor (e.g. losing the use of a limb, complete inability to talk), or visceral (e.g. pseudo–malaria, severe headaches, or coughing fits).

The second type of hysterical neurosis is commonly referred to as the dissociation type. Although less common than the conversion type, the symptoms are even more theatrical. There are several types of hysterical dissociative disorder including multiple personality states (i.e. patient holding two or more distinct personalities), amnesia and fugues (i.e. inability to recall events – coupled with a "flight" from problems in the fugue state), and somnambulism (i.e. sleepwalking to perform certain acts in connection with his or her dreams).

EATING DISORDERS

The eating disorders include anorexia nervosa, bulimia nervosa and obesity. Anorexia nervosa is the relentless pursuit of thinness through dieting to a pathological and sometimes life–threatening degree. Bulimia nervosa is characterised by bouts of binge eating followed by force vomiting of the food. Like anorexia nervosa, obesity seems to involve a misuse of the eating function and results in afflicted individuals being conspicuous by their appearance. Obesity is often viewed as the clinical counter-part of anorexia nervosa but it is not a psychiatric condition per se. Although it is often thought that obesity results in part from psychological factors, there is little evidence to support this assumption. Cooper and Cooper (1988) have pointed out that despite considerable research there is little evidence that obese people differ from those with normal weight with respect to rate of eating, susceptibility to external eating cues, emotional arousal or even amount of food consumed. Genetic factors appear to be of considerable aetiological significance in obesity and the condition is essentially a physical disorder which does not have the same psychiatric correlates as anorexia nervosa or bulimia nervosa.

More women than men develop both anorexia and bulimia and both are particularly prevalent in adolescent girls (Slade, 1982).

There is wide agreement about the essential diagnostic criteria for the identification of anorexia nervosa. Garrow and his associates (1975) succinctly stated their view of the essential diagnostic criteria as a morbid fear of fatness and weight gain together with a self-inflicted severe loss of weight, often by food avoidance, abuse of purgatives, excessive exercise, and self-induced vomiting. In addition, anorexia generally precipi-tates a secondary endocrine disorder which results in amenorrhoea in women and loss of sexual interest in men.

The appropriate diagnostic criteria for bulimia nervosa are less clear and this creates considerable difficulties in interpreting the research literature.

PERSONALITY DISORDERS

Over the years there have been many descriptions of personality disorders but a great deal of confusion and controversy still remains. One of the main objections is that labels have often been used to describe the whole person rather than merely the condition which a person possesses. In a useful discussion, Millon (1981) has identified three behavioural characteristics which appear to discriminate between normal and abnormal personalities. First, pathological personality types have few strategies for adapting to and coping with stress and those which do exist are practised in a rigid way. Second, pathological personality types tend to perpetuate existing problems and instigate new ones by their behaviour. Third, individuals with disordered personalities are fragile and lack resilience under stress.

Personality traits which are both inflexible and maladaptive tend to create conditions in which the person or surrounding others begin to suffer and it is at that point that these traits constitute personality disorders. The ICD-9 identifies eight categories of personality disorder and the DSM-111 identifies eleven although there is a great deal of overlap between the descriptions of both classifications. Since the DSM 111 is the most commonly used and up-to-date classification it will be used as the basis or discussion here. The eleven categories will not be discussed separately but, in line with Millon's (1981) approach, as variants of five basic personality patterns. It must be remembered that many of the characteristics listed below occur in people without any personality disorder.

DEPENDENT AND HISTRIONIC DISORDERS

Those with a dependent personality disorder are characterised by passively allowing others to assume responsibility even for important areas in their lives. Typically, they are compliant and self-sacrificing, lacking in self-confidence and have a fear of being alone. Histrionic disorders are characterised by excitability and overreaction, intensely expressed self-dramatisation, vanity, shallowness and proneness to suicidal threats. In Millon's (1981) scheme both dependent and histrionic personality disorder are characterised by a strong dependence on others. The dependent personality adopts a passive, submissive strategy whereas the histrionic personality actively seeks attention from others.

NARCISSISTIC, PARANOID AND ANTISOCIAL DISORDERS

The person who is pathologically narcissistic has some of the following characteristics; a grandiose sense of uniqueness and self-importance, a preoccupation with fantasies of outstanding success or power, a lack of empathy and an extraordinary need for attention and adulation. Their interpersonal relationships are often characterised by intense swings, between over-glowing and over-derogatory views of others, and they tend to be exploitative, envious and driven by rage.

Paranoid personality types are often suspicious, mistrustful, and guarded and are inclined to be over-sensitive and easily slighted. They often exaggerate difficulties, lack humour and sentimentality and like to take pride in their objectivity and rationality.

There is an extensive literature on psychopathic or antisocial personality and since space precludes any detailed discussion, the reader is referred to Blackburn (1984) for a fuller account. Antisocial disorders are identified by a detailed set of criteria which relate to the violation of other people's rights; typically, these delinquent and irresponsible behaviours occur before the age of fifteen. Millon suggests that the major criteria for this category are vindictiveness, hostility, rebelliousness and a disregard for danger and considers that "aggressive" may be a more appropriate term for this category of personality disorder.

In Millon's scheme both narcissistic and aggressive personalities have a common need for independence and self reliance but the narcissistic individual passively relies on an exaggerated image of self-worth whilst the aggressive individual actively attempts to dominate others. Although paranoid individuals share some features with compulsive individuals, they also reveal characteristics of the narcissistic and aggressive personality types. Generally, the paranoid disorder presents itself as some combination of exaggerated self-importance, extreme mistrust of others and externalised hostility.

COMPULSIVE, PASSIVE–AGGRESSIVE AND BORDERLINE DISORDERS

Those with a compulsive personality disorder tend to be excessively conscientious, perfectionist and stubborn with a desire to make others do things their way. They have little ability to express warm emotions and are often unable to gain real pleasure from interpersonal relationships.

The passive–aggressive personality tends to be sullen, irritable and pessimistic, and resists the real or assumed demands of others by procrastinating, forgetting, inefficiency, or by making irrelevant excuses. Passive–aggressive disorders are among the least reliably identified personality disorder and have not really been recognised outside America.

The individual with a borderline personality disorder has some of the following attributes; marked instability in moods and behaviour, unstable and intense relationships, identity disturbance, extreme vulnerability to stress, and chronic feelings of emptiness and boredom.

According to Millon, both compulsive and passive–aggressive personality disorders stem from over- or under-reliance placed onthe self or on external demands. The compulsive opts for a conforming, over-controlled approach while the passive-aggressive vaciliates between despondency and malice. The borderline condition overlaps with every other personality disorder with the exception of the schizoid and the antisocial disorder. It is best not seen as a distinct type of disorder but rather as representing extreme forms of concurrent personality types. Consequently, Millon partitions the borderline personality into subtypes such as "borderline–histionic", "borderline–dependent" and so on.

SCHIZOID, SCHIZOTYPAL AND AVOIDANT DISORDERS

The DSM–111 criteria for schizoid disorders include emotional blandness, emotional coldness and indifference to others, few close relationships, and an absence of severely eccentric thoughts or behaviours. In contrast, the person with a schizotypal personality disorder although sharing some of the attributes of a person with a schizoid personality disorder, has persistent eccentricities of perception, thought, speech or overt behaviour. These aberrations may include "magical" thinking (superstitiousness or clairvoyance), vague, depressive or circumstantial speech, recurrent illusions, depersonalization, bizarre habits and hypersensitive reactions. Avoidant disorders are characterised by a hypersensitivity to rejection or criticism, unwillingness to enter into relationships without a strong guarantee of acceptance, painful shyness coupled with a strong desire for affection, low self-esteem and extreme self-doubt.

In Millon's scheme, both the schizoid and avoidant personalities are characterised by a detachment from others distinguished by passive detachment in the schizoid type and active detachment in the avoidant type. Either set of behaviours may be exhibited in schizotypal disorders which are additionally associated with cognitive eccentricities as their most significant feature.

FUNCTIONAL PSYCHOTIC DISORDERS

The World Health Organisation (1977) has defined psychoses in the following way;

> "mental disorders in which impairment of mental function had developed to a degree that interferes grossly with insight, ability to meet some ordinary demands of life or to maintain adequate contact with reality."

Typically, the psychotic is seen as suffering from something outside normal experience whereas the neurotic is seen to be "like us" in our fears, doubts and conflicts but experiencing these to a greater degree. Jaspers (1963) made the interesting observation that neurotic thinking and behaviour is ultimately understandable by others whereas psychotic thinking and behaviour cannot be really understood even by the most empathetic therapist.

Generally, those with psychotic rather than neurotic disorders are clinically distinguishable on the basis of several broad criteria including, greater extent of problem denial, less contact with reality, greater degree of disorientation and a higher likelihood of causing harm to the self or to others. Unlike the neurotic, the psychotic individual is more profoundly disturbed and normal social functioning is often severely impaired. Whereas the neurotic struggles to cope, the psychotic has lost contact with reality and may withdraw into his or her own fantasy world sometimes overreacting to events in a grossly exaggerated fashion. Often the psychotic experiences delusions or hallucinations and requires protective care in a sheltered environment. The two most prevalent functional psychoses are schizophrenia and the affective psychoses and these are respectively discussed in a little more detail in the subsequent sections.

SCHIZOPHRENIC DISORDERS

The term schizophrenia was coined by the Swiss psychiatrist, Bleuler (1911) and referred to the splitting of thought and emotion from external reality; the populist idea that schizophrenia refers to a "split" or "multiple personality" is misleading. Schizophrenia is a major psychosis and tends to appear in adolescence or young adult life; it is relatively rare in middle life and if it does occur tends to be of the paranoid type. Schizophrenia is a significant mental health problem, afflicting about one per cent of the population, and accounting for nearly one-third of patients admitted to mental hospitals. More than half of psychiatric hospital beds are occupied by schizophrenics and this is because a minority of schizophrenics become long-term chronic patients.

Thought disorder is a central characteristic of schizophrenia and reveals itself in a variety of ways in the sufferer's behaviour. Typically, the schizophrenic appears to be withdrawn, emotionally blunted, apathetic and listless. Stupor, semi-rigid muscle states, stereotypic behaviours (e.g. rocking, pacing up and down) can sometimes occur. Speech may be lucid at some times and, at other times, vague, illogical and meandering. Schizophrenics may feel that thoughts are crowding into their mind or that their thought are becoming blocked in some way. Problems in maintaining concentration and attention are common and sometimes delusions and hallucinations occur (in particular "hearing voices").

The variability of schizophrenic symptoms probably means that the label is being indiscriminately applied to a number of essentially different disorders. Historically, a distinction has been drawn between simple, hebephrenic, catatonic and paranoid types of schizophrenia. Simple schizophrenia is characterised by emotional blunting ("flatness of affect") and an inability to make decisions or act on them ("lack of volition"). Hebephrenic schizophrenia is characterised by thought disorders and inappropriate emotional responses ("incongruity of affect"). Catatonic schizophrenia is characterised by psychomotor disturbances such as remaining in a fixed position for many hours. Paranoid schizophrenia is characterised by the predominance of delusions (usually of grandeur and/or persecutions) and the experience of hallucinations in clear consciousness.

This fourfold typology is no longer in common usage, due largely to difficulties in diagnosis. The paranoid type appears to be the most homogeneous and is relatively easily diagnosed, leading many to believe that the paranoid/non-paranoid distinction is the only viable distinction in this domain. Other pragmatic distinctions have been drawn between "process" and "reactive" schizophrenics, and between "acute" and "chronic" psychosis. The process–reactive distinction appears to be strongly related to prognosis. Process patients are those who become schizophrenic without unusual stress and often experience a slow insidious deterioration in their condition. Prognosis is much better for reactive patients who are precipitated into the illness by episodic problems (Neale and Oltmanns 1980). Acute schizophrenia manifests itself between three to six months following initial personality disturbances whereas in chronic schizophrenia the period of time from the beginning of personality change to overt psychosis is generally longer than six months.

There have been many suggestions about the causes of schizophrenia and genetic, biological, psychological and social factors have all been implicated. As yet, the causes remain to be clearly identified. The reader is referred to Cutting (1985) for a discussion of the breadth of issues involved. Although it is generally agreed that both biology and experience play an important part in schizophrenia, most theorists have tended to plump for either the biological/genetic "camp" or the experience/environmental "camp". Confusingly, the same evidence may be used to support each perspective. For example, a child with one or more schizophrenic parents has a much greater chance of developing the disorder (by a factor of ten for one schizophrenic parent and by a factor of forty for two schizophrenic parents) and this may be seen either as evidence of genetic defect or as a learned response through repeated exposure to the parent.

AFFECTIVE PSYCHOSES

Affective disorders are those where the primary disturbance is associated with disorders of mood ranging from severe depression on one hand to elation or euphoria on the other. This distinguishes affective disorders from other disorders such as schizophrenia in which the affective component may be seen either as a symptom or as secondary to the primary disturbance of thought disorder.

Mild or reactive depression is presumed to occur as a response to stressful life events and is usually seen as synonymous with neurotic depression which has been discussed previously. In contrast, affective psychosis is more severe and is presumed to be caused by a genetic predisposition or malfunctioning biochemistry.

The affective disorders are further characterised by a periodicity in their appearance, although the "manic-depressive" who swings from mania to normality to depression is uncommon as is mania itself although it's less acute form hypomania is occasionally encountered. There are therefore three types of affective psychosis; mania, depression and manic-depression. The symptoms of mania include a denial of problems, elation, excitement, excessive talkativeness, decreased need for sleep, increased sex drive, and excessive self-conceit. In contrast endogenous depression is associated with the following symptoms; complaints of sudden loss of interest, loss of appetite, decreased sex drive, early morning wakening, self-deprecation, depressed mood unaffected by environmental change, slowing of thought processes and delusional guilt.

There are many potential causes and a variety of types of depressive condition. Psychological, physiological and neurochemical factors all seem to play a part although the relative importance of these components within different types of depressive condition is not yet well understood.

CONCLUDING COMMENT

The chapter has briefly and selectively touched upon several areas of abnormal psychology and related disciplines in order to present some explanations and perspectives on abnormal behaviour. Although many topics have not been discussed, it seems clear that the enormous variety of abnormal experiences and behaviours cannot be encompassed by any single psychopathological model or theory.

These disparate theories about human behaviour are vital not only for making sense of how and why people behave but also are essential if scientific progress is to be made. Although it is critical to revise old theories and develop new ones, there is always the danger that the plethora of different approaches may lead to confusion. There is a real and urgent need for progress in understanding abnormal behaviour although many of the current theories in the area of abnormal psychology have limited practical value. One major problem appears to be the lack of experimental testing of different theories under real-world conditions. It is only through this endeavour that the prospect of effectively applying psychology to the complex problem of dealing with abnormal behaviour may become fully realised.

REFERENCES

American Psychiatric Association (1980). *Diagnostic and Statistical Manual of Mental Disorders – DSM 111.* 3rd edn. APA: Washington DC.

Blackburn, R. (1984). The Person and Dangerousness. In D.J. Muller, D.E. Blackman & A.J. Chapman (eds) *Psychology and Law.* Wiley: Chichester.

Bleuler, E. (1911). *Dementia Praecox or the Group of Schizophrenias.* International Universities Press: New York.

Carr, A.T. (1978). The Psychopathology of Fear. In W. Sluckin (ed) *Fear in Animals and Man.* Van Nostrand: London.

Cochrane, R. (1983). *The Social Creation of Mental Illness.* Longman: England.

Cochrane, R. & Stopes-Roe, M. (1979). Psychological Disturbance in Ireland, in England and in Irish Emigrants to England: A Comparative Study. *Economic and Social Review,* 10: 301–320.

Cochrane, R. & Stopes-Roe, M. (1980). Social Class and Psychological Disorder in Natives and Immigrants to Britain. *International Journal of Social Psychology,* 27: 173–183.

Cooper, Z. & Cooper, P.J. (1988). Classification and Diagnosis. In E. Miller & P.J. Cooper (eds) *Adult Abnormal Psychology,* Churchill Livingstone: UK.

Cutting, J. (1985). *The Psychology of Schizophrenia.* Churchill Livingstone: London.

Davison, G.C. & Neale, J.M. (1982). *Abnormal Psychology.* 2nd edn. Wiley: New York.

Gale, A. & Chapman, A.J. (eds) (1984). *Psychology and Social Problems. An Introduction to Applied Psychology.* John Wiley & Sons Ltd.

Garrow, J.S., Crisp, A.H., Jordan, H.A. *et al.* (1975). Pathology of Eating, Group Reports. In T. Silverstone (ed) *Dahlem Konferenzen. Life Sciences Research Report 2 Berlin.*

Hanley, I. & Hodge, J. (1984). *Psychological Approaches to the Care of the Elderly.* Croom-Helm: London.

Ilfield, F.W. (1978). Psychological Status of Community Residents along Major Demographic Dimensions. *Archives of General Psychiatry,* 35: 716–724.

Jaspers, K. (1963). *General Psychopathology,* translated from German, 7th ed. Hoenig, J. & Hamilton, M.W., Manchester University Press: Manchester.

Kaplan, H.B. (1972). Toward a General Theory of Psychosocial Deviancy: The Case of Aggressive Behaviour. *Social Science and Medicine,* 6, 593–617.

Kendall, R.E. (1983). The Principles of Classification in Relation to Mental Disease. In M. Shepherd & O.L. Zangwill (eds) *Handbook of Psychiatry: 1. General Psychopathology.* Cambridge University Press: Cambridge.

Kraepelin, E. (1896). *Lehrbuch der Psychiatrie,* 5th ed. Barth: Leipzig.

Laing, R.D. (1967). *The Politics of Experience.* Ballantine: New York.

Levy, R. & Post, F. (1982). *The Psychiatry of Later Life.* Blackwell: Oxford.

Mackay, D. (1975). *Clinical Psychology: Theory and Therapy.* Methuen & Co. Ltd.: London.

Meehl, P.E. (1962). Schizotaxia, Schizotypy, Schizophrenia. *American Psychologist,* 17, 827–831.

Miller, E. & Morley, S. (1986). *Investigating Abnormal Behaviour.* Weidenfeld and Nicholson, London.

Miller, E. & Cooper, P.J. (1988). *Adult Abnormal Psychology,* Churchill Livingstone: U.K.

Millon, T. (1981). *Disorders of Personality: DSM-III, Axis II.* Wiley: New York.

Neale, J.M. & Oltmanns, T.F. (1980). *Schizophrenia.* Wiley: New York.

Prins, H. (1990). *Bizarre Behaviours: Boundaries of Psychiatric Disorder.* Tavistock/Routledge: London & New York.

Rachman, S.J. & Hodgson, R.J. (1980). *Obsessions and Compulsions.* Prentice-Hall: New Jersey.

Rivett, P. (1972). *Principles of Model Building. The Construction of Models for Decision Analysis.* John Wiley and Sons.

Schmidt, H.G. & Fonds, C. (1956). The Reliability of Psychiatric Diagnosis. *Journal of Abnormal and Social Psychology,* **52**: 262–267.

Sims, A. (1983). *Neurosis in Society.* Macmillan Free Press Ltd: London.

Slade, P.D. (1982). Toward a functional Analysis of Anorexia Nervosa. *British Journal of Clinical Psychology,* **21**: 167–179.

Slater, E.T. (1976). What is Hysteria? *New Psychiatry,* **2**: 14–15.

Steele, R.E. (1978). Relationships of Race, Sex, Social Class and Social Mobility to Depression in Normal Adults. *Journal of Social Psychology,* **104**: 37–47.

Szasz, T.S. (1961). *The Myth of Mental Illness.* Harper & Row: New York.

Turner, F.J. (1984). Mental Disorders in Social Work Practice. In F.J. Turner (ed) *Adult Psychopathology: A Social Work Perspective.* The Free Press: New York.

Warr, P. (1984). Job Loss, unemployment and Psychological Well-Being. In V.L. Allen & E. Van De Vliert (eds) *Role Transitions.* Plenum: New York.

Warr, P. & Jackson, P. (1985). Factors influencing the Psychological Impact of Prolonged Unemployment and Re-Employment. *Psychological Medicine,* **15**: 795–807.

Warr, P. & Parry, G. (1982). Paid Employment and Women's Psychological Well-Being. *Psychological Bulletin,* **91**: 498–516.

Weissman, M.M. & Klerman, G.L. (1985). *Gender and Depression. Trends in Neurosciences.* **8**: 416–419.

Williams, J.M.G., Watts, F.N., MacLeod, C. & Mathews, A. (1988). *Cognitive Psychology and Emotional Disorders.* John Wiley & Sons: London.

Woods, R.T. & Britton, P.G. (1985). *Clinical Psychology with the Elderly.* Croom-Helm: London.

World Health Organisation (1977). *International Statistical Classification of Diseases, Injuries and Causes of Death,* 9th Revision, W.H.O., Geneva.

6

ASSESSMENT AND THERAPY IN CLINICAL PSYCHOLOGY

S.P. LLEWELYN

INTRODUCTION

This chapter explores the professional contribution made by clinical psychologists in the assessment and therapy of their clients, who are normally patients in hospital or the community. An illuminating place to start this exploration is a careful examination of the competencies of clinical psychologists, so we can see what it is that clinical psychologists actually do at work, and how psychology as an applied discipline plays its part in the treatment of those in need of clinical help. Two different psychological perspectives which may be used in both the assessment and therapy of patients will be discussed, and illustrated by cases studies. The chapter will also include an examination of future developments which seem likely to occur in the practice of clinical psychology, which offer the exciting prospect of synthesising a number of different perspectives in a way that should benefit both the discipline and those who ask clinical psychologists for help. Because of limitations of length of the chapter, the area of adult mental health will be chosen to illustrate the differing perspectives which may be taken.

THE ROLE AND CONTRIBUTION OF CLINICAL PSYCHOLOGY

What are clinical psychologists, and what do they do? Put most simply, a clinical psychologist applies psychology within a clinical context, usually a hospital, medical or community setting, with people (patients or staff) who consider themselves to be in need of a psychological perspective on their lives. In practice, the majority of clinical psychologists contribute to the assessment and treatment of people who see themselves as having psychological problems, such as those with mental health difficulties, but they also work with the handicapped, families, those with learning difficulties, and more widely, with staff and organisations. As shown in a later chapter in this volume, they also work with the neurologically impaired.

Within any particular hospital or community service such as a unit for adults with learning disabilities, or day hospital for those with mental health problems, there are likely to be a number of professional staff, including nurses, social workers, counsellors and doctors, who aim to provide treatment and care for the patients or residents. Only a very small minority will be qualified psychologists. It is important therefore to be clear about the particular and possibly unique contribution that can be made by a clinical psychologist. One way of clarifying this question is by looking at the competencies which properly qualified clinical psychologists should possess, by virtue of their training and experience. Becoming clear about this should allow us to become clear about what clinical psychologists are trying to do, and why their contribution to the clinical care and treatment of patients or clients is an important one.

THE TRIADIC MODEL OF A CLINICAL PSYCHOLOGIST'S COMPETENCE

One way of specifying what clinical psychologists do is to draw up a list of all the skills they have, such as the ability to administer psychometric tests or interview patients. This might be known as the psychologists' clinical skill competence. Another way is to specify all the places psychologists work or the types of clients or patients they work with, for example with long-stay psychiatric patients in psychiatric hospitals, or the staff of community homes. This might be known as the psychologists' clinical context competence. Yet another way would be to specify all the theories or types of evidence used by psychologists in carrying out their psychological work, for example, the applications of behaviour therapy, or the implications of evidence concerning factors which may impede recovery from head injury. This might be known as the psychologists' theoretical or academic knowledge competence. Yet none of these three competencies on its own distinguishes clinical psychologists, nor does it adequately describe what a competent clinical psychologist actually does.

A more adequate way of conceptualising clinical psychology is to use an integrative model, which proposes that clinical psychologists are acting as competent professional psychologists when they operate at the confluence of the three competencies already mentioned, namely, skills, awareness of clinical contexts, and theoretical or academic knowledge. What distinguishes the clinical psychologists, then, is not the ability to behave in a skilled way towards patients, nor familiarity with a particular context, syndrome or theory, but the ability to apply theoretical models or knowledge, in a clinical context, through the operation of clinical skills.

Without diminishing the contribution of clinical skills and awareness of context, this triadic model implies that the academic or research base of clinical psychology is extremely important: what competent clinical psychologists bring to their work is the ability to use and apply the academic knowledge base of the discipline in an applied clinical context. This means that theoretical knowledge is of fundamental importance, as is the commitment of clinical psychologists both to carry out research, and to modify their working practices in the light of research findings.

Bearing in mind the equal importance of these three competencies, much of the remainder of this chapter will be concerned with the ways in which different psychologists have developed their theories, clinical skills, and knowledge of clinical groups, and applied them in the assessment and therapy of patients. Although the key competence is the ability to integrate all three competencies, for the sake of clarity, each competency will be considered separately, before the main perspectives in assessment and treatment are considered.

The triad of core competency: 1. Clinical skills

There are a number of clinical skills which should be possessed by any competent clinical psychologist, first and foremost of which is the ability to assess the nature of the problem presented by the patient or client. Irrespective of the type of problem involved, or the particular theoretical perspective employed (see subsequent sections) a number of basic skills are needed, including the ability to engage the client's co-operation; the ability to take a clear history of the problem (when it started, what makes it worse or better, what steps have already been taken to attempt to solve the problem, etc.); the ability to observe accurately the behaviour of the client; and the ability to administer and use psychometric assessment techniques. Assessment is not something that occurs only when a patient is initially seen; it is a continuing process throughout the patient's contact with the psychologist. Secondly, the psychologist normally needs some core or generic intervention or therapeutic skills, including the ability to formulate the problem in terms of hypotheses about how the problem arose, and what is maintaining it; the ability to plan an intervention designed to modify the problem; and the ability to use a number of specific intervention skills which are derived from theoretical models. Last, but of crucial importance, is the ability to monitor, record and evaluate what has been achieved, and if necessary, to modify any subsequent intervention.

Other clinical skills which would normally be expected of clinical psychologists include the ability to work in groups or teams, teaching skills, research skills, managerial skills, and a wide range of other professional skills. None of these is of direct relevance at this point however, and will not be discussed further in this chapter.

The triad of core competency: 2. Clinical context

The range of contexts, clinical problems or clients with which a clinical psychologist is expected to be familiar, at least at the level of basic training, is extensive. It may range from work with the neurologically impaired or those with gynaecological problems, to therapy with autistic children, to the provision of support for staff working with trauma survivors. The core of a psychologist's work, however, is likely to be with mental health problems, children and families, those with learning disabilities, and the elderly. The range of abnormal behaviour seen by clinicians is described in other chapters in this book. But as already noted, this chapter will take the area of adult mental health as an example by which to demonstrate the different perspectives which are normally used by clinical psychologists.

The triad of core competency: 3. Theoretical and research underpinnings

There are a vast number of different theoretical perspectives in clinical psychology, matched by an enormous literature on the assessment and treatment of every clinical condition imaginable. But it is probably true to say that there are, broadly speaking, four major approaches to assessment and treatment: psychodynamic, cognitive/behavioural, client-centred and systems. Because some of these perspectives are considered in more detail elsewhere in this book, only the first two will be covered in any depth in this chapter. In each case, the basic assumptions will be described, followed by some details of the application of each perspective in practice. Then a case study will give an even clearer account of what it is like to work in each way. Further details about different approaches can be found in Dryden (1984).

Different perspectives: 1. Psychodynamic therapies

Clinical psychologists have in the past decade or so become increasingly interested in the potential contribution of psychodynamic therapies to their clinical work. This has occurred for a number of reasons, perhaps most important of which is the growing willingness of psychodynamic therapists to submit their work to empirical research. In addition psychodynamic therapists have shown themselves prepared to adapt their practice to the demands of brief, focused therapeutic work. In Britain for example this has meant that some psychodynamically oriented clinical psychologists now work within the National Health Service, such that psychodynamically oriented therapy is now in theory available to anyone who needs it. Elsewhere in Europe and in the United States, many clinicians work almost entirely from a psychodynamic perspective. Hence it is no longer the case that psychodynamic therapy is seen as solely the prerogative of private clients.

The essential assumptions of the psychodynamic approach.
Despite the heading of this section, it is probably inaccurate to speak generically of "the psychodynamic approach", since there are many schools of thought within the psychodynamic tradition, and, as with many areas of human endeavour, different schools of thought tend to grow, splinter and divide over seemingly insignificant points of dogma. But it is certainly the case that all psychodynamic therapies can be traced back to the work of Freud, although nowadays some psychodynamic therapists operate in ways which would seem scarcely recognisable to Freud himself. In common to all psychodynamic approaches is the belief in the importance of unconscious factors which have a significant effect on behaviour, and the need to understand these factors if neurosis is to be relieved. As described elsewhere in this volume, neurotic behaviour is seen as resulting from defences against conflicts of which the person may not be conscious, and which need to be made conscious in order to relieve the need for the neurotic behaviour. The therapist will seek to understand the unconscious conflicts by analysing the defences shown by the patient, and to bring the patient to an understanding of the underlying conflict which he or she is avoiding. Having obtained insight into the conflict, the path is then clear for the patient to try to resolve it in a healthy, rather than an unhealthy, or neurotic way.

The original Freudian approach postulated that the personality was subdivided into three parts: the id, the ego and the super-ego, roughly being equivalent to instinctive, primitive drives; the observing and more rational part of the personality; and the conscience. Freud also suggested that the individual developed through different psycho-sexual stages, from the oral, though the anal, phallic, and latent stages, to the Oedipal. Problems were assumed to arise when an individual failed to progress satisfactorily through one of these stages. Sexuality was seen as the main drive which fueled behaviour in conflict with the demands of reality and of the conscience. In his later work, Freud also postulated the existence of a death instinct, although this has remained controversial.

Another basic belief held by all psychodynamic therapists since Freud is that there is no clear dividing line between those who are "normal" and those who are "abnormal" or "neurotic". Freud firmly believed that we are all, to some degree or another, neurotic, meaning that we all sometimes act in self-defeating ways, and often appear to be prone to repeating our mistakes especially in the relationships which we have with other people. Psychological health in modern-day psychodynamic thinking is usually defined as the ability to make good relationships, which are based on both self-love and love of another, and which are reasonably free from anxiety, guilt or abuse.

Beyond this, however, there is disagreement amongst the many followers of the psychodynamic tradition. Strictly speaking, the word "psychoanalysis" should be reserved for close followers of Freud, who stick fairly rigidly to the theories and practices described by Freud, whereas the term "psychodynamic" is a looser word, which can be applied to any therapy which is based on the notion that behaviour is at least in part motivated by unconscious forces. In Britain, most modern psychodynamic thinkers are allied with the Object Relations school; in the USA this is known as the Personal Relations school. Important workers in this tradition include Fairbairn, Klein and Guntrip (see for example Segal, 1979). Also highly influential is the work of Malan who has been particularly helpful in adapting psychodynamic therapy to brief work. Malan has written a number of accessible books which can be recommended for further reading (for example Malan, 1979) in which he describes a model for use in structuring brief therapy, known as the Two Triangles, which will be described in more detail below.

Psychodynamic assessment

The main assessment tool used by most psychodynamically oriented psychologists is the clinical interview, that is, the therapist tries to gather as accurate a picture as possible of the patient's life and the symptoms which have brought the patient to therapy. This assessment may follow a standard pattern, in which case it will consist of a life history, an account of the symptoms, and in particular, an assessment of how far the patient is likely to be able to make use of the psychodynamic approach. This is usually done by the therapist making a trial interpretation of the patient's behaviour, to see how the patient responds. If the patient appears to be prepared to take the therapist's comments on board, and to be willing to think about them, then the patient may be suitable for dynamic therapy. If however the patient is excessively defensive, for example by denying the relevance of the therapist's interpretation, then it is unlikely that therapy which seeks to look at unconscious motivations will succeed.

In addition to this obviously subjective form of assessment, the therapist will usually assess the patient on a number of more objective variables, to see whether he or she is likely to be able to cope with the demands of therapy. For example, it is often thought desirable for the patient to have a reasonably high level of ego strength, in other words, an ability to function fairly adequately in the world without a tendency to "act out", that is, to react impulsively or aggressively to frustration or intense feelings. Many therapists also stipulate that a patient should have some areas of their life which is functioning well, such as a job or a steady relationship. (This is so that the patient does not become over-dependent on therapy, which might quickly become the only regular commitment in his or her life.) A history of drug abuse or alcohol abuse is also contra-indicative.

Other forms of assessment in psychodynamic therapy include the administration of projective tests, such as the Rorschach (ink blot) test, or the Object Relations Test. In these tests patients are shown pictures or ambiguous patterns and asked to describe their reactions to the designs. These reactions are assumed to reveal some of the unconscious conflicts, and to indicate the level of psychopathology experienced by the patient. Such tests are however notoriously difficult to interpret in any reliable way, and many clinical psychologists, who have been trained to question the properties of any psychometric instrument, are rather wary of using them.

More recently, some researchers have tried to develop more accurate ways of assessing the symptoms experienced by patients, in order to give therapists a clearer picture of the patient's unconscious conflicts. One such example is the Core Conflict Relationship Theme (Luborsky and Crits-Christoph, 1990). This is a measurement of the themes repeatedly expressed by patients, albeit in different guises, during therapy sessions, and it takes the form of an assessment of the patient's wishes and the reactions he or she fears receiving from others. For example, a patient may desire intimacy, but fear rejection. Judges are asked to rate transcripts of tape recordings of therapy sessions, and to identify these themes. As yet, however, techniques such as these have been used more for research purposes than as a routine part of assessment.

The practice of psychodynamic therapy

The therapeutic work of psychodynamically oriented therapists usually aims to remove the patient's symptomatic (distressing) behaviour by uncovering unconscious conflicts. Therapists will use a number of techniques as part of this process, perhaps most important of which is interpretation. The therapist first attempts to understand and formulate the patient's feelings, thoughts and behaviour in terms of a theoretical model (such as the Two Triangles, see below). Next the patient is offered an interpretation of his or her behaviour in terms of this formulation. The patient's response to this interpretation is then used to refine the formulation made by the therapist, and another interpretation may be offered, until the patient starts to gain a greater understanding of the underlying conflicts which fuel the neurotic behaviour. When the patient understands and applies the therapist's formulation, on an emotional as well as an intellectual level, the patient is assumed to have obtained insight, and can start to change his or her behaviour. The interpretation offered by the therapist usually concerns a link between the patient's current behaviour and feelings, and some situation in the past, or it may concern the relationship between the therapist and the patient (known as a transference interpretation).

The Two Triangles model proposed by Malan offers a way of thinking about the conflicts. The patient is assumed to be experiencing anxiety because the defences which he or she has established against the hidden feelings are no longer working (the Triangle of Conflict). The anxiety is what drives the patient into seeking therapy: if the defences were working adequately the person would not be aware of having a problem. The therapist's job is to discover the hidden feelings and bring them into awareness. However, this is not done by telling the patient what those feelings are; they are hidden precisely because they are too painful or difficult to face. Therefore the therapist has to approach them gradually, by discussing the defensive system of the patient first.

The Triangle of Person represents significant people in the patient's life, and the relationships between them and the patient. The task of the therapist is to help the patient to see the way in which he or she is trapped by relationships, into repeating patterns which have failed, or conflicts which have not been resolved. Links are drawn by the therapist between the patient's relationships in the past and present, firstly between the patient's relationship between people in life at the moment and in the past; secondly between the therapist and people in the patient's current life; and thirdly, between the therapist and significant people in the patient's past, usually the patient's parents. This latter link (transference) is often assumed to be the most powerful of all, because the emotions we have towards our parents are assumed to be the most heavily censored or defended against. The aim of making all these links, or interpretations, is to help the patient to see that current relationships may be over-determined by unresolved conflicts from the past, and that the only way to become able to have relatively healthy relationships in the present is to come to terms with issues from the past. This may mean facing up to feelings of, for example, intense anger towards a parent. In therapy these feelings may be uncovered and re-experienced towards the therapist, who may be felt as being in a similarly powerful position vis-a-vis the patient, as the parent was towards the child.

Case study: Tom
This is perhaps best illustrated by an example. Tom, a thirty-two year old single man, came to therapy complaining of feeling lonely and out of touch with those around him, particularly women. He lived on his own, and had few friends, apart from one or two colleagues at work. He presented as a tense and detached individual, with a marked tendency to talk intellectually about himself and his problems. He was especially careful to check out the therapist's qualifications, and was more than a little suspicious of the fact that she was a woman. During his first interview at the Department of Psychology, Tom described a history of parental deprivation and neglect: his father had left when he was three years old and his mother had then lived with a series of men, some of whom had physically assaulted her. He was taken into care at the age of ten, and had lived with a number of foster parents. Since then he had had sporadic contact with his mother, who tended to want to see him only when she was short of money. Despite all of this, Tom did well at school and now had a steady job as a lecturer at a College of Further Education.

Given this account, the therapist's clinical assessment was that Tom was a man who feared he was not adequate or lovable as a person. She suspected that he simultaneously wanted to be close to others, yet feared, on the basis of his past experiences, that he would be rejected by others. She hypothesised that Tom, who was intellectually able, sought to impress others (hence to gain approval or love) by displaying his erudite knowledge.

During therapy sessions, it emerged that Tom's over-intellectual style sometimes succeeded in winning him admiration, although he still seemed unable to form close relationships. Faced with a potentially intimate situation, Tom retreated into his well-established pattern of intellectual debate, which soon drove away potential friends. In therapy itself, Tom attempted to engage the therapist in a discussion about the theoretical underpinnings of psychoanalysis, and actively strove to avoid her attempt to discuss his feelings about his difficulties in life, or about being in therapy.

A psychodynamic therapist, seeking to understand Tom's behaviour, would probably see his neurotic behaviour (excessive intellectual talk) as a defence against some hidden conflict (the desire to be emotionally close to someone and yet the fear of being rejected). His current unhappiness would be seen as resulting from the failure of his defence to protect him from the welling up of some feelings of loneliness. These dynamics can be represented by the Triangle of Conflict.

Having formulated his neurotic behaviour as a system of defence against unwanted unconscious feeling, the therapist then, by pointing to the inadequacy of his defensive system, needed to help Tom to become aware of the feelings of fear and love, which he was hiding from himself, and to accept them, thus removing the need for the neurotic behaviour. One particularly potent tool which she had available to help her in this process was Tom's current relationship with her, the therapist. While it is possible, in the abstract, to talk in therapy sessions about Tom's difficulties in relating to others, and inadequate defensive systems, the therapist had a clear example of these difficulties, there and then in the therapy room. Whenever she tried to probe into his emotional life, he retreated from her questions into intellectual talk.

The therapist started, therefore, by pointing out the link between his behaviour with her, and his behaviour with others in his life (the Triangle of Person). She also pointed out that by talking intellectually, he was not only avoiding talking about other things, but was also seeking to ensure that she would not reject him, by trying to impress her by his intellectual prowess (the Triangle of Conflict). She then went on to point out that Tom felt towards her as he felt towards his mother, which was a combination of fear of rejection, desire for her love, and anger and hatred for her for rejecting him (again the Triangle of Person). The therapist pointed out that this was shown in Tom's repeated attempts to demonstrate his intellectual superiority over his therapist.

Obviously, such an interpretation may well fall on deaf ears, if the patient is not yet willing to look at his or her behaviour and feelings in such a way. But psycho-dynamically oriented therapists usually attempt to time their interpretations carefully: they will only make such interpretations if there is already a reasonably strong bond of liking and trust between therapist and patient, and if the patient has already demonstrated a willingness to accept such interpretations. In addition, any competent therapist will probably phrase interpretations in a tentative way, demonstrating a readiness to adapt the formulation if the patient is not yet ready to hear it. The therapist also has to accept that the patient cannot bear insight into too much hidden material at once: for example Tom might have been able to accept, and feel, the sadness he had about the rejections he has suffered as a child, but he might not have been willing, yet, to accept that he felt anger and hatred towards his mother for the way in which she treated him.

In Tom's case, the interpretations made by the therapist were accepted and used by the patient, and they spent many months together working through the implications of what this meant to him. Gradually he became more able to express his need for love, as well as his anger and disappointment with his mother (and all women). His over-intellectualisation began to diminish, and he reported being able to establish closer relationships with people at work, including women.

Benefits and drawbacks of psychodynamic therapy
While the issue of the effectiveness of psychodynamic therapy will be considered in more detail below, it is worth considering here some of the benefits and drawbacks for

clinical psychologists of taking a psychodynamic approach. Perhaps of most immediate concern to those working in the public sector is the fact that only a small number of patients can be seen at any one time. Although therapy duration is very considerably less than it was when originally practised by Freud and his followers, it is still a lengthy process: many therapists want to see patients for a minimum of six months, and more probably for one year or longer. Sessions tend to last for an hour or so, which means that the case load of psychologists working in this way will be relatively small.

Another issue which is of great concern to clinical psychologists is the scientific status of the theory which they are using as the basis of their work. It has often been said that psychodynamic theory is as much an art as a science, a situation which is hardly acceptable to psychologists trained to respect the scientific status of their subject. It is certainly the case that many of Freud's fundamental ideas are extremely difficult to subject to scientific scrutiny, and are in addition probably open to mis-use by some therapists. Nevertheless, many clinical psychologists also feel that psychodynamic work deals with more fundamental issues than other therapies do, and that there is a greater potential for understanding human behaviour through a psychodynamic approach than through any other approach yet devised. Hence they accept the charge that the theories have not yet been scientifically validated, but still feel that they have an enormous amount to offer in the understanding and therapy of individual patients. It is clear that the growing acceptance by psychodynamic therapists of the need to evaluate their work has made it more acceptable to clinical psychologists, who place great weight on the need for evidence on the question of effectiveness.

One last drawback of the psychodynamic approach is that it does not suit everybody: in fact it has been suggested that psychodynamic therapists only choose to work with those who are mildly disturbed, and who would probably get better of their own accord. It is certainly the case that psychodynamic therapy works best with neurotic patients: it has had very little success with the seriously disturbed or psychotic.

Developments of the psychodynamic approach
While most of the work described above is based on individual therapy with adult patients, some psychologists work using this approach with children and adolescents. The work of Melanie Klein and Anna Freud has been very influential in this area (see Segal, 1979). In addition, some therapists have applied psychodynamic ideas in group settings (a method which partially deals with the problem of the limited number of patients who can be treated). One approach which is particularly widely used is Interpersonal Therapy (Yalom, 1975) in which the relationships between psychotherapy group members becomes the main focus for analysis and interpretation. In this form of therapy, the group therapist takes a less prominent role than in individual therapy, and seeks to help group members to resolve their interpersonal relationship difficulties in the "here and now" of the group.

Different perspectives: 2. Cognitive behavioural therapy

Although a substantial minority of clinical psychologists are interested in the psychodynamic approach, by far the majority of psychologists work primarily from a cognitive/behavioural perspective. It is by now difficult to separate the two approaches, although historically they developed along rather different lines. Behaviour therapy first emerged in the fifties, and acted as the passport for clinical psychologists to become involved in the treatment of patients, rather than merely in assessment and diagnosis. The emphasis on the observable and measurable within behaviourism initially excluded consideration of cognitive phenomena, so that behaviour therapists were concerned largely with the objectively observable behaviour or symptoms of patients, rather than what they thought or felt about their difficulties. Operant and classical conditioning models were used to explain the establishment and maintenance of neurotic behaviour. For example, a phobia of dogs would be assumed to have arisen though classical conditioning by the pairing of a dog with an unpleasant stimulus (such as loud barking), and maintained though operant conditioning, by the provision of reinforcement (attention and sympathy from others) when a dog appeared and was avoided.

Behaviour therapists therefore aimed to control the factors in the patient's environment which gave rise to, maintained or reinforced the neurotic or maladaptive behaviour. Behavioural analysis was used, which sought to specify the antecedents and consequences of target behaviours, and systematically to modify these. It was assumed to be unnecessary to try to understand any underlying meaning for the symptoms, but rather to remove the symptoms, hence to alleviate neurotic suffering. Initial reports suggested that behaviour therapy was very successful, especially with patients with phobias and other behavioural problems.

The growing emphasis on cognitive variables within mainstream psychology eventually encouraged clinicians to include a consideration of patients' cognitions in their assessment and therapy. The ideas of Bandura (1977) on self-efficacy also became important. These suggested that people are primarily concerned with mastering their environment, and are striving continuously to retain control over their current lives and futures. Hence what they think about is of primary importance. Psychological problems are said to arise when people hold cognitions which are negative about themselves and their ability to control their lives. According to Beck et al (1979) for example, depression results when a person holds a triad of negative cognitions about self, the world, and the future ("I am worthless, there is nowhere that things are any better, nothing is ever going to change for the better"). Likewise, Bandura (1977) suggests that anxiety or depression results from a lack of a sense of mastery, based on failure or traumatic experiences which are then inappropriately generalised to all other experiences.

The essential assumptions of the cognitive/behavioural approach
The essential assumptions of the cognitive/behavioural approach are that behaviour and cognitions can be modified without recourse to esoteric explanations such as those used by psychodynamic theorists. The main aim is to establish and hence to control the links between behaviour and its consequences. The relationship between therapist and patient should be collaborative, and whilst it is widely acknowledged that a positive and warm therapeutic relationship usually enhances the success of the therapy, concepts such as transference are not seen as helpful. A careful attention to the factors which are maintaining the dysfunctional behaviour or cognitions is seen as crucial, hence assessment plays an essential and continuing role in the work of cognitive/behavioural clinical psychologists.

A number of models or theories are used which underlie the therapeutic procedures employed. One example is the two factor theory of anxiety (Wilson, 1982). This predicts that if a given situation provokes anxiety and fear, then uncontrolled exposure to that situation will foster avoidance and further fear of that situation. As a consequence, therapists must make sure that exposure to the feared object is gradual, or controlled, and that patients must be able to see clearly that their fears (for example that they will not be able to cope) have not been realised. Another example is the learned helplessness model of depression (Seligman, 1975). This predicts that individuals will become depressed if they have little or no control over events. One implication of this model is that therapists must endeavour to set up situations in which patients are able to establish some connection between their actions and the consequences of those actions. One last example is Beck *et al.*'s (1979) theory of depression: this postulates that depressed people systematically distort information about their own actions and the world in a way which reflects badly upon themselves. They also attribute negative outcomes to their own stable, global characteristics. The therapist's task is therefore to challenge these attributions, for example by identifying errors in thinking and the setting of homework tasks which are likely to have a positive outcome.

Assessment in cognitive/behavioural therapy
Many clinical psychologists see the initial period spent in assessing the patient to be the most crucial, during which time a full behavioural analysis is carried out of the symptoms which are causing distress to the client. The patient's cognitions are also explored, so that the therapist can learn what maladaptive thoughts may be defeating any positive behaviours. Formal assessment techniques which are routinely used by cognitive/behavioural psychologists include various psychometric tests, such as the Beck Depression Inventory (BDI). This is a standardised measure of depressive symptomatology (Beck *et al.*, 1979) which gives an indication of symptoms (such as suicidal thoughts) which might warrant immediate intervention. Other psychologists may use tests such as the Symptom Check List (SCL-90; Derogatis, 1973). Also frequently used are rating scales, some of which may be designed specifically for each client, which allow the psychologist and client to monitor the frequency of certain target behaviours or thoughts. In addition, patients are often encouraged to keep diaries, in which they record their thoughts and behaviours, so that both they and their therapists can begin to see the underlying connections between mood and cognitions, and between cognition and behaviour.

The practice of cognitive/behavioural therapy
A number of specific techniques are used in cognitive/behavioural therapy, which are based on empirically established procedures. Very commonly used with anxiety disorders is systematic desensitisation, whereby the patients' fears are arranged in a hierarchy, and presented gradually, at a rate which is perceived by the patient as non-threatening. Often the patient is taught some self-control procedure, such as progressive muscle relaxation, to assist in the desensitisation. This form of therapy is often used for patients with phobias such as agoraphobia or fear of examinations, and it may be done "*in vivo*" for example by the therapist accompanying the patient around a busy supermarket, or it may be done in imagination; for example, by the therapist asking the patient to imagine him or herself taking an important examination. Sometimes the therapist will use the two approaches in combination.

If the problem presented is one of impulse control, such as a compulsion to gamble, or self-exposure, a technique such as covert sensitisation may be used. Here an aversive thought or consequence is paired with the target behaviour, so that the patient is taught to link ideas of (for example) being physically sick with approaching gambling arcades. For obsessional and complusive symptoms, techniques such as thought stopping are used, whereby the patient is taught to bring their thoughts under control, by using some pre-arranged signal, or by using self-talk. For depressed patients, as already noted, therapists will encourage the recognition and challenge of automatic thoughts (such as the belief "nobody likes me") by pointing out the self-defeating nature of such thoughts, and the need to seek for alternative explanations of depressing experiences. Other frequently used techniques include role-playing (for social skills problems), self-instruction (for fears and phobias, see Meichenbaum, 1975), self-control and problem-solving techniques (for destructive behaviours such as violence), and communications training (for marital problems and social skills problems).

Of course the techniques used will vary, according to the nature of the presenting symptoms, but they all have in common the aim of helping the patient to regain a sense of control and mastery, which it is assumed will allow the patient to live a more productive and happy life in the future.

Case study: Angela
At least some of these procedures can be illustrated by a case study. Angela was a 27 year old woman referred to the Department of Clinical Psychology for help with feelings of panic when she left home on her own. She lived in a small house some way from local amenities with her husband and three year old daughter. Before her daughter was born, Angela had worked as a clerk in a building society, a job which she had enjoyed and had felt sorry to leave. Since the child's birth, Angela had become rather isolated, and had tended to wait for her husband's return from work before going out on joint shopping trips. She came from what appeared to be a close family, although she said she had never got along well with her mother. She said that her childhood was a reasonably happy one, although she had few memories before the age of ten.

Because of Angela's fear of going out alone, she was at first visited at her home by the clinical psychologist. He took a careful history of her symptoms, and asked her to complete various psychometric tests. He noted that she had an elevated score on the Beck Depression Inventory, as well as a significant level of anxiety on various anxiety check lists. He then carried out a comprehensive behavioural analysis of Angela's problematic behaviour. This established that her feelings of panic were most likely to emerge when going into large supermarkets, and when visiting her family by bus. Her panic symptoms include profuse sweating, feelings of breathlessness, a pounding heart and dizziness. When she felt the panic starting, she would attempt to leave the supermarket, or dismount the bus. At this point the anxiety would subside, and she would turn round and go home, often by taking a taxi.

The therapist then attempted to assess Angela's cognitions about leaving home, and found that she was preoccupied by the thought that it was "not safe" away from home. She pointed to evidence on the television and in the newspapers to substantiate her beliefs that the world is a dangerous place, especially for women and children. She was also convinced by her physical symptoms that she would suffer a heart attack if she did not avoid the situations which she feared.

The therapist decided to start to work behaviourally with Angela, so he taught her a standard relaxation procedure which he asked her to practice every day. When she became reasonably proficient in this, they jointly constructed a hierarchy of feared situations, from standing at her door looking outside (to which Angela gave an anxiety rating of 1) to queuing up at the check-out with a full trolley of shopping in a busy supermarket on a Friday night, on her own (to which Angela gave an anxiety rating of 10). In between these two extremes were items concerned with travel by bus, and visiting Angela's mother. The therapist then accompanied Angela as they worked their way systematically through the first few items on the hierarchy, and when she felt the panic developing, he reminded her to use her relaxation technique until she could cope adequately in the situation.

All progressed well until the therapist started to explore in more detail Angela's cognitions about being out on her own, and her feelings of vulnerability. Around this time the therapist and Angela were also approaching the items on the hierarchy of feared situations which concerned visiting Angela's family. Careful questioning by the therapist then allowed Angela to tell him about some memories which she had previously denied, about a sexual assault which had occurred when she was about eight, in the garden of her home. The perpetrator was an uncle, who was at that time living at Angela's mother's home. Besides seeking to establish whether there was any evidence that this uncle might still be a risk to other children, the therapist then explored with Angela her feelings about the assault. It emerged that Angela had always assumed that she was to blame, and that she must in some way have invited the attack, since all the family always spoke so highly of this uncle. Angela also indicated that she believed that she was tainted and dirty, and that others would never like her if they knew what had happened to her. She also said that she believed that no-one else in the world could be as bad as she was.

Angela's therapist then started to examine Angela's cognitions in some more detail, and to challenge what he saw as irrational and dysfunctional beliefs. He did this by asking her to think rationally about the evidence for what she thought, for example by giving Angela a number of books to read written by survivors of childhood sexual abuse (in order to reduce her sense of being unique). He pointed out to her that many children who have suffered abuse erroneously take the blame upon themselves, seeing themselves as having in some way invited the assault, and because of the threats often made by the perpetrator, they often fail to check out with anybody else whether these perceptions are accurate. Angela began to feel less isolated, and her depression started to lift. She then began to realise that she was frightened of going to her mother's house partly because it reminded her of the assault. Being more aware of her distorted cognitions, she was able to challenge them, and her fears of visiting her mother began to subside. The therapist also pointed out that her fears of having a heart attack were not realised, and that she was in fact starting to master her anxieties. This set up a positive set of cognitions, and she began to reconsider her view of herself as being simply a victim of her past and of her anxieties.

Therapy with Angela lasted several months. After the first two months, Angela was able to visit the therapist in the Department of Psychology rather than needing a home visit, and after three further months she was able to go shopping by herself. Some marital problems then became evident, connected with the memories of the sexual assault, and the therapist suggested the involvement of another female therapist in joint marital therapy. These sessions lasted for about six weeks, by which time Angela was largely symptom-free. Her score on the Beck Depression Inventory was within the normal range, as were her scores on the anxiety check-lists. Some evidence of distorted cognitions remained, but these did not appear to interfere significantly with Angela's mood or behaviour.

Benefits and drawbacks of the cognitive/behavioural approach
The issue of outcome will be considered below, but before this, it is important to consider some other aspects of the cognitive/behavioural approach. Firstly, in contrast with practitioners of the psychodynamic approach, cognitive/behavioural therapists use techniques which are relatively easily specified, and open to empirical investigation. On the whole, these techniques originated in the laboratory, and are continuously subjected by researchers to further refinement, based on experimental study. Some might argue, therefore, that this approach is a more truly psychological approach than the psychodynamic one, since it relies more heavily on procedures which have been empirically validated. As such, it could be suggested that this is the perspective of choice for a competent clinical psychologist, who is trying to make consistent use of empirically based research and theory.

Secondly, the time needed for effective therapy to take place is usually less than is the case of psychodynamic therapy, even if this means that the issues covered during therapy are less far-reaching. The range of patients who can be helped is also wider, as these methods can be applied to the relatively inarticulate, as well as to the more verbal. Furthermore it is relatively easy to teach the techniques developed by clinical psychologists to members of other professions, hence increasing the number of patients who can be treated by psychological means.

Another considerable advantage of the cognitive/behavioural approach is that its goals are usually very clearly specified. Vague statements are avoided, therefore it is relatively easy for both therapist and patient to agree on the focus of therapy, as well as to assess progress.

Nevertheless, there are critics of this approach. Some claim that the meaning of the symptoms for the patient is ignored by these theories, and also that real social or political issues (such as poor housing or lack of opportunity) which may contribute substantially to a problem such as depression, are not explored. Others claim that these methods are essentially reductionist, and are based on an over-mechanistic view of people. Yet others have pointed out that the combination of behavioural and cognitive theories is really a marriage of convenience, and that there are numerous theoretical problems and contradictions involved in amalgamating the two approaches.

Developments of the cognitive/behavioural approach
The emphasis on the importance of environmental stimuli for maintaining maladaptive behaviours has led a number of behavioural therapists to try to maximise their control over these stimuli, either by working in groups, or in families. Bennun (1987) for example has outlined the potential which this approach has for distressed couples, and advocates the use of techniques such as communications skills training and problem-solving approaches. He stresses that marital therapists need to be "skilled in modifying both overt behaviour and overt cognitions. The myopic tendency to focus on one or the other results in a less extensive intervention and does an injustice to the complex interactive nature of marital distress and treatment". Other areas where work is in progress includes the modification of the behaviour of sex offenders, and the treatment of addictive behaviours.

REVIEW OF EVIDENCE ON OUTCOME

The question of outcome is obviously crucial: as noted earlier it is part of the key competence of clinical psychologists to evaluate the effectiveness of the procedures they use. Initial reports (e.g. Eysenk, 1952) suggested the superiority of behavioural over psychodynamic methods; however these studies were flawed and are no longer widely accepted. During the last few decades there have been a large number of studies which have compared the outcomes of different types of therapy, although cognitive/behavioural researchers have probably been more diligent in carrying out research than psychodynamically oriented therapists. Common problems in this area of research have been that the quality of the therapy carried out has not always been monitored, the measures of outcome used have not been equally appropriate for the types of therapy being compared, and adequate time has not been allowed for follow-up. In addition, much of the work, particularly with behavioural therapies, has been done using analogue studies, for example using students with snake phobias who may bear little resemblance to patients with real life clinical problems.

The technique of meta-analysis, whereby the results of a large number of well-conducted studies are combined together, have clarified the picture somewhat. The evidence now seems to suggest that both psychodynamic and cognitive/behavioural therapies are significantly more effective than no therapy, and that about two thirds of patients treated are helped (Luborsky *et al.*, 1975; Shapiro and Shapiro, 1983). It may well be the case that different types of patients are suited to different types of therapy: for example some studies suggest that behavioural methods are slightly better for phobias, and psychodynamic therapies for relationship difficulties. Nevertheless, there is still a wide variation in outcome, and researchers are still unclear about what specific type of problem should be prescribed for what type of patient. What has been agreed, however, is that "global" questions such as "does therapy work?" are not helpful; rather we should ask "What type of therapy for what type of patient under what circumstances for what type of patient?" (after Paul, 1967).

A key issue which presents problems for researchers who are trying to compare types of therapy is the suggestion that it is something about the relationship between the patient and the therapist which is central to the effectiveness of therapy, not the specific techniques of a particular type of therapy. It is very difficult to rule this suggestion out, since it is virtually impossible to carry out any form of therapy without the presence of some of the so-called "non-specific" factors, such as simply being in therapy, receiving encouragement, and liking the therapist, and so on. Some researchers (for example Frank, 1989) have suggested that patients improve primarily as a result of these non-specific factors, and that techniques such as those described earlier in this chapter are not as important as the provision of a therapeutic relationship, with a socially sanctioned therapist who provides some form of explanation for, and way out of, the patient's unhappiness. As noted, it is difficult to exclude these factors, since they undoubtedly do contribute very significantly to any effective therapy. Other researchers have also suggested that the therapy simply represents a vehicle for persuasion by a powerful therapist, and that some process of social influence is probably part of the reason for any therapist's effectiveness. However, other researchers (as reviewed by Stiles, Shapiro and Elliott, 1986) have suggested that we still do not have enough information, and that, given time and enough keen researchers, eventually we should be able to answer Paul's (1967) superficially simple question.

Another related problem for therapy researchers is the possibility that what works for one therapist-patient pair might not work for another. Likewise it could be the skilfulness or the personality of the therapist which is crucial, or perhaps the motivation of the patient. The study by Shapiro and Firth (1987) was an attempt to address these issues. In their study, forty patients were given two periods of therapy, of equal duration, first from one perspective (broadly psychodynamic) and then from another (broadly cognitive/behavioural), each from the same therapist who was equally well trained in both types of therapy. (Half the sample received the two treatments in the reverse order.) This meant that the personalities and motivations of both patients and therapists were controlled, as was the skilfulness of the therapists in using the specific techniques. Results again showed a broad similarity in outcome between cognitive/behavioural and psychodynamic therapies, although with slight advantage to cognitive/behavioural approaches. Hence even after sophisticated research designs such as this one, it is still not clear why some patients improve when others do not, nor is it clear why apparently different techniques seem to have broadly similar results.

Nevertheless, researchers are still trying to establish ways of increasing therapeutic success. Because of the lack of clear evidence on outcome, much of the effort has now turned away from a "horse race" between the different perspectives, to an attempt to understand the process of therapy, that is, how therapy actually works. Some of these researchers (for example Elliott and James, 1989; Llewelyn, 1988) have tried to use the experience of participants in therapy to find out what are the most helpful and unhelpful events in therapy, and hence to discover the crucial ingredients in successful therapy, irrespective of perspective taken. Others have tried to focus on specific types of therapeutic event, such as insight, or assimilation (Stiles et al., 1990). Studies such as these have focused not on the features which distinguish between therapy types, but rather on the processes by which change occurs. For example, Stiles et al. have suggested that assimilation is a process whereby problematic experiences (experienced by the patient who comes into therapy as painful feelings or thoughts) are gradually incorporated into the patient's existing schemata, by passing through a reasonably predictable series of stages: from being merely painful feelings, to being puzzling (semi-assimilated) experiences, to being understood, and hence, eventually, to being mastered. Stiles et al. stress that this process occurs in any type of therapy, and as such is pan-theoretical.

INTEGRATIVE APPROACHES

Another particularly fruitful approach has been to try to integrate different perspectives, hence to maximise the effectiveness of what is offered to patients. Given the evidence on equivalence of outcome, yet diversity in technique, this seems hopeful. In recent years a number of researchers have attempted to synthesise what they see as the most effective aspects of different perspectives in clinical psychology to create new, more promising approaches to assessment and therapy. Although there have been a number of such attempts, only one will be described here, the work of Ryle (1990).

Ryle's approach, known as Cognitive-Analytic Therapy (CAT) is based on the observation that cognitive/behavioural techniques do indeed seem to be very effective in helping people to remove troublesome behaviours and resolve symptoms; yet they do not always appear adequate in describing the complexities of the interpersonal traps and dilemmas which people experience. Ryle's work is based on a procedural sequence model, which suggests that mental and behavioural processes (or procedures) are organised hierarchically, with the implication that change at one level will have effects on other levels. Hence for example change in the procedure by which a person makes judgements about the friendliness of others will have an effect on the behaviour of that person towards other people, and vice versa. Procedures may be more or less conscious, and may be more or less useful to the patient; neurotic procedures are conceptualised as those which are persistently used despite being harmful or ineffective. Exactly where the therapist chooses to make a therapeutic intervention therefore depends on accessibility, or the simple proposition "push it where it moves!"

In Cognitive-Analytic Therapy, a full assessment is carried out with the patient, using psychometric tests, but also using the therapist's clinical judgement of the nature of the dynamics of the patient's interpersonal relationships, as revealed by the transference. This assessment is shared with the patient, in the form of a written or diagrammatic reformulation, which also contains a list of the goals of the therapy. Therapy consists of work on these goals, which are usually described as the modification of procedures which are ineffective or harmful, but which the patient is finding it hard to abandon. The therapist may use techniques drawn from both cognitive/behavioural and psychodynamic therapies, depending on the particular procedures recognised as problematic during the assessment. Thus, for example, a patient such as Tom might be asked to participate in some social skills therapy, as well as looking at his relationship with his therapist, and a patient such as Angela might be asked to look at the transference she has towards her therapist as a way of getting in touch with her feelings about her mother for not having protected her from sexual abuse, as well as using systematic desensitisation to deal with her agoraphobia. Evidence on the effectiveness of this approach is as yet limited, but it seems promising.

CONCLUSION

In this chapter we have only been able to touch upon two key perspectives in clinical psychology, but they have illustrated the way in which competent clinical psychologists try to integrate clinical skills, familiarity with clinical phenomena, and knowledge of academic or theoretical research, in carrying out their professional work. A therapeutic or assessment intervention which is carried out without a secure foundation in academic research and evidence may indeed by chance have some value for some individual patients, but it is not likely to be as effective or helpful as an intervention which has some carefully worked out theoretical underpinning. Furthermore, interventions which are carried out in ignorance of theory do not have the potential to feed back into any research and academic tradition, and as such, the results of such interventions are not available to the community of psychologists who are trying to increase the effectiveness of clinical work.

Clinical psychology as a profession and as an academic discipline has passed through many changes since its inception; doubtless there will be many changes to come. But its major strength lies in the fact that it very effectively combines the three competencies described in this chapter, and therefore it brings to the job of assessing and treating patients the triad of academic rigour, clinical skill and knowledge of clinical contexts, no matter which particular theoretical perspective is taken.

REFERENCES

Bandura, A. (1977). Self-efficacy: toward a unifying theory of behavioral change. *Psychological Review*, **84**, 191–215.

Beck, A.T., Rush, A.J., Shaw, B.F. & Emery, G. (1979). *Cognitive Therapy of Depression*. New York: Guildford Press.

Bennun, I. (1987). Marital dysfunction: investigation. In S. Lindsay & G. Powell (Eds.), *A Handbook of Clinical Adult Psychology*. Aldershot: Gower.

Derogatis, L., Lipman, R. & Covi, M. (1973). SCL-90, an out-patient rating scale. *Psychopharmacology Bulletin*, **9**, 13–20.

Dryden, W. (Ed.) (1984). *Individual Therapy in Britain*. Milton Keynes: Open University Press.

Elliott, R. & James, E. (1989). Varieties of client experience in psychotherapy: An analysis of the literature. *Clinical Psychology Review*, **9**, 443–467.

Eysenk, H. (1952). The effects of psychotherapy: an evaluation. *Journal of Consulting Psychology*, **16**, 99–144.

Frank, J.D. (1989). Non-specific aspects of treatment: the view of a psychotherapist. In M. Shepherd and N. Sartorius (Eds.). *Non-specific Aspects of Treatment*. Hans-Huber.

Llewelyn S.P. (1988). Psychological therapy as viewed by clients and therapists. *British Journal of Clinical Psychology*, **27**, 223–237.

Luborsky, L., Singer, B. and Luborsky, L. (1975). Comparative studies of psychotherapies. *Archives of General Psychiatry*, **32**, 995–1008.

Luborsky, L. and Crits-Christoph, P. (1990). *Understanding transference: the CCRT method*. New York: Basic Books.

Malan, D. (1979). *Individual Psychotherapy and the Science of Psychodynamics*. London: Butterworth.

Meichenbaum, D. (1975). A self-instructional approach to stress management. In C. Speilberger and J. Sarason (Eds.), *Stress and Anxiety*, Vol 2. New York: Wiley.

Paul, G. (1967). Strategy of outcome research in psychotherapy. *Journal of Consulting Psychology*, **31**, 109–118.

Ryle, A. (1990). *Cognitive Analytic Therapy*. Chichester: Wiley.

Segal, H. (1979). *Klein*. Brighton, Sussex: Harvester.

Seligman, M. (1975). *Helplessness: On depression, development and death*. San Francisco: Freeman.

Shapiro, D.A. and Firth, J. (1987). Prescriptive vs. exploratory psychotherapy: Outcomes of the Sheffield psychotherapy project. *British Journal of Psychiatry*, **151**, 790–799.

Shapiro, D. and Shapiro, D.A. (1982). Meta-analysis of comparative therapy outcome studies: A replication and refinement. *Psychological Bulletin*, **92**, 581–604.

Stiles, W., Elliott, R., Llewelyn, S., Firth-Cozens, J., Margison, F., Shapiro, D. and Hardy, G. (1990). Assimilation of problematic experiences by clients in psychotherapy. *Psychotherapy*, **27**, 411-2420.

Stiles, W., Shapiro, D. and Elliott, R. (1986). Are all psychotherapies equivalent? *American Psychologist*, **41**, 165–180.

Wilson, G.T. (1982). The relationship of learning theories to behavioural therapies: problems, prospects and preferences. In J.C. Boulougouris (Ed.), *Learning Theory Approaches to Psychiatry*. New York: Wiley.

Yalom, I. (1975). *The Theory and Practice of Group Psychotherapy*. New York: Basic Books.

7

CLINICAL NEUROPSYCHOLOGY

P. BROKS

Since behaviour and experience are rooted in the workings of the brain, damage to the brain through physical trauma or disease often has consequences which are best understood in psychological terms. Clinical neuropsychology, broadly defined, is the application of psychological knowledge and principles in the diagnosis, description and management of such neurological disorder. It is a branch of clinical psychology and, as such, draws on the same body of psychological knowledge as its parent profession. To some extent though, it also looks beyond this into the territories of neurology (the branch of clinical medicine concerned with diseases of the nervous system) and the neurosciences, and in this sense it is a discipline whose boundaries are not easily defined.

The main objective of this Chapter is to outline the practical role of the clinical neuropsychologist and to summarise the skills and knowledge required for professional practice in the field. But to gain a proper appreciation of neuro-psychological work it is also necessary to grasp some of the important conceptual issues at the heart of the discipline, and to understand that the term "neuro-psychology" itself subsumes a range of scientific attitudes and approaches. I hope to show that the practice of clinical neuropsychology demands a clear understanding of such issues and that it draws on a variety of basic science traditions. The later sections therefore focus on some fundamental theoretical issues. First, though, a broad brush account of what the clinical neuropsychologist actually does.

THE PRACTICE OF CLINICAL NEUROPSYCHOLOGY

Many clinical psychologists will from time to time do work which might be classified as neuropsychological. Those who specialise in work with the elderly, for example, generally have a significant case load of clients with senile dementia, or some other neurological condition prevalent in old age such as stroke. Likewise, child psychologists routinely conduct assessments and treatment interventions with children who are known or suspected to have a neurological disorder of some kind, for example epilepsy. In both cases the psychologist is working with an age-defined client group and, partly for that reason, will be exposed to a relatively narrow range of neuropsychological disorders. Also, of course, he or she will devote much of their time to work of a purely psychological, rather than neuropsychological, nature.

By contrast, clinical neuropsychologists specialise in the psychological evaluation and treatment of neurological disorder, spend the bulk of their time with neurological patients and, typically, gain experience in dealing with a wide variety of neuropsychological problems. Some neuropsychologists are based in general hospitals and have a special responsibility for the provision of psychological services to neurology and neurosurgery departments, as well as taking referrals from other sources. Others are attached to rehabilitation hospitals or to units specialisng in the treatment of particular neurological conditions. In Britain there are in fact relatively few people who fully specialise in clinical neuropsychology—exact figures are difficult to ascertain but, at the time of writing, perhaps fewer than fifty out of a total of around 1500 clinical psychologists working within the National Health Service in England. Consequently, the need for neuropsychology services outstrips the supply, a point made in a recent British Psychological Society report on the provision of psychological services for people with acquired brain damage (British Psychological Society, 1989). The position is somewhat different in certain other countries such as the United States, where neuropsychology has historically formed a more prominent strand within the clinical psychology profession.

Assessment and Intervention

As with other branches of clinical psychology, the work of the neuropsychologist has a number of different aspects which fall to either side of the broad division between "assessment" and "treatment". On the assessment side a distinction is often made between diagnostic and descriptive evaluations, although in practice there is a considerable overlap between the two. In diagnostic assessments the following sorts of issue are considered: Does the patient in question have an organic brain disorder? If so, what type of disorder is indicated? If not, what might be responsible for the presenting signs and symptoms? In descriptive assessments, on the other hand, the patient's diagnosis is not in doubt. What is required is a detailed account of the ways in which psychological functioning is affected (if any) and, following from this, an evaluation of the implications for the clinical management of the patient's condition. If appropriate, recommendations regarding the possible role of psychological treatment interventions will be made.

Such interventions can be pitched at a number of different levels. At the most general level, patients and their relatives might be offered counselling to help in their adjustment to illness. This might entail advice on coping with the acute stresses that follow in the wake of a sudden illness such as stroke, or advice on coming to terms with a chronic, but stable, disability. Sometimes it is appropriate for counselling to be directed principally towards the relatives, for example in cases where the patient's condition will inevitably deteriorate as the result of a degenerative condition such as Alzheimer's disease.

In cases where there is an identifiable "general" psychological disorder associated with the patient's illness (such as an anxiety disorder, or depression) more specific psychological or behavioural therapies will be called for. Such disorders may be secondary to neurological illness but, as will be seen, psychological distress can also be at the root of certain "neurological" symptoms.

At the most specific, "neuropsychological" level, a treatment intervention will take the form of a rehabilitation programme geared to the remediation of "focal" neuropsychological deficits, such as memory or perceptual disorders. For example, a variety of methods have been used to treat memory disorder, which is one of the most common and debilitating consequences of brain injury. The least effective of such methods has been the use of repetitive exercises and drills, thus confirming the futility of treating a poor memory like an out of condition muscle. Some modest success has been gained through teaching patients mnemonic strategies (e.g. visual imagery techniques) but improvements achieved in structured clinical settings rarely generalise to "real world" situations. However, the use of more ecologically relevant external aids, tailored to the individual patient's needs, can be a valuable means of circumventing the practical difficulties arising from memory disorder. Such aids might range from strategically placed labels and signs around the patient's home, to the use of electronic diaries and alarm devices programmed to generate reminders and prompts. Some success has also been achieved in teaching amnesic patients "domain-specific" knowledge with a wide potential application, such as elementary microcomputer skills (for reviews of this and other approaches, see Glisky and Schacter, 1989). In short, efforts at restoring cognitive function have been largely disappointing but, on the basis of an appropriate analysis of the problem, it is often possible to devise means of alleviating the difficulties arising from cognitive disorder.

Finally, it is worth noting that there is also scope for the use of psychological treatments in the management of neurological conditions which may not generally be recognised as having a psychological dimension. For example, there is growing interest in the possibility of using cognitive-behavioural techniques in the control of epileptic seizures (see Goldstein, 1990).

Knowledge Base

Some, at least elementary, knowledge of the structure and functions of the brain is essential for the clinical neuropsychologist, as is some basic knowledge of neuropathology and its typical behavioural manifestations. As noted, neuro-psychological observations often serve a diagnostic function and so without some knowledge of the brain and its disorders the psychologist would clearly not be in a position to offer any opinion as to the nature of the patient's problem. Also, in cases where the patient's diagnosis is not in doubt, such knowledge facilitates the selection of appropriate assessment and treatment methods. Clinical neuropsychology has traditionally been mainly concerned with the so-called higher cerebral functions (language, thinking, perception, memory, purposeful action) mediated by the brain's outermost layer, or cortex. Increasingly, however, it has come to be appreciated that other forebrain structures, such as the basal ganglia, play an important role in sustaining cognition and that different forms of neurological disease can damage such structures (and therefore cognitive function) selectively. It is also important to realise that damage to hindbrain and midbrain structures can profoundly affect a patient's cognitive functioning and behaviour because of the role they play in maintaining basic arousal and attentional mechanisms. For these reasons the neuropsychologist's interests are not confined to the cerebral cortex, although it remains true that disorders of cortical function are the most common reason for referral to a clinical neuropsychologist.

Some common neurological disorders are outlined briefly in the next section. However, no attempt will be made to cover the complex field of functional neuroanatomy. For those who wish to pursue the matter, Kolb and Whishaw (1990) provide a comprehensive and accessible general survey of functional neuroanatomy for the neuropsychologist, and Walsh (1987) offers an excellent introduction to the field from the perspective of clinical neuropsychology.

CAUSES OF NEUROPSYCHOLOGICAL DISORDER

Neurological/Neurosurgical cases

Neuropsychological disorders can arise from a wide range of medical conditions. The nature of the disorder, in terms of the profile of psychological impairment, will obviously depend to some extent upon the nature of the injury or disease. For example, the effects of a severe head injury are likely to be quite different from those of a more circumscribed lesion due to a small cerebral haemorrhage or tumour. However, there can be great variability in the way that a given neurological disorder is expressed psychologically, and it must also be borne in mind that there is considerable overlap between different aetiologies in terms of their psychological consequences. For example, different forms of dementia (global intellectual deterioration) may be due to quite different disease processes but be similar in terms of their psychological effects. The neuropsychologist must therefore be aware of the characteristic patterns of psychological disorder associated with different neurological conditions, but at the same time recognise that such knowledge provides only a loose frame of reference.

The major forms of neurological disorder giving rise to psychological impairment are summarised below. This should give some idea of the variety of disorders that clinical neuropsychologists encounter. Lishman (1987) offers a substantial and authoritative review of organically-based psychological disorder, and both Lezak (1983) and Walsh (1987) provide a sound introduction to neuropathology for psychologists. A comprehensive review of neurological disorders is provided by Scadding (1990).

Head Injury

Epidemiological studies indicate that, in England and Wales, around 140,000 people per year are admitted to hospital with head injuries (Field, 1976). Road traffic accidents are the most common cause. Among young adults and children such injuries are the commonest form of brain damage. The advances in critical care medicine in recent years have meant that increasing numbers of accident victims are surviving with serious head injuries, the consequences of which range from mild cognitive or affective disorders through to devastating impairments of intellectual, emotional, and social functioning.

Cerebrovascular Disorders

The term cerebrovascular disorder refers to a disruption of the brain's blood supply. This can have a number of causes, including disease of the cerebral arteries, heart disease, and disorders of the blood. The commonest cause is atheroma, which involves a degeneration of the walls of the arteries due to the accumulation of fatty deposits and scar tissue. Cerebrovascular disorder in the form of a blocked or burst artery can cause an abrupt onset and rapid development of neurological deficits, an event referred to as a cerebrovascular accident (CVA) or, more commonly, stroke. Depending on the location and extent of the damage, stroke can give rise to a wide range of psychological disorders, including sometimes quite specific (focal) impairments of memory or perceptual function. Stroke survivors constitute about a quarter of all severely disabled people in the community (Harris, 1971), but many survivors achieve good physical and psychological recovery.

Intracranial Tumours

The term tumour can refer to any abnormal swelling but is usually applied to abnormal tissue growth. As with tumours in other parts of the body, intracranial (i.e. within the skull) tumours may be malignant or benign. The neuropsychological effects of a tumour will depend on its size, location and rate of growth. Meningiomas, which are benign tumours arising from the coverings of the brain, may grow slowly over a period of many years causing few if any symptoms until they exert significant pressure effects on the brain. Other types of tumour developing within the substance of the brain may produce severe symptoms at an early stage if they encroach upon key structures or neural pathways.

Infectious Diseases

A wide range of infections of the central nervous system can give rise to disturbances of psychological function, ranging from mumps to AIDS (Lishman, 1987). Some, such as measles encephalitis, can cause a global deterioration of intellectual functions as well as severe physical disability. Others may have devastating neuropsychological effects with little or no residual physical disability. For example, herpes simplex encephalitis (which is caused by the common cold sore virus) has a predilection for brain structures crucially involved in memory and others involved in regulating certain apects of social behaviour. Typically, the patient is left with a dense amnesia (memory disorder) and often with a tendency to behave in a socially disinhibited fashion.

Epilepsy

Epilepsy is not so much a disease as a range of symptoms that can have a variety of underlying causes. Sometimes it is associated with identifiable structural damage to the brain caused by, say, head injury or tumour, but the cause is often unknown. The hallmark of the condition is the recurrence of episodes of acute, transitory brain dysfunction which are characterised by abnormal electrophysiological activity. The resulting seizure can take a variety of forms, with a broad distinction drawn between generalised and partial (or focal) types. Tonic-clonic fits (grand mal, major fits), which involve severe generalised convulsions and loss of consciousness, fall into the first category, as do petit mal attacks which entail a brief loss of consciousness (absence) without convulsions. Such generalised seizures arise from structures deep within the brain. By contrast, partial seizures may have their focus in any region of the cerebral cortex, the nature of the fit being determined by the point of origin of the discharge. So, for example, fits arising in the motor cortex will be characterised by convulsive twitching on one side of the body, whereas abnormal discharges in the sensory areas of the brain will cause sensory disturbances. The temporal lobes are the commonest partial seizure site, and neuropsychologically the most problematic. Seizures arising in the temporal lobes can give rise to severe disturbances of sensory, affective, behavioural and cognitive function (especially memory and language functions).

Dementia

Dementia is defined by a progressive and unremitting deterioration of intellectual function. A number of different neurological conditions can give rise to dementia but the most common cause is Alzheimer's disease, which affects perhaps one in twenty people over the age of sixty-five. The cause of Alzheimer's disease is unknown and it is, as yet, incurable. Enormous research efforts are currently underway to find an effective treatment, much of which is following early leads which suggested that the disease is characterised by specific neurochemical deficits and therefore might be treated pharmacologically. Psychological signs of disorder (e.g. forgetfulness, poor concentration) almost invariably precede neurological signs and so neuropsychological assessment plays an important part in the diagnostic process. (Unless the patient is subjected to a brain biopsy, which is rarely justifiable, Alzheimer's disease cannot in fact be diagnosed with certainty until post-mortem examination reveals the characteristic pattern of "plaques and tangles" in the brain). It is important to distinguish "probable Alzheimer's" from other possible causes of intellectual decline. For example, severe depression can mimic dementia quite closely ("depressive pseudodementia") and some apparent dementias may be due to organic disorders which are potentially treatable (e.g. certain vascular disorders). Other conditions, such as multi-infarct dementia which is caused by a succession of small strokes, may not be reversible but benefit from treatments inappropriate for Alzheimer's disease.

Movement Disorders

Movement disorders such as Parkinson's disease often have significant affective (especially depression) and cognitive components. Intellectual decline associated with such diseases is sometimes referred to as subcortical dementia because of the brain structures primarily involved (basal ganglia) and to distinguish it from cortical dementias such as Alzheimer's disease. The majority of people with Parkinson's disease, however, do not suffer a dementia but many may show mild impairments in certain areas of cognitive functioning.

Demyelinating Conditions

Demyelinating disease is characterised by degeneration of the fatty myelin sheath covering nerve fibres, which leads to disruption of the transmission of nerve impulses. Essentially, it is thus a disease of the connective white matter of the central nervous system rather than the grey matter. Multiple sclerosis (MS) is the most important of the demyelinating conditions. Because the pathology can occur at any central white matter sites, the clinical presentation and course of MS are variable, as are the psychological sequelae.

Other Conditions

A wide range of other medical conditions can give rise to neuropsychological disorder, including various endocrine diseases, metabolic disorders, vitamin deficiences, and toxic disorders (for review see Lishman, 1987). In addition, neurosurgical interventions (e.g. for the removal of a tumour) will often have significant neuropsychological consequences.

Psychiatric and "Quasi-Neurological" Cases

To broaden the definition of the neuropsychologist's role given earlier, it should be pointed out that it is not limited to work with patients who fall neatly into the neurological category. The neuropsychologist is sometimes called upon to examine or treat patients whose primary disorder is psychiatric rather than neurological, for example people with a schizophrenic illness or depression. In such cases, doubts may have arisen about the original diagnosis and a neuropsychological opinion is sought to clarify the issue; or it may be that a detailed description of the patient's cognitive abilities, of the type that a neuropsychological assessment yields, is required in order to plan a programme of treatment or rehabilitation.

There is also a sizeable group of patients who present with neurological symptoms but, on investigation, turn out to have no detectable signs of neurological dysfunction. One might call these "quasi-neurological" cases, although they are more commonly referred to as "functional" disorders. The so-called "hysterical conversion disorders" would fall into this category. In such cases a person may suffer paralysis of the limbs, blindness, or some other disability of an ostensibly physical nature for which no organic cause is discernible, but which occurs in the context of severe psychological distress or unresolved conflict which is presumed to be ultimately responsible for the condition. Conversion disorder is a form of "illness behaviour" over which the patient is believed to have little or no conscious control. In other cases it may be in an individual's interests to fake a neurological condition deliberately, for example if there is financial compensation, or perhaps some emotional gain at stake. Neuropsychological methods can play a role in exposing such malingering. There are other forms of illness behaviour which occur in the context of an established neurological disorder. For example, a small minority of patients with epilepsy exhibit "pseudoseizures" in addition to having genuine fits. Such pseudoseizures are sometimes (although not always) difficult to distinguish from the real thing on grounds of clinical observation alone, but they lack the characteristic paterns of electrophysiological activity associated with genuine fits. The neuropsychologist may be requested to try and identify and treat the possible psychological causes.

There are still other stress-induced conditions whose symptoms seem to mimic those commonly seen with neurological disease. For example, chronic psychological stress may be accompanied by physical, "neurological", symptoms such as limb weakness, loss of sensation or dysarthria (slurred speech), and by psychological symptoms such as impaired memory and concentration. With other conditions such as the "occupational cramps" (e.g writer's cramp) the neurological basis continues to be debated, but in many cases there appear to be contributory psychological factors (and, whatever the cause, behavioural methods have sometimes been used successfully in treating such conditions).

Neuropsychologists play a role in the assessment and treatment of each of these types of problem. Certain conditions in this category are also of potentially great theoretical interest, in so far as they raise some interesting conceptual issues concerning the distinction between neurological and psychological levels of explanation.

CATEGORIES OF NEUROPSYCHOLOGICAL DEFICIT

So far, we have discussed neuropsychological disorders from a broadly medical viewpoint, i.e. in terms of the underlying neurological condition. This is inescapable in neuropsychological practice since the medical and psychological issues are so closely intertwined. For practical purposes this sort of "aetiological" categorisation of disorders gives an essential frame of reference. Just as the motor mechanic's job of understanding a fault is make easier by a prior knowledge of the "signs and symptoms" of different categories of engine failure, so the neuropsychologist's work is facilitated by a basic understanding of the common neurological disorders. Aside from the question of assessment, any recommendations concerning the patient's future management must take prognosis into account (i.e. the likely outcome of the illness) which, of course, will depend on aetiology (i.e. its root cause).

An alternative, or rather complementary, way of looking at things is from the psychological perspective. Here, categories of psychological disorder, rather than categories of disease, provide the frame of reference. At first sight, the classical division of psychological domains into the cognitive ("thinking and perceiving"), the affective ("feeling"), and the conative ("doing"), seems a reasonable starting point for the classification of neuropsychological disorders. The effects of brain disorder can extend into any or all of these areas of functioning and, certainly, a neuropsychological evaluation failing to give proper consideration to each of them would be incomplete. It is also the case that, quite often, patterns of impairment do appear to fall predominantly into one or other division of the classical triad: for example, one patient's problems may be primarily cognitive (e.g. memory disorder); for another, disturbances of affect may be the primary disorder (e.g. irascibility); still other patients exhibit pronounced behavioural ("conative") disorders (e.g. sexual disinhibition). However, such a three-way classification is too broad to be of much practical use because of the great diversity of disorders found within each division, and because some disorders are due to a combination of deficits from two or more of these broad divisions. For clinical descriptive purposes, the numerous subcategories of cognitive, emotional, and behavioural disorder provide a more appropriate point of departure.

Cognition

Cognitive disorders have received the most clinical and scientific analysis but, even so, there is no firmly established taxonomy. The areas of cognitive functioning which typically come under the scrutiny of the clinical neuropsychologist reflect conventional, "textbook chapter", areas of inquiry: attention, perception, thinking, memory, language, motor skills, etc. Partly, this is because the neuropsychologist brings to the job a conventional, academic, approach; and partly because the breakdown of psychological function through brain disorder often faithfully honours the chapter headings! Thus, a patient may exhibit deficits which appear to fall within a single one of these domains, others remaining untouched. The dysfunction might be confined to the language domain (e.g. speech production difficulties—"expressive dysphasia") or to some aspect of attention (e.g. a failure to attend to sensory information on one side—"unilateral inattention"). Often the pattern of deficits will embrace two or more functional domains, but it would be rare, if not unheard of, for all of them to be seriously compromised (with the possible exception of advanced states of dementia). This makes it possible, and useful, to construct a "neuropsychological profile" on the basis of an individual's capacities in each of the major domains of function.

This sort of "textbook taxonomy", while clinically useful, is nevertheless still rather crude because, of course, for each domain of cognitive functioning there are numerous subdomains which can be affected selectively by damage to the brain. Different forms of brain disorder can cause language, perception, memory etc. to break down in a variety of different ways. As we shall see, the ways in which particular aspects of cognitive functioning "fractionate" as a consequence of brain disorder can be highly informative in terms of our theoretical understanding of the organisation of normal cognition, as well as shedding light on the nature of brain-behaviour relationships.

In terms of the clinical evaluation of a cognitive disorder, the more fine-grained the analysis of dysfunction the better but, in practice, there are invariably limitations on what it is possible to achieve within the constraints of a routine clinical assessment. The "textbook taxonomy" therefore continues to serve a useful purpose in providing a framework for the description of cognitive disorder. However, it is important to retain scope for flexibility and innovation in the neuropsychological examination.

There are certain disorders of cognition which do not fit easily into any of the categories referred to so far. These might best be understood in terms of failures of self-awareness or self-monitoring. Some neurological patients show a marked lack of insight into the nature of their disabilities. This can range from, say, a patient's failure to appreciate the extent of a relatively mild, but significant, perceptual disorder (leading to overestimation of their capacity to resume everyday activities such as driving) to total denial of a gross physical disability such as a paralysed limb ("anosagnosia"). It is generally agreed that such lack of insight or denial represents a cognitive rather than an "emotional" disorder. In other words it is not the result of an unconscious retreat from a harsh reality to be explained in psychodynamic terms. Impairments of self-monitoring are often accompanied by a wider impairment of social perceptiveness and so may represent a more general disorder of social cognition.

Emotion

All forms of acquired brain disorder carry emotional consequences, whether "general" (in terms of the individual's response and adjustment to illness) or "specific" (in terms of disorders attributable to damage to brain areas directly involved in the regulation of emotional responses). As already indicated, the neuropsychologist's role is not limited to the assessment and treatment of specific disorders, but will also involve working with patients whose problems are, in the neuropsychological sense, non-specific. The emotional sequelae of brain disorder have received considerably less research attention than cognitive disorders and, consequently, the taxonomy of emotional disorders is poorly developed. Some disorders fit readily into conventional psychiatric categories such as depression or mania, but others are harder to accommodate. For example, following certain types of stroke (in particular when the brain's limbic structures have been damaged) it is quite common for patients to exhibit what is sometimes referred to as "emotional incontinence". This is a state of emotional volatility in which the patient appears to be hypersensitive to emotional stimuli and will, usually with considerable embarrassment, continually burst into tears in response to certain words, tones of voice, facial expressions or other triggers such as sentimental music. There are also other forms of emotional volatility, including acute irritability and lowered anger thresholds.

Behaviour

Acquired brain damage can cause profound alterations of personality and behaviour. Such behavioural changes, which are often associated with damage to the frontal lobes of the brain, may severely disrupt social functioning and family relationships, and thus carry implications which sometimes far outweigh the significance of more circumscribed physical or cognitive disabilities.

Broadly speaking, the behavioural disorders can be classified as either negative or positive. The negative syndromes are characterised by apathy, inertia, lack of spontaneity and inflexibility. The patient is inclined to become socially withdrawn and, if left undisturbed, might sit mute in an armchair for hours on end. There seems to be a fundamental lack of drive and such disorders are sometimes conceptualised as a motivational dysfunction. The positive disorders take a variety of forms. Some previously well-adjusted individuals develop aggressive and anti-social traits, sometimes leading to criminal behaviour. Others may become uncharacteristically fatuous, garrulous or histrionic. Some patients become socially and sexually disinhibited. At one end of the spectrum this might take the form of habitual sexual suggestiveness in casual verbal exchanges, but in more extreme cases an individual may show a tendency to masturbate in public places or make unsolicited physical advances to strangers and acquaintances. It is, incidentally, no coincidence that certain features of the positive disorders are also characteristic of people who are drunk, as alcohol appears to have a predilection for the frontal lobes.

NEUROPSYCHOLOGICAL EXAMINATION

There is no such thing as a "standard" neuropsychological examination. The particular procedures adopted will vary according to the reasons for referral, the patient's medical condition and general capabilities, the range of test materials and equipment available, and the expertise and biases of the examiner. However, all assessments proceed in some way from observation to interpretation, and the following general framework accommodates most facets of clinical neuropsychological inquiry.

Methods and Procedures

1. Case appraisal, clinical interview and observation

Aims: To gather background information about the patient (including social, educational, occupational, and medical/psychiatric history), and about the nature and history of the presenting problem. Such information sets the context for subsequent examination procedures.

Methods: Inspection of relevant case notes; interview with patient, interview with patient's relatives and/or carers; observation of patient's behaviour (e.g. on the ward).

2. Formal neuropsychological screening

Aims: To determine the patient's general level of intellectual functioning and to judge whether this is consistent with probable premorbid (i.e. "before the illness") capacity. To determine whether impairments are evident in any of the major functional domains (memory, perception, language etc.).

Methods: Quantitative: standardised psychometric testing. Qualitative: clinical examination techniques. (See below).

3. Hypothesis testing

Aims: To investigate further any deficits revealed by the formal screening procedures so as to provide a more fine-grained analysis of the problem.

Methods: Failure in a given task may be investigated further by examining the patient's performance in subsequent tasks which tap particular elements of the original. For example, poor performance in constructional tasks might be due to perceptual disorder or an incapacity to formulate a plan of action; each of these aspects might be tested separately.

4. Interpretation

Taking all of the above into account, an opinion is formed as to what kind of disorder (if any) is indicated. For example, is it likely that the condition has an organic basis or might it be "functional"; if there is evidence of an organic disorder, is the damage focal (confined to a specific region of the brain) or diffuse (widespread throughout different brain regions)? Opinions will also be offered as to whether further investigations are advisable (medical or psychological) and whether any psychological contribution might be made to treatment or rehabilitation.

Neuropsychological tests

Methods used to investigate neuropsychological function range from the simplest paper-and-pencil tests, through highly structured psychometric instruments, to sophisticated computerised assessments. With appropriate interview and behavioural observation techniques the experienced examiner will actually gain a great deal of information about a patient's neuropsychological status at the bedside, without recourse to any formal test materials. A thorough neuropsychological examination will combine formal psychometric procedures with clinically-derived interview and observation techniques. The "clinical" and "psychometric" approaches should be seen as complementary.

My own approach to assessment combines the use of, (1) well-standardised, commercially available psychometric tests; (2) tests derived from the clinical and experimental literature for which normative data may (or may not) be available; (3) "bedside" clinical tests for which normative data are inapplicable or unavailable; (4) test procedures currently "under development"; (5) Novel tasks devised to examine specific hypotheses.

Examples of well established psychometric instruments which are widely used by neuropsychologists would be the Wechsler Adult Intelligence Scale—Revised (WAIS–R) (Wechsler, 1981), which yields valuable information about specific verbal and non-verbal capacities as well as general intellectual level, and the Warrington Recognition Memory Test, which tests recognition memory for words and for faces (Warrington, 1984). The Cognitive Estimates Test (Shallice and Evans, 1978) provides an example of a task which is fairly widely-used by neuropsychologists but which is poorly established by conventional psychometric standards. In this test, which appears to be sensitive to frontal lobe damage, the subject is required to venture various estimates of speed, size, weight etc. (e.g. 'How fast does a race horse gallop?'). The lack of adequate norms hardly seems to matter when wildly inaccurate estimates are proffered (e.g. "Five hundred miles per hour" in response to the above question) but mildly eccentric responses are more difficult to interpret.

There are numerous clinical (as opposed to psychometric) assessment procedures which rely for their interpretation almost entirely upon that elusive quality "clinical judgement". Amongst these would be included various routines for the assessment of different forms of dyspraxia (inability to execute purposeful or skilled actions), and for the evaluation of "somaesthetic" disorders such as loss of body position sense, or impairment of the ability to identify objects by touch ("astereognosis"). Various aspects of visual-perceptual function and attention are also amenable to purely "clinical" assessment procedures. For example, evidence for unilateral visual inattention can be elicited by the method of confronting the patient with simultaneous visual stimuli (e.g. finger movements) in different regions of the visual field.

In addition to the psychometric and clinical approaches mentioned above, it is also sometimes appropriate to use experimental test procedures which have little or no track record in clinical neuropsychology. For example, there are as yet no standard clinical procedures for the assessment of sustained vigilance, but I find certain experimental methods extremely useful for this purpose (e.g. the sustained attention task devised by Wilkins *et al.*, 1987).

Finally, if an assessment enters a "hypothesis testing" phase, it may be necessary to improvise tasks which will focus explicitly on the patient's presumed deficit.

Space prohibits a more detailed account of the many and varied procedures employed in neuropsychological examination. The standard reference work by Lezak (1983) is highly recommended as a comprehensive introduction to neuropsychological assessment methods, including an extensive compendium of tests. The clinical (as distinct from psychometric) approach is best exemplified by Christensen's introduction to the methods developed by A.R. Luria (Christensen, 1974).

SOME THEORETICAL ISSUES

Varieties of neuropsychology

For much of the time it is appropriate for psychologists to disregard the fact that human performance and experience have a biological dimension. It is possible to deal profitably in the theoretical constructs of psychology without the need to consider any underlying anatomy and physiology. Thus behavourists and cognitivists have both, in their different ways, treated the human organism as a black box. For those in the behavioural tradition the contents of the black box are of no particular interest. All that matters is a specification of its inputs and outputs in terms of stimulus and response. For the modern cognitive psychologist the black box seethes with the invisible activity of a complex information processing system and the challenge is to define the components of the system and specify its operation. Just as a software engineer requires no specialist knowledge of the computer's hardware, so it is possible to approach an understanding of human cognition without reference to the brain.

In contrast to these approaches, it has traditionally been the business of experimental neuropsychology to delve into the biological hardware in an attempt to specify what relationships hold between psychological constructs (perception, memory, thinking, emotion etc) and the physical systems of the brain. However, even among neuropsychologists there are great differences in terms of the importance attached to the investigation of underlying brain mechanisms. For some, the primary task for the science of neuropsychology is the mapping of psychological functions to particular regions of the brain. Others, characterised by Shallice (1988) as the "ultra-cognitivists" appear to disown the neurological tradition altogether, preferring to concentrate their efforts on constructing models of cognition to account for the observed effects of brain damage regardless of its underlying nature. Between these two approaches lies a broad spectrum of neuropsychological science, some with more of a biological emphasis and some whose perspective is primarily cognitive. The latter variety, as an outgrowth of mainstream cognitive psychology, has become widely influential in recent years, an influence that can be expected to grow in clinical neuropsychology. Biological neuropsychology, caught up in the current wave of interest in the neurosciences, is also experiencing a period of unusual vitality. For these reasons it is worth spelling out the differences in emphasis of the two approaches.

Cognitive neuropsychologists investigate the performance of the damaged brain as a means of testing and refining theories of normal cognitive function. An essential feature of this approach is that models of normal cognition are taken as the point of departure. Within the framework of a particular model, hypotheses are formed concerning the patterns of dysfunction that might result from brain disorder. The model gains support to the extent that a patient's experimental task performance conforms with its predictions. On the other hand, the emerging data may challenge the original model, forcing its modification or abandonment. The nature of the underlying neurological disorder is largely, perhaps entirely, irrelevant in this enterprise. Regardless of neurological factors, what matters is the extent to which particular models of normal cognition are able to accommodate observed patterns of cognitive disorder. In this way, significant contributions have been made in a number of areas, notably psycholinguistics and perception (for reviews see Ellis and Young, 1988; Shallice, 1988; McCarthy and Warrington, 1990).

Other neuropsychologists *are* interested in the brain systems underlying cognitive function and a variety of methods have been employed in their investigation. Such methods have included observations of the behaviour of animals subjected to experimental lesions of the brain as well as studies of patients who have suffered brain lesions as a result of disease or surgery. Brain-behaviour correlations are established by analysing the functional consequences of damage to particular regions of the brain. Studies of the effects of drugs on cognitive function are another means of investigating the relationship between brain systems and cognition (see Stahl *et al.*, 1987).

It should be emphasised that the biological and cognitive approaches to neuropsychology are not (or certainly need not be) mutually antagonistic. They ought to be complementary. It is true that the goals of cognitive neuropsychology can be pursued in virtual ignorance if the anatomy and physiology of the brain, and some purists would regard such considerations as an irrelevance. But the fruits of the cognitive neuropsychologists' labours are of vital importance to those, including clinical neuropsychologists, who have an interest in the structure and functions of the brain. In order to know how psychological functions are represented across different neural structures one must first have the functions themselves clearly delineated.

The clinical neuropsychologist, daily confronted with cases where cognitive functions (and/or emotional and social functioning) are impaired by damage to the brain, draws on both traditions. Because different neurological diseases and patterns of brain damage can have widely differing psychological consequences, it is not sufficient for the clinician to rely on psychological knowledge and principles alone. The assessment and treatment of patients is greatly facilitated by knowledge, so far as this is available, of the relationship between brain systems and behaviour. Although as "scientist-practitioners" it is skills and knowledge drawn from the cognitive and behavioural sciences that clinical neuropsychologists routinely apply, it is important to keep sight of the neurological dimension.

In fact, the state of the art for experimental neuropsychology is still fairly primitive and, in many respects, knowledge about brain-behaviour relationships is lacking. For this reason clinical neuropsychology is a discipline whose pure and applied aspects are complementary. As we have seen, there are features of the neuropsychological examination that are very close in spirit to basic experimental methodology. Every so often in conducting an examination for purely clinical reasons one comes across aspects of a patient's cognitive functioning for which there is no clear precedent in the clinical and scientific literature. On clinical grounds alone there is an obligation to investigate such anomalies systematically in as much detail as is practicable—the better the description of a patient's disorder the more confidently can the guidelines for management of the problem be drawn. But there can be important spin-offs for basic science too, and significant theoretical insights have been gained by following up interesting leads initially revealed through clinical assessment. Thus, aside from their clinical role, neuropsychologists are uniquely placed to contribute to the advancement of basic knowledge about cognitive functions and the neurological structures that support them.

Basic theoretical assumptions of clinical neuropsychology

Most, if not all, clinical neuropsychologists would share the following basic assumptions about brain-behaviour relationships.

A) The mind (or cognitive system) has some form of modular organisation.
B) This modularity is represented in the physiology and anatomy of the brain.
C) The corollary is that specified brain lesions will have predictable functional consequences.

Regarding the first assumption, the term "modularity" is used here fairly loosely. All it implies is that "the mind" (or, if you prefer, cognitive system) is composed of a confederation of subsystems of perception, memory, language and action which are to some degree functionally independent. Independent, that is, to the extent that the operation of certain systems (say, those involved in recalling the name of an object) do not depend on the integrity of others (say, those involved in recognising a familiar face).

Another way of stating the second assumption is that different systems of the brain subserve different psychological functions. But this apparently innocent statement, which is really the central tenet of neuropsychology, actually leaves some important questions begging. For instance, what is a "brain system", and how does one define a "psychological function"?

Defining brain systems

The Russian neuropsychologist A.R. Luria helped to clarify such issues by distinguishing between "functions" and "complex functional systems" in the brain (see for example, Luria, 1973) A simple function can be exemplified by the highly specific role played by the pyramidal cells of the motor cortex – it is the *function* of one group of cells to generate the motor impulses required to initiate the sequence of nervous and muscular activity that results in a movement of the thumb, whereas another specific group of cells is involved in movements of the index finger. If you want to wiggle your finger you cannot help but use certain well specified neuronal pathways with a behavioural repertoire restricted to finger wiggling. The notion of a *complex functional system* comes into play when, from a wider perspective, one takes into consideration the processes leading up to and beyond the movement of the finger. An example of a complex functional system would be the integrated involvement of distinct cortical (and subcortical) regions in co-ordinating the movement of a musician's index finger on a piano keyboard. Moreover, the combination of brain regions involved would differ according to whether the musician were playing from memory or reading a musical score.

In this view there is only a very limited sense in which one can talk of higher psychological functions being "localised" neuroanatomically, rather they are *distributed* across different brain areas. However, the elementary subcomponents of a distributed system *are* strictly localised to particular neuroanatomical zones so that, for example, specific regions of the brain involved in processing basic visual attributes of a stimulus (colour, movement, position, depth) are dedicated to that function (Cowey, 1985).

This kind of analysis offers the clinical neuropsychologist a useful perspective from which to view the relationship between psychological (dys)functions and the hardware of the brain, but it is really just a starting point. What is further required is some understanding of the "anatomy" of cognition.

Defining psychological functions

Essentially, neuropsychologists have used three different forms of evidence in trying to define psychological functions and to determine their relation to brain structures and processes: associations, dissociations and double dissociations.

Associations

It is commonplace to observe that a patient who is impaired in the performance of one task (e.g. identifying photographs of objects) will also be impaired in the performance of certain others (e.g. drawing pictures of the objects). It seems reasonable at first sight to suppose that there is a functional overlap between the tasks, i.e. that there is some underlying process that they have in common. If so, it might be possible to "triangulate" basic psychological functions by examining associations between symptoms. Whilst it is often the case that clusters of symptoms (syndromes) are bound by a common functional thread, such associations can be misleading in terms of their significance for *psychological* processes. Syndromes can equally arise because brain lesions straddle anatomical boundaries. Suppose that the performance of task 1 depends crucially on the integrity of anatomical area A, task 2 on area B and task 3 on area C. If the three areas happen to be adjacent then damage to any one of them is likely to affect the other two, thus disrupting the functions of all three. A certain syndrome might therefore be neurologically significant but uninformative with regard to an analysis of psychological processes. For this reason associations, whilst often clinically significant (in so far as they might indicate the location of a lesion) are not greatly valued by the cognitive neuropsycologist (who is interested purely in the analysis of cognitive functions).

Dissociations

If a patient is impaired in the performance of task 1 but performs competently on task 2, then the dissociation between the two tasks can be taken as evidence that they depend upon different functional processes. For example, supppose the patient performs well in a word learning task but poorly in a task requiring the memorisation of a complex visual pattern. On this evidence it would seem reasonable to postulate that the "memory system" is normally composed of at least two independent subsystems, one concerned with verbal information, the other with non-verbal, and that our patient has suffered damage to one of these subsystems but not the other. If we are about the business of "defining psychological functions", this would appear to be a useful first step towards a delineation of the constituent elements of "memory".

Unfortunately, there are other possible interpretations of such a dissociation. It could be that tasks 1 and 2 are of unequal sensitivity, i.e. that one is for some trivial reason easier than the other. The apparent "dissociation" could then be due merely to the fact that our patient's memory deficit is relatively mild and does not affect easy tasks.

Double Dissociations

The most reliable means of delineating independent functional domains ("cognitive modules") is by way of double dissociations. If patient A performs poorly on task 1 but competently on task 2, whereas patient B shows the reverse pattern, we can with more justification infer that the performance of the first task (say, verbal memory) depends upon the operation of cognitive processes not required for task 2 (say, spatial memory). Double dissociations are important for two related reasons: first, they can help define the structure of the normal, intact, cognitive system; second, they lead to knowledge of how cognitive processes map onto the anatomy and physiology of the brain. Effective clinical practice demands some knowledge of both.

PROSPECTS

I have attempted in this chapter to give an idea of the nature of clinical neuropsychological work and to chart some of the theoretical currents that run into neuropsychology as an applied science. The challenge for the clinician is to keep pace with, and exploit, the rapid expansion of knowledge in cognitive and experimental neuropsychology. Such calls for a closer partnership between theoretical and applied psychology have become something of a cliché, so much so that one hesitates to echo them (they are usually ignored anyway). I would suggest, though, that a closer convergence of theoretical and applied interests in neuropsychology is not only desirable but also inevitable and, in this respect at least, the future of clinical neuropsychology looks healthy. This optimism stems from advances on each of the main basic research fronts.

Recent years have seen some important developments in experimental/biological neuropsychology. Neuropsychological techniques have contributed significantly to the advancement of functional neuroanatomy and, as a consequence, we are approaching a clearer understanding of the relationship of brain systems and behaviour. For example, the combination of neuropsychological analysis with innovative neuroanatomical tracing methods is shedding light on the neural and functional interconnections of different brain regions (Goldman-Rakic, 1987). Animal models of neuropsychological disorder have also contributed to an understanding of the neuroanatomical basis of human cognitive function, Mishkin's work on the anatomy of memory serving as an elegant example (Mishkin and Appenzeller, 1987). Interest in the neuropsychology of memory has, in fact, been particularly vigorous, and the growing complexity of contemporary psychological models is mirrored by the elaboration of theories about the neural systems subserving memory (reviewed by Mayes, 1988). Much of the emerging knowledge is of direct relevance to an understanding of cognitive disorders seen in the clinic and, in turn, clinical observations will continue to stimulate basic research. The advancement of neuropsychological knowledge will also be facilitated by the increasing availability of neuroimaging techniques such as nuclear magnetic resonance imaging (MRI) and single photon emission computerised tomography (SPECT). Such techniques yield information about the anatomy and physiology of the living brain with which to correlate psychological data.

Another cause for optimism has been the growth of cognitive neuropsychology during the past two decades. Closer collaboration between cognitive psychologists and clinical neuropsychologists is of benefit to theoreticians and clinicians alike. As noted earlier, theoretically interesting neuropsychological conditions often come to light during the course of routine clinical assessments. Close contacts between clinicians and researchers ensure that the researchers are alerted to potentially interesting cases. With the consent of the patient, an individual can then undergo further experimental investigations. What the clinician stands to gain is a clearer understanding of the patient's cognitive deficits and, in the long run, a wider range of practical assessment techniques and a firmer theoretical foundation from which to conduct clinical investigations. Cognitive neuropsychologists have focused almost exclusively on the breakdown of cognitive functions following brain damage, but they are beginning to appreciate that there is much to be learnt from the processes underlying recovery of function. It is reasonable to hope that a better theoretical understanding of the recovery process will eventually lead to significant clinical advances in the area of cognitive rehabilitation.

The future of the profession of clinical neuropsychology, of course, ultimately depends upon an adequate supply of well-trained practitioners. Here, from a British point of view at least if not elsewhere, there is perhaps less cause for optimism. An adequate commitment to the training of clinical neuropsychologists is often sadly lacking in post-graduate clinical psychology courses. This is partly a reflection of the fact that clinical psychology has traditionally been most strongly linked with services for the mentally ill and learning disabled rather than other aspects of healthcare. In its early history the profession was widely perceived as being merely ancillary to psychiatry. Times have changed, and the role of clinical psychology has greatly diversified (Watts, 1989) but, nevertheless, the majority of psychologists continue to work primarily with the mentally ill or handicapped, and it remains possible to gain professional credentials in clinical psychology having had no experience in neuropsychology. It is now widely acknowledged that clincal psychology can make a much broader contribution to healthcare, and that the trend will be towards further diversification (Management Advisory Service, 1989). It is to be hoped that, in line with such developments, the teaching and promotion of clinical neuropsychology will in future be treated with due seriousness.

REFERENCES

British Psychological Society (1989). *Services for young adult patients with acquired brain damage.* (Working party report). Leicester: British Psychological Society.

Christensen, A.-L., (1974). *Luria's neuropsychological investigation.* Munksgaard.

Cowey, A. (1985). Aspects of cortical organisation related to selective attention and selective impairment of visual perception: A tutorial review. In M.I. Posner & O.S. Marin (Eds.), *Attention and Performance* (Vol. 11). Hillsdale, N.J.: Erlbaum.

Ellis, A.W. and Young, A.W. (1988). *Human cognitive neuropsychology* Hove: Lawrence Erlbaum Associates.

Field, H.J. (1976). *Epidemiology of head injuries in England and Wales with particular reference to rehabilitation.* London: HMSO.

Glisky, E.L. and Schacter, D.L. (1989). Models and methods of memory rehabilitation. In F. Boller and J. Grafman (Eds.), *Handbook of neuropsychology – Volume 3.* Amsterdam. Elsevier.

Goldman-Rakic, P.S. (1987). Circuit basis of a cognitive function in a non-human primate. In S.M. Stahl, S.D. Iversen and E.C. Goodman (Eds.) *Cognitive neurochemistry.* Oxford: Oxford University Press.

Goldstein, L.H. (1990). Behavioural and cognitive-behavioural treatments for epilepsy: A progress review. *British Journal of Clinical Psychology*, **29**, 257–269.

Harris, A.I. (1971). *Handicapped and impaired in Great Britain. Part 1.* Office of Population and Census Surveys. London: HMSO.

Kolb, B. and Whishaw, I.Q. (1990). *Fundamentals of human neuropsychology (3rd Edition)* New York: W.H. Freeman.

Lezak, M.D. (1983). *Neuropsychological assessment.* (2nd Edition) Oxford, Oxford University Press.

Lishman, A.L. (1987). *Organic psychiatry.* (2nd Edition). Oxford: Blackwell Scientific Publications.

Luria, A.R. (1973). *The working brain.* Harmondsworth: Penguin.

Management Advisory Service (1989). *Review of clinical psychology services* (report by Management Advisory Service to the NHS, May, 1989).

Mayes, A.R. (1988). *Human organic memory disorders.* Cambridge: Cambridge University Press.

McCarthy, R.A. and Warrington, E.K. (1990). *Cognitive neuropsychology: A clinical Introduction* San Diego/London: Academic Press.

Mishkin, M. and Appenzeller, T. (1987). The anatomy of memory. *Scientific American* **256** (6), 62–72.

Scadding, J.W. (1990). Neurological disease. In R.L. Soulhami and J. Moxham (Eds.) *Textbook of medicine.* Edinburgh: Churchill Livingstone.

Shallice, T. and Evans, M.E. (1978). The involvement of the frontal lobes in cognitive estimation. *Cortex*, **14**, 294–303.

Shallice, T. (1988). *From neuropsychology to mental structure.* Cambridge: Cambridge University Press.

Stahl, S.M., Iversen, S.D. and Goodman, E.C. (Eds) (1987). *Cognitive neurochemistry.* Oxford: Oxford University Press.

Walsh, K.W. (1987). *Neuropsychology – A clinical approach.* (2nd Edition). Edinburgh: Churchill Livingstone.

Warrington, E.K. (1984). *Recognition Memory Test.* Windsor; NFER Nelson.

Watts, F.N. (1989). The efficacy of clinical applications of psychology: an overview of research. In *Review of clinical psychology services.* Report by Management Advisory Services to the NHS, May 1989.

Wechsler, D. (1981). *Wechsler Adult Intelligence Scale – Revised* San Antonio: The Psychological Corporation, Harcourt Brace Jovanovich. (British version distributed by NFER Nelson).

Wilkins, A.J., Shallice, T. and McCarthy, R. (1987). Frontal lesions and sustained attention. *Neuropsychologia*, **25**, 359–365.

8

RECRUITMENT AND SELECTION

V. SHACKLETON

OVERVIEW

Personnel recruitment and selection has a long-standing history in applied psychology. Systematic studies of the employment interview were being conducted in the early 1900s, for example. It is a major part of what the British call occupational psychology, continental Europeans call work psychology and North Americans call industrial and organizational psychology.

At its most basic, recruitment and selection aims to find and match individuals with jobs, "fitting the person to the job" as it used to be known, and so concerns itself with two sides of an equation, individuals and jobs. Because of this, it has strong links with many other topics of psychology. On the individual side, personnel selection is based on an understanding of the psychology of individual differences, on assessment techniques (see Chapter 5) and on the theories and techniques of psychometrics, to name just a few. On the job side, it presupposes an understanding of tasks, jobs and careers, based on such techniques as job analysis, job descriptions and person specifications.

Traditionally, personnel selection has taken a predominantly organizational or managerial perspective. As such, it aims to select the best person or persons for a job. "Best" may mean a reduction in the time required to train that person, or an increase in the chance of selecting a productive worker, or one who will stay with the organization, or refrain from stealing, or any of a host of other objectives. It is concerned, then, with organizational outcomes. Yet for a long while enlightened employers have recognized that a "good fit" between employee and job is in the interests of both parties, the job incumbent and the organization. Many employers accept responsibility for the quality of working life of their employees. They are interested not only in productivity and profitability, but also in the health and well-being of their employees. Employees, for their part, often value work which gives them an opportunity to use their skills and abilities and which coincides with their interests, values and preferences. They are less likely to find such work if the organization makes a poor job of selection.

More recently, psychologists have stressed the dual interest nature of the selection process even more strongly, particularly in the selection interview. Peter Herriot has been at the forefront of this movement (see Herriot, 1989, for example). He has stressed that the interview is a two-way process, involving mutual exploration, negotiating, contracting and agreeing on what each side expects and wants from the eventual successful outcome, a job offer and job acceptance. This is a view we will return to later in this chapter, but the reader can see that the "seat of power" switches markedly under this perspective. Traditionally, it is the organization or the employer who holds all the cards. It is the employer who insists on the candidate jumping through the hoops of application form, interview, tests, leading to the final offer of a job or the rejection letter. Under the social exchange view of Herriot and others, the employer may still have the administrative power since it manages the selection procedure and determines which selection tools are used. But the candidate has supply or labour market power, able to offer or withhold their labour, especially when labour is scarce.

Now that we have had a chance to briefly overview the purpose of personnel recruitment and selection, and some contrasting perspectives, we need to get down to practicalities. This involves examining the key steps in the process, main techniques and the issues of debate. It is to these that the chapter now turns.

THE PROCESS OF RECRUITMENT AND SELECTION

The way that organizations go about selecting people to work in them is essentially a process. This process involves a number of steps and a feedback loop, as shown in Figure 8.1. In this chapter we will concentrate on a few of the steps, primarily the middle ones in the figure. Yet it is important to realise that selection is only one part of a system which aims to effectively manage people (the "human resources") in an organization.If the best people are chosen, we may nevertheless find that they do not give of their best, or they leave, or they feel dissatisfied, because other parts of the system are less than adequate. Some of the other parts of the system are mentioned in other chapters in this book and include job design and the working environment. Conversely, the best working environment, or design ofjob, or training scheme, may be doomed to failure if the individuals selected are unable to do the job or cannot profit from the training. Very often occupational psychologists are brought into an organization with requests to improve the existing personnel selection techniques because of, say, high labour turnover, when it is other parts of the system, such as the quality of the supervision or the pay rates, which are at fault. So it bears repeating that one cannot and should not think of selection as an isolated event but as part of a system for effectively managing people in organizations.

In particular, two parts of the system are closely coupled to selection and are often considered together with it. These are recruitment and placement. **Recruitment** refers to the process of attracting applicants to apply for the available job or jobs by means of advertisements or recruitment agencies of various kinds. Obviously it makes selection easier, up to a point, if a large number of well qualified applicants are available from whom to select. But only up to a point. Thousands of applicants for just a few jobs throws more work onto the screening, or pre-selection part of the process. This is likely to be a particular problem for organizations in times of high unemployment. But even this is preferable, as far as organizations are concerned, to a very tight labour market where employers compete for scarce, specialised employees. In such cases,

THE RECRUITMENT AND SELECTION PROCESS

MANPOWER PLANNING
|
JOB ANALYSIS
JOB DESCRIPTION/PERSON SPECIFICATION
|
RECRUITMENT ADVERTISING
|
SCREENING
|
TESTING/INTERVIEWING
|
SELECTION
|
PLACEMENT
|
TRAINING

APPRAISAL/REVIEW
(WITH FEEDBACK TO MODIFY STEPS ABOVE)

FIGURE 8.1

recruiting becomes an expensive priority. Recruitment thus involves providing the selector with what is known as a favourable **selection ratio**. This is the ratio of number of applicants to number of available jobs. A favourable ratio for a selector would be a large number of suitable applicants for each job available. Good recruitment provides it. But it is interesting to note that a favourable selection ratio for an employer (lots of candidates per job) is just the opposite, and highly unfavourable; for the candidate.

Placement, or classification, is the process of deciding where to place an applicant once hired. Obviously if there is only one job then placement is not an issue. An applicant is either accepted or rejected for that job. But sometimes there is more than one opening and the question of which job is most suitable for an applicant has to be considered. Placement is commonly an issue for large organizations, such as the armed forces or the police, with large numbers of applicants for numerous openings year after year.

Despite the importance of recruitment and placement to the success of the selection process as a whole, it is the testing, interviewing and selection decision steps of Figure 8.1 on which psychologists have concentrated most of their research. But before we consider this research and the practical lessons that have been learned, we need to spend a few minutes considering earlier steps in the chain.

Manpower planning is a vast topic in its own right (see Fyfe and Hornby, 1988, for a discussion) but in a selection context it refers to such questions as: how should the work be divided into jobs; how many people does the organization need to do the job of work; do we need people to do it at all (could it, or a part of it, be better and more economically performed by a machine, for example) and what should people do? **Job analysis** likewise has a large literature describing methods and techniques (see Pearn and Kandola, 1988, for example). In a recruitment and selection context it involves analysing the job into its components so as to be able to describe the tasks, duties, responsibilities, levels of authority, and so on, of the job. The resulting picture becomes the job description. Only then can a person specification for the target job be drawn up. The **job description** is, as the name suggests, a description of the job, whereas the **person specification** is a description of the job in "people" terms. That is, a specification of the attributes (behaviour and ability requirements) of a person considered suitable for the job. These attributes or characteristics are those considered typical of effective job performance. In addition, they must include appropriate characteristics as predictors of future work performance.

Strictly speaking, the job description should be written only after an exhaustive job analysis. In practice, the personnel manager, a line manager, or the job incumbent draws up the job description from knowledge of the job. Sometimes no formal job description is available for the recruiters. Even if it is, and even if it is up to date and accurate, it is all too common for there to be no person specifcation for the job and so little information is available to guide the selection phase. The field of personnel selection is full of cases where accepted "good practice" and actual day-to-day practice are poles apart.

In this examination of the stages preceding the decision to accept or reject a candidate, we have taken an organizational perspective on recruitment and selection. This might lead you to believe that the individual candidate is somehow a passive part of the process. This is not so. The individual is very much an active participant. A candidate selects an organization just as much as an organization selects a candidate. Selection is a dynamic, two-way process. The applicant and the organization communicate and negotiate. The situation is a social exchange, where either party has the opportunity to withdraw at any stage.

CRITERION MEASURES

The heart of the process, from the organization's point of view, should be the criterion measures.

The organization's aim in selection is to make a predictive decision—that this candidate will be able to learn the job or stay for an acceptable length of time, or perform the job to the necessary standard. It aims, then, to predict criterion measures. The criterion can be defined as an evaluative standard used to measure a person's work performance, attitude or behaviour and usually includes productivity, absenteeism, accidents or supervisors' ratings. It can be seen that the criterion is defined from an organizational point of view. Rarely does it take in addition a perspective from the other side of the relationship, that of the employee. The measures are usually the *satisfactoriness* of the worker with scant regard for his or her *satisfaction*.

Criterion measures lie at the heart of selection. Without them, we cannot validate any aspect of the selection process, be it tests, interviews or the whole recruitment, selection and placement system. The problem is that there are considerable difficulties in obtaining worthwhile and meaningful criterion scores.

One element of the problem is deciding what kind of performance to measure. There is rarely one obvious measure. Take the example of the university lecturer. Should we measure teaching ability, publications, research contracts, administrative ability, pastoral responsibilities, reputation, or what? All are presumably important, but their relative importance varies with who is asked the question. To a student the most important function may be teaching skill, while to a head of department it might be amount of contract money earned for the university, to the vice chancellor it might be publication record and to peers it might be ability or willingness to accept administrative tasks. For some jobs, such as manager, just defining performance may be even harder.

There is often the additional problem of variations or fluctuation in performance on a day-today or week-to-week basis, with different moods or different people to deal with. In the lecturer example, someone might be a superbly interesting and stimulating teacher with a small postgraduate class and yet be far too erudite, pompous or confusing to a large undergraduate one.

Assuming we can define performance, there are few, if any, situations in which a single measure of performance constitutes an adequate criterion. Rather, the result is likely to be a number of output variables, as in the lecturer example. So there is the problem of weighting and combining them into some "super criterion" or composite criterion such as the long-range profitability of a commercial or industrial organization. Alternatively, we may keep the multiple criteria separate and correlate predictors with separate criteria (although this approach is more often adopted for research purposes, where just understanding is sufficient, rather than for practical, applied studies). Rarely can valid measures of this ultimate, long-range criterion be obtained. So we are thrown back on more immediate, easy to-obtain criteria. Hardly surprising, then, that the majority of studies report just one global, immediate and obvious criterion such as supervisors' ratings.

The problem with performance competencies rated by supervisors or line managers is that they tend to be notoriously unreliable and heavily coloured by human error. Moreover, they tend not to make differentiations among aspects of performance. Their ratings of distinct and different aspects of work performance, such as "persistence" and "oral communication" are usually highly correlated with each other. This reflects a uni-dimensional view of an employee as "good" or "poor". Since job performance is almost always multi-dimensional, it is doubtful whether a single measure is at all useful. More is known about the problem than about how to improve the results, but behavioural checklists, self appraisal and training in both the human and technical aspects of the rating process can help. (See Chapter 5 for more on rating problems).

The implications of the "criterion problem" for selection are profound. Without adequately reliable and valid criteria, no predictor is going to show a strong and consistent relationship with the criteria. Simply put, how can we state that a test or measure predicts success if we cannot define and measure success?

Criterion-related validities

Since selection is about making predictions, we need some method of establishing how successful our predictions are. Only then are we able to compare one method, such as interviews, with another, say test results. Only then are we able to establish how good the selection procedure is as a whole. Methods of gathering data about candidates, such as tests and interviews, give us predictor scores or, more strictly speaking, the scores on *potential predictors*. Establishing the validity of predictors, in the context of selection, involves relating predictor scores to criterion measures. This is known as establishing the **criterion-related** validities of the predictors.

There are two types of criterion-related validity: concurrent validity, sometimes called the present-employee method, and predictive validity, sometimes known as the follow-up method. Both involve analysing the job to establish the person specification, described earlier. Suitable tests and measures are then selected based on this analysis. It is at this stage that much intuition and subjective judgement are usually used by personnel psychologists. For a responsible job involving considerable social skill and technical knowledge, for example, a lengthy procedure involving tests, interviews and group discussions may be required. For a less demanding position, a mechanical aptitude test or a work sample test may be all that is needed. The tests or measures are then administered and measures of job performance collected. Statistical procedures, typically correlations, are employed to provide validity coefficients for the criteria. It is quite rare to find validity coefficients greater than about 0.5, that is explaining only 25 percent of the variance and most researchers consider validities around 0.3 or 0.4 as acceptable (explaining 16 percent or less of the variance), though this depends on the selection ratio.

The difference between the concurrent and predictive validity methods is largely one of timing. With concurrent validity, measures of criterion performance are obtained around the same time as the test scores and on the same people. These people are *currently employed* by the organization. Predictive validity involves a rather longer time scale. The procedure is:

1. Test candidates for the job using the chosen measures.
2. Select candidates without using the results of the tests.
3. Obtain measures of criterion performance at some later date.
4. Calculate the predictor-criterion relationship.

The advantages of the concurrent validity method is that it is quick. One does not have to wait around for at least six months, and often much longer, before criterion data can be collected. This advantage means that it is by far the more common method in practice in organizations. Management usually wants to evaluate selection methods and to effect changes immediately, and so wants to have the results straight away, not in a year's time. Yet the predictive validity model is much superior methodologically. For one reason, the motivation of the testees is different in the two methods. In the concurrent case, they are already employed and so are taking the tests for research purposes. They are likely to have different motivation, perhaps being less keen to do their best, when compared with testees in the predictive validity case. The latter testees are *candidates*, and so likely to have similar test-taking attitudes to those on whom the methods will later be used, assuming acceptable validity coefficients are obtained. Secondly, present employees have experience of the job which candidates do not have and which may affect test results. This can be crucial. Imagine how much more knowledgeable and skilled a person is after having done the job for a year or so, compared with before they were taken on. This knowledge or skill may well be picked up by test results. The resulting correlation between test score and criterion performance may have been very different without this source of contamination. Thirdly, in the concurrent study we have no results on those who have left the organization. If those who remain are representative of those who have left on our predictor scores, then it may not matter too much. Perhaps, though, the "best" or "worst" employees have left. Such restriction of range (the loss of employees at the two extremes) will affect the predictor-criterion relationship. So, it should be obvious why the predictive validity model is to be preferred.

Validity generalization

Since 1980 there has been a sea-change in the field of validity. This has been brought about by meta-analysis and validity generalization analysis.

Meta-analysis is a method of pooling the results of a large number of separate research studies, so as to estimate the validity coefficients based on samples of thousands, not the 50 or 70 of a typical individual study.

Early work using meta-analysis by Ghiselli (1966) and others in the 1970s were taken to show that the validities for selection techniques were a feeble correlation of around 0.2 or 0.3, ranging from 0.05 for personality questionnaires to around 0.35 for cognitive abilities (see Table 8.1).

TABLE 8.1
Comparison of Validity Coefficients for Training and Proficiency Criteria by Type of Test

Type of test	Mean Validity Training	Coefficient Proficiency	No. of pairs of coefficients
Intellectual abilities	.35	.19	38
Spatial and mechanical abilities	.36	.20	28
Perceptual accuracy	.26	.23	15
Motor abilities	.18	.17	24
Personality traits	.05	.08	2
All tests	.30	.19	107

Adapted from Ghiselli (1966)

Traditional wisdom was that even these poor validity coefficients were suspect. Much depended on the specific organization in which the job was performed. The standard recommendation in occupational psychology text-books was to revalidate the methods in every organization in which they were used.

So, although meta-analyses were extremely useful in validity studies, they still left a confused and rather depressing picture. However, it now seems that these earlier views were far too pessimistic and that validities are higher than the measly figures gathered by Ghiselli. Moreover, it seems as if these validities are fairly stable across similar occupations, especially where cognitive abilities are being tested. This change of heart has come about by taking into account the limitations of a typical validity study. Schmidt, Hunter and others (eg Schmidt and Hunter, 1981; Schmidt *et al*, 1985) have shown that the earlier observed differences in validities in different organizations can be explained by sampling error due to small sample size, differences between studies in criterion reliability and restriction of range on the predictor.

1. *Sampling error.* The typical validity study tests a small sample (around 68 on average). Correlations calculated on small samples are very unstable, meaning reported correlations can vary widely.
2. *Criterion reliability.* As we have seen earlier in this chapter, criterion measures can vary in reliability. This will cause variations in validity coefficients. Uncorrected validities of tests results can never exceed the reliability coefficient.
3. *Restricted range.* Validities ought to be calculated from a sample of applicants. In practice, they are based on *successful* applicants. This restricts the range, because only applicants with good scores on the selection techniques are employed, which depresses the correlation with the criterion. Range restriction varies from study to study causing further variations in validity coefficients.

Validity generalization analysis is a complex process. It estimates how much error variance in a sample of validity coefficient these sources of error *could* account for, then compares this estimate with the actual variance (variation about the mean) to see if there is any "residual variance" left to explain. If residual variance is zero, then the hypothesis of situational specificity can be rejected. Validity generalization analysis also corrects mean validity for test and criterion unreliability, and restriction of range, to find estimated mean true validity. The validity of cognitive ability tests can easily rise from an uncorrected mean validity coefficient of 0.20 to a "true" validity of 0.75 when corrected for these errors. Meta-analysis in the area of validity generalization has truly revolutionized our picture of personnel selection methods.

These fundings imply that the validity of a test, for example, is much less situationally specific than has been thought, and it is not necessary to repeat a validity study where there is validity information on the same or similar test in a similar job. Simply put, most tests are valid in most situations. The crucial question becomes, "is the job similar?", which in turn leads to the concept of job families (Pearlman, 1980) and an emphasis on job analysis and job classification techniques.

Work on validity generalization has led to a revival of interest in the concept of synthetic **validity** (eg Hamilton and Dickinson, 1987). Synthetic validity can be defined as:

1. Inferring the validity in a specific situation by analysing jobs into their elements
2. Determining the test validity for these elements
3. Combining validities for each element into a whole.

So, there is a key difference between validity generalization and synthetic validity. Validity generalization refers to the transportability of validity results to similar jobs within or across organizations. It is the whole job which is of concern. Synthetic validity refers to the transportability of validity for specific job elements or components. It is most useful in situations where sample sizes are too small to conduct a validity study, or in situations where the job content changes rapidly, or in new jobs for which there are no workers as yet.

PREDICTORS: THE TOOLS OF SELECTION

Selection is fundamentally concerned with the prediction of job performance. In order to decide whether to select or reject an applicant for a job, we need to have information upon which to base the decision. Dozens of methods have been used. They range from palmreading or astrology, which we can dismiss for selection purposes, through graphology (hand-writing analysis) which is of very doubtful usefulness (Klimoski and Rafaeli, 1983) to climbing mountains and building bridges. The many and various ways of gathering data on candidates are often grouped under the heading of predictors. All aim to predict future behaviour. As we will see, some are better than others at this task. And some are more popular than others. Shackleton and Newell (1991) conducted a survey of methods used by large companies in Britain and France to select managers. In both countries, interviews were extremely popular, followed by psychometric tests. But there were some major differences between the two countries. France relied much more heavily on graphology, while Britain was more fond of references.

So let's look at some of the most popular tools of selection.

Application Forms and Biographical Data

The function of an application form in selection is to gather biographical information relevant to the decision to accept or reject an applicant. Generally speaking, it does this job poorly. It is designed with little thought and used haphazardly. Often it is merely scanned before the interview to give the interviewer ideas for questions to ask. This is a pity, since research has shown that properly used it can be among the most reliable and valid of all selection instruments. To use it properly, one must design the application form to include questions that potentially predict job performance, or any other work behaviour that is considered important. The application form items are then item analysed, which involves computing correlations between each item and a measure of job success. Where there is a significant correlation, the item can be used to select future candidates.

One version of this method is a **Weighted Application Blank** (WAB) where specific items are given weights based on their relationship to criteria of job success.

Table 8.2   Long and Short-Tenure Office Employees

Application Form Items	Short-tenure group %	Long-tenure group %	Weight assigned to response
Address:			
With city	39	62	+2
Suburbs	50	36	−2
Age:			
20	35	8	−3
21–30	46	34	−1
31–35	7	10	0
36+	11	48	+3
Age of Children:			
Preschool or			
Public School	65	37	−3
High School			
or Older	35	63	+3

Adapted from Fleishman and Berniger (1960)
Totals not always 100% due to missing data or rounding errors.

Table 8.2 gives an example of an early weighted application form study by Fleishman and Berniger (1960). There were two criterion groups of female office employees, a long-tenure group (those who stayed with the organization for more than two years) and a short-tenure group (those who left within two years). Three clusters of items predicted tenure. These were address, the age of the employee and the age of her children (although the latter two are obviously correlated). Weights were assigned according to item analysis, with items not predicting tenure given a zero weight. The correlation between overall score on the items and tenure was 0.57. The table shows clearly that a "good risk" from the organizations's point of view are applicants living within the city who are 35 or older and have children old enough to be in secondary school. It is important in studies like these that the results are cross-validated on a new sample (as Fleishman and Berniger did) to check that the results are generalizable.

However, there are problems with this method. One is the intensely practical one of using such findings to offer a job to one candidate rather than another. Just because there are group differences doesn't mean that findings will apply to specific individuals. There are undoubtedly large overlaps between groups. So it is difficult to justify making a decision about *one* candidate purely on the basis of a statistical relationship with a *group* of candidates. Secondly, there are ethical problems. Suppose that the statistics showed differences according to race or sex. Should we use the findings and so discriminate in favour of one group? One answer is to seek other predictors and other criteria apart from just biographical data but the issue of fairness in selection is one to which we shall return. Thirdly, empirically derived weights tend to be specific to the situation in which they were developed. So a set of weights may predict life insurance sales peoples' performance but not that of computer sales people. Finally, the method cannot be placed in any theoretical background and so the reasons for its predictive successes are not always evident. The classic WAB was based on simply analysing the application form (or "blank"). Its advantage is that it is cheap and quick to complete and generally yields honest answers, which in any case can often be verified. Its use is based on the well-accepted tenet of psychology that past behaviour predicts future behaviour.

Since the 1960s the classic WAB has given way to biodata (also known as Life History Data). This uses a questionnaire format with multiple-choice answers but again largely based on "biographical data" items. Biodata has been used successfully to predict a range of jobs including scientists, researchers, bus drivers, police officers, and sales staff. Lots of evidence suggest it is among the best predictors, with meta-analysis showing validities above 0.30 and sometimes around 0.40. Moreover, biodata validities can generalize across major job families and may not be specific to particular organizations (Rothstein *et al*, 1990). As with the WAB, *why* biodata predicts isn't always clear. However, there have been attempts to relate life history data to future performance, notably in the assessment centre context which go beyond more item analysis and attempt a more theoretical approach to biodata. Owens and Schoenfeldt (1979) have provided explanations of the predictive nature of biodata, and Drakeley (1989) a useful review of the topic. As yet, though, theory is lacking.

A variation on biodata, known as the "accomplishment record" has been developed by Hough (1984). The method is based on self-reported descriptions of past accomplishments, which are matched with job-related dimensions of behaviour. Correlating scores with job performance gave validity coefficients of 0.23. Hough claims that the resulting scores are not related to traditional measures of aptitude, and so may be adding unique information to the selection process.

The Interview

A series of reviews of the psychological literature concerned with selection interviews has appeared at regular intervals over the last 40–50 years. Each has come to largely the same conclusions. The interview, as it is normally carried out, has poor reliability and validity. Reliability here refers to how consistent is the information obtained on a candidate. The conclusion is that the interview has poor inter-rater reliability, that is, different interviewers arrive at different judgements about a candidate. Moreover, because the interview is so unreliable, whatever it is supposed to measure it cannot be measuring with any validity. A wide range of criteria has been used in the case of the interview including absenteeism, leaving rates, success in training and measures of performance such as supervisors' ratings or amount of sales. Generally they have been shown to be very poorly predicted by interviews. Meta-analysis of typical unstructured interviews demonstrates that their validity rarely rises above 0.20 (eg Wiesner & Cronshaw, 1988).

Why is the typical selection interview unreliable? Summaries of the literature show that there are a number of reasons:

(a) In unstructured interviews, material is not consistently covered and interviewers wander from one half covered point to another.

(b) Interviewers are unable to reliably and validly assess traits other than intelligence (which anyway is much more cheaply, easily, reliably and validly measured by tests).

(c) Interviewers are influenced more by unfavourable than by favourable information about a candidate.

(d) Interviewers do not reliably agree on what is favourable or unfavourable information.

(e) Interviewers tend to make up their mind about a candidate early in the interview, before they have much information. This is after as little as four minutes (Anderson and Shackleton, 1990). They then seek information consistent with their first impressions and decisions.

(f) Interviewers weight the same information differently in arriving at a decision.

(g) Interviewers' evaluations are influenced by situational factors such as contrast (ie. the quality of previous candidates) as well as by personal feelings, the race, sex and nonverbal communication of the interviewee.

Yet there is a hopeful side to this dismal picture. In some situations with some interviewers, the interview is reasonably valid. Reliable and valid interviews are more likely when:

1. The interviewer is trained, is familiar with the job and uses the person specification as a guide.

2. The interview has a structure or plan.

3. There are a number of interviewers, such as with board or panel interviews, or sequential interviews by a number of individuals.

4. Interviewer ratings are combined with other information (eg. from tests) using a statistical predictor model rather than a subjective, clinical "impressionistic" model.

5. The interview is used to assess specific factors, such as personal relations (the ability to "get along with people") and the motivation to work.

Unfortunately, these conditions are rarely found in current practice.

Structure is particularly important. A high degree of structure improves the interview considerably, especially when accompanied by formal job analysis and mechanical scoring systems. Meta-analysis shows estimated validities of 0.39 (Wright et al, 1989). However, structured interviews move the interview process firmly into the camp of other psychometric instruments and away from the negotiation and exchange view of the interview, mentioned earlier.

An interesting innovation has been the development of situational interviews (Lathan and Saari, 1984). These use the results of job analyses to produce job-related incidents. The incidents are then turned into interview questions in which candidates are asked to say how they would behave in the incident or situation described. Although only a small amount of research has yet been published on this method, what has been reported shows validity coefficients of up to 0.35.

References

Another very common source of data on an applicant is a reference report, usually requested from a previous employer. Because previous behaviour is a good predictor of future behaviour, we might expect references to be a useful and valid aid in selection. Unfortunately, this is not so. One problem is leniency. Reference reports are rarely even slightly negative. Some of the reasons for this are that employers are reluctant to commit negative evaluations to paper and that, in some cases, they are delighted at the prospect of getting a poor employee off their hands and so don't want to put a prospective new employer off. But leniency is not the only difficulty with references. A second problem is their lack of reliability. Reviews of the literature have found that reliability coefficients rarely exceeded 0.40 and Muchinsky (1979) concluded his review by noting that references are poor selection devices. Similarly, Reilly and Chao (1982) reviewed evidence on the validity of references. They found average correlations of 0.18 with rating criteria and 0.08 with turnover. The average validity was 0.14. They concluded that reference reports have low validity in employment settings.

Yet, if used differently references could be useful. One way is to structure the reference report around specific question areas, such as time-keeping or honesty. Alternatively, telephone references instead of written ones can be used, to allow probing by the questioner so that they begin to reflect well conducted interviews. Yet, just like the interview, the unreliable, invalid, unstructured reference form continues to be a favourite method among selectors.

Tests

Tests, even more than interviews, have occupied centre stage as assessment techniques in the field of individual differences. Along with biographical information, psychological tests as selection devices are generally smiled upon by applied psychologists. The reason for this is the same as the reasons for distrusting references and interviews, namely on the grounds of reliability and validity. Research has shown that many tests are good predictors of performance in jobs. Cognitive abilities in particular show acceptable validities. Hunter and Hunter (1984) found an average validity of 0.49 for cognitive tests. Personality measures generally show lower validities, and therefore some psychologists argue that they should not be used in selection (see *Personnel Management*, September 1991, for a debate on this issue).

Personality measures are less suitable for selection than ability tests for another reason, and that is faking. When being selected for a job, candidates naturally want to appear at their best. Not only are they likely to put on their smartest clothes and most radiant smile, but they are also motivated to portray a favourable image when tested. This means faking the results in the direction believed appropriate. Faking is no problem for the selection psychologist with test of intelligence and aptitude, since it is impossible to "fake good". You can either do the question or you can't. But with questions of typical or preferred behaviour, such as interest and personality questionnaires, it is quite possible to paint a particular picture of yourself which may not be typical. Moreover, there is evidence that candidates *do* fake.

It should be noted that many studies quote figures relating to single tests given to predict specific outcomes. Yet tests are often used in combination with one another in a test battery. There are various ways of using the battery, but one common way is to require a candidate to obtain an acceptable mark in all the component tests. This can increase the predictive validity of tests considerably.

Work samples

This involves a candidate in performing tasks which have a direct relevance to the job in question. Sometimes they are small parts of the job the applicant will perform if selected. There are a number of different types of work sample tests. One type is psychomotor, involving such tasks as sewing or assembling components. Another is situational, such as the In-Tray or In-Basket exercise. Here the applicant must work through a series of tasks similar to those of a manager's, including answering letters, arranging meetings, making decisions under time-pressure, and so on. A third type is group discussion, where groups of approximately six candidates discuss an issue, watched and assessed by observers. All the methods aim at throwing light on the skills, abilities and temperament considered important for the job.

Although they are costly, the validity of work samples and situational tests tends to be high when compared with alternative methods (see the review by Robertson and Kandola, 1982, for example). Schmitt *et al.* (1984) report an average validity coefficient of 0.38 in 18 studies over the eighteen-year period, 1964–82.

Assessment Centres

So far, we have considered methods of gathering data on candidates one at a time. However, it is well accepted in selection psychology that multiple assessment methods are superior to one technique alone. Assessment centres (they are methods, not places) are attempts to combine a number of methods to achieve better predictive validities. They were first used by the German military in the 1930s for choosing potential officers. The British War Office Selection Board borrowed and developed the technique in the 1940s for the same purpose and the US Office of Strategic Services used it to select secret agents during the Second World War.

The method was essentially abandoned after the war until adopted by American Telegraph and Telephone (AT&T) in the 1950s who launched its ambitious

Management Progress Study of the careers of more than 400 young executives (Bray *et al.* 1974). This longitudinal study was the largest and most comprehensive investigation of managerial career development ever undertaken. Its purpose was to attempt to understand what factors are important to the career progress of employees as they move up through the organizational hierarchy.

Selected recruits spent three-and-a-half days at an assessment centre run each year from 1956 onwards by trained assessors. They were rated on 25 dimensions using a variety of techniques. Additionally, yearly information was collected from the men's companies and from the men themselves. No information about any man's progress at the assessment centre was ever passed to their companies, which meant no contamination of the subsequent criterion data by the assessment results. Criterion data included management level and current salary.

When the initial results were made available in 1965, Bray and his colleagues found the reliability and validity of the assessment centre predictions to be high. Of the 125 college men and 144 non-college men included in the sample, 58 had been promoted to middle management positions. Of the college men who had been promoted, the assessment centre staff had correctly identified 82 percent. Similarly, 75 percent of the promoted non-college men had been correctly identified. Of the 72 men who had not been promoted, the assessment centre had correctly identified 94 percent. These were very encouraging findings.

Not surprisingly, therefore, the method spread rapidly, particularly in the USA. In Britain, assessment centre use is mostly confined to large organizations but is slowly becoming more generally popular. While assessment centres usually concentrate on identifying management potential or talent, they have been used for several other purposes as well. These include selection of non-managers, promotion, placement and career development (Shackleton, 1992). A review of the published literature by Gaugler *et al.* (1987) confirmed that assessment centres are generally useful in predicting management potential and future performance, as well as other outcomes. Yet Gaugler and her colleagues showed that they are not equally valid for all purposes. They seemed to be most successful when used for the early identification of managerial talent, as in the AT&T studies. They were least successful when used to determine who should be promoted. In addition, assessment centres were more successful in predicting future potential than in predicting ratings of current job performance. Lastly, they were more successful when trained professionals, such as psychologists, served as assessors, rather than colleagues, managers or supervisors.

Although research suggests that an assessment centre can be a useful technique, giving valid and practical outcomes, they are not without problems. They are expensive to set up and run, and negative ratings, if revealed to participants, can have a very demotivating effect. Properly designed and handled, though, they are a very useful selection tool.

SELECTION FAIRNESS

An issue which has occupied the minds of many personnel specialists, particularly in the USA, over the last 20 years has been the topic of fairness or bias in selection procedures.

In one sense, the issue of fairness has always been with us. We pointed out at the beginning of the chapter that selection is about choosing on the basis of predictions. Since the methods, however rigorously developed and applied, are unlikely ever to give perfect prediction, they will be unfair to those who would have succeeded in the job had we not predicted they would fail and so rejected them. Yet the issue of fairness is much more than that. The suggestion is that selection methods, principally tests, may unfairly discriminate against particular groups such as women or ethnic minorities. The effect is known in the USA as "adverse impact", meaning that minority groups are not selected at the same rate as majority groups. If a subgroup is rejected on grounds which are not relevant to performance on the job, indirect discrimination may be occurring.

In Britain, discrimination in recruitment and selection, as well as in other personnel areas, is illegal under the terms of the Sex Discrimination Act of 1975 and the Race Relations Act, 1976. Both Acts make "direct" and "indirect" discrimination on grounds of gender or race illegal. Indirect discrimination is defined as applying a requirement or condition, whether intentional or not, which affects adversely a larger proportion of one race or gender than another, and which cannot be justified as job-relevant. Unjustifiable height or clothing regulations are examples (see Shackleton, 1989, for others).

Studies following the 1976 Race Relations Act have continued to show evidence of racial discrimination in personnel selection. One example showed many more black applicants than whites with similar experience and qualifications not invited for interviews for a range of white collar and skilled manual jobs. On the positive side, many organizations have firmly adopted equal opportunities policies, and evaluate these by the recommended methods of ethnic or gender monitoring.

Concerning the selection procedures themselves, much of the research in the USA has focused on the validity of selection instruments and their impact on different subgroups. Recent research has not upheld the earlier blanket view that tests lead to unfair discrimination. Most validity coefficients are not significantly different across subgroups. Assessment centres, self assessments and work samples seem to have the best combination of moderate or high validity combined with small subgroup differences. Ability and cognitive tests offer a combination of moderate validity and moderate subgroup differences.

The implications of this research is clear. Valid methods, including tests, should be used, especially if the alternative is sole reliance on interviews or other methods with low validity. And shortlisting and interviewing procedures should be improved through training, to make selection criteria more job relevant.

COMPUTER-ASSISTED RECRUITMENT AND SELECTION

Increasingly, microcomputers are being used to save staff time in the recruitment and selection process. Some software packages attempt to help handle virtually the whole administration from logging responses to advertisements, sending out application forms, screening applicants on selected criteria, administering tests and sending out letters of job offer or rejection. The computer can collate all the information from application forms, references, test scores, exercises, interview reports and give it due weight without lapses of memory, fatigue, boredom or distortion through prejudice As far as personnel psychologists are concerned, the computer's greatest impact in selection has been in computer-assisted testing (CAT) (see French, 1986, for a discussion). It is a topic which is likely to grow both in extent and in controversy, since CAT has its committed advocates and its hardened sceptics.

Most CAT packages are software versions of existing paper tests, since computers are ideal for the routine administration, scoring and interpreting of such tests. A typical software system enables a recruiter to choose a specific battery of ability and personality tests for a target job, administers the tests on-screen to the candidate, scores them, loads the resulting scores into a database to build norms for this job in this organization, and prints out a report.

In addition, the computer enables testing that is difficult or impossible to do by traditional means. They offer the possibility of new tests measuring abilities not reliably measured before. The most obvious application stems from making tests dynamic. Computer graphics allow test items to move, rotate, fade, change colour, and so on. One system, used to select aircraft pilots, shows moving displays and gives direct feedback on decisions the candidate has made.

Adaptive testing is another area which will continue to greatly benefit from the computer. Adaptive testing is a form of ability testing where only relevant items offering maximum assessment information are presented. The testee answers just a few questions, which, depending on which ones and how many were right or wrong, allows the computer to home in on the intellectual level of the individual being tested, adapting its questions to the individual concerned. It then concentrates its questions on this narrow intellectual band to arrive at a final text score. In this way, lengthy testing with bored or frustrated candidates is eliminated. Such branching and fine tuning of questions would be virtually impossible without the computer's ability to hold hundreds of questions in memory, and select just those required with speed and accuracy. Adaptive testing has so far been confined to large users of ability tests, such as the armed forces. But it has considerable potential for wider use in the future (see Bartram, 1989, for further information).

Finally, even on the more traditional form of tests, computers can process more responses than simply recording the answer given. Measures of speed of response, difficulties in reading, conservatism, alignment errors and guessing are all far more simply gathered in the normal process of testing by computer than they are by paper and pencil methods.

In the early days of CAT, concerns were expressed that computerized tests would not necessarily have the same validities as their paper and pencil versions, or that candidates would object to the "impersonal" nature of computerized tests. These fears have proved to be largely groundless. Reviews of the literature have mostly agreed on the following points:

1. Computerized tests tend to correlate highly with the paper versions, and are as valid.
2. Testees are not averse to CAT if it is well presented.
3. Standardization and control of administration are increased.
4. Costs can be reduced by up to 50 percent, especially in the case of adaptive testing.

Although computerized versions of tests correlate highly and seem to be as valid as paper and pencil ones, there is still the problem of equivalence. That is, the scores may not be equivalent in the interpretations that can be made from them. The computer version usually needs to be renormed, especially for ability tests where speed of response is critical. Moreover, if there are different displays or response methods on different machines, scores may change again, necessitating new norms. This is a tedious and time-consuming process.

UTILITY ANALYSIS

At the beginning of this chapter we talked about good recruitment and selection as benefitting both job holder and employing organization. The claim that spending money on good recruitment is money well spent can be shown empirically to be true by the technique known as utility analysis. Utility analysis can be defined as the process which involves describing, predicting and explaining the usefulness or desirability of decision options, and analysing how that information can be used in decision making. It allows us to calculate the consequences of decisions (concerning recruitment, selection, training or control of labour turnover, for example) on performance-related outcomes (such as sales, benefits or reduced costs).

So utility models are a decision aid. In the context of recruitment and selection, the method allows a cost-benefit analysis of different selection procedures to be estimated financially. Early work by Schmidt *et al*, (1982) provided equations which give a direct monetary value of a selection system. This is:

Monetary value   = average length of service of employees (years)
               × difference in job performance between selected versus non-selected employees
               × the standard deviation of job performance in dollars of the unselected group

The *net* monetary value can be obtained relatively simply by subtracting the costs of selection. It is the final part of this equation, how to calculate one standard deviation in criterion levels of performance (usually known as SDy), which has proved difficult and controversial. Note, though, that utility analysis focuses on the decision of whether or not to install a new selection procedure, rather than on a decision about each applicant. It allows us to calculate the costs and benefits of, for example, a testing programme for clerical staff or an assessment centre for managerial selection, rather than whether this clerk or this manager is worth taking on. Implementing a new selection procedure is of benefit to an organization if it increases the correctness of the decision to accept a candidate in ways that more than offset the costs of the new procedure.

There are lots of different models of selection utility but Boudreau (1989) points out that each takes account of three main attributes. These are quantity, quality and cost.

1. Quantity reflects the quantity of employees recruited and the time period affected by the selection programme.
2. Quality reflects the consequences (per person and per time period) associated with the programme.
3. Cost reflects the resources of time, money and people needed to implement and maintain the programme.

The financial outcome, or payoff, from the selection programme is calculated by taking the product of Quantity and Quality and then subtracting Cost.

Until recently, psychologists have mostly concentrated on the Quality component, with an emphasis on mean predictor scores of selected individuals, research studies of predictor validity and standard deviation of performance. Boudreau notes that this can underestimate the utilities by not giving sufficient attention to the number of employees selected and their average length of tenure (the "number of time periods affected"). However, including the quantity component of the model makes important assumptions (Sackett, 1989). These are:

1. Multiplying utility per selectee per time period by the average number of time periods an employee stays at the job assumes that the standard deviation of performance, SDy, remains constant across these time periods. One possibility is that variability increases over time. While both high and low performers benefit from training and experience, high performers might benefit more, so increasing the SDy. If performance variability increases, treating it as a constant produces a conservative utility estimate. Conversely, if variability decreases, treating it as a constant inflates the utility estimate.
2. Multiplying utility per person per time period by the number of time periods affected assumes that validity remains constant over time. Because a test correlates 0.40 with first year performance doesn't necessarily mean that it will correlate 0.40 in ten year's time, if ten years is the average tenure.
3. Multiplying utility per selectee per time period by the number of time periods affected assumes that there is no systematic relationship between turnover and performance. If the average tenure of high performers differs from that of low performers, utility estimates will be inaccurate. Evidence on whether this happens in practice is mixed. A review of the literature by Jackofsky (1984) showed some studies reporting higher turnover among high performers, others showing higher turnover among low performers, and others showing no difference. This suggests that automatically assuming no performance-turnover relationship in any situation may be misleading.

The *costs* of selection procedures including pay, training, retraining, absenteeism, interview time, test materials, etc. can be relatively easy to calculate. Some costs are harder to estimate, though, such as the opportunity cost of not hiring a good applicant who performs excellently for a competitor or the costs of a poor public image through inefficient or unfair selection procedures. Similarly, some benefits may be easy to calculate, such as sales revenue or number of items produced, but generally benefits are more difficult to calculate. This is because one is trying to estimate the worth of an individual's performance, when there is often no direct relationship between performance and financial benefits.

There have been numerous attempts at measuring an employee's worth to the organization. Some use an individualised estimation technique which converts some measurable characteristic of each individual in the sample, such as pay or sales activity, into money using average salary or average sales. One example of this technique is CREPID, the Cascio-Ramos Estimate of Performance in Dollars (Cascio and Ramos, 1986). This method breaks a job into its important "principal activities". Then each activity is rated on four dimensions (time/frequency, level of difficulty, importance and consequence of error). The ratings are multiplied to give an overall weight to the activity. The proportion of total weights becomes the final importance weight assigned to each activity. To assign a monetary value (say dollars) to each activity, average salary earned in the job is divided among the activities according to their weights. Once this "job analysis" phase is complete, supervisors are asked to rate employees' performance on each principal activity, using a 0 to 2 scale. These ratings are then multiplied by the dollar value of that activity so that each employee has a dollar value for each activity. These activity values are summed to give the total money value for the yearly performance for that employee.

A more simple approach to individualised estimation involves asking supervisors to directly assign monetary values to each employee, based on their performance. Ledvinka *et al*, (1983), for example, used total payroll plus benefits divided by the number of insurance claims as the value per claim, and then multiplied this value by the standard deviation of claims processed.

The problem with individualised estimation methods is that they make certain basic assumptions which may not be supported in practice. CREPID is based on the assumption that the average wage equals the average productivity, which will not hold true in organizations with pay systems based on rank, or tenure based systems where earnings are based on length of time in the job or many hourly-paid wage systems. Sales-based methods assume that sales are an accurate reflection of performance differences. This ignores the importance of certain tasks, such as training, which reduce an individual's sales but increase sales in the group as a whole.

Some researchers have cut through the difficulty and complexity of methods such as individualised estimation by suggesting proportional rules. This method involves multiplying average salary in a job by some proportion of that salary (say 40 percent or 6Q percent) to derive the SDy estimate.

Hunter and Schmidt (1982) reviewed empirical studies and concluded that the average for SDy fell somewhere in the range of 40 percent to 70 percent of average salary. They recommend a conservative estimate for SDy of 40 percent of mean salary, in virtually all situations. A later review of 64 utility studies (Boudreau, 1989) revealed 17 SDy estimates below 40 percent of salary, 18 estimates within the 40 to 70 percent range and 29 estimates above 70 percent of salary. These results therefore broadly support the conservative Hunter and Schmidt decision rule. However, the proportional rule approach may produce such conservative estimates that new selection systems or other human resource programmes will not be undertaken. These programmes might have had considerable financial benefits if their utilities had been more accurately measured.

So is it worth investing in selection methods with higher validities (such as structured interviews) rather than those with lower ones (such as unstructured interviews)? The answer from utility analysis is a resounding Yes. Boudreau (1989) reviewed empirical studies with 39 different utility values. Virtually every study produced financial outcomes that clearly exceeded costs. In every case the more valid selection procedure, although more costly to implement, produced the greater utility. The largest utility values are in those cases where large numbers of individuals are affected by the selection programme. Studies dealing with many employees can produce utility values of $20 to $30 million.

Even using conservative estimates, selection utility analysis research has shown that large utility values are obtained. Virtually every study has shown positive, and often extremely large, payoffs from investing in effective selection systems. Almost always, using a more valid selection technique is worth the extra costs. And it discriminates more fairly, which, you will remember, is what personnel recruitment and selection is all about.

REFERENCES

Anderson, N. & Shackleton, V.J. (1990). Decision-making in the graduate selection interview: A Field Study. *Journal of Occupational Psychology.* 63 (1), 63–76.

Bartram, D. (1989). Computer-based assessment; in P. Herriot (Ed) *Assessment and Selection in Organisations.* Wiley.

Boudreau, J.W. (1989). Selection utility analysis: A review and agenda for future research; in M. Smith & I.T. Robertson (Eds) *Advances in Selection and Assessment.* Wiley.

Bray, D.W., Campbell, R.J. & Grant, D.L. (1974). *Formative Years in Business: A long-term AT&T study of managerial lives.* New York: Wiley.

Cascio, W.F. & Ramos, R. (1986). Development and application of a new method for assessing job performance in behavioural/economic terms. *Journal of Applied Psychology,* 71, 20–28.

Drakeley, R.J. (1989). Biographical data; in P. Herriot (Ed) *Assessment and Selection in Organizations,* Wiley.

Fleishman, E.A. & Berniger, I. (1960). One Way to Reduce Office Turnover. *Personnel,* 37, 63–69.

French, C.C. (1986). Microcomputers and psychometric assessment. *British Journal of Guidance and Counselling,* 14, 33–45.

Fyfe, J. & Hornby, P. (1988). Manpower planning and development; in E. Sidney (Ed) *Managing Recruitment,* Gower.

Gaugler, B.B, Rosenthal, D.B. Thornton, G.C. & Bentson, C. (1987). Meta-analysis of assessment centre validity. *Journal of Applied Psychology,* 72, 493–511.

Ghiselli, E.E. (1966). *The validity of occupational aptitude tests.* New York: Wiley.

Hamilton, J.W. & Dickinson, T.L. (1987). Comparison of several procedures for generating J-coefficient. *Journal of Applied Pscyhology,* 72, 49–54.

Herriot, P. (1989). Selection as a Social Process; in M. Smith & I.T. Robertson (Eds) *Advances in Selection and Assessment,* Wiley.

Hough, L.M. (1984). Development and evaluation of the "Accomplishment Record" method of selecting and promoting professionals. *Journal of Applied Psychology,* 69, 135–146.

Hunter, J.E. & Hunter, R.F. (1984). Validity and utility of alternative predictors of job performance. *Psychological Bulletin,* 96 (1), 72–98.

Hunter, J.E. & Schmidt, F.L. (1982). Fitting people in jobs: the impact of personnel selection on national productivity. In M.D. Dunnette & E.A. Fleishman (Eds), *Human Performance and Productivity,* Vol 1, Hillsdale, N.J., Erlbaum.

Jackofsky, E.F. (1984). Turnover and job performance: an integrated model. *Academy of Management Review,* 9, 74–83.

Klimoski, R.J. & Rafaeli, A. (1983). Inferring personal qualities through handwriting analysis. *Journal of Occupational Psychology,* 56, 191–202.

Lathan, G.P. & Saari, L.M. (1984). So people do what they say? Further studies on the situational interview. *Journal of Applied Psychology,* 69, 569–573.

Ledvinka, J., Simonet, J.K., Neiner, A.G. & Kruse, B. (1983). The dollar value of JEPS at Life of Georgia. Unpublished technical report.

Muchinsky, P.M. (1979). The use of reference reports in personnel selection: a review and evaluation. *Journal of Occupational Psychology,* 52, 287–97.

Owens, W.A. & Schoenfeldt, L.F. (1979). Towards a classification of persons. *Journal of Applied Psychology,* 64, 569–607.

Pearlman, K. (1980). Job families: A review and discussion of their implications for personnel selection. *Psychological Bulletin,* 87, 1–28.

Pearn, M. & Kandola, R. (1988). *Job Analysis: A practical guide for managers.* Institute of Personnel Management: London.

Robertson, I.T. & Kandola, R.S. (1982). Work sample tests: validity, adverse impact and applicant reaction. *Journal of Occupational Psychology,* 55, 171–183.

Reilly, R.R. & Chao, G.T. (1982). Validity and fairness of some alternative selection procedures. *Personnel Psychology,* **35,** 1–62.

Rothstein, H.R., Schmitt, F.L., Erwin, F.W., Owens, W.A. & Sparks, C.P. (1990). Biographical data in employment selection: Can validities be made generalizable? *Journal of Applied Psychology,* **75,** 175–184.

Sackett, P.R. (1989). Comment on selection utility analysis; in M. Smith & I.T. Robertson (Eds) *Advances in Selection Assessment,* Wiley.

Schmidt, F.L. & Hunter, J.E. (1981). Employment testing: Old theories and new research findings. *American Psychologist,* **36,** 1128–1137.

Schmidt, F.L., Hunter, J.E. & Pearlman, K. (1982). Assessing the economic impact of personnel programs on workforce productivity. *Journal of Applied Psychology,* **35,** 333–347.

Schmidt, F.L., Hunter, J.E., Pearlman, K. & Hirsh, H.R. (1985). Forty questions about validity generalization and meta-analysis. *Personnel Psychology,* **38,** 697–798.

Shackleton, V.J. (1989). *How to Pick People for Jobs,* Fontana.

Shackleton, V.J. (1992). Using a competency approach in a business change setting; in R. Boam & P. Sparrow (Eds) *Designing and Achieving Competency: A Competency Based Approach to Developing People and Organizations.* London: McGraw Hill.

Shackleton, V.J. & Newell, S. (1991). Management selection: A comparative survey of methods used in top British and French companies. *Journal of Occupational Psychology,* **64,** 23–36.

Wiesner, W.H. & Cronshaw, S.F. (1988). A meta-analytic investigation of the impact of interview format and degree of structure on the validity of the employment interview. *Journal of Occupational Psychology,* **61,** 275–289.

Wright, P.M., Lichtenfels, P.A. & Pursell, E.D. (1989). The structured interview: Additional studies and a meta-analysis. *Journal of Occupational Psychology,* **62,** 191–199.

9

ASSESSMENT AND APPRAISAL

P. HERRIOT

INTRODUCTION

In the previous chapter, Shackleton made two very important points. First, we cannot look at human resource systems such as selection or appraisal in isolation; we have to see them in their organisational context, and, in turn, the organisation within the environmental context. Second, we cannot take a solely managerialist point of view – we cannot look at selection or appraisal only from the perspective of the organisation's interests. We have to consider the individual's interests as well.

The importance of context cannot be over-emphasized. Individual instruments of assessment have to be seen in the context of the system of selection, appraisal, or reward of which they are part. Systems themselves cannot be analyzed in isolation from each other – whom you select has implications for how they are trained. And human resource strategies as a whole cannot be understood only in terms of how their systems relate to each other; they have to be integrated with the business strategy of the organisation. Finally, strategy doesn't occur in vacuum. It is in reaction to, or more rarely, in anticipation, of, environmental changes in the commercial, social, economic political and industrial environments.

My previous paragraph, however misses out the most important elements in organisations – people. The two dominant traditions in psychology have given us theories and methods to look at individuals first as individuals, and second in relation to each other and to organisations. The psychology of individual differences and their measurement enables us to assess individuals along a variety of dimensions; social and organisational psychology helps us understand relationships. One of the mistakes we have made in applying psychology in organisations is to over-emphasise the former tradition at the expense of the latter. Consequently, we know quite a lot about how organisations may assess individuals, but not so much about the relationship between individuals and organisations in the assessment setting. For example, what effects does assessment have on individuals? Who owns assessment data? To what purposes is it put, and with whose consent?

A final general issue is about the status of work in organisational psychology and human resource management. The dominant mode slips easily from descriptive analysis aimed at understanding what goes on in organisations to prescriptive accounts of "best practice"; from what is to what ought to be. This is particularly true in the area of assessment, where text-book recommendations and messy reality are often miles apart.

The present chapter is about assessment, a general process, and appraisal, a specific human resource system. Assessment can be of performance, long-term potential, suitability for a job or other things. It can be of an individual or a work-group. It can be made by top management, bosses, colleagues, subordinates, customers, psychologists, or by one self. It can provide information for decisions about selection, promotion, training, or rewards. As such, it is one of the basic processes through which the organisation manages its employees. The way in which it is used are a strong indication of an organisation's culture (of which more later).

Appraisal, on the other hand is a system. Just as a selection system has certain functions, so the appraisal system of an organisation is designed with certain functions in mind. It may serve to assess previous performance in order to allocate performance-related pay; to set performance objectives for the following year; to elicit training and development needs; to predict long-term potential; to discuss career. These functions fit in to an overall approach to human resources – a human resource strategy.

Business Trends

So we have clarified the chapter title. Let us return to our initial emphases; those of context, and of interests. Psychologists in the applied setting have always run the risk of becoming psycho-technologists; of being experts in one particular technology which is placed at management's disposal to achieve its ends. This is because psychometrics has been construed as the particular area of expertise to which psychologists have an exclusive claim. As a consequence, assessment, especially for selection purposes, has been a favourite area for psychologists. Historically, psychological testing and the study of individual differences has provided the technical basis for these applications.

However, technical competence in designing and using specific tools of assessment is not enough. There are many organisations which use certain technically excellent assessment tools which do not meet the organisation's current needs. Psychologists working in applied settings have to use a range of psychological theories and techniques. In particular, psychologists working in organisations need to understand their social psychology. Katz and Kahn's (1978) classic book on the subject is entitled "The *Social* Psychology of Organisations" (my emphasis).

So to understand the roles of assessment and appraisal, we have to look at the organisation which is their context, and also at the environment in which the organisation is operating. Let us bring the discussion down to less general terms, then, and consider the key current organisational trends. These are admirably reviewed by Kanter (1989), and may be summarised as follows:

- organisations are becoming more international
- alliances and mergers are more frequent
- successful organisations rely upon a few core competencies
- goods and services become rapidly obsolescent
- they have to be customised to meet the need of market segments
- knowledge is the key commodity, not finance, or plant

- competition is becoming keener, especially in new products and services
- responsibility for decisions is decentralised to local levels
- there are less levels in the organisational hierarchy.

Human Resource Strategy

All of these trends have implications for the human resource strategies which organisations need to employ. Given such corporate directions, what sort of people do organisations need, and what sort of systems do they require to manage them?

There are certain general expectations which organisations will have to make of their employees. They will want specialist skills and knowledge, and, more important, the willingness and capacity to keep them up to date. But they will also expect cooperation across the functions of the organisation; R and D people, designers, production people, marketers, salespeople and those who actually serve the customer or client all need to combine in developing new and innovative products and services. Organisations will expect decision makers at local level who understand all aspects of the business sufficiently well to manage their own budget; and they will want people to understand other cultures, both organisational and national, and work with them. Such will be the competition for scarce specialists that their attraction and retention will be a key issue. At the same time, the development of other staff to enable them to adapt as quickly as the rate of change itself will be a key requirement.

Over the last decade, organisations have begun to realise that their strategies for change have to be informed and supported by a human resource strategy (Fombrun, Tichy and Devanna, 1984). A recent survey (Brewster and Smith, 1990) showed that about 40 per cent of UK organisations have a written human resource strategy, compared with around 60 per cent which have a written corporate strategy. A human resource strategy addresses such questions as:

- in order to achieve our corporate strategic objectives, what sort of people do we need, in approximately what numbers?
- where will we get them from (from inside or outside the organisation?)
- how will we attract, retain, develop, and reward them?

The Human Resource Cycle

This last question implies the second basic requirement of an HR strategy. Not only must it serve and inform corporate strategy. It should also result in a coherent set of systems which are likely to help the organisation carry the strategy through. One configuration of systems, "The human resource cycle" suggested by Fombrun *et al.* (op cit), can be seen in Figure 9.1. The point to be made here is that this system of systems is designed as a whole. The purpose is to help the organisation achieve an improvement in its performance. In many organisations, systems have grown up in isolation from each other, by historical accident. Typically, a psychological consultant may have designed a state of the art assessment centre for selection purposes, while decisions about development are based on entirely ad hoc short-term considerations. The results of the assessment centre might well have been useful in helping the individual and organisation decide on his or her training and development needs. But

The Human Resource Cycle

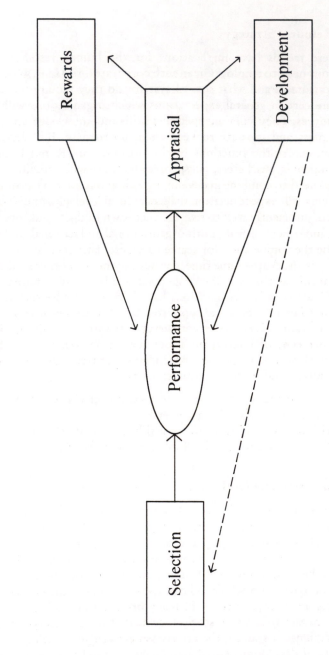

FIGURE 9.1 The Human Resource Cycle (from Fombrun, Ticby and Devanna, 1984)

its results were seen as relevant to selection only, and entirely different people, who don't communicate with each other, were probably in charge of the two systems (selection, and training and development).

The Psychological Contract

So the first point made in Chapter 4 of this volume – that any system has to be seen in its context – is of even more importance in the present decade. The second major point was that it is inappropriate to look at human resource systems solely from the organisation's point of view. Indeed, the whole idea of "using human resources" carries a certain connotation of people being like raw materials or financial resources. Of course, part of the initial impetus for the adoption of the term "human resources" rather than "personnel" was to emphasise how valuable people were, and how corporate plans had to include people as well as money.

The fact that employees have expectations of organisations as well as the converse has been nicely captured by Argyris (1960) in the idea of the *psychological contract*. This concept suggests that the employment relationship is not only characterised by a formal employment contract, but also by a series of usually unwritten and often even unspoken understandings. For example, until the last decade, the expectation of bank employees was of a job for life, and the bank expected in return loyal and consistent service. The psychological contract implies some compromise where expectations are incompatible, or else one of the other party breaks off relations. It is worth noting that the organisation's power to make the employee redundant may be matched by the employee's marketability; it all depends on the labour market in this employee's skills and knowledge. Re-contracting is also a major periodic feature of the psychological contract, as both organisations' and individuals' expectations change over time. Organisations might expect more and more international mobility; individuals who would have welcomed such developmental opportunities ten years ago are now more concerned about their children's education (Herriot, 1992; Mayo, 1991).

Hence organisations' human resource strategies cannot consist of a set of systems designed to do things to people. They have to involve employees and take account of their expectations and objectives. Before we consider the assessment process and the appraisal system, therefore, we have first to consider how best to design human resource systems in the light of human resource strategy and the psychological contract.

Designing Assessment Systems

The Design Cycle
Roe (1989) gives a clear account of the design process derived originally from the engineering model. The process is represented in Figure 9.2. In the first stage:

Definition, we ask the crucial question "What functions or purposes is the system designed to fulfil?" As we shall see when we look at appraisal systems, some functions may be incompatible with others: you cannot achieve both within a single system.

Analysis, the next stage of the design cycle, requires us to look at the requirements the system should meet, and the constraints within which they have to be met. Assessment centres may meet the requirements of reliability and predictive validity

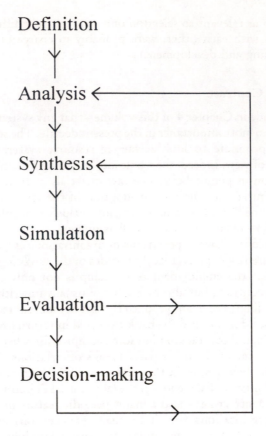

FIGURE 9.2   The Design Cycle (from Roe, 1989)

quite well (see p. 165), but they may exceed the constraining budget limit set by the organisation.

Synthesis is the next stage; in the light of our purposes, and in accordance with the requirements and constraints, we have to create a preliminary design or prototype of the system we are designing. One way of helping on this creative activity is to try to list the specifications of the system; what is it going to look like, what features is it going to have to have, if it is going to achieve its functions? When designing an appraisal system, for example, if the purpose is to discover the development needs of individuals, the system is going to have to encourage them to assess their own strengths and weaknesses. This can only be done in a non-threatening situation which carries no connotations of the award or withholding of rewards.

Simulation involves trying out the prototype system, and *evaluation* means seeing how well it achieves its functions within the constraints set. Finally, *decision* requires us to choose whether to put the prototype into operational use, or whether to go through the synthesis stage again. We may even decide after several failures that our analysis of the requirements and constraints was mistaken. Or we may in the end conclude that we cannot in principle achieve the purposes we started out with.

One problem with the design cycle is that it tends to result in a system which fulfils the stated functions well; but which may not be amenable to change when the stated functions change. For example, in the 1970s many organisations designed excellent appraisal systems whose prime function was to discover development needs. However, during the 1980s, many adopted performance-related pay schemes. Despite the fact that the basic function of the appraisal system had changed to one of assessing performance, few consciously redesigned their systems – most merely grafted the new function on.

A second and more fundamental problem with the design cycle is that it fails to specify who should be involved in designing the system. Instead of involving employees, the tendency is to see it as a technological issue to be addressed by specialists in human resources. The origin of the design cycle idea in engineering runs the risk of the technological fix at the expense of the psychological contract.

Organisational Culture

One of the most important contextual constraints on the design of systems is the organisation's culture. Schein (1985) suggests that an organisation's systems are like artifacts of a culture. Anthropologists and archaeologists examine these in order to draw conclusions about the nature of the society which produced them; Roman roads tell us something about the Roman empire. In just the same way, an appraisal or selection system can tell us a great deal about the underlying values and assumptions prevalent in the organisation which produced it.

Here is a list of assumptions which might underlie two different organisations' systems:

1. People don't change much.
2. You can predict how they will perform.
3. People's views of themselves predict their behaviour.
4. You can measure the characteristics of people.
5. Jobs are constantly changing.
6. People are individually entirely responsible for their performance.
7. It is difficult to measure individual performance.
8. Jobs consist of tasks.
9. Employees select organisations.
10. The main purpose of assessment is to predict performance.
11. People can change the nature of the job they are in.
12. Assessment results in a mutually acceptable agreement.

Try and divide the twelve assumptions into two groups of six which belong to each organisation. Numbers 1, 2, 4, 6, 8 and 10 imply a very different set of beliefs about people and jobs than numbers 3, 5, 7, 9, 11 and 12.

Neither set is either right or wrong. The first set might be appropriate for a stable organisation in a predictable environment where jobs and tasks remained much the same over the years. Indeed, it was for such organisations that the traditional selection and assessment systems described in applied psychology tests were devised. However, if the impact of change is as great as I argued at the beginning of this chapter, then for most organisations the second set of assumptions in the list above is more appropriate. Their cultures will be changing to incorporate these new assumptions, and the functions for which they wish to design their systems will change also. They will be looking more to help people develop their knowledge and skills and to be ready for career opportunities within the organisation.

Functions, Requirements and Constraints

So our next task is to explore in more detail the various functions which organisations are wishing to serve in their use of assessment systems. What might they be trying to achieve? Here is a list of 15 – there may be more.

1. Prediction of long term potential, and of the overall contribution an individual is likely to make.
2. Prediction of turnover.
3. Information to individuals about their aptitudes, personality, interests, values, and preferred styles.
4. Information to individuals about the job and the organisation.
5. Initial placement of individuals in positions.
6. The formation of effective work groups.
7. Assessment of suitability for promotion or sideways movement.
8. Feedback to individuals or groups about their performance.
9. The allocation of rewards based on performance.
10. The discovery of training needs.
11. The assessment of training outcomes.
12. The discovery of directions for the development of individuals and for their career paths.
13. The audit of the skills, knowledge and experience available in the organisation.
14. Assessment of poor performance.
15. Prediction of job performance.

Within this list, numbers 1, 4, 7, 8, 9, 10, 12 and 14 have all been seen at one time or another as purposes of the appraisal system of an organisation. Which of these functions an organisation wishes its appraisal system to serve will, of course, depend on its strategy. Many organisations during the 1980s wanted to ensure that they had a cadre of highly developed and broadly experienced high-fliers ready to fill senior management positions as they fell vacant. One of the major functions of their appraisal system was therefore to identify the extent of long-term potential as assessed by the individual's line manager. Those thus identified would then be sent to an assessment centre to assess more reliably the extent of this potential. Assessment centres are particularly useful for this purpose, for they permit assessees to try to solve problems derived from jobs much higher up in the organisation than their present position. So here we have a case where an element of human resource strategy (development of a high-flier cohort) is a purpose of a human resource system (appraisal) in the design of which a particular instrument (assessment centre) was most appropriate to achieve the purpose.

We have summarised some of the *functions* which assessment systems might serve. Now let us examine the next stage of the design cycle. What are the *requirements and constraints* which they have to meet? Here is a list, some of the items of which repeat requirements mentioned in Chapter 4.

- *Validity.* The methods used must assess what they claim to assess (construct validity). If they are used to predict an outcome, they must do so to an acceptable level (criterion validity). If they sample the job, they must do so in a representative manner (content validity).

- *Acceptability.* Users should find the methods acceptable in the sense that they do not harm them, appear to be useful, and do not violate their personal or professional standards.
- *Usability.* Users should be skilled enought to use the methods or be capable of being trained to do so. The assessment obtained should be in a form suitable for giving feedback and/or for aiding subsequent decision-making. The methods chosen should not need a lot of time in preparation, administration and analysis.
- *Fairness.* Methods have to be fair and be seen to be fair. The spirit as well as the letter of the laws regarding discrimination in employment have to be followed.
- *Generality.* It is extremely useful if the same methods can be used for different levels of employee. It is a lot cheaper.
- *Utility.* The individual methods must each contribute to a system which is cost-effective.
- *Availability.* Methods and systems which depend upon rare professional skills and knowledge for their continued use (as opposed to their design) are less preferable. This is because organisations can be held to ransom by experts and become dependent upon them.
- *Serendipity.* Some methods have unexpected beneficial outcomes, others have less welcome and unintended consequences. Possible outcomes should be predictable, which implies knowledge of previous usage of the method.
- *Consistency.* Methods should not be at variance with the methods used in other Human Resource Systems than the ones being designed. It's no good mixing authoritarian and participative systems. There should be a general organisational policy regarding criteria for the design of systems. This will take account of the culture of the organisation.
- *Context.* Methods and overall design should also take account of the overall context. For example, the state of the labour market and its impact on organisation objectives should exercise a major influence.

Synthesis and Simulation

Given all these considerations, it's amazing that people ever succeed in completing the third stage of the design cycle: *synthesis.* The only way to appreciate the nature of this process is to try to do it oneself. Assuming my readership consists mostly of students who have had vacation employment, give yourself the task of designing an annual appraisal procedure for someone in the position you occupied (bar staff? check-out operator?). Don't forget to think first about the organisation. What are the functions which such an organisation is likely to want of its appraisal system? What will the system look like? How will you represent it on paper – by a flow diagram? What documentation will the system need and what will these documents look like? What will be the input to the process – what information should the appraiser and the appraisee start off with? What should be the outcomes or products of the system, and who should own them?

Having designed a prototype, decide what you think might be some of the unexpected consequences if you tried it out in a *simulation*? Could the consequences of a critical review of employees' past performance actually demotivate them for the future? Could the process of setting the appraisee's objectives for the next year have the incidental advantage of helping him or her to understand the appraiser's own job better?

APPRAISAL SYSTEMS

Functions of Appraisal

Now let us move on to discuss appraisal systems in particular. This will anchor the generalisations we have been making so far in some specific research and practice. The most useful sources are Fletcher and Williams (1985) and Dulewicz and Fletcher (1989).

First, let us return to Figure 9.1, the human resource cycle of Fombrun *et al.* (1984). Appraisal occupies a pivotal role in the cycle. It can be used to evaluate how well the selection system is working, through its assessment of the performance of those who have been selected. It can be used to inform individuals about their performance, and enhance it by such feedback. It can provide evidence upon the basis of which performance–based rewards can be allocated. It can set objectives and plan work for a future period of time. It can point to training and development needs and help ensure they are met. And it can provide the evidence on which promotion decisions may be made (dotted line). In addition, appraisal information can contribute to a human resource data base on the basis of which planning decisions may be made. Finally (and not represented in Figure 9.1) appraisal can act as a signal of the organisation's culture; for example, if work groups rather than individuals are appraised, cooperative rather than individualistic values are being signalled.

Such a pivotal role has brought its problems, as Fletcher and Williams (op cit) point out. Specifically, the different functions which appraisal is asked to perform are often mutually incompatible. As McGregor (1957) and Maier (1958) recognised very early on, it is terribly difficult to act as a judge of people's past performance and also as a helper for the future. In particular, it is next to impossible to get people to admit to weaknesses and thereby identify training needs and at the same time to assess their performance for such purposes as allocating performance bonuses.

So appraisal systems are likely to have problems at the first stage of the design cycle, that of establishing what *functions* they are to serve. It is worth noting, though, that systems can be designed which meet different functions on different occasions using different appraisers. But thus far we have been considering the functions of the system from the organisation's point of view. What about the employees? Perhaps the functions of appraisal from their points of view are rather different. As Dulewicz and Fletcher (1989) point out, they may wish to present themselves in a favourable light, for all sorts of psychological and other reasons. They may want to keep in with the appraiser (often their boss). And appraisers, too, may have different objectives for appraisal from the official ones. They may want to retain the person being appraised in their own team, rather than allowing development needs to dictate a move to another Department. They may wish to avoid confrontation (Ilgen and Favero, 1985) or to get unmerited rewards for their proteges. So not only is it important to keep the evaluative and the developmental functions separate from the point of view of the organisation. It is also important to recognise that different parties have different objectives, and therefore that all should buy into the system from the start. This requirement is likely to necessitate involving appraisers (line managers, usually) and appraisers as well as human resource people in the design process.

Analysis and Synthesis

Which brings us on to the second stage of the design cycle – analysis of requirements and constraints. George (1986) suggests in addition the following six requirements. An appraisal system must:

- have the support of senior managers
- meet real organisational needs
- be acceptable to users
- be administratively convenient
- fit the organisational culture
- be supported by training and development

To which should be added:

- fit in with other systems in the HR cycle.

As far as the *synthesis* stage of the design cycle is concerned, there are major problems. What on earth is an appraisal system going to look like which might serve all or most of the functions which are typically required of it? And even if we limit the number of functions, are there tools which enable us to meet even these? Consider the assessment of performance for the sake of allocating rewards. We would tend to assume that people's performance needs to be compared with that of others for differential rewards to be allocated (though this assumption may not be justified). The usual way to compare performance is by means of a rating scale, completed by line managers of the appraisees. However, there are major problems with rating scales. As Saal, Downey and Lahey (1980) convincingly demonstrate, all sorts of errors creep into the use of rating scales: the halo effect, for example, which is the rater's failure to discriminate among different aspects of a ratee's behaviour; the leniency or severity error, which speaks for itself; the error of central tendency, that is, the failure to use the extremes of the scale; and restriction of range, the tendency to cluster ratings round any one point of the scale.

Big efforts have been made to redesign rating scales so as to reduce these errors. For example, the development of behaviourally anchored rating scales (BARS) requires a lengthy and complex job analysis in order to be able to give examples of behaviour which would justify a particular rating. So instead of having scales which rate on a six point scale from "ineffective with people" to "effective with people", a BARS scale would be far more specific. For example, "Upsets people needlessly, sours the atmosphere, drains other people's enthusiasm, dampens morale and hinders team achievement" (example from Handyside, 1989). You may wish to ask whether these are actual behaviours, or their consequences. One would hope that the use of BARS would result in more reliable and valid rating, but the research evidence offers little encouragement. We would expect there to be less restriction of range than in Handyside's (1989) research. He found that on a simple overall rating scale without behavioral anchors, 4.7 per cent of 8,000 plus employees were rated outstanding; 55.2 per cent very good; 34.1 per cent good; 5.5 per cent fair; 0.4 per cent not quite adequate; and 0.05 per cent unsatisfactory!

Landy and Farr (1980) conclude, unfortunately, that characteristics of the rater are much more predictive of error variance than aspects of the rating scale. Typically, 4–8 per cent of variance in ratings is explained by the format of the rating scale, while over 20 per cent by characteristics of rater and ratee (such as ethnicity and gender) which are irrelevant to the behaviour being rated. All sorts of implicit theories of personality and attributions are involved. Why for example, should we assume that an individual's performance is a consequence of their effort and ability? It might be attributable to matters largely outside their control, e.g. the opening up of an entirely new market by chance.

So what tools are we to use at the synthesis stage of the design cycle? If we want to assess performance, we may want to do it by looking at the extent to which people achieved the objectives which had been agreed at the previous appraisal. But as Fletcher and Williams (1985) point out, a job can't always be expressed in terms of objectives; and if one person's objectives are harder than another's to achieve, comparisons are impossible.

So the synthesis stage might come up with a set of different appraisal situations, each designed to serve one or two of the many functions. For example, long-term potential, often assessed by a single rating scale at the end of an appraisal form, might be more validly assessed by an assessment centre using exercises from a higher organisational level. Development needs might be discovered more appropriately by self-ratings, since we know that one of the properties of self-ratings is that they distinguish between different behaviours very well – we are good at drawing a differentiated profile of ourselves (Mabe and West, 1982). And so on. But if we were to design an appraisal system in this way, it would never see the light of day in organisations. They have the utmost difficulty in persuading line managers to conduct one appraisal interview per annum. There are constraints of time and cost.

Current Appraisal Practice

Which brings us to the question of what actually happens in UK appraisal practice, rather than what is good professional practice. Fletcher and Williams (1985) give an "Identikit" picture of a British appraisal system. Typically, the aims of the scheme are several, including assessment of training and development needs; of performance; and of promotability and potential. It has been driven by the personnel function. It occurs annually, and the appraiser is usually the appraisee's immediate boss. Top management and secretarial and clerical staff and operatives are not appraised. There is some training for appraisers. The form which they complete lists the objectives towards which the appraisee has been working, comments on the extent to which they have been achieved, and identifies any obstacles in the way of performance improvement. An overall performance rating follows, and a section for training and development needs. All these parts of the form are shown to the appraisee and discussed in an interview. A final part of the form which is not shown is a rating of promotability and long-term potential. The interview may take half an hour.

Difficulties of incompatibility of purposes are apparent. So is the absence of such likely interests of the appraisee as the possible direction for their career within the organisation. Overall, the idea of the psychological contract in which both parties' expectations are discovered is woefully absent from the identikit picture. On the other hand, some organisations are developing career interviews entirely separate from appraisals.

Looking at some more formally derived surveys of the UK practice, we may note that Long (1986) asked 230 organisations what were the main purposes of their appraisal schemes. There were three purposes shared by almost every scheme: to review past performance (98 per cent), to improve current performance (97 per cent) and to assess training and development needs (97 per cent). For 81 per cent the objective was to set performance objectives, for 75 per cent to assist career planning decisions, and for 71 per cent to assess future potential or promotability. Of relatively lower frequency was to assess increases or new levels in salary (40 per cent). So the identikit picture seems to reflect accurately the evidence of a multiplicity of objectives. As we might have predicted, however, when appraisees were asked what had been covered in the appraisal, performance weaknesses and training needs were only discussed in one half of the cases (Fletcher and Williams, 1985). So practice does seem to fall well short of intention.

The Applied Psychologist

What contributions can an applied psychologist make to such a situation? Looking at things "from the bottom up", we should have something to contribute to the specific elements of the appraisal system. If a rating scale is used, we should know enough about the psychometrics of scale design to optimise chances of avoiding various measurement errors. We should also be sufficiently familiar with the theory and research on person perception and judgement to be aware of the biases likely to be operative. If an interview is used, we need to understand the nature of the social processes involved, and be aware of the need to maintain self-esteem on the part of the appraisee. If we design a training course for appraisers, we have to establish training needs, and plan a program which takes account of the way people learn. So at the level of the tools of the trade, a wide variety of psychological theory and practice is required.

But applied psychologists are more than designers and users of specific instruments. As we have seen, the overall appraisal system has to be designed. Apart from the creativity required at the synthesis stage (see Figure 9.2), the applied psychologist has to understand the functions, requirements, and constraints of the system. This requires a dialogue with the client, which may involve not just understanding what they want but helping them discover what they need. Such help cannot be given unless the psychologist understands the organisation as a whole. Psychologists have to be able to understand business strategies and their implications for human resources strategies if they are to operate at this level.

But perhaps most important of all, applied psychologists have to wrestle with the problem of who is their client. It is the organisation which pays them for their work; but it is all the employees involved whose interests and welfare are affected. Part of the answer, but only part, is to respond that human resource systems are most effective when they are based on a psychological contract; therefore it is in both parties' interests to design such systems. The reality, however, is that the very strong ethos of "management's right to manage" which characterised the 1980s will inhibit the development of psychological contracting during the next decade.

REFERENCES

Argyris, C. (1960). *Understanding Organisation Behaviour*. Homewood, Illinois: Dorsey.

Brewster, C. & Smith, C. (1990). Corporate Strategy: A no-go area for personnel. *Personnel Management*, **22** (7), 36–40.

Dulewicz, V. & Fletcher, C. (1989). The context and dynamics of performance appraisal. In Herriot, P. (ed) *Assessment and Selection in Organisations*. Chichester: Wiley.

Fletcher, C. & Williams, R. (1985). *Performance Appraisal and Career Development*. London: Hutchinson.

Fombrun, D., Tichy, N.M. & Devanna, M. (1984). *Strategic Human Resource Management*. New York: Wiley.

George, J. (1986). Appraisal in the public sector: Dispensing with the big stick. *Personnel Management*, May, 32–35.

Handyside, J. (1989). On ratings and rating scales. In Herriot, P. (ed) *Assessment and Selection in Organisations*. Chichester: Wiley.

Herriot, P. (1992). *The Career Management Challenge*. London: Sage.

Ilgen, D.R. & Favero, J.L. (1985). Limits in generalisation from psychological research to performance appraisal process. *Academy of Management Review*, 10, 311–321.

Kanter, R.M. (1989). *When Giants Learn to Dance*. New York: Simon & Schuster.

Katz, D. & Kahn, R.L. (1978). *The Social Psychology of Organisations* (2nd ed.). New York: Wiley.

Landy, F.J. & Farr, J.L. (1980). Performance rating. *Psychological Bulletin*, **87**, 72–107.

Long, P.A. (1986). *Performance Appraisal Revisited*. London: IPM Press.

Mabe, P.A. & West, S.G. (1982). Validity of self-evaluation of ability: a review and meta-analysis. *Journal of Applied Psychology*, **67**, 280–296.

Mailer, N.R.F. (1958). Three types of appraisal interview. *Personnel*, March/April, 32–40.

Mayo, A. (1991). *Managing Careers*. London: IPM Press.

McGregor, D. (1957). An uneasy look at performance appraisal. *Harvard Business Review*, **35**, 89–94.

Roe, R. (1989). Designing selection procedures. In Herriot, P. (ed) *Assessment and Selection in Organisations*. Chichester: Wiley.

Saal, F.E., Downey, R.G. & Lahey, M.A. (1980). Rating the ratings: Assessing the psychometric quality of rating data. *Psychological Bulletin*, **88**, 413–428.

10

ORGANISATIONAL PSYCHOLOGY

F. BLACKLER

INTRODUCTION

Popular culture provides many images of organisations. Government agencies are presented as benign and helpful in the radio soap opera "The Archers"; Kafka's novels present bureaucracies as impenetrable; in films such as "Robocop" big business is stereotyped as ruthless and machine-like; and television shows like "Spitting Image" attribute much to the personalities of key policy makers. Such a variety of images is hardly suprising: organisations pervade modern societies. Most of us are born in an organisation and are likely to die in one; we are educated in organisations, find employment within them, and throughout our lives we depend upon them, not only for the luxuries of life but also for essentials such as water, power, security, employment, health, and communications.

The smooth functioning of complex, modern organisations is something that we take for granted most of the time. This too is not suprising; organisations can be defined in terms of the relatively enduring, integrated and co-ordinated patterns of activities that take place within them. Nonetheless managerial incompetence, technical failure, industrial unrest, or political upheaval can, quite suddenly, starkly expose how dependent the quality of modern life is on effective organisations. There is no natural law which governs the operation of complex social systems; social order is not God-given, organisational routines have no inevitability. Organisations are man-made and the effectiveness and acceptability of their operations results from the actions of those who participate within them.

This chapter introduces the distinctive contribution that organisational psychology is making to the study and management of behaviour in organisations. The subject stands as a bridge between theory and practice, embracing as it does both the concerns of academics and those of managers and consultants; moreover it is uniquely positioned intellectually, at the junction of micro- (psychological) and macro- (sociological, political, economic) studies of behaviour. The argument of this chapter is that organisational psychology addresses some of the central practical and intellectual issues of our time.

Table 10.1   Key Developments in Organisational Psychology

Dates	Issues	Approaches
1910	Unskilled American workforce, but rapid industralisation.	Taylor's "Principles of Scientific Management", and the possibilities of task fragmentation and financial motivation.
1914–18	Need for rapid production of ammunitions.	Study of working conditions and productivity in munitions factories.
	Placement of army conscripts.	Application of statistical methods to psychological testing.
1930s	Economic depression.	The Hawthorne studies and recognition of interpersonal factors.
1938–45	Development of radar and advanced fighting machines.	Developments in ergonomics.
	Placement of army conscripts.	Officer selection techniques.
1960s	Expanding economies, and changing attitudes to authority.	Decision making and leadership styles.
	Management training and employee motivation.	Group processes and organisation development. Job design and worker motivation.
1970s	Trade union power.	Influence strategies in organisations.
	New technologies and changes in business environments.	Organisations as complex systems.
1980s	New information technologies.	Technology design as organisational intervention.
	Changing patterns of world trade.	Theories of organisation culture and leadership.
Early 1990s	Disjunctive political and social changes	Human resources management and business strategy.

THE DEVELOPMENT OF ORGANISATIONAL PSYCHOLOGY

An overview of key developments in the emergence of modern organisational psychology is presented in Table 10.1.

It is normally assumed that the history of any specialist area should focus principally on its disciplinary origins and internal theoretical developments and, as is discussed later in this chapter, it certainly is true that the distinctive contribution that the social sciences can make is intimately related to the strength of their methodologies and the insights that their concepts and theories can provide. Nonetheless, as Cherns (1979) pointed out, in the case of an applied social science consideration of such factors alone would provide an inappropriately inward-looking introduction to its development. Advances in the applied social sciences certainly do depend on developments in theory and method, but they are inextricably linked also to prevailing social problems and to current ideologies.

As Table 10.1 indicates, the origins of organisational psychology can be traced to the early decades of this century when America was rapidly industrialising with a poorly educated work-force. In this situation the efforts of an engineer, Frederick Winslow Taylor, to develop what he rather unfortunately called a "scientific" approach to management were dramatically successful. Taylor believed that inefficiency in people should be dealt with by carefully selecting and controlling workers, management should take responsibility for planning and monitoring their efforts, and workers' behaviour should be channelled by carefully administered financial incentives. This kind of approach was widely adopted (Henry Ford's mass-production methods of car assembly provide an early example); indeed, the image Taylor promised of organisations as smooth-running machines, controlled from the top and rationally utilising both their human and material assets was to have a lasting appeal. In recent years, of course, the problems of organising in such a way have been well publicised and, as will become clear, much modern organisational psychology can be presented as an attempt to develop alternatives to the de-humanised approaches to management that are associated with Taylorism. Nonetheless in the early decades of this century Taylor's guiding assumptions largely passed unquestioned. His work appealed to his contemporaries because his approach accorded well with the prevailing belief of the time that the righteous should prosper through hard work.

Similar social and cultural influences can be identified in later key developments in the emergence of organisational psychology. The crisis of the first world war prompted research into the productivity of ammunitions workers and the placement of large numbers of conscripts to the army; research into both worker fatigue and selection tests was firmly guided by a philosophy of individualism. Next, the discovery between the wars at the Hawthorne factory in Chicago that workers are at least as responsive to their immediate work group as they are to the exhortions of their superiors led to a recognition of the importance of human relations factors at work; "human relations" approaches accorded well with the growing wish of the times that workers should be contented as well as hardworking. Similarly, theories of participative leadership and interpersonal styles were to resonate with concerns in the 1950s and 1960s that alternatives to authoritarianism had to be found, and the theories of intrinsic worker motivation of the 1960s and 1970s were to complement the general expectation that improved levels of worker self-determination were desirable. Then, as trade union power in many Western countries appeared to challenge management prerogatives, the economies of the West were to be shaken in the 1970s and 1980s by the rise of Japanese industry. New technologies based on micro-electronics promised radical change, and the emerging ideology of the enterprise culture legitimated renewed interest in the practice of leadership, entrepreneurism and competition.

Outlooks within organisational psychology have, then, developed very significantly in recent years. The emphasis on business and military organisations that characterised early work has been overtaken by an involvement in organisations of all types. Moreover, as the complexity of real-world problems have become better appreciated a broad analytical orientation (influenced by sociology, economics and other social sciences) has emerged, which has complemented the strong emphasis organisational psychologists have continued to place on the development of usable techniques. Indeed, as the following discussion will illustrate, helping clients learn to solve their own problems has emerged as one of the central goals of the field.

KEY AREAS WITHIN ORGANISATIONAL PSYCHOLOGY

An inventory of topics considered relevant to organisational psychology nowadays would be long, and would need to include job analysis, section (see Shackleton's chapter in this volume), training (see Patrick's chapter), assessment and appraisal (see

Herriot's chapter), working conditions and rewards, information technology (see below, and also Sheehy's chapter) job design, stress, health and safety, motivation and morale, group development, leadership theory, industrial relations psychology, organisation change, organisation structure, organisation culture and human resources management.

At least two things distinguish organisational psychology from cognate disciplines. First, the level of analysis developed within the subject is distinctive. It neither focusses on individuals in isolation from their environments (as does some experimental psychology) nor on the social context in isolation from individuals (as does some sociology and economics); rather, organisational psychology explores the interrelationships between individuals and their immediate contexts. Second, as has already been noted, organisational psychologists place a strong emphasis on the development of usable theories and methodologies in their work; the subject is strongly pragmatic.

To illustrate these points developments in two areas of central importance will be described: job design theory, and organisation change. *Job design* has been a particularly fruitful area for psychologists and research has produced a battery of approaches that provide clear alternatives to Taylorism. Part of the fascination of the field arises, however, from the difficulties that have been encountered in attempts to encourage general adoption of these ideas; the recent advent of a powerful new generation of workplace technologies, based on micro-electronics, has made such an issue all the more important. Such issues raise basic questions about the management of *organisational change*. The need to understand reactions to changes has long been recognised as a topic of importance in this area, but the startling variety of developments affecting organisational life at the present time have made this one of the key social issues of the moment.

Job Design and the Quality of Working Life

The methods of job design pioneered by F.W. Taylor involve the "rationalisation" of jobs into small task units, the technical streamlining of production methods, and strict use of time. Dramatically successful as it has been in certain instances, for some time now it has been recognised that Taylorism produces disillusioned workers and high levels of absenteeism and turnover. Despite this it was only in the 1960s and early 1970s (when such issues became particularly important) that serious efforts were made to build alternative approaches to job design.

The first approach was initially developed in America by Herzberg (1959). The starting point for his theory was a study of job satisfaction amongst accountants and engineers. Herzberg asked the people he studied to think of times when they had been very satisfied with their work, and times when they had been very dissatisfied. Content analysis of their accounts suggested that, in general, the causes of good and bad times differed fundamentally. Causes of job satisfaction were factors intrinsic to work, such as interesting tasks, achievement, responsibility, recognition, learning, or job advancement. On the other hand instances of job dissatisfaction tended to be associated with factors extrinsic to the job, including unpleasant colleagues, poor relations with superiors, inadequate financial reward, poor working conditions or job insecurity. Herzberg concluded that the causes of job satisfaction are different from the causes of job dissatisfaction. Factors intrinsic to the job, he thought, might lead people to be satisfied but their absence would not cause active dissatisfaction; extrinsic factors on the other hand, can promote active dissatisfaction when when they are not acceptable, but in other circumstances they will not of themselves promote active satisfaction.

The detail of Herzberg's research has not been accepted by all psychologists (his method has been criticised on the grounds that people tend to attribute success to their own efforts but to blame other people or external causes for their disappointments). Nonetheless the thrust of his argument was similar to theories which were already well regarded. In particular Abraham Maslow's theory of human needs pointed in the same direction. Maslow proposed that a heirarchy of motives influences behaviour: to begin with physiological needs dominate behaviour, as these become satisfied concerns with safety become predominant, then social needs; later the higher order needs for self respect and then self fulfillment may come into play. Both Herzberg and Maslow pointed, therefore, towards the problems of treating people at work in a partial way, both predicting that approaches to work organisation which deny people the opportunity to self actualise, and merely rely on their needs to avoid pain or discomfort, would not create an involved, motivated work force.

In applying this approach to work design, Herzberg argued that opportunities for workers to exercise their discretion should systematically be (re-)introduced to jobs, reversing the process of job simplification that Taylor had recommended. "Job enrichment" was the term Herzberg coined; not that workers were to be paid more according to early formulations of this approach; it was the content of jobs that was to be enriched, with increased motivation developing out of the stimulus of more interesting and responsible work roles.

Herzberg's prescriptions proved attractive to many managers, and in the 1960s a number of well publicised attempts were made to put his ideas into practice. The theory of job enrichment was, however, couched in rather general terms; in his work terms such as responsibility, recognition, interesting work remained little more than slogans, as the specific characteristics which distinguish motivating jobs from alienating ones had not been explicitly identified in his theory. Later researchers were to address this issue and in 1975 Hackman and Oldham proposed a model to summarise relevant research. This is summarised in Figure 10.1. Core motivating characteristics of jobs include, the model suggests: opportunity to use a variety of skills, the identity of the task, its significance, the opportunities it provides to exercise autonomy, and the presence of information about results. Motivating jobs can therefore be created by combining previously fragmented tasks together in the same job, forming new work groups around related tasks, establishing direct relations between workers and the client groups they serve, delegating authority from more senior decision makers in the heirarchy, and providing performance data directly to workers for them to monitor their own performances.

Helpful as these insights were, however, some loose ends still remained. Hackman and Oldham pointed out that although the interest people have in what they do is often underestimated, not all workers place high store on interesting, responsible work; a qualification of their theory is the acknowledgement that some people show little interest in interesting jobs and may respond less positively to enriched jobs than others. Since Hackman and Oldham published their model, however, further research

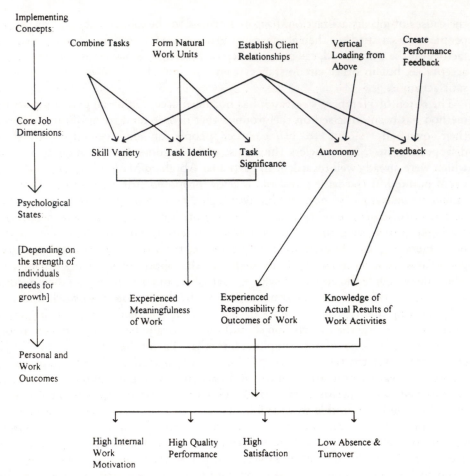

FIGURE 10.1   The Job Characteristics Model of Work Motivation (adapted from Hackman and Oldham, 1975)

has been undertaken into the consequences of impoverished work, some of which throws light on this issue. The popular image of stressful work, of course, is of fast-moving, ulcer-inducing executive jobs. As Fletcher and Payne (1980) reported in their summary of stress research however, it does appear that this is something of a myth, for the people who suffer the most from stress related diseases are employees of low socio-economic status engaged in low-level routine jobs. Over time, it would appear that repetitive, routine jobs (especially machine-minding jobs) are particularly injurious of health. People employed in such jobs who are also experiencing difficulties in their lives outside work are especially likely to be at risk. For them, apathy caused by the experience of chronic stagnation in their jobs over many years, the lack of opportunities to move on, coupled perhaps with poor housing, financial problems, unhealthy patterns of eating, drinking and smoking can produce a cycle of deprivation, leading to reduced ambition and abilities to cope, therefore to increased stressors, a high incidence of maladaptive responses, and finally to a higher incidence of stress related disease and lowered life expectancy. Many pyschologists interested in work redesign theory are not content, therefore, merely to accept that a simple distinction can be drawn between workers who show an interest in intrinsic job design factors and those who do not. The situation is more complicated for the meanings that work comes to have for different people are learned and will reflect their particular life experiences.

The second alternative to Taylorism is socio-technical systems theory. This was first proposed after detailed study of the introduction of mechanised methods of coal mining in Britain in the 1950s (Trist *et al.*, 1963). Coal mining has always been a dangerous affair. Before automation small, self-selected teams (often involving family members) worked in close proximity at the coal face. Together, in near darkness, they hacked the coal, shifted the pieces and loaded it in trucks, and fixed roof supports as they progressed. Theirs was a common pay packet. If injury occured to any member of the team it was normal for the others to support him and his family until a return to work was possible. Automation profoundly disrupted this situation. In traditional industrial engineering style a system was introduced which disrupted the autonomous mining groups, dividing the job into separate tasks. A three shift system was designed: one group of forty or fifty would supervise the coal cutting machinery, another group would shift the coal out, out, the third shift would place roof supports, extend rail lines, move the machinery forward, etc. Within this new system great emphasis was placed on the role of supervisor. Consequences of the new system included greatly increased rates of absenteeism and accidents. Morale amongst the miners became poor, and acrimonious relations developed between the different shifts.

Later, a pit was studied where, although the same equipment had been installed, different working arrangements had been tried. In this case multi-skilled teams had been created, workers rotated around the shifts, and payment was made to each shift as a unit. Production rates, absenteeism and morale were all significantly improved under this system.

Socio-technical systems theory generalises from such observations. It argues that work technologies influence the organisation of work in significant ways but, typically, the effects of different technologies are not predetermined and choices do exist about how to use them. In particular, the theory suggests that social and psychological considerations should be given as much weight as technological concerns. Rather than dividing jobs into fragmented tasks the logic of socio-technical systems theory is to build self-managing work groups around a significant cluster of activities that have a recognisable unity.

Efforts to refine socio-technical theory have focussed in large part on the practicalities of organising around such semi-autonomous groups. Such groups, it is now recognised, should not be too large or they will fragment into sub-groups. The group should be, at least partly, self regulating. Different degrees of self-management are possible, of course, concerning who does what, when and how; what is essential is that the group should judge itself (and be judged) in terms of the results it achieves. Payment systems will need to reflect this. Clearly, such a method of organising requires a level of social skills amongst employees where Taylorism required none. Equally important, such an approach requires changes in the role of management; rather than being concerned with supervision and monitoring the key role of management becomes to ensure that such groups have sufficient resources to solve their own problems.

Brief though this review has been it should be clear that job enrichment and socio-technical systems theory articulated a new outlook for management, emphasising the advantages of self direction and collaborative working relationships, highlighting the existance of technological choices and the advantages of building work systems around the skills and abilities of those who use them. By the early 1970s therefore, the issue had become less how to develop such an approach and more how to encourage others to use it. A loosely knit but very active international network of academics and consultants interested in such ideas, the "Quality of Working Life Movement", emerged (see Davis and Cherns, 1975). Early efforts to encourage new approaches to organisation tended to follow a similar pattern: pilot experiments were introduced to demonstrate the potential of new approaches, in the light of their outcomes managers, trade unionists and perhaps government would be encouraged to invest resources in further work, with academic and consultant psychologists making themselves available as expert advisors. Early expectations were that diffusion of the new approaches would occur first in the organisations where demonstration projects had been successful, then in other organisations.

Some individual successes were achieved through such an approach but in general, to the disappointment of many of those involved, diffusion of new approaches to work organisation did not take place on the scale, or at the rate, that had been expected. Subsequent studies of what did happen identified two key reasons for these early disappointments. First, it became clear that new approaches to job design need to be understood in terms of the broad impact they have on the management system where they are introduced. Walton (1975) demonstrated that it is not enough merely to communicate the potential advantages of the new work methods to those involved. Even if the new approaches do offer advantages over existing structures they may threaten existing managerial norms. It has already been noted that if work groups are to be reorganised according to job redesign theory a change in the role of management will be required: local autonomy is significantly increased under such systems, first line supervisory jobs may become redundant, middle managers may feel they are losing control. Moreover, the very effectiveness of the new work systems can also cause problems: increases in productivity in one section may put strains elsewhere in the organisation. Pay differentials may also become disrupted. One interesting additional point is that trade unions have not always been supportive of experiments in job redesign, feeling that the success of new work methods can lead to job reductions.

A second key lesson about the process of introducing new approaches to organisation concerned the role of organisational psychologists. Put directly, it is a mistake to assume that practitioners will readily accept what self-styled behavioural experts have to say. People learn most readily from others whom they respect (typically, people like themselves or like they would like to be). Psychologists interested in encouraging new approaches to job design, therefore, have tended to move away from strategies for introducing change that depend on their expert advice, and to develop techniques to help people learn for themselves. In the section on action research below we return again to this point.

Job design and information technologies

The significance of theories of work design has been underlined in recent years by the advent of advanced work systems based on micro-electronics. Advanced computing and communications systems cover an extraordinary range of work-place technologies from robots and integrated manufacturing systems, to advanced office systems, to systems designed to simulate or support complex decision making. Given all the publicity such systems have received it is perhaps surprising to recall that they are still very recent; experiences with them are still in relative short supply, and misunderstandings about them remain common.

In the early 1980s the extraordinary performance characteristics of these technologies were much discussed. The speed with which new information systems could process data lead many to assume that, at a time of growing international competitiveness, it was essential that organisations should rapidly adopt these technologies (in the early 1980s government exhortations for people to adopt these technologies included the slogans "Automate or Liquidate" and "Modernise or Fossilize"). It was assumed that the benefits the technologies offered would follow their introduction more or less automatically. How the new generation of technologies could be grafted onto organisations as quickly as possible seemed to be the key task. Stiff resistance was anticipated as established work practices would, it was felt, be disrupted. Accordingly, close direction from the top of organisations in introducing the technologies was generally thought to be a good thing.

These assumptions are summarised in Table 10.2, and contrasted to an alternative series of assumptions suggested by job redesign theory. Experiences in the 1980s have supported the validity of these alternative assumptions rather strongly (Blackler,

Table 10.2 Changing Assumptions about High Technology Work Systems (adapted from Blackler, 1988)

Common Expectations about Information Technologies and Organisations	Revised Expectations about Information Technologies and Organisations
Technologies based on micro-electronics are merely machines and gadgets.	Work technologies are patterns of social relationships.
They are deterministic in their efforts.	Information technologies are exceptionally flexible and can be applied in a variety of ways.
	Positive effects on performance are not guaranteed.
They can be grafted onto existing work organisations.	Traditional assumptions about organisation (e.g. regarding patterns of authority, job demarcations, departmental boundaries, and career expectations) may not provide the best guiding assumptions.
Technological innovation must be managed from the top.	Technological change typically requires wide understanding, participation, incremental introduction, and significant inputs to training.
	The introduction of new technologies inevitably involves "political" behaviour.

1988). Rather than conceiving of work place technologies in terms of "nuts and bolts" work technologies should be thought of in terms of the social relationships they support. Moreover, key choices exist in how the social and the technical can be interlinked; technologies built on micro-electronics are exceptionally flexible and may facilitate significant changes in conventional approaches to work organisation. Technological change is not something that can simply be managed by senior managers, but it requires widespread participation by people who will use any new system. Finally, the process of organisational change needs to be understood not only as a process governed by rational planning, but as a social process which takes time, requires resourcing, and prompts people to manoeuvre in their own interests.

It is difficult to overstate the continuing significance of these points. A great many new work systems have been built because people are fascinated by technological possibilities rather than because they understand user needs, skills, abilities and resource requirements. Detailed studies of how new work systems have been conceived and introduced suggest that, unless conscious efforts are made to the contrary, design techniques tend to remain strongly Tayloristic (Bjorn-Anderson *et al.*, 1986). Design engineers, for example, tend to conceive of their task in terms of engineering specifications rather than its impact on users, and to underestimate the uncertainty and problems users will experience with new systems. Questions that a user-oriented approach would encourage (including: How do people ask for advice? What is the best way for a computer to present it? How will the needs of novices differ from those of experts? How should tasks be divided between people and machines? How can machines be used to support more convivial social arrangements? How can they be used to support involved, capable staff?) seem only rarely to be asked.

As a post-script to this discussion it should perhaps be noted that psychologists who have worked with design engineers report that they often do take criticisms of the inadequacy of their approaches rather seriously. It is not, in other words, that engineers generally turn their backs on a psychological approach, dismissing the very idea of a user centred approach. In practice though, even when they are sympathetic towards a user-centred orientation they may display little ability to use one. Design engineers need, it would seem, constant reminders and guidance about what a human-centred approach means for their practices. What they are good at is using structured design methods which encourage an analysis of the logic of information characteristics. This raises important questions about tacit skills and taken-for-granted assumptions that have yet to be fully understood.

Organisational Psychology and the Management of Change

Important as it is, new technology is not the only source of changes in work organisations at the present time. Changes are being stimulated because, amongst other things, of the shifts in the world economy, new relations in the European community and in Eastern Europe, the ideology of the enterprise culture, new approaches to public sector management, demographic changes, and changing attitudes towards the environment. The pattern of such developments has not been coherent and different sectors have been affected differently. Nonetheless changes such as these are raising considerable problems of management and policy making. Collectively they are disturbing vested interests and are requiring shifts in priorities, new relations between government and business, and new approaches to organisation.

Ever since Marx it has been recognised that capitalist societies are societies of change. What does seem unusual at the present time, however, is the rate and extent of changes. "Post-industrialism", "post-Fordism", and "post-modernism" are some of the terms that social commentators have used to try and encapsulate the significance of a constellation of changes that appears to be transforming industrialised Western countries. While there are key differences in such scenarios they share the common message that present experiences of uncertainty will not be replaced by more tranquil times. The message of the times is: uncertainty today, uncertainty tomorrow.

Organisational psychologists have long shown an interest in the management of change and, in the light of current developments, in recent years there has been considerable activity in this area. In this section the style of theorising that characterises contributions from organisational psychology to the topic are illustrated. To begin, reactions to change at the individual level of analysis are considered, then change at the level of groups, then at the level of organisations. After introducing the implications of such insights for practice more recent approaches to managing rapid changes by manipulating organisational cultures are reviewed.

Approaches to understanding individuals' reactions to changes have been greatly helped by Peter Marris's (1974) account of bereavement. The loss of a loved one is a distressing experience which leaves people shocked, physically distressed, and vulnerable to illness. The anguish of yearning and the release of weeping can last for many weeks; feelings of anger, rage and bitterness are common. Grieving individuals are unwilling to surrender the past and the loved one who was such an important part of it. They may brood, cling to the possessions of the dead, perhaps cultivating reminders of his or her presence, mulling over memories in an apparently fruitless way.

Various factors appear to be associated with different patterns of grief, important amongst them are conflicts and doubts in the relationship with the lost person, early experiences of attachment and loss, opportunities to prepare for the loss; and events after it. Yet while the details of grieving are unique for each person, common patterns can be identified. Grieving people typically show a number of apparently contradictory inclinations. They may complain they have no-one to talk to, yet rebuff sympathisers; may say they have nothing to live for, yet rush back to work; may feel lonely, yet avoid others; may want to forget their pain, yet cultivate reminders of the person they have lost. Such contradictions express the conflict that all bereaved people have to have to face between, on the one hand, the wish to return to the time before the death and remain faithful to the memory of the one who has been lost and, on the other, the emerging need to move forward and build a new life without the loved one. It is through the process of grief and mourning, Marris argues, that these contradictory impulses can become resolved. Grief enables lives to be rebuilt; a re-integration of self is achieved where the past is neither forgotten nor clung to, but where past meanings are rehabilitated to inform a new future.

Marris takes such insights to develop a more general model to understand reactions to change. The web of meanings that inform peoples' lives, he points out, is constructed cumulatively through time; feelings cannot be commanded and the significance that events have for people may not easily be revised. This style of analysis suggests that not all change will be resisted, but changes that threaten peoples' key purposes and attachments will be. The implication is that it would be wrong to think that resistance to change is necessarily a bad thing; attempts to protect key meanings are, according to this analysis, as healthy as adaptability itself.

Analysis of reactions to change at the group level of analysis builds on this kind of insight. Since the Hawthorne experiments a very considerable amount of time and energy has been spent researching group pracesses and much of significance in this area has been summarised by Schein (1983) and Hackman (1976). Schein points out that the small groups people identify with serve a number of important psychological functions. These include providing an opportunity for people to explore and validate their interpretations of reality, providing an outlet for affiliation needs, helping people develop a sense of their own esteem and, through shared endeavours, increasing individuals' power and abilities to get things done. Two implications for the management of changes will be clear: the formation of informal friendship groups in organisations is inevitable in organisations, and the way individuals react to changing circumstances may be explained in part by the norms of the groups of which he or she identifies.

Group norms develop around behaviours that are found useful in the group and often take some time to develop. Not all group norms apply equally to everyone, of course, as different group roles become differentiated. People will not always be able clearly to articulate the norms of the groups of which they are a member, norms will only rarely be explicitly articulated and appreciation of them may remain tacit. Nonetheless when changes threaten the key norms of a group, a group defender is likely quickly to emerge and his or her concerns can be of great value in revealing the nature of the system under threat. There is much truth in the maxim that if you want to understand the true nature of your organisation, try changing it. In connection with such thinking psychologists interested in applying group theory to the analysis of organisational change have found it useful to develop the theatrical overtones of the concept of "role". Mangham (1978), for example, develops the analogy that can be drawn between dramatical performances and social interactions: actors learn their parts, prepare their props and make-up, and act out the drama before an assembled audience; in the same way, in their everyday interactions, people cooperate in enacting and improvising a social script, carefully managing the way they present themselves to each other. The notion of "situation script" helps explain the effectiveness with which people co-operate in the enactment of complex social interactions. Moreover it draws attention to the political nature of organisational life; prevailing social scripts tend to operate for the benefit of some people more than others and they can be very difficult to re-write, intermeshed as they become with the cultural fabric of an organisation.

At the organisational level of analysis three key points need to be recognised. The first relates to the ease with which organisations of different types find they can adjust to changes and much has been written about the inflexibility of bureaucracies. In everyday usage the term bureaucracy has come to imply red-tape and excessive rules and regulations. However, as originally analysed by the sociologist Max Weber (1947) the term refers to a form of organising which helps account for the emergence of the modern industrialised state. A key element of bureaucracies is that employees within them are not expected to act in their own selfish interests but to act rationally, that is, in accord with impersonal rules and regulations. Procedures within a bureaucracy are carefully defined according to abstract rules, a division of labour and a management heirarchy. They enable routine functions to be allocated, routines enacted predictably and consistently, and problem cases to be passed to higher authorities for special attention. Rules do not equate with excessive regulations, as good rules will be developed from past experiences and will have been formulated to ensure efficiency and equity. Moreover within a bureaucracy, typically, rules will have been formulated to govern the arrangements under which people are employed, providing them with stable terms and conditions of employment.

Summarised in this way it is evident that to a greater or lesser extent most organisations in the modern world show some of the characteristics of bureaucracies (one reason, perhaps, why the image of organisations as machines remains so influential). Nonetheless, not all aspects of bureaucracies are functional. Taylorist approaches to work design are typical of jobs in bureaucracies; they tend to suffer from all the problems of motivation already reviewed. Moreover such methods of organisation rely heavily on communications downward and a lack of trust between different levels in the heirarchy is common. When key features change in the environment that a bureaucracy has been fashioned to serve begin to shift, therefore, problems can quickly develop. The role orientation that is characteristic of such organisations provides a poor training ground for open debate and problem solving and in times of change different sections of a bureaucracy are likely to manoeuvre against other sections in defence of their localised interests.

Table 10.3   Organisational Structures and Responses to Change

Bureaucracies	*Organisations Built Around Semi-Autonomous Work Groups*	*Organic Structures*
Tasks fragmented according to Tayloristic principles.	Individuals are assigned to the tasks of a group.	Overlapping work roles. Continuous adjustment of roles as circumstances require.
Clear hierarchy of command, based on formal authority.	Group representatives liaise with other groups, and senior managment.	Networks of authority based on expertise, commitment and social skills.
Patterns of communications are predominantly vertical.	Fluid communications within groups. Mutual problem solving and negotiations between groups and coordinating staff.	Communications are open and extensive. Advocacy combined with evaluation and criticism. High tolerance of differences.
Loyalty is to the organisation.	Loyalty to the group and its task.	Loyalty to the mission of the organisation. A strong results orientation.
Skills specific to the bureaucracy are valued most highly.	Skills needed in the group for internal flexibility and task needs are valued most highly.	Professional and "cosmopolitan" skills are valued most highly.

Not all organisations need find it as hard to adjust to changes. In Table 10.3 key features of bureaucracies are compared with socio-technical systems approaches discussed in the last section, and a third approach to organising that has been labelled the "organic" approach to organisation structure. "Organic" forms of organising were first described in the electronics industry, where firms were facing both rapid technological developments and fast changing customer requirements; in such circumstances the best performers operated very flexible working structures (Burns and Stalker, 1966). While it will be clear that the fluid and changing social relationships that exist in organically structured organisations can make them stimulating places to work in, the demands they make on peoples' social skills and abilities to deal with ambiguity can, however, prove demanding and stressful.

Earlier in this chapter the problems of introducing new approaches to job design highlighted how, in addition to reorganising work roles, job enrichment can affect such things as management roles, promotion prospects, control and information systems, training requirements, and payment systems. The second key point about organisations and change is, therefore, that different parts of an organisation interact with others in complex ways; the tasks to which people are assigned, the roles they enact, the technologies with which they are equipped, and systems of command, control and reward, are all interdependent in their effects. In this sense complex organisations are dynamically conservative, changes in one area may have unanticipated and perhaps undesirable consequences elsewhere.

Finally regarding the organisational level of analysis, it is important to recognise that different sub-groups within an organisation are likely to develop different objectives. Disputes about how best to work towards shared goals are common; different goals will be given different priority; different groups may develop incompatible goals. It is important to recognise that the goals top management espouse are unlikely to be the only ones which exist within an organisation, a plurality of goals is likely. When resources are limited disputes between different groups will quickly surface. At their most extreem they will involve direct confrontation, but much of the time such differences will be acted out less dramatically, through organisational politics and interpersonal influence processes.

In reviewing the implications of these ideas for the managemgnt of change it is interesting to begin by discussing what they imply should one wish to resist proposals for changes in an organisation. Unwelcome changes can be imposed on people in many ways; arguments for change are often supported by the more or less overt use of superior power and authority. Given that most organisations do not cultivate an atmosphere of equality, openness and debate, direct and immediate opposition to proposals for change may not always be the most successful way to prevent them.

In such circumstances the notion of the dynamic conservatism of organisations, theories of the ways in which groups resist disruptions to valued behaviours, and accounts of how individuals resist changes which threaten, all provide a possible starting point. They suggest that it is not always necessary actively to declare an opposition to undesirable proposals for change; many novel ideas die a death simply because of the inertia of complex social systems. It is not an unknown, of course, for people to give inertia a helping hand by, for example, forgetting to pass on messages or to leaving memos unanswered. If, however, things do seem likely to go ahead one unobtrusive oppositional tactic is to begin to draw attention to the disruptions it may cause to established routines. A similar tactic would be to draw attention to the complexities of whatever is being proposed. If arguments such as these fail to have the desired effect a more overtly "political" tactic would be to undermine the credibility of whoever is making the new proposals. This requires careful handling; a whisper of doubt about the credentials or track record of an outside consultant can, however, can do much to undermine a doubtful proposal. Finally, if more concerted opposition is needed, one tactic is to choose to argue with the particulars of the change proposals in such a way that any lack of detailed insider knowledge of the workings of the organisation are starkly exposed. (Further discussion of such tactics can be found in Keen, 1985, who discusses ways in which people can undermine the introduction of new technologies. The tactics of collective resistance are outlined in Walton, 1965).

Much intervention theory in organisational psychology has been developed specifically with the intention of overcoming tactics such as these. In the light of theory of individual, group and organisational reactions to changes, the thrust of theory in this area has been to encourage participative approaches to change management (see Blackler and Shimmin, 1984). The ideas presented in this section suggest that changes will be introduced smoothly if people feel their needs are being met, if open discussion of the ideas is encouraged and the primary proposers are respected, and if objectives are clearly communicated and are relatively specific. In addition, projects are more likely to meet with success if changes are introduced incrementally or on a pilot basis to enable emerging problems to be addressed; rewards for involvement must be adequate; and sufficient resources should be made available to support the time and energy that the change process itself will itself consume.

Managing disjunctive changes

As noted above, in recent years the rate of change affecting organisations has increased dramatically. One problem with participatory and incremental approaches has become very clear: they require both time and patience. This raises the the disturbing possibility that perhaps demands on organisations to change may have outstripped the abilities of organisations to respond.

A number of efforts have been made in recent years to deal with this issue, in particular attention has been drawn to the suggestion that a key barrier to rapid organisational change is the way that "taken-for-granted" systems of thought and action become entrenched. Attention has focussed therefore on ways in which "organisational cultures" might be managed. The concept of culture has been adopted in modified form from anthropological theory, and in this case is intended to refer to the specific features that distinguish one organisation from another. Schein (1985), for example, uses the term to refer to "the deeper levels of basic and assumptions and beliefs that are shared by members of an organisation, that operate unconsciously, and that define in a basic, 'taken-for-granted' fashion, an organisation's view of itself and its environment". Stories and myths that members of an organisation share provide clues about the nature of such assumptions, formal management statements about mission or achievements can be similarly revealing. An organisation's culture is more than these things however, and is best understood as the expressive and affective dimension of organisational life, its shared system of language, symbols, values and ideologies.

The core issue here, of course, is how far an organisation's culture can be consciously manipulated. Cultures have their roots in history and custom; to an extent an organisation's culture is what an organisation is, and is not a separate variable that can easily or comprehensively be manipulated. Moreover, organisations are pluralist and in all probability will contain a variety of cultures. Nonetheless, as was stressed at the start of this chapter, organisations are social creations and are sustained by the actions and interactions of those who participate in them. Although, as we have already seen, organisations tend to be somewhat resilient by nature a particular organisational culture has no inevitability.

Studies of organisation cultures have identified some of the processes through which taken-for-granted assumptions emerge and are sustained. The aims and values of key figures in the early years of an organisation often provide a lasting influence. Emerging structures and practices will have a strong effect, and the distinctive competencies of the organisation are also likely to provide clear models. Out of such factors "strategic recipes" emerge, that is, characteristic modes of thinking, which provide a model about appropriate objectives for the organisation, appropriate ways of meeting them, and the kinds of criteria that should be used to judge effectiveness (Hinings and Greenwood, 1988). Studies of successful attempts to change the strategic recipes of major companies (see especially Pettigrew, 1985, and Child, 1987) have provided useful insights into processes through which this may be achieved. The vision of senior managers is undoubtedly a key factor; similarly, the stimulus of a changing environment and the availability of new ideas and exemplars about how to respond are both important. Nonetheless the incubation of significant new ideas is likely to take time and, if new ideas are to be adopted, a variety of management actions are likely to be necessary. Amongst these: networks within the organisation of people supporting strategic change should be cultivated; as should contacts with outside organisations moving in similar directions so that their lessons can be understood. Moreover, in addition to ensuring good communications and encouraging open discussion about new ideas, what senior leaders concentrate on, the role models they provide, the criterea for reward and recruitment that they insist upon, and how they react to crises are likely to particularly important factors.

To conclude this section, approaches from organisational psychology indicate that three core tasks must be addressed if significant changes within organisations are to be managed successfully. The first is that it is essential to manage continuity with the past. People preoccupied with the need to encourage a redirection of effort sometimes forget this, but analysis of individual, group and cultural changes confirm the need for continuity. Indeed, paradoxical as it may first seem, organisations that succeed in maintaining a consistency with the past by, for example, being clear about their core strengths, publicising these internally, investing in the continuing development of basic skills, and placing an emphasis on stable, helping relationships, are more likely to be able to change radically than are organisations which have a less obvious sense of their own identity. In addition, however, it is important that organisations should seek also to manage creativity. Managers need, for example, to encourage interest in new ideas through education, recruitment, and the use of outside advisers. They need also to encourage new ideas from all levels in the organisation, and to value experimentation (this means they must accept that their staff will make mistakes). It is unlikely that a climate such as this cannot be introduced quickly; rather, it needs to be nurtured over a period of time. Finally, organisations need also to manage specific periods of rapid transition. Here senior leaders have an important role to play in articulating a common vision, encouraging genuine debate, and communicating key messages.

TABLE 10.4 Differences Between the Perspectives of Theorists and Practitioners

Aims, Orientations:	Theorists:	Practitioners:
General Aims:	Understanding	Accomplishment
	Valid knowledge	Effective action
	Abstract and general theory	Contingent and specific guidelines
Problem Orientation:	Long-term time perspective	Short-term, immediate issues
	Objectivity	Involvement
	Vary inputs, study outputs	Vary inputs to control outputs

Action Research and Consultancy

One theme of this discussion has been the relevance of organisational psychology to practical problems; another has been the difficulties that can arise in gaining acceptance of new ideas. As early disappointments in encouraging the adoption of new approaches to job design illustrate and as discussion of the problems of managing organisational change explain, people do not always accept what experts recommend. This is, indeed, a very common experience: professional advisors of all kinds who research management problems then write a report detailing their recommendations, very often find that their suggestions are received politely by their client, but are soon forgotten. To conclude the chapter therefore the issue of the utilisation of organisational psychology is discussed directly. A major attempt, action research, to develop a method to overcome problems of acceptance is first described and evaluated. Then the advantages and disadvantages of alternative approaches for encouraging the utilisation of psychological ideas are reviewed.

It has long been recognised that there are significant differences in perspective between academics and practitioners and that communication barriers between the two groups can be considerable. Table 10.4 summarises such differences. Theorists typically adopt detached, abstract, approaches to problem solving and are primarily interested in the development of general concepts; practitioners, on the other hand are involved, interested in specific issues, and concerned about particular outcomes. A project that goes wrong provides data for the theorist, for the manager it will signal failure.

There are, moreover, a number of problems associated with the relevance of mainstream methods in psychological research for studying real-life problems. Traditional experimental methods can be difficult to use in organisational situations, indeed many have argued that experimental approaches are not only difficult to use outside a laboratory, they are inappropriate. Argyris (1968) for example, compared the climate created in experimental settings with bureaucratic approaches to organising. Organisations that are strongly heirarchical, with key decision making clustered at the top and mindless task execution at the bottom, tend to alienate their junior staff he pointed out, making them dependent on their superiors in the heirarchy, and encouraging sullen hostility and interpersonal mistrust. Experimental settings are not dissimilar in their effects. Like senior managers the experimenters unilaterally decide what is best; like shop-floor workers experimental subjects are asked to engage in silly tasks that are not properly explained to them, usually in return for payment. The behaviours such settings produce, Argyris argued, are largely the outcomes of such situations: dependency, hostility, mistrust and an instrumental orientation to activity. Experiments on human beings, in other words, create a milieu with its own behavioural dynamic.

Action research should, therefore, be understood as an attempt to develop an alternative to traditional experimental approaches within psychology. Action research projects normally fall into different phases. To begin is the initial problem identification phase. This requires researcher and client should work together to achieve an agreed orientation to the problem under investigation. Next, a data collection phase will take place. This might include interviews and questionnaire surveys, but depending on the research aims that are pursued, the use of participant observation techniques, and systematic approaches to the collection of data, could all be regarded as legitimate. Feedback of such data to those involved will, once again, involve joint interpretation of its significance. The fourth phase would be the creation of a plan of action. Ideally this would itself be followed by attempts to take action, and by a subsequent review and evaluation.

As used by some researchers and consultants, this approach to research is best understood as a collaborative orientation to enquiry that makes use of the insight that an incremental, participative approach is an effective way of introducing change. Such approaches can be highly effective (see French and Bell, 1983, for a discussion of approaches associated with this style of working). Nonetheless other psychologists believe that there should be more to action research than merely smoothing the way for acceptance of new ideas. For them, action research differs from conventional orientations in substance as well as in style.

This point of view has been developed by, amongst others, Susman and Evered (1978). Their starting point is to emphasise how the logic of traditional approaches in science are inappropriate when

> "the unit of analysis is, like the researcher, a self-reflecting subject, when relationships between subjects (actors) are influenced by definitions of the situation, or when the reason for undertaking the research is to solve a problem which the actors have helped to define".

Traditional scientific methods in psychology emphasise the importance of observed behaviours; this provides the raw data for which explanations are developed. Such an approach however, can only assume that the behaviours which the experimenter records were inevitable for, in the absence of and understanding of the meanings that informed peoples' actions, no insights can be provided into the alternative behaviours that people might have considered (or, indeed, might come to consider). The point is that conventional experimental methodologies in psychology deal only with the social world as the researcher finds it; they enable theories to be built about what presently happens, but often fail to provide an insight into alternative possible behaviour patterns. For these to be understood less emphasis should be placed on the essentials of positivist methods, namely deduction, induction, prediction, and detachment; more emphasis should be given to conjecture, understanding, engagement and learning.

Seen in this way action research is more than merely a way of securing receptivity to new ideas, rather it is an essentially collaborative approach to enquiry, emphasising both practical and theoretical issues, and highlighting the importance of encouraging the people directly involved to develop "self-help competencies" for themselves.

To illustrate the workings of action research a project in the area of job design undertaken by Elden (1985) provides links with the discussion earlier in this chapter. Elden was asked to work in an aluminium smelting plant and to study effects of technological changes from a trade-union point of view. He might have chosen to have undertaken a study himself, simply reporting its outcome to the people concerned. He decided, however, to approach the problem in a collaborative, action research mode, and to work with a project group of employees. Over a two day workshop he introduced social science theory about the quality of working life to the group. Group members were then asked to identify for themselves satisfying characteristics of jobs found in the plant, to review the history of technical changes in its twenty five year history, and to consider how these had effected the experience of work. An empirical study followed (lasting about twelve months) in which, working with Elden, the project group compared job descriptions from throughout the plant to the criteria of satisfying work that the group had itself developed. People from different sections of the factory were interviewed as well. It was to emerge that while technological change had increased both the quality and quantity of production in the plant, fewer people were now employed and the jobs that remained were less satisfying than they had been. In particular, jobs now involved less worker discretion, control, opportunities for learning and social contact in work. While this project was somewhat unusual in that the action researcher worked with a trade union rather than with a management client, it demonstrates three characteristics of a good action research project: the research process was controlled jointly by the client group and the researcher; it produced new knowledge relevant to social science theory (in this case, knowledge concerning the relevance of job satisfaction theory to the aluminium plant); and it contributed significantly to the skills and understandings of the client group involved, alerting them to possible adverse consequences of technological change and encouraging them to take a long-term view in future discussions with management.

It should be emphasised that action research is no panacea: access to people who may be willing to work in an action research mode can be difficult to obtain, and action research projects are often demanding of resources difficult to manage to a tight timetable. Yet the approach offers certain clear advantages to organisational psychology. Action research has:

(a) drawn attention to the way in which the abstract and remote nature of much academic work renders it irrelevant to the concerns of people facing immediate "concrete" problems.

(b) exposed a number of institutional shortcomings within psychology, in particular the failure of conventional approaches to emphasise the importance of the applicability of research projects. (When research papers are considered by scientific journals, for example, practical relevance is only rarely used as a criterion for selection).

(c) analysed the problems of approaches to behavioural enquiry which treat people as if they were passive "subjects".

(d) led to an awareness of the difficulties of working in a collaborative mode.

Elaboration of this latter point provides a suitable conclusion to this section. In the early days action researchers underestimated the problems associated with the development of genuinely collaborative approaches to research. For example, it was sometimes assumed that people in organisations can be expected to subscribe to an identical set of priorities and that organisational psychologists could regard the organisation as a whole as the client. Decisions about the research needs of an organisation are not reached by reason alone however; has already been noted, organisations contain a plurality of interest groups and priorities which are identified in any particular case will reflect the ways in which the values of different interest groups are reflected in the ways problems are interpreted and the effectiveness with which people have argued their cases. One implication of this is that there are clear limitations to the extent to which powerful members of an organisation are likely to feel committed to encourage the development of certain "self-help competencies" amongst groups whose intentions they mistrust. This is not to argue that attempts to develop collaborative approaches through action research are impossible. It is to point out that action researchers have limited opportunities to operate outside the dominant ideology of existing social systems.

Short term acceptability versus long term relevance

Discussion of the problems of developing an applied psychology of organisations inevitably leads to issues concerning the short term acceptability of psychology projects, versus their potential relevance to new, long term policies.

Earlier, reference was made to the common image of organisations as machines, austerely effective, with individual parts integrating effectively to produce a smoothly functioning performance. Consistent with this image are assumptions about decision making in organisations: the process, it is assumed, is highly rational; when managers are taking decisions they will be aware of the significance of what they are doing; will deal with particular issues in a purposeful way; and will endeavour to calculate carefully the pros and cons of alternative courses of action.

If the process of making decisions really was like this the job of developing an influential organisational psychology would be easy. Research into specific policy issues could be undertaken, knowledge codified, then when managers were considering policy options relevant theory and data could be presented to them. In fact, decision making is only exceptionally as focussed and as logical as popular assumptions about the process assume.

Weiss (1986) has offered a useful summary of research into how policy makers actually do make decisions; the process is complex and varied. First, frequently, policy makers rely on precedent to provide possible pointers as to how to proceed; custom and implicit rules can provide powerful models for action, at other times managers will improvise around standard approaches. Second, if other parties are likely to be affected by particular decisions a process of mutual adjustment would be normal, anticipating how others might respond; overt political manoeuvring between different interested parties can also occur; formal negotiations may also take place. Third, sometimes decision making occurs by default with new policies emerging as by-products of other decisions. Finally, sometimes managers seize a window of opportunity to try out ideas they have been interested in for some time. In short, while decision making clearly involves logical elements, Weiss' description accords well with analysis offered earlier in the chapter of organisations as complex social and cognitive systems. Popular imagery of organisations as machine-like and rational fall very short of reality.

The question arises, what are the implications of this insight for the development of an influential organisational psychology? Two possible alternative courses of action can be identified. The first would be designed to achieve short term acceptability, the second to achieve long term relevance. Short-term acceptability can be obtained by working within the dominant general decision-making paradigm of an organisation. Four key tasks can be identified:

- psychologists should demonstrate a strong task, or results orientation in their work (i.e. they should not present themselves as interested in employee satisfaction or morale alone) seeking to demonstrate the psychology's relevance to specific issues. This could involve the development of techniques that others could apply for themselves.
- psychologists working in this mode need also to work within the prevailing power realities of the organisation; this normally means they will work on problems sanctioned by senior management.
- in conducting their work, it is necessary that they should adopt a systems' perspective, working with those affected by the problem, anticipating how changes in one aspect of the organisation may have ramifications elsewhere.
- standard solutions to problems are rarely appropriate; it is necessary to avoid pre-packaged prescriptions and to be creative and eclectic in developing recommendations for change.

Short term acceptability is one thing, long term impact may be something else. It is unlikely to be advisable for an applied social science to become too preoccupied with immediate results; the long-term relevance of organisational psychology is likely to be related to its ability to encourage people to re-frame their understandings and develop unfamiliar approaches. Key tasks necessary for organisational psychology to develop a long-term policy orientation can be specified as follows:

- independence of thought is something that must be preserved.
- it is essential that conceptual and theoretical sophistication is nurtured.
- problems relevant to broad policies should be studied (albeit that these are often the most difficult to tackle).
- disciplined method and critical self-reflection (that is, "rigour" in its broadest sense) is indispensable.

Despite the differences in emphasis between what is required to make organisational psychology acceptable in the short-term and what will ensure its long-term relevance, perhaps it would be a mistake to force a choice between the two orientations. In some cases it may be possible to pursue both at the same time (action researchers would certainly like to think so). In others, success in the one may may assist success in the other, simply by helping develop a good reputation for the subject. What is crucial, however, is that those involved with organisational psychology must recognise that both approaches are essential.

SUMMARY AND CONCLUSIONS

To summarise the chapter, organisational psychology has developed considerably in recent decades. Work in the area of time and motion studies, working conditions, selection and equipment design has broadened to include studies of interpersonal behaviour, motivation, technologies, structures, cultures and corporate strategies. Developments in the subject have been driven by changing perceptions of social problems as well as by a growing theoretical and methodological sophistication. New approaches to organising have been developed; theories of job design, for example, have provided a new exemplar for management. Analysis of the social and cognitive processes which provide the basis of organisational behaviour have provided a series of insights into how organisational change can be managed. Moreover, developments within the subject have underlined the importance of approaches that enable psychologists to work with people rather than sirnply studying them.

It is not easy to predict how the subject will develop further over the coming years. Yet, as this review has indicated, many of the issues that need to be faced are clear. What is needed is a subject that is both pragmatic and theoretical, oriented towards intervention but concerned with methodological rigour, and relevant to broad policy issues but in touch with every-day problems. This is a tall order, but as this chapter has illustrated, some progress has already been made in these matters. At its best, organisational psychology promises to be a genuinely emancipatory social science. The extent to which it becomes so will depend on the extent to which those involved with it choose to address emerging, unfamiliar issues and on their skills in blending theory with practice.

REFERENCES

Argyris, C. (1968). Some unintended consequences of rigorous reseach. *Psychological Bulletin, 7*, 185–197.
Bjorn-Anderson, N., Eason, K. & Robey, D. (1986). *Managing Computer Impact: An International Study of Management and Organisation.* Norwood N.J.: Ablex.
Blackler, F. (1988). Information technologies and organisations, lessons from the 1980s and issues for the 1990s. *Journal of Occupational Psychology,* **61**, 113–127.
Blackler, F. & Shimmin, S. (1984). *Applying Psychology in Organisations.* London: Methuen.
Burns, T. & Stalker, G.M. (1966). *The Management of Innovation.* London: Tavistock.
Cherns, A.B. (1979). *Using the Social Sciences.* London: Routledge & Kegan Paul.
Child, J. & Smith, C. (1987). The context and process of organisational transformation: Cadbury Ltd. in its sector. *Journal of Management Studies,* **24**, 565–594.
Davis, L.E. & Cherns, A.B. (1975). *The Quality of Working Life, Volumes 1 and 2.* New York: Free Press.
Elden, M. (1985). Democratising organisations: a challenge to organisational development. In R. Tannenbaum, N. Margulies & F. Massarick (eds). *Human Systems Development.* San Francisco: Jossey Bass.
Fletcher, B.C. & Payne, R.L. (1980). Stress at work: a review an a theoretical framework. *Personnel Review,* **ix**, 1, 19–29; ix, 2, 5–8.
French, W. & Bell, C. (1983). *Organisational Development: Behavioural Science Interventions for Organisational Improvement.* Englewood Cliffs N.J.: Prentice Hall.
Hackman, J.R. (1976). Group influences on individuals. In M. Dunnette (ed). *Handbook of Industrial and Organisational Psychology.* Rand McNally.

Hackman, J.R. & Oldham, G.R. (1976). Motivation through the design of work. *Organisational Behaviour and Human Performance,* 16, 250–279.

Herzberg, F., Mausner, B. & Snyderman, B. (1959). *The Motivation to Work.* New York: Wiley.

Hinings, C.R. & Greenwood, R. (1988). *The Dynamics of Strategic Change.* Oxford: Blackwell.

Keen, P. (1985). Information systems and organisational design. In E. Rhodes & D. Wield (eds). *Implementing New Technologies: Choice, Decisions and Change in Manufacturing.* Oxford: Blackwell.

Lewin, K. (1951). *Field Theory in Social Science.* New York: Harper & Row.

Mangham, I. (1978). *Interactions and Interventions in Organisations.* Chichester: Wiley.

Marris, P. (1974). *Loss and Change.* London: Routledge & Kegan Paul.

Pettigrew, A. (1985). *The Awakening Giant.* Oxford: Blackwell.

Schein, E. (1980). *Organisational Psychology.* Englewood Cliffs N.J.: Prentice Hall.

Schein, E. (1985). *Organisational Culture and Leadership.* San Francisco: Jossey Bass.

Susman, G. & Evered, R. (1978). An assessment of the scientific merits of action research. *Administrative Science Quarterly,* 23, 582–603.

Trist, E.L., Higgin, G., Murray, H. & Pollock, A.B. (1963). *Organisational Choice.* London: Tavistock.

Walton, R. (1965). Two strategies of change and their dilemmas. *Journal of Applied Behavioural Science,* 1, 2, 167–179.

Walton, R. (1975). The diffusion of new work structures: explaining why success didn't take. *Organisational Dynamics.* Winter, 3–22.

Weber, M. (1947). *The Theory of Social and Economic Organisation* edited and translated by A.M. Henderson & Talcott Parsons. London: MacMillan.

Weiss, C. (1986). Research and policy-making: a limited partnership. In F. Heller (ed). *The Use and Abuse of Social Science.* London: Sage.

11

TRAINING

J. PATRICK

INTRODUCTION TO TRAINING

Training is a challenging and developing area of applied psychology. The psychological basis of good training practice is gradually changing together with the nature of the real world problems which training addresses. This chapter attempts to highlight the activities of the applied psychologist involved in training. Given the range of these activities, this chapter has to be selective in its discussion and more comprehensive reviews can be found in Goldstein (1986), Morrison (1991) and Patrick (1992).

In a review of training, Goldstein (1980) defined training as:

> "the acquisition of skills, concepts or attitudes that result in improved performance in an on-the-job environment." (p. 230)

The goal of training therefore is to improve performance mostly in a job situation although sometimes it may be in a non-occupational context (e.g. training a sportsperson or a person with some disability). This is achieved by applying psychological principles to both the analysis of the tasks/skills which require training and to the design of a training programme. The applied psychologist attempts to delicately "engineer" an optimal learning environment for the tasks which have to be mastered. Some training takes place off-the-job in which case the learning gains made during training need to be translated into effective performance in the job situation. This requirement might apply to, for example, off-the-job training using a space vehicle simulator or to a management training course. However, the consequences of ineffective training in these two situations may have dramatically different consequences for on-the-job performance. This highlights the importance of the training context.

Training occurs in all types of industry and recent emphasis has been not only on training 'raw recruits' but also on retraining existing staff for new tasks and jobs as a consequence of technological change. Training is also a vital activity of the armed services in which jobs and tasks are subject to constant change from hardware developments and manpower turnover. Training is concerned with the full spectrum of jobs including: relatively "unskilled" manual workers; clerical and administration jobs; and professional and management positions. The number and type of tasks comprising these jobs will vary although quite frequently similar tasks may be performed in apparently different contexts under different job titles. The applied psychologist should not be influenced by superficial job distinctions such as job titles and should analyse the requirements of a job/task in order to devise an effective training programme.

Application of new technology in industry is having various consequences. The development of perceptual-motor skills is of diminishing interest as many repetitive manual tasks are now automated if they involve procedures which can be specified and programmed. Engineers, technicians and instrument mechanics are more frequently required to use problem-solving skills in order to rectify machine or equipment malfunctions. These skills have to be versatile and applicable to many pieces of equipment in which novel faults might occur. Nowadays operators monitor complex, largely automated industrial processes and are rarely required to intervene although when they are, any ineffective actions may have costly consequences (e.g. Rasmussen, Duncan and Leplat, 1987). Information technology not only creates its own training problems but can assist in providing training solutions through Computer-based training (CBT) and Intelligent Tutoring Systems (ITSs) which are mentioned later. CBT and ITSs offer a means by which various skills which are used infrequently can be maintained and updated alongside the job.

SYSTEMS APPROACHES TO THE DEVELOPMENT OF TRAINING

The development of effective training programmes can be facilitated in two ways:

(a) by identification of the functions which have to be fulfilled in the development of training.
(b) by application of principles from psychology which promote efficient skill acquisition, transfer and retention.

In the former case the development of training is viewed as a system and this system is divided into its sub-systems, each of which performs a function which contributes to the overall objective of the system, i.e. the production of good training. This systems approach makes *logical* distinctions between different functions involved in the development of training and shows how they interrelate. These functions are the same irrespective of whether instruction is being developed in either a "training" or "educational" context. Models which specify these different functions in the development of training are known as Instructional Systems Development (ISD) models and the main ones are discussed by Patrick (1992).

Applied psychologists have to prescribe *how* these functions can best be performed. A function might involve deciding either how a task should be analysed or how an effective training programme should be designed, in terms of its structure, the sequence of the training material, and the nature of the advice provided to the trainee. These decisions essentially involve *psychological* expertise and are considerably more difficult to make. A few of these issues are discussed later in the chapter.

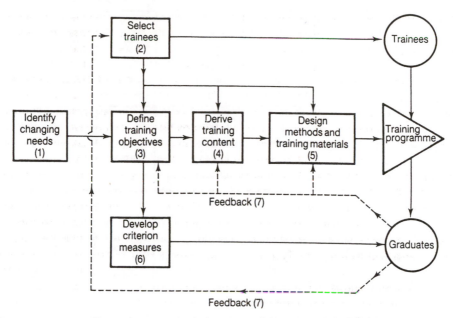

FIGURE 11.1   Different functions and their interrelationships in the development of training (Patrick, 1980).

Instructional Systems Development (ISD) Models

Functions in the development of training are represented in Figure 11.1. Their interaction with personnel selection (2) is also indicated because there is often a need to select *for* retraining (given the current high level of unemployment and the rapidly changing job demands which frequently require a more intellectual component). Therefore the tradeoff between selection and training is an important one. There are six remaining functions within the training development system (Figure 11.1). The first identifies some actual or potential problem situation in an organisation which involves a training need (1). This may be a consequence of: the introduction of new technology or revised procedures; staff changes and development; and unacceptable levels of production in terms of quantity and/or quality. In order to identify this training need (1), it is necessary to specify clear and unambiguous behavioural or performance objectives (3) which the trainees should achieve as a consequence of training. This will also enable appropriate criterion measures (6) to be developed which can be used to evaluate trainees' performance as 'graduates' of the training programme.

In order to define the training objectives for a job or a set of tasks (3) and to derive training content (4) for these objectives to be met, some form of job or task analysis has to be carried out. The final stage before running a training programme involves the design of training (5). The applied psychologist has to synthesise psychological principles affecting skill acquisition, transfer and retention and advise how they can be incorporated into a training programme. Not all principles derived from laboratory studies have sufficient power and generality to be used in the design of training. Sometimes it may be necessary for the applied psychologist to carry out

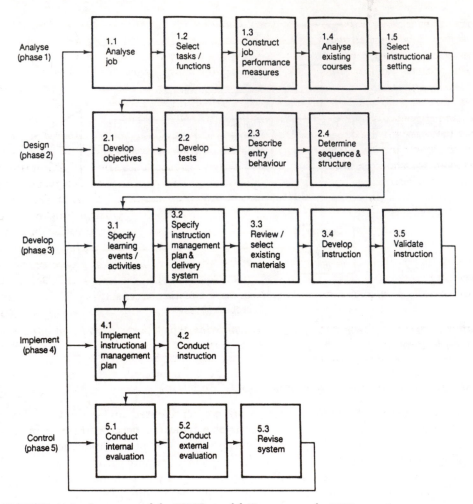

FIGURE 11.2 Summary of the IPISD model (Branson et al., 1975).

some research in order to solve a specific training problem. Finally the training development system should be capable of modifying and improving itself and this is achieved on the basis of the feedback loops (7) which stem from various forms of evaluation of the training programme and its "graduates". The effects of training can be evaluated by: reactions of trainees to the programme; changes in skill and knowledge from before to after training; improvements in job performance; and ultimately in positive effects on the organisation, e.g. higher productivity, less damage to equipment. Evaluation may indicate that modifications are needed in the training objectives, training content and the design of training.

An influential Instructional Systems Development (ISD) model developed in the context of the United States military training is known as IPISD—Interservice Procedures for Instructional Systems Development (Branson, Rayner, Cox, Furman, King and Hannum, 1975). The model consists of five main phases: analyse; design; develop; implement; and control; which are divided further into more detailed functions (see Figure 11.2). Such a model can be viewed as providing a useful set of

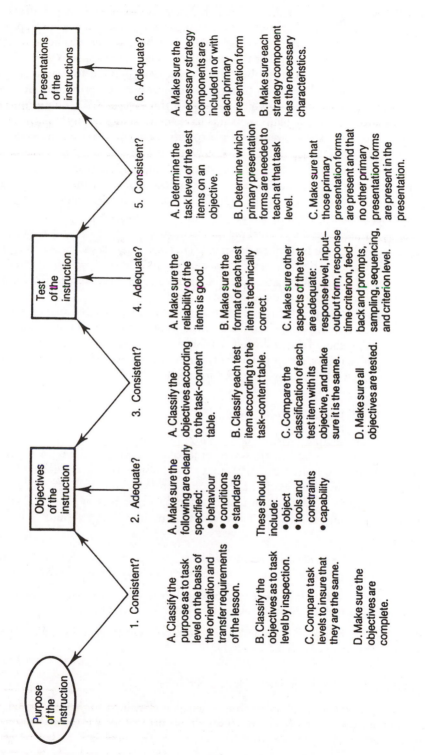

FIGURE 11.3   *Summary of the aspects analysed by the Instructional Quality Profile (Merrill, Reigeluth and Faust, 1979).*

prompts to the developer of training which generalise to any training context. One criticism is that this model represents a rational top-down view of the development of training which may obscure the idiosyncratic and bottom-up activities which are involved. Another criticism is that this model and similar ones specify "what" has to be accomplished but fail to prescribe "how" these development functions should be performed. Some work has begun to remedy this problem by providing aids for the "authors" of training materials which map onto the various ISD functions. This is difficult because on the one hand such aids have to generalise to any training context and on the other hand they have to provide specific prescriptions for the developer. In this tradition O'Neal, Faust and O'Neal (1979) described a training course for authors of instructional materials which included classifying instructional objectives and designing training for the acquisition of rules, concepts and procedures. Merrill, Reigluth and Faust (1979) discussed the Instructional Quality Profile which is aimed at ensuring that aspects of training development are both consistent with each other and adequate from logical and technical perspectives. Figure 11.3 provides a summary of this technique which can be broken down into six areas: purpose-objective consistency; objective adequacy; objective-test consistency; test adequacy; test-presentation consistency; and presentation adequacy. (Note that presentation refers to information given in training i.e. training materials.)

   In conclusion application of the systems approach and associated author aids to the development of training is likely to have considerable benefit. It is not suggested that any one system should be followed slavishly. Nevertheless an awareness of the functions involved in the development of training and how they interrelate provides an important framework for those engaged in training.

Specification of Training Objectives

One initial and essential element of training development, which has already been mentioned, is the use of correctly stated objectives. A great deal has been published about the specification and use of different types of objective (e.g. Davies, 1976) whilst some criticisms have been made of this approach (MacDonald-Ross, 1973). Mager (1962) provided the classic account of developing objectives which, he argued, are primarily for communicating instructional intent. They should have three components:

> "*First*, identify the terminal behaviour by name; you can specify the kind of behaviour that will be accepted as evidence that the learner has achieved the objective.
>
> *Second*, try to define the desired behaviour further by describing the important conditions under which the behaviour will be expected to occur.
>
> *Third*, specify the criteria of acceptable performance by describing how well the learner must perform to be considered acceptable."
>
> (Mager, 1962, p.12)

An example provided by Mager of an objective is:

> "Given a DC motor of ten horsepower or less that contains a single malfunction, and given a standard kit of tools and references, the learner must be able to repair the motor within a period of 45 minutes." (p.39)

Mager insisted that objectives should reflect the *actions* which the trainee should be able to perform after training, the *conditions* under which they are to be carried out and the *standards* of performance which have to be achieved. Slight changes in any of these three components can change the skills required and therefore the nature of the training programme. Perhaps the most important component of a training objective is a verb to describe performance which is both concrete and action-oriented. This will avoid the ambiguity inherent in such verbs as "to know" and "to understand". When performance objectives are being developed, a set of action verbs should be defined. Such an approach was adopted in a study by Fredericksen and Freer (1978) of the basic electronic skills of maintenance personnel. They provided a list of twelve action verbs which made distinctions in maintenance functions (e.g. to inspect, to adjust, to test) with associated definitions. It is then possible to ensure that training objectives can be communicated effectively not only to those involved in the development of training but also to the trainees at the beginning of training.

ANALYSING JOBS AND TASKS

Some form of systematic breakdown of a task (or job) is important because it reveals the activities required by a task which form the focus of the training programme. This section is divided into three parts and is based on accounts by Patrick (1991, 1992). Firstly, different types of analysis and how they differ are discussed (for a more wide ranging treatment of job analysis methods, see McCormick, 1979). Secondly, two taxonomies are described which help to distinguish between the differing psychological demands of tasks. Thirdly, one type of task analysis, namely, Hierarchical Task Analysis developed by Annett and Duncan (1967), is discussed in the context of training applications.

Types of Analysis

The terms job and task analysis are both used to describe methods of breaking down an area of work. Patrick (1991,1992) adapted Wheaton's (1968) ideas concerning how behavioural taxonomies can vary in order to identify dimensions along which job and task analyses differ. For our present discussion it is useful to consider the following five dimensions: (a) nomenclature; (b) purpose; (c) descriptive base; (d) structuring and classification procedures; and (e) data collection methods.

Nomenclature
The term "job analysis" is a more general and widely used term within occupational psychology. In contrast the term "task analysis" usually refers to techniques used within the context of training. This is exemplified by the following definition of task analysis by the Department of Employment's Glossary of Training Terms (1971) as:

> "A systematic analysis of the *behaviour* required to carry out a task with a view to identifying areas of difficulty and the appropriate training techniques and learning aids necessary for successful instruction." (p.28).

It is difficult to define the terms "job" and "task" although there is agreement that "job" is at a higher level and refers to all the tasks which occur within a person's prescribed duties of employment. IPISD, (Branson *et al.*, 1975) defined a task as "the lowest level of behaviour in a job that describes the performance of a meaningful function in the job under consideration" (p.171). However, Wheaton (1968) distinguished two dimensions along which even task definitions may differ. The first of these involves the breadth or scope of the definition with respect to the general work environment whilst the second is whether a task is considered to have some objective reality of its own or whether it is intrinsically linked to the perceptions and values of the person who therefore subjectively defines it.

Purpose

Job and task analysis techniques can be viewed as providing the means to achieve certain goals and should therefore be judged by how effectively they accomplish them. Some job analysis techniques are multi-purpose and might be used for various occupational problems including job evaluation, personnel selection, performance appraisal and vocational guidance. This is true of techniques such as the Position Analysis Questionnaire (PAQ – McCormick, Jeanneret and Mecham, 1969) and Functional Job Analysis (Fine and Heinz, 1958) part of which has been incorporated into the Dictionary of Occupational Titles (DOT) which is a classification of types of job in the United States economy. Part of DOT involves dividing a worker's function into three functional levels consisting of activities with respect to data, people and things. In each of these three areas a hierarchy of activities exists such that the higher ones subsume the lower ones. For example with respect to data one might be synthesising, coordinating, analysing, computing, copying or composing, proceeding from the highest to the lowest activities. In a similar tradition, is Smith's (1973) work on Generic Skills which suggests that work can be analysed into basic categories such as mathematics, communication, reasoning, interpersonal and manipulative skills. These can be further subdivided into various job elements.

It is doubtful whether these broadbased job analysis techniques provide useful information for training purposes. Despite considerable efforts to define categories rigorously, it is inevitable that a considerable amount of information is lost in the process of classification which cannot be retrieved easily without a re-examination of the job. This is partly because judgement of the involvement of a job element is made with respect to *all* the tasks involved in that job rather than each one. The resulting information is too gross for training purposes. It is not surprising therefore that multi-purpose job analysis techniques will be less effective for training than techniques specifically designed for such a purpose, for example, Hierarchical Task Analysis, discussed later on.

Descriptive base

Morgan (1972) provided a useful review of occupational classification and the type of variables which can be used to describe jobs. A job (or task) might be analysed in terms of its content, context and the requirements of the job holder. One important distinction made by many writers is that between *task-oriented* descriptive variables and *person-oriented* (or psychological) variables. Patrick (1980) stated that:

"Task-oriented descriptions concern the goal of performance, the equipment or conditions in the work situation or the observable activities associated with a task.

Person-oriented descriptors relate to the cognitive capacities used or required by the person performing the job." (p. 56).

If we reconsider the functions of the training system (Figure 11.1) it is evident that both types of description are necessary. In order to derive the objectives and content of the training programme detailed task-oriented descriptions or analyses are necessary. On the other hand, it is necessary to describe the task demands in person-oriented terms in order to select potential trainees with the necessary qualities, to design training in a psychologically expedient manner, and also to analyse the skill or expertise involved in task performance. It is not surprising therefore that considerable discussion has focused upon how these different types of description can be systematically linked. For a more detailed account of these issues the reader is referred to Dunnette (1976), Patrick (1980) and Peterson and Bownas (1982).

Structuring and classification procedures

The descriptive variables used in any analysis can be structured and classified on the basis of theoretical distinctions, practical categories and statistical manipulations.

The most common theoretical distinctions used by analysis techniques are from the information processing approach. The Position Analysis Questionnaire (PAQ) Form B (McCormick, Jeanneret and Mecham, 1969) is made up of 194 job elements which are organised into six divisions, covering information input, mental processes, work output, relationships with other workers, job context and other job characteristics. Alternatively the elements or tasks involved in a job can be grouped into categories which have some practical significance in that domain, e.g. start-up, operating and maintenance procedures.

Statistical techniques are frequently used to structure the output from job and task analyses. This is particularly so when the tasks or job elements have been rated with respect to their applicability, frequency of use, importance or criticality to the job. For example Christal (1974) developed a task inventory, comprising a large number of task statements, which was used to monitor changing training requirements, career patterns etc. in the United States Air Force. Tasks were rated in terms of relative time spent on each and a suite of computer programs performed various statistical analyses (e.g. cluster and regression analyses) which provided job analysis data in useful formats. Another commonly used statistical technique is factor analysis (e.g. McCormick used factor analysis to derive underlying job "dimensions"). Whilst such statistical techniques are useful in reducing and organising data, they nevertheless make a variety of statistical assumptions and the resulting output does not necessarily have psychological validity.

Data collection methods

There are many methods for collecting job or task analysis information. These include the use of existing documentation (such as operating manuals), observation, interviews, questionnaires, simulation, experimentation, and discussion (with job incumbents, supervisors and experts). Each of these methods has various well documented advantages and disadvantages. In order therefore to ensure that information is reliable, it is desirable to use as many methods as possible. In situations which depend upon a trained job analyst synthesising the relevant information or a person rating the job, the use of more than one analyst or rater together with the calculation of reliability measures are necessary safeguards against biased and unreliable data.

Taxonomies for Training

Taxonomies can facilitate the analysis of a job or task by providing categories for classifying their psychological demands. One type of taxonomy uses the information processing paradigm (e.g. Miller, 1974) whilst another distinguishes between the types of learning required by a training programme (e.g. Gagné, 1970; 1985).

R.B. Miller, in various publications since the 1950s, has attempted to pinpoint potential training difficulties associated with what would now be termed the "cognitive processes" required by the trainee in performing the task. His classification is based upon an information processing model of skilled performance. In this input-processing-output model, Miller (1974) identified twenty-five categories such as detect, identify, interpret, store, decide, and plan. (A useful source for this work is Fleishman and Quaintance, 1984.) Miller suggested that each task should be examined with respect to his twenty-five categories in order to identify which aspects of task performance are likely to be most difficult and require the focus of training. Some tasks may make demands primarily in the perceptual domain (e.g. recognising an aircraft) whilst others may make them in decision-making (e.g. controlling a nuclear power plant).

One advantage of using information processing categories is that they are applicable to any type of task (i.e. are context independent) and can therefore be used to compare the psychological demands between different tasks. One criticism is that information processing taxonomies neglect two issues. Firstly they decompose a task into categories and do not indicate how these interact dynamically in task performance. Secondly, most except some recent cognitive taxonomies, ignore the "higher level" cognitive processes which are the hallmark of the performance of experts. Another criticism is that it is difficult to identify the psychological demands of a task except on a subjective basis although perhaps the ultimate criterion of such taxonomic schemes is whether or not they are useful as Miller himself proposed. A final criticism is that the categories of such taxonomies are not linked explicitly to different training solutions. Nevertheless they do provide a useful framework for the analyst attempting to unravel the nature of a task.

A rather different taxonomic approach has been proposed by Gagné (e.g. 1970; 1985) who has distinguished different learning categories. Five varieties of learning outcome exist according to Gagné: intellectual skills, verbal information, cognitive strategies, motor skills and attitudes. Gagné's important proposition is simple: different types of learning require different learning conditions. Hence from a training perspective the taxonomy is not only concerned with the analysis of a task/job but also the design of training. In the area of intellectual skill, Gagné has suggested a "hierarchy" such that more complex intellectual skills can only be mastered if their prerequisite sub-skills have been acquired. So, for example, problem solving requires as prerequisites that certain rules have been mastered which require as prerequisites some concepts which in turn require as prerequisites some discriminations, etc. More complex intellectual skills can only be developed when their lower level components have been mastered. This therefore has implications for not only the analysis of a task but also the sequence of training activities. Despite some criticism, Gagné's ideas have been very influential in the area of training.

Another taxonomy of types of learning has been described by Merrill (1983) in his Component Display Theory (CDT). CDT identifies types of learning by combining two dimensions: one concerns the type of content to be learned (facts, concepts, procedures and principles) and the second identifies the level of performance required (remember, use and find). This results in ten permissible combinations or learning types, each of which is linked by Merrill to a different training objective, using Mager's prescriptions discussed earlier.

Hierarchical Task Analysis

Hierarchical Task Analysis (HTA) was developed by Annett and Duncan (1967) and has been described by Annett, Duncan, Stammers and Gray (1971), Patrick (1992), and Shepherd (1985). (It should not be confused with Gagne's hierarchical analysis of intellectual skills.) It is useful for identifying training needs, specifying training objectives and identifying the outline of training content. As its name suggests, Hierarchical Task Analysis utilises task-oriented descriptions to decompose a task into a hierarchical array of sub-tasks. It is a logical rather than a psychological technique. The analysis begins by considering a general task or job and then progressively breaks it down into a series of sub-tasks which logically comprise and exhaust the higher level task. There are essentially four features of this technique: the process of hierarchical breakdown; the specification of "operations" (tasks) and "sub-operations" (sub-tasks); the description of their "plans"; and a stopping rule which specifies when further breakdown of the task(s) is not necessary. The two main advantages of Hierarchical Task Analysis from a training perspective is that the logical decomposition process should ensure that *all* of the sub-tasks are analysed. Secondly rather than depending upon a fixed number of levels of analysis it is possible, at least in theory, for it to tailor its level of description to the target population of trainees (through its stopping rule).

Formally Annett *et al.* (1971) described tasks as "operations" which are:

"any unit of behaviour, no matter how long or short its duration and no matter how simple or complex its structure which can be defined in terms of its objective." (p.3)

The analysis of operations is guided by application of the $p \times c$ stopping rule. This requires an estimate to be made of the probability of inadequate performance without training (p) and the costs (in the widest sense) of such inadequate performance (c). If either of these estimates is unacceptable and a training solution cannot be identified, then the operation is analysed further. Figure 11.4 represents the analysis of a task in the chemical processing industry which is divided into five sub-tasks, 1.1–1.5. Sub-task 1.1 is straightforward and does not require further analysis whereas, for example, sub-task 1.4 does because both the probability of inadequate performance and its associated cost are unacceptable.

The concept of a "plan" is a necessary complement to that of an "operation". Just as there is a hierarchy of operations, so there is also a hierarchy of plans. A plan specifies when and in which sequence the operations (or sub-tasks) should be performed. Some plans are straightforward and involve fixed procedures as are often found in the start-up and shut-down procedures for machines or equipment. Plans 1.2 and 1.4 in Figure 11.4 represent simple procedures. Trainees can easily be trained to master such simple plans if indeed it is necessary to do so. On the other hand some plans may be more complex and involve various decisions which will dictate the sequence of operations to be followed (e.g. Plan 1 in Figure 11.4). Another example of this would be an algorithm

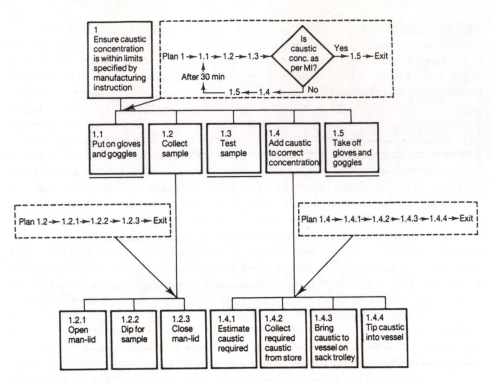

FIGURE 11.4   *Hierarchical Task Analysis of a task in the chemical processing industry (Patrick, Spurgeon and Shepherd, 1986).*

which might specify the sequence in which operations should be performed to diagnose a fault efficiently in a piece of equipment. Shepherd and Duncan (1980) described the analysis of a complex task in which a "controller" of a chlorine plant had to "balance" the production of gas from various units with consumer demand. The primary problem in the task analysis was to identify and specify the plans and sub-plans involved which could not be easily inferred by the analyst or verbalised by the skilled controllers.

Finally in order to improve the reliability of any task analysis, as discussed previously, it is worthwhile using not only more than one analyst but also as many different methods of data collection as possible. It is likely that the analysis will proceed iteratively through three stages: data collection; assimilation of information into a coherent structure; and finally verification that the task analysis represents accurately activities required by the job. Collaboration with technical experts and job incumbents will be necessary not only for the initial data collection but also for the final phase in which the operations and plans are agreed as correct and comprehensive.

In conclusion Hierarchical Task Analysis enables training objectives to be identified because operations are described in this manner. The output from a Hierarchical Task Analysis, as represented in Figure 11.4, provides a framework for the development of training content. The taxonomies for training can be used to classify the types of learning and information processing requirements of the tasks identified by such an analysis.

DESIGN OF TRAINING

It is unfortunate that at the present time no comprehensive set of principles exist which dictate how training should be organised for various types of subject matter and different trainees. Some piecemeal principles and theories do exist in diverse publications in the areas of education, training and instruction and these are reviewed by Patrick (1992). Theories of training design are also discussed by Reigeluth (1983). Training design is concerned with how to "engineer" an optimal learning environment and includes the provision of training material and advice during training; the sequencing, organisation and adaptivity of the training materials; and the selection of the appropriate means of "delivering" training. The last issue concerning which training media should be adopted is more of a practical one and is discussed by, for example, Romiszowski (1981) and Briggs and Wager (1981). Other training design issues inevitably depend not only upon our perspectives of how people acquire new or modified skills but also how they transfer and retain them. Consequently relevant theoretical perspectives and some aspects of training design are discussed below. This discussion has to be highly selective and a more comprehensive treatment can be found in Patrick (1992).

Theoretical Perspectives

Skill acquisition

Psychological theories of learning have changed radically over the past fifty years. Behaviourism focused upon learning being "effected" as a result of the principles of reinforcement. Consequently training regimes were concerned with the optimal organisation of the task in order to elicit the correct behaviours from trainees which could then be reinforced. The trainee was essentially a passive recipient of information provided by a training programme. Subsequently in the sixties and early seventies an information processing model of skill became popular which detailed the various stages which might intervene between stimulus input and response output. Miller's taxonomy, discussed previously, is in this tradition and provides a set of categories to identify the information processing stages where difficulties can arise in learning a new task. Gradually, what became known as cognitive psychology shifted from a predominant interest in how information was structured, for example, in long-term memory, to questions of how people acquire new knowledge. This focus on the dynamics of learning is reflected by the contributors to *Cognitive Skills and their Acquisition* edited by J.R. Anderson (1981). Greater emphasis was placed on the *active* role of the learner who uses general and specific cognitive strategies in both learning and performing new tasks. Therefore the role of training is to ensure that appropriate cognitive strategies are used not only in learning but also in subsequent task performance. Glaser and Bassok (1989) have provided a useful review of recent work in this vein.

During skill acquisition both *quantitative* and *qualitative* changes occur in trainee's behaviour. Trainees become faster and more accurate at performing a task with increasing amounts of training. A review by Newell and Rosenbloom (1981) identified the relationship between speed of performance and amount of training which extends to many tasks. This is known as "the power law of practice". During the early stages of

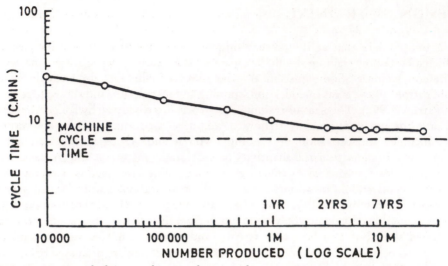

FIGURE 11.5   *Speed of cigar making as a function of practice (Crossman, 1959). Each point is the average machine cycle time.*

training there is a rapid improvement in performance although later on more and more training is required to achieve the same improvement. Hence there are diminishing returns from extended amounts of training. The most famous data which illustrate this phenomenon were provided by Crossman (1959) in his study of cigar-making by female operators (Figure 11.5). Performance improved dramatically over the first year of practice and although improvements were still taking place with up to two years of practice, these were extremely small. Whether or not extended training is worthwhile will depend upon the cost savings associated with improved performance which in turn depend upon the particular training context. The power law of practice and its equations are described fully by Newell and Rosenbloom (1981) and provide an opportunity for the developer of training to at least calculate how much training is required to achieve a specified standard of performance.

Two theories which describe the *qualitative* changes which occur during skill acquisition are those by Fitts (1962) and Anderson (1982, 1987). Both theories propose three stages of learning although Anderson is concerned with the *cognitive* basis of skill whereas Fitts' ideas were couched more in terms of the development of stimulus-response connections for perceptual-motor skills. Anderson (1982) proposed that as learning progresses, "declarative" knowledge (i.e. facts) is gradually transformed into "procedural" knowledge through the process of "knowledge compilation". Initially a trainee receives information concerning the requirements of a new task situation. (This corresponds to Fitts' "cognitive phase".) Skilled behaviour during this early stage is fairly crude as general rather than specific procedures have to be used to apply this information to perform the new task. However with practice this knowledge is converted into a procedural form which is directly relevant to task performance. This is achieved through the process of knowledge compilation which involves the subprocesses of composition and proceduralisation. (Knowledge compilation is equivalent to Fitts' "associative phase".) Anderson then described how learning continues by further "tuning" of these task-specific procedures which is similar to

Fitts' "autonomous phase". From a training perspective Anderson's theory suggests that training will be more effective to the extent that the skill or procedures required by task performance can be identified and captured in detail by a training programme. That is why the analysis of a task/skill, discussed earlier, is so important. Training can never be too specific because, as Anderson's theory points out, each task requires at least some unique elements. Also this "procedural knowledge" can only be developed by *doing* i.e. training must enable the trainee to practise the task in order for the skill to be compiled. Unfortunately both Fitts' and Anderson's theories are more descriptive than predictive and do not enable us to predict when these qualitative changes will occur and how training should be managed to optimise these transitions.

During the initial stage of skill acquisition trainees are heavily dependent on instructions and feedback concerning the nature of their performance. Trainers should recognise that at this stage high demands are made of working memory as trainees are often bombarded with too much information as they struggle to comprehend what is required by a task. In contrast when skill has developed, the task makes fewer demands of the trainee's resources and behaviour becomes "automatic" with the trainee knowing what to attend to, how to interpret information and what course of action is required.

Cognitive strategies

The view that a person's cognitive strategies in manipulating information associated with a task are important has gathered momentum over the past twenty years. The information processing model of skill tended to suggest that information inevitably processed through such intervening stages as perception, memory and decision making which might impose various capacity limitations. This preoccupation with structure tended to ignore the influence of "strategies" which an individual might utilise. Underwood (1978) was one of many to suggest that the cognitive strategies adopted by a learner are likely to be of supreme importance in the encoding and retrieval of material. The idea that the learner adopts strategies can be traced back to the influential work of Bruner, Goodnow and Austin (1956) on concept learning. Bruner characterised the strategies which subjects adopted in attempting to identify a concept as either testing the attributes involved in the concept (focusing strategies) or testing hypotheses about the concept (scanning strategies).

Pask (1976) examined the nature of the strategies adopted in a "free learning" situation in which exploration of the subject matter is under the learner's control. In learning hypothetical topics he has made the well-known distinction between learners' strategies which are classified as "holist" and those which are "serialist". The former strategy tends to focus initially on the overall breadth of the material to be mastered whilst the latter concentrates on the lower levels of detail. Some degree of instructional intervention is necessary as neither strategy leads to a complete mastery of the material. Pask and Scott (1972) have suggested that there is some advantage in attempting to match the teaching strategy with that normally used by the learner.

An illuminating theoretical account of how instruction might be better designed to ensure that the appropriate cognitive strategies are used by the trainee to master different types of subject matter is provided by Rigney (1978). Rigney provided the following definition of cognitive strategy:

"Cognitive strategy will be used to signify operations and procedures that the subject may use to acquire, retain and retrieve different kinds of knowledge and performance . . . .

Cognitive strategies involve representational capabilities of the student (reading, imagery, speech, writing and drawing) selectional capabilities (attention and intention) and self directional capabilities (self-programming and self-monitoring)." (p.165).

Rigney observed that the traditional approach to training has been to provide specific content and hope that appropriate cognitive strategies will be generated by the trainee. An alternative and potentially more incisive approach is to train these strategies either directly or indirectly through the use of what Rigney termed "orienting tasks". As the term suggests "orienting tasks" induce the trainee to adopt and develop the necessary cognitive strategies. The role of the applied psychologist is therefore to develop effective orienting tasks.

The work of Dansereau and his colleagues exemplifies the attempt to train learning strategies independently of any particular training programme. They developed a "learning strategy training programme". This comprised instruction intended to improve what were termed "primary" and "support" learning strategies (Dansereau *et al.*, 1979; Dansereau, 1985). Primary strategies included comprehension techniques (such as paraphrasing using visual imagery and analysis of key ideas) and retention techniques (such as means-end analysis). Various support strategies were identified, such as, cultivating a positive learning attitude, concentration (coping with internal and external distractions) and self-monitoring of the learning process. This research has been confined to the comprehension of text and whilst evaluations have been encouraging, they have not examined the contribution of individual strategy components. There is also now a general view that such learning strategies are better trained if they are "embedded" in training programmes. This avoids some of the transfer difficulties which occur because trainees do not know how or when to apply these learning strategies to new situations.

Rigney (1978) discussed orienting tasks aimed at developing appropriate learning strategies which are embedded in the subject-matter to be learned. One example of this is where questions are interspersed in text which are intended to provoke the reader into processing the information in a particular manner. A review of the literature concerning the effect of the different types, positions and frequency of such questions in reading text is provided by Rickards and Denner (1978). An example of an embedded orienting task in an industrial training situation is provided by a study by Marshall, Duncan and Baker (1981). Training was concerned with diagnosing plant failures and in one training condition information concerning various indicators was "withheld" until requested by the trainee. This training condition produced superior diagnostic performance compared to one in which information was "presented" and available. The "orienting task" of requiring trainees to request information enabled the instructor to ensure that the trainees were using the appropriate diagnostic rules during training.

Transfer and retention

Existing skills can either facilitate (i.e. positive transfer) or hinder (i.e. negative transfer) the development and performance of new ones. Transfer is relevant to various aspects of training:

● Trainees' skills existing prior to training determine how new ones are acquired during training.

- Transfer has to take place from various training exercises to unaided performance at the end of training.
- Skills acquired during training have to transfer to performance of a job or task in its natural setting.

Training should be designed to maximise the amount of positive transfer in all of these situations. Theoretical notions of transfer have remained largely unchanged since Thorndike and Woodworth (1901) who proposed that transfer was determined by the extent to which two tasks shared "identical elements". In the behaviourist tradition these elements were seen as stimuli and responses whereas more recently cognitive psychology has interpreted them as cognitive elements which, according to Anderson (1987), are the rules constituting the procedures of cognitive skill.

There are various practical reasons why the extent to which skills are retained over periods of no practice is important to training. The need for astronauts to retain skills associated with space missions and landings led to a literature review by Gardlin and Sitterley (1972). Annett (1977) re-examined the evidence concerning skill loss in the context of the provision of training for both employed and unemployed persons. The importance of retention of skill in military contexts has been emphasised by Hagman and Rose (1983) who provided a review of results from thirteen studies of "real" tasks including donning gas masks, visual aircraft recognition, machine-gun disassembly/assembly and testing pieces of equipment. The findings from these reviews, and others, is that retention characteristics depend upon the task. In order to avoid such apparently obvious statements, vain attempts have been made to identify "categories" of task, which are associated with different retention characteristics. For example dichotomies frequently cited have been "discrete" versus "continuous" tasks, "motor" versus "verbal" tasks and "integrated" versus "non-integrated" tasks. Unfortunately from an academic perspective comparison of such types of task is often confounded by various other factors which themselves affect retention. These factors relate to the comparability of the tasks in terms of performance measures, the amount of training and the difficulty of the task. Consequently differences in retention characteristics do not necessarily imply *intrinsic* differences between these types of task but rather differences between the manner in which training was organised and performance measured.

Despite this academic debate it is nevertheless possible to find skill-retention situations in which there is an apparent rapid skill loss and others where there is not. The traditional literature concerning "continuous" perceptual-motor tasks (such as driving and tracking) suggests that skills of this sort are well retained even over many years of no practice. Any loss which does occur is recovered very quickly. On the other hand tasks which involve a series of "discrete" steps, such as in a procedure, can be quickly forgotten unless there is an opportunity for the trainee to rehearse the task during the retention period. Unfortunately there is little available evidence concerning the retention of more cognitive skills. One exception is a study by Duncan (1971) using an industrial search task. People were trained to locate a fault using a decision tree and were then tested for retention and transfer using a similar task after periods of 6, 58 or 182 days. There was no deterioration in transfer whilst surprisingly retention only declined for low ability trainees. Duncan suggested that this may be evidence that high ability trainees learned a more general search skill which could be well retained over long periods of time. Further skill retention studies are needed which break down performance into the planning, reasoning and decision-making components of skills and investigate how and which components decay with no practice.

Other generalisations which emerge from the retention literature are important but not startling. For example, the best single predictor of retention is the amount of original learning. Consequently as Gardlin and Sitterley (1972) concluded:

> "the type of training which produces the highest level of performance will also produce the best initial retention test performance." (p.14)

Not surprisingly increasing the duration of the retention period will tend to affect recall adversely although this will depend upon the specific task being trained and how it is measured, as noted above. Some degree of overtraining will inhibit a retention deficit although increasing the amount of overtraining, as with training itself, is associated with diminishing returns. Schemes which permit some sort of rehearsal or refresher training will mitigate against skill loss.

Issues in Training Design

The following four issues in training design are discussed briefly:

* Pretraining
* Instructional support
* Simulation
* The role of computers in training

Pretraining

Providing the trainee with information concerning the content of a subsequent training programme has both cognitive and motivational benefits. Some time ago Ausubel advocated that a trainee needs to have available a relevant conceptual framework which will facilitate the absorption of subsequent information (Ausubel, 1960). He proposed that this conceptual framework be provided to the trainee by an advance organiser which is at a "higher level of abstraction, generality and inclusiveness than the learning task". There are two types of advance organiser: an expository organiser which provides a sort of overview of novel material and a comparative organiser which distinguishes the similarities and differences of new information from that already known. Advance organisers are typically used in connection with learning technical material and are usually composed of prose although this is not inevitable. There are various methodological problems concerning how such organisers are developed and reviews have suggested that their positive effects are not so clearcut (Barnes and Clawson, 1975; Hartley and Davies, 1976). On the other hand there is general agreement that using advance organisers as a form of pretraining is beneficial and Mayer (1979) has attempted to specify parameters of the learning situation which determine their effectiveness.

These notions have been extended by Reigeluth and Merrill into the Elaboration Theory of training design (Reigeluth, Merrill, Wilson and Spiller, 1980; Reigeluth and Stein, 1983). This theory suggests that the sequence of training should proceed from the general to the specific, beginning with an "epitome" (or advance organiser) which is progressively elaborated into various types and levels of detail. The analogy provided is that of a "zoom-lens" camera in which:

"the student starts with a wide-angle view of the subject matter and proceeds to zoom in for more detail on each part of that wide-angle view, zooming back out for context and synthesis."

(Reigeluth, Merrill, Wilson and Spiller, 1980, p.217)

The theory attempts to specify how training should be organised at the "macro" level for the learning of concepts, theories and procedures. These intriguing ideas deserve evaluation particularly in the context of the efficiency of different training sequences and the extent to which the trainee should be given control over exploration of the training material.

Instructional support

Some training principles are concerned with providing the trainee with sufficient support during training. They apply irrespective of whether training is on-the-job or off-the-job and whether training is provided by a human or computer.

One idea can be traced back to the programmed learning and instruction movement in the 1960s in which the function of an "adaptive controller" was important. This function judged whether trainees had mastered a particular sub-task and could proceed to another more difficult sub-task or whether some form of remedial training was necessary. Ideally therefore level of difficulty and the nature of the new information could be tailored to the trainee's developing competence. Such individualised adaptive training is highly beneficial (e.g. Atkinson, 1972; Bartram, 1988) and might be delivered by an instructor or by some computer-based device.

Another principle of instructional support which is almost the *sine qua non* of learning concerns the provision of feedback (or knowledge of results) to the trainee during the learning process. The most common training "method" is to provide the trainee with practice coupled with feedback which enables performance to be improved. This applies to any kind of learning whether it involves simple facts, concepts, procedures, problem solving and indeed learning how to acquire and implement cognitive strategies. Feedback to the trainee may be given: verbally by an instructor during on-the-job training; written after some test or exercise in a lecture room; and via some automated device. It is important that such information is available to the trainee *before* the next attempt at the task. Some other important features and dangers of this feedback information are described by Wheaton, Rose, Fingerman, Karotkin and Holding (1976):

"Effectiveness is greatest when the information is clearly and simply related to the action performed. Any distortion or equivocation in the information fed back to the trainee will reduce its effectiveness.

Unduly full or complex information may be partly ignored or may confuse the trainee.

The information given should indicate the *discrepancy* between what is required and what has been achieved, rather than merely give a reminder of requirements or some broad measure of achievement.

The trainee must have *some* cues to the results of his actions if he is to perform accurately at all and training procedures will be effective insofar as they help him to observe and use such cues as are inherent in the task for which he is being trained. They will fail insofar as they provide him with extra cues on which he comes to rely but which are not available when he changes from training to the actual job."

(Wheaton, Rose, Fingerman, Karotkin and Holding, 1976, p.78 – The word trainee has been substituted for S in this quotation.)

It is a relatively straightforward matter to provide feedback which complies with these recommendations for simple tasks and the evidence is that it will improve learning substantially. For complex tasks in which there is a variety of means of tackling the task and the trainee is required to reason or problem solve, it is more difficult to provide the trainee with appropriate feedback. Consider a trainee technician attempting to troubleshoot some malfunctioning equipment or a student trying to understand a geometry proof. Before being able to provide feedback, the tutor (man or machine) has to diagnose the trainee's weakness or misunderstanding from his initial actions. This will not be obvious if a variety of misconceptions on the part of the trainee can sustain the same performance. Consequently research has been concerned with how to pinpoint trainees' weaknesses and how instructors might be trained in good strategies of diagnosis. Provision of the necessary help and advice to the trainee then becomes feasible. This is of course vital in the context of computer-based training and intelligent tutoring systems in which a sensitive tutorial dialogue has to be generated. In this regard Collins (1985) and Collins and Stevens (1983) have provided a fascinating account of the strategies used by good teachers in tutorial dialogue.

Providing the trainee with information in *advance* of practice can also be effective. A demonstration of part or all of a task can be useful where verbal instructions cannot describe adequately what is required. This technique has been used for training not only supervisory skills in which say a manager has to deal with a difficult situation but also cognitive skills where a trainee has to learn the sort of questions to ask in order to comprehend a text passage. A trainer or expert can act as a "model" for the trainee by demonstrating how the task should be performed. In the training of some sports and gymnastic skills, it is beneficial if the trainee is guided through the pattern of movements which have to be learned. All of these approaches are effective and provide trainees with information *before* they have to generate their own actions.

Simulation
It might be argued that any form of training which occurs "off the job" inevitably involves some form of simulation. In this broad sense simulation can be viewed as an attempt to represent some characteristics or features of the real task and to incorporate them into an effective training environment away from the job. The key issue therefore is to devise simulation training which will result in a high transfer of training when the trainee performs in the real work situation.

There are many reasons why some form of simulation (or simulator) may be desirable or necessary for training. These include the need to reduce the costs of "on-the-job" training, to provide a more effective training environment and to provide training for tasks which either do not currently exist or for some reason are inaccessible. Flight simulators have long been used for training pilots and not only provide considerable reductions in operating costs compared with real aircraft but also reduce the potentially high cost of lost equipment due to trainee error. In 1983 Orlansky and Chatelier estimated that United States military flight simulators run at approximately 8% of the operating costs of aircraft although even these simulators are not cheap and procurement costs of simulators are about 275 million dollars per year. By using some form of simulation during training it is possible to both change and add features to the simulated task which can be beneficial to learning. Stressors can be eliminated which will allow the trainee to master the task before encountering them in the real situation. It is possible to speed up and slow down a simulated task. Trainee technicians can be presented with a comprehensive range of simulated faults to diagnose which otherwise might take a life-time to experience on-the-job. Feedback (or knowledge of results) can be provided during practice with a simulated task and it is possible to "freeze" a display and discuss with trainees their current task performance and identify mistakes or misconceptions. Many complex simulations of, for example, nuclear power plants are computer driven. The computer can provide speed and flexibility in being able to generate and display different types of information for the trainee. Such facilities were embodied in the Generalised Maintenance Trainer Simulator which was a general purpose device which could simulate various pieces of equipment for training purposes (Towne, Munro and Johnson, 1982). Other researchers have developed a system for training air traffic controllers by means of computer generated simulations of pilot speech used in conjunction with a simulated flight path being presented on a VDU.

Simulation is an important technique for training not only tasks involving complex equipment but also various "management" skills. Behaviour role modelling is an approach advocated by Goldstein and Sorcher (1974) for training supervisory and interpersonal skills. The trainee is presented with a model of key behaviours via perhaps a film and then rehearses them in the context of feedback from the trainer. Also "business games" attempt to train the decision making of managers via the use of simulated situations. Similar approaches have been adopted to train the tactics and strategies of military personnel in complex war scenarios.

The key question to be answered in the context of simulation for training is how to decide what characteristics or features of the task should be *represented* in the simulation in order to achieve high transfer of training. One solution to this problem in the area of flight simulation has been to devise a comprehensive research simulator which permits different simulation designs to be evaluated for various training situations (Simon, 1979). The degree to which a simulation represents the real situation has been termed its "fidelity" and this has been interpreted traditionally to refer to the degree of realism or physical fidelity of the training device. However transfer is determined by the extent to which a simulation represents the psychological aspects of a task rather than its physical appearance. Such psychological fidelity can often be achieved without a high degree of physical fidelity. This has been found for the training of both procedures and, not surprisingly, cognitive skills. Cox, Wood and Boren (1965) found that simulations of low physical fidelity can produce effective training for a 92-step procedure associated with a control panel. This study found that training with even photographs and cardboard models of the control panel was as effective as training with the real equipment which was considerably more expensive. Similarly the training of fault-finding skills can be accomplished successfully with various simulations of low physical fidelity which nevertheless capture the psychological requirements of the task (Fink and Shriver, 1978; Patrick and Stammers, 1981). For example Marshall, Scanlon, Shepherd and Duncan (1981) used a magnetic board to represent specific plant instruments and their readings in order to train operators to diagnose malfunctions in an oxidation plant.

It must be remembered that any simulation per se will be ineffective unless it also provides the trainee with sufficient instructional support. Also given our previous discussion of skill acquisition, different types of simulation are likely to be required at different stages of training although this idea has not yet been investigated by research studies.

The role of computers in training

A computer can be used to perform various training functions. This becomes evident if we reconsider the various functions identified by a systems approach to the development of training, discussed earlier. Each of these can be performed by computer, human or a mixture of the two.

A computer might be employed to generally "manage" the overall training system (termed "computer-managed learning" – CML). In this role a computer can schedule trainees through various training exercises performed off-line, record progress, administer tests and provide summaries of such information to the instructors involved in training. This administrative role is particularly useful in large scale organisations which have a high turnover of trainees and need to coordinate and schedule many training activities.

Alternatively a computer might be used in various support roles for trainers and subject-matter experts who are required to produce training materials. A computer-based training package could be designed to train the trainers in, for example, how to utilise different training methods. Similarly a computer might instruct the authors of training materials in how to construct good test items and how to specify training objectives, or it might monitor and assess the level of reading difficulty of some training text. It is also possible that a computer program might itself generate a training package. An example of this approach is given by Braby, Parrish, Guitard and Aagarg (1978) where a program named AUTHOR was designed to organise and output materials for the training of symbol recognition. It was developed by the US Navy and generated pretests, tutorial exercises, criterion tests and suggestions for refresher training for any new set of symbols.

The more conventional role of a computer is to provide all or part of a training programme for a particular task. This role began with the programmed instruction movement in the 1960s and was subsequently labelled "computer-based training" (CBT) in the 1970s. More recently artificial intelligence techniques have been used to develop what are known as "intelligent-tutoring systems" (ITSs) (e.g. Sleeman and Brown, 1982; Wenger, 1987). A computer has been used for training various skills including auditory and visual identification, keyboard and tracking skills, administrative procedures, problem diagnosis, social skills and technical information (Patrick and Stammers, 1977). In large-scale commercial or administrative organisations which already have computer networks, it is possible to "piggyback" CBT packages onto the existing computer system. Staff can be quickly trained and updated in new procedures without the requirement to attend training courses at centralised locations. Indeed as computer networks are extended both within and between organisations, oppotunities for such applications will increase.

The computer might provide a display of a simulated task and various types of instructional support associated with practice and mastery of the task. One CBT study by Hillelsohn, Rosenblatt, Price and Seidel (1976) involved training letter sorting machine operators in the United States Postal Service. A VDU was used to simulate different types of computer generated envelopes with different handwriting styles. Trainees progressed through a variety of self-paced on-line training modules in order to learn to identify different postal codes. Performance measures dictated when trainees progressed to different modules although instructors were able to override the programmed sequence. Crawford and Crawford (1978) reported an interesting CBT study which evaluated the feasibility and effectiveness of using an interactive graphic simulation of part of an anti-submarine aircraft system for training. Trainees were able to input various commands via a touch panel on a PLATO terminal and the system would respond in a similar manner to the real equipment. Evaluation indicated that CBT was superior to conventional workbook methods using various performance criteria. Such studies illustrate the possibility of using computer-based part-task training which is considerably cheaper than using a full-scale realistic simulator.

It is therefore misleading to characterise the use of a computer for training as *one* form of training. A computer can perform various functions even alongside conventional methods and it can be used for training various tasks. A computer is a potential solution to an instructional problem and therefore needs to be designed with the necessary instructional support to promote efficient learning. Unfortunately both CBT and ITSs have been poorly evaluated in terms of both the criteria used and the conventional training methods with which they have been compared. There is a need to examine in a more microscopic manner the different training functions which a computer can fulfil by comparing, for example, different configurations of CBT and ITSs.

SUMMARY

It has been suggested that the area of training is changing as a consequence of the new problems being faced and the changing perspectives of psychology. This process is a gradual one and developments in cognitive psychology have not yet been translated into training applications which might result ultimately in a coherent body of training principles. In the absence of a strong theoretical basis for training, it is helpful if training activities are structured by a systems approach to the development of training. This identifies two important functions which are concerned with the requirement to *analyse* a job or task before proceeding to design the necessary training programme. Some of the methods by which jobs can be analysed have been discussed in this chapter. The design of training should be influenced not only by psychological perspectives concerning the acquisition, transfer and retention of skill but also by principles emanating from research studies concerning training design. Four training design issues have been discussed briefly: pretraining; instructional support; simulation; and the role of computers in training. One important responsibility for the applied psychologist in training is to collate, synthesise, implement and develop as many useful psychological findings as possible in order to improve training practice.

REFERENCES

Anderson, J.R. (1981). (Ed). *Cognitive skills and their acquisition.* Hillsdale, New Jersey: Lawrence Erlbaum.

Anderson, J.R. (1982). Acquisition of cognitive skill. *Psychological Review,* **89**, 4, 369–406.

Anderson, J.R. (1987). Skill acquisition: Compilation of weak method problem solutions. *Psychological Review,* **94**, 192–210.

Annett, J. (1977). *Skill Loss. A review of the literature and recommendations for research.* Coventry: Department of Psychology, University of Warwick.

Annett, J. and Duncan, K.D. (1967). Task analysis and training design. *Occupational Psychology*, **41**, 211–221.

Annett, J., Duncan, K.D., Stammers, R.B. and Gray, M.J. (1971). Task analysis. Training Information No. 6. London: HMSO.

Atkinson, R.C. (1972). Ingredients for a theory of instruction. *American Psychologist*, **27**, 921–931.

Ausubel, D.P. (1960). The use of advance organisers in the learning and retention of meaningful verbal material. *Journal of Educational Psychology*, **51**, 267–272.

Barnes, B.R. and Clawson, E.U. (1975). Do advance organizers facilitate learning? Recommendations for further research based on an analysis of 32 studies. *Review of Educational Research*, **45**, 4, 637–659.

Bartram, D. (1988). The design and evaluation of a computer-based training system for foreign destination coding desk operators. In Patrick, J. and Duncan, K.D. (Eds). *Training, human decision making and control*. Amsterdam: Elsevier.

Braby, R., Parrish, W.F., Guitard, C.R. and Aagarg, J.A. (1978). Computer aided authoring of programmed instruction for teaching symbol recognition. TAEG Rep. No. 58. Orlando: Naval Training Equipment Center.

Branson, R.K., Rayner, G.T., Cox, L., Furman, J.P., King, F.J. and Hannum, W.H. (1975). Interservice procedures for instructional systems development. Executive summary and model. Tallahassee: Center for Educational Technology, Florida State University. Distributed by Defense Technical Information Center, Alexandria, Virginia.

Briggs, L.J. and Wager, W.W. (1981). *Handbook of procedures for the design of instruction*. 2nd edition. Englewood Cliffs, New Jersey: Educational Technology Publications.

Bruner, J.S., Goodnow, J. and Austin, G. (1956). *A study of thinking*. New York: Wiley.

Christal, R.E. (1974). The United States Air Force Occupational Research Project. Technical Report AFHRL-TR-73-75. Texas: Occupational Research Division. Airforce Human Resources Laboratory.

Collins, A. (1985). Teaching reasoning skills. In Chipman, S.F., Segal, J.W. and Glaser, R. (Eds). *Thinking and learning skills, Volume 2, Research and open questions*. Hillsdale, New Jersey: Lawrence Erlbaum.

Collins, A. and Stevens, A.L. (1983). A cognitive theory of inquiry teaching. In Reigeluth, C.M. (Ed). (op.cit.).

Cox, J.A., Wood, R.D. Jr. and Boren, L.M. (1965). Functional and appearance fidelity of training devices for fixed procedure tasks. Technical Report 65. Alexandria, VA: HUMRRO.

Crawford, A.M. and Crawford, K.S. (1978). Simulation of operational equipment with a computer-based instructional system: A low cost training technology. *Human Factors*, 20(2), 215–224.

Crossman, E.R.F.W. (1959). A theory of the acquisition of speed-skill. *Ergonomics*, 2, 153–166.

Dansereau, D.F. (1985). Learning strategy research. In Segal, J.W., Chipman, S.F. and Glaser, R. (Eds). *Thinking and learning skills. Volume I: Relating instruction to research*. Hillsdale, New Jersey: Lawrence Erlbaum.

Dansereau, D.F., Collins, K.W., McDonald, B.A., Holley, C.D., Garland, J., Diekhoff, G. and Evans, S.H. (1979). Development and evaluation of a learning strategy training programme. *Journal of Educational Psychology*, **71**, 1, 64–73.

Davies, I.K. (1976). *Objectives in curriculum design*. London: McGraw Hill.

Department of Employment (1971). *Glossary of training terms*. 2nd Edition. London: HMSO.

Duncan, K.D. (1971). Long-term retention and transfer of an industrial search skill. *British Journal of Psychology*, **62**, 4, 439–448.

Dunnette, M.D. (1976). Aptitudes, abilities and skills. In Dunnette, M.D. (Ed). *Handbook of industrial and organisational psychology*. Chicago: Rand McNally.

Fine, S.A. and Heinz, C.A. (1958). The functional occupational classification structure. *Personnel and Guidance Journal*, **37**, 180–192.

Fink, C.D. and Shriver, E.L. (1978). Simulators for maintenance training; some issues, problems and areas for future research. AFHRL-TR-78-27. Texas: Brooks Air Force Base.

Fitts, P.M. (1962). Factors in complex skill training. In Glaser, R. (Ed). *Training research and education*. University of Pittsburgh. Reprinted 1965 – New York: Wiley.

Fleishman, E.A. and Quaintance, M.F. (1984). *Taxonomies of human performance*. Orlando: Academic Press.

Fredericksen, E.W. and Freer, D.R. (1978). Basic electronics skills and knowledge. Research Note 79-5. Alexandria, Virginia: US Army Research Institute.

Gagné R.M. (1970). The conditions of learning. New York: Holt, Rinehart and Winston.

Gagné, R.M. (1985). The conditions of learning and theory of instruction. New York: CBS College Publishing.

Gardlin, G.R. and Sitterley, T.E. (1972). Degradation of learned skills – review and annotated bibliography. Report No. D180-15080-1. US: Boeing Company.

Glaser, R. and Bassok, M. (1989). Learning theory and the study of instruction. *Annual Review of Psychology*, 40, 631–666.

Goldstein, A.P. and Sorcher, M. (1974). *Changing supervisory behavior*. New York: Pergamon.

Goldstein, I.L. (1980). Training in work organisations. *Annual Review of Psychology*. 31, 229–272.

Goldstein, I.L. (1986). *Training in organisations. Needs assessment, development and evaluation*. Monterey, California: Brooks Cole.

Hagman, J.D. and Rose, A.M. (1983). Retention of military tasks: A review. *Human Factors*. 25, 2, 199–213.

Hartley, J and Davies, I.K. (1976). Preinstructional strategies: The role of pretests, behavioral objectives, overviews and advance organisers. *Review of Educational Research*, 46, 2, 239–265.

Hillelsohn, M.J., Rosenblatt, R.D., Price, P. and Seidel, R.J. (1976). Task analysis of multiple position letter sorting machine operator's job. RP-ED-76-18. Alexandria, VA: HUMRRO.

MacDonald-Ross, M. (1973). Behavioural objectives–a critical review. *Instructional Science*, 2, 1–52.

Mager, R.F. (1962). *Preparing instructional objectives*. Palo Alto: Fearon Publishers.

Marshall, E.C., Duncan, K.D. and Baker, S.M. (1981). The role of withheld information in the training of process plant fault diagnosis. *Ergonomics*, 9, 711–724.

Marshall, E.C., Scanlon, K.E., Shepherd, A. and Duncan, K.D. (1981). Panel diagnosis training for major-hazard continuous process installations. *The Chemical Engineer*, February.

Mayer, R.E. (1979). Twenty years of research on advance organisers: Assimilation theory is still the best predictor of results. *Instructional Sciences*, 8, 133–167.

McCormick, E.J. (1979). *Job analysis: Methods and applications*. New York: Amacom.

McCormick, E.J., Jeanneret, P.R. and Mecham, R.C. (1969). A study of job characteristics and job dimensions as based on the Position Analysis Questionnaire. Report No. 6. Purdue, Lafayette: Occupational Research Center, Purdue University.

Merrill, M.D. (1983). Component display theory. In Reigeluth, C.M. (Ed). *Instructional design theories and models: An overview of their current status*. Hillsdale, New Jersey: Lawrence Erlbaum.

Merrill, M.D., Reigeluth, C.M. and Faust, G.W. (1979). The instructional quality profile: A curriculum evaluation and design tool. In O'Neill, H.F. (Ed). *Procedures for instructional systems development*. New York: Academic Press.

Miller, R.B. (1974). A method for determining task strategies. Technical Report No AFHRL-TR-74-26. American Institute for Research.

Morgan, T. (1972). Occupational description and classification. Report E-D-19. Air Transport and Travel Industry Training Board.

Morrison, J.E. (1991). (Ed.) *Training for performance: Principles of applied human learning*. Chichester: Wiley.

Newell, A. and Rosenbloom, A. (1981). Mechanisms of skill acquisition and the law of practice. In Anderson, J.R. (Ed). *Cognitive skills and their acquisition.* Hillsdale, New Jersey: Lawrence Erlbaum.

O'Neal, H.L., Faust, G.W. and O'Neal, A.F. (1979). An author training course. In O'Neil, H.F. (Ed). *Procedures for instructional systems development.* New York: Academic Press.

Orlansky, J. and Chatelier, P.R. (1983). The effectiveness and cost of simulators for training. *IEE Conference Publication,* **226**, 297–305.

Pask, G. (1976). Styles and strategies of learning. *British Journal of Educational Psychology,* **46**, 128–148.

Pask, G. and Scott, B.C.E. (1972). Learning strategies and individual competence. *International Journal of Man-Machine Studies,* **4**, 217–253.

Patrick, J. (1980). Job analysis, training and transferability: Some theoretical and practical issues. In Duncan, K.D., Grunberg, M.M. and Wallis, D. (Eds). *Changes in working life.* Chichester: Wiley.

Patrick, J. (1991). Types of analysis for training. In Morrison, J.E. (Ed). *Training for performance: Principles of applied human learning.* Chichester: Wiley.

Patrick, J. (1992). *Training: Research and Practice.* London: Academic Press.

Patrick, J., Spurgeon, P. and Shepherd, A. (1986). *A guide to task analysis: Applications of hierarchical methods.* Birmingham: Occupational Services.

Patrick, J. and Stammers, R.B. (1977). Computer-assisted learning and occupational training. *British Journal of Educational Technology,* **8**, 3, 253–267.

Patrick, J. and Stammers, R.B. (1981). The role of computers in training for problem diagnosis. In Rasmussen, J. and Rouse, W. (Eds.). *Human detection and diagnosis of system failures.* New York: Plenum.

Peterson, N.G. and Bownas, D.A. (1982). Skills, task structure and performance acquisition. In Dunnette, M.D. and Fleishman, E.A. (Eds.). Volume 1. *Human Capability Assessment.* Hillsdale, New Jersey: Lawrence Erlbaum.

Rasmussen, J., Duncan, K. and Leplat, J. (1987). *New technology and human error.* Chichester: Wiley.

Reigeluth, C.M. (1983). (Ed). *Instructional design theories and models. An overview of their current status.* Hillsdale, New Jersey: Lawrence Erlbaum.

Reigeluth, C.M., Merrill, M.D., Wilson, B.G. and Spiller, R.T. (1980). The elaboration theory of instruction: A model for sequencing and synthesising instruction. *Instructional Science,* **9**, 195–219.

Reigeluth, C.M. and Stein, F.S. (1983). The Elaboration Theory of instruction. In Reigeluth, C.M. (Ed). (op.cit.).

Rickards, J.P. and Denner, P.R. (1978). Inserted questions as aids to reading text. *Instructional Science,* **7**, 313–346.

Rigney, J.W. (1978). Learning strategies: A theoretical perspective. In O'Neil, H.F. (Ed). *Learning strategies.* New York: Academic Press.

Romiszowski, A.J. (1981). *Designing instructional systems.* London: Kogan Page.

Shepherd, A. (1985). Hierarchical task analysis and training decisions. *Programmed Learning and Educational Technology,* **22**, 3, 162–176.

Shepherd, A. and Duncan, K.D. (1980). Analysing a complex planning task. In Duncan, K.D., Gruneberg, M.M. and Wallis, D. (Eds). *Changes in working life.* Chichester: Wiley.

Simon, C.W. (1979). Applications of advanced experimental methodologies to AWAVS training research. Tech. Rep. NAVTRAEQUIPCEN 77-C-0065-1. Orlando: Naval Training Equipment Center.

Sleeman, D.H. and Brown, J.S. (1982). (Eds). *Intelligent tutoring systems.* New York: Academic Press.

Smith, A.D.W. (1973). *General skills in the reasoning and interpersonal domain.* Prince Albert, Saskatchewan: Training Research and Development Station.

Thorndike, E.L. and Woodworth, R.S. (1901). The influence of improvement in one mental function upon the efficiency of other functions. *Psychological Review*, 8, 247–261, 384–395, 553–564.

Towne, D.M., Munro, A. and Johnson, M.C. (1982). Generalized maintenance trainer simulator: Test and evaluation. Technical Report 98. Los Angeles: Behavioral Technology Laboratories, University of S. California.

Underwood, G. (1978). Concepts in information processing theory. In Underwood, G. (Ed). *Strategies of information processing.* London: Academic Press.

Wenger, E. (1987). *Artificial intelligence and tutoring systems.* Los Altos, CA: Morgan Kaufman.

Wheaton, G. (1968). Development of a taxonomy of human performance; A review of classificatory systems relating to tasks and performance. Technical Report 1. Washington: American Institute for Research.

Wheaton, G., Rose, A.M., Fingerman, P.W., Karotkin, A.L. and Holding, D.H. (1976). Evaluation of the effectiveness of training devices: Literature review and preliminary model. Research Memo 76-6. Washington: US Army Research Institute for the Behavioral and Social Sciences.

12

APPLIED COGNITIVE PSYCHOLOGY

J. ELLIS AND D. JONES

INTRODUCTION AND BACKGROUND

In this chapter we examine the nature and scope of applied cognitive psychology by first, outlining the main characteristics of the discipline, its theoretical presuppositions and its emergence as a major force in contemporary psychology. We acknowledge a series of tensions about the appropriate methodology, in particular the degree to which an applied discipline may rely on laboratory studies and the role which theory can play in explicating practical problems. Rather than provide an exhaustive and necessarily tedious list, we discuss the methods of applied cognitive psychology by illustration. We provide four case studies which we consider to be representative of the range of contemporary concerns. While we are conscious that some areas are under-represented and that a distorted picture might emerge, the accompanying references point to material which is a good deal broader than can be encompassed here. We begin with a broad-based definition of cognitive psychology.

What is Cognitive Psychology?

In a seminal work, Ulric Neisser defined cognitive psychology as 'the processes by which the sensory input is transformed, reduced, elaborated, stored, recovered, and used' (Neisser, 1967). From this straightforward definition, we may see that the province of cognitive psychology is large. It covers those activities such as thinking and awareness, which makes it almost all-embracing, since arguably these activities can be said to cover most of mental life. Notice that it does not specify a class or range of activities in the world or classes of visible behaviour, but focuses instead on processes, of transformation, of elaboration and so on. Thus, it does not just include those processes of which we are consciously aware, such as the act of multiplying two numbers together or remembering the name of the current Wimbledon champion, but it also is concerned with those processes of which were not aware or may only be aware of indirectly. A moment's reflection will reveal the need for such scope. It is perfectly clear, for example, that an individual may not be able to describe the rules governing the production of language but such rules may nevertheless govern the production of language by that individual. This distinction is prominent within the discipline and is usually described as one between *declarative* and *procedural* knowledge. In other words, the distinction is between 'knowing that' and 'knowing how'. The task of cognitive psychology is to reveal the models which best describe both classes of process.

Cognitive psychology specifies a way of understanding how these mental activities may be accomplished. This we can more properly refer to as cognitivism. This refers generally to the conviction that the key to understanding behaviour rests with knowing how information is represented and transformed within the brain. Some approaches to psychology hold that nothing need be inferred about the 'internal workings' of the person, that is, the linkages between stimulus and response. All behaviour may be explained by contingencies between input and output, each of which of course is an observable event. This is the main characteristic of behaviourism. Cognitivism, by contrast, specifies that certain intervening mechanisms may be inferred from the relation between stimulus and response. In more detailed terms, cognitive psychology seeks to establish the path taken by the information, the constraints imposed by how much information can be handled, the form in which it is held, what transformations it may undergo and what limitations there are to its access. (See Eysenck and Keane, 1990, for a general review of cognitive psychology).

Even with the binding power of cognitivism, cognitive psychology is not a coherent monolith, rather, a range of sub-areas have grown within it, not all of them contented bed-fellows. We may distinguish, cognitive neuropsychology, cognitive social psychology, cognitive ergonomics, and so forth. The area of applied cognitive psychology is no less a part of this proliferation. Like other applied areas there is a dilemma about the extent to which the discipline should be laboratory or field based. On the one hand we may be extremely conservative and exclude from it evidence which is laboratory-based, admitting only evidence from field work using representative individuals in natural settings. However there are purists who sometimes argue that all data gathered in the applied setting are worthless and that the only adequate way of advancing knowledge is to undertake work in the laboratory. Most psychologists interested in applied work take the middle way by advocating a compromise between these extreme views and suggest that one may gather evidence from a wide-range of sources. In this context laboratory research serves as a means of developing a theory with good predictive power which can then be deployed (and if possible tested) in a practical setting. Applied work can also act as a stimulus for theory, and lead to predictions which can be tested in the laboratory. There are advantages to each approach which may be summarised as follows (see Banaji and Crowder, 1989; Neisser, 1976 for further discussion):

(i)   Laboratory studies allow control over extraneous variables whereas in the field the variable of interest may be under the influence of unidentified or uncontrollable variables. But the very isolation of variables brings with it a number of difficulties, first there is the problem of ensuring that the important variable has been isolated and second the potential difficulty that the degree of interplay of variables and their impact on actual behaviour in the practical setting will be underestimated. It is rare to find a practical setting in which only one variable is at work, others tend to modify its action. Factors not acting in isolation can either augment or diminish each others' action. Moreover, this effect can be more than the sum of each factor acting alone.

(ii) Field studies may only provide a restricted range of variability; this means that establishing a lawful relation between two variables (which could usefully be applied in other settings) is more difficult to establish. However, this charge may be countered by the claim that values of variables outside the range of normal experience constitute a novel setting for the individual and lead to behaviour that is unrepresentative of that individual or of that setting.

(iii) Even well-developed theories are insufficiently specified to establish what should happen in a field setting, which argues for applied research looking at the variables of interest on a common-sensical basis. If a precise answer is required a carefully conducted study should be mounted. Time and funds however, do not always permit such studies to be undertaken and in this case it could be argued that a weak theory is better than sheer conjecture.

Much of the trend toward applied work stems from a movement in the nineteen-seventies toward making cognitive psychology ecologically valid. Ulric Neisser was in the vanguard of this movement, which espoused applied work and emphasised the importance of using models of cognition to inform and enrich our understanding of people's lives. Perhaps its greater contribution has been to extend the domain of the discipline, in widening the scope and pointing to human activities that are ubiquitous and important.

Origins

The history of cognitive psychology is rather short, with its main growth in the mid nineteen fifties. But its antecedents can be discerned as early as the nineteen thirties in the work of Frederick Bartlett. He was particularly influential in guiding interest away from studying the very simple materials which had very little resemblance to activities undertaken in everyday life, by then the stock-in-trade of experimental psychology. In his study of remembering, rather than use lists of nonsense syllables such as 'JUX', and 'WUZ', which are devoid of meaning, he used narrative passages rich in complexity and ambiguity. He studied not just the single recall by an individual but the way in which the original story was transformed as it was retold by one reader after another. The types of transformations did not yield a single convenient index of what was remembered in memory. Indeed, any simple measure like the number of words recalled would have missed the important feature of the data: that within memory the meaning of the passage was altered so as to be consonant with what the person already knew, with what Bartlett termed schemata. These schemata were mental representations which perform the extremely useful task of allowing the person to interpret the world but which also imposes the constraint that new information is made consistent with the person's expectations. This work anticipated much of what was to follow in the 1970s and 1980s in which our understanding of processes such as reading, listening and memory employed the notion of a schema.

The second world war gave particular impetus to the development of applied cognitive psychology: This was mainly due to the increasing complexity of military operations both in speed, sophistication and complexity, not to say devastation.

Mechanical machines, then the immediate precursors of electronic computers, also increased the mental load of those for whom they provided information. One major area of endeavour which was created as the result of much of this work was ergonomics. Its motto was fitting the job to the person'. Initially this meant that the demands of the workplace should not exceed the physical capacities of the individual: that not only should machines be within easy reach of the individual, but that also the requirement that the sensory requirements of the work should be within the scope of the human's sensitivity and tolerance, and that the duration of work was not too taxing in psychological or physical terms. As work became more complex, the emphasis shifted, quite properly, from physical limitations to those of the cognitive load placed upon the individual. More than anything else the advent and development of the general purpose digital computer has done much to hasten the growth of cognitive ergonomics. Arguably, for rich countries of the West at least, these machines have relieved the physical burden of work and in turn sophisticated machines have created a new burden, this time on the limits to the speed and accuracy of human information processing.

That the growth of cognitive psychology has paralleled that of the electronic computer is no accident: it has served to change the nature of work so that more of it involves thought rather than physical labour and so in turn there has been an increasing emphasis on understanding cognitive processes. The computer also played an important role in advancing cognitive psychology: it provided a metaphor for describing the brain's cognitive activity. Just as Sigmund Freud in the age of steam saw human action as the result of transformations of psychic energy, the prevailing computer technology of the fifties and sixties provided a model for describing human behaviour. If computers handled large quantities of complex symbol manipulation via registers, stores and by coding information in special ways, why not humans too? Cognitive psychologists were not so fanciful as to suppose that these were directly analogous to structures in the brain, but such a metaphor might prove to be an extremely powerful way of describing cognitive processes. The computer also now plays a third pivotal role within cognitive psychology: it provides a means for modelling human thought and for testing whether theories of cognitive psychology can be made to simulate behaviour.

CASE STUDIES

We now outline four areas which are illustrative of applied cognitive psychology. They cannot do justice to the richness and variety of the discipline, but we have attempted to show that a well-developed conceptual framework, not simply a descriptive account, is crucial to the success of the enterprise. One of the most promising areas of cognitive psychology relates to neuropsychological aspects of cognition in which very many interesting advances have been made. However, we do not include it as one of our case studies since the topic is covered in Chapter 16 of the present volume.

Working Memory

Although much of what we remember may be retained for some considerable time, often without much loss, much of what we see and hear needs only to be remembered for a relatively short period of time. A system having two types of memory, one for short periods and the other for long periods, is especially useful if the person is constantly bombarded by information and must be selective about what is to be remembered. This sort of system allows some facts to be discarded after a short period (such as a telephone number) while others may be usefully retained for very long periods. This enables the person to respond to short-term demand and to events which are essentially ephemeral without 'gumming-up' the brain with useless facts, as it were. Immediately, one can see the immense practical issues which emerge from this simple distinction, for reading, for learning, and for the performance of a whole range of complex tasks.

In fact, current models of memory are a good deal more complicated than the two-part model just described. For example, it seems there are many more parts or sub-systems than was first thought. The notion that the mind is comprised of modules is one which is frequently encountered in cognition. This is the idea that the mind is comprised of quasi-autonomous parts, each of which has a separate and distinct function, the products of each being interchanged by being passed on to other modules. The important feature of this idea is that each module is functionally autonomous. Each of the various modules has a characteristic way of holding information, not just the time over which material may be held (long or short) but also in the way that information is represented within it. Indeed, the very reason we know from experiments that these parts exist is that they act as *functionally independent* enties. Part of the enterprise of theory is to specify the number and nature of such modules.

One of the most powerful models to emerge in recent years is the working memory model of Baddeley and Hitch (1974). The primary feature of the model in practical terms is that it can account for a range of phenomena associated with the way that errors are produced in settings which require large amounts of information to be held for a short period. Moreover, it also predicts how well we can do two things at a time, such as driving and dialling a mobile telephone.

The essential feature of working memory is that of a temporary store which comprises three components: a central executive which directs attention and manages resources of the system; an articulatory loop, through which material can be rehearsed in speech-like form; and a visuo-spatial sketch-pad which is dedicated to holding information about the position of objects in space. The critical feature of the articulatory loop component of the model is that its capacity is affected by how long it takes to say the words being held. Straightforwardly this predicts that fewer long words than short words can be held within it.

If we compare the intelligence of two groups who speak different languages then we must be careful to make sure that the length of time it takes to speak the digits in each language is the same. For example, in Welsh it takes longer to articulate digits and hence one might expect the estimate of span (and hence intelligence) to be less when the person is tested in Welsh. Bi-lingual children were studied by Ellis and Hennelly (1980) who found that indeed it was the case that it took longer to recite the digits in Welsh and that also the span was lower for these children in Welsh. The model strongly suggests that although Welsh-speaking children appear to have poorer intelligence as measured by memory span, this is illusory and their intelligence is comparable to their monoglot English-speaking counterparts.

The model also suggests that spatial tasks, those activities largely connected with the physical attributes of objects and not with their meanings or names, may be performed independently of verbal tasks, such as remembering lists of words. Morris (1987) undertook a series of studies with a task that could not be done by translating any of its components into a verbal code. Experimental subjects had to remember the position of a dot on each of five successive displays. If the subjects were asked to perform one of a number of other tasks at the same time a consistent pattern of interference appeared. For example, memory for the position of dots was immune to any effect of articulatory suppression (saying 'the' repeatedly to oneself while the dot displays were being chosen) but if subjects undertook a tracking task (in which subjects had to traverse by touch alone a simple repetitive pattern over a key-pad repeatedly) then there was an appreciable deterioration in the memory for the position of dots. Morris argued that this was because the two tasks shared the same level of coding within the visuo-spatial sketch-pad. If the same tasks were tried not with dot position but with a task which required remembering a list of consonants in the order in which they were presented, a quite different pattern of interference emerged. Here, articulatory suppression brought about a deterioration in performance on the memory for dots. However the tracking still had an effect on verbal memory though smaller than that with spatial memory and this was ascribed to the action of a central executive in organising the complex interleaving of the two tasks.

This functional separation is helpful in understanding those applied settings in which a person has to perform several tasks at once. Consider the fighter pilot flying at very low altitude and very high speed. This is an uncomfortable and dangerous environment made more inhospitable by the very high workload. The work of controlling the aircraft is primarily spatial. Our knowledge of working memory sub-systems suggests that the workload can be increased without endangering the pilot by increasing the burden of verbal processing but not spatial processing. If, for example, we required the pilot to use a keyboard or to reach out for a series of switches when the burden of spatial processing is already high then overall efficiency is likely to be impaired. Similarly if we display a message on a screen (even one which does not draw the eyes away form the windscreen, such as is provided by so-called 'head-up' displays) then again the load of spatial processing is increased.

However, if instead of keyboards and displays we provide verbal information via speech, then the likelihood of interference is very much diminished. So, in order to input data we provide a speech recognition system rather than one which requires some kind of spatial-manual control. Also, instead of a visual display we can provide the pilot with synthesized or digitized speech to relay messages either form the ground or form systems on board the aircraft (see Jones and Hapeshi, 1990, for further discussion).

Autobiographical Memory: The Organisation and Retrieval of Personally Relevant Information

In the foregoing section we have used the concept of memory in a rather narrow way. Indeed, much of the theoretical base to the work arises from laboratory tasks which call upon memory for lists of digits of consonants and so forth. However, during the course of our everyday lives many of the tasks that we undertake depend on using information relating to skills, events, concepts and factual information that we have acquired or experienced in the past. In addition to the short-term memory phenomena considered earlier, research has also examined retention over extended intervals ranging from minutes to years. While these topics have been studied extensively by cognitive psychologists the focus of such studies has tended to be on the retention, organisation and retrieval of information presented in a form that is designed to strip it of personal meaning and relevance.

Autobiographical memory research, in contrast, is the study of information related to the self. The study of autobiographical memory provides examples of each of two frequently used interpretations of applied cognitive psychology: extending the nature and domain of conventional experimental research and the application of its findings in understanding real-world problems. It also provides examples of the extension, refinement and development of different methodological approaches.

Not since the work of Sir Francis Galton in the late 1800s has autobiographical memory received systematic scrutiny. Research in this area re-emerged in the 1970s using a modified version of Galton's 'cueing technique' in which subjects are asked to read a list of words and to recall a personal memory associated with each word (Corvitz and Schiffman, 1974). On completion subjects provide an estimate of the date of occurrence of each recalled memory thus enabling the researchers to examine the distribution of the recalled memories across the life span. This remarkably simple technique, applied to personally relevant memories, initiated the study of the availability of such memories over time, thus allowing examination of the robustness of experimental 'forgetting functions' for greatly extended retention intervals (years rather than days) and for events rather than, for example, items in a word list.

Linton's (1975) study, by contrast, involved the author recording information on two or three relatively distinct events from her life each day, for a period of six years. At the end of each month, items from her 'pool' of events were selected (non-systematically) and she attempted to date and recall information pertaining to these events. Linton, therefore, employed a form of 'diary' to record and examine retention and retrieval of event memory in everyday life. Unlike Crovitz and Schiffman's technique, this provides a veridical record of personal events, and their absolute age. Linton's study, however, examines only a small sample of such events in relation to the lifetime period potentially available in studies such as that of Crovitz and Schiffman.

Reviewing these and other, more recent studies in the area, Conway (1990) points to a clear discrepancy between the findings from 'cueing' and 'diary' studies. The former suggest that, if all other factors are held constant, retention varies as a function of time; that is, most memories are recalled from more recent time-periods and least from remote time-periods. Findings from 'diary' studies, in contrast, indicate that very few memories captured by this technique are totally forgotten – forgetting is not a monotonically decreasing function of time. It is suggested that these differences can be explained by the operation of two main factors in retrieval – cue specificity and retrieval strategy. When the cues used to search memory are general (e.g., word prompts as in 'cueing' studies) subjects may be biased towards adopting a 'backward-search' strategy thus accessing more recent memories. When a cue is more specific (for example, relates directly to a particular subject's life as in 'diary' studies) the effects of this strategy appear to be reduced by the increased accessibility of memories across lifetime periods, leading to a constant forgetting rate of approximately five per cent of memories per year (Conway, 1990). It should be noted however that, across a range of different retrieval tasks, more memories of recent than remote events are recalled. This may be due to additional factors such as knowledge about, and distinctiveness of an event, and the lifetime-period within which it occurs.

As Robinson and Swanson (1990) point out, there is general agreement among researchers in this area that information about autobiographical events is organised at several levels of abstraction. Most theorists have proposed schemes that describe broadly hierarchical structures of relations between events in which more general activities (e.g: trips to the cinema) contain both information that is common to most instances of that activity (selecting a film/cinema, queuing for a ticket, choosing a seat and so on) and that may directly access specific instances of that activity (e.g. the time I went to see film X with my cousins). There is also some indication that auto-biographical memories may also be organised in larger-scale event structures that cover extended periods of time, for example 'when I was at college'. The retrieval of specific autobiographical memories may be influenced in part by the general event/activity category they fall into and in part by personal time periods. When asked to access a particular memory of a cinema visit, for instance, one might first access a period in which such visits were common, and then attempt to recall a particular instance of these visits.

A general, and consistent finding in autobiographical memory research is that the recall of specific events is better when an event is unique (e.g. if I had only been to see one film on one occasion with my cousins) than if it occurs on many similar occasions (e.g. I have seen several films with my cousins over the years). This is commonly explained using some form of schema theory which suggests that repeated experience of broadly similar events leads to the abstraction of their common features to form an event/activity schema. However, many other factors may influence this phenomenon, for example, the length of time for which the material is stored in memory and the order in which the material is presented.

Individual differences in the ability to retrieve memories of specific events, and variation in the content of memories that are retrieved have been employed recently by some clinical psychologists to study cognitive factors in patients experiencing clinical disorders. Research by Teasdale and his colleagues, for example, suggests that depression may result in biasing autobiographical memory retrieval (e.g. Clark and Teasdale, 1982). Their studies indicate that memories of negative events are more frequently recalled as subjects become more depressed and that positive memories are less likely to be recalled. Teasdale describes this as a 'vicious circle' in which the bias towards retrieving negative memories exacerbates or perpetuates the experience of depression. More recent research by Williams and his colleagues suggests that both depressed patients and suicide attemptors, who are more emotionally disturbed and confused than depressives, also tend to retrieve negative events more rapidly than memories of positive events (e.g. Williams and Broadbent, 1986). Moreover, there is some indication that these patients are more likely to recall 'general' (e.g. visits to my mother) than specific (visit to mother last Tuesday) memories of events. As Conway (1990) suggests this apparent 'clouding' of autobiographical memory may serve an adaptive function by protecting a patient from recalling details of negative events.

Control of Action: Organising Current and Future Events and Activities

As Neisser (1982) pointed out, in ordinary language we use the word 'remember' in at least two different senses – to remember what we must do as well as what have just done. Memory for future plans and actions rests not only on the recall and organisation of personal and other forms of information but also on the control and organisation of actions and events and, most critically, on the formation, encoding and retrieval of intentions. Examples of these range from intentions to 'go and make a cup of coffee', or 'telephone a colleague after we have completed our current conversation' to 'attending a meeting next month'. Success or failure on such tasks carries implications in real life for one's self-concept, perceived reliability and effectiveness and general ability to function satisfactorily at work – particularly in complex and demanding environments.

Research on these types of tasks has been very limited perhaps because of the difficulties involved in adequately capturing them in a laboratory situation. Most traditional memory tasks for example rely upon a subject learning (incidentally or intentionally) some information provided by an experimenter. The experimenter then reminds the subject of this 'learning' experience and asks them to relate the previously encountered information. A characteristic of intentions, however, is the need to self-initiate retrieval of a particular intention at some appropriate moment in the future and to prevent oneself from being distracted or diverted from the desired action by other competing possible actions or activities. Such a task seems, superficially at least, to be far removed from conventional memory studies.

For these, and other reasons research in this broad area has often been conducted in the 'real world' using subjects' self-reports of different events and experiences. One of the earliest and most important studies to use and develop this technique was carried out on the occurrence and characteristics of naturally-occurring 'action-slips' (see Reason, 1984). Reason defines action–slips as 'actions-not as-planned'; that is, instances where one intends to carry out one particular action (e.g. to make a cup of coffee) but instead performs another action that was not specified or implied by the original intention (e.g. make a cup of tea). Typically the research uses structured 'diary studies' in which subjects are asked to maintain a structured, record (answering a series of standardised questions) on their action-slips during a two-week period.

The findings from these studies indicate that in general, action-slips tend to occur in highly familiar surroundings while performing tasks that have been frequently and recently executed and that tend to be conducted relatively 'automatically'. Many of these slips also appear to involve intrusions from other, similar such tasks; for example, pouring boiling water into the kettle and not, as intended, into a saucepan. Finally, these situations are often further characterised by reported feelings of either preoccupation with unrelated thoughts or being distracted by some external event; stressors, such as being upset, unwell etc. are judged to be relatively unimportant.

An important, and possibly counterintuitive finding from these and other studies is that slips appear to occur during the performance of highly practiced, skilled pieces of behaviour. In general, experimental research leads us to expect a decrease in errors with increased practice and familiarity. Explanations of these findings, while differing in detail and specificity, suggest two modes of controlling and selecting actions and action sequences (see, for example, Norman and Shallice, 1980). One mode controls the routine selection of routine behaviours and is believed to operate without the need for deliberate direction or continuous conscious control. This is thought to be sufficient for the execution of most learned actions in many situations (i.e. 'automatic' behaviour). The other mode is said to be qualitatively different and to involve the modification of these acquired action sequences by a centralised system that is responsible for programming, regulating and monitoring behaviour. This mode of control is required for poorly-learned or novel situations and tasks (i.e. 'controlled' behaviour). It includes the application of conscious attentional processes to modify and bias the former, more usual mode of operation. The advantage of the first, 'routine' or 'automatic' mode of control, is that it does not require the continuous and exclusive allocation of attentional resources in order to complete a task. Unfortunately, however, this can lead to errors as it leaves us free to attend to other, unrelated tasks i.e. 'to think about something else'. In these situations we may, for example, 'find ourselves doing something else'; that is, committing action-slips.

Diary studies such as those conducted by Reason have led to the inclusion of action-slips in both research and theory development – they have helped to extend and refine both the subject matter of cognitive psychology and theoretical accounts of cognitive processes. This research has also been extended by consideration of action-slips and other forms of error that unfortunately tend to have greater consequences than those committed in ordinary everyday life, such as accidents, disasters and so forth. While empirical investigations into the nature, form and underlying causes of everyday errors have helped inform understanding of these undesirable events, investigations of the latter suggest not only that the performance of skill-based action-slips is important but also that knowledge- and decision-based errors often lie dormant in, and are a consequence of, particular organisational or group environments. Again, these and similar studies in the 'real-world' may lead us to extend and modify current research and theory. These points are considered further in the final section of this chapter.

Research on action-slips has tended to focus on the control and performance of current routine actions. Often, however, we wish to carry out intentions at some future, delayed time or occasion – for example, to return a book to the library this afternoon or to give a message to someone when they return to the office. Studies of our ability to carry out these types of task are often included under the rubric of 'everyday memory', and more specifically 'prospective memory' – memory for future actions and events. Investigations of these phenomena have tended to be conducted in subjects' home environments – in part due the difficulties of simulating considerable delays ('retention intervals') between forming and carrying out an intention in a laboratory, and in part because of the contrast that is often drawn between this form of remembering and that commonly studied in laboratory tasks of memory (cued recall of past experience – see above).

Common tasks in this area include requesting subjects to post letters to, telephone, or turn up for an appointment with an experimenter at prearranged times and/or days (for a review of many of these tasks see Harris, 1984). More recently, these have been extended by attempts to construct similar tasks in an experimental setting (Einstein and McDaniel, 1990) and the study of naturally-occurring intentions (Ellis, 1988). While systematic study of these phenomena has only recently begun, current research does point to some general factors underlying success or failure such as motivation, and the context in which these intentions are planned and realised (social, physical, and activity-related influences). Such research emphasises the importance of cognitive skills other than memory (attention, planning, decision-making etc.) and the role of factors that extend beyond the individual mind. The study of prospective memory tasks, therefore, has implications for the understanding of processes that govern the way we plan, organise and modify both short and long sequences of action and behaviour and thus for the performance and co-ordination of activity at home and work.

Natural Reasoning

For our fourth example, we look at an area in which natural behaviour is observed and examine what implications there are for our understanding of cognitive psychology in general as well as the practical limitations.

The strategy here is to give people problems rather like the ones they normally encounter in everyday life. The person's response to such problems can be judged either against a solution based on careful reflective reasoning, or by comparison with objectively-collected data that indicate the correct solution or by comparing it with a solution suggested by mathematical theorems that make an objective assessment of the problem.

A series of studies by Kahneman and Tversky (e.g. 1973) has been instrumental in showing how such decisions are made and most importantly perhaps how wrong people can be, even about really rather important matters. They discovered that people used rules of thumb, so-called heuristics they deployed whenever they had to make a quick judgement in conditions where the available information was rather meagre. Often these heuristics are accurate, but occasionally they are inaccurate and from the point of view of cognitive psychology, fairly predictable. Cynics about the human condition will be comforted to know that the more inappropriate and incorrect heuristics are often accompanied by a great feeling of confidence that the outcome is correct.

One of the most powerful heuristics which they observed was the *representativeness* heuristic. This describes the tendency for people to compare the case before them with some prototype, model or schema, derived from similar settings and compare how close the current case is to the prototype. If the difference appears to be rather small they infer that the current setting is just like the prototype and make the assumption that the outcome is the same. This is rather useful and accurate if a set of correlated events or signs form a syndrome. A decision may be made by noticing the degree of correspondence between the events being judged and the pattern specified by the syndrome. Such a process has the advantage that the decision maker can take into account many more factors than would otherwise be the case – the syndrome forms a mental framework within which the events may checked. Otherwise, memory would be overwhelmed by the number of events and their combination. However, in making this match what usually happens is that the prior probability of an outcome is usually ignored. For example, there is a tendency for a physician to diagnose a disease only on the basis of whether its symptoms fit the pattern suggested by the syndrome. A far better strategy would be to make the diagnosis using a combination of the fit with the syndrome and the likelihood of occurrence of the disease. So, even though a disease may be extremely rare it may be diagnosed because the symptoms presented by a patient appear to be more representative than a more frequently encountered disease, for which the symptoms make a less good fit.

In cognitive terms we can see two complementary processes at play in the representativeness heuristic. One is the role of schemata as organising forces within long-term memory; they constrain the accuracy of the decision making at the expense of the very great economy of bringing a distilled account of previous experience to bear. The other process is the difficulty which the individual has of bringing information about the likelihood of an event to bear (and, too, the sluggishness with which new information about the likelihood of that event occurring anyway, without the presence of some specified condition, the base rate, is incorporated).

The *availability* heuristic is based on the ease with which information can be brought to mind and reflects the fact that reasoning is influenced by the availability of material in memory. For example, a person is asked to estimate the proportion of words in English that begin with a k and the proportion of words which k is the third letter. One way of doing this is to recall instances of each type and to make a judgement of their relative frequency. However, the availability heuristic contaminates this estimate: it is much easier to search through memory for instances of words beginning with a particular letter than when embedded in a word. Usually the person will report that a k at the beginning of a word is much more common, but in fact a k appearing as the third letter is three times more likely to occur. We seem to believe that the contents of memory are a good reflection of the events in the world. Deployment of the availability heuristic means that events which are recent, noticeable and frequent have undue weight in the decision making process, but in complex settings such as the control room of a nuclear power station these may not be the events which are most diagnostic. Of course, the way in which the information is presented may in part overcome the bias in the way the information is processed.

The way in which decisions are worded can lead to widely different outcomes. Consider the framing of medical decisions studied by McNeil, Pauker and Tversky (1988). They presented people with the choice between surgery and radiation therapy as treatments for hypothetical case of lung cancer. They were given estimates of the effectiveness of the two therapies immediately after treatment, after one year, and after five years. Objectively, on the basis of these data it would be safe to conclude that surgery offers tougher life expectancy but that it also entails much greater risk of immediate death. However, when presented to experimental subjects the estimates could either be framed in terms of mortality or in terms of survival. So in terms of survival the outcome was couched in the following terms:

> 'Of 100 people having surgery, 90 will live through the surgery, 68 will be alive af the end of the first year, and 34 will be alive at the end of 5 years. Of 100 people having radiation therapy, all live through the treatment, 77 will be alive at the end of the first year, and 22 will be alive at the end of 5 years.'

A different group of people were given a format which couched the same information this time in terms of mortality:

'Of 100 people having surgery, 10 will die during the treatment, 32 will have died by 1 year, and 66 will have died by 5 years. Of 100 people having radiation therapy, none will die during treatment, 23 will die by 1 year, and 78 will die by 5 years.'

The results were stunning in their clarity: of those people presented with the survival format 18% preferred radiation treatment, in contrast, of those presented with the mortality format 47% favoured radiation treatment. Here, the same basic information, through the effect of framing, can have markedly different consequences. Such a result has profound implications for the way in which information is presented to patients so that they may make a balanced and informed judgement about the choice of treatment. It is worth noting at this juncture that biases are not only found in patients but also in professional persons among them doctors, field marshals and even cognitive psychologists!

The essential feature of decision making in everyday life is that is not a static once-and-for-all matter, rather, evidence may have to be accumulated about a hypothesis, as might be the case with finding a fault in a television set. Here again we witness bias in human reasoning which leads to sub-optimal decision making. First, people tend to seek out information that confirms their initial hypothesis, especially if they are under time pressure or other type of stress. There is a tendency for people not to actively seek out evidence which might go against their opinion, this is called confirmation bias. Even when presented with negative evidence the person will not use it to an adequate degree in counteracting the prevailing hypothesis.

What can be done in a practical way to overcome the improper use of heuristics? One way is to ensure that the decision maker is not overwhelmed by information. This can be done by arranging that only a *relevant* sub-set of all information is shown. Part of the difficulty in decision making is filtering out irrelevant information. Providing the decision maker with a small set of items on which to base the decision is relatively easy to achieve when the information can be controlled by, for example, computer displays. Another tactic is to provide the person with aids that reduce the burden on short–term memory. The bias against negative evidence can be partly overcome by forcing the decision maker to consider an array of evidence.

Training can also help considerably. One tactic is to make the operator more aware of the likely pitfalls of employing heuristics in a particular setting. Another approach is to provide feedback so that the decision makers are aware of the outcome of decisions and the relative success and failure of the heuristic they employed.

FUTURE DIRECTIONS

The domain of applied cognitive psychology has been interpreted recently in two different, but complementary ways:

(i) the application of findings from conventional laboratory tasks, and resultant theories, to understanding and advising on real-world problems and tasks, and

(ii) studies of naturally-occurring behaviours and of experimentally designed behaviour in real-world settings that extend and refine the nature and domain of conventional experimental research and theory.

The review of case studies has been necessarily selective. This may have given the impression of a truncated range of interest in the subject. However, in our suggested readings we have pointed to some general texts which should allow the reader to follow up any general or specific points. In the remainder of this section we look at what developments we might see within applied cognitive psychology and examine emerging themes within the discipline.

Indications of future directions come from a number of related research domains. Somewhat surprisingly, given the combative and eclectic nature of psychological research, they point to similar problems and suggestions for ameliorating these difficulties. The problems arise from difficulties encountered, when dealing with real-world tasks or personally-relevant material, in attempting to model cognitive processes independent from other relevant aspects of psychological experience and from the context in which these processes are applied. Conway (1991), for example, suggests that cognitive approaches to the study of autobiographical memory are led, by current findings, to '...consider the role of the self, emotion and personal meaning...' and that these considerations may soon extend into more general areas of cognition. He points to the inadequacy of cognitive models that use abstracted symbolic representations which fail to capture these 'internal' characteristics. Brown (1990) extends this critique by pointing to the several strands of research (from diverse fields such as linguistics, connectionism and human-computer-interaction) that emphasise a view that much of meaning (supposedly captured in mental representations or symbols) appears to be located 'in the world' rather than 'in the head'. An interesting empirical question that follows from this concerns the nature of the relation and inevitable trade-off between these informational sources in natural behaviours and experience.

A closely related concern has also been expressed by the use of the term 'situated action'. Situated action is viewed as an emergent property of moment-to-moment interactions between an individual and their (social and physical) environment rather than as the product of pre-formed mental constructs. It represents an attempt to capture the dynamic and opportunistic nature of human activity in a partially unpredictable environment. Research in this area has tended to focus on the role of verbal communication in dyadic interactions – conversation, however, is clearly only one of many means of communicating in a social world. A complementary approach to human behaviour, and one that has influenced many researchers interested in investigating situated action, comes from Russian activity theory. This distinguishes between activities, actions and operations. Activities are assigned to the collective ventures of various groups; actions are the conscious acts of the individual defined, in part, by their perception of the relevant activity; and operations are the individual's means of realising an action. This notion of activity focuses on the socio-culturally defined context in which we operate which has only rarely been considered in contemporary cognitive psychology. It assumes that an individual's repertoire of actions and operations evolves continuously and is based on experience gained both as an individual and as part of a group; situated in the social and material environment. Scribner and her colleagues (see for example, Stevens, 1988) have attempted to elaborate the implications of activity theory for cognitive research by developing a methodology which takes account of these – particularly in the cognitive aspects of work. This includes the use of observation, laboratory simulations or quasi-experimental intervention at work, and established laboratory procedures. In this way they hope to create a reciprocal exchange of data between practical or situated action and experimental research. Studies indicate that focusing on an activity allows one to both take account of and investigate inter-relations between the content and structure of the social and work environment and the use that an individual makes of this in the pursuance of different actions within that activity.

Recent research on 'distributed cognition' (see, for example, Hutchins, 1987) also develops this theme and in so doing offers a further bridge between cognitive (individual-based) and social (group-based) psychological theorising and research. It also acknowledges and incorporates the relation between knowledge 'in the (physical) world' and knowledge 'in the head'. The theory of distributed cognition indicates a pattern of co-operation and co-ordinating between individuals and their activity. On one level this pattern can be seen as a structure for sharing and processing information and on another level can be seen as a system in which shared cognition emerges as a system level phenomenon. It focuses on the flow of information through a group of individuals and their activities, the interactions between internal and external representations, and the distribution of activities between individuals. It suggests that this pattern of co-ordination and knowledge distribution may be crucial determinants of an activity in ways that cannot be fully captured by focusing on any one individual's actions.

Clearly the importance of these considerations depend on the circumstances in which a particular activity is situated – these almost certainly vary along a continuum from those primarily centred on an individual, on the one hand, to those primarily collective on the other. We should remember however that even actions that seem to be primarily centred on an individual, such as retrieving a previously formed intention or recalling a past event in one's life frequently involve other people, particular locations, specific periods in one's life etc. These factors are almost always present at the time of experiencing or encoding an event or intention. There are also, however, a wide range of factors that can influence retrieval – recollection rarely takes place outside of a social and/or activity-related context. For those activities that are primarily concerned with the operation and co-ordination of tasks within group in a work setting the factors identified in distributed cognition, and other related constructs, are of prime importance in understanding and modelling cognitive processes. They have been recently addressed in a collection of work on distributed decision-making (Rasmussen, Brehmer and Leplat, 1991). Several contributors identify the need, following failures to adequately capture decision-making at work using conventional methods, to analyse decision-making at several levels within the context of the activity in which it is embedded.

Future directions for research in applied cognitive psychology therefore appear to point to the adoption of genuinely interdisciplinary research. This work could then feed into the construction of suitably broad theoretical frameworks that allow analyses to proceed at several levels, using a variety of methods, and that acknowledge the constraints and demands of the general activity as it is perceived by concerned participants.

REFERENCES

Banaji, M.R. & Crowder, R.G. (1989). The bankruptcy of everyday memory. *American Psychologist*, **44**, 1185–1193.

Baddeley, A.D. (1990). *Human memory: theory and practice*. London: Erlbaum.

Baddeley, A.D. & Hitch, G. (1974). Working memory. In G.A. Bower (Ed.), *Recent advances in learning and motivation. Vol. 8*. New York: Academic Press.

Brown, G.D.A. (1990). Cognitive science and its relation to psychology. *The Psychologist*, **3**, 339–343.

Clark, D.M. & Teasdale, J.D. (1982). Diurnal variations in clinical depression and accessibility of memories of positive and negative experiences. *Journal of Abnormal Psychology*, **91**, 87–95.

Conway, M.A. (1990). *Autobiographical memory: An introduction*. Buckingham: Open University Press.

Conway, M.A. (1991). Cognitive psychology in search of meaning: The study of auto-biographical memory. *The Psychologist*, **4**, 301–305.

Crovitz, H.F. & Schiffman, H. (1974). Frequency of episodic memories as a function of heir age. *Bulletin of the Psychonomic Society*, **4**, 517–518.

Einstein, G.O. & McDaniel, M.A. (1990). Normal ageing and prospective memory. *Journal of Experimental Psychology: Learning, Memory, and Cognition*, **16**, 717–726.

Ellis, J.A. (1988). Memory for future intentions: Investigating pulses and steps. In M.M. Gruneberg, P.E. Morris & R.N. Sykes (Eds.) *Practical Aspects of Memory Vol. 1: Current Research and Issues*. Chichester: Wiley.

Ellis, N.C. & Hennelly, R.A. (1980). A bilingual word-length effect: Implications for intelligence testing and the relative ease of mental calculation in Welsh and English. *British Journal of Psychology*, **71**, 43–52.

Eysenck, M.W. & Keane, M. T. (1990). *Cognitive psychology: A student's handbook*. London: Erlbaum.

Harris, J.E. (1984). Remembering to do things: A forgotten topic. In J.E. Harris & P.E. Morris (Eds.) *Everyday memory, actions and absent-mindedness*. London: Academic Press.

Hutchins, E. (1987). *In search of the navigators*. New York: Wiley.

Jones, D.M. & Hapeshi, K. (1989). Monitoring speech recognizer feedback during data entry from short-term memory: A working memory analysis. *International Journal of Human-Computer Interaction*, **1**, 187–209.

Kahaneman, D. & Tversky, A. (1982). On the study of statistical intuitions. In D. Kahneman, P.Slovic, & A. Tversky (Eds.) *Judgements under uncertainty: Heuristics and biases*. Cambridge: Cambridge University Press.

Linton, M. (1975). Memory for real-world events. In D.A. Norman & D.E. Rummelhart (Eds.) *Explorations in cognition*. San Francisco: Freeman.

Morris, N. (1987). Exploring the visuo-spatial scratch pad. *Quarterly Journal of Experimental Psychology*, **39A**, 409–430.

Neisser, U. (1967). *Cognitive psychology*. New York: Appleton-Century-Crofts.

Neisser, U. (1976). *Cognition and reality*. San Francisco: W.H. Freeman.

Neisser, U. (Ed.) (1982). *Mermory observed: remembering in natural contexts*. San Francisco: Freeman.

McNeil, B.J., Pauker, S.G., & Tversky, A. (1988). On the framing of medical decisions. In D.E. Bell, H. Raffia & A. Tversky (Eds.) *Decision making*. Cambridge: Cambridge University Press.

Norman, D.A. & Shallice, T. (1986). Attention to action: Willed and automatic control of behavior. In R.J. Davidson, G.E. Schwartz & D. Shapiro (Eds.) *Consciousness and self-regulation, Vol. 4*. New York: Plenum Press.

Rasmussen, J., Brehzner, B. & Leplat, J. (Eds.) (1991). *Distributed decision making: Cognitive models for co-operative work.* Chichester: Wiley

Reason, J.T. (1982). Lapses of Attention. In R. Parasuraman & D.R. Davies (Eds.) *Varieties of attention.* Orlando, Fla.: Academic Press.

Stevens, J. (1988). An activity theory approach to practical memory. In M.M. Gruneberg, P. E. Morris & R.N. Sykes (Eds.) *Practical aspects of memory: Current research and issues (Vol. 1).* Chichester: Wiley.

Williams, J.M.G. & Broadbent, K. (1986). Autobiographical memory in attempted suicide patients. *Journal of Abnormal Psychology,* 95, 144–149.

13

PSYCHOLOGY AND INFORMATION TECHNOLOGY

N.P. SHEEHY AND A.J. CHAPMAN

WHAT IS INFORMATION TECHNOLOGY?

Information technology is concerned with the acquisition, processing, storage and communication of information. Information technology (IT) has been made possible by an application of science and engineering to the modelling, processing and retrieval of information. It has evolved as a separate technology by the convergence of data processing techniques and telecommunications. Advances in electronic engineering have provided resources for the storage and manipulation of information on a very large scale. Telecommunications has made possible the technology for the transmission of very large quantities of information in different formats. Affordable applications of advances in science and engineering to the production of information technology have been made possible by the availability of complex, reliable, low-cost microelectronic components.

How can psychology be applied to what seemingly is an engineering discipline? The answer lies in the nature of the material on which the technology operates – information. Information refers to facts and opinions which are discovered, created and communicated. Information can be coded in different formats: acoustic (speech, music), visual (pictorial, graphic), textual or numerical. Information technology can capture information in each of these formats. People combine facts and ideas with have been communicated to them with ideas of their own and thereby generate new information. The manipulation and transmission of information has changed dramatically with the availability of economical technological innovations and psychology can make an important contribution in trying to ensure that the technology is accessible for its intended users.

IT: A BRIEF HISTORY

In order to communicate information it is necessary for societies to develop information storing techniques which are external to, and not directly dependent on, human memory. Palaeolithic cave drawings constitute representations of ideas from pre-historic times coded and stored in a format external to human memorial capabilities. The development of pictographic languages reflects the expanding conceptual world of the human race. For example, modern Chinese comprises more than 50,000 ideographs and represents an outgrowth of this development. Of course the visual spatial relationships between the ideographs and their referents have become obscure and the semantics of ideographs has come to be founded on a set of conventions for their interpretation. As the relationship between the visual appearance of ideographs and their referents became more obscure so the conventions for the interpretations of ideographs became increasingly arbitrary. These conventions are no longer intuitively obvious but must be learned through skills of reading and writing.

The invention of the written phonetic alphabet is believed to have taken place in the Tigris–Euphrates valley about 4000 BC. Sounds, rather than pictures, began to be represented as an alphabet of arbitrary graphic symbols. The principle advantages of alphabetic over pictographic writing systems have been apparent at least twice in the present millennium. The first was linked with the invention of the moveable-type printing press in the fifteenth century. This early information technology facilitated an enormous expansion in the recording, production and communication of facts, ideas, beliefs, doctrines and values. The second major technological advance was associated with the development of the electronic computer during the 1940s and 1950s. This prompted a further expansion in the production, dissemination and creation of information. Within the past decade there has been a third qualitative expansion through the inter-linking of different information technologies; specifically the coupling of computing and telecommunication technologies. This third innovation has made it possible to use technology not only to communicate and store information but also to manipulate the information automatically.

As a consequence of these developments information has acquired two functional connotations. First, it has come to be regarded as an economic resource. People buy and sell information in much the same way as labour, material and capital is bought and sold. Information is transacted commercially because its possession and application are considered to increase the effectiveness of physical and human resources. For instance possession of climatological information facilities judicious use of natural resources, improves the cost-effectiveness of the agricultural industry and thereby enhances standards of living and quality of life. Second, information is regarded as a commodity. The information service sector is associated with industries concerned with exploration, innovation and design, planning, and financial management.

Although information is regarded as a resource and a commodity it has a number of social psychological attributes which distinguish it from other economic entities. First, it is intrinsically diffuse. Second, it reproduces through use; it is not consumed in the way other commodities are consumed. In this sense 'consumers' of information are agents for its reproduction and expansion. Third, information can only be shared, it cannot be transacted. Someone who supplies or communicates information is not automatically dispossessed of it. This greatly complicates commerce in information and introduces a range of psychological and social processes into economic transactions.

INFORMATION PROCESSING SYSTEMS

Computer engineering has enabled the construction of machines capable of operating on information automatically. Consequently information processors have come to be regarded as intelligent – they have the capacity to discriminate between significant and non significant signs. This is an abstract way of thinking about information processors but it is useful because it encompasses both physical and biological information processing systems. For example immune systems constitute biological information processors capable of detecting objects which threaten the organism. Inanimate information processors such as electronic computers can sense and process some objects, such as alphanumeric symbols, but not others, such as those associated with processors for the object signs – the stimuli – associated with smell and touch.

Electronic computers are digital processors; they work by means of a formal code, such as logic or mathematics, which can be executed using stepwise procedures. Logical or mathematical symbols are discretely different from one another which means they can be processed by digital computers which are themselves composed of electronic circuits which can change their state (discrete on/off switches) at great speed. On the other hand biological information processors are usually thought of as analogue computers; they do not operate by coding objects into a symbol system. Instead they manipulate continuous physical variables; a change in one physical variable (such as electrical activity in a group of neurones) induces transformations in another physical variable (such as a chemical change in part of the endocrine system). One might be tempted to think of digital and analogue computers as similar at an abstract level but radically different at a physical level. The reality of information technology challenges this thinking. For instance, bio-informatics is concerned with biological information systems, including the design of biological computers, that can behave like symbol-manipulating digital computers. The application of positive and negative micro-volts to some single cell organisms can cause the nucleus to migrate to different ends of the organism without destroying it. This causes these micro-organisms to behave like digital switches in a computer – migration to one end of the organism is denoted 'off' and to the other end as 'on'. The distinction between analogue and digital processes is also becoming increasingly fuzzy in telecommunications where fibre optic cable is used to transmit pictures, sounds, numbers and words by modulating a continuous stream of electromagnetic radiation which is released into fine glass fibre filaments.

Figure 13.1 describes a schematic structure for a generic information processing system which was proposed by Newell and Simon (1972). An information processing system has a set of receptors which are used to detect stimuli or signs in the external environment. In the case of a digital computer this might entail sensing signals at a keyboard capable of generating an acceptable or 'meaningful' set of symbolic expressions. These are passed to a processor which has four major functions. First, it applies elementary processes to symbolic expressions (e.g. mathematical operations are applied to expressions denoting numbers). Second, it provides a temporary or short-term information store for handling symbolic expressions for input and output. The processor has a limited memory store. This is often regarded as analogous to the limited capacity of human short-term memory. Third, it is responsible for scheduling the execution of information processes. This can be considered akin to human

Environment

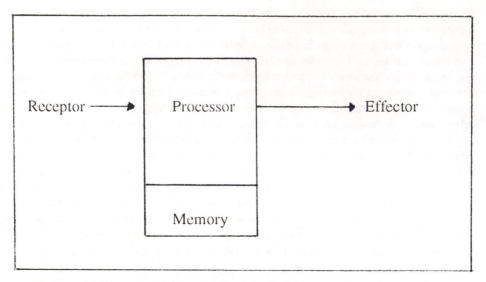

FIGURE 13.1   Architecture of a generic information processor

planning. Fourth, it can manage the sequence of operations to be performed according to the complexity of the task. This is analogous to human problem solving. The memory component stores long, complex strings of symbolic expressions, such as programmes. The only restriction on its size is imposed by the capacity of the processor to index the location of the stored information and to retrieve it rapidly and accurately. The effector is the means by which the system transmits processed structures into the environment. In the case of a digital computer these might be letters or numbers on a computer screen.

It is often thought that the design of digital information processors must have been influenced by psychological theories and in particular by evidence on the structure and function of human memory and reasoning. While similarities can be found in the terminology used to describe computer technology and human cognition (e.g. input-output, short-term memory, long-term memory, executive processor etc.) it would be wrong to conclude that the design of electronic information processing systems mirrors the architecture of human cognition. Analogies can be drawn and the strongest of these apply to computer architectures that mirror the structure of neural systems but even here the architecture in current neural computers represents a tiny sample of the interconnection architectures to be found within biological nervous systems (Orchard and Phillips, 1991).

APPLICATIONS OF IT

There are many ways of categorising IT. For example one might distinguish between 'intelligent' IT, such as computer-based technology for supporting medical diagnosis, and 'dumb' IT, such as that supporting library catalogues stored on computers (Claus and Schwill, 1992). More useful, from a psychological perspective, would be to adopt an applications-oriented approach and consider the variety of uses to which IT has been put. Viewed in this way one can see that information technologies have been applied in four major sectors of human activity:

Command and Control Systems (CCS): these are information systems used by those in policy-related roles to facilitate planning and strategy in order to achieve organisational goals. These systems have been applied extensively in military establishments where they are referred to as command and control systems because they permit their users to monitor and manage personnel and ordinance. However they can be applied in any organisation whose leaders or senior executives manage very large amounts of diverse multivariate data.

Management Information Systems (MIS): these are very similar in structure and function to CCSs but they are applied at lower levels of an organisational hierarchy to facilitate day to day resource management. MISs include project management technology which is intended to permit users to specify resource databases, goals and deadlines and monitor progress on a large number of individual tasks.

Service-oriented Information Systems (SIS): this is a very large category of IT tools directed to facilitating the activities that are the reason for an organisation's existence. There are three main kinds of SIS: Expert systems, manufacturing systems and transaction systems. Expert systems offer users decision support and advice. These are considered in greater detail later in this chapter. Manufacturing systems are intended to facilitate the manufacturing process and include, for example, robotic production lines for vehicle assembly. Transaction systems are at the core of the financial services industry. They facilitate the purchase and selling of stocks, shares and money by networking very large numbers of savers, investors, bankers and borrowers.

Public Information Utilities (PIU): these are information services for mass consumption. They include, for example, teletext information services and home banking services. TV catalogue shopping is an application of IT made possible by linking computer technology with TV technology.

Each of these sectors present different problems because the requirements of users vary. Equally the involvement of psychologists varies according to the nature of the application. The generic architecture of information processors described in Figure 13.1 provides a template on which to locate the differing roles for psychology in the design and implementation of information technology. Psychologists have a role to play in relation to each of the main components of the information processing system and these are summarized in Table 13.1

Within the environment in which information technologies function psychologists are principally concerned with issues of work design, organisational practice and the quality of life of users of IT. From an environmental perspective IT can provide tools to facilitate the users' tasks and the principal evaluation criteria are guided by considerations of task-defined usefulness.

The receptor and effector parts of the system are embraced within the term 'user interface' – the physical configuration of the technology as users encounter it. Here

TABLE 13.1
Distribution of applications of psychology to information processor design and use

Information Processor Component	Application of Psychology
Environment	Work design Organizational practice Quality of life
Interface (Receptor & Effector)	Hardware ergonomics Cognitive ergonomics Psycholinguistics
Processor	Pattern recognition Reasoning Learning and memory Knowledge representation
Memory	Memory and forgetting Knowledge representation

psychologists are concerned with the ergonomic design of devices for in-putting and receiving information from the processing system. They are also concerned with the kind of images these systems conjure up in the minds of their users. For instance, a very large database may be made more accessible if its visual appearance prompts users to imagine themselves journeying through its complex structure seeking navigational guides. Users of IT are often frustrated in their efforts by difficulties associated with learning to use the technology. Often they are required to learn a new mini-language to interact with the technology and they regard the technology as 'unfriendly' and obscurantist (Shneiderman, 1987). This has prompted psychologists, linguistics and computer scientists to consider how computers might be programmed to interact in the natural languages of their users and to apply basic rules of good conversation (Schank, 1986).

The central processor is at the heart of any piece of IT and considerable efforts have been made to improving the range and complexity of the tasks that processors can perform. Artificial intelligence is partly concerned with ways of extending the reasoning capabilities of information processors. The sub-discipline of cognitive science is partly concerned with applying ideas and techniques from cognitive psychology to improve the reasoning and problem solving abilities of computers. This has involved formalising parts of theories and hypotheses about human cognition. These efforts may not always prove helpful to the designers of information processing systems but very useful to psychologists who may find that some of their theoretical ideas are not as well defined as they had thought (Sharples *et al.*, 1989).

The memory part of the information processing system contains both operating programmes for the information processor and, more importantly from the users' perspectives, the library of data and information that they wish to access. The memory part if analogous to long term memory and capable of storing vast amounts of information in much the same way that the human unconscious seemingly stores limitless experiences. The difficulty is to design information technologies that can remember where information has been stored so that it can be retrieved quickly. Usually users want information to be stored in collections of conceptually related things. For an information processor to do this it must be capable of reasoning on the content of the information it places in memory. This is a complex problem. For

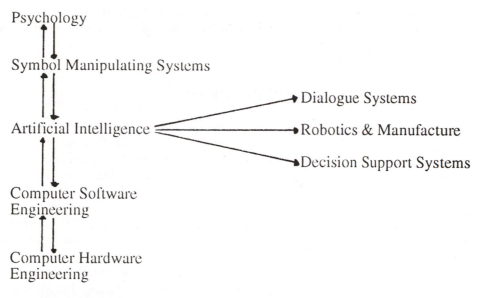

FIGURE 13.2   Role of Psychology in IT Design

example, if the stored information is in pictorial form, such as x-ray (e.g. lung, skull), it contains significant medical information (e.g. haemorrhage, fracture). Psychologists have an important part to play in designing ways for information technology to analyse the data it is handling in order to facilitate parsimonious storage and retrieval.

Attempting to enhance the sophistication of IT is not the province of any one discipline. Research and design problems in IT do not observe disciplinary boundaries and the field has become associated with inter-disciplinary theory and research. The contribution of psychology, as it is often seen by other disciplines, is schematically depicted in Figure 13.2.

The right hand side of the figure lists three application areas: (1) Dialogue systems which are designed to facilitate communication between computers and their users; (2) Robotics and manufacturing systems which are designed to promote product development and sales; and (3) Decision support systems intended to advise users of possible gaps, inconsistencies and flaws in their problem solving activities. Computer scientists are concerned with the production of hardware and software technology. Psychologists are concerned with the specification of human requirements. This entails formulating a representation of the symbolism contained in human communication and cognition with regard to the formal constraints imposed by available technology. The field of artificial intelligence (AI) occupies a central role, translating psychological knowledge into workable software while also taking cognisance of contributions from other disciplines. For example, in relation to the design of dialogue systems AI is concerned with the logical or formal integration of principles of conversational structure (from psychology), theories of grammar (from linguistics) and the requirements of programming languages (software engineering). The design of manufacturing robots requires the formal integration of principles of motor skill (from psychology) cybernetic theory (from engineering) and the requisites of programming languages. The design of decision support systems requires the integration of principles of problem solving and explanation (from psychology), axioms and rules (from the application domain) and programming stipulations (Yazdani, 1986).

DESIGNING IT: FROM THE INSIDE OUT

The most important goal of IT design and development is the production of tools which can store and reason on information processing tasks which would otherwise consume creative human resources. Thus, IT can be thought of as a complex tool that can be used to support human decision making, problem solving and creativity. Computer engineering, artificial intelligence (AI) and psychology can be applied to improve the processing of data and information through the design of information processors capable of very fine discriminations between object signs. This is what is meant by 'intelligent' IT (cf. Simon 1980 for a discussion on artificial intelligent systems).

Information technologies that can perform high level reasoning tasks and monitor their own performance provide their users with opportunities to spend more time in creative enterprises. AI makes it possible to produce knowledge from data and information by logical inference and deduction and thereby 'to go beyond the information given', just as humans do (Bruner, 1973). For example, AI makes it possible to create expert systems: computer programmes that can perform complex reasoning tasks such as medical diagnosis, electronic fault finding and weather forecasting. Some computer systems are intended to model accurately a specific feature of human knowledge and reasoning. However the majority do not have this as their primary objective but rather the emulation human experts by reaching the correct answer in common problem cases. For example, in medicine expert systems can be used to correctly diagnose a disease condition by reasoning on the data contained in symptoms and medical tests. These kinds of expert systems are designed from 'the inside out' and the human-computer interaction aspect is a secondary object in their development; the primary objective is for the system to compute the right answers (Sharples *et al.*, 1989).

Expert systems have three parts: (1) an interface which allows users to formulate queries and read answers, advice or explanations that the system might offer; (2) a knowledge base comprising facts (axioms) and rules for making inferences from these facts; and (3) a computer programme that invokes the reasoning or inferencing process. In order for computer systems to compute correct answers it is necessary to use a framework to construct the knowledge base. A knowledge representation framework is a method of encoding knowledge according to the style in which it is to be applied to solve problems. This means that knowledge (1) must be elicited from human experts, and (2) represented in a format that allows it to be encoded in a computer programme (Taylor, Corlett and Simpson, 1987). Psychologists have an important role here, mediating between human expertise and the formal restrictions of computer programming. Conventionally this involves eliciting both the information that experts use to solve a problem and the rules they use to organise that knowledge.

This approach to knowledge elicitation is limited in two main ways. First, the literature in human problem solving indicates that while people may be able to organise and express their knowledge as procedural rules it does not mean that reasoning and problem solving skills are rule governed. People may enumerate a complex set of rules to report their knowledge but in any particular instance they may violate those rules, create new rules or apply a different set of rules. Second, knowledge representation frameworks incorporate constraints which reflect the limitations of computer programming science. This may lead to significant knowledge omissions since it may be that a particular domain of expertise cannot be compiled into the chosen framework. Expert systems developed according to this approach may place limitations on the capability of a system to deal with problem cases that are slightly unusual but not uncommon. The 'inside-out' approach to building expert systems may defeat its primary objective of building robust problem solving programmes (Hayes-Roth, Waterman and Lenat, 1983). In this regard psychologists can play an important role as knowledge engineers: they can facilitate the construction of expert systems which can report limitations on their own reasoning capability. By knowing the ways and extent to what an expert system fails to capture expert knowledge one can facilitate its judicious use and acceptability by users.

DESIGNING IT: FROM THE OUTSIDE IN

If expert systems illustrate the problems with developing IT from the inside out then user interface design illustrates the issues that arise when designing from the outside in. The success of any technology will be partly dependent on its useability. Elegant systems for helping with decision making will remain unused if those for whom they are intended perceive them to be difficult to operate. Because of the complexity of information technology considerable effort has been directed towards ensuring that it is usable and a substantial part of the research and development has been undertaken by psychologists. Of course psychologists can play a significant part in designing any piece of technology but the prominence and importance of their work for IT design arises partly from the nature of that technology – the manipulation and transmission of symbolic data. Information comprises symbols and signs and as such can be dynamically structured and made to appear in different ways. In order to develop computer hardware and software capable of dynamically structuring information it has been necessary to consider how people can do this. There is an added advantage in knowing how people model and manipulate information because we can use that knowledge to ensure that users are given the information in ways in which they find it most useful.

The user interface refers to devices and procedures which users encounter when accessing a system, including the software which cannot be seen by the users but which is intended to facilitate useability. The tangible parts of the interface include the devices available to the user (mouse, keyboard, light pen etc.) and the device (normally a VDU) used to display information to the user. The software part of the interface, which is not directly observable, is often referred to as the user modelling component. The tangible parts of the interface are normally concerned with the human factors and ergonomic elements of the system and the covert parts are concerned with the cognitive ergonomics of the system and with user modelling. This distinction has largely been driven by practical considerations: the development of user modelling

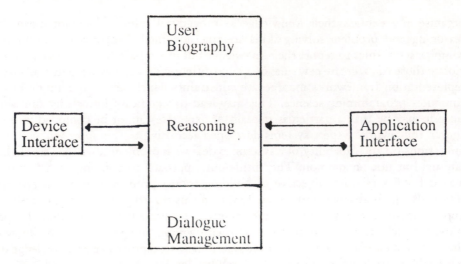

FIGURE 13.3   Conceptual model of a user interface

capabilities has proved more difficult to implement than the design of functional devices with which users can interact with the technology (Long and Whitfield, 1989). Figure 13.3 describes a conceptual model of user interface and its principal elements. The reasoning part of the system (the processor) takes inputs from the user interface device and relates this to existing information about the user – requirements, preferences and so on. The processor retrieves the appropriate information from the application (e.g. a database) and presents it to the user through the device interface, taking account of rules for good dialogue management. The dialogue management part ensures that the user receives a reply (even if that is to say that there are no data available) that is readily intelligible in the context of the query posed.

It is possible to develop an IT system which looks and feels good yet proves difficult to access in terms of its task support capabilities. There are theoretical and practical challenges posed in ensuring that this will not happen. For instance, a medical registrar and a staff nurse can pose an identical question to a senior consultant: 'Why does the patient's blood pressure fail to respond to medication?' The medical expertise of the nurse and registrar are different and the consultant will almost certainly take this into consideration when appraising (1) the urgency of problem posed by the question; (2) the meaning of the question; and (3) the requirements for an appropriate answer. One can say that the consultant creates a mental model of the person asking the question and constructs an interpretation of the question and the requirements for a satisfactory answer with reference to that model (Johnson-Laird, 1983). Now consider that some of the consultant's expertise has been captured in a computer and the staff nurse and the registrar enter the same query. How can the computer ensure that a satisfactory response is given in the context that anything less may contribute to the patient's death? The computer will need to construct at least six models: (1) a model of the user; (2) a model of the patient; (3) a general model of the patient's disease; (4) a specific model of the progress of the disease in the patient; and (5) a general model of the treatment protocol; and (6) a biographical model of the protocol for the patient in question. These models need not be particularly elaborate in order to be effective. The user model can refer to the identification and medical grading of the person asking the question. The patient model can contain information about age and gender, and so on for the other models. There are several ways of classifying user models (Rivers, 1989; Trenouth and Ford, 1989) but however one views user models there are three questions to be answered:

- What aspects of the user are to be modelled?
- How are these aspects to be detected by the system with which the user is interacting?
- What effects will the user model have on the behaviour of the system and the user?

These are psychological questions and, in principle, can be answered in a form that software engineers can use to develop a working system (Johnson-Laird, 1983).

Even when the component models are very simple there remains the problem of their interrelationship. In interpersonal dialogue all of these considerations are combined, integrated and weighted in complex ways in order to produce an answer that ensures that the patient survives and hopefully recovers. Expertise is valued over encyclopaedic knowledge because it carries functional, operational and procedural implications – about why, when and how to do things. IT systems will become increasingly accessible when psychologists can describe the reasoning processes used in answer questions in a form that can approximate human competence in this area.

For practical reasons the development of user interfaces has tended to proceed on a modular basis, reflecting the practical difficulties associated with translating psychological knowledge into a form that software engineers can work with. However, it would be wrong to think that system development proceeds in a fragmented fashion. It is vital that the different parts of the user interface function together but interlinking the constituent parts is often not easy. For instance, the 'Put that there' experimental system (Bolt, 1980) was designed to allow a user to speak the words 'put that there' while point to an object on a visual display. A system with this capability would, in principle, make a user's task of moving objects such as folders and documents a good deal easier and more natural. The challenge of interlinking the different parts of such a system is considerable. For example, imagine a situation where a user instructs the systems to 'put that there' but nothing happens on the screen. The failure may have arisen for several reasons: (1) The speech recognition part of the system might not have discriminated the different parts of the utterance. The person may have spoken too quickly, too slowly, too softly or with a strong accent; (2) Speech recognition systems respond to acoustic energy and the utterance may have been masked by a background noise detected by the system but unnoticed by the speaker; (3) The precision with which users point to 'that' and 'there' varies, and individual users may vary the precision of their pointing over time; (4) The referential parts of the utterance ('that' and 'there') can be more or less synchronised with the pointing gesture and the synchronisation may vary even with a single utterance-gesture pairing. In order to allow the system or its users to identify the origins of the fault it is necessary to have a higher level, reflective model of the interaction – a perspective on the actions of the user interacting with the system and the system's responses. The development of such models will present considerable challenges to psychological theory (Sheehy and Chapman, 1986).

Finally it is important that the development and implementation of technology should not be dissociated from the context in which it is intended to function. Technological innovations invariably carry a learning and operational over-head and it is important to determine these in advance. Information technology is characterised by increasing integration of previously separate devices and functions. The dispersion of tasks by machine type often provides an important aid to the organisation of work. For instance, the planning and scheduling or work can be accomplished by compiling and preparing work to be: (1) photocopied, (2) faxed, (3) filed, (4) mailed and so on. Each task is executed in a location corresponding to the placement of the requisite technology. When technologies become integrated useful environmental cues disappear. Quality assurance becomes more difficult too and integrated technologies bring new sources of error and new challenges to overcome them. For instance, in a conventional, busy office it is comparatively easy to check that tasks have been completed by recollecting the sequence of incidental events linked with it:

(1) A letter is typed
   [Memory of using the word processor]
(2) The letter is printed
   [Memory of collecting the paper from the printer]
(3) The letter is faxed
   [Memory of going to and using the fax machine]
(4) The letter is filed
   [Memory of filing the letter]

In a word processor with integrated telecommunications facilities there are fewer incidental events to aid recollection of whether or not all parts of the task have been completed. For instance, in a machine with an integrated fax the sequence might become:

(1) A letter is typed
   [Memory of using the word processor]
(2) The letter is filed
   [Step (4) above becomes step (2)]
   [Filing is performed by key press; the paper record and memory cue disappear]
(3) The letter is faxed
   [Faxing is performed by key press and becomes indistinguishable from the word processing task and the filing task]

The challenge for designers and developers is to provide psychologically rich environments capable of supporting the variety of tasks workers will be expected to perform while also providing easily accessible audit mechanisms to support planning and quality assurance (Bailey, 1983). In practice this may entail recreating aspects of the clutter, decoration, irrelevance and nuisance factors characteristic of conventional offices which provide a continuous stream of environmental cues to aid scheduling and prompt accurate recollection. In this regard there is considerable interest in the opportunities promised by three dimensional interfaces, virtual reality and cyberspace. Part of their potential lies in the manner in which they can place the user in a visualisation of the information environment they wish to explore and thereby support high level problem solving where interaction with the technology carries minimal learning overheads; the technology becomes transparent (Fisher, 1990).

Systems, like people, will always fail but they will continue to be used if there is some way of determining why they failed in order that the interaction may be repaired. The availability of error recovery strategies ensures that the technology continues to be regarded as accessible and usable. This is particularly important as user interfaces become increasingly sophisticated and elaborate, creating an illusion of technological transparency. Persuading people to suspend disbelief about the useability of technology will prompt users to increase their expectations of system versatility and functionality. Once again the key issue is one of designing with a view to managing the interaction between user expectations and experiences and psychologists can make important contributions by developing models of how interactions fail and how they can be repaired (Reilly, 1987).

DESIGNING IT: GOOD PRACTICE

There is no best way to design a new technology but there are principles of good practice which have been derived from experience. The development of information technologies can usually only proceed on the basis of a combination of bottom-up and top-down design activities (Gardiner and Christie, 1987). High level tasks in the design process comprise:

- An analysis of the application domain (the tasks, the people and the organisation).
- An assessment of available and 'affordable' information technology with regard to its suitability for meeting existing organisation needs and projected increases.
- A matching of organisational requirements and technology suitability leading to a functional specification for the new IT system.
- Interaction of the functional specification with other developmental activities, particularly hardware and software development, to produce system prototypes.
- An iterative design and build process tied to an explicit evaluation programme.

The concept of iterative designing-and-building is central to the application of IT. It involves a number of sequential steps with feedback loops which are intended, among other things, to keep user requirements at the centre of the design process. These steps are summarized in Figure 13.4.

It is often thought that feedback loops are costly and for this reason there are pressures to reduce them. Certainly they require time to complete but it is apparent from Figure 13.4 that the loss of just one feedback loop will have the effect of marginalizing the involvement of IT users in the design and development process. Psychologists have a significant role to play at steps 1 (identifying users' needs), 2 (establishing a precise list of requirements for the IT tool), 5 (eliciting and applying users' criteria), 7 (introducing the IT tool to the work place, including user training) and 8 (helping workers to integrate the new technology with other aspects of their tasks). Psychologists can also play a crucial role in the feedback loops which couple users' needs and requirements to later steps in the design cycle. Unfortunately their research methods are sometimes perceived to be cumbersome and slow. Design methodologies usually place time at a premium – on minimising the time required to design and deliver a system to its users. This means that it is often impossible to

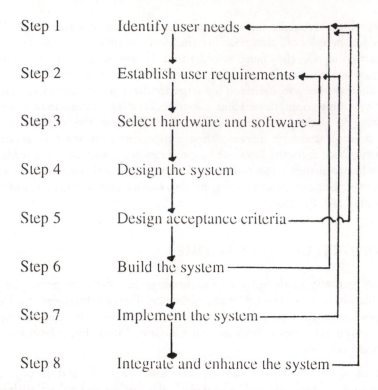

Step 1   Identify user needs

Step 2   Establish user requirements

Step 3   Select hardware and software

Step 4   Design the system

Step 5   Design acceptance criteria

Step 6   Build the system

Step 7   Implement the system

Step 8   Integrate and enhance the system

FIGURE 13.4   Design Cycle of an Information Technology Tool

conduct extensive field studies at each step in the design cycle. Designers and users may not tolerate full-blown experimental trials and may prefer to proceed through a series of pilot studies supplemented by psychologists' qualitative, professional judgements about what is likely to work and what is not.

The criteria against which IT tools are most commonly evaluated are multiple and varied and the primary psychological issues form only a part of a bigger picture. The most commonly used evaluation criteria include the following:

- Device Independence: the extent to which a piece of software can be moved from computer to computer.
- Reliability Completeness: the extent to which the technology captures the requirements of a task in a complete or comprehensive form.
- Accuracy: the extent to which the technology performs a task accurately.
- Consistency: the degree to which the technology uses uniform notation and terminology.
- Task Efficiency: the speed at which the technology completes its task.
- Device Efficiency: the degree to which the technology places requirements on resources for other tasks. For example, the degree to which an automated machine requires human supervision and maintenance.
- Human Factors: The extent to which the technology incorporates ergonomic considerations.
- Comprehensibility: the extent to which the technology performs in a comprehensible fashion. For instance, early speech recognition systems were known to mistake

a word such as 'letter' for 'number' and it was difficult for users to imagine how 'letter' could be uttered to make it sound less likely to be confused with 'number'.

● Modifiability: the technology should be capable of accommodating expansion and upgrading on a componential basis.

The list of criteria can be ordered in different ways and psychological criteria may not always be paramount. Psychologists form part of a multi-displinary design team and the discourse and process of the design group is like that of all groups: it is strategic and ill structured. It is particularly important for psychologists to recognise this because they can assist design teams in understanding the dynamics of their group and its tasks and help them understand how and why their innovations succeed and fail. This is particularly important when innovations fails due to causes not directly attributable to the team. Seemingly elegant innovations may be rejected by their users, perturb organisational procedures and hinder organisational goals. This pattern of response may perplex and dismay design teams who may feel that their best efforts to improve organisational efficiency through the provision of IT tools are misunderstood, undervalued or ignored. If psychologists can clarify why this may happen they can have an important role in improving the effectiveness of the design team.

To elucidate why apprently good innovations fail it is useful to view social organisations as strategic structures in the sense that their existence is based on the dynamic, opportunistic solution of strategic problems. Strategy is concerned with the employment and distribution of limited resources. A strategy is a continuous organisational process which attempts to structure the relationship between means and ends. Inevitably this entails agenda setting and this means that some issues come to be regarded as central and others are treated in a marginal way. The implementation and evaluation of IT takes place within a strategic context. Consequently the acceptability of the technology is affected by implications for the distribution of organisational resources. This means that those concerned with the implementation of IT tools should be cognisant of the events that preceded a decision to seek improvements in organisational effectiveness through information technology. Organisational psychologists have sentient skills which can promote this awareness. The 'best' IT solution to an information processing problem is likely to be one which is pragmatically guided by a balance of organisational requirements and technological sophistication. Evaluations of information technology by experts are concerned with issues of validity, reliability and durability. Evaluations by users determine its utility. Thus, even if a new piece of information technology is developed within budget, delivered on time and adequately meets the requirements of the functional specification, a client may be unhappy with it for several reasons. The client may regard the technology as unwanted, as failing to meet new and more important task requirements, or as difficult to integrate with other organisational requirements.

DESIGNING IT: REFLECTIVE PRACTICE

Most people, at one time or another, feel that technological developments proceed at a pace faster than they can comprehend and this can sometimes be recognised in apprehensive attitudes or downright resistance to the technology. It is sometimes thought that this reluctance to embrace new technology reflects intolerance, unwillingness or inability to learn. This explanation is simplistic. In most cases reluctance to use innovative technology arises from the fact that it challenges long established, well tested ideas for making sense of the world of technology at work. For example, most workers would understand a word processor to consist of a computer: there is a one-to-one mapping between the machine and the task that can be performed with it. This view is reinforced in many organisations where machines are dedicated to supporting specific risks. Problems can arise when the mapping of task to machine becomes more complex, as happens when a single machine can support word processing, spread-sheet calculations, invoice preparation and so on. For some the challenge is almost too great and otherwise competent word processor operators can find it difficult to make sense of the idea that 'their word processor' can undergo an unimagined transmogrification and 'become a spreadsheet' or whatever. These challenges and confusions are likely to increase rather than diminish as the integration of technology is correlated with its 'de-materialisation': the fax machine need not be a separate device but can be integrated within the computer; the laser printer need not be separate from the photocopier but integrated within it. Psychology has an important role to play in helping the innovators understand that their ideas and solutions may seem confusing to those who have just come to terms with one set of 'common sense' ideas about the technology of work.

While psychology and information technology have developed an important symbiotic relationship at the level of design, development and implementation the contribution of psychology extends beyond these practical considerations. Psychology has another and wider contribution to offer in providing a theoretical framework with which to step back from research and development programmes and reflect on fundamental questions about the relationship between technology, people and work. For instance, theory and practice in relation to human computer interaction has implicitly adopted the concept of **work station** as a reference model for design and development. The term has become part of the vocabulary of office systems. However the 'work station' concept appears to rest on several restrictive assumptions about the nature of work practices and structures. It implies that work is conducted at fixed, physical stations, by individual workers using their own machines. However, the overwhelming finding to emerge from studies of organisational communication is that the principal focus of activity for professionals, administrators, clerks, technicians and secretaries is communicating with people and that rates of communication are rarely affected by physical aspects of the work context, such as office size (Klemmer and Snyder, 1972). The organisation of work is made possible through dialogue among workers. If psychologists were to limit their involvement with IT to the design and development of work stations they would miss an important opportunity to explore the life of technology users beyond the confines of the work station. The need to adopt such a reflective stance is illustrated by the fact a majority of text books on psychology and information technology contain pictorial illustrations depicting personnel working alone or inter-connected exclusively at the level of task inter-relationships. A new challenge for the design of the next generation of information technology lies not in determining whether interface ergonomics can be generalised to many different physical contexts but rather in providing support for workers who will increasingly rely on telecommunications for quality maintenance of the organisation of their work (Huws, Korte and Robinson, 1990).

MANAGING THE USERS OF IT

Communication is at the heart of work, it is how people construct and maintain the organisation of their work. Computer supported co-operative work can provide opportunities for workers to improve their communications networks both for the purpose of completing specific tasks and for the management of their organisation. There are new challenges here because computer mediated messaging systems impose particular requirements on users and have been shown to have special characteristics:

- Participants engage in less overt agreement and more opinion giving than comparable face-to-face groups (Hiltz and Turoff, 1985).
- Computer-mediated group discussion is less likely to produce polarisation or shifts to extremes on a risk-caution dimension than in face-to-face interaction (Hiltz and Turoff, 1985).
- North American findings suggest a greater incidence of swearing, insults, name calling and hostile comments than occur in comparable face-to-face exchanges (Kiesler, Siegel and McGuire, 1984). British findings suggest the contrary (Wilbur, Rubin and Lee, 1986).

While computer mediated dialogues are characterised by high levels of task related interaction one cannot conclude that computer mediated conversations are entirely task governed. In one Fortune 500 company 40% of all message traffic was ostensibly unrelated to work – 'ostensibly unrelated' because the creation and maintenance of social contacts is crucial to effective co-ordination and task accomplishment (Sproull and Kiesler, 1986). Knowing who one's co-workers are extends beyond a definition based on competence-on-task and it is vital to the maintenance of the work organisation.

The challenges are more complex than the provision of flexible electronic messaging systems. How are managers to identify troubled staff? People who become seriously stressed in their work can often convey this to others in the manner in which they conduct themselves in conversation. Computer-mediated dialogue is unlikely to eliminate the expression of stress through dialogue and people may learn to use the technology in new ways in order to signal their troubles. A small number of studies have explored how people can display signs of stress through 'addiction' to computer-based conferencing systems and the following indicators have been identified (Bezilla and Kleiner, 1980):

- Logging on unnecessarily many times in a day
- Excessive irritation when the system is inaccessible
- Preference for composing thoughts on line
- Logging on 'just one more time' before stopping work.

These indicators of 'symptoms' are not unique to computer-based systems. Exactly the same kinds of behaviour can be detected in face-to-face dialogue where one of the speakers is stressed: they pursue seemingly unnecessary conversations with the same person several times a day; they become excessively irritated when their preferred co-worker is temporarily unavailable; they develop a preference for composing thoughts 'as they come' in conversation and so on. The development of good management practice and the fostering of a healthy social climate for workers is founded on the acquisition and application of skills for detecting and avoiding impending trouble.

Many troubles can be detected and repaired through conversation. Computer-mediated dialogue removes most visual and acoustic cues for detecting impending difficulties but the technology has its own operating characteristics which are likely to capture aspects of a user's broader intentions and needs. In other words, users may learn to convey both propositional content (*what* they say) **and** illocutionary force (*how* they say it) in their interactions with other system users. We do not know what these operating characteristics are for different tele-computational devices nor are we yet in a position to describe features which can be used reliably to allow managers and other system users to identify and resolve impending task- and personnel-related difficulties.

CONCLUSIONS

Information is a social production; it is created and shared by people interacting and organising their behaviour. Information technology provides new tools for conviviality. Psychologists have played a number of roles in both the design and the evaluation of IT tools and will continue to do so in the future. Both psychology and IT have yet to realise the potential in this relationship. There is a wide variety of automated IT products available on the market and while many of these products (e.g. decision support systems, project management systems etc.) have relatively limited and specialised capabilities they demonstrate that it is possible to construct intelligent information processing tools at an affordable price. Predicting future developments in IT is difficult because of the uncertainty of its acceptability. One of the largest barriers to the acceptability of many IT tools is the learning curve associated with their use. New tools often require the acquisition of new sets of skills and frequently there are limited opportunities for skills transfer across tools.

Future developments in IT are likely to proceed in at least four main ways. First, there is likely to be an increased effort to develop standardisation metrics to minimise the skills acquisition overhead associated with the use of the diverse tools already available and yet to be developed. If users can be assured that learning to use one set of IT tools can facilitate the use of others the demand for these technologies is likely to increase. Second, there are likely to be significant improvements in the design of user interfaces. The development of interfaces which permit users to work with their native language, which conform to basic conversational rules for turn-taking and which can detect user difficulties at an early stage, is likely to become a priority. There are important roles for psychologists in the design of these interfaces (Sheehy and Chapman, 1986). However, the application of ideas and principles from psychology is never easy because psychological theories are not formulated in a manner which facilitates their application to the design of intelligent IT tools. For example, attempts to identify design guidelines which flow from psychological theories have not proved successful (Shneiderman, 1987). Guidelines are most useful when taken as providing a general orientation to an information processing problem. They are less useful when treated as recipes for designing the 'best' solutions.

Third, the availability of IT has been largely restricted to applications with uniform data sets. For example, there are systems for storing and retrieving pictures, numbers, text and music. There are no commercially available systems which can integrate visual, numerical, verbal and acoustic data in the ways humans do. Physicians, for example integrate verbal, acoustic and numerical data when interpreting the meaning of a pattern of heartbeats. Some IT tools can juxtapose different data formats but they cannot perform cross-modal reasoning in the way humans do when they think about the problems they are attempting to solve. Many IT tools do not yet take adequate account of the diverse information formats which their users are accustomed to dealing with. It is often the case that the success of IT tools more accurately reflects the adaptability of their users than the versatility of the tools themselves.

Fourth, the work station has provided an important reference model for theory and practice in human computer interaction. While the model has been shown to have some important yet largely unnoticed restrictions it remains of central relevance to the expansion of most industries. However it needs to be extended and supplemented, specifically by taking greater account of the significance of ostensibly 'off task' communication in quality maintenance of the organisation of work. The provision of communications work stations for supporting co-operative work presents an important challenge in this regard.

The application of psychology has contributed to significant developments in usable information technology. Many of these benefits reflect back to psychology in a number of ways. First, much of the technology is directly usable by psychologists in their teaching and research. The reader may already be familiar with computer-based instructional software for planning and running psychological investigations (and with the limited teaching competence of such systems; Sleeman and Brown, 1983). Second, the technology challenges psychological theories to be precise. In practice it can be extremely difficult to translate psychological theory into precise software specifications. However in attempting such a translation psychologists can acquire new understanding of the limitations of their theory and use these insights in the pursuit of better paradigms and development of more intelligent and intelligible information technology. This evolutionary cycle is unending; human creativity has always been too extensive to be encapsulated within the technology it creates.

REFERENCES

Bailey, R.W. (1983). *Human Error in Computer Systems.* Englewood Cliff, New Jersey: Prentice-Hall.

Bezilla, R. & Kleiner, A. (1980). Electronic network addiction. Paper presented at the National Computer Conference, Arnheim, California.

Bolt, R. (1980). 'Put that there': Voice and gesture at the graphics interface. *Computer Graphics,* 14, 262–270.

Bruner, J.S. (1973). *Beyond the Information Given.* New York: Norton.

Claus, V. & Schwill, A. (1992). *Encyclopaedia of Information Technology.* London: Ellis Horwood.

Fisher, S.S. (1990). Virtual interface environments. In B. Laurel (Ed.), *The Art of Human-Computer Interface Design.* New York: Addison-Wesley.

Gardner, M.M. & Christie, B. (Eds.) (1987). *Applying Cognitive Psychology to the User-Interface Design.* Chichester: Wiley.

Hayes-Roth, F., Waterman, D.A. & Lenat, D.B. (Eds.) (1983). *Building Expert Systems.* Reading, Mass.: Addison-Wesley.

Hiltz, S.R. & Turoff, M. (1985). Structuring computer mediated communications systems to avoid information overload. *Communications of the ACM, 28*, 680–689.

Huws, U., Korte, W.B. & Robinson, S. (1990). *Telework: Towards the Elusive Office.* Chichester: Wiley.

Johnson-Laird, P.N. (1983). *Mental Models: Towards a Cognitive Science of Language. Inference and Consciousness.* Cambridge: Cambridge University Press.

Kiesler, S., Siegel, J. & McGuire, T.W. (1984). Social psychological aspects of computer-mediated communication. *American Psychologist, 39*, 1123–1134.

Laurel, B. (Ed.) (1990). *The Art of Human-Computer Interface Design.* New York: Addison-Wesley.

Long, J. & Whitfield, A. (Eds.) (1989). *Cognitive Ergonomics and Human-Computer Interaction.* Cambridge: Cambridge University Press.

Newell, N. & Simon, H. (1972). *Human Problem Solving.* Englewood Cliffs, New Jersey: Prentice Hall.

Orchard, G. and Phillips, W.A. (1991). *Neural Computation: A Beginner's Guide.* London: Erlbaum.

Reilly, R. (Ed.) (1987). *Communication Failure in Dialogue and Discourse.* Amsterdam: Elsevier/North Holland.

Rivers, R. (1989). Embedded user models – where next? *Interacting with Computers, 1*, 14–30.

Schank, R.C. (1986). *Explanation Patterns: Understanding Mechanically and Creatively.* Hillsdale, New Jersey: Erlbaum.

Sharples, M., Hogg, D., Hutchison, C., Torrance, S. & Young, D. (1989). *Computers and Thought.* London: Bradford and MIT Press.

Sheehy, N.P. & Chapman, A.J. (1986). Nonverbal behaviour at the human-computer interface. *International Reviews of Ergonomics, 1*, 159–172.

Shneiderman, B. (1987). *Designing the User Interface: Strategies for Effective Human-Computer Interaction.* New York: Addison-Wesley.

Simon, H. (1980). Cognitive science: the newest science of the artificial. *Cognitive Science, 4*, 33–46.

Sleeman, D. & Brown, J.S. (Eds.) (1983). *Intelligent Tutoring Systems.* London: Academic Press.

Sproull, L. & Kiesler, S. (1986). Reducing Social Context Cues: Electronic Mail in Organizational Communication. *Management Science, 32*, 1492–1512.

Taylor, N.K., Corlett, E.N. & Simpson, M.R. (1987). Problems of knowledge acquisition for expert systems. In E.D. Megaw (Ed.), *Contemporary Ergonomics.* London: Taylor and Frances.

Trenouth, J. & Ford, L. (1989). User modelling. In M. McTear & T. Anderson (Eds.), *Understanding Knowledge Engineering.* Chichester: Ellis Horwood.

Wilbur, S., Rubin, T. & Lee, S. (1986). A study of group interaction over a computer-based message system. In M.D. Harrison & A.F. Monk (Eds.), *People and Computers: Designing for Usability.* Cambridge: University Press.

Yazdani, M. (Ed.) (1986). *Artificial Intelligence: Principles and Applications.* London: Chapman and Hall.

14

ECONOMIC PSYCHOLOGY: AN INTRODUCTION TO A NEW INTERDISCIPLINARY FIELD

S.E.G. LEA AND P. WEBLEY

ECONOMIC BEHAVIOUR AND ECONOMIC PSYCHOLOGY

Economic psychology is one of the newest forms of applied psychology. So far, it has been relatively little studied, and many textbooks of psychology (and many psychology courses) will not even mention it. Yet it is potentially one of the most important fields of psychology.

Economic psychology sets out to answer two major questions. First, we aim to understand what psychological processes underly individuals' economic behaviour. It is fairly obvious what we mean by economic behaviour, though it is possible to argue about it at the margins. In a modern society, anything that involves the exchange of goods or services for money is a kind of economic behaviour, so working for an employer, buying things from shops, and saving money in banks or building societies, are all included. Less obvious examples include giving money to charities or as presents to friends and relations; gambling, whether through a commercial organization such as a betting shop, or informally with friends; paying tax to the government; and watching, or deciding not to watch, advertisements on television.

Some important cases are not at all clear-cut. Is following a course of study economic behaviour? It may improve your career prospects in the future. What about doing the housework? If you paid someone else to do exactly the same job, that would certainly be an economic transaction. When people choose how many children to have, is that an economic decision? It certainly has economic consequences, for children are expensive to keep while young, but may support you economically in your old age. Fortunately, we don't need to resolve all these difficult cases. The important point is that they show how a successful analysis of economic behaviour might turn out to have wide psychological implications.

Our second major question concerns the effect that the economy has on individuals. 'The economy' here means the whole network of economic activity within a nation, the sum total of millions of people's economic behaviour, working, buying and selling, advertising, investing, importing and exporting, not to mention the government's attempts to control and influence all of that activity. The economy is a major aspect of the social environment in which we all live. It is obvious that it is a very different experience to live in the advanced capitalist economies of Western Europe or North America, compared with living in the socialist economies that until recently held sway in Eastern Europe. It is very different again to live in the less developed economy of a country like India or Zaire. What psychological effects will follow from these massive economic differences? On a smaller scale, any given economy shows variation over time. We are all familiar with times of economic growth and stagnation, times of inflation and recession, or in general with good times and bad times at the economic level. What psychological effects will such economic processes have on the individuals who live within the economy?

Both these questions show how important economic psychology must be. We spend a large proportion of our waking hours engaged in economic behaviour, certainly if we count the work we do for our employers into the equation. Even if we leave that out, as belonging more to occupational psychology than to economic psychology, a large part of our remaining time is involved with buying and consuming goods that are produced through the economy, not to mention the other kinds of economic behaviour outlined above. Similarly, it is hard to imagine a more drastic transition than moving from (say) Zaire to (say) the United States; and even if we stay in one country, the state of its economy can make the difference between having a job and being unemployed, or between a young couple being able to rent a flat and set up house on their own and their having to live with in-laws. These are the kinds of differences that can have profound psychological effects.

THE HISTORICAL DEVELOPMENT OF ECONOMIC PSYCHOLOGY

Economics and psychology share common intellectual roots. Within the English-speaking world, both can trace their origins to the group of seventeenth to nineteenth century philosophers referred to as the 'British empiricists'. However, economics developed as an independent academic and practical discipline earlier than psychology, and it developed in a different way. As we shall discuss in more detail below, it has tended to take a theoretical and mathematical approach where psychology has been more empirical and pragmatic.

Nonetheless, the idea that these two neighbouring social sciences should be brought together is not a recent one. The well-known French social psychologist Gabriel Tarde published a two-volume work called *La psychologie économique* in 1902, and other early twentieth century psychologists such as William McDougall also took an interest in economics. Mainly, though, their approach was to criticise the way economic theory is based on the assumption of rational choice. We discuss the substance of this issue below, but it will be obvious enough that attacking the core assumptions of economics was not the best strategy if the aim was to encourage productive interdisciplinary collaboration.

Modern economic psychology has its origins in more practical concerns. During the second world war, the Hungarian-born psychologist George Katona found himself involved in the United States' efforts to manage a war-time economy without producing the high inflation that so often accompanies wars. He argued that war-time inflation can be understood in terms of psychological processes, which the government could address by both economic and other means (e.g. by publicity campaigns). In the immediate post-war period, he extended this idea by collecting survey data on consumer and business attitudes, and attempting to use them to predict the future development of the economy. At a time when the available conventional economic indicators were predicting a recession, Katona correctly predicted an economic boom. He thus began a long career of using psychological survey data within economic forecasting, and also of trying to account for his results by integrating economic and psychological theory.

Although not all economists agreed that his 'soft' data could really add anything to economic forecasting techniques, Katona's work became well known both in economics and psychology. Nonetheless, economic psychology did not develop quickly in the United States, and it remained closely identified with Katona and a few colleagues. There was more development in continental Europe, where Pierre-Louis Reynaud in France, Gery Van Veldhoven in the Netherlands, and Karl-Erik Wärneryd in Sweden were among those who picked up and developed Katona's ideas. With a handful of other colleagues, they founded the European Group for Research in Economic Psychology, which held its first international symposium in Tilburg, the Netherlands, in 1976. This informal group has since grown into a formally constituted learned society, the International Association for Research in Economic Psychology (IAREP), which holds conferences every year, sponsors the publication of the *Journal of Economic Psychology*, and generally works to encourage interdisciplinary research.

To begin with, most people who described themselves as 'economic psychologists' were originally psychologists rather than economists by training. That is no longer true. Similarly, although France, the Netherlands and Scandinavia originally provided the founders of the discipline in its modern form, economic psychology is now much more widely accepted. In fact, it is no longer a predominantly European idea: the majority of the papers published in the *Journal of Economic Psychology* now come from the United States or Australasia.

Three recent developments have enhanced this trend for economic psychology to become a truly international and a truly interdisciplinary subject. The first is the rapid development of an experimental school in economics, until recently thought of as a wholly non-experimental science. Hey (1992) provides an excellent introduction to this area. Although experimental economists still feel themselves as somewhat under suspicion by their more traditional colleagues, their techniques are rapidly becoming part of mainstream economic thinking. But they also have very pointed reasons for seeking collaboration with psychologists, with their much longer tradition of experimental work.

The second is the wide acceptance within economics of the importance of some modifications of the assumption of rational choice. We discuss this assumption and psychological criticisms of it below. Typically, such criticisms have been either ignored or resisted by economists. Recently, however, the decision theorists Kahneman and Tversky (1979) have succeeded in establishing some very reliable ways in which rationality appears to fail when people take decisions under risk, and their explanation of why these occur, 'prospect theory', has become widely known and respected among economists.

The third is the sudden emergence of a new field of study under the title of 'socioeconomics'. This school of thought drew its inspiration in particular from Amitai Etzioni's book *The Moral Dimension* (1988). Many of those who have now started calling themselves socioeconomists are highly critical of the dominant 'neoclassical' school of economic theorising. They seek a theoretical standpoint that draws on more realistic principles of human behaviour, and they are also concerned that theories should be tested against actual data. As its name implies, socioeconomics is more concerned with the interface of economics with sociology than with psychology. Nonetheless, the boundaries between socioeconomics and economic psychology are ill-defined and not of great importance, and the rush of interest in socioeconomics, especially in the United States, can only strengthen economic psychology.

Because of the short history of economic psychology as a (relatively) independent field of study, much of the research on which we have to call in this chapter was done by economists, or consumer scientists, rather than by psychologists. It is likely to be quite inaccessible, intellectually and possibly also practically, to the psychology student. For this reason, we have generally not given bibliographic references to the original research, but to review papers and books which go some way to interpreting the results for an interdisciplinary audience. We have made an exception for the most recent research, which has not yet been reviewed in this way. Otherwise, most of the material presented here can be found in expanded form in the substantial texts on economic psychology that have now begun to appear (e.g. Lea, Tarpy and Webley, 1987; Van Raaij, Van Veldhoven and Wärneryd, 1988). These books mark a turning point in the development of economic psychology: the beginning, perhaps, of a more general recognition that it is an important branch of applied psychology.

THE RELATION OF ECONOMIC PSYCHOLOGY TO OTHER KINDS OF APPLIED PSYCHOLOGY

Nonetheless, economic psychology is different, in several ways, from most of the other kinds of applied psychology introduced in this book.

Economic Psychology is not a 'Professional' Discipline

Some kinds of applied psychology, like clinical psychology, or criminological and legal psychology, are mainly concerned with the use of psychology in a particular practical context. Thus clinical psychologists are trying to help particular people whose behaviour or mental experience is distressing (to themselves or, sometimes, to others); criminological psychologists are trying to understand and modify the behaviour of particular people who have broken the law; and so on. Of course research goes on in all these fields, both at the academic level (within universities, polytechnics, and research institutes) and as part of the day to day practice of the subject. The main emphasis, however, is on using the general psychological knowledge we have in order to help particular individuals.

Economic psychology, on the other hand, is mainly a research discipline, at least as a student is likely to experience it; it is concerned with general laws rather than particular instances. It is true that some of the findings of economic psychology may be relevant to the formation of economic policy. Furthermore, quite a lot of its methods, and some of its findings, may be used by particular economic agents (mainly firms, either as employers or as sellers of goods). But the information such firms generate is unlikely to come into the public domain: if a firm discovers an efficient way of marketing its goods, it is not going to publish the results in a scientific journal for its competitors to read. At the moment, therefore, the main aim of economic psychology as an academic discipline is to understand the two-way relation between the psychology of individuals and the workings of the economy.

Research in Economic Psychology May Have Commercial Value

Just because economic psychology deals with economic behaviour, the results it obtains may have economic consequences. Put more simply, it may be possible to make money, or to make more money, by knowing the regularities in other people's economic behaviour. This complicates the academic study of economic psychology in two ways.

First, as has already been mentioned, research is likely to be carried out by active economic agents, who will have no incentive to publish their results. They may even have an incentive to mislead the wider community about the extent and conclusions of their research. Although we have never encountered a case of this sort, we have, for example, encountered a large financial organization that was in a position to monitor a substantial proportion of all the consumer purchases made in the United Kingdom, and was doing so. Its staff were understandably not interested in sharing their observations with academic researchers.

The second complication is more subtle. Suppose we discover a regularity about, say, the way people bid at auctions (the subject of some interesting current research: Smith, 1989; Thaler, 1988). It may then become possible to become a more effective bidder, and make more money, by behaving in a way that breaks the 'law' we have just discovered. We see, therefore, that formulating a 'law' in economic psychology may in fact undermine it. This is an example of what has been called the 'uncertainty principle' that applies in all human sciences: if a prediction about behaviour is communicated to the subjects of the prediction, they may be induced to change their behaviour, if only because they resent being predicted. Where economic behaviour is concerned there may be a financial advantage, as well as sheer cussedness, to induce people to violate our predictions. Economics itself suffers from this problem, of course, but to a lesser extent, because it tends to base its predictions on an assumption of rational behaviour and it is rarely financially advantageous to behave irrationally. Economic psychology is more vulnerable, because it is open-minded about rationality.

Economic Psychology Involves Interacting with Another Academic Discipline

Economic psychologists are not the only people interested in understanding how individuals and the economy interrelate. This is the major concern of economics, which is at least as well established as a social science as psychology itself. As far as theory goes, indeed, economics is much more integrated and advanced than psychology. Economic theory has something to say about every kind of economic behaviour, and about the way people at large behave as a result of economic changes. And although empirical investigation is more difficult in economics than in psychology, economists have collected various kinds of data which give us a lot of information about the details of economic behaviour.

Economic psychology certainly must not ignore this valuable source of information. In fact, it is and has to be part of economics as well as part of psychology: if it is to be successful, it needs to be a fully interdisciplinary subject, drawing on the strengths of both economics and psychology. This makes some part of economic psychology quite hard to study, because economists are used to working with complicated mathematically expressed theories, of a sort that have had much less influence in psychology.

Important Parts of Economic Psychology Fall Within Other Branches of Applied Psychology

The two most important kinds of economic behaviour, in terms of the amount of time we spend on them during our daily lives, are working and buying. Each of these has its own branch of applied psychology already, and so their status as parts of economic psychology is ambiguous.

Work is the subject matter of occupational psychology (often known in North America as industrial and organizational psychology). That is an important enough branch of applied psychology to account for four chapters in the present book, and almost any treatment of applied psychology would see it as one of the major branches. Buying is a slightly different case. Quite a lot of research has been devoted to the study of 'Consumer Behaviour', and it is not uncommon to find books, or courses, on 'Consumer Psychology'. This is both a research area and a professional area. Consumer psychologists often work for the marketing departments of large firms, or for advertising agencies, and a few also work for consumer organizations. As well as studying buying itself, consumer psychologists are interested in the psychological mechanisms of advertising and other marketing strategies. Consumer psychology isn't as well developed a specialism as occupational psychology, and there isn't a separate chapter about it in this book. Here, therefore, we treat it as just part of economic psychology. Like occupational psychology, it is really a bigger subject than economic psychology itself, in the sense that there are probably more people in the world who think of themselves as consumer psychologists than there are who think of themselves as economic psychologists.

Logically, both occupational psychology and consumer psychology are parts of economic psychology, because working and buying are both kinds of economic behaviour. Of course, economic psychologists are not interested in trying to take over what is already being worked on, successfully, by someone else. Most people who call themselves economic psychologists do so because they are interested in more than just work, or more than just buying and advertising. Some are mainly interested in one or more of the other kinds of economic behaviour, which aren't 'big' enough to have a branch of psychology all to themselves. But most are interested in economic behaviour as a whole: how the various kinds of economic activity (including working and buying, but also including saving, giving, taxpaying, and so forth) interact with one another, and how they add up together to influence the economy as a whole.

Also, the second main question of economic psychology, the ways in which the economy influences the individual, has not been given very much attention within either occupational psychology or consumer psychology. A few areas have been explored: for example, times of economic depression tend to lead to high levels of unemployment, and occupational psychologists have contributed a great deal in recent years to our understanding of the psychological effects of unemployment (e.g. Jahoda, 1982). It is equally true, however, that times of economic boom lead to changes in people's buying behaviour, and consumer psychologists have not paid these much attention. Economic psychologists have generally been more willing to look at these 'macro' phenomena.

THE VEXED QUESTION OF RATIONALITY

As we have already explained, one of the unusual things about economic psychology is that it involves us in working together with specialists in another area, that is, with economists. This is actually quite difficult to do, because the history of economics, as an academic discipline, has been rather different from that of psychology. In psychology, we tend to find a large number of competing theories, and a general willingness to resort to data to decide between them. The data may come from formal experiments, from observations in the field, or from the experience of professional applied psychologists; but when we learn about psychology, what we learn first are these facts about human behaviour. Only later do we try to give an account of them in terms of some kind of theory.

Economics is different. When you first learn economics, you start by learning its theory, and understanding how behaviour in a variety of different economic situations can be predicted from a fairly simple set of basic ideas. Only later (if at all) do you come to consider whether the data are consistent with your theoretical deductions; often no data seem to be available to check them at all. To a psychologist, this seems a strange way of proceeding, and what seems even stranger is that the basic assumptions of economics have a very psychological look about them. They are assertions about how people will choose between simple alternatives; they seem to be open to direct psychological tests, for example by quite simple experiments; and they also seem very likely to be wrong.

According to economic theory, if we want to predict how people will behave in a given economic situation, we must start by working out how it would be most profitable for them to behave. Any economic situation has some kind of constraints: for example, each of us has only a limited income, each of us has access to only a limited range of shops selling a limited range of goods, and so forth. Given all the constraints in a particular situation, though, we normally have at least some limited freedom of choice, so we can still ask how a rational person would behave. By a rational person, we mean one who fully understands the situation, has all the information that is relevant to a decision, and wants to get the maximum amount of money, or money's worth, or satisfaction, out of it. Economists then assume that people will, by and large, behave like this ideally rational individual. This is called the *assumption of rationality or of utility maximization*. Of course we have given a very simplified version of it; it is usually put into a much more complicated, mathematical form. For a recent survey of rationality theory, see Hargreaves Heap, Hollis, Lyons, Sugden and Weale (1992).

Many psychologists have seen the task of economic psychology as being to attack the assumption of rationality. If economics is founding itself on false assertions about individual behaviour, surely it must come to false conclusions? Some economists have taken the same view, and have looked to psychology for an improved theory of choice. One way of approaching economic psychology is therefore to look at each kind of economic behaviour, and see whether it is consistent with the assumption of rationality.

However, we believe that this approach is misguided (see Lea *et al.*, 1987, Chapter 5), for two reasons. First, it leads to a marginalisation of psychology in relation to economic behaviour. Whatever behaviour can be understood as rational the economists will keep for themselves; psychology ends up with the odd few irrational bits that are left over. Secondly, Rachlin has shown that, in principle, any consistent pattern of behaviour can be made to be consistent with the assumption of utility maximization, because the concept of utility is only defined in a rather weak way.

Our view is that economic psychology should be concerned with the whole of economic behaviour, whether or not we can see a 'rational' explanation of it. If people do behave in a way that obviously maximizes their utility, we want to understand the psychological mechanisms behind their behaviour. And if behaviour seems irrational, we still want to know what mechanisms are at work, and we may also be able to use psychology to discover more about people's sources of satisfaction, and so explain how behaviour is after all consistent with the rationality assumption.

SOME EXAMPLES OF INDIVIDUAL ECONOMIC BEHAVIOUR

This section gives some of the best established facts and theories about three different kinds of individual economic behaviour. We look briefly at work, and in rather more detail at buying. Both these sections involve picking out one or two interesting points from very large bodies of research. Finally we consider what is known about the psychology of saving; here there has been much less research so far, and we give a more comprehensive overview.

Work

As we have already explained, the psychology of work is dealt with in more detail in the chapters of this book which deal with different aspects of occupational psychology. Here we will just draw attention to some issues that have been of more concern to economic psychologists than to occupational psychologists as such.

A key question in the psychology of work is, of course, the motivation for working. While earning money may be the normal and 'manifest' reason for seeking employment (Jahoda, 1982), going to work has other, 'latent' functions. The simplest economic analyses of work ignore these factors, concentrating on the trade-off between leisure and consumption (paid for by earnings). More sophisticated economic analyses do take into account 'non-pecuniary motivations', and show that they can affect choice of a job. Economic psychologists are seeking to address this question by looking at the behaviour of people who are working but not being directly paid for it (e.g. voluntary workers, housewives or househusbands, and students). For example, recent research by Sharon Lapham in our department has shown that although voluntary workers do not much mind that they are unpaid, a major motivation for them is developing their skills or confidence for paid work they will take up later. Having something to organize their time, one of Jahoda's latent functions of work, was also important for them.

Another area of current research is the psychological effects of taxation and social security payments (see Lea *et al.*, 1987, Chapter 11; Lewis, 1982). If taxes are increased, or social security payments are decreased, one of two things can happen. People might work harder, or longer hours, to restore their incomes to its previous level; or they might work less, because there is less incentive. Economic theory is unable to say which will occur. Economists, psychologists, and economic psychologists have been trying to look at this question, using a number of different approaches. There are statistical studies of the effects of the relation between take-home pay and hours worked (summarized by Brown, 1980, Chapters 5, 7), studies based on experimental manipulations of the social security system (such as the well known New Jersey Income Maintenance experiment), and even a series of experimental studies, by Battalio, Kagel and their colleagues, using rats who are 'paid' for performing simple responses by food rewards. All these studies agree that the incentive factor is much weaker than might be expected. Particular groups may be strongly affected by tax or social security changes; for example, in the New Jersey experiment, it was found that women do tend to leave the labour market if social security payments are increased. This is hardly a surprising result, especially since nearly all the women in the sample had dependent children; such women are in any case the least likely to be in paid employment (see the survey by Baxter, 1988, Chapter 4). In a more recent study done in Britain, James, Jordan & Redley (1992) have shown that married women tend to leave the labour market if their husbands become unemployed, because of the peculiar structure of the British tax and social security system.

Economic theory also finds it difficult to predict when people will seek to evade or avoid paying taxes. Economic psychologists have studied this question in two rather different ways, through surveys (reviewed by Lewis, 1982) and though experiments (Webley, Robben, Elffers & Hessing, 1991). Both methods have their problems (cf. Hessing, Kinsey, Elffers & Weigel, 1988). In surveys, you are asking people to tell you about behaviour which is probably illegal, and the answers often do not correlate well with what we can find out about tax evasion from the tax authorities themselves. The most usual experimental technique involves using computers to simulate the situation of earning money and declaring it for tax; its problem is the risk that participants will just treat it like a computer game.

In both cases, however, good results can be obtained given careful design, and this is a field in which there has been some most ingenious research. The best studies of both types agree that

(i) perceived unfairness of the tax system is more likely to be an after-the-fact justification than a real motivation for evasion;
(ii) receiving a refund from the tax authorities, which is seen as a gain, reduces evasion;
(iii) opportunity to evade is one of the most important factors in explaining evasion.

A third area where economic psychology has made an interesting contribution is in the study of entrepreneurial behaviour (reviewed by Wärneryd, 1988). In contemporary political discussion, much has been made discussion of the importance of entrepreneurship for the health of the economy. Psychologists, too, have seen entrepreneurs as the key figures in economic development; McClelland's (1961) elaborate theory of the rise and fall of nations as economic powers depended on a socio-psychological theory of the origins of entrepreneurship.

Current research is rather more realistic in tone. Ronen argued that there are two personality dimensions that predispose people to become entrepreneurs, novelty-seeking and purposefulness of action. Wärneryd points out that much of the psychological work has argued that preference for risk is the crucial personality factor, and suggests considering all three dimensions together. In either case, we can see that entrepreneurs are not some distinct kind of human being, but rather that different people will have stronger or weaker preferences for an entrepreneurial role. Whether they take up such a role will depend on many other factors.

Among the most important factors will be the alternative opportunities available to them, and the economic advantages or disadvantages of entrepreneurship in a given economy. The economic psychology of entrepreneurship therefore needs to take into account economic analyses of the costs and benefits of running one's own business. Casson (1982) has given a stimulating analysis from the economist's point of view. More recently, the rapid changes now under way in the economies of eastern Europe give us a unique opportunity to study how people respond to new opportunities for entrepreneurial careers (and, perhaps, declining opportunities for more bureaucratic roles). Many distinguished Eastern European psychologists, such as Tadeusz Tyszka in Poland and Zbyněk Bureš in Czechoslovakia, are currently trying to investigate the psychological processes involved in the economic transformations in which their countries are now embroiled.

Buying

Within consumer psychology, there has been an immense amount of research on why people buy particular products in particular quantities. Often, its main concern has been with how people can be persuaded to buy more of a product, or more of one brand than another. A product is a class of goods, which may be quite general (breakfast cereals), or more specific (cornflakes); whereas a brand is a particular make of that product, and possibly of other products, e.g. Kellogg's.

Although consumer psychology has generated some very complex theories (e.g. Howard & Sheth, 1969), these are open to severe criticism. They incorporate many different psychological processes, and can fit in with almost any conceivable pattern of data. It is not easy to make strong general statements about buying behaviour, other than the most obvious (people buy more of nearly all products when their incomes go up, and less when prices go up, for example).

In some ways, the clearest facts about buying concern its variability. Marketing psychologists devote much effort to *market segmentation* – trying to find different groups within society who will have different levels of interest in particular products or brands, will react differently to advertising, and above all, who will have different probabilities of purchasing goods. Segmentation is often based on the obvious demographic variables of age, sex and social class, or on economic variables of which the most important is income. But it may also be based on more psychologically interesting variables such as personality or, more usually, attitudes. For example, Karns (1987) has described a psychographic approach to segmenting financial markets on the basis of individuals' acceptance of financial risk. This involves classifying people according to their preferences with regard to the variability of the financial return of an investment and whether they prefer to take their own decisions or follow the advice of experts. This gives four rather zoological segments, from 'mice' (who like low variability and follow experts) through 'squirrels' and 'thoroughbreds' (who favour high variability and follow experts) to 'bulls'. The resulting classification can be used to predict various kinds of financial behaviour: as a very simple example, thorough-breds own the most credit cards and mice the least.

Economic psychologists, as distinct from consumer psychologists, have also posed more general questions about buying. The heart of the economic theory of supply and demand is the derivation, from a few assumptions about the way individuals choose, of a complex theory of the relation between prices, incomes, and the quantities of different goods that people will buy. Economic psychologists have been interested in this theoretical structure at a number of levels.

First, as we have already pointed out, the economists' assumptions about individual choice behaviour seem psychologically implausible. Are they nonetheless correct? A number of experiments have been done to test this. For example, a key assumption is transitivity, which can be explained by a simple example. If a person would rather have an apple than a banana, and would rather have a banana than a cabbage, what will happen if we offer him or her a choice between an apple and a cabbage? The principle of transitivity says that the apple will always be preferred; if someone prefers the cabbage, that is called an *intransitive* choice. Put like that, transivity seems a reasonable idea, but is it reliable? Even if it holds for the majority of choices, will it hold for all? Davis gave male students a series of choices between imaginary marriage partners, and he found that the great majority of choices were in fact transitive. However, Tversky subsequently showed that if the objects to be chosen between have many different properties, so that each one is better in some ways and worse in others, there are some conditions where intransitive choice will occur reliably. These and other experiments on the choice axioms are summarised by Lea *et al.* (1987, Chapter 5).

A second way of investigating the theory of supply and demand is to look at its results rather than the principles on which it is based. Do people in fact react to price and income changes by buying more or less of the goods concerned, in the way suggested by theory? It is quite difficult to test this, but it is not impossible. One approach is to use animals in experimental models of the economy, and in this way, Kagel, Battalio and their colleagues have tested many deductions from the economic theory of supply and demand. In general they have found results that are consistent with utility maximizing principles, and they have been able to go on to examine details not specified by the basic theory, such as the functional form of demand curves (e.g. Battalio, Dwyer & Kagel, 1987).

A third approach is to look at data obtained by market researchers. Gabor and his colleagues invented a technique for finding out whether people would buy a product following a possible price change. Not surprisingly, they found that, as predicted by demand theory, people are generally much less likely to buy when price increases. They also made the interesting discovery that people regularly refuse to buy because prices are too low (e.g. Sowter, Gabor & Granger, 1971). Economically speaking, price simply serves as a barrier to acquisition. Psychologically, it is also a signal of quality and desirability.

The research on buying discussed so far concentrates on the purchase of individual products. What about the *aggregate* tendency to buy: the net result, over the entire economy, of the buying decisions of all the consumers in the nation? This is a variable of great economic importance, since aggregate consumer demand can make the difference between growth and stagnation, or between inflation and stability. It was this variable that George Katona was concerned with in the studies that were so important in the development of modern economic psychology. Katona constructed a psychological test called the Index of Consumer Sentiment, which asks people how they feel about the current state of the economy. Panels of volunteers have completed this test at regular intervals since 1952 in the United States (see, for example, Katona, 1975, Chapter 5), and since the early 1970s in the European Community (Vanden Abeele, 1983). The average value of the Index correlates well with the future level of activity in the economy, and at least in its early days, it was a better predictor of recession or growth than any economic statistics then available (Katona, 1975, Chapter 6).

Saving

Saving is almost the direct opposite of buying: whatever money we do not spend, we almost by definition save. Consumer psychologists have done far less research on saving than on buyer behaviour. However, the economic psychology of saving turns out to be particularly interesting. Research by economists and psychologists has been summarised by Lea *et al.* (1987, Chapter 8) and Wärneryd (1989).

Katona was particularly interested in saving, and one of his first insights was that the simple symmetry between spending and buying breaks down at the psychological level. Psychologically, there is a big difference between what he called contractual, discretionary, and involuntary saving. Contractual saving involves setting up an agreement that 'forces' us to save: making regular payments into a savings plan linked to life insurance or a pension, for example. Even repaying a debt such as a house mortgage is a form of contractual saving from the economic point of view. Discretionary saving involves a specific decision to set aside a specific sum of money there and then. Involuntary saving is the saving we do by accident, for example by having some salary left over at the end of the month, or by paying too much tax, which is subsequently refunded. This last is a very common behaviour in the United States, as has been shown by very recent research by Cordes and his colleagues (e.g. Cordes, Galper & Kirby, 1990).

Economic theorists have recognised that the psychology of saving is important. The reason is that if we look only at the most obvious economic variables, the function of saving must be to let the pattern of our spending deviate from the pattern of our income. People who do not want to go on working in their old age must therefore save when they are younger and have a good income (economists call this 'hump saving'). However, if this is the target of saving, people rarely hit it at all accurately. Put crudely, we save much too little while we are young, and quite a bit too much when we are old. Katona found that most households save, every year, less than they had planned. On the other hand, in a study of wills that had been proved in the state of Wisconsin, Menchik and David found that the longer people live after retirement, the more money they have to leave. This must mean that people who have retired on a pension, and are therefore already living on what they have saved, go on adding to their savings until their death. It follows that 'hump saving' cannot be a full explanation of saving behaviour.

Some psychological research has concentrated on people's limitations as savers. The parallel with the difficulty of 'delaying gratification' has been widely noted. In a long series of experiments, Mischel and his colleagues have shown that if you offer people a small reward now or a larger one later, they are likely to take the small, immediate reward even when it would be more profitable to wait. The extent of delayed gratification varies between groups of people, and some of these differences correspond to differences in saving behaviour. For example, working class children are less likely to delay gratification than their middle-class peers, and this corresponds to the class difference in saving which has been widely proposed by sociologists such as Weber (1904, 1976). However, Katona's research shows that, although overall saving increases with income, the wealthiest people in society are also those most likely to run down their savings by large purchases. Clearly a complex of different motivations lie behind the decision to save.

A different psychological approach, therefore, has been to look at how children learn to save. Although young children find it very difficult to defer gratification in experiments like Mischel's, they are often formidable savers out of their pocket money. Saving is encouraged by parents in a variety of ways, so that it becomes almost a moral principle to save. In an experiment simulating a series of shopping and saving opportunities of children, Sonuga-Barke and Webley (1993) found that the major changes in saving occurred between the ages of 6 and 9. At age 4 the use of the 'bank' was essentially random. To the 6-year-old it appeared that money saved was money lost, and if children of this age did save, it seemed to be due to the fact that saving was a thing they believed that they ought to do. In contrast, 9-year-olds viewed saving strategically and were aware that savings could be used for expenditure in the future and that savings and expenditure were related, not distinct, activities. The belief of many 6-year-olds that money saved is money lost is not unreasonable given that children of this age do not have access to money put in banks or building societies on their behalf. These results show the need to see children's saving in context; saving is just one possible budgeting strategy among many and a 'spend, spend, spend' approach, where children spend all their money and then ask their parents for more, may in some cases be more profitable.

This is not a complete survey of the psychology of saving. What it does show is how psychological and economic theory can work together, and also how economic psychology uses a mixture of data, some from traditional psychological experiments, others from surveys of what happens in an entire economy.

THE ECONOMY AS AN INDEPENDENT VARIABLE IN PSYCHOLOGY

The study of individual economic behaviour is only half the story of economic psychology. It is just as important to look at the way the economy acts on individuals. Primarily, of course, the economic environment will affect economic behaviour, but that is not all it affects. For example, Padgett and Jorgenson argued that threatening economic conditions lead to increasing interest in astrology and mysticism (they based their conclusions on an analysis of the content of magazines and newspapers in Germany during the inter-war years).

The Economic System

One way to look at the effects of the economic environment is to compare very different economies. In the socialist economies that dominated eastern Europe from 1945 until 1990, people's behaviour was very different from what we were used to in capitalist western Europe. We are now in the middle of a historical experiment to see the effects of a radical change. It is difficult to isolate the economic factor when it is linked to a complex of social and political conditions, as it is in this example and as it inevitably always will be. Nevertheless, it is worth the effort of trying to understand the psychological effects of the economic system, because they are likely to have a serious effect on the process of transition.

The same considerations apply if we contrast, not eastern and western Europe, but European/North American models with Japanese and east Asian ones. The rapid rise to predominance of the economies of Japan, South Korea, Singapore and Taiwan has been popularly linked to aspects of 'oriental psychology'. More serious literature has been concerned with the traditions of management, particularly in large firms (e.g. Pascale & Athos, 1982), though these are of course themselves products of the wider culture.

Finally, we can contrast 'North' and 'South', the developed world with the less developed countries of Africa, south Asia and South America. Munro (1983), for example, argues that the psychology of work motivation needs a thoroughgoing re-write if it is to apply to conditions in Africa; it is not that the concepts developed in Europe and North America do not apply, but the situation is so different that the kinds of behaviour we predict cannot be the same.

In all three of these cases, we are not interested only in the psychological effects of the economic system. There is also a vital interest in the effects that psychological processes might have in bringing about economic change. Applying psychology in this way is not easy (Sinha, 1983), and from our point of view it falls more into the class of looking at the economic effects of individual behaviour than of considering the economy as an independent variable. But it is potentially extremely important.

The State of the Economy

It is rather easier to look at the effect of economic fluctuations within one country. It is well established that nation-wide indicators of mental disorder increase in times of economic hardship (Brenner, 1973; Dooley & Catalano, 1980). The reasons for this are a matter of dispute; perhaps economic depression just allows mental illness that was always present to come to light. More likely, however, difficult economic conditions put the most vulnerable people in society under stress. People who are already economically disadvantaged are the ones most likely to lose their jobs, slide into serious poverty, or have a justified fear of such developments. They are also the ones most at risk from most mental disorders, as indeed from most physical illnesses (Dohrenwend & Dohrenwend, 1969).

Milder economic adversity may actually benefit people. A study by Elder and Liker (1982) illustrates this neatly. In 1969–70, they and their colleagues traced a group of 81 women from the town of Berkeley, California, who had all given birth to children during 1928–29. They looked at the mental and physical health of women whose husbands had lost their jobs in the depression of the early 1930s. Among working-class women, the adverse effects of this economic shock could still be seen: these women had poorer health than comparable women whose husbands had managed to stay in work. Among middle-class women, however, the effect was reversed. Elder and Liker argued that these women had been forced into more independent, stimulating roles by their husbands' unemployment.

Advertising

The economic environment has, of course, many facets. For example, the level of advertising to which consumers are exposed varies between times and between places. It is often argued that, as well as inducing people to buy specific goods, the all-pervading presence of advertising may induce general psychological change in people, especially in children. It might, for example, make people more materialistic, more concerned about owning large numbers of goods. Williamson (1978) argues that advertising serves to confuse people about the real economic relations in society. Many writers have pointed to the way advertising may reinforce, or even create, social stereotypes about minority groups, or women. At least until recently, women in advertisements were almost invariably shown in dependent, uninformed roles, and this kind of biased presentation certainly can affect behaviour. Jennings and his colleagues showed women college students simulated television commercials in which the roles had been reversed, so that the powerful, well-informed parts were taken by women. Compared with other students who saw advertisements with the original sex roles intact, the students were more independent and self confident when asked to take decisions and make a speech in public shortly afterwards. These and related studies are discussed further by Lea *et al.* (1987, Chapter 13).

Money

Money serves almost as a metaphor for the economic factor in our lives, yet most of the cultures that have developed in the world have done without money, and our western money of coins and notes (and, more recently, computer records operated on by plastic cards) is only one of many forms that money has taken. Clearly, the sort of money we now use is a very successful invention, because it has come to dominate economic exchanges wherever it has been introduced. What psychological difference does it make to live in an economy that has money, compared with living in one that does not?

Money makes possible exact calculation of what goods or services are worth. In so-called primitive economies, in which there is no money, trade occurs through a process of barter. Sahlins (1974, Chapter 6) analyses in detail three such examples of primitive trade. For example, the aboriginal people of northern Queensland trade spears, made near Cape York in the extreme north, for axes, made at a quarry 400 miles further south. In a rough and ready way, the usual economic laws of supply and demand do apply to these exchanges, so one axe may be traded for several spears near Cape York, but several axes must be given for one spear further south. However, prices are much less precisely determined by economic conditions than in a modern economy. The possibility of exact calculation may be one reason why we have found, in a series of surveys, that even in a modern economy money is often unacceptable for the exchange of gifts among close friends and family. This is one of the oldest forms of economic exchange, and perhaps 'primitive' social rules still apply to it.

Similarly, when we are paid money for doing some kind of work, this gives us an exact estimate of how much that work is worth to our employers; it also gives us an exact reason for doing the job, rather than the nebulous feelings of enjoyment or obligation which bind us to unpaid work. In experimental situations, paying people to perform simple tasks may make them less likely to repeat the task in the future (Lepper & Greene, 1978). Social psychologists have argued that this is because the external, precise, money reward undermines any intrinsic satisfaction the task may have given. It gives people a simple explanation for the fact that they were performing the task, so they no longer believe that they enjoyed it. Extending this analysis to everyday life, Pearce (1983) has shown that, when volunteers work alongside paid workers doing the same job, the voluntary workers feel more motivated by the characteristics of the job itself: paid workers claim to be motivated largely by the money they receive.

CONCLUDING COMMENTS

This very brief survey has only given an idea of the kinds of questions that interest economic psychologists. A more detailed introduction, which goes further than this chapter but is not too difficult for a beginner, is the book by Maital (1982). Much fuller accounts are now available (e.g. Lea et al., 1987; Van Raaij et al., 1988), while the *Journal of Economic Psychology* provides the natural means to keep pace with new research.

Economic psychology has now begun to develop much more rapidly, and both economists and psychologists are showing increasing interest. The range of its potential applications is wide. At the moment, the chief users of economic psychology are the commercial organizations who employ consumer psychologists to help them understand their customers. Clearly, governments also need to understand how individuals' economic behaviour affects the state of the economy, and the effects that changes in the economy may have on individuals. Our hope is that economic psychology will also be useful to the individuals who live in the economy: to you and to us. We need to understand how economic forces act on us, and how powerful economic organizations (the government, the firms that employ us, and the firms that try to sell to us) try to mould our behaviour. A full understanding of our own economic psychology would greatly increase our power to choose our own economic behaviour.

REFERENCES

Battalio, R.C., Dwyer, G.P. & Kagel, J.H. (1987). Tests of competing theories of consumer choice and the representative consumer hypothesis. *Economic Journal*, **97**, 842–856.

Baxter, J.L. (1988). *Social and psychological foundations of economic analysis.* New York: Harvester Wheatsheaf.

Brenner, M.H. (1973). *Mental illness and the economy.* Cambridge MA: Harvard University Press.

Brown, C.V. (1980). *Taxation and the incentive to work.* Oxford: Oxford University Press.

Cordes, J.J., Galper, H. & Kirby, S.N. (1990). Causes of overwitholding: Forced saving or transactions cost? Paper read at the conference of the Society for the Advancement of Socio-Economics Washington DC, March.

Dohrenwend, B.P. & Dohrenwend, B.S. (1969). *Social status and psychological disorder: A causal enquiry.* New York: Wiley.

Dooley, D. & Catalano, R. (1980). Economic change as a cause of behavioral disorder. *Psychological Bulletin*, **87**, 450–468.

Elder, G.H. & Liker, J.K. (1982). Hard times in women's lives: historical influences across forty years. *American Journal of Sociology*, **88**, 241–269.

Etzioni, A. (1988). *The moral dimension.* New York: Free Press.

Hargreaves Heap, S., Hollis, M., Lyons, B., Sugden, R. & Weale, A. (1992). *The theory of choice.* Oxford: Blackwell.

Hessing, D.J., Kinsey, K.A., Elffers, H. & Weigel, R.H. (1988). Tax evasion research: measurement strategies and theoretical models. In W.F. Van Raaij, G.M. Van Veldhoven & K.-E. Wärneryd (Eds), *Handbook of Economic Psychology* (pp. 516–537). Dordrecht: Kluwer.

Hey, J.D. (1992). Experiments in economics – and psychology. In S.E.G. Lea, P. Webley, & B.M. Young (Eds.), *New directions in economic psychology* (pp. 65–98). Cheltenham: Edward Elgar.

Howard, J.A. & Sheth, J.N. (1969). *The theory of buyer behavior.* New York: Wiley.

Jahoda, M. (1982). *Employment and unemployment: a social-psychological analysis.* Cambridge: Cambridge University Press.

James, S., Jordan, W.O. & Redley, M. (1992). Labour market decisions in low-income households. In S.E.G. Lea, P. Webley, & B.M. Young (Eds.), *New directions in economic psychology* (pp. 243–259). Cheltenham: Edward Elgar.

Kahneman, D. & Tversky, A. (1979). Prospect theory: An analysis of decision under risk. *Econometrica,* **47**, 263–291.

Karns, D. (1987). Market segments in flux: the psychographic segmentation of financial markets. In F. Ölander & K.L. Grunert (Eds), *Understanding Economic Behaviour.* Århus: Handelshojskolen.

Katona, G. (1975). *Psychological Economics.* New York: Elsevier.

Lea, S.E.G., Tarpy, R.M. & Webley, P. (1987). *The individual in the economy.* Cambridge: Cambridge University Press.

Lepper, M.R. & Greene, D. (Eds) (1973). *The hidden costs of reward.* Hillsdale, NJ: Erlbaum.

Lewis, A. (1982). *The psychology of taxation.* Oxford: Martin Robertson.

Maital, S. (1982). *Minds, markets and money.* New York: Basic Books.

McClelland, D.C. (1961). *The achieving society.* Princeton: Van Nostrand.

Munro, D. (1983). Developing *'la conscience professionelle'* in cultures with a history of vocational disadvantage. In F. Blackler (Ed.), *Social psychology and developing countries* (pp. 51–69). Chichester: Wiley.

Pascale, R.T. & Athos, A.G. (1982). *The art of Japanese management.* Harmondsworth: Penguin.

Pearce, J.L. (1983). Job attitude and motivation differences between volunteers and employees from comparable organizations. *Journal of Applied Psychology,* **68**, 646–652.

Sahlins, M. (1974). *Stone age economics.* London: Tavistock.

Sinha, D. (1983). Applied psychology and problems of national development. In F. Blackler (Ed.), *Social psychology and developing countries* (pp. 7–20). Chichester: Wiley.

Smith, C.W. (1989). *Auctions: The social construction of value.* London: Harvester Wheatsheaf.

Sonuga-Barke, E.J.S. & Webley, P. (1993). *Children's saving.* Hove: Erlbaum.

Sowter, A.P., Gabor, A. & Granger, C.W.J. (1971). The effect of price on choice: A theoretical and empirical investigation. *Applied Economics,* **3**, 167–81.

Thaler, R.H. (1988). The winner's curse. *Journal of Economic Perspectives,* **2**, 189–202.

Van Raaij, W.F., Van Veldhoven, G.M. & Wärneryd, K.-E. (1988). *Handbook of economic psychology.* Dordrecht: Kluwer.

Vanden Abeele, P. (1983). The Index of Consumer Sentiment: predictability and predictive power in the EEC. *Journal of Economic Psychology,* **3**, 1–17.

Wärneryd, K.-E. (1988). The psychology of innovative entrepreneurship. In W.F. Van Raaij, G. M. Veldhoven, & K.-E. Wärneryd (Eds.), *Handbook of economic psychology* (pp. 404–447). Dordrecht: Kluwer.

Wärneryd, K.-E. (1989). Improving psychological theory through studies of economic behaviour: the case of saving. *Applied Psychology: An International Review,* **38**, 213–236.

Weber, M. (1976). *The Protestant ethic and the spirit of capitalism* (2nd ed., T. Parsons, Trans.).

London: Allen & Unwin (Originally published 1904).

Webley, P., Robben, H.S.J., Elffers, H. & Hessing, D.J. (1991). *Tax evasion: an experimental approach.* Cambridge: Cambridge University Press.

Williamson, J. (1978). *Decoding advertisements.* London: Marion Boyars.

15

ENVIRONMENTAL PSYCHOLOGY

A. HEDGE

We spend about 90% of our lives inside building, and much of our behaviour is shaped by this experience of the built environment. We live in houses; work in factories, hospitals, offices; study in schools and colleges; shop in supermarkets; dine in restaurants; take holidays in hotels, and so on. Buildings provide for our basic needs, giving protection against the elements, shelter and security. They are functional spaces allowing us to perform work, learn, and play, irrespective of prevailing climate conditions. Yet they can also affect our feelings, e.g. marvelling at the grandeur of St. Paul's. They can signify extensions of ourselves either as individuals, e.g. how we decorate and maintain our homes, or as organisations, e.g. the formal grandeur of the Houses of Parliament creates an image unmistakably British. Buildings are an integral part of our cultural heritage and future development. Yet it is not the "bricks and mortar" of buildings that interest environmental psychologists, but the way in which any physical setting can facilitate or inhibit those behaviours which give meaning to the setting and which make it either a success or a failure.

Environmental psychologists study the interactions between people and their physical settings, and they generate knowledge to improve environmental design so that this better meets people's needs and desires (see Canter and Donald, 1987, for an historical overview of British environmental psychology). To do this requires information about spaces, places, and most importantly, their cultural context. How we use verbal and nonverbal cues, orient and posture our body, and manage distance in interpersonal interactions all vary within and between cultures, and all are affected by the spaces in which they occur. Similarly, the symbols we learn which signify how a space should be used, together with any past experiences of what happens in the space, combine to give us a culture bound sense of place. Knowledge of sociospatial behaviours and their cultural context is of fundamental importance in environmental psychology, although to date most of what we know is based on studies of Western settings, particularly those in North America. How far many of the current concepts can be generalized to other cultures remains to be tested.

Sociospatial Behaviour

The anthropologist, Edward Hall, called the study of sociospatial behaviour "proxemics", and he defined this as "the study of interrelated observations and theories of Man's use of space" (Hall, 1966). Hall developed a simple taxonomy of spaces based not on their size or location but on their social functions.

At the macroscopic level space is categorized as "fixed-feature", which is expressed in the design of buildings and the layout of villages, towns and cities, and it reflects the ways in which the activities of individuals and groups are organised. If you have travelled abroad you will be aware of how the character of each country is reflected in its buildings, and the layout of its towns and cities. Fixed-feature space, once constructed, is expensive to alter or raze to the ground (in the absence of war or natural catastrophe), and therefore it is a relatively enduring aspect of space, e.g., consider how many of us still live in dwellings that are more than 50 years old, or how many British roads can be traced back to Roman times.

On a smaller scale space can be thought of as "semi-fixed feature". Research on the influences of alternative layouts in psychiatric hospitals showed the behavioural effects of two alternative arrangements:

sociofugal space – layouts which tend to inhibit interaction by keeping people apart, e.g., the fixed row of seats of an airport gate waiting area.

sociopetal space – layouts which tend to facilitate interaction by bringing people together, e.g., the flexible seating layouts in a pub.

Examples of these layouts are shown in Figure 15.1.

Sociofugal space   Sociopetal space

FIGURE 15.1   *Hall's classification of semi-fixed feature space (Hall, 1966)*

Numerous studies have shown that changes in the layout of spaces can influence social interaction patterns. Office filing cabinets placed in lines between rows of desks modify communication patterns among workers by reducing worker interactions between each row but increasing worker interactions within each row. Psychiatric patients behave in a less institutional, more sociable manner when their ward layout is altered from being sociofugal to sociopetal. When a traditional lecture room layout is rearranged from sociofugal to sociopetal (see Figure 15.2), its popularity among

Traditional layout   'Softened' layout

FIGURE 15.2   'Softening' the classroom (Sommer and Olsen, 1980)

students increases, students ask more questions and contribute more views in discussions, and students make more frequent informal use the room between lectures.

Some spaces appear to be "pseudo-fixed feature" spaces, i.e. peoples' behaviour suggests that the space is fixed but isn't. One of my favorite demonstrations of this involves rearranging tables and chairs in a teaching room so that they appear to have been left in a sociopetal arrangement by a previous student group. Invariably when new students enter the room they will rearrange the tables and chairs to conform to the stereotypical sociofugal layout for a class! Similar fixations on how layouts should be arranged also can be found in many other settings. In open plan offices, the potential flexibility of the space often is constrained by our images of how traditional enclosed offices should be configured. In a two storey house, we expect a sink and a cooker in a kitchen, which is at ground floor level, and we expect to sleep in a bedroom, which is on the first floor. If we chose to sleep in the kitchen and cook in the bedroom our behaviour would be judged as strange.

At the microscopic level of the individual, Hall describes space as "informal", and this is further subdivided into four interpersonal distance zones each of which as a "close" and a "far" distance. These four zones are public distance, social distance, personal distance, and intimate distance (see 15.3).

Public speaking, such as a politician addressing a meeting, usually places one at the far phase of public distance. At this distance the finer facial features of the speaker cannot be discerned by the audience, and consequently the speaker relies heavily on gross body gestures, e.g. shaking a fist, pointing a finger, waving, and on voice loudness, to convey an appropriate emotional context for what is being said. A formal lecture typifies the close phase of public distance, and here personal exchanges of information usually are not expected until an appropriate time e.g. question time at the end. In a formal lecture gross body nonverbal cues are used to convey additional meaning to what is being said (notice how the front rows of lecture rooms are often the last seats to be filled because these place people closer to the speaker than normal public distance dictates).

The far phase of social distance is characterised by formal interaction between strangers, e.g. a formal interview across a desk, and the face-to-face distance typically

PUBLIC DISTANCE

Far (more than 8m) - public speaking

Close (3.5-8m) - lecture

SOCIAL DISTANCE

Far (2-3.5m) - formal interaction

Close (1.25-2m) - strangers interacting

PERSONAL DISTANCE

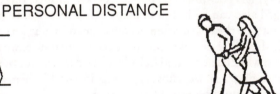

Far (.75-1.25m) - friends interacting

Close (.5-.75m) - holding hands

INTIMATE DISTANCE

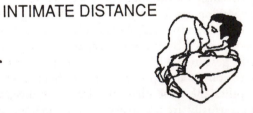

Far (.15-.5m) - intimate exchanges

Close (less than .15m) - embracing

FIGURE 15.3   Examples of close and far distances for the four zones of informal space.

exceeds 2 meters. The close phase describes interactions between strangers, e.g. asking street directions. In both these situations only formal information is expected to be exchanged.

Personal distance is based on the concept of personal space (Sommer, 1969), and the far phase is typified by informal interaction between friends. Now distances are sufficiently close that facial features can be clearly discriminated and used to augment verbal communication. At the close phase of personal distance some kind of body contact also is often established, e.g. a couple holding hands while walking. At intimate distances our patterns of communication change. At the far phase we may exchange intimate information, e.g. holding a confidential conversation spoken in a subdued voice. Touching becomes more frequent and prolonged, e.g. putting your arm around someone all evening while sitting in a pub, and either smell or the lack of it becomes very important, hence the popularity of perfumes, aftershaves, and deodorants. The close phase of intimate distance is typified by behaviours like embracing, lovemaking, and wrestling. Greater emphasis is placed on tactile sensations, stroking, kissing, hugging, caressing, and less emphasis on verbal or visual exchanges, indeed eyes are often closed a good deal of the time.

These categories of interpersonal distance do not describe an absolute set of distances, but they describe how our relative use of distance is an important component in the nature and success of our interpersonal interactions, and much research has shown that interpersonal distancing varies between cultures. Consequently, when designing any setting, in addition to its physical functions, we need to ask questions about its social functions in terms of the interpersonal behaviours to be facilitated or inhibited. The layout which is ultimately designed can either directly support these social functions, or indirectly support these by giving individuals the opportunity to rearrange the layout as required.

The importance of this kind of behavioural approach to design was highlighted by the American psychologist Robert Sommer. In his book entitled "Personal space: the behavioural basis for design" Sommer (1969) shows how concepts of individual distance and personal space can be applied to environmental design thus, "individual distance and personal space interact to affect the distribution of persons. The violation of individual distance is the violation of society's expectations; the invasion of personal space is an intrusion into a person's self boundaries. Individual distance may be outside the area of personal space – conversation between two chairs across the room exceeds the boundaries of personal space, or individual distance may be less than the boundaries of personal space – sitting next to someone on a piano bench is within the expected distance but also within the bounds of personal space and may cause discomfort to the player. If there is only one individual present, there is infinite individual distance, which is why it is useful to maintain a concept of personal space, which has also been described as a portable territory, since the individual carries it with him wherever he goes although it disappears under certain conditions, such as crowding." (p. 27).

Sommer describes how alternative layouts influence people's behaviour in hospitals, in offices, in prisons, in airports, and in schools and colleges, and he shows how the type of interaction may even affect the choice of seating positions at tables (see Figure 15.4), but he emphasizes that as well as personal space, design values such as variety, flexibility, and the ability to personalise space also must be emphasized. To support this view, Sommer (1974) distinguishes "hard" architecture, characterised by building designs which reflect an impermeable, impersonal, and impregnable mentality; and "soft" architecture, where emphasis is placed on the personalisation of places, on providing an individual with personal control over changes to this, and where the environment can become a legitimate extension of an individual's personality. He proposes that the solutions to many current social problems, such as vandalism, may lie not in adopting "harder" architectural solutions which make the environment even harsher and more secure than it presently is, but rather in changing and "softening" places by allowing more opportunity for personalisation, thereby encouraging the acquisition of more caring and responsible attitudes to the environment.

Territoriality is another sociospatial influence on behaviour. Altman (1975) sees territorial behaviour as "a self/other boundary regulation mechanism that involves personalization of a place or object and a communication that is owned by a person or group." The term territory describes the spatial expression of territorial behaviour. Unlike informal space which is always egocentric around a person and has invisible boundaries which change relative to the position of that person. A territory is always stationary, has visible boundaries, and is place centred, often around a building, e.g. a house. A territory implies that someone or some organisation has responsibility for jurisdiction over or ownership of that space. Territories can be ephemeral, such as a seat in a library which you might mark by personal belongings, such as your coat, bag, or books, or relatively permanent, such as a house in which someone has lived most of their life. Thus we display territorial behaviours in a wide variety of settings throughout our life. Altnan suggests that there are three types of territories:

Primary territories – private places clearly identifiable as exclusively owned and used by individuals or groups; they are controlled on a relatively permanent basis and they are central to the day-to-day lives of the occupants, e.g. a person's home, or workplace. Temporary access by others to primary territories is carefully regulated and often depends on their behaviour closely following the rules of that place, e.g. no smoking in my office, taking muddy boots off in my home.

Secondary territories – semi-public places where we can interact with friends, neighbors, or forge new acquaintances, e.g. local pubs, coffee bars, youth clubs, churches. Regular users may personalise such places even though there is no real ownership of these, and such personalisation signifies jurisdiction to other groups of users. When personalisation is absent conflicts between user groups can occur in these places and little control over access can be exercised.

Public territories – spaces which are usually easily accessible by others, e.g. a local park, a shopping precinct, and although there is usually some attempt at regulating behaviour via rules, such as "Keep off the grass" or "No ball games" or via some system of authority, e.g. park wardens, police officers, careful control is normally difficult to achieve.

Altman's typology of human territories has been tested in repertory grid studies of urban and suburban subjects, and children and adults, to see how subjects categorize the names or photographs of places. Urban and suburban subjects categorize places into the three of types territory, as do adult subjects, but these differences are less clear for the young children who appear to use a simple territorial model in which secondary and public territories are not distinguished so precisely.

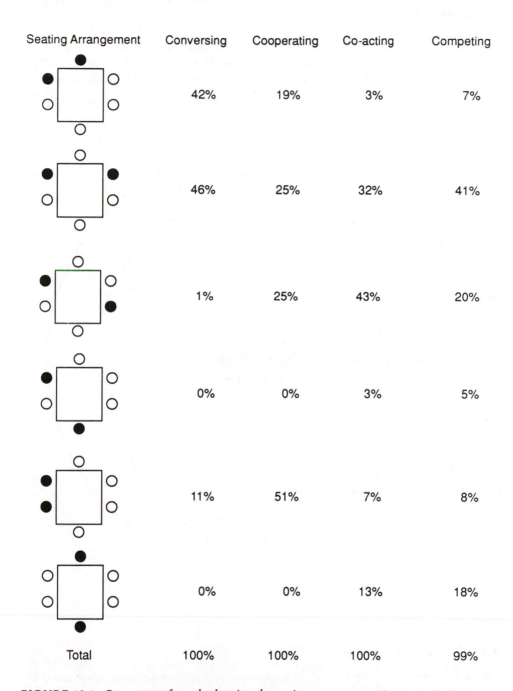

Seating Arrangement	Conversing	Cooperating	Co-acting	Competing
	42%	19%	3%	7%
	46%	25%	32%	41%
	1%	25%	43%	20%
	0%	0%	3%	5%
	11%	51%	7%	8%
	0%	0%	13%	18%
Total	100%	100%	100%	99%

FIGURE 15.4   Percentage of people choosing the seating arrangement (Sommer, 1969)

Environmental Psychology in the Workplace: the Design of Office Environments

Driven by the growth in the white-collar workforce and the widespread introduction of computers into offices, environmental psychologists have extensively researched office design issues, such as how the spatial organisation of the office affects worker behaviour, and what kind of ambient conditions (temperature, ventilation and air quality, light, sound) are most comfortable and healthy (see Figure 15.5).

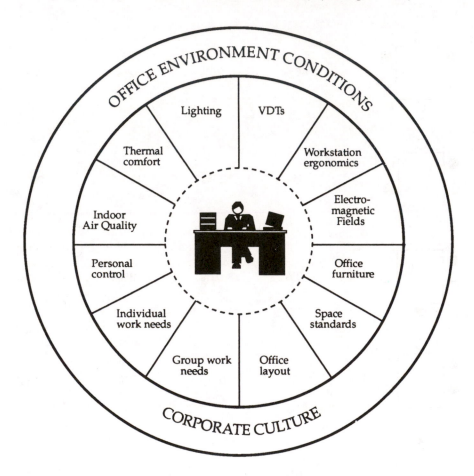

FIGURE 15.5   Factors to be considered in office design (Hedge, 1992)

Research on office layouts

Office buildings are costly to rent, buy, or construct, and maximizing space use is an economic necessity. With the increasing automation of routine office tasks and the need to integrate new office technology and office practices into existing spaces, researchers have studied how to optimise relationships between office workers, their work demands, and the organisation of their work environment.

In the UK, research into the psychological impact of offices began in the 1960s when the West German concept of office landscaping (Bürolandschaft) and open-planning began to radically transform office interiors. Office landscaping uses plants to bring more greenery into interior spaces, and office open-planning replaces internal walls and private offices, characteristic of conventional buildings, with moveable screens, and furniture clusters, supposedly to facilitate communication between all levels of workers. Open-plan layouts can be configured to optimise work flow and encourage inter-personal communication, thereby increasing the social cohesiveness of the workforce and improving their productivity. Large interior open spaces also enable uniform ambient conditions to be provided throughout the building. The use of flexible furniture (including systems furniture) increases the sensitivity of the layout to changing organisational needs so that as particular work groups expand and others contract, or as organisational structures are revised more drastically, the layout can be speedily and inexpensively changed, and around 20% of the costs of creating and maintaining office space can be saved. Not surprisingly, when these ideas were originally voiced they were enthusiastically received by designers and managers alike. Such was the pace of change in West Germany that by 1977 it was estimated that about 90% of white-collar staff worked in open-plan or landscaped offices. Yet by 1981, research conducted for the Department of Labour in West Germany condemned such designs as being inhumane and unhealthy environments in which to work (Hedge, 1986).

Numerous evaluation studies of open-plan offices have documented a range of problems experienced by workers (for a good overview see Wineman, 1986). Brookes and Kaplan (1972) showed that employees who moved from a conventional, cellular office to a landscape office found this no more functional or efficient than the conventional office, and in terms of visual and aural privacy, noise, other disturbances, and security, the landscape office was judged significantly worse. Although the landscape office was seen as more attractive and more sociable, no increases in worker efficiency were shown. Nemecek and Grandjean (1973) compared 15 offices and found that workers in open-plan complained of problems of disturbances, difficulties in concentrating on work, and loss of privacy, particularly for confidential conversations. However, managers found their surroundings less satisfactory than staff at lower levels in the organisation, who typically reported more positive attitudes to their workplace because of improved sociability. Hedge (1986) showed that in a large open-plan office managerial staff reported greatest job satisfaction but complained most of loss of privacy, disturbances and lower personal productivity, compared with clerical workers who complained of frequent boredom at work, but viewed working conditions more favorably because of increased opportunities for informal social interaction. Similar findings on the problems of open-plan offices have been reported in many other studies (see Sundstrom, 1986; Wineman, 1986).

Many of the problems which organisations and their employees have experienced with open-plan and landscape offices, have resulted from the inappropriate fit of this design to the needs of the organisation, work, and workers. In particular, open-planning has proved unpopular because it minimizes individual control over the work environment. Workers usually have minimal control of ventilation, heating, and lighting, of visual and aural privacy, and of the type and frequency of social interactions. Also, workers find it difficult to delimit their workspace and personalise this. Although open-plan offices may be economical to plan, modify, and maintain, unless good environmental psychology is applied in their design, the office layouts often

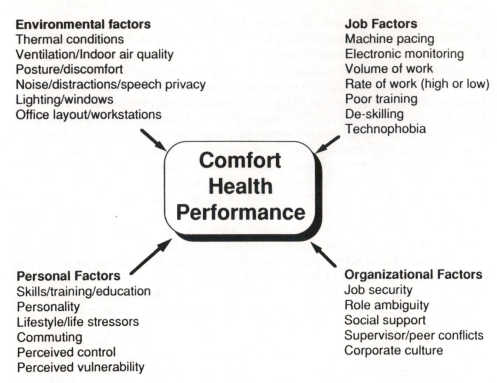

Environmental factors
Thermal conditions
Ventilation/Indoor air quality
Posture/discomfort
Noise/distractions/speech privacy
Lighting/windows
Office layout/workstations

Job Factors
Machine pacing
Electronic monitoring
Volume of work
Rate of work (high or low)
Poor training
De-skilling
Technophobia

Comfort Health Performance

Personal Factors
Skills/training/education
Personality
Lifestyle/life stressors
Commuting
Perceived control
Perceived vulnerability

Organizational Factors
Job security
Role ambiguity
Social support
Supervisor/peer conflicts
Corporate culture

FIGURE 15.6   *Environmental, occupational and personal factors affecting well-being and performance*

fail to satisfy the personal requirements of workers, and can even be a source of stress. Indeed, there is growing evidence that modern offices can be unhealthy workplaces.

Ambient conditions in buildings

Today's office buildings are technologically sophisticated and expensive structures which use heating, ventilation, and air-conditioning systems to maintain thermal comfort and good indoor air quality, and fluorescent lighting to illuminate the workplace. The belief in a "one shoe fits all" approach to designing ambient conditions is enshrined in standards for thermal comfort zones, ventilation, and lighting. But getting these ambient conditions "just right" for all employees is difficult if not impossible because the relationship between the physical conditions and a worker's sensation, comfort, performance, and well-being are complex (see Figure 15.6). Mediating variables, such as the influence of the social setting, of individual roles, and of personal control over conditions, modify the relationship between ambient conditions and behaviour.

(a)   Thermal conditions

Because we are warm blooded, our bodies constantly strive to balance the heat gained from or lost to the environment with that generated by metabolic processes. If we lose more heat than we can generate we feel cold. If we cannot lose the heat we generate, or we gain an excess of heat, we feel hot. Either way we experience discomfort, and usually behave to compensate for this. When too cold we may put on warmer clothes, thereby conserving body heat, or we may turn on a heater, thereby reducing the rate of heat loss by warming the environment. Conversely, when too hot we may remove clothing, to increasing body heat loss, or cool our environment in some way, such as sitting in the shade or turning on a fan or air-conditioning. We gain or lose heat from the environment via one of four processes – *radiation:* heat loss from a warmer to a cooler body, e.g. from a fire to our body, from our body to air; *convection* – heat loss from the movement of air or water past the body, e.g. wind blowing past the skin will cool this – the "wind chill" factor; *evaporation:* heat loss via the evaporation of body fluids, e.g. via breathing, sweating; *conduction:* heat loss by direct transfer from body contact with another body or surface, e.g. standing on a cold floor, sitting on a cold seat. Losses due to conduction are usually negligible and therefore most research has focussed on the effects of radiation, convection, and evaporation, which together account for most lost heat. Two other factors also affect thermal balance. *Activity* is usually expressed as the metabolic heat production per unit surface area of the body (Watts meter^{-2}) and this varies considerably, e.g. for office work this is around 75 Wm^{-2} while for digging the garden it may be 320 Wm^{-2}. The surface area of a young adult's body is between 1.3–2.2m^2, so the average young office worker is producing around the heat equivalent of a 100–150 watt light bulb, which is why the ventilation system in many buildings has to be able to cool as well as heat the air. *Clothing* acts as thermal insulation, and its effectiveness is measured in clo's (1 clo = 0.16 m^{2o} CW^{-1}). A light, sleeveless dress over cotton underwear has an insulation value of around 0.2 clo, whereas trousers, vest, long sleeved shirt, and a jacket together have an insulation value of around 1.0 clo. With some products, such as a duvet, insulation is rated in togs (1 tog = 0.645 clo).

A number of factors influence thermal sensation and thermal comfort, consequently the relationship between physical measures of thermal conditions and reported thermal comfort can be very variable. Some studies have shown that a wide range of air temperatures (20°C–30°C) and relative humidities (15%–85%) can be judged comfortable in certain circumstances (McIntyre, 1980). Several studies have found no significant sex differences in thermal comfort under laboratory conditions, where clothing, activity, and climate are standardised (Fanger, 1972), but field surveys typically have reported significant differences between men and women in their ratings of thermal comfort (Hedge, 1986; Schiller *et al.*, 1988). Whether these results are due to clothing differences between men and women, differences in activity levels at work because in offices women more often perform sedentary clerical or secretarial jobs, or to physiological differences between the sexes needs further investigation.

Building standards specify that air temperatures between 20°C–26°C and relative humidities between 50–70% define the thermal comfort zone for sedentary workers wearing normal clothes (0.5–0.1 clo), but localized thermal conditions in buildings often exceed these limits, and a large number (49%) of office employees in air-conditioned offices say that thermal conditions at work are uncomfortable (Schiller *et al.*, 1988). Consequently, a number of new designs for ventilation systems recently have been developed, and these incorporate controls for individual workers to regulate thermal conditions so that they can more appropriately adjust these to suit their requirements. How well these systems work in practice to improve thermal comfort for office workers remains to be tested.

(b)   Indoor air quality

Since the 1970s all buildings are constructed to be more energy efficient and many older buildings have been renovated to improve their energy efficiency, e.g. installing roof and wall insulation. However, a number of comparative studies of different types of office buildings have shown that in modern, sealed, air-conditioned offices, problems of the *sick building syndrome*, which include headaches, sore and irritated eyes, sore throats, and cold-like symptoms, are much more prevalent than in conventional, naturally ventilated offices. To date, similar findings have been reported for buildings in the U.K., Canada, U.S.A., Finland, Germany, Sweden, Denmark, and Holland (Hedge, 1989). Poor indoor air quality is known to cause *building-related illnesses*, like the 1989 outbreak of Legionnaire's disease at the BBC which killed 9 people, as well as the *sick building syndrome* where frequent problems of headaches, eye, nose and throat irritation, lethargy and fatigue, and sometimes dizziness and nausea are reported (Hedge, 1989). Some researchers have suggested that many of these symptoms might be alleviated by using negative air ionisers, which supposedly improve health and increase alertness and performance. Negative air ions are charged complexes of water molecules which may by biologically active, however, recent studies have found no evidence to support these claims (Finnegan *et al.*, 1987; Hedge and Collis, 1987).

Indoor air quality is influenced by a number of factors: the outdoor air quality, contamination from the ventilation system, contamination from building materials, technology, workers, and their activities (Hedge, 1987). As air-conditioned buildings are made more airtight and more new synthetic materials are used which can "offgas" irritating volatile organic chemicals, e.g. formaldehyde from plywood, chipboard, caulking, adhesives, etc. so the possibility of indoor air pollution is increased. To conserve energy while maintaining comfortable thermal conditions in winter, ventilation systems usually circulate a mix of around 15–25% outdoor air with 75–85% recirculated indoor air, and this can result in an accumulation of air pollutants released within the building.

Ventilation is consistently highly ranked as being important to comfort by both office workers and executives. The current ventilation standard recently was doubled to 10 L/sec/person to increase the amount of air for dilution ventilation. Two other strategies which work in conjunction with dilution ventilation are being used: *source control* and *breathing-zone filtration*. Source control describes ways of controlling, removing or encapsulating pollution sources, such as restricting smoking in buildings or removing asbestos from buildings. Breathing-zone filtration re-circulates air in each person's breathing zone (the air layer 0.75–2 metres above the floor) through a coarse filter, to remove larger particulates, a high efficiency particulate arrester (H.E.P.A.) filter, to remove 99.97% of fine particulates $> 0.5\ \mu$ m, and an activated-carbon filter, to remove volatile organic contaminants. This provides localized air filtration and a continuous supply of clean air at each worker's desk (see Figure 15.7). This system works independently of the office ventilation system and it can be easily installed in either existing or new construction offices. The additional localized filtration is equivalent to an increase in the ventilation rate of up to 13 air changes per hour. Research shows that breathing-zone filtration significantly reduces levels of volatile organics, fibers and particulates in indoor air, all of which have been associated with the sick building syndrome.

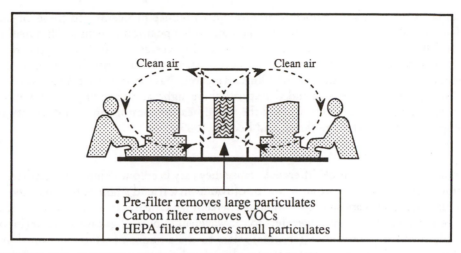

Clean air   Clean air

• Pre-filter removes large particulates
• Carbon filter removes VOCs
• HEPA filter removes small particulates

FIGURE 15.7   Schematic of a breathing-zone filtration system

(c)   Lighting

Vision is our dominant sense and studies of how variations in light influence behaviour have been conducted throughout this century. Most lighting in buildings is a combination of daylight and artificial light. Workers generally express strong preferences for daylight, and studies in offices show that even those distant from windows greatly overestimate the proportion of daylight falling on their desks (Boyce, 1981). Windows also are desirable for the external view, and high levels of satisfaction will be expressed with a window area of 25–30% of the wall area. Unfortunately, daylight is an unpredictable light source and on short winter days it is often unavailable in work time, consequently modern buildings also must have artificial lighting. But how much lighting should be provided for office workers? Studies have investigated the effects of changes in *illuminance* (the amount of light falling on a surface), and of *luminance* (the brightness of a light source or a surface) on visual task performance. In general, increasing the level of illumination for a task requiring a given level of visual acuity (the ability to discriminate between closely spaced lines) improves speed and accuracy of performance when initial illumination is low, however with additional increments of illuminance, these improvements in performance become progressively smaller and above a certain level of illumination subsequent performance changes are negligible (Boyce, 1981). The reflectances of room surfaces affect perceived luminance because pale surfaces reflect more light than dark surfaces and textured surfaces scatter more light than smooth surfaces. These considerations are important when painting and decorating spaces. With high levels of illumination or bright point light sources, e.g. a bare light bulb, glare problems with high reflectance surfaces, such as glossy magazines or computer screens, can interfere with visual performance and be a source of visual discomfort. Two common types of glare are found in buildings: *disability glare* which is direct glare from a bright light source, e.g. direct sunlight through a window, and *discomfort glare* which is indirect glare from uncomfortably bright reflections, e.g. specular reflections of ceiling light fixtures in a computer screen. Screen reflections can be a source of distraction and discomfort, and they can detrimentally affect complaints of eyestrain, which are now the most common health problems reported among office workers. New lighting standards have been developed in an attempt to reduce problems and these include advice on light fixtures and on office layouts which position screens so that neither ceiling lights nor windows create glare (I.E.S., 1989). However, just changing the office layout to resolve problems often is impractical because of the large window areas and general configuration of the building. Research has shown that using *lensed-indirect lighting*, where suspended fixtures shine light at the ceiling, creates more uniform illumination which benefits the visual health, comfort and productivity of computer workers (Hedge, Sims, and Becker, 1989).

(d)   Colour

Similar settings often look different because they vary in colour. Think of the different colours of the rooms in your house, or of rooms in a friend's house, or the different colours our houses are painted. Colour is a percept which arises from the integration of three separate dimensions: *hue* refers to the wavelength of the light for a colour (in the visible spectrum); *saturation* (chroma) refers to the amount of white contained in a colour, e.g. red is more saturated than pink; *value* (brightness or reflectance) refers to the degree of lightness or darkness of the colour relative to a white-to-black scale of brightness. Some colours have no spectral equivalents, e.g. there are no wavelengths in the visible spectrum for browns, and colour judgments can vary between individuals. Of particular interest to architects and designers is that certain colours are believed to evoke affective connotations which influence our experience of interior spaces: blues and greens are "cool" colours (blue associated with water, green associated with vegetation), and yellows, oranges and reds are "warm" colours (yellow associated with sunlight, orange and red with fire). Studies of colour preferences consistently have shown that blues and greens tend to be preferred to yellows, oranges, and reds, and that saturated colours tend to be preferred to unsaturated colours. Preferred temperature was slightly elevated (+0.4°C) for subjects in an environmental chamber illuminated with extreme blue rather than red light, although another environmental chamber study found no differences in thermal comfort for subjects who wore either red-tinted, blue-tinted, or clear goggles. Other research has shown that subjects rate colour slides of rooms decorated with darker colours as "richer" and "more expensive" but "less spacious" than those of the same room decorated in lighter colours. Unfortunately, in these studies either colour manipulations have been very unnatural with all interior surfaces appearing to be red or blue, or environments have been obviously artificial, and whether these findings apply for real rooms remains to be established.

(e)   Acoustic conditions

With the exception of some factories or urban noise sources such as airports, roads or railway lines, loud noise is seldom a major problem in buildings. In many buildings acoustic problems arise because it is too quiet so that nearby conversations, telephones ringing, typewriters or printers working become distracting noises. Acoustic problems can be tackled in three ways. First, noise sources can be isolated or insulated, e.g. putting an acoustic hood over a printer, moving noisy machinery into an unoccupied room. Second, sound absorbing surfaces can be used to reduce reverberations or reflections, e.g. putting sound absorbing tiles on the ceiling, thick pile carpet on the floor, and partitioning open spaces with sound absorbing panels. Third, distracting noises can be masked to reduce their intelligibility by increasing the background level of meaningless sound either by *sound masking* (adding random "pink" or "white" noise to the setting) or by *music conditioning* (playing music or Muzak in the setting). Numerous studies have been conducted to test whether in addition to masking distracting noises, background music might also increase people's satisfaction and performance at work, but most have not shown any large effects in output, although decreases in output with music never occur. Research has shown that workers need quiet conditions to perform strenuous mental tasks which demand a high degree of concentration, but when performing less demanding work, more tolerance is shown for music, especially light music rather than classical, pop, radio, or sterile (synthesized) music. The evidence that music adds to rather than detracts from performance at work is poor, and Sundstrom (1986) concludes that people in offices and factories may only prefer music to the extent that their capacities are not absorbed by their work.

(f) Electric and magnetic fields
Electric and magnetic fields (EMF) from power lines and from appliances, such as electric blankets, microwaves, and TVs, may increase the risk of nervous system cancers and leukemia (Nair, Morgan and Florig, 1989). Unlike microwaves (non-ionizing radiation which causes tissue heating) and X-rays (ionising radiation which breaks chemical bonds), EMF may affect the electric field at cell membranes, which in turn may influence biochemical processes involved in cancer growth. There is conflicting evidence on the health effects of EMF, both from household appliances and from computers, but there is a growing public concern about this issue. If a computer is placed on a non-conducting surface, such as a wooden desk, then keeping the screen and systems unit at least at arms length away should lower the field strength to a level which may not pose a risk. More carefully controlled studies are needed to test whether EMF poses a serious health risk.

ENVIRONMENTAL PSYCHOLOGY AND THE DESIGN OF INSTITUTIONAL ENVIRONMENTS

The impact of the design of institutional environments on the behaviour of psychiatric patients was instrumental in the establishment of environmental psychology. To date, research studies have focussed on total institutional settings, e.g. hospitals, old people's homes, and prisons, although some research on other settings, e.g. schools, university residences, has been reported.

Therapeutic settings

Research on therapeutic settings mainly has been conducted in psychiatric hospitals and old people's homes, although some studies have looked at the design of general hospitals (see Canter and Canter, 1979). This is because residents in psychiatric and geriatric settings are longer term residents, compared with the average short stay hospital patient, and their treatment often involves behavioural programming which is sensitive to the effects of environmental design. These effects can work for or against the success of therapeutic intervention and the well-being of residents. In the 1950s psychologists demonstrated that the traditional design of psychiatric hospitals encouraged institutionalized behaviours among residents, and institutionalized patients characteristically were introverted, submissive, withdrawn, passive, and attempted only minimal social interaction with others.

Since that time, therapists understand that the layout of the institution and its organisational climate both influence patient behaviour. Traditional long corridor dormitory/ward style facilities dramatically reduce patient's opportunities for privacy, and sociofugal furniture arrangements decrease social intimacy. Conversely, the provision of private or semiprivate bedrooms with individual doors plus small rooms or alcoves for conversations and sociopetal furniture arrangements facilitate social intimacy and feelings of personal privacy. Indeed, the frequency of social interactions can be doubled simply by reorganising a dayroom in a psychiatric ward from a sociofugal to a sociopetal layout. Also, the lack of privacy often found in traditional psychiatric settings detrimentally affects the rapport between counsellor and client, and the loss of privacy experienced by patients can be felt by nursing staff if they lack important interaction settings, such as their own social room, individual offices, and separate washrooms.

In addition to improving privacy and social interactions, changes in layout can also be used to foster residents' personal, self care skills along with any hobbies or interests. Residents' independence can be improved by designing small group units with private or semi-private bedrooms around common facilities, such as a dining room, lounge or kitchen, within a larger facility such as a hospital wing, or as an independent nursing facility, e.g. nursing home.

Prisons

In many respects, prisons and psychiatric settings are alike: they both function to contain those whose behaviour is not normally considered acceptable, the environment is usually designed to benefit the staff and the organisation not the inmates, and they both purport to "rehabilitate" residents (Spurgeon and Thomson, 1979). However, unlike those in other institutions, people in prison must serve mandatory sentences and society perceives the goal of a prison as one of punishment rather than care or treatment as is the case for a psychiatric hospital.

Although research is difficult to conduct in a prison setting, several investigators have examined how variations in design affect prisoner well-being. Studies have compared measures of stress (blood pressure, pulse rate) for prisoners in dormitory style and cell accommodation. Compared with single or two-person cells, dormitories can increase the lack of privacy, the difficulty in marking out a "territorial" area, and crowding (the number of prisoners in the setting). More illness was reported by prisoners in dormitories compared with those in single or two-person cells, and this difference may be due to greater stress induced by dormitory living. Unfortunately, prisoners are not randomly allocated to different settings and whether prisoners perceive dormitories as more crowded remains to be tested. One study measured perceived crowding and blood pressure differences between prisoners in two, three and six-man cells. Those in two-man cells rated their environment as less crowded than those in three or six-man cells and they also had the lowest blood pressures. However, prisoner allocation was not random. While these studies may suggest that the layout and spatial density of prison accommodation affect the stress experienced by prisoners, none have considered institutional factors which might systematically have biased allocation to accommodation, and other evidence suggests that when these are controlled then clear cut links between design, perceived crowding, and psychological stress do not emerge.

Each year reported crimes increase and new prisons and correctional facilities are under construction. In describing traditional prison design, Sommer (1974) maintains that "no one can argue that prisons improve a man or a woman any more than a zoo cage reforms captive animals." (p. 52). Instead, he argues that prison environments should be "softened", e.g. by changing colour schemes, furniture arrangements, and cell design, to create more humane settings which will reinforce appropriate behaviours. However, Sommer says that this does not mean that prisons should be built which are "just like home", in fact he says that "a prison can never be like home... There is no logic in a correctional facility trying to approximate the inmate's previous physical environment any more than in trying to duplicate his previous social environment, both of which may have been pathogenic. But this does not mean that a correctional facility cannot provide the inmate with a humane environment rather than cold, sterile, institutional quarters. Warm colours, soft furnishings, and the amenities of a home situation are desirable without attempting to duplicate the inmate's previous home environment." (p. 48). British environmental psychologists are influencing the design of prisons (see Canter and Donald, 1987), but there is still considerable scope for expanding the involvement of environmental psychologists in the design of correctional facilities.

Schools

Over the history of education, the design of schools has changed dramatically. The introduction of the comprehensive education system led to many smaller schools merging into larger schools, thereby changing the environmental scale of the school setting. In many of these larger schools there was also an important organisational change. Whereas previously teachers (relatively small in numbers) moved around the school between lessons to teach most of the lessons in the pupils' own classrooms, now pupils (relatively large in numbers) move around the school to different lessons, and consequently, school buildings have suffered a marked increase in "wear-and-tear".

Another change has been the testing of open-plan schools, particularly at the primary level, in which traditional classrooms are replaced by flexible internal space (a parallel with open-plan offices). Just as with open-plan offices, the success of open-plan schools depends on how the space is used and how teachers adapt their teaching style, e.g. dividing classroom space into discrete functional areas for different activities which sometimes occur simultaneously, such as reading stories, art, study. The more informal atmosphere created by open classrooms and the greater range of functional spaces can offer each child a broader range of possible educational experiences. Although these ideals of open-plan schools sound attractive, studies of the practicality of working in such settings have shown many problems. Noise levels can be particularly disruptive to teaching, especially with very young pupils. The lack of walls and doors also creates a more visually distracting environment and children are more likely to accidentally wander into other's spaces or to hold conversations across functional areas. Whether the open-plan school benefits or detracts from children's learning has proved difficult to establish and evidence on this is conflicting.

Considering the importance of education relatively little attention currently is being paid to evaluating alternative designs of educational settings, although this may change as educationalists become more aware of work in environmental psychology.

ENVIRONMENTAL PSYCHOLOGY AND THE DESIGN OF RESIDENTIAL ENVIRONMENTS

Housing Research

In any country where there is rapid urbanisation and population growth the provision of housing is a major concern. Avoiding the rapid growth of shanty towns, slum accommodation, and homelessness requires a comprehensive housing policy based on needs rather than wealth. To meet housing needs in the post-war years in the UK, and to some extent in the USA, housing policy supported massive slum clearance programmes and the construction of large public housing projects to be occupied by rental tenants. In Birmingham in 1960 there were 58,000 families on the waiting list for public housing and by 1978 this had been reduced to 8,000 families. At its peak, post-war public housing comprised about one-third of all housing in the UK.

For many architects and planners the post-war era offered an opportunity to implement new design philosophies, such as that of the Swiss architect Jean Edouard Jeanneret, better known as "Le Corbusier". In a series of books published in the 1920s and 1930s, Corbusier argued for the re-design of cities along simple geometrical, rational, and functional lines. In his vision of the city of the future, 95% of the land area was to be open park for recreational use, people were to be housed in towers up to 17 storeys high (these were to be arranged in geometric block patterns), office buildings were up to 60 storeys, pathways and roads were to follow straight lines, everything was to be ordered and rational. So vehemently did Corbusier criticise existing architecture and planning in Western cities and so persuasively did he argue his case that when the opportunity presented itself in the late 1940s, 1950s, and 1960s, with the exception of a few sociologists, no one seriously questioned the validity of his views. In keeping with Corbusier's vision of the city, the tower block became the symbol of post-war public housing in many countries. In the UK the first tower block was completed in 1954, yet by 1967 the British government had ended public housing tower block construction, and the last public residential tower block was completed in 1971 . Other than a few cases of structural problems with these buildings, the reasons for ending their construction stemmed from the many social and psychological problems experienced by residents.

The demise of high-rise public housing

For most residents the quality of the physical amenities provided in tower blocks was vastly superior to that which previously had existed in the slums from which they moved. Yet what Corbusier and others had neglected to consider were the disruptive social effects of this vertical design on the patterns of social interaction in the re-housed communities, and the diffculties of raising children in this type of accommodation.

By the late 1960s and early 1970s many of these social problems had been carefully documented by UK sociologists who were studying families in high-rise flats in

Birmingham, and by US planners studying the residents of housing projects such as Pruitt-Igoe in St. Louis. These studies found that high-rise living was impersonal and socially isolating, it fostered anonymity, it denied parents any close surveillance of their children's outdoor play, and buildings were easily vandalised, expensive to maintain, and in many cases dangerous, with cases of children and mothers either accidentally falling or jumping to their death.

In the USA the Fruitt-Igoe project, a forty three eleven storey block project hailed as a masterpiece of design, became a notorious example of vandalism and crime, and several high-rise blocks were abandoned. In 1976, some twenty years after its opening, these abandoned blocks were demolished. Similar examples of abandonment and demolition occurred in the 1970s and 1980s in the UK, although because of high costs, architects generally have favored looking for ways of modifying rather than destroying these buildings.

Studies of public housing projects have investigated how physical changes to the environment can be made which facilitate the development of territorial feelings and territorial behaviours in residents, and which convey these clearly and unambiguously to strangers, especially potential criminals. After studying a number of housing developments across the USA, Newman (1972) concluded that many acts of vandalism and other felonies in multi-family public housing were committed in the public spaces within the buildings and that these were crimes of opportunity. Therefore he argued, the environment can be modified to decrease such opportunities. Based on his comparative research he advocated four basic design guides for the creation of *defensible space*:

Perceived zones of territorial influence – the sub-division of the residential environment into zones toward which residents can develop proprietary attitudes, and the unambiguous definition of paths and grounds as semi-public or semi-private areas.

Surveillance opportunities – the improvement of residents' capacity to casually and continually survey the non-private areas of their indoor and outdoor living environment.

Reduce perceived stigma – changing the external appearance of public housing so that it blends with the surrounding private accommodation rather than standing out as unique or isolated from this.

Geographical proximity with "safe-zones" – the construction of new projects so that these are adjacent or close to low crime areas.

In addition he also recommended that tenant populations should be homogenous, e.g. all older people, to make it easier for them to identify and challenge strangers, and that where possible families with young children should not be housed in this accommodation. Not surprisingly, these apparently simple solutions to complex social problems has brought a wealth of criticisms of Newman's work and ideas, and critics have accused him of making errors in calculations, of deliberate bias in project selection, and of architectural determinism, i.e. the belief that the form of the built environment directly causes certain behaviours. If nothing else, Newman's work has served as a provocative stimulus to subsequent studies!

(a) Defensible space

Throughout the last decade many studies have explored various aspects of defensible space, including subsequent work by Newman himself, and what these studies have shown is that social factors rather than purely physical factors can mediate crime in public housing. Newman and Franck (1980) conducted an extensive survey of the relationship between social, physical, and project managerial characteristics with crime rates, fear of crime, and community stability of residents in 63 federally assisted housing developments. They found that the four factors which emerged as having the largest and most consistent effects were those of building size; accessibility of buildings and apartments to intruders; percentage of one-parent families, families on welfare, and mean household income; and the teenager/adult ratio in the resident population. Newman and Franck also showed that community instability appears to be primarily related to building size and household income, such that when income is low and the building large then instability is greatest. Fear of crime increased when the teenager/adult ratio was high and household income low, but burglary rates were primarily related to the ease of accessibility. They also found that the degree of resident control over space outside the apartment was an intervening variable mediating the relationship between building size and fear of crime and crime rates. Thus, while Newman and Franck conclude that this supports the basic tenets of defensible space, social and economic factors like the teenager/adult ratio and income level also are important. In the U.K. this result was confirmed by Wilson (1980) in a study of 285 blocks of dwellings on 38 inner London housing estates. Wilson examined the relationship between physical and defensible space dimensions, social parameters, and the incidence of vandalism. Her results failed to show any overall direct relationship between physical and defensible space dimensions and vandalism rates, but rather child density was the single most potent predictor of vandalism, and most of the vandalism was at ground level in areas where children played. There was, however, some evidence that a relationship between defensible space and vandalism might exist at low child densities, but at high child densities increased defensible space had little effect. Research has shown that burglaries are less likely if private housing incorporates defensible space principles (Brown and Altman, 1981).

(b) Defended space

Merry (1981) describes an extensive survey of residents' perceptions and their use of defensible space and the relationship of this to actual and perceived crime rates and also to criminals' perceptions of the space. She studied a project which housed a racially heterogenous population of 1200 people in 500 apartments and 100 housing units which appeared to have good defensible space, yet the crime rate in the project was high and over 50% of reported robberies occurred in apparently "defensible" areas. She concluded that several factors, such as fear of retaliation, lack of effective police intervention, and fear of crime mediate the development of defensive behaviours in defensible space. Consequently residents develop a norm of nonintervention. Newman had originally argued that any housing project can only tolerate a certain proportion of families on welfare (social security) before there is a breakdown of social order. However, Merry's findings challenge this assumption. It seems that any housing project can only tolerate a certain proportion of passive, apathetic and frightened residents, and once this proportion has been exceeded even active and assertive individuals will cease to intervene because they feel that they are acting alone.

Ironically, Merry also showed that those areas perceived as most safe, such as the space in front of the apartment or house, turn out to be the places where most of the robberies actually take place! From interviews with some of the criminals she found that although they were aware of the architectural features which constitute good defensible space, they also considered other environmental design features, such as the provision of escape routes, and social factors, such as the likelihood of being challenged, being recognised, or of the police being called, to be more important. These criminals clearly distinguished between defensible space, the design features, and defended space where the necessary social support processes operate. Merely providing good defensible space design can create a necessary but not sufficient condition for crime prevention unless social processes also operate to adequately support and defend this space.

(c) Offensible space
Application of defensible space principles in public housing projects has been limited because of a lack of consensus about potential benefits and budget constraints on housing authorities. Ironically, a recent survey of 21 well known crime sites in South Florida found that US drug dealers were applying defensible space principles of surveillance, territoriality, and access control to create *offensible space*, i.e. a safe space which resists intrusion by law enforcement officers and other outsiders (Atlas, 1990).

FUTURE DIRECTIONS FOR ENVIRONMENTAL PSYCHOLOGY

This chapter is a brief and limited review of environmental psychology. Environmental psychologists study many topics not covered here, such as how people acquire cognitive maps of the environment, what factors influence perception of the environment and of hazards, and how urban settings influence behaviour. By studying people's behaviour in physical settings environmental psychology can help to improve environmental design. As skilled practitioners, environmental psychologists can help architects and designers to better understand user requirements which helps improve the design programming process. Here, the environmental psychologist's role may be that of an "environmental counsellor", helping people to articulate and recognize their own requirements and communicating these to designers in unambiguous language. Ideally, such involvement should occur at the conceptual design stage, although at present it is more common for an environmental psychologist to be consulted after building construction, and then only after occupants have vigorously protested about environmental problems! Comprehensive evaluations of buildings and occupants can be conducted by environmental psychologists, and problems and their solutions often can be identified. However, such treatment clearly is less effective than prevention, and one benefit of the early involvement of an environmental psychologist to anticipate problems is that these can be designed out of the building.

As a field of applied psychology, one goal of environmental psychology is to improve the design of places to better support healthy behaviours. But environmental psychology is still a young field of applied psychology, and as it continues to mature and influence design so the success of buildings of the future will be judged by the extent to which they reflect a humane approach to architecture which gives people greater control and choice over their physical environment, and which creates healthful environmental conditions wherever people learn, work, play and live.

REFERENCES

Altman, I. (1975). *The environment and social behavior.* California: Brooks/Cole.

Atlas, R. (1990). "Offensible space" – law and order obstruction through environmental design. In *Proceedings of the Human Factors Society 34th Annual Meeting,* Vol. 1, 570–574.

Boyce, P.R. (1981). *Human factors in lighting.* London: Applied Science Publishers.

Brookes, M.H. & Kaplan, A. (1972). The office environment: Space planning and affective behavior, *Human Factors,* 14, 373–391.

Brown, B. & Altman, I. (1981). Territoriality, defensible space, and residential burglary: An environmental analysis. *Journal of Environmental Psychology,* 3, 203–220.

Canter, D. & Canter, S. (Eds.) (1979). *Designing for therapeutic environments: A review of research.* Chichester: Wiley.

Canter, D. & Donald, I. (1987). Environmental psychology in the United Kingdom, In D. Stokols & I. Altman (Eds.) *Handbook of environmental psychology.* Vol. 2, chap. 36, New York: Wiley, pp. 1281–1310.

Fanger, P.O. (1972). *Thermal comfort.* New York: McGraw-Hill.

Finnegan, M.J. Pickering, C.A., Gill, F.S., Ashton, I., & Froese, D. (1987). Effect of negative ion generators in a sick building. *British Medical Journal,* 294, 1195–1196.

Hall, E.T. (1966). *The hidden dimension.* New York: Doubleday.

Hedge, A. (1986). Open versus enclosed workspaces: The impact of design on employee reactions to their offices. In J. Wineman (Ed.) *Behavioral issues in office design.* New York: Van Nostrand Reinhold.

Hedge, A. (1987). Office health hazards: An annotated bibliography. *Ergonomics,* 30, 733–772.

Hedge, A. (1989). Environmental conditions and health in offices, *International Reviews of Ergonomics,* 3, 87–110.

Hedge, A. (1992). Ecological ergonomics: the study of human work environments, *Impact of Science on Society,* 165, 53–64.

Hedge, A. & Collis, M.D. (1987). Do negative ions affect human mood and performance? *Annals of Occupational Hygiene,* 31, 285–290.

Hedge, A. Sims, W.R. Jr. & Becker, F.D. (1989). Lighting the computerized office: A comparative field study of parabolic and lensed-indirect lighting systems, *Proceedings of the Human Factors Society 23rd Annual Meeting,* Vol. 1, 521–525.

I.E.S. (1989). *VDT Lighting.* I.E.S.RP-24-1989, New York: Illuminating Engineering Society.

McIntyre, D.A. (1980). *Indoor Climate.* London: Applied Science Publishers.

Merry, S.E. (1981). Defensible space undefended: Social factors in crime control through environmental design, *Urban Affairs Quarterly,* 16, 397–422.

Nair, I., Morgan, M.G. & Florig, H.K. (1989). *Biological effects of power frequency electric and magnetic fields-background paper,* U.S. Congress, Office of Technology Assessment, OTA-BP-E-53, Washington D.C.: U.S. Government Printing Office.

Nemecek, J. & Grandjean, E. (1973). Results of an ergonomic investigation of large space offices, *Human Factors,* 15, 111–124.

Newman, O. (1972). *Defensible space.* New York: MacMillan.

Newman, O. & Franck, K.A. (1980). *Factors influencing crime and instability in urban housing developments.* U.S. Department of Justice, National Institute of Justice.

Schiller, G. Arens, E., Benton, C., Bauman, F., Fountain, M. & Doherty, T. (1988). *A field study of thermal environments and comfort in office buildings.* Final Report, ASHRAE 462-RP, January 1988, CEDR —04-88. Berkeley, Ca.: Center for Environmental Design Research, University of California, Berkeley.

Sommer, R. (1969). *Personal space: the behavioral basis of design.* California: Brooks/Cole.

Sommer, R. (1974). *Tight spaces: Hard architecture and how to humanize it.* California: Brooks/Cole.

Sommer, R. & Olsen, H. (1980). The soft classroom, *Environment and Behaviour*, **12**, 3–16.

Spurgeon, P. & Thomson, M. (1979). Institutionalization: hospitals and prisons, In W.T. Singleton (Ed.) *The Study of Real Skills, Vol. 2, Compliance and excellence*, Blackburn: MTP Press, pp. 117–134.

Sundstrom, E. (1986). *Workplaces: The psychology of the physical environment in offices and factories.* New York: Cambridge.

Wilson, S. (1980). Vandalism and 'defensible space' on London housing estates. In R.V.G Clarke & P. Mayhew (Eds.) *Designing out crime.* Chap. 4, London: HMSO, pp. 39–62.

Wineman, J. (Ed.) (1986). *Behavioural issues in office design.* New York: Van Norstrand Reinhold.

16

HEALTH PSYCHOLOGY

J. WEINMAN

INTRODUCTION

Health psychology is one of the newest disciplinary areas of psychology, even though many of its core themes can be traced back to earlier times. It is concerned with the application of psychological methods to understanding human behaviour in the context of health and illness. The most widely used definition of the field has been provided by Matarazzo (1980), who described health psychology as the "aggregate of specific educational, scientific and professional contributions of the discipline of psychology to the promotion and maintenance of health, the prevention and treatment of illness, and the identification of aetiologic and diagnostic correlates of health, illness and related dysfunction". In the present overview the field of health psychology will be divided into six broad areas which fit well with the range of topics outlined by Matarazzo.

The disciplinary emergence of health psychology can be traced back to the 1970s and a task force which was set up by the American Psychological Association (APA) to assess the role of psychology in relation to health and health care. In the report of this task force it was concluded that psychologists should become more involved in research on aspects of health and illness and in developing applications to bring about improvements in the maintenance of health, the prevention of illness and the delivery of health care. Consequently the APA formed a separate division of health psychology and shortly after this the first specialist books and journals started to appear.

In the United States there have been considerable developments in undergraduate teaching and in postgraduate training in health psychology. The postgraduate programs have taken a number of contrasting approaches. Some have adopted a 'Clinical Health Psychology' approach in which the major emphasis is on acquiring skills in applying clinical interventions, typically for individuals or small groups for preventive or treatment purposes. Other programs have developed a more research–based, disciplinary approach and a third group of programs have concentrated on a preventive/public health orientation with an emphasis on the maintentace of good health and the prevention of health problems.

Similar developments are now taking place in a wide range of other countries, where health psychology is slowly becoming a part of the undergraduate curriculum, although not always as a required component. There are a small but growing number of postgraduate training programs, mainly with a research orientation (see, Jansen and Weinman, 1991 for an overview). Finally there have been the other usual markers of progress such as the formation of national and international societies and the emergence of journals and books to serve the fast growing field.

This chapter will begin by providing an outline of the main research strategies adopted in health psychology research. Following this there is an overview of the main content areas, identifying some of the key issues and important empirical findings. Since it is not possible to describe any of these content areas in any detail, one area has been selected for a more detailed coverage in order to demonstrate the range of issues and approaches. Finally there is an attempt to anticipate future developments in the field.

HEALTH PSYCHOLOGY RESEARCH APPROACHES

In broad terms, research studies in health psychology fall into three categories: descriptive, explanatory and intervention-based. These are not mutually exculsive categories since some research clearly involves two or even three of these but this provides a general classification.

The first category involves studies which aim to describe some aspect of health or illness-related behaviour. For example, many studies have examined what people do when they experience particular physical symptoms or when they are diagnosed as having a certain illness. This research would attempt to describe their thoughts, feelings or behaviours, particularly their coping behaviours (see below). Other descriptive research may be more concerned with the relation between two variables. For example many studies have attempted to describe the relation between specific psychological variables, such as mood or stress and either physiological changes (e.g. in heart-rate or immune system functioning) or changes in actual health status (e.g. in occurence of specific symptoms or in the progression of an ongoing disease). This type of descriptive study may also produce tentative causal conclusions and hence overlaps with the second category of research study.

The second, more powerful type of research study aims to not only describe health or illness-related behaviour, or a link between behaviour and health, but also aims to provide an explanation. For example many studies have attempted to find out why people do not follow medical treatment or why people cope in apparently irrational ways with threats to their health. Greater care needs to be taken with the design of these studies in order to ensure that the causal interpretations which are made are justifiable in terms of the data. Thus it may often be necessary to use carefully chosen control or comparison groups and to use more elaborate designs (e.g. prospective) in order to establish the nature of the process being investigated and to be confident that the causal explanations are not confounded by other factors. For example in examining the links between stress and health, it becomes important to know not only that particular stressors are associated with adverse health but also what factors are responsible. Is it because stress directly affects certain physiological processes which then give rise to illness or is it because stress increases the level of health risk behaviour (e.g. smoking or alcohol use), which in turn has detrimental health outcomes? In reality, both factors may be involved and ideally the chosen research design should allow for this and permit an evaluation of the relative contribution of each. Typically this level of research gives rise to or makes use of theories or models.

An important third category of study in health psychology involves the evaluation of an intervention. Many explanatory studies identify the need for interventions to facilitate health-related behaviour (e.g. to improve attendance for health screening) or to improve the delivery of health care (e.g. reduce anxiety before surgery; provide information about treatment etc). Interventions may be concerned with primary prevention in that they seek to prevent or reduce known health-risk behaviours or they may have a more secondary or tertiary preventative aim by facilitating recovery or reducing the risk of re-occurence.

THE MAIN AREAS OF HEALTH PSYCHOLOGY

For convenience, the diverse contents of health psychology can be divided into six broad areas. There are many overlaps between the areas and, within each, all three categories of research described about are found. Thus in each area, there are many basic findings, concepts and measures, as well as various interventions and, less frequently, theoretical models. These main areas are shown in Table 1 and are described more fully below.

TABLE 16.1
The Main Areas of Health Psychology

(i)	Behavioural Risk Factors in Disease
(ii)	Health Protective and Enhancing Behaviours
(iii)	Health/Illness Cognitions
(iv)	Communication and Decision-Making
(v)	Psychological Responses to Investigations and Treatments
(vi)	Coping with Illness/Disability

In each area: Basic findings, measures, concepts
Some Theories
Interventions

Behavioral Risk Factors

The behavioural risk factors refer to a wide range of behaviours which epidemiological and other studies have identified as carrying increased risks to health, either generally or in reference to particular diseases. Perhaps the best known example here is the evidence on the role of "Type A" behaviour in the aetiology of coronary heart disease.

The Type A behaviour pattern was orginally described by two cardiologists, interested in the role of psychological factors in heart disease. It was characterised by competitiveness, time urgency, hostility and related behavioural factors which were found to be correlated with a significantly increased risk of coronary heart disease. Although the earlier studies in the 1960s and 1970s were very encouraging, more recent work has complicated the picture. Some studies have notably failed to find any relation between Type A and heart disease and it is now thought that only certain components of the original Type A formulation are 'pathogenic'. Moreover experimenters have sought to identify the types of physiological changes (e.g. in heart-rate, blood pressure or stress hormone levels) together with the types of environmental stressor which elicit these changes.

Research on Type A behaviour pattern falls into the three categories of research described in the previous section. Thus an important strand of Type A research is concerned with describing and measuring the key components. A second area of work has been concerned with understanding and explaining the links between Type A and heart disease. It is important to note that, despite the uncertainty about its exact role in heart disease, there have been a number of successful interventions to modify aspects of Type A in order to prevent the reoccurence of heart disease.

There are many behaviours such as smoking and high alcohol use which have very clear detrimental effects on many aspects of health. Some behaviours may carry very specific risks for particular diseases and a current example of this is the category of so called "high risk" sexual behaviours (e.g. unprotected sexual intercourse) in the context of the spread of HIV and AIDS.

Probably the most general psychosocial pathogen is that of stress, a rather loose term which is used to describe situations in which individuals are faced with environmental or other demands which exceed their immediate ability to cope. Stressful situations are typically those which are novel, unpredictable and uncontrollable as well as those involving changes or loss. Very often these situations produce adverse psychological and physiological changes and sometimes they are associated with a disease outcome. However the problem for health psychologists is to understand the way in which stress is associated with the development of illness. The evidence to date indicates that there is not a single route involved here. Thus stress may result in adverse health outcomes by increasing levels of risk behaviour (e.g. smoking; alcohol consumption), by direct effects (e.g. increases in blood pressure, muscle tension or gastric motility), affecting the individual's resistance to disease as the result of immunosuppresion, or by exacerbating or triggering a disease process in an already vulnerable individual.

In attempting to make sense of the stress/illness relationship, considerable progress has been made in understanding the sorts of social and occupational situations which have stressful effects. For example, the deleterious effects on health of loneliness and poor social support have been consistently demonstrated.

Other research has focused on behavioural responses shown by individuals as they attempt to cope with stressful situations. Similarly there is increasing knowledge of the neuroendocrine and immunological changes which are related to acute or chronic stressful episodes. During stressful episodes, releasing factors from the brain cause the pituitary to release adrenocorticotropic hormone (ACTH) which gives rise to the release of corticosteroids from the cortex of the adrenal glands. In addition to producing a number of well-known changes associated with the mobilisation of both short and longer term physical resources (e.g. release of adrenaline or noradrenaline; release of glucose; activation of endorphins/encephalins etc.), it is now known that these steroids can have effects on the immune system. Moreover recent experiments show that the central nervous system can affect the immune system and that it is possible to increase or decrease levels of immune functioning by classical conditioning. Thus fairly acute stressors, such as exams, and more chronic stressors, such as caring for a dependent elderly relative, can lead to deleterious immunological changes and increased incidence of illness (see Kiecolt-Glaser and Glaser, 1987).

There are too many specific factors here to enable a comprehensive list to be presented and the ones mentioned above provide a selection of examples. Similarly there are many different types of intervention which have been developed for modifying risk behaviours and only a selection will be mentioned. Many of the interventions in this area have been developed as part of community-based programs designed to reduce risk behaviours as well as promote healthy behaviours (see Ingham and Bennett, 1990). Whereas these programs have attempted to reduce risk behaviour and hence disease incidence on a community basis, other interventions have used more individual or small-group based techniques with specific groups (e.g. Type A individuals) or in specific settings, such as the worksite. Many of these interventions make use of stress-management techniques and relaxation training as basic components of the change process. These can be applied to 'healthy' individuals in stressful situations to reduce the likelihood of deleterious consequences or to individuals recovering from illness such as ischaemic heart disease.

Health Protective and Health Enhancing Behaviours

This encompasses those behaviours which have been identified as beneficial to health. The widely quoted behavioural factors (7–8 hours sleep; eating 3 regular meals each day, including breakfast; moderate body weight; not smoking; limited alcohol intake; regular physical activity) identified by the Alameda County study (Breslow and Enstrom, 1980) provide some indicators of basic behaviours which can have a positive (or negative) influence on health. This large study examined the relation between the health practices listed above and subsequent levels of health. It was found that the adoption of all or most of these health practices was associated with significantly lower mortality in the following five and ten year follow-up periods. Many so called "behavioural immunogens" may arise from or reflect the absence of factors which may be injurious to health, such as unemployment, poor housing or social support (see below). However here the emphasis is on the positive associated aspects of such factors as good social support as well as the ability to exert control over life situations, the ability to relax and to express emotion.

There is now a growing body of evidence to indicate that regular exercise has a beneficial effect on physical and psychological health. For example the benefits of exercise have been shown to reduce the incidence of physical health problems in the elderly, and to facilitate recovery from heart attack. However, this picture is not universally rosy since some studies have failed to show clear benefits and there are significant problems in ensuring that exercise programs are adhered to. These considerations mean that any intervention needs to be carefully planned and delivered by appropriately skilled individuals. This is a general problem for interventions aimed at promoting healthy behaviour since it has been found to be extremely hard to give up risky behaviours and to adopt more healthy life-styles. Providing information is usually insufficient to promote change since it is necessary to alter cognitions (see next section) and to influence social networks as a basis for bringing about changes in health related behaviour.

Interventions in this area often involve attempts at health promotion, typically those aiming to change or influence the behaviour of whole communities. However there is a great deal of current interest in programs which are targeted at a particular group (e.g. schoolchildren) or make use of a particular context (e.g. the worksite).

Health/illness cognitions

This area is concerned with beliefs, perceptions and attributions which patients hold about their health and illness and which play a role in determining their behaviour. In health psychology, work in this area has been influenced by studies of attitudes and beliefs, social learning theory and attribution theory as well as by information-processing approaches (Marteau, 1989 – for an overview).

Within this area, the health belief model (HBM) is the oldest and most widely used approach. The HBM was orginally developed in the 1950s to explain the low levels of uptake of various preventive health services, such as innoculations or screening. According to the model people will only engage in certain health behaviours in response to specific cues (e.g. a letter from the doctor inviting the patient to attend for cholesterol screening) if they hold certain beliefs. The beliefs are concerned with their own vulnerability or susceptibility to the health problem in question (e.g. heart disease) and the seriousness of the disease. Their willingness to take action will also depend on their perception of the relative costs (e.g. time, incovenience etc.), the potential benefits (eg avoiding serious illness) and the effectiveness of the treatment or procedure involved.

Although HBM has not been entirely successful as an explanatory model, it has nevertheless identified different sorts of beliefs which sometimes help to predict different health-related behaviours, such as preventive practices and adherence. However it is bedevilled by the general problem within psychology of the relatively poor predictive power of beliefs in relation to behaviour. As a result, other models, such as the Theory of Reasoned Action have focused on the role of personal and normative (i.e. peer group) beliefs about different health behaviours as determinants of behavioural intentions, which in turn may give rise to specific behaviours. The Protection Motivation Theory also goes beyond the HBM by adding the concept of self-efficacy expectancy (i.e. beliefs in one's ability to carry out a particular behaviour such as quitting smoking) and uses this as a way of attempting to improve the explanatory power of health beliefs.

Although the HBM and other models attempt to explain health-related behaviours in terms of individual beliefs, one of the most consistently powerful predictors of future behaviour is past behaviour which means that it may be valuable to concentrate on those cognitive processes which are used by the individual to make sense of their past experiences. Thus there is now a great deal of interest in the way individuals search for causal explanations for health or illness experiences. Similarly, when individuals become ill, many useful insights into their illness behaviour (e.g. coping; adherence to treatment) can be gained by understanding more about the way in which they make sense of their illness and the internal representations which they generate (e.g. Leventhal, Meyer & Nerenz, 1980).

The interventions in this area are less clear cut. However an important aim of some mass media health campaigns can be to change someone's perceptions either of their vulnerability to a certain illness or of its severity in the hope of changing their behaviour. Similarly valuable health outcomes can be achieved by changing the causal attributions which some individuals may make. For example, it has been found that if elderly people can be encouraged to attribute causes of their health problems to specific factors, such as infections, rather than to global factors such as the ageing process, they adapt better to these. Finally it is important to mention that many psychological interventions in the health field (e.g. stress management packages; preparations for stressful medical procedures) may have an important cognitive component since they will seek to identify and change specific cognitions which individuals may hold and which are precursors of their emotional responses. (See section on cognitive/behavioural therapy in chapter by Llewelyn.)

Communication and decision making

This area focuses on individual behaviours in the health setting, particularly those involving the interaction between the health care professional (HCP) and the patient. Many studies have examined aspects of communication between HCPs, particularly doctors, and patients with a view to explaining the all too often disappointing outcomes (see Ley, 1988). Typically it has been found that patients complain that they are not given sufficient information or that their doctors do not seem interested or concerned. Moreover, it has been found that patients may find it difficult to understand or remember information which they have been given. Not surprisingly therefore there is quite widespread evidence of patient dissatisfaction with communication.

Much of the earlier work in this area failed to take account of important individual differences in the two parties involved in this interaction (i.e. patient and HCP). More recent work has shown that patients differ in their perceptions of the role of the doctor as well as in their beliefs, coping styles and informational needs (Miller, Brody & Summerton, 1988) and that these differences can determine not only the extent to which medical help is sought but also the process and outcome of medical encounters. Similarly doctors are not a homogeneous group since they show consistent and characteristic differences in their overall approach and in their consultation style. A number of problems have been described in the outcomes of medical encounters and, of these, the two most widely investigated have been the low levels of patient satisfaction and the low rates of adherence to advice or treatment. Causes of these problems are quite diverse but many relate to aspects of the communication process and the failure of the HCP to attend to and discuss the needs and concerns of the patient. This has inevitably led to the most obvious intervention in this area, namely that of communication skills training for HCPs, particularly during their early training. Some of these training interventions have aimed to improve general communication skills whereas others have been designed for work with particular types of patients or particular situations (e.g. giving "bad news").

In an attempt to understand the processes involved in medical decision-making, cognitive psychologists have provided models of medical problem-solving and decision-making. Increasingly these models together with evidence from studies of the nature of medical expertise are being used in the development of computer systems for the diagnosis and management of different diseases. Some implications of these developments are discussed at the end of this chapter.

Finally in this section, it should be mentioned there has been a large amount of work attempting to understand as well as improve patient's adherence with medical advice or treatment. Many communication factors can influence a patient's level of adherence and there are an increasing range of psychological interventions being devised to improve adherence. These are described in more detail later in this chapter.

Psychological responses to investigations, treatments, etc.

This area focuses on the effects on patients of different investigations, treatments and environments which they may encounter in the health care setting. Many studies have demonstrated the stressfulness associated with investigative or treatment procedures. As a result there have been attempts by psychologists to provide interventions to prepare patients for hospitalisation generally or for a specific unpleasant procedure within the hospital setting. Preparation for hospital admission has mostly been confined to work with children but the preparations for stressful procedures have been developed for both children and adults. These interventions work at a number of levels. Some essentially provide information as to what will happen to the patient, in terms of the nature of the procedure and its likely effects. Others attempt to reduce anxiety, either generally using relaxation training or by identifying and dealing with specific fears or concerns and facilitating appropriate coping behaviours. With children there has been the successful use of videotapes of other children undergoing the same investigations or treatment, allowing the child to model itself on the child in the video. The interventions have had a mixed success in helping patients cope with the procedures and in improving the outcome in terms of such factors as speed of recovery and pain experience (Weinman & Johnston, 1988).

One problem with the work on psychological intervention for stressful medical procedures is the fact that interventions are not always well specified and may involve a number of components (e.g. information; relaxation; cognitive – behavioural approaches). Similarly there are many different sorts of outcomes which can be investigated (e.g. pain; anxiety; speed of recovery, etc.) and it is probable that some interventions are better for achieving particular outcomes. Moreover, accumulating research is indicating that it may be necessary to match the amount and type of intervention to the patient's coping style and informational needs. However when the better controlled studies are scrutinised, it would appear that cognitive-behavioural approaches produce better outcomes than other types of interventions on both behavioural and self-report measures.

In addition to considering how patients respond to different medical environments, health psychologists have also been concerned with understanding how different health care professionals are affected by their work environment. There are widespread reports of job stress amongst HCPs and a number of factors appear to contribute to this. These include the stressfulness of the work, the lack of support and the working conditions and long hours worked by many HCPs. Thus it is important to understand more about the way in which different components of health care work and health care work settings can have adverse effects on staff. Increasingly psychologists are becoming involved in offering interventions for preventing and combating these deleterious effects by running staff support or stress management groups.

Coping with illness/disability

This area focuses on the psychological concerns and responses of patients with chronic, disabling or terminal conditions which are now the most widespread and demanding healthcare problems. A great deal of this work has been concerned with understanding the way patients cope with the different demands of their illnesses. In contrast to older work which tended to indicate that the demands were illness-specific, more recent studies show that coping depends very much on the individual's perception of the threats and demands as well as on the social circumstances in which the illness is experienced (Burish and Bradley, 1983).

There is a growing interest in the way patients perceive and interpret their illnesses. This was discussed in the earlier section on 'health cognitions' and is central to understanding the determinants of coping behaviour. *Coping* is a general term which describes the wide range of responses used by individuals to deal with the threats and demands of their health problem. Although the concept of coping seems straightforward, there is still considerable disagreement and uncertainty about its nature and measurement as well as about its effects on emotional and physical outcomes (Cohen, 1987). Most researchers now agree that coping is not a static process in the context of chronic illness since it can change over time as the perceptions, demands and social implications of the illness change. However the debate is primarily over the generality or specificity of coping behaviours and their relation to the patient's quality of life. Some researchers prefer to use very broad dimensions of behaviour (e.g. approach vs avoidance) to characterise individual differences in coping behaviour whereas others focus on much more specific behaviours in order to describe the range of responses shown by patients. It is also unclear whether coping determines psychological or physical well-being or whether this relationship is a more two-way process. A great deal of the coping research has been based on the assumption that coping determines various outcomes, such as emotional state but there are increasing indications that coping can also be a consequence of emotional state.

It is also increasingly recognised that the individual's social circumstances may be of particular importance not only in determining the way in which a patient copes but also in the degree of success which coping strategies can have in regulating well-being. The most widely used concept here is that of *social support* which refers not only to the access which one has to other individuals but also to their perceived value or adequacy in actually providing support to the patient. As with coping, there are conceptual and methodological issues associated with social support. Social support does not always produce a beneficial outcome for the patients (see Schwarzer and Leppin, 1989) and it is important to understand the relationship between different types and sources of support and different physical and psychological outcomes for the patient. Despite these emerging complexities, there is still agreement that social support can have significant direct and indirect effects on the well-being of individuals with chronic illnesses and disabilities. Thus those indviduals with little or no effective social support are likely to show a poorer response to illness or treatment.

The increasing understanding of the nature and role of such processes as coping and social support are particularly important for developing interventions in this area. Training for health professionals on these topics can promote the delivery of more effective health care by increasing the awareness of and responsiveness to the needs of patients. An important part of this can be achieved by improving communication and listening skills, which in turn will allow patients' needs to be identified. More specific psychological interventions have also been developed for helping patients cope better with certain aspects of their illness. Also there is now a range of psychological approaches for the management of chronic pain which is a very common component of chronic or disabling conditions.

With many chronic illnesses, behaviour change may be critical in preventing reoccurrence or exacerbation. For example, in patients recovering from heart disease, approaches such as stress management can be valuable to facilitate better coping with stressors. It may also be necessary to change such behaviours as diet, exercise and smoking which can play an important role in their illness The use of counselling (see Chapter by Pickard and Caroll) and support skills by health professionals are also important in helping patients adjust to and cope with the demands of an illness and any behaviour changes. Moreover there is an increasing emphasis on the value of self-management approaches for patients with chronic illnesses (Holroyd and Creer, 1986), and these make use of many different approaches, including health education and social learning theory. These interventions involve teaching specific self-management skills, developing cognitive changes which facilitate effective skill performance and adherence, as well as the mobilisation of social support to provide an optimal context for all this to occur.

THE EXAMPLE OF ADHERENCE

While the above overview provides a sense of the breadth of approaches and applications in health psychology, it obviously does not give an in-depth account of any area. Moreover by separating the field into component areas it may generate the erroneous impression that these areas are quite separate. In reality much work in health psychology cuts across these areas. The example of adherence to treatment or advice is selected to illustrate this and to present one topic in a little more depth.

Health psychologists have had considerable interest in measuring and understanding different aspects of adherence as well as in developing different sorts or interventions to facilitate adherence (Meichenbaum & Turk, 1987). Adherence refers to the extent to which an individual follows recommended treatment or advice. Older studies tended to use the term compliance but the term adherence is now preferred for a number of reasons. It refers to quite a broad range of behaviours including adherence to specific medications and following advice about health-related behaviour change such as dietary change, quitting smoking or increasing levels of exercise. Thus adherence can be seen as a potentially health-enhancing behaviour but more typically non-adherence or low adherence is construed as a potential health-risk behaviour.

There are very many studies which have assessed levels of adherence in different contexts and they reveal significant but very variable levels of non-adherence. There are also quite fundamental associated measurement problems since it is often difficult to know exactly the extent to which an individual has adhered to medication or advice and whether this represents a serious problem. A range of procedures have been used to monitor or measure adherence and it is clear that none are perfect. Moreover some, such as diary keeping can also serve to affect levels of adherence, thereby confusing measurement and outcome.

Despite these inherent difficulties, the results from these studies indicate high levels of non-adherence across a range of treatments and treatment settings. Very typically findings are that some 40–50% of patients do not adhere to treatment or advice in a way which is clinically significant. The level of adherence is quite markedly affected by the type of treatment and the clinical condition. In general, lowest rates of adherence are found in patients with chronic conditions and in those taking medication for preventive purposes. In contrast patients receiving such treatments as chemotherapy for cancer show very high levels of adherence, even though the treatments may be quite unpleasant, in terms of side effects.

Although factors associated with the nature of the illness and the demands of the treatment influence patient adherence, many studies have also identified the contribution of communication and patients beliefs. The quality of communication between doctor and patient has a strong influence on patient satisfaction which, in turn, plays a role in determining adherence levels. As was discussed earlier, quality of communication depends not only on the doctor's ability to listen and respond effectively to the patient's problems but also on the way information is presented.

One aspect of effective communication, with implications for adherence, concerns the ability to elicit the patients own beliefs about their state of health and about the treatment or advice which has been offered. Much early work on adherence pointed to the importance of the health beliefs, described earlier. Thus if patients perceive their condition is serious and believe in the efficacy of the treatment, they are more likely to adhere to it. For adherence to recommendations to avoid or reduce health risk behaviours such as smoking, or to adopt potentially health protective behaviours such as 'safe sex' practices, there is increasing evidence that 'normative beliefs' are particularly important. These are the beliefs held by the individual about the views or attitudes held by their social peers. These more socially based beliefs can affect response to treatment or health-related advice in a number of ways.

Since a range of psychological factors can influence adherence, it not surprising to find that psychologists have devised a variety of interventions to facilitate adherence. Some of these are based on communication training for health professionals in order to improve their basic communication skills as well as their ability to present information concerning treatment. More focused interventions encourage the doctor to share decision making and treatment planning with the patient in order to agree treatment goals, anticipate any barriers and encourage adherence.

Hopefully this overview has demonstrated that important topics, such as adherence, cut across all the major areas of health psychology. Adherence describes one aspect of the patient's response to treatment but the level of adherence can have positive or negative effects on health. Moreover an understanding of the reasons for non-adherence must depend on an analysis of communication processes occurring in the consultation as well as on the beliefs held by the patient. Also it can be seen that the three levels of health psychology research are also represented here since psychologists have not only developed research to measure, describe and explain non-adherence but they have also produced various interventions to facilitate adherence.

FUTURE DEVELOPMENTS IN HEALTH PSYCHOLOGY

Any attempt to make accurate forecasts of future developments, particularly in such a rapidly growing area as health psychology, will inevitably be selective and speculative. The shape of health psychology in the next decade will be influenced and determined by many factors including the needs of society and developments within medicine as well as by pressures within the discipline. Some of these influences and determinants are overviewed to provide a picture of the range of issues involved.

Social Needs

The World Health Organisation (WHO) have recommended the need to achieve "health for all by the year 2000". As a basic step in meeting the WHO challenge, health psychologists will need to continue producing good research identifying the health risks associated with different behaviours and social conditions. This data should then be used in attempts to lobby politicians and other policy makers since it is clear that political, economic and social changes will have to occur in attempting to eliminate conditions such as poverty, unemployment and loneliness, all potent sources of ill health. Since many high risk individual behaviours (e.g. smoking; poor diet; high alcohol consumption) are often associated with these adverse social conditions, it will be quite inappropriate for health psychologists to pursue individual models of behaviour change as the only way of achieving 'health for all'. It will be necessary to adopt community-based approaches and to develop a better understanding of the social meanings of different risk behaviours and of the norms and value systems which underpin and maintain them (Ingham and Bennett, 1990).

Another major societial need arises from the changing demographic structure of industrialised societies during this century and the very significant increase in the proportion of elderly people. Health psychologists will need to devote a clear research priority to the investigation of health cognitions, health behaviour and health needs in older people. It will also be necessary to understand more about the influence of social contexts, to develop greater insights into the problems experienced by the carers of elderly people and to develop effective interventions. Moreover, to obviate the various problems associated with cross-sectional studies, it will be vital to initiate longitudinal studies of behaviour and health. In this way it will be possible to become more confident that our prescriptions for such healthy life-style changes as regular exercise actually do result in positive health outcomes in old age, as is being currently predicted.

Another very different social trend has been the increased awareness of environmental or 'green' issues, all of which have radical implications for our future health. Here the major changes will clearly have to come from governments and industrial companies but we should not underestimate the power of effective lobbying. Health psychologists can contribute by producing research demonstrating effects of adverse environmental conditions and toxins on health and behaviour. Moreover, there is a very practical role to be played in increasing public awareness of the extent to which individual behaviour change can produce positive environmental outcomes.

Developments in Medicine

Here again a brief selection of trends and issues will serve to provide different examples of some future directions for the development of health psychology. Thus this section will focus on important health problems, emergent medical technologies and on better ways of evaluating patients, quality of life and responses to treatment.

It is very likely that the most salient health problem in terms of medical research and public interest will continue to be in the area of Human Immunodeficiency Virus (HIV) and the Acquired Immune Deficiency Syndrome (AIDS). Psychologists should be able to make a contribution to two distinct aspects of HIV/AIDS. The first is in the area of primary prevention, particularly since this is currently the major option for limiting the spread of the disease. Attempts to do this have involved a range of mass media campaigns which have achieved some change in the knowledge of sexually active young people but generally there has been little significant behaviour change directly resulting from such campaigns. Thus there is a major challenge for health psychologists to become involved in the planning of effective preventive campaigns. A second challenge is to understand the role of behavioural factors in the progression of HIV/AIDS. There have been some studies of the effects of life events on people with AIDS and there is growing evidence of the potential contribution of such factors as relaxation, dietary change and coping. Here good, longitudinal studies are needed to evaluate the extent to which psychological variables can affect both emotional and biological outcomes. These, in turn, can provide the basis for developing effective psychological interventions for improving coping and, hopefully, delaying the progression of the disease. It also may provide valuable insights for the growing field of psychoneuroimmunology, a new field which is concerned with understanding the nature of psychological influences on the immune system. The development of this field will also provide very important data for understanding how stress can play a role in causing or exacerbating different diseases, as was discussed earlier in this chapter.

An undoubted second major development in medicine, with implications for health psychology, is in the practical application of the so-called 'new genetics', which involves the use of genetic probes either to identify individuals who are 'at risk' of developing major diseases or for prenatal diagnosis. There are many considerations here and the task for health psychologists will be to investigate the various psychological issues associated with this type of screening and to understand more clearly how individuals make sense of and cope with the information which is revealed. This will be needed to facilitate the difficult decision-making tasks involved (e.g. whether to plan a family; to terminate a pregnancy, etc.) and to provide good counselling approaches which are appropriate for dealing with these complex questions.

Another major technical advance in medicine which offers scope for challenging psychological research is in the area of medical computing. Computers are being used increasingly for the storage of medical records, automating laboratory analyses and for interviewing patients and providing diagnostic information. It is the latter task which is of most interest and concern to psychologists and should draw upon the expertise of cognitive and health psychologists. Cognitive scientists are already engaged in the task of studying and defining medical expertise so that this expertise can be transformed into viable computer programs. Health psychologists will need to provide insights about the different functions of the medical consultation and to investigate the effects of human computer interaction on patients and staff. It will be necessary to know whether an interrogation by computer gives rise to qualitatively and quantitatively different data and to find out how the decisions made by computers are evaluated by patients as well as the extent to which they are implemented and acted upon.

The final area in medicine in which psychologists will need to make a key contribution is in the evaluation of 'quality of life'. Increasingly the development of new treatments calls into question their effects on the patient's quality of life. It is no longer sufficient to simply evaluate a treatment in terms of its effects on a specific biological process (e.g. tumour growth; cardiac functioning, etc) but it is also vital to know whether it gives rise to a significant improvement in the way in which someone lives. This growing realisation should open the door for some important psychological research to identify the important components of life quality, as well as the need to develop valid new measures for assessing this (see Fallowfield, 1990).

Developments within Health Psychology

For its disciplinary development, it will be important for health psychology to generate and apply coherent models of health and behaviour. One basic requirement is the need to construct core models of health cognitions as a basis for understanding health behaviours. For this it may well be necessary to borrow concepts and methodologies from cognitive psychology and social psychology.

There is also a real need for health psychologists to begin to reach some consensus as to the nature and measurement of the core concepts in the discipline. Concepts such as coping, social support and life stress are used and assessed very differently across studies which means that it is often difficult to compare or combine findings. Although it is necessary to try out and develop new ways of conceptualising and measuring important processes it is also worthwhile for time and effort to be spent carrying out good meta-analyses and critical reviews (e.g. Cohen, 1987; Schwarzer and Leppin, 1989). Hopefully this will result in a greater awareness of the strengths and weaknesses of different methodologies and measures which, in turn, will lead to a more consistent and coherent research base.

A final major area of development is in the area of training at three distinct levels. First it will be important to ensure that health psychology courses or their equivalent can be routinely introduced as part of undergraduate training in psychology. This is happening in the United States and to some extent elsewhere and undergraduates do seem very interested in the general area. Thus a major task for health psychologists is to make their discipline an accepted part of undergraduate training and to demonstrate its links with other areas of psychology.

To increase the likelihood of good future research and to create the possibility of a professional status for health psychology, coherent postgraduate training at the Masters and Doctoral level must be initiated. In doing this, many issues and questions will come into focus. For example, should such courses be primarily aimed at producing researchers or should they be geared more to developing practitioner skills? Similarly, should the focus of such courses be mainly on primary prevention at the community level or should equal weight be given to work involving people with health problems in treatment settings? Clearly good courses must incorporate all these themes and approaches in order to equip future health psychologists to meet a broad range of challenges. However the immediate priority is to establish a strong research base in the discipline and one upon which any future practical applications can be based with confidence. A number of authors have considered this issue and the interested reader is referred to their work (see Jansen and Weinman, 1991).

In planning future training initiatives, it is vital not to overlook the training of other health professionals in health psychology. Health psychology cannot exist in isolation from other branches of health care and health research. Also, many of the most ambitious research programs may involve collaboration with medical or nursing colleagues on the one hand and other biomedical researchers on the other. Effective teaching for these other groups will certainly not be achieved by offering a few one-off lectures in their training courses. It will be necessary to build on the experiences of these other groups and to bring about changes in their models of health and illness and hence in their perception of the role and value of health psychology.

CONCLUSION

Health psychology is a new and exciting branch of psychology (Gatchel, Baum & Krantz, 1989; Sarafino, 1990). Its emergence in the last ten years has been rapid and influential and it seems highly likely that this will continue. It has a broad focus and is concerned not only with patients but also with health care professions and with healthy individuals as they make decisions or take actions which relate to their present or future health status. An attraction of the field is that it provides many possibilities for harnessing a wide range of psychological theories and methods for describing, explaining and sometimes for changing different health-related behaviours.

At present there are many postgraduate opportunities in research and teaching, particularly in the recent expansion of degrees for the professions allied to medicine since these usually place considerable emphasis on psychological aspects of health and health care. At present it is primarily a disciplinary area with an emphasis on research. However, with the implementation of appropriate postgraduate training, health psychology may well have a separate professional identity and play an important role in the prevention of health problems and in delivering specific types of health care in community and hospital settings.

REFERENCES

Breslow, L. & Enstrom, J. (1980). Persistence of health habits and their relationship to mortality. *Preventive Medicine*, **9**, 469–483.

Burish, T.C. & Bradley, L.A. (Eds) (1983). *Coping with Chronic Disease: Research and Applications*. New York: Academic Press.

Cohen, F. (1987). Measurement of coping. In S.V. Kasl & C.L. Cooper (Eds), *Stress and Health: Issues in Research Methodology*. Chichester: John Wiley.

Fallowfield, L. (1990). *The Quality of Life: the missing measurement in health care*. London: Souvenir Press.

Gatchel, R.J., Baum, A. and Krantz, D.S. (1989). *Introduction to Health Psychology*, 2nd Edition, New York: Random House.

Holroyd, K.A. & Creer, T.L. (Eds) (1987). *Self-Management of Chronic Disease*. New York: Academic Press.

Ingham, R. & Bennett, P. (1990). Health Psychology in Community settings: models and methods. In P. Bennett, J. Weinman & P. Spurgeon (Eds), *Current Developments in Health Psychology*. London: Harwood Academic.

Jansen, M. & Weinman, J. (Eds) (1991). *The International Development of Health Psychology*. London: Harwood Academic.

Kiecolt-Glaser, J.K. & Glaser, R. (1987). Psychological moderators of immune function. *Annals of Behavioural Medicine*, **9** (2), 16–20.

Leventhal, H., Meyer, D. & Nerenz, D. (1980). The common-sense representation of illness danger. In S. Rachman (Ed), *Medical Psychology*, Vol. 2, New York: Pergamon Press.

Ley, P. (1988). *Communicating with patients: improving communication, satisfaction and compliance*. London: Croom Helm.

Marteau, T.M. (1989). Health beliefs and attributions. In A.K. Broome (Ed), *Health Psychology: processes and applications*. London: Chapman & Hall.

Matarazzo, J.D. (1980). Behavioural health and behavioural medicine: frontiers for a new health psychology. *American Psychologist*, **35**, 807–817.

Meichenbaum, D. & Turk, D.C. (1987). *Facilitating Treatment Adherence: A Practitioner's Guidebook*. New York: Plenum.

Miller, S.M., Brody, D.S. & Summerton, J. (1988). Styles of coping with threat: implications for health. *Journal of personality and social psychology,* **54**, 1, 142–148.

Sarafino, E.P. (1990). *Health Psychology.* New York: J. Wiley.

Schwarzer, R. & Leppin, A. (1989). Social support and health: a meta-analysis. *Psychology and Health,* **3**, 1, 1–16.

Weinman, J. & Johnston, M. (1988). Stressful medical procedures: an analysis of the effects of psychological interventions and of the stressfulness of the procedures. In S. Maes, C.D. Spielberger, P.B. Defares & I.G. Sarason (Eds), *Topics in Health Psychology.* Chichester: J. Wiley.

17

PSYCHOLOGY AND LAW

A.J. CHAPMAN, N.P. SHEEHY AND M.S. LIVINGSTON

PSYCHOLOGY AND LAW

Psychology and law share common interests in the way people behave and the factors governing that behaviour. But the perspectives of psychology and law are different: psychology endeavours to describe and explain human behaviour and experience in scientific terms; the law is concerned with regulating behaviour and enforcing social prescriptions for the conduct of individuals and groups in Society. The law is a system of rules for application. Psychologists study rules as part of their effort to describe, explain and predict how people conduct their affairs; and, as part of that enterprise, psychologists are concerned with the assumptions which underlie legal norms and rules.

The application of psychological principles to the operation of the legal system is not straightforward; and, in general, relationships between psychology and law are not simple. There is a host of complicating matters, some of a definitional nature, and others to do with social, moral and political questions. Any psychologist with interests in law must have a clear understanding of what is meant by "the legal system". For example, it would be grossly misleading to conceive of the legal system as a closed system of rules and procedures. Then again, when one considers problems to do with criminal behaviour, it has to be appreciated that crime is a societal problem: it cannot be contained and resolved within the legal system. That system reflects, and is sustained by, the prevailing philosophy about the form and elements of criminal conduct. Also, it is important to guard against scientific and professional imperialism: hence, for example, the legal system is not the exclusive province of lawyers and judges. Psychologists and lawyers are members of Society, and inevitably they base their professional views on received and shared wisdom about what it means to live in a modern, complex society. Neither profession operates independently of the prevailing social, moral and political climate, and in the final analysis both are publicly accountable.

To some extent it may be because of imperialist and dismissive attitudes that we have been slow to realise the advantages attached to inter-disciplinary contact between psychology and law. For instance, some lawyers may have discarded psychology before attempting to assess its relevance: rather than recognising it as an empirical and applied science, they may see psychology as little more than astute awareness of individual and group processes – an awareness which they might maintain is readily accessible to the intelligent or sensitive layperson through self-reflection and observation. Psychologists for their part may point disparagingly to contradictions between legal 'commonsense' and established psychological principles. However, existing barriers have not been constructed merely through negative prejudice, and nor are they founded purely or primarily upon emotional reactions. They have arisen, in part, because psychology and law are enormously complex areas of enquiry. Hence, within each discipline, there are numerous specialisms, and intensive and broad training is required in order to achieve satisfactory levels of professional accomplishment: the legal system embraces persons in disparate occupational roles – members of the police force, the courts and the prison service; and psychology encompasses several major sub-disciplines, such as clinical, industrial and physiological psychology. Thus, when psychologists talk to lawyers about psychological data they must be precise about the parameters of their analyses and their application.

As psychologists we may hold some naive ideas about the legal system, just as judges and lawyers often seem to be badly informed about psychology. In a short chapter such as this it is not possible to provide even the most cursory guide to the legal system and its administration. However, one should bear in mind three occupational divisions: academic scholars who study and teach law; members of the senior judiciary who monitor laws and advise Parliament of appropriate changes; and legal practitioners, such as lawyers, barristers and judges. When we talk of introducing psychology to enhance 'law' we have to be clear about the level at which it is proposed to introduce change. For example, academic lawyers might show an interest in psychologists' ideas about the mental elements in crime (e.g. 'mens rea' or guilty mind), and they may inform their students of these views. However, the courts could not address fundamental questions of a corresponding nature: changes in the elements of 'mens rea', say, could only be introduced after thorough review by the senior judiciary who would then, in Britain, advise Parliament of the appropriate changes. Major legal innovations cannot be sustained exclusively on psychological grounds: relevant moral, social and legal implications must be debated.

The occupational division raises a more general point about the ways psychologists can contribute to the legal process, and there are in fact two distinct styles of research. There is applications-driven research which aims to solve specific problems: for example, in the absence of relevant theory Court Magistrates in the City of Leeds used an experimental design to evaluate two judicial procedures commonly employed in truancy cases (cf. Berg, Hullin and McGuire, 1979). Then there is theory-driven research which proceeds by applying established psychological principles to relevant areas of the legal process: applications of psychological theories of memory to witness testimony is an example of this kind of approach (cf. Loftus, 1979). Figure 17.1 presents a simplified model of the way theory- and applications-driven research are informed by different kinds of source issues. The contribution of both is integrated in Legal-Forensic Psychology which organises contributions to the legal process through three available channels: training, policy research and expert testimony.

In the remainder of this chapter we consider how insights in some areas of psychology might be applied at specific levels to some areas of the legal system. We

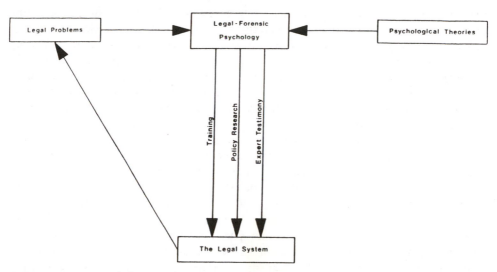

FIGURE 17.1   *Psychology's Input to the Legal System through Training, Policy Research and Expert Testimony.*

concentrate on five main areas which provide a representative range of coverage: *viz.* the criminal personality, witness testimony, jury-decision making, judicial sentencing and expert testimony.

THE CRIMINAL PERSONALITY

People hold radically differing views about the relative importance of personal and situational determinants of crime. Traditionally psychology has been especially concerned with the role of individual factors, and the bio-social theory of crime, proposed by Eysenck, is one of the best articulated theories to have emerged in psychology (e.g. see Eysenck, 1984). The theory considers the biological aspects of human behaviour, both criminal and non-criminal, in the context of the social environment in which people are reared. Despite criticisms that the theory is overly simplistic it does have the merit of drawing together genetic, personality and criminality variables, and hence one can contemplate predicting the 'dangerousness' levels of particular individuals.

Feldman (1977) draws on social learning theory (see Bandura, 1977) to offer an important alternative to the bio-social theory of crime. Learning results both from an individual's direct experiences and from his/her observations of significant others (termed 'models'). According to the social learning theory of crime, criminal behaviour is far from confined to particular social groups or classes. Certain social settings may influence the acquisition of criminal behaviours, perhaps because of exposure to persuasive communication from established criminals or exposure to models of criminal behaviour, but this is not the whole picture. Feldman believes that to understand the nature of crime fully we need to address three basic issues: (1) the method by which criminal behaviour is acquired; (2) the rewards and punishments that affect its occurrence; and (3) the social and environmental variables that cue its occurrence in a given context. He maintains that criminal behaviour is acquired through a combination of a person's own experiences and his/her observation of the behaviour of significant others. Observational or vicarious learning can result in the emergence of new patterns of behaviour, the strengthening or weakening of previously learned inhibitions, and the facilitation or weakening of previously-learned responses (Feldman, 1980). For observational learning to occur, repeated exposure to a model is required plus the correct perception and selection of certain behaviours. Criminal behaviours, for example, may be practised in public or private and will lead to either positive or negative consequences.

As well as being exposed to models for criminal behaviour, people are also exposed to verbal attempts at persuading them to break the law. The verbal enticements can take place in one-to-one settings or in groups. In the latter cases peer-group pressure may facilitate the adoption of criminal behaviour: group members approve group-standards of behaviour, and they sanction departures from those standards, whether the standards are generally accepted by Society or not. Whether the individual continues to engage in criminal behaviour is partly governed by the long-term schedule of reinforcement. For most offences, particularly minor ones, the offender is likely to be rewarded. As Feldman (1980) has noted, crime does seem to pay, especially autotheft and shoplifting, and benefits are not measured simply in terms of material gain; perpetrators can enjoy the enhanced attention and friendship of fellow offenders. Once criminal behaviour is incorporated into a person's behavioural repertoire, criminal acts occur when particular combinations of social cues arise: an offence against property, for example, is most likely to occur when detection is unlikely, punishment is anticipated as being minimal, incentives are high, there is a lack of legitimate options, little skill is necessary, the owner/victim is a stranger to the offender and unlikely to report the offence, and when self-esteem is low (Feldman, 1977).

Whether particular clinical practitioners are advocates of the bio-social theory, the social learning theory or some other, rival theory, they may be called upon to judge the dangerousness of individuals and to offer their views to a court of law. These judgements play a crucial role in assessments of bail applications and in weighing the potential risks in releasing a person from custody. The concept of 'dangerousness' is complex and is not readily operationalised in psychometric procedures. The accuracy of judgements of dangerousness is a function of the individual clinician making the judgement of the person about whom the judgement is made, and the generality of the behaviour criteria adopted in formulating the judgement.

In order to examine the accuracy of clinical predictions of dangerousness Sepejak, Webster and Menzies (1984) had a panel of mental health professionals – comprising a psychologist, a psychiatrist, a social worker, a psychiatric worker and a probation officer – assess the dangerousness of 598 accused persons. Their predictions were recorded against a four-point scale ('no', 'low', 'medium' and 'high'), and accuracy was assessed during a follow-up period of two years. Four criteria were adopted: further criminal charges, misconduct during imprisonment, events precipitating contact with psychiatric services, and behaviour during hospitalisation in a psychiatric unit. It was found that psychiatrists could accurately predict dangerousness at a level significantly above chance. Nevertheless, about forty per cent of their predictions were found to be wrong. The predictions offered by the psychologists and the psychiatrists were most accurate, with the probation officers next best, followed by the nurses and social workers. However, there were considerable *individual differences* in the accuracy of judges within each professional group. Also judges were better at predicting dangerousness for individuals in particular categories of accused persons, and they were notably better for those with psychiatric histories. In addition, accuracy was dependent upon whether the measurement criterion was taken to be the single most dangerous subsequent incident or a composite of all subsequent incidents. Thus, 'dangerousness' is a complex concept, composed of a large number of elements, and its prediction is equally complex.

Sepejak and co-workers found that biographies of psychiatric disorders were powerful indicators of judges' predictions of dangerousness. The relationship between 'mental illness' and 'criminality' is complex, and the stigma of double deviance (e.g., 'criminally insane') is especially strong. In order to examine perceptions of the relationship between insanity and criminality Howells (1984) invited eighty subjects to read a number of fictitious newspaper reports in which the seriousness of an alleged offence was paired with a reported history of mental illness. For the less serious offence attitudes towards the accused were more tolerant and the predominant response was that 'medical treatment' is a more attractive alternative than penal servitude. However, in the case of a serious crime, namely murder, the history of mental illness was linked with the crime in the concept of 'dangerousness', and punishment was the preferred measure. A further finding was that subjects with higher levels of formal education took relatively greater account of the mental illness factor in less serious than in more serious crime, whereas subjects with lower education backgrounds *only* took account of mental illness when judging the more serious crime. Similar findings emerged in a replication study and these suggest that the association between mental illness and crime is not unambiguously negative. Lay-persons generally adopt an attitude similar to that adopted by mental health professionals: they seem to believe that evidence of previous criminal offences is a better index of potential dangerousness than is mental illness on its own.

A widely held belief is that personality, mental illness and criminality are interrelated. Physical appearance is also held to be an important element: hence, according to received wisdom, 'one can spot a criminal by his appearance' (cf. Bull, 1982). In an early test of this view Thornton (1939) showed twenty photographs of criminals to a large audience of adults who were asked to write down which of four crimes each of the twenty criminals might have committed. (Thornton took the precaution of selecting his sample of photographs randomly from crime archives: otherwise his selection may have been biased, in that he might have chosen photographs to conform with his personal expectations of what criminals look like). He found that members of his audience could match faces to crimes more reliably than would be expected by chance.

Three decades later Masters and Greaves (1969) catalogued facial deformities in a population of eleven thousand convicts and concluded that sixty per cent of criminals had facial deformities compared with twenty per cent of the non-criminal population. There are methodological weaknesses with this study which exemplify the difficulties normally encountered in investigating relationships between appearance and criminality. For instance, it seems likely that the individuals who made the judgements about facial deformities for Masters and Greaves knew that they were looking at photographs of convicts, and their judgements were presumably influenced by shared stereotypes about the appearance of criminals.

It may be that some physically deformed individuals are encouraged into criminal ways because Society as a whole effectively rejects those individuals through its response to their deformities. If that is the case it is feasible that surgical correction may help to reform such individuals, and this is a possibility to which Meyer, Hoopes, Jabaley and Allen (1973) have turned their attention. They collected a large body of psychological data on twenty-one youths between the ages of twelve and twenty who were formally designated 'delinquent' or who came from a socio-economic and family background with a 'high risk' of delinquency. Fourteen of the twenty-one were given plastic surgery, and fresh data were gathered one year later. On the psychological measures Meyer *et al.* were not able to detect any significant improvements in the fourteen who had undergone surgery, and similarly there were no differences between the surgery and no-surgery groups. Although this cannot be regarded as a definitive study (e.g., 'high-risk background' was not defined), it would not be surprising to find that cosmetic surgical intervention fails to produce reductions in criminal activity: crime is a complex social problem, not a surgical problem.

Nevertheless, a case has been made for a link between facial deformity and criminality. It is the direction of causation which has yet to be determined: certainly facial disfigurements can sometimes arise during the course of a violent criminal career, but we have no evidence that congenital deformities can precipitate such a career. The issue of causation has wider generality when considering evidence pertinent to the predicted associations between crime and factors such as personality, appearance and mental illness. In the absence of large-scale longitudinal studies, which are expensive and problematic to administer, it is difficult to determine which of various individual factors cause crime and which emerge because a criminal style of life is pursued.

Individual factors appear to help precipitate particular kinds of crime in particular kinds of social circumstances. Psychologists have tended to concentrate their attention on violent crimes and other overt crimes, such as theft. However, some of the most serious thefts are covert (e.g. embezzlement) and some of the most violent crime is covert (e.g. arising from illicit importing and selling of narcotics). These kinds of covet crime attract a wide variety of criminal persons, including a selection from wealthy economic circumstances and stable social backgrounds. Hence separate theories of criminal pre-disposition may be required, or theories broader than those currently salient. In general we must resist developing theories which embody prevailing social stereotypes. For example, according to one such stereotype, crime emanates from the lower social classes: but, then, individuals with personality and physical defects may gravitate to the lower classes, wherein there may be a concentration of such individuals.

PSYCHOLOGY OF TESTIMONY

Although interest in some of the relationships between psychology and law are new, historiographers remind us that the psychology of testimony can be traced to work in the nineteenth century (cf. Sporer, 1982). Some of the conceptual issues raised long ago remain pertinent to contemporary debate.

One way of studying the psychological variables underlying accurate and reliable testimony has been to examine, through simulation techniques, the impact of witnesses attitudes on their testimony – for example, the impact of stereotyped attitudes about the appearance and personality of criminals. Studies of this kind have shown us that witnesses' accounts of what they experienced are biased by their preconceptions. For example, Yarmey (1982) found that elderly subjects were more likely than younger subjects to identify an innocent bystander as an observed assailant if that bystander 'looked like a criminal'. Yarmey, Jones and Rashid (1984), in a simulation of an attempted rape, found that younger subjects recalled more details when the assailant wore jeans and a leather jacket.

In describing psychological research on testimony it has sometimes been found useful to draw a dichotomous distinction between 'system variables' and 'estimator variables'. System variables are those that can be manipulated by the police and the courts: they include, for instance, appropriate procedures for the conduct of identification parades. Estimator variables are those variables which cannot be controlled, such as the age, sex and racial identity of an accused person. The dichotomy is simple but not always easy to operationalize. In practice it can be difficult to categorise variables as *either* system *or* estimator variables: for instance, in the case of identity parades, one may have little insight into witnesses' identification strategies, yet is is crucial to know about those strategies in order to manipulate system variables effectively.

An alternative conceptual arrangement is advocated by Hall, Loftus and Tousignant (1984) who use a three-stage experimental paradigm to identify how witnesses' memories for an incident can be changed by post-incident experiences. In the first stage – 'acquisition' – subjects witness a simulated crime or accident. In the second stage – 'retention and change' – subjects are exposed to new experiences which may interact with the previously acquired information. In the third stage – 'retrieval' – memory of the original event is tested. (This three-stage process corresponds to events outside a research context: in everyday life people witness incidents; they think about what they have witnessed; and subsequently they are questioned about what they have witnessed). Typically, research using this paradigm shows that people have difficulty in differentiating between initial and subsequent experiences.

An example of this mode of research is the study by Loftus, Miller and Burns (1978) of witnesses' accuracy in recalling details of a staged car accident. First, slides were shown of a car accident. Second, each subject was asked a set of questions; but, for some subjects, their questions contained potentially misleading information (e.g. one question was 'Did another car pass the red Datsun while it was stopped at the stop sign?', when in fact the subject had seen slides in which was shown a *yield* sign). Some time later, in the third stage, subjects were questioned about their recollections of the stop/yield sign. Nearly 60% of recollections were influenced when a false detail was introduced during the second stage. The information which has already accrued from research of this kind can help us design procedural protocols which guard against memory distortion.

It has long been thought that 'leading questions' can dramatically alter the content of witnesses' recollections; and hence such questioning is prohibited in most courts. Systematic research confirms the wisdom of this policy. For example, Read and Bruce (1984) showed subjects two pieces of film, one depicting a traffic accident and the other a fistfight. The subjects were adults, in three groups. They were invited to complete a questionnaire, comprising three categories of questions: (1) four 'presupposition' questions in which the existence of an object was indirectly presupposed — i.e. through a question about another object; (2) four questions in which the existence of an object was directly presupposed; and (3) four questions which did not mention any presupposed object. Results indicated that the indirect presupposition questions elicited more false information than the questions which contained no presuppositions. In subsequent experiments it was found that the biasing effects of leading questions can be reduced, and sometimes eliminated entirely, by giving subjects additional background information about the incident. The improved performances may be due to subjects spending less time trying to place the incident in a context and thus attending more to the thematic content of the film. It was found, too, that providing subjects with information about the fallibility of witness testimony reduced the amount of false information elicited in their accounts.

Whether or not a criminal investigation is solved may rest upon the quality of the eyewitness account (Rand Corporation, 1975). However, eyewitness accounts, as already mentioned, are known to be often incomplete, unreliable and partially constructed, and they may be malleable during the questioning procedure (Clifford and Hollin, 1983; Loftus, 1975, 1979; Loftus Miller and Burns, 1978; Wells, Ferguson and Lindsey, 1981). Although researchers have begun to report new procedures for gaining eyewitness testimony, chief among these being the Guided Memory Interview (Malpass and Devine, 1981) and the Cognitive Interview Procedure (Gieselman, Fisher, Firstenburg, Hutton, Sullivan, Avetissian and Prosk, 1984), the Standard Interview Procedure (SIP) is still being used routinely by police and lawyers. The standard procedure involves a period of free recall about the event followed by specific questions on the information generated during the free recall (Roy, 1991). Although the SIP in all its guises is widely used by lawyers and law enforcement agencies its efficacy is rarely questioned.

Geiselman and his colleagues based the Cognitive Interview Procedure (CIP) upon the Guided Memory Interview. The CIP utilises four retrieval-mnemonics. The first mnemonic requires mentally reinstating the context, both environmental and personal, as it existed at the occurrence of the to-be-remembered event (Bower, Gilligan and Monterio, 1981; Davies and Thomson, 1988; Malpass and Devine, 1981; Smith, 1979). Mentally reinstating the context that surrounded the crime has been shown to be a powerful memory aid in laboratory experiments, and it is usually preferable to returning to the scene of the crime (e.g. because important elements in the scene of the crime often change with time).

The second mnemonic involves the witness reporting absolutely everything that may be regarded as having an association with the event under examination (Smith, 1983). The recalling of all information, regardless of the perceived importance of this information, is important for two main reasons: (1) witnesses may not know what information has investigative value; and (2) striving for comprehensiveness in the recall of the to-be-remembered event may lead to the witness remembering important details which occurred with the unimportant ones.

The third mnemonic requires the event to be recalled in various orders (Burns, 1981; Loftus and Fathi, 1985; Mingay, 1986; Whitten and Leonard, 1981). For example, the witness may be required to go through the event in reverse order, and then to try starting with the item or incident that impressed him/her most in the event, and then go from there moving forward and backward in time. Initially the events are recalled in the order they occurred, but then manipulating the order of events sometimes unearths additional and valuable data on the to-be-remembered event. Recalling events in reverse order serves to force witnesses to scrutinize their memory record, looking for important events to facilitate the backward recall. When events are recalled solely in forward order, some people reconstruct what they imagine must have occurred based upon outcomes and/or knowledge of previous, similar crime scenarios, and this can lead to incomplete and/or inaccurate reports.

The fourth mnemonic device involves the witness recalling the event from a variety of perspectives (Anderson and Pichert, 1978; Firstenberg, 1983). For instance, a witness may be encouraged to try placing him/herself in the role of a prominent character in the event and to think about what he/she must have seen. This technique is again useful in enhancing the accuracy of a report.

Outside a research context most witnesses may initially have a variety of perspectives on the to-be-remembered event, but they may have the opportunity to report only from a unitary, static perspective. Yet several empirical studies by Geiselman and others have established that CIP increases the amount of correct information and may sometimes decrease the amount of incorrect information about a to-be-remembered event (e.g. Fisher, Geiselman, Raymond, Jurkevich and Warhaftig, 1987; Geiselman, Fisher, Mackinnon and Holland, 1985, 1986; Chapman and Perry, 1992). Geiselman and colleagues suggest that the CIP elicits between 40–70% more information than an SIP, although it should be noted that the two types of interview often do not differ on amounts of incorrect items produced.

In addition to the four main mnemonics, there are a number of supplementary CIP techniques which can aid recall. For example, Mackinnon, O'Reilly and Geiselman (1990) developed a means of supplementing the recall of car number plates. This technique involved the witness forming an image of the context in which the car was seen and then focusing on the rear end of the car including the lights, bumper and the number plate itself. For example, the cognitive interviewer might ask:

'Did the plate have any special characteristics that stood out?'
'Do you think the numbers were high or low?'
'Did the letters or numbers remind you of any words or things?'

The CIP is a practical part-solution to the important problem of eyewitness memory enhancement, but two main criticisms have been levelled against it. The first is that the CIP's benefits may simply be an artefact of more questions being asked and greater time spent questioning, or a result of heightened interviewer or subject motivation; but the work by Geiselman, Fisher, MacKinnon and Holland would seem to undermine these possibilities. The second criticism is that the CIP makes the witness more suggestive to biased or misleading questions. Geiselman *et al.* (1986) tested this claim and reported that as long as the cognitive interview techniques were presented prior to the leading questions, the cognitive interview did not increase witness susceptibility to leading/misleading questions; rather, the CIP seemed to provide a degree of insulation against such forms of question.

The CIP may have special application in gathering information from child witnesses. Children have consistently been found to recall information less accurately than adults (e.g. Goodman, Aman and Hirschman, 1987). However, Chapman and Perry (1992) found that children in three age groupings (4/5-year-olds, 9/10-year-olds and 14/15-year-olds) produced more accurate reports on road accidents when interviewed with the CIP than when a standard interviewing procedure was used. In addition the 4/5- and 14/15-year-olds also produced less inaccurate information when interviewed using the CIP. This obviously has implications for interviewing child victims of physical and sexual abuse, where recall of events may be difficult and painful for the interviewee.

Witnesses' accounts provide indispensable pieces of evidence, and the courts' willingness to accept that evidence hinges on the credibility of the witness. 'Credibility' is conceptualized as having at least two components. The first component is accuracy of recall; that is, the perceived ability of the witness to recall details of an observed incident. The second component relates to the perceived willingness of the witness to tell the truth; and an important factor here is the interpretation of the witness' role in the alleged crime.

Most of the theory and research bearing on witness testimony refers to the first of these components. It attempts to assess the reliability of reports against conventional scientific and legal standards: it asks whether one can know if a witness' testimony is accurate.

In the courtroom, jurors do not directly question witnesses but are an audience to interactions between witnesses, barristers and judges. Their estimates of witness confidence and credibility are a complex function of those somewhat scripted interactions. The 'scripts' are produced by examining and cross-examining counsel, and they substantially affect the performance of witnesses and the styles of their testimony. Surprisingly, psychological research on witness testimony has largely neglected to consider the counsels' roles. The majority of investigations have sought to determine whether the most confident witness is also the most accurate. An answer to this question is obviously invaluable whenever witnesses offer conflicting testimony such that only one can be telling the truth.

A separate 'confidence' issue is that bearing on individual witnesses' estimates of their own confidence: the issue is the extent to which witnesses' estimates of their own confidence vary systematically with their perceptions of the accuracy of their testimony. Confidence *per se* may play little part in a witness' decision about what evidence to give. For example, in first identifying a person in a line-up, confidence may not be important; but it may assume considerable importance after the initial decision has been made. Stephenson (1984) has shown that the relationship between confidence and accuracy is always positive for individual witnesses, but that there is considerable variation: in general terms, the more confident a given individual, the more accurate is likely to be the evidence. By contrast, across a group of people, the confidence-accuracy relationship is often negative: within a group of people, those who are most confident may not be those who are most accurate. Thus, discussions about confidence and accuracy must spell out whether they are concerned with within-group or within-individual relationships.

Laboratory research has not only demonstrated that witness testimony can be highly inaccurate but that the inaccuracy is often a function of the questions posed to the witness. Largely because researchers are in the privileged position of knowing exactly what has been witnessed, they are able systematically to vary their questions according to relevance, informativeness, bias, and so forth. In the courts, the counsels enjoy comparatively few corresponding advantages, and the witnessed incidents are often farther removed in time. It is reasonable to assume that interrogators who themselves know the precise details of incidents ask questions differently, and ask different sorts of questions, to interrogators who have no first-hand knowledge. Hence the kinds of inaccuracies identified in the laboratory may bear little resemblance to 'real-world' inaccuracies; and, to the extent that laboratory research sometimes focuses on details which are of marginal concern to the courts it may paint a pessimistic picture of witness fallibility. Then again, witnesses in courts of law are generally questioned on a relatively confined set of issues: for example, a witness to a traffic accident would probably not be asked much about the physical circumstances of the accident because accurate information will have been recorded by police officers at the scene of the accident.

Questions about assessing witness truthfulness, separate from accuracy and reliability, have rarely been addressed empirically. It is common knowledge that in practice the courts generally judge the truthfulness of a testimony through an assessment of the witness' character and the possible involvement of that witness in the alleged crime. However, in psychology, theoretical analyses and clinical practice have shown that 'personality' and 'character' are elusive constructs, and we know that people can portray different aspects of themselves according to the roles and situations in which they find themselves.

As far as possible research into eyewitness testimony must not be mis-directed and, in the context of judging truth, researchers should bear in mind that, at least in criminal cases, the final arbiters are the jurors. As noted earlier, jurors do not communicate directly with witnesses and it could well be that they assess evidence in ways that are different from those of the judge and courtroom protagonists.

Within the burgeoning literature on psychology and law, a corpus of theory and research is developing which is specifically concerned with jurors' decision-making processes. We believe that the issues in 'jury decision-making' are intrinsic to the assessment of 'witness testimony' and, therefore, the distinction drawn between these two topics is superficial and less than helpful.

JUROR DECISION MAKING

Judges and jurors do not always agree on what judgement to return in specific cases, and this is illustrated, for example, in a study by Kalven and Zeisel (1966). Using postal questionnaires they elicited judges' reactions to 3,576 criminal cases tried before a jury. The judges agreed with the jurors' decisions in 78% of cases, and jurors' judgements were more lenient in 16% of cases. This may suggest that defendants fare better with jury trials, but that would be a rather sweeping general conclusion to draw from isolated studies.

Although there is a high level of agreement between the verdicts of judges and jurors, they arrive at decisions in different ways: judges offer individual, professional judgements while jurors offer group, lay judgements. Psychologists are particularly interested in the ways jurors arrive at their decisions. This is because jury deliberations are a specific case of group decision making and, within social psychology, there is a large body of theory and empirical research relating to group decision making. Special psychological theories have traditionally concentrated on the cost-benefit analysis in which people are thought to engage when working towards a decision.

For the juror, one 'cost' of advocating a guilty verdict would be the risk of convicting an innocent person, and a 'benefit' would be convicting a guilty person. But there is a large number of costs and benefits to be weighed up before reaching a verdict. Decisions are difficult because jurors must consider the nature and significance of the 'facts' before them, and usually they must negotiate a unanimous verdict with fellow jurors who sometimes will not perceive and interpret the evidence in identical fashion.

In arriving at a verdict probably the most difficult cognitive task for jurors is to assign relative weightings to cost and benefit elements. It is difficult because the costs and benefits are both intrinsic and extrinsic to the immediate trial: costs are largely intrinsic – a false conviction or false acquittal undermines the justice principle and does not reach the criminal behaviour to which it is directed; benefits are largely extrinsic – a correct verdict reinforces Society's confidence in the legal system and does reach the behaviour to which it is directed. Thus, jurors must offer verdicts based on individual and then group analysis of variables located on three dimensions: alternative verdicts (convict/acquit), accuracy of verdict (correct/incorrect), and the costs and benefits associated with the four combinations of verdict type and verdict accuracy.

Nagel, Lamm and Neef (1981) have pointed out that juror decision making may follow one of three main courses: (1) arrival at a standard of guilt (according to the judge's instructions); perception of defendant guilt, and then a decision to convict or acquit; (2) arrival at a tentative decision to convict or acquit, acceptance of the standard of guilt, and then adjustment of one's perceptions of defendant guilt to conform with the tentative decision and the standard of guilt; or (3) arrival at a tentative decision to acquit or convict, perception of the defendant's guilt, and then adjustment of one's perception of the standard of guilt. These three different courses illustrate the intimate relationships that exist between the sharing of information among jurors and the process of negotiating a verdict. Within social psychology the 'risky shift' phenomenon is well established – individuals in a group tend to modify their judgements so that the overall group decision is riskier than that of individual members – and there is evidence that risky shift occurs in juror decision making (Kaplan and Schersching, 1981). The shift seems to be a consequence of the way the jurors order and distribute the factual evidence rather than a consequence of any normative pressure exerted on the members to reach a unanimous verdict rapidly.

Evidently individual differences play an important part in juror decision making. Sealy (1979) has reported that a minority of jury members contribute most of the discussion leading up to a verdict. The most vocal jurors may be the most dogmatic and prejudiced and they may permit their personal biases to colour their own judgements and those of similarly minded jurors. Sealy has concluded that there is no evidence for a correlation between jurors' personality characteristics and their verdicts, but this does not mean that personality factors can be discounted. The relationship between personality and specific individual and group verdicts is neither simple nor direct, and verdicts may not be sensitive indicators of personality influences. Personality characteristics are likely to influence the kind of evidence jurors consider relevant and important.

In deciding on a legal standard of guilt it is obviously crucial that jurors should understand the judge's instructions and guidelines. However, psychological studies have cast doubt on the common assumption that judges' instructions are sufficiently unambiguous to permit jury members to reach a verdict in a proper manner. Comprehension levels of 50% or less have been found for mock jurors and representative samples of jurors (Buchanan, Pryor, Taylor and Strawn, 1978; Charrow and Charrow, 1979; Elwork, Sales and Alfini, 1977, 1982; Imwinkelreid and Schwed, 1987; Severance and Loftus, 1982; Strawn and Buchanan, 1976). For example, only half the jurors in a Florida sample understood that the criminal defendant did not have to produce any evidence of innocence (Strawn and Buchanan, 1976). While Severance and Loftus (1982) found that juror comprehension levels for legal concepts explained in patterned instructions were not significantly different from jurors who had received no instructions. Even when jurors offer assurances that they understand the instructions given, low-levels of comprehension of patterned instructions still appear commonplace (O'Mara and von Eckartsberg, 1977).

Content analysis of jurors' requests for clarification has helped identify some specific problem areas (Severance and Loftus, 1984). First, jurors often have doubts about the elements of criminal acts, particularly the relationship between behavioural acts (*actus reus*) and mental states (*mens rea*). Second, they have doubts about the nature of decision criteria, particularly the meaning of 'reasonable doubt' in criminal cases. Third, where multiple charges are involved, jurors are often uncertain about the procedures they ought to adopt when arriving at verdicts.

Although jurors' instructions are naturally designed to emphasize legal accuracy, they are not simple to follow and, as Elwork and Sales (1985) have pointed out, incomprehensible jury instructions severely affect the quality of the verdict reached in three crucial ways: (1) legally inappropriate topics or issues are more likely to feature in jury deliberations; (2) there is an increased likelihood that juries will neglect to discuss important points of law; and (3) because of the ambiguity of a judge's instructions, one or two jurors may claim expertise and come to exert a disproportionate influence. But legal accuracy and effective communication are not mutually exclusive objectives. Severance and Loftus (1984) have shown that it is possible to transform legal jargon into the language of the layperson without loss of legal accuracy, and this overcomes many of the comprehension problems encountered regularly by jurors. Possibly legal accuracy and effective communication could be improved by presenting jurors with written rather than oral instructions (Hastie, Penrod and Pennington, 1983; Kassin and Wrightsman, 1979, 1985). Regrettably most committees charged with the responsibility for compiling comprehensible, legal, accurate instructions do not include psychologists and linguists amongst their membership.

Jury studies typically use role-playing simulations in order to investigate juror decision-making processes, but the fidelity of the method has often been criticized (e.g. Konečni and Ebbesen, 1981). Critics point out that experimental settings cannot adequately embrace the richness of the moral, legal and social dimensions which characterize the deliberations of real juries. Some investigators have successfully employed alternative methods. Bridgeman and Marlowe (1979), for example, used an interview technique with sixty-five people who had previously served as jurors in ten trials, and thus they retrospectively examined relationships between a number of demographic variables and trial outcomes. No significant relationships were observed, and this can be interpreted as an encouraging outcome: it suggests that jurors are conscientious citizens who determine their verdicts on the material evidence presented to them rather than on the basis of personal prejudices and hunches.

EXPERT WITNESSES

Two general questions emerge when considering the potential of psychologists as expert witnesses. First, in whose interests should evidence be given? Should the psychologist invariably act in the role of an independent and neutral witness, or are there circumstances where it is appropriate for the psychologist to act as advocate for one party against the other? Second, what expectations should the psychologist have about the proffering and examining of evidence, and what are the implications for expressive style on the witness stand?

To illustrate the difficulties encountered in trying to answer the first of these questions – about whose interests the psychologist should serve – let us consider parental disputes involving children. In divorce cases, the psychologist might be expected to comment on child custody; and that may entail an explicit analysis of the complex and troublesome concept, 'the best interests of the child'. 'Interests' is value laden: here, it assumes meaning in the context of a set of beliefs and values relating to childhood. The conceptual difficulties cannot be circumvented, for example, by reverting to the child's orally reported wishes. Clearly children can be unfairly influenced by one or both parents, and they can often experience difficulty articulating their feelings, wishes, fears and desires. Above all, they may not appreciate sufficiently the long-term consequences of pursuing a particular course of action. How can the expertise of the psychologist inform the judgements of the courts? Some commentators have suggested that the psychologist should actively articulate and represent the child's point of view (cf. Hayden, 1984). Rather than contest the arguments of the disputants, the psychologist would then act to present the nature of the child's needs in the context of an established developmental framework, and attention would be drawn to the special features of the family circumstances. Thus, as child advocate, the psychologist pieces together the various accounts of the parents in the context of the child's needs and wishes. There is no implication that the psychologist should act to reconcile the parents: that may not be in the best interests of the child.

The second question – regarding the conduct and demeanour of the psychologist in the witness box – requires an understanding of the social psychological structure of courtroom order. The role of the expert witnesses will obviously vary according to the circumstances in which testimony is solicited. For instance, cases brought before Magistrates' Courts tend to be well prepared, and over 90% of the defendants plead guilty or are found guilty. The expert witness in a Magistrates' Court is, therefore, in a different context to the expert in a Crown Court, where convictions are less frequent and where presumably expectations of convictions are proportionately diminished.

Haward (1979) has identified three roles for the expert psychologist: experimental, actuarial and medical. The experimental role involves investigating and evaluating variables which the courts consider important in the trial of particular cases: for example, Haward (1964) showed that a policeman who was said to have recorded the registration numbers of four speeding motorcycles could not have done so under the lighting and weather conditions prevailing at the time. The actuarial role refers to the probabilistic estimation of associations between psychological variables: for example, psychologists are called to give an assessment of the effect of neurological damage to long-term healthy cognitive functioning. The medical role is usually supplementary or complementary to other medical evidence: for instance, the psychologist will often be able to assist the courts in assessing a defendant's capacity to give evidence and in estimating dangerousness for purposes of bail setting.

The expert witness does not control the subject matter of the court's enquiries, and this can make for uneasy exchanges in the courtroom – for psychologists as much as for any other class of expert. The psychologist – like any other witness, expert or not – is expected to give evidence which the court has invited and hence is liable to be interrupted if he or she is seen to be digressing from the court's questions. The judges and examining counsel are not engaged in a conversation with the expert witness, and the principles which govern interrogatory exchanges in the court are radically different to those which apply in routine conversations. Acquiring competence as an expert witness in court is akin to acquiring a new set of social skills.

Many expert witnesses speak from a written report. This is usually regarded as acceptable precisely because the expert is not there to engage in a conversation. He or she is there to participate in an informed meeting with other interested professionals and, in choosing to speak from a well-researched and well-prepared report, there may be less of a danger of slipping into technical language and thereby becoming incomprehensible to the court.

Although expert witnesses are privileged in being allowed to report professional *opinions*, poorly supported or indirect evidence is likely to be challenged on the grounds of hearsay, and quite properly so. It is imperative that professional opinion should be based on established, replicated empirical evidence, rather than on novel research findings which may prove to be unsound; and it should be borne in mind that the courts are likely to know of controversy surrounding the validity of some psychological theories (e.g. they may know something about the so-called 'Burt controversy'). Because the courts seem slow to embrace expert psychological testimony, it should not be imagined that they are necessarily closed to its contribution. The courts are right to be hesitant about introducing 'expertise' until they are certain that it is not ill-founded: they need to be confident that evidence will not subsequently be shown to be wrong, or in need of significant qualification.

For the individual it is chiefly practice that brings familiarization with the role of expert witness, but preliminary training can be designed, drawing on points already made. Training is akin to socialization. It provides the novice with a basic set of social skills which facilitate conformity to acceptable standards of courtroom conduct; otherwise, sophisticated skills are acquired through uncomfortable and expensive trial-and-error methods. But the training itself must be based upon a recognition of the sophistication of court proceedings. Analytic studies of courtroom interaction have repeatedly demonstrated that the formal rules of conduct are not simple, and they do not account for the range of conduct which can be observed in court sessions. To understand the procedural variations, and to judge how best to react, it is important to acquire and apply the appropriate set of analytic skills. Contingent upon these skills is one's capacity to function effectively: without such skills it is difficult to envisage the expert remaining sufficiently composed while handling technical questions in the labile atmosphere of the court.

The problems confronting the psychologist as expert witness can sometimes be exacerbated by everyday professional circumstances. For example, Ward (1981) has noted that clinical psychologists are often hampered in preparing legal submissions by a lack of forensic services through which they can conduct appropriate tests with defendants. Also, as intimated earlier, fundamental problems can arise in communicating with non-psychologists, and some of these problems are different in kind to those experienced by other professional people endeavouring to communicate with persons outside their profession. One important problem is that some psychological terms are used non-technically in everyday conversation, and it is sometimes inescapable that the psychologist as expert witness respectfully defines (or re-defines) the meaning of such terms for the benefit of the court. Another important problem is that psychological information is sometimes presented to courts by non-psychologists. For example, it can find its way into the medical reports of psychiatrists serving as expert witnesses. This occurs when psychological evidence is extracted from case reports, and when that happens the psychologists' notes are often used in ways for which they were never intended. The danger in by-passing the psychologist becomes acute when, in the court's deliberations, the non-psychologist is expected to interpret the information or to elaborate upon it and extrapolate from it.

Important ethical problems can arise bearing on (1) the confidentiality of clients' disclosures to a psychologist and (2) the communication of psychological information to the courts. The principal problem emanates from role ambiguity and is not easily resolved: when acting as expert witness should the psychologist serve the best interests of his/her client or the best interests of the court? The second ethical issue is more general and relates to the presentation of psychological testimony. Often the professional objectives of the psychologist are not entirely congruent with the professional objectives of the judge and barristers. For example, the therapeutic emphasis of the psychologist's testimony is likely to be substantially disregarded. Thus, the psychologist must decide whether information should be volunteered knowing that it could well be used in a manner which runs counter to professional objectives which are well-established and well-supported.

JUDICIAL SENTENCING

While the behaviour of jurors has been a special interest of psychologists, the behaviour of judges, which is central in any court case, has received surprisingly little attention. In arriving at a decision on any case the judge is governed by the letter and spirit of the law and by personal conscience. However, the unguided use of discretion may lead to the imposition of substantially different sentences for similar offences and offenders.

There are three main methods available to investigate sentencing disparity. The first of these is archival, and it has high ecological validity because the data used are from real court cases. However, when the focus of interest is disparity in sentencing, there is a need for a large number of similar cases within various crime categories. As far as the archival method is concerned, it is unfortunate that even crimes falling within a single category incorporate large differences: every criminal incident has its unique features, and obviously each alleged offence is tried on the 'facts' as presented to the courts.

Archival-based studies have usually culminated in feedback to judges about their sentencing decisions, and thereby the researchers have endeavoured to promote greater uniformity through norm-referenced sentencing decisions. The feedback has been channelled in two ways. Sometimes it has operated through the introduction of a sentencing-guidelines model which attends to the *structure* of sentencing decisions: the model allows for some variation in the sentences imposed, but where any particular sentence exceeds the normal range the judge is invited to give an account of the legal basis to that decision. Second, feedback has been given more directly, in the form of statistical summaries of sentences handed down for the various kinds of crime. This feedback arrangement is used, for example, in Victoria, Australia; and Lovegrove (1984) has reviewed its effectiveness in that state. One point made by Lovegrove is that statistical analyses of archive material are not designed to throw light on the way judges actually come to their decisions: because statistical reviews are based on group data, they can tell us nothing about individual thought processes, and that is a serious limitation. Another point of criticism is that even the most sophisticated statistical analysis may call attention to factors which are not actually pertinent to the judges' sentencing patterns. For instance, a review of robbery-with-violence cases may reveal that black defendants receive stiffer sentences than white defendants. However, unemployment and other factors might also be strongly correlated with race, and so one cannot know whether it is race or some other factor which is most salient in judges' decisions.

A second method of investigating sentencing disparity is through sentencing councils, and these too are intended to reduce disparity through the provision of feedback to judges. In sentencing councils judges discuss their proposed sentences with other judges before delivering final sentence (cf. Sporer, 1984): professional opinion on legal issues are thereby communicated to the trial judge, and those opinions are taken into account as that judge deems fit. This arrangement has features in common with the system of appeal courts, but in the latter system the consultative process is introduced later and only if an appeal is lodged against the imposed sentence. In any method designed to reduce disparity one must be careful that a sentence is not judged purely on statistical grounds – that is, where the sentence falls in relation to others – rather than on the facts and circumstances of the crime: the underlying objective in providing feedback is to eliminate a form of error – *viz* unintended variations in sentencing; the objective is *not* to eliminate sentencing discretion.

The third method of studying sentencing is to use experimental simulations. These are high in ecological validity to the extent that they approximate the kinds of cognitive behaviour intrinsic to the judging of real cases. Researchers can systematically manipulate variables and generate data about fictitious cases which can then be presented to judges for 'sentencing'; and, of course, identical cases can be presented to a number of judges, and/or sets of judges can be presented with cases which vary in known ways. However, the external validity of this method may be low. Although the cognitive processes used by judges in real and simulated cases are essentially the same, the motivational, moral, social and legal circumstances are quite different. Cognitive functioning is not independent of other forms of psychological functioning; and, in any given situation, we do not know to what extent it may be influenced by those other factors. Clearly one needs to exercise caution in generalizing from simulations.

Using simulation Palys and Divorski (1984) presented five cases, in questionnaire format, to 206 Canadian judges. The judges were first asked to impose sentences on six accused persons and later to indicate (1) the facts relevant to their sentencing decisions and (2) the legal objectives of their decisions. Wide discrepancies were found, both with regard to the relative importance of particular facts and in sentencing objectives. Lawrence (1984) has worked with practising magistrates and used in-depth questioning to investigate their judicial judgement and sentencing processes. This 'interview' approach shares some of the characteristics of the archival method: judges are encouraged to talk about their cases, and these cases are in public records. It also has similarities with the simulation approach: judges identify regularities in their decision-making processes which they believe characterize their sentencing policies. Lawrence noted that many magistrates have difficulty in conceptually organising the multitude of variables which they regard as influencing their decisions. While these difficulties do not invalidate the data generated through a paradigm such as Lawrence's, they do suggest that researchers should be organised and directed in their questioning of judges.

Archival research, experimental simulation and in-depth interviewing are complementary methods of investigation. The method, or methods, chosen should depend upon the information sought and the questions to be asked. Archival research is particularly appropriate for describing judicial sentencing characteristics; and experimental simulations are particularly useful for investigating sentencing disparity and sentencing error. In-depth interviews are of most benefit when the focus of attention is on either the kinds of personal factors which influence legal decisions or the purpose and legal objectives of those decisions. As for current knowledge about sentencing disparities, it is regrettable that psychological research has not yet progressed to a point where it can usefully supplement Diamond's (1981) conclusion: 'Disparity arises under a variety of circumstances and disagreements in a particular case may derive from a number of sources' (p. 406).

CONCLUSION

We can exploit various avenues of communication in order to disseminate our ideas about the importance of psychological variables in the legal system. In endeavouring to 'give psychology away' we inevitably enter forums of public debate in which our contributions will be challenged and tested on non-psychological grounds. For example, psychologists often debate the generalizability of simulation studies among themselves; but some of these academic debates can be seen to have extremely important legal implications. In our legal system it is axiomatic that justice should be done and that it should be seen to be done. We believe that until such time as psychological evidence is seen by the courts and by the public to be relevant to the legal system, the principle that 'justice must be seen to be done' will not be satisfied. Persuading the courts and the public that psychology is relevant to law is not just a problem for empiricists.

Psychologists already influence the legal system indirectly in many ways. For example, through involvement in police training, in other professional roles (perhaps as probation officers, for example) and in informal communication with judges, solicitors and barristers outside court settings. We have a public and professional responsibility to communicate empirical evidence and theoretical ideas in a direct and balanced manner, and we must resist embarking on professional crusades. In the final analysis psychology is for Society, and Society must be the final arbiter of psychology's value to judicial equity.

REFERENCES

Anderson, R.C. & Pichert, J.W. (1978). Recall of previously unrecallable information following a shift in perspective. *Journal of Verbal Learning and Verbal Behavior*, 17, 1–12

Bandura, A. (1977). *Social Learning Theory*. Englewood Cliffs, N.J.: Prentice-Hall.

Berg, I., Hullin, R. & McGuire, R. (1979). A randomly controlled trial of two court procedures in truancy. In D.P. Farrington, K. Hawkins & S.M. Lloyd-Bostock (eds), *Psychology, Law and Legal Processes*. London: Macmillan.

Bower, G.H., Gilligan, S.C. & Monteiro, K.P. (1981). A multicomponent theory of the memory trace. In K.W. Spence & J.T. Spence (Eds.), *The Psychology of Learning and Motivation.* New York: Academic Press.

Bridgeman, D.L. & Marlow, D. (1979). Jury decision making: An empirical study based on actual felony trials. *Journal of Applied Psychology,* **64**, 91–98.

Buchanan, R.W., Pryor, B., Taylor, K.P. & Strawn, D.U. (1978). Legal communication: An investigation of juror comprehension of pattern jury instructions. *Communication Quarterly,* **26**, 31–35.

Bull, R.H.C. (1982). Physical appearance and criminality. *Current Psychological Reviews,* **2**, 269–281.

Burns, M.J. (1981). Witness evidence: Conclusion and prospect. In S.M. Lloyd-Bostock & B.R. Clifford (Eds), *Evaluating Witness Evidence.* New York: Wiley.

Chapman, A.J. & Perry, D.J. (1992). Applying the Cognitive Interview Procedure to road accident witnesses. *The Psychologist,* **5**, 55–56.

Charrow, R.P. & Charrow, V. (1979). Making legal language understandable: A psycholinguistic study of jury instructions. *Columbia Law Review,* **79**, 1306–1374.

Clifford, B.R. & Hollin, C.R. (1983). The effects of discussion on recall accuracy and agreement. *Journal of Applied Social Psychology,* **13**, 234–244.

Crowe, R.R. (1972). The adopted offspring of women criminal offenders: A study of their arrest records. *Social Science Review,* **39**, 165–171.

Davies, G.M. & Thomson, D.M. (Eds.). (1988). *Memory in Context: Context in Memory.* Chichester: Wiley.

Diamond, S.S. (1981). Exploring sources of sentencing disparity. In D.B. Sales (Ed.), *The Trial Process: Perspectives in Law and Psychology,* Volume 2. London: Plenum.

Elwork, A., Sales, B.D. & Alfini, J.J. (1977). Juridic decisions: In ignorance of the law or in light of it? *Law and Human Behavior,* **1**, 163–169.

Elwork, A., Sales, B.D. & Alfini, J.J. (1982). *Making Jury Instructions Understandable.* Charlottesville, VA: Michie.

Elwork, A. & Sales, B.D. (1985), Jury instructions. In S.M. Kassin & L.S. Wrightsman (Eds), *The Psychology of Evidence and Trial Procedure.* Beverly Hills, Ca: Sage.

Eysenck, H.J. (1984). Crime and Personality. In D.J. Müller, D.E. Blackman & A.J. Chapman (Eds.), *Psychology and Law.* Chichester: Wiley.

Feldman, M.P. (1977). *Criminal Behaviour.* Chichester: Wiley.

Feldman, M.P. (1980). The making and control of offenders. In P. Feldman & J. Orford. *Psychological Problems: The Social Context.* NY: Wiley.

Firstenberg, I. (1983). The role of retrievability variability in the interrogation of human memory. (Doctoral dissertation, University of California, Los Angeles, 1983). *Dissertation Abstracts International,* **44**, 1623B.

Fisher, R.P., Geiselman, R.E., Raymond, D.S. Jurkevich, L.M. & Warhaftig, M.L. (1987). Enhancing enhanced eyewitness memory: Refining the cognitive interview. *Journal of Police Science and Administration,* **15**, 291–297.

Geiselman, R.E., Fisher, R.P., Firstenberg, I., Hutton, L.A., Sullivan, S., Avetissian, I. and Prosk, A. (1984). Enhancement of eyewitness memory: An empirical evaluation of the cognitive interview. *Journal of Police Science and Administration,* **12**, 74–80.

Geiselman, R.E., Fisher, R.P., MacKinnon, D.P. & Holland, H.L. (1985). Eyewitness memory enhancement in the police interview: Cognitive retrieval-mnemonics versus hypnosis. *Journal of Applied Psychology,* **70**, 410–412.

Geiselman, R.E., Fisher, R.P., MacKinnon, D.F. & Holland, H.L. (1986). Enhancement of eyewitness memory with the cognitive interview. *American Journal of Psychology,* **99**, 385–401.

Goodman, G.S., Aman, C. & Hirschman, J. (1987). Child sexual and physical abuse: Children's testimony. In S.J. Ceci, D.F. Ross & M.P. Toglia (Eds.), *Children's Eyewitness Memory.* New York: Springer-Verlag.

Hall, E.F., Loftus, E.F. & Tousignant, J.P. (1984). Post-event information and changes in recollection for a natural event. In G.L. Wells & E.F. Loftus (Eds.), *Advances in Eyewitness Research*. Cambridge: Cambridge University Press.

Hastie, R., Penrod, S.D. & Pennington, N. (1983). *Inside the Jury*. Cambridge, MA: Harvard University Press.

Haward, L.R.C. (1964). Psychological experiments and judicial doubt. *Bulletin of the British Psychological Society*, **17**, 5.

Haward, L.R.C. (1979). The psychologist as expert witness. In D.P. Farrington, K. Hawkins & S. Lloyd-Bostock (Eds.), *Psychology, Law and Legal Processes*. Guildford: Macmillan.

Hayden, B. (1984). In the best interests of the child: The psychologist as child expert and child advocate. In D.J. Müller, D.E. Blackman & A.J. Chapman (Eds.), *Psychology and Law*, Chichester: Wiley.

Howells, K. (1984). Public perceptions of mentally ill offenders. In D.J. Müller, D.E. Blackman & A.J. Chapman (Eds.), *Psychology and Law*, Chichester: Wiley.

Imwinklereid, E.J. & Schwed, L.R. (1987). Guidelines for drafting understandable jury instructions: An introduction to the use of psycholinguistics. *Criminal Law Bulletin*, **23**, 135–150.

Kalven, J. Jr. & Zeisel, H. (1966). *The American Jury*. Boston, MA: Little Brown.

Kaplan, M.F. & Schersching, C. (1981). Juror deliberation: An information integration analysis. In B.D. Sales (Ed.), *The Trial Process: Perspectives in Law and Psychology*. Volume 2. London: Plenum.

Kassin, S.M. & Wrightsman, L.S. (1979). On the requirements of proof: The timing of judicial instruction and mock juror verdicts. *Journal of Personality and Social Psychology*, **37**, 1877–1887.

Kassin, S.M. & Wrightsman, L.S. (Eds.) (1985). *The Psychology of Evidence and Trial Procedure*. Beverly Hills, CA: Sage.

Konečni, V.J. & Ebbesen, E.B. (1981). A critique of theory and method in social-psychological approaches to legal issues. In B.D. Sales (Ed.), *The Trial: Perspectives in Law and Psychology*, Volume 2. London: Plenum.

Lawrence, J.A. (1984). Magisterial decision making: Cognitive perspectives and processes used in courtroom information processing. In D.J. Müller, D.E. Blackman & A.J. Chapman (Eds.), *Psychology and Law*. Chichester: Wiley.

Loftus, E.F. (1975). Leading questions and eyewitness report. *Cognitive Psychology*, **7**, 560–572.

Loftus, E.F., Miller, D.G. & Burns, H.J. (1978). Semantic integration of verbal information into a visual memory. *Journal of Experimental Psychology: Human Learning and Memory*, **4**, 19–31.

Loftus, E.F. (1979). *Eyewitness Testimony*. Cambridge, MA: Harvard University Press.

Loftus, E.F. & Fathi, D.C. (1985). Retrieving multiple autobiographical memories. *Social Cognition*, **3**, 280–295.

Lovegrove. A. (1984). Structuring judicial sentencing disparity. In D.J. Müller, D.E. Blackman & A.J. Chapman (Eds.), *Psychology and Law*. Chichester: Wiley.

Mackinnon, D.P., O'Reilly, K. & Geiselman, R.E. (1990). Improving eyewitness recall for license plates. *Applied Cognitive Psychology*, **4**, 129–140.

Malpass, R.S. & Devine, P.G. (1981). Guided memory in eyewitness identification. *Journal of Applied Psychology*, **66**, 343–350.

Masters, F. & Greaves, D. (1969). The Quasimodo complex. *British Journal of Plastic Surgery*, **20**, 204–210.

Meyer, J.K., Hoopes, J., Jabaley, M. & Allen, R. (1973). Is plastic surgery effective in rehabilitation of deformed delinquent adolescents? *Plastic and Reconstructive Surgery*, **51**, 53–58.

Mingay, D.J. (1986). Memory of Eyewitness Materials: Improving and Predicting Performance.

Unpublished PhD, University of Cambridge.

Nagel, S., Lamm, D. & Neef, M. (1981). Decision theory and juror decision making. In B.D. Sales (Ed.), *The Trial: Perspectives in Law and Psychology*, Volume 2. London: Plenum.

O'Mara, J.J. & von Ecartsberg, R. (1977). Proposed standard jury instructions – Evaluation of usage and understanding. *Pennsylvania Bar Association Quarterly*, **48**, 542–556.

Palys, T.S. & Divorski, S. (1984). Judicial decision-making: An examination of sentencing disparity among Canadian Provincial Court judges. In D.J. Müller, D.E. Blackman & A.J. Chapman (Eds.), *Psychology and Law*. Chichester: Wiley.

Rand Corporation (1975, October). The criminal investigation process (Vol. 1–3). Rand Corporation Technical Report R-1776-DOJ, R-1777-DOJ, Santa Monica, CA.

Read, J.D. & Bruce, D. (1984). On the external validity of questioning effects in eyewitness testimony. *International Review of Applied Psychology*, **33**, 33–49.

Roy, D.F. (1991). Towards improved recall by an eyewitness – a review of the cognitive interview and other interview techniques. Paper presented at the First Annual Conference of The British Psychological Society Division of Criminology and Legal Psychology, Canterbury.

Sealy, A.P. (1979). The contributions of psychology to legal processes: An analysis of jury studies. In D.P. Farrington, K. Hawkins & S.M. Lloyd-Bostock (Eds), *Psychology, Law and Legal Processes*. Guildford: Macmillan.

Sepejak, D.S., Webster, C.D. & Menzies, R.J. (1984). The clinical prediction of dangerousness. In D.J. Müller, D.E. Blackman & A.J. Chapman (Eds.), *Psychology and Law*. Chichester: Wiley.

Severance, L.J. & Loftus, E.F. (1982). Improving the ability of jurors to comprehend and apply criminal jury instructions. *Law and Society Review*, **17**, 153–197.

Severance, L.J. & Loftus, E.F. (1984). Improving criminal justice. *International Review of Applied Psychology*, **33**, 97–119.

Smith, M. (1983). Hypnotic memory enhancement in witnesses: Does it Work? *Psychological Bulletin*, **9**, 387–407.

Smith, S. (1979). Remembering in and out of context. *Journal of Experimental Psychology: Human Learning and Memory*, **5**, 460–471.

Sporer, S.L. (1982). A brief history of the psychology of testimony. *Current Psychological Reviews*, **2**, 323–339.

Sporer, S.L. (1984). Sentencing Councils: A social-psychological analysis. *International Review of Applied Psychology*, **33**, 121–136.

Stephenson, G.M. (1984). Accuracy and confidence in testimony: A critical review and some fresh evidence. In D.J. Müller, D.E. Blackman and A.J. Chapman (Eds), *Psychology and Law*. Chichester: Wiley.

Strawn, D.U. & Buchanan, D.V. (1976). Jury confusion: A threat to justice. *Judicature*, **5a**, 478–483.

Thornton, G. (1939). The ability to judge crimes from photographs of criminals. *Journal of Abnormal and Social Psychology*, **34**, 378–383.

Ward, E. (1981). Problems of the clinical psychologist as expert witness. In S.M. Lloyd-Bostock (Ed.), *Law and Psychology*. Oxford: SSRC Centre for Socio-Legal Studies.

Wells, G.L., Ferguson, T.J. & Lindsay, C.C.L. (1981). The tractability of eyewitness confidence and its implications for triers of fact. *Journal of Applied Psychology*, **66**, 688–696.

Whitten, W. & Leonard, J. (1981). Directed search through an autobiographical memory. *Memory and Cognition*, **9**, 566–579.

Yarmey, A.D., Tressilian Jones, H.P. & Rashid, S. (1984). Eyewitness memory of elderly and young adults. In D.J. Müller, D.E. Blackman and A.J. Chapman (Eds), *Psychology and Law*. Chichester: Wiley.

Yarmey, A.D. (1982). Eyewitness identification and stereotypes of criminals. In A. Trankell (Ed.), *Reconstructing the Past*. Deventer, The Netherlands: Kluwer.

18

FUTURES FOR APPLIED PSYCHOLOGY

A. GALE

ON THE RELATIONSHIPS BETWEEN PURE AND APPLIED PSYCHOLOGY

Application is based on science?

"Meaningful applications of psychology must be based on a sound scientific foundation. Consequently, ethical application of psychological principles to social problems must await the development of relevant theory that has been tested by empirical research. In addition to a thorough knowledge of scientific facts and theory, practitioners of applied psychology must also have the requisite personal qualities that will enable them to work comfortably and effectively with a wide range of clients" (Spielberger, 1984, p. xi).

The views expressed by Spielberger will be echoed by other authors in this volume. Part of the public acceptability of professional psychology must be based on the notion that psychologists are scientists and that they have scientific evidence to back up their claims of competence. The notion of the scientist conjures up images of white coats, laboratories, scientific conferences and scientific journals, an imagery which owes much to the public's views of the natural, hard, or traditional sciences and the undoubtedly successful and beneficial application af science in medicine and engineering. In addition, the public is protected by a professional ethic which resists application in the absence of scientific evidence for efficacy. To what extent is such a view supported by the facts?

Is application in psychology based on a two-stage model?

According to Schönpflug (1992) applied psychology has an historical existence relatively independent from pure or academic psychology. Although applied psychologists might wish to claim that they have a sound scientific basis for social interventions such a causal relationship is rare. In other disciplines a two stage model applies because important applications arise from basic discoveries; thus for example, research into the characteristics of lasers was pursued for largely theoretical reasons, and extensive application of laser technology came later. Such relations between science and technology (the two-stage model) are easy to demonstrate, but Schönpflug claims that parallel examples from psychology are elusive. He demonstrates that behaviour modification techniques and intelligence testing, examples which are often cited as major achievements in psychology, were not based historically on basic scientific discoveries, either about the impact on behaviour of reward and punishment or on the nature of thinking and problem solving.

Thus Xenophon, who lived some 2,500 years before Skinner, described ways in which the obedience of slaves could be guaranteed by deploying techniques well established in the training of pets and wild animals:

> "... in dealing with slaves the training thought suitable for wild animals is also a very effective way of teaching obedience; for you will do much with them by filling their bellies with the food they hanker after. Those of ambitious disposition are also spurred on by praise, some natures being hungry for praise as others for meat and drink ...." (cited by Schönpflug, 1992).

In this extract Xenophon displays an understanding of three contemporary psychological principles: that there is continuity in basic principles of learning between species, that positive reinforcement is a powerful means of shaping behaviour, and that individuals vary in the modes of reinforcement to which they are maximally responsive.

Schönpflug suggests that several authorities, like Xenophon, Aristotle, or Machiavelli, used shrewd detailed observation and intelligent reflection on personal experience to offer pragmatic advice within a lay psychological framework, in treatises and practical manuals which cover many aspects of personal and interpersonal behaviour. In a historical sense, therefore, applied psychology appeared well before academic or pure psychology. Human problems in child-rearing, animal husbandry, education, work, legal settings, politics, and interpersonal relationships were too important to wait for the scientific development of psychology in the twentieth century. Thus the contemporary notion that pure psychology is theory driven and applied psychology is problem driven (Middleton and Edwards, 1985) has historical precedent.

Spielberger (1984) cites intelligence testing and psychometrics as an example of applied psychology's contribution to the solution of major social problems, such as the appropriate allocation of educational resources or the selection of personnel in two world wars. The science behind mental testing came from Galton's work on individual differences and Cattell's doctoral studies in experimental psychology at Wundt's laboratory in Leipzig. However, Schönpflug argues in contrast that intelligence testing has always been a pragmatic affair: Binet knew little about psychological models of problem solving but given a problem to solve created a pragmatic and workable scheme for educational selection; subsequently, Gestalt notions of the nature of problem solving had little impact on testing; and after 80 years of mental testing it is still not clear whether intelligence tests actually predict ability or competence for real-life problem solving. The actual psychological processes which lead to different test scores are still to be elucidated.

Therefore, the particular relationship between basic theory and research in psychology on the one hand, and successful application on the other, appears not to have followed the two-stage route of other disciplines. Are there in fact sufficient commonalities between pure and applied psychology to resist this historical trend and to change the future nature of this relationship?

Distinctions Between Pure and Applied Psychology

Middleton and Edwards (1985) explore the various ways in which pure and applied psychology have been differentiated. They say the stereotypical view of the distinctions to be drawn is as follows. Pure psychology is theory driven, while applied psychology is need driven. Secondly, pure psychology operates in artificially contrived laboratory type situations while applied psychology operates in the real world. This means, thirdly, that pure psychology is concerned with experimental control, replicability and generalisability while applied research uses a variety of methods dictated by the need to be met, under circumstances militating against generalisability, and focuses on the daily life of people.

Such distinctions are reflected in judgmental factors which make pure research of higher status and esteem and those who engage in it are seen as rigorous, hard-nosed and objective. Middleton and Edwards say "... 'pure' involves purity, cleanliness, normality health and goodness. Anything opposed to it is by implication abnormal, inferior, dirty or contaminated (p. 150)." Thus the language used to describe the two psychologies helps to sustain the stereotype.

Middleton and Edwards prefer to use the terms *theory-driven* and *need-driven* to 'pure' and 'applied'. They suggest that when academics claim to be doing applicable work they are often accused of having a cavalier attitude both to applied experts and to the realities of the real-world, for with insensitivity and lack of tact, they can ride roughshod over existing beliefs and practices, failing to appreciate the complexities of relationships which operate in the field. Finally, academics are seen to cloak their private academic world behind an applied smokescreen, by focusing on particular groups like persons suffering from schizophrenia, the elderly and so on, caring more for the development of theory than for the wellbeing of the group studied. Middleton and Edwards are clearly dissatisfied by this state of affairs:

> "There is currently a sense in which 'pure' psychology *is* psychology, while the 'applied' field is the point where psychology meets the real world. Such a conception is ruinous both of theory and of practice" (p. 148).

This tension has had interesting consequences for psychological research in British universities. During the Thatcher revolution (1979–1991) which depended so strongly on the concept of usefulness and the commercial metaphor, psychologists might have been tempted to exploit such criteria of worth and make major claims about applicability. There has been a temptation to join an applied research bandwaggon to sustain personal careers and gain access to limited research resources. Thus there has been a perception that pure psychology can obtain research money more easily if fervent claims are made for the field applicability of laboratory findings. Yet as this chapter is being prepared institutions of higher education in Britain have been told that pure science will be funded from the public purse, while application must be funded by the customer. The tensions within psychology are reflected in conflict within a broader context. The apparent worth of basic science and application is to be reflected in differential patterns of funding of institutions.

However, British psychological scientists may be fighting a losing battle. The world trend in the development of psychology indicates a progressive reduction in academic/research fields (comparative, developmental, educational, experimental, personality, physiological, psychometric, quantitative, and social psychology) and a rapid growth in health service provider fields (clinical, counselling, health and school psychology) (Rosenzweig, 1992). Thus the purity of academic psychology is likely, through distillation, to become even more pure.

A Multidimensional Approach

The Scientific Affairs Board of the British Psychological Society (1988) when considering such fundamental tensions, also sought to define the alleged distinctions between pure and applied psychology and the relationships between them. A multidimensional approach was proposed in which the following relatively independent dimensions or continua were identified: the context of the investigation (including laboratory studies of field measures and field applications of laboratory techniques); the nature of the problem (theoretical, atheoretical or problem-driven); the practical relevance of the outcome; generalisability across situations; generalisability across individuals or classes of individuals; and, generalisability across tasks. This multidimensional framework can be applied to particular examples, to demonstrate the relative importance or salience of each dimension. Such a dimensional approach thus challenges the stereotypical dichotomies which Middleton and Edwards (1985) condemn.

Because the careers of psychological scientists are in part dependent upon funding for their work, the apparent chasm between pure and applied psychology is a source of contention and even bitterness. In the Scientific Affairs Board report, one respondent expressed concern on five counts: (a) because of the way academic departments are funded, applied research can only be carried out at the expense of pure research; (b) there is little evidence that scientific advance arises out of attempts to solve 'real-world' problems; (c) pure and applied research require a "rather different mentality and ... it is not particularly easy to switch from one to the other"; (d) without fundamental research there would be a dearth of knowledge to apply; and (e) when the public realises that psychologists do not in fact use specifically psychological research in solving real-world problems, funding for psychological research in general will dry up (Scientific Affairs Board, 1988, p. 20). Thus, this particular academic respondent expressed the powerful view that applied psychological research can actually threaten the very existence of psychological research in general.

Readers will have observed in Chapter 1 of this volume how two World Wars both stimulated and shaped the nature of psychology; current social demands, for health, reduction of poverty, pollution and the need to husband the world's resources, might also be expected to shape the future of psychology in the twenty first century. As health replaces science as the new social religion the debate between pure and applied psychologists might become harsher.

A cynical reaction to this debate is that self-interest is a primary concern rather than science or the public benefit, or that the expressed views of psychologists on either side of the fence are exhortations in the absence of evidence, motherhood statements, or mere wishful thinking. Only a careful historical argument (such as that developed by Schönpflug, 1992), or a sophisticated analysis of future trends (always a hazardous endeavour) can provide appropriate evidence. Few psychologists have been concerned with the history of the discipline or projecting forward to the future (Haggard and Weinreich-Haste, 1986, see below).

A Working Example of a Happy Marriage Between Pure and Applied Psychology

However, it is possible to identify individual examples which demonstrate a good level of collaborative enterprise between pure and applied approaches. A contemporary example of the complex interplay between laboratory based work and field application is the use of the cognitive interview in securing testimony in young witnesses (Gieselman and Fisher, 1988). Such work has been stimulated by an increasing public interest in child abuse and the problem of securing adequate and reliable information retrieval from young children in particular as well as enhancing investigative interviewing in general.

A variety of techniques has been developed for this and related investigative purposes: mental reinstatement of context, recollection from a variety of perspectives, instruction to report everything, and recall of events in different chronological order. While it might be tempting to claim that such a list of techniques arises from basic work on memorial processes and retrieval in particular, the notion of reinstatement of context (probably the most effective of these techniques) is associated with centuries-old mnemonic devices for retrieval, notwithstanding the fact that it has been demonstrated experimentally. The other three techniques seem to owe more to innovatory insight than to solid principles of the psychology of memory.

Memon and Bull (1991) in a succinct review of the literature, show that it is not clear how or why particular techniques or aspects of them are effective, which techniques are associated with more or less omission or commission errors, and which are the least sensitive to suggestibility. Yet what Memon and Bull demonstrate is that the pure/applied distinction is hard to sustain, for they call for a mixture of laboratory studies with field applications to aid the development of the technique.

Here we can see how the multi-dimensional approach is easily demonstrated: research studies involve controlled laboratory investigations, field observations, laboratory simulations, controlled field studies, interventions to improve field performance by both psychologists and police investigators, comparisons between groups of witnesses (adults versus children), comparisons across types of crime and situations, and constant reference back to theoretical models of memory developed within laboratory settings. Nevertheless, it must be said that research on cognitive interviewing could also be cited as a further illustration of Schönpflug's claim that the two-stage model rarely applies in psychology; given the considerable research effort devoted to memorial processes we might have imagined that some of the complex problems identified by Memon and Bull should have already yielded to more straightforward answers.

However, this example and the analysis of problems in the field of cognitive interviewing offered by Memon and Bull, demonstrates also the limits of Schönpflug's argument. While persisting problems in human affairs which arise from human nature, might well have stimulated intelligent observers like Xenophon to formulate basic laws of behaviour, the experimental tradition was only recently established. Thus, the psychology of learning goes well beyond Xenophon's formulations and in a systematic and question-driven manner, explores the limits of the application of the basic laws, the conditions under which principles of reward and punishment are most effective and the precise relationships between individual action and the application of reinforcement.

While lay psychology may identify psychological facts, only scientific psychology can test the validity of such facts through systematic enquiry. This applies of course both in laboratory contexts and in the field, since contemporary psychology, as developed in the twentieth century, is orderly, logical and constrained by rational argument. While the overlap between formal psychology and lay psychology cannot be denied, only formal psychology knows how to put those appropriate questions which will take knowledge forward beyond simple assertions of basic principles or commonsense truisms.

Lay Psychology and Competition for Influence

The use of psychological theory, methods and research to enhance the everyday work of police staff provides a nice example of the way in which psychology can be applied in real-life situations, without competing with other specialists or professional groups. In contrast, the application of psychology within the classroom, in social work, or in counselling, clearly involves competition for resources, since in those fields there are long traditions of working in particular ways and with particular assumptions. Claims that psychological approaches are more effective clearly offer a threat to other established professions.

In Britain for example, the British Psychological Society recently set up a Scientific Section on Counselling which rapidly became one of the largest sub-systems within the Society. It is inevitable that this Section will be translated into a Professional Division, encompassing qualified practitioners, with a registration certificate that permits practice and obliges the holder to abide by a code of personal and professional conduct and potentially can subject the holder to disciplinary procedures in the event of failure to behave in accordance with the code. Such disciplinary procedures, designed to protect the general public, can lead to dismissal from the Society, loss of the ability to practise as an applied psychologist, and loss of a means of earning an income. A standard for entry to membership is set by the establishment of a Diploma in Counselling and a board of examiners. There are of course many counsellors and indeed many psychotherapists who are neither members of the Society nor qualified psychologists.

The justification for such a formal threat to others seeking to occupy a common niche (to provide counselling to persons in distress) is a mixture of several claims: that psychological counselling is founded in sound psychological theory; that the efficacy of psychological counselling can be demonstrated; that a qualification in academic psychology is a precondition for professional training; that professional training is orderly, systematically monitored and properly examined; and that this basis in science, formal training and professional monitoring serves to protect the public against exploitation and abuse. In a zero-sum game, where different professions are competing for a common resource, psychology's claim to be a scientific discipline must surely be seen to be a powerful hand to play?

Is Applied Psychology Relevant to Others But Not to Psychologists?

The notion that in the not-too-distant future, psychological counselling will be recognised as a regulated profession, different in quality and professional discipline from other competitors in the field, leads us to ask whether in all spheres of psychological activity, psychologists are willing to impose an equal discipline on themselves.

Gale (1990a), in a Presidential Address to the British Psychological Society, asked whether psychologists actually apply psychology to themselves. He accused academic psychologists, who teach psychology to students, of failing to apply psychological knowledge to their own professional practice. He identified several areas of teaching and the teacher's interaction with the student, which could benefit from the application of psychological expertise: selection of students, counselling of students, principles of learning and instruction, assessment, feedback on both staff and lecturer performance, and staff development.

If we take the first of these, student selection, it is clear that in spite of half a century of advance in psychometrics, most psychology departments in Britain select their students through performance in public examinations putting a firm belief in results in the Advanced Level examination. Few departments do more than cream off the best candidates on the basis of examination potential; other characteristics which might guarantee the best cohorts of graduates and potential researchers/practitioners, are ignored. Thus there has been no task analysis, job description or job specification relating either to psychology students or their teachers. The lack of predictive validity of selection criteria or any measure of external validity is partly due to the absence of appropriate outcome criteria or process variables. Should we not be in a position to answer the question: "What makes a good psychologist" and provide the psychological technology to ensure that we both select and create appropriate individuals?

Psychologists engaging in psychology teaching may also be shortsighted in failing to keep in touch with the growing literature on innovation and evaluation of psychology teaching (Gale, 1989). Again, concepts from organizational psychology and research on group atmosphere and group performance could also be applied to the management and enhancement of psychology departments. The apparent failure to apply psychology to ourselves reveals yet a further potential gap between academic and applied psychology and the apparent failure of psychological organizations to recognize their own pathology (de Board, 1978).

Conclusion

There is clearly substance in Schönpflug's claim that the relationship between basic science and application in psychology is not a straightforward one. Lay psychology over several centuries has presented a commonsense view of human problems. In present times, claims to demonstrate that applied psychology arises from basic scientific investigations are somewhat tenuous. The alleged clear-cut dichotomy between pure and applied psychology is also difficult to sustain, while a multi-dimensional basis for drawing such distinctions is to be preferred. Nevertheless, given the view that academic psychologists and applied psychologist have a different world-view and think and act differently, there is considerable potention for division. A multi-dimensional approach also demonstrates that there are key differences between lay psychology and formal psychology, the latter offering a systematic and orderly development of concepts and techniques, in which there is a constant interplay between bench and practice. The apparent scientific superiority of psychology can be used as a means of protecting the applied professions and supporting psychology's role as a cuckoo in the well established nests of other professions. At the same time, psychologists do not always turn their psychological knowledge on themselves; this is particularly the case in the teaching of psychology and the organisation and delivery of the degree in psychology.

It is possible to accept Schönpflug's account of the historical development of the relationship between pure and applied psychology but suggest that he would be guilty of the fallacy of historicism if he were to suggest that the same pattern of relationships will continue in the future. The rate of gain of psychological knowledge and our growing confidence in applying psychology in a variety of contexts (as demonstrated by the foregoing chapters in this volume) means that the future need not be dictated to by the past. The Scientific Affairs Board report (1988) details several excellent examples which demonstrate the effectiveness of applying psychological know-how in a variety of social settings, including cognitive therapy, occupational stress management, health screening, assessment centres, destigmatization, manufacturing technology, instrument design, quality control, and machine pacing. Such applications have helped to alter public attitudes, change people's view of themselves, and affect manufacturing technology and ways of working.

In the next section we consider whether current practices within professional psychology might serve to inhibit the application of psychological expertise. The practice of educational psychology is examined as a special case.

FRAGMENTATION IN PROFESSIONAL PSYCHOLOGY IN BRITAIN

Can Communality be Achieved?

The parting of the ways of scientific and professional psychologists in the USA and the constitutional consequences for the American Psychological Association, which literally split apart, remind us of the dangers of the divisions between pure and applied psychology which Middleton and Edwards (1985) both identify and exhort us to reject.

Gale (1983), Gale and Chapman (1984), and Gale (1990b) suggest that there are also unjustifiable divisions between the various branches of applied psychology in Britain. Gale and Chapman (1984) suggest that titles such as clinical, occupational and educational psychologist owe more to the context in which such professional psychologists work, the needs specified by employers, and the historical development of psychological contributions within that context, than to a psychological analysis of need. Furthermore, they claim that a psychological analysis (or task analysis) of the work of professional psychologists demonstrates a great deal of communality of actual or potential approach.

The quotation from Spielberger (1984) at the beginning of this chapter ended with a comment on the need for special personal skills on the part of professional psychologists if they were to work effectively with clients. Such a view indicates that applied psychological sciences call upon a broader range of skills than do the pure psychological sciences, exposed as the professional psychologist is both to the client and to the complex social worlds which the client occupies.

The following list of the attributes and skills of professional psychologists is taken from the analyses offered by Gale (1983), Gale and Chapman (1984), and Gale (1990b) who over a period of years have refined and augmented it to provide a picture of generic and all-encompassing characteristics. The author is grateful to colleagues on the British Psychological Society's Professional Affairs Board Task Force on the Implications of the Changing Trends in Professional Psychology, for their constructive comments on the taxonomy.

Space is not available to enable us to amplify the many conceptual and methodological issues which each item entails. It will be seen that items refer to competencies, skills, belief systems and attitudes and form a general description of the practice of professional psychology. Nevertheless, every item can be subjected to a specifically psychological analysis. While many of these attributes are displayed separately in the practice of many professions, the work of the applied psychologist displays all of these attributes, and seeks to relate them to a particularly psychological account of individual, inter-personal and group behaviour.

Such a combination of overlapping skills, makes applied psychology potentially very powerful as a profession, for it draws upon years of expertise and experience gained elsewhere as well as drawing upon the particularly psychological components.

Core Skills, Beliefs, Values and Commitments in Applied Psychology

Problem solving. All applied psychology involves the analysis of problems into their component parts. All problems are multiply determined. Particular theories of the origins or causation of human conduct will guide the particular nature of problem analysis.

Change. Change is a feature of all psychological interventions. Clients seek it. Measurement and attribution of change is relevant in all branches of professional psychology.

Quality of living. An implicit commitment is to improving the quality of life of clients, whether this be in terms of feelings, relationships, efficacy, or performance.

Devising interventions. Psychological principles and skills guide the psychologist in devising interventions as a means of creating conditions for change. Such interventions are designed also in the light of an awareness of what is feasible in a particular context; thus effective application is of crucial importance.

Training and education. Although different terms are used in different contexts, education and training imply conveying knowledge and skill to the client so that the client learns new ways of doing things.

Coping mechanisms. Life is rarely problem-free. Both the psychologist and his or her clients need to develop adaptive or functional means of coping with stress and associated problems.

Observation, measurement and report. This is an important aspect of all psychological work, whether in relation to individuals or to groups. It relates both to the psychological definition of a particular problem and to communicating recommendations or outcomes following interventions.

Explaining and reporting to non-psychologists. Special skill is needed in transmitting information to others. Psychologists need to set up noise-free channels of communication and send clear messages along them.

Evaluation of interventions. This must be sine qua non of all interventions if the psychologist is to be accepted as a practitioner–scientist, and is an essential aspect of public accountability.

Rights and responsibilities. Clients will have rights and responsibilities which society can at times redefine. Thus the relationship between psychologist and client is regulated by broader social, cultural and legal norms.

Moral and ethical consequences. Working with people gives psychologists access to private and confidential information; it also involves defining who exactly the client is and may involve making decisions for others.

Values. Sensitivity is necessary to appreciate (a) the psychologist's own implicit values (say, about how we should live); (b) the value system of the client, and (c) the impact of cultural and religious variations on the individual's view of what is proper and improper conduct. Skills of reflexivity are a valuable asset in assessing one's own value system and beliefs.

Autonomy. Psychologists and psychology have no special insight into how we should live or what is right or wrong for the individual or for the group. Thus psychologists need to be sensitive to the temptation to impose their own values on others. Somehow, the client needs to make decisions about what is right or wrong for them.

Advocacy. In several situations, the psychologist might find themselves in the role of advocate for the client. This may involve challenging the power and authority of those who have some degree of control over the client.

Social networks. Clients belong to a variety of social networks (family, religion, ethnic, political affiliation, etc.) which will influence their beliefs about themselves and others. Psychological interventions need to be tailored to the client's belief system, and the factors which will influence the client.

Organizations. Both psychologists and their clients work and live within organizations (work, family, institutional settings). The psychologist needs to understand the role of organizations both in creating problems for individuals and as agencies of change. Organizations have their own rule and role systems. Psychologists have to appreciate how to work the organization to achieve appropriate aims. Analysis of organizations and an audit of their strengths, weaknesses and potential is often essential to effective intervention.

Other professional groups. All psychologists work in association with other groups. To be effective, psychologists must appreciate how such colleagues see their own profession and how they view psychology. In some situations, psychologists find themselves vying with other groups for resources, power and influence.

Teamwork. In most working contexts, psychologists work in teams involving other psychologists or other professionals. Effective teamwork is often essential to the effective delivery of service to clients.

Legislation. Few jobs in psychology do not involve a need to appreciate and keep in touch with relevant legislation, affecting both psychological practice and the context in which the client works or lives.

Resource allocation. Psychologists are paid by others. They also need cash to do their work and to deliver services to clients. Thus there is a need to appreciate how resources can be acquired, the prioritizing of expenditure, and the processes of decision-making which lead to resource allocation. In resource allocation, as in other contexts, bargaining and negotiation skills are essential.

Updating and personal development. Without updating, the psychologist cannot maintain psychological competence, nor can a totally adequate service be delivered to clients.

Gale (1983) argues that if such a list can indeed be compiled which applies to all applications of psychology, then there are profound implications for both training and practice. If generic skills are evident, should there be generic training? If generic training is available, what justifies the specialist labelling of particular applied psychological professions? Where and how should applied psychologists be trained and prepared for their work or receive updating to enhance their skills? How long should such training be and what is the appropriate relationship in education and training between pure and applied psychology?

Should particular contexts in which psychologists work (i.e. hospitals, clinics, schools, prisons, workplaces and so on) dictate the type of psychologist who should be working there? Are human problems and human situations so general that a specifically psychological approach overrides differences in context and differences in perceived need? Indeed, if the client drives the construction of the problem will the psychologist's approach be limited to the causal attributions and worldview of the client? Clearly, the answer to such questions goes well beyond a purely formal analysis and impinges on long-entrenched tradition, vested interests and the amour propre of established orthodoxy.

Let us conclude this section by considering how such a broadened view of applied psychological expertise might influence the ways in which one particular profession might operate, namely educational psychology.

An Example: Broadening the Scope of Educational Psychology

The following description is taken from the careers leaflet published by the British Psychological Society:

"Educational Psychology is the application of psychological science and theory to the learning and behaviour, social and emotional problems of children and young people in the educational context. This work takes place in nurseries, schools, colleges, special units and schools as well as the home or hospitals. Educational psychologists are largely employed by local authorities who offer a well-defined career structure. Most psychologists spend a large amount of time working directly with individual children, assessing their progress, their academic and emotional needs, helping them by counselling, applying behaviour analysis and curriculum programming, whilst others take a more consultative role and work indirectly with children through their work with parents, teachers and others who have more regular contact with the child".

This description of the educational psychologist's role (although it displays some broadening in the latter half of the final sentence) is very much a traditional, but accurate account of the status quo, which focuses primarily on clinical work with individual children.

Gale (1991, 1992) argues for a different conception, claiming that the interests of both children and teachers should be the focus of concern for educational psychologists and that their aim should be the amelioration of the educational system as a whole rather than to intervene on a fire-fighting basis when an individual child appears to be in difficulty. The argument is that a systemic, organizational approach to the school and those who work in it, will in the longer run create a superior environment in which children can thrive.

To this end, the skills of clinical and occupational psychologists are just as relevant to the school as are the delimited skills of the educational psychologist as specified by the British Psychological Society's careers leaflet and by current practice. If the reader examines our list of core skills, it will be apparent that all apply to the school context; if that is the case then there is no reason why the educational psychologist should not be capable of providing a much broader range of expertise. Thus psychologists should and could advise schools on all aspects of management, staff selection procedures, staff development, job satisfaction, group decision-making, organizational and individual stress, assessment, counselling, resource management, health education, attitude change, family interventions, and so on, over and above the present set of functions. If psychological ergonomists can provide input into industrial design both of hardware and software, why should they not be involved in the design of instructional devices (such as books), the creation of good quality environments (the buildings) or in ensuring that equipment (for example in workshops, laboratories, or in the gymnasium) is safe and easy to use?

Clearly, the school is a place of work and thus psychological interventions designed for the workplace should be just as appropriate as they are for the industrial organization or office. Similarly, the school represents a sample of the population at large, so that all the problems of society are somehow encapsulated within the school. In a sense, the teacher is at the same time a teacher, trainer, counsellor, social worker, psychiatrist, police person and prison warder. Indeed, all the previous chapters in this volume should have applicability within the school context.

This brief exhortation to change the practice of educational psychologists, could be equally applied to other psychological professions. The current resistance to such change stems in part from the fact that psychologists accept the model of the person offered by the client. Thus the child as emotional misfit or incompetent learner dominates professional practice. In contrast, alternative models see the child and the classroom as only sub-systems within a complex social hierarchy in which the potential for positive change is actually much greater if one tackles dysfunction much higher in the structure (Gale, 1992).

BROADER ISSUES: THE EXTENSION OF PSYCHOLOGY'S INFLUENCE

Psychology and Social Policy

How high up the social structure should applied psychology venture? What is the limit to the extension of psychological intervention? Such questions raise moral and ethical questions of a wider nature. In an examination of the ethics of socially sensitive research Sieber and Stanley (1988) point to the impact on society and social policy of past psychological research. For example, they claim that only public concern with the realities and impact of child abuse has served to undermine Freudian views of women's sexuality, which in spite of fifty years of failure to provide corroborative evidence, persist in the public mind and shape our view of women. Again, Mead's work on adolescence, her naive belief in inherent goodness, combined with American optimism, served to undermine child-rearing practices, and in their view, ruined a generation through indulgence and failure to set limits. Thus psychology is no less capable of influencing society than is atomic physics. Psychologists should therefore: (a) cease pretending that they can work in a vacuum with little impact on social policy; (b) should recognise how their work has an effect on the images of the person conveyed in social consciousness; and (c) should evaluate their work ethically, in advance, to anticipate its consequences.

There is no doubt that psychological research and texts on the elderly have served to sustain negative public images of the old and to assist in stigmatization (Schaie, 1988; Whitbourne and Hulicka, 1990). The reason for this is that psychologists, like everyone else, absorb current social beliefs; thus they set up research which focuses on needs and deficits rather than strengths, limiting the potential outcome of the research and discovering what they set to find out. Whitbourne and Hulicka demonstrate, in an analysis of 139 texts, that recent research is under-reported, space devoted to the elderly (one third of our lives?) in developmental texts is minimal, the emphasis on outdated research is to underline incompetence and weakness, and that the language used describes predominantly negative aspects of ageing and ageing as a problem. Thus the stigma held about the elderly by the general public, politicians, professional workers, the families of the elderly, and indeed, as an oppressed group, the elderly themselves, is reinforced in the published psychological literature which in turn, enters the consciousness of the students who read the texts.

In relation to ethnicity, race and gender, Scarr (1988) accuses fellow psychologists of moral cowardice. Rather than confront public reaction to findings on race and gender, psychologists avoid carrying out the actual research needed to create appropriate knowledge so that underrepresented groups can actually be supported and facilitated in achieving true social equality.

Does Psychology Sustain the Status Quo?

The most stirring recent attack on psychology's failure to tackle major social issues has been mounted by Prilleltensky (1989) who accuses psychology of supporting the status quo. His argument is as follows. Every society has a ruling elite which retains power over economic and political resources by setting up appropriate social structures and cultural mechanisms. People then accept these cultural mechanisms as fact and reality rather than appreciating they are constructions designed to maintain social stability. Psychologists, without being conscious of their socialization, pass through various rites de passage during their personal development which serve to reinforce their place within the social structure, and then, incorporating social beliefs into their own research, create empirical descriptions which are in truth socio-political *prescriptions*.

Thus rather than aid the welfare of fellow human beings, psychologists confirm the current ideology and keep people in their place. Prilleltensky lists several ways in which this is apparent: (a) seeing causes of behaviour within the individual, thus setting up a false distinction between self and society, drawing attention away from social causation and seeing solutions to social problems in the form of intervention with individuals; (b) sustaining the view that technology rather than moral or political change will solve human problems; (c) forcing the myth that psychology is value-free, neutral and depoliticised, thereby giving greater weight to psychological viewpoints which are in fact saturated with value judgements and social norms; (d) the influence of several theoretical approaches all of which cast a veil over political influence and social evil: humanistic psychology, radical behaviourism, genetic approaches to individual differences, cognitivism, which focus respectively on apparent human goodness, the immediate environment as reinforcer, the biological and physiological causes of personal conduct, and the internal representation of reality. Prilleltensky argues that psychologists should be more aware of their role in society, reject it, and become active in promoting human wellbeing and "the good society".

Psychology as the New Religion

The view that psychology is naive, and is an instrument in maintaining inequality in society ("the richman in his castle, the poor man at his gate, God made them high or lowly and ordered their estate"), is particularly important as we enter the twenty first century, when psychology is likely to take over many roles previously fulfilled by religion. In what ways is that so? The parallels are considerable. Psychology has offered various images of the person and increased our understanding of the human condition. Secondly, among its explanations are those for good and evil (crime, antisocial behaviour, violence and child abuse). Thirdly psychology has sought to counsel at critical times in the life cycle: contraception, childbirth and childrearing; education; adolescence, coming of age and the emergence of sexual behaviour; stress in life crises such as work stress, marital stress, surgical operations; terminal illness and bereavement. Wherever, in the past, you may have found a priest, now you will find a health psychologist. Whether the ethics, and the broader moral responsibilities of such roles have been fully explored as yet, is questionable (Gale, 1993). As psychology becomes less modest about its scope it needs to recognise the fundamental reciprocal principle, that power also implies responsibility. Only relatively recently have the housejournals of the APA and BPS, the two largest psychological societies in the world, begun to contain articles on matters of social policy and public responsibility.

The expectation that psychology will intrude in important aspects of living is reinforced by the *scene de la vie future* study of Haggard and Weinreich-Haste (1986). They asked a sample of British psychologists what the world would be like in the year 2010. In a two stage study, they developed a questionnaire which was then redistributed. Factor analysis of responses from a large sample of distinguished psychologists revealed three key factors (representing 43, 24 and 14 percent of the variance): (a) intervention to reduce stress, support social welfare, coping, training and health; (b) reluctance to deal with Third World issues, increased professionalisation, dealing with society's casualties, not influencing social policy; and (c) increased understanding of psychophysiology, attitude change, personnel selection and training, curriculum design, and criminal behaviour. The Haggard and Weinreich-Haste survey could be interpreted as an empirical reinforcement of Prilleltensky's views. Factor (c) is more of the same thing and represents continuity of current concerns, with a clear focus on individuals and intra-personal explanation. Factor (a) reflects trends in health psychology and increasing intervention as a health change agent, while Factor (b) shows a defence of the value-free, professional approach, blinded to major world concerns. Prilleltensky would argue that such findings clearly demonstrate the naivete of psychologists and their lack of awareness of the roles they have had set out for them.

Psychology on the World Stage

To what extent are the predictions of the Haggard and Weinreich-Haste respondents reflected in current data about world trends? Rosenzweig (1992) conducted a world-wide review of the status of psychology. He shows that over a ten year period, the total number of qualified psychologists in the world doubled to half a million, being about one twelfth of the total number of physicians. In the USA the ratio of physicians to psychologists is much less, at 5:1. While the ratio of researchers to practitioners is shrinking worldwide, the same trend is demonstrated in terms of priorities within research, when developed and developing countries are compared: "The mean level for research activity for industrialized countries was about 30 percent greater in the academic/research fields than in the health service provider fields: Conversely, for the developing countries, the mean level of research activity was 23 percent higher in the health service provider fields than in the academic/research fields" (Rosenzweig, p. 720).

Thus we see how the development of psychology is shaped by social trends and public need; in developing countries, health and well-being must be primary priorities, or in Maslow's terms, must be a prepotent need, before psychology can be seen to indulge in specialized and idiosyncratic research, carried out for its own intrinsic value. Presumably, as the health base of developing countries becomes more established and food production and sanitation are in place, the emphasis will then move to education, work, economic psychology and factors affecting productivity.

In the West, the key thrust for the psychology of selection, training and ergonomics, was provided by two World Wars. In developing countries, the key motive must be continued survival. It is unfortunate that so few psychologists in the developed world show any interest or enthusiasm for psychology in the developing world.

Conclusion

Whatever the formal relationship between pure and applied psychology, or the actuality, historical or contemporary, of that relationship, professional psychologists do claim that part of their legitimised authority comes from their origins within the psychological sciences. An analysis of the common facets of professional psychology reveals a set of skills, attitudes, beliefs and values which go beyond science towards a conception of society in which the psychologist is facilitating individuals and groups in achieving positive states and high levels of competence. Such an analysis becomes a challenge to present patterns of training and working, by demonstrating the communalities among the contexts in which professional psychologists are employed.

But a systems-based approach to personal and social problems need not stop at the level of the individual organization. Alternative models of social stress point to socio-political and economic factors as principal determinants of the individual's world view, their sources of anxiety and their concepts of what is right and wrong. The implications of the broader responsibilities which psychologists are taking on, as they stretch their influence deeper into individual lives, have yet to be recognised or confronted. There is little evidence that psychologists (and particularly the learned and professional societies which protect their interests) appreciate the role they might have in sustaining social inequality.

My intention in preparing this contribution to the present volume is to demonstrate that compartmentalisation, either between pure and applied psychology, or between the various professions of psychology and the skills they have developed, could prove to the detriment of both clients and the profession. A similar compartmentalisation between psychology as scientific and value-free on the one hand and social awareness and social responsibility on the other creates a number of moral and ethical dilemmas of which we are only just becoming aware.

REFERENCES

British Psychological Society (undated). Opportunities and careers for psychology graduates and chartered psychologists. Leicester: British Psychological Society.

de Board R. (1978). *The Psychoanalysis of Organizations: A Psychoanalytic approach to behaviour in groups and organizations.* London: Tavistock Publications.

Gale, A. (1983). Jobs for psychologists: A radical view. *Occasional Papers of the Division of Educational and Child Psychology,* **12**, 51–54. Leicester: British Psychological Society.

Gale, A. (1989). Psychology as God's gift: How ungrateful can you be? A critical evaluation of the psychology degree and its failings. In J. Radford and D. Rose (eds) *A Liberal Science: Psychology education past, present and future.* Milton Keynes: Society for Research Into Higher Education and Open University Press.

Gale, A. (1990a). Applying psychology to the psychology degree: Pass with first class honours or miserable failure? *The Psychologist,* **11**, 483–488.

Gale, A. (1990b). Core skills, values, beliefs and commitments in applied psychology. *Counselling Psychology Review,* **5**, 24–25.

Gale, A. (1991). The school as organisation: New roles for psychologists in education. *Educational Psychology in Practice,* **7**, 39–45.

Gale, A. (1992). Psychology in schools: the rights of children and teachers. Public lecture presented at the University of Warwick, February, 1992.

Gale, A. (1993). Ethical issues in psychological research. In A.M. Colman (Ed.) *Encyclopedia of Psychology,* London: Routledge.

Gale, A. and Chapman, A.J. (1984). The nature of applied psychology. In A. Gale and A.J. Chapman (eds) *Psychology and Social Problems: An introduction to applied psychology,* Chichester and New York: John Wiley and Sons.

Gieselman, R.E. and Fisher, R.P. (1988). The cognitive interview: An innovative technique for questioning witnesses of crime. *Journal of Police and Criminal Psychology,* **2**, 2–5.

Haggard, M. and Weinreich-Haste, H. (1986). One generation after 1984: The role of psychology. *Bulletin of the British Psychological Society*, **39**, 321–324.

Memon, A. and Bull, R. (1991). The cognitive interview: Its origins, empirical support, evaluation and practical implications. *Journal of Community and Applied Social Psychology*, **1**, 291–307.

Middleton, D. and Edwards, D. (1985). Pure and applied psychology: Re-examining the relationship. *Bulletin of the British Psychological Society*, **38**, 146–150.

Prilleltensky, I. (1989). Psychology and the status quo. *American Psychologist*, **44**, 795–802.

Rosenzweig, M.R. (1992). Psychological science around the world. *American Psychologist*, **47**, 718–722.

Scarr, S. (1988). Race and gender as psychological variables: Social and ethical issues. *American Psychologist*, **43**, 56–59.

Schaie, K.W. (1988). Ageism in psychological research. *American Psychologist*, **43**, 179–183.

Schönpflug, W. (1992). Applied Psychology: Newcomer with a long tradition? *Applied Psychology: An International Review*, **42**, 5–66.

Scientific Affairs Board (1988). *The Future of the Psychological Sciences: Horizons and opportunities for British psychology* Leicester: British Psychological Society.

Sieber, J.E. and Stanley, B. (1988). Ethical and professional dimensions of socially sensitive research. *American Psychologist*, **43**, 49–55.

Spielberger, C.D. (1984). Foreword. In A. Gale and A.J. Chapman (eds) *Psychology and Social Problems: An introduction to applied psychology*, Chichester and New York: John Wiley and Sons.

Whitbourne, S.K. and Hulicka, I.M. (1990). Ageism in undergraduate psychology texts. *American Psychologist*, **45**, 1127–1136.

INDEX